Development Challenges of Pakistan

Jamil Nasir

Development Challenges of Pakistan

Constraints and Choices

palgrave
macmillan

Jamil Nasir
Federal Board of Revenue (FBR)
Revenue Division
Islamabad, Pakistan

ISBN 978-981-97-3063-6 ISBN 978-981-97-3064-3 (eBook)
https://doi.org/10.1007/978-981-97-3064-3

This Palgrave Macmillan imprint is published by the registered company Springer Nature Singapore Pte Ltd.
The registered company address is: 152 Beach Road, #21-01/04 Gateway East, Singapore 189721, Singapore

Preface

Why Pakistan is unable to put itself on the trajectory of long-term sustainable growth? This question, being an issue of utmost significance concerning the lives of over 240 million people, begs serious debate for searching out the constraints on economic growth and ways to remove them. The book in hand is an attempt to analyze and answer the posed question. Generally, discussion on economic issues in Pakistan does not go beyond fiscal numbers like balance of payments, current account deficit, taxes, and public debt, et cetera. These numbers are important per se as they reflect upon the income and expenditure of a country. And every nation, just like a household, would always be concerned about its earnings and expenses. Discussion on numbers is, however, a hallow debate and would lead nowhere unless constraints and structures hidden beneath these 'bad numbers' are analyzed, debated, and fixed.

The concept of economic growth suffers from some misconceptions particularly in Pakistan. For instance, growth is considered a result of some mechanical process which it is not. Economic growth is a complex process which is embedded in the socio-economic and political structures of the society. It is not only about economic factors. Rather some non-economic factors and variables like culture, institutions, patience, political stability, eagerness to welcome new ideas, and quality of leadership are also its important determinants. Another misconception is that prerequisites for initiating and sustaining economic growth are the same.

A distinction needs to be appreciated between growth initiating conditions and growth sustaining conditions. A country can initiate economic growth by giving special treatment to certain segments of the population but economic growth would be difficult to sustain for long if its dividends are not widely distributed for poverty alleviation and provision of quality public goods.

Pakistan witnessed high growth in 1960s. It enjoyed some reasonable growth, though in a boom-bust pattern, till 1990 that is before losing its policy sovereignty to IMF's neoliberal policies imposed as conditionality. In 1960s, the world was betting on Pakistan that it would continue to show high economic growth in the coming decades. Some renowned economists were all praise for the economic progress Pakistan had made in terms of numbers like growth in large-scale manufacturing, investment, and agricultural production. They predicted that Pakistan shall show grow at higher growth rates in comparison to South Korea and Taiwan. Their predictions, however, did not come true. The roads diverged between the East Asian countries and Pakistan. The reasons of this divergence are multiple and are liable to debate. For instance, it can be argued that South Korea used industrial policy tools profusely and picked up winners. So did Pakistan. It established institutions like Pakistan Industrial Development Corporation, Pakistan Industrial Credit and Investment Corporation, Investment Promotion Bureau, and Industrial Development Bank of Pakistan. It picked up industries like sugar, textiles, jute, cement, and cigarettes for protection. It initiated schemes like export vouchers, duty drawbacks, export processing zones, et cetera, for export promotion but the results of such policies were quite different from those of East Asian countries.

The argument of this book is that Pakistan was able to initiate economic growth like East Asian countries but it failed to sustain it broadly due to inequitable distribution of resources, lack of focus on human resource development, and continuation of outmoded colonial governance structure. The distribution of initial endowments was highly skewed in Pakistan compared to South East Asian countries. The situation could be improved through redistribution of land on the pattern of South Korea and Taiwan but land reforms in Pakistan remained ineffective. Investment in human resource could be another route to reduce inequities but HR development also did not become a priority with the ruling elite. Pakistan waited for the trickledown to happen. The result simply was that economic growth sharpened regional and class divisions.

On the other hand, the East Asian countries prioritized human resource development and equitable distribution of wealth. They kept Gini under control through investment in education, training, and health of the people. Consequently, social, economic, and political gaps did not widen. And the result was hope in the future and trust in the government. The equitable distribution of wealth and development-oriented policies created a sense of solidarity and with solidarity came socio-political stability, an important prerequisite for long-term high growth.

On the contrary, Pakistan remained content with aggregate numbers and did not recognize socio-economic fissures hidden beneath them. The disaggregated numbers as 'who was getting what' were not given serious consideration in the formulation of socio-economic policies. The aggregate numbers, despite being reasonable, did not have reflection in the lives of the people. Human development indicators of Pakistan are among the worst in the world. A large number of children are out of school. The quality of learning is low. The poor of Pakistan are the poorest in terms of health indicators in comparison with the poor of the low middle-income countries (LMICs) that is countries of same income level. Poverty incidence is high and inequalities are multiple. Access, coverage, and quality of public service delivery are poor. The result of uneven growth and neglect of human resource is that the majority is neither included in the dividends of development nor it is contributing to the development process. Further, the elites have created narratives in the name of ideology which have no relevance with the real-life issues of the people. Threat of common enemy, bogey of conspiracy, and overemphasis on religion-based ideology were some of the strategies adopted for nation building. Public service delivery and human development which are the real-life issues were neglected. Result is that skills and productivity of Pakistani workers are low, confirmed by International reports on competitiveness and ILO estimations.

The case, made out in this book, for the failure of growth in Pakistan revolves around low human development, inequitable distribution of productive assets, and weak governance capacities. These themes run concurrently throughout the book. Several other factors like geo-political environment of the region, historical baggage, military-dominated leadership, et cetera, can also be discussed as culprits responsible for low growth and underdevelopment. In the majority of the books and papers written on Pakistan, by the local as well as foreign commentators, said factors are invariably given much significance and space while searching out answer to the question of underdevelopment. These factors do give some explanation but it would not be fair to lay all the blame of Pakistan's woes on such factors. If the geo-political environment constrained Pakistan's development, its geostrategic location was not all bane. Being located at the fulcrum of huge market with enormous potential for international trade, it could capitalize on its location by making prudent choices. Geography certainly confers certain advantages but economic growth does not ooze out of it automatically.

Similarly, military-dominated leadership is considered by many analysts in Pakistan as a big constraint on long-term economic growth and development. The quality of leadership does matter for shaping the destiny of a nation but even democratic leadership does not necessarily guarantee prosperity if the political system is marred by instability and bad governance and if democracy is just a plaything for the few families with power and privilege. Strangely, high economic growth in countries like South Korea and China took place under non-democratic regimes. Coincidently, Pakistan also witnessed high economic growth rates under military regimes. Some empirics also show that the type of regime is neutral for economic growth. If a democratic regime does not ensure good governance, it would, in all probability, fail on the promise of high economic growth. For instance, the decade of 1990s was a big disaster for Pakistan from the perspective of economic growth despite democratic rule in the country.

The book is predominantly academic in nature but coming from the hands of a practitioner of economic policy, implications, and policy suggestions shall also flow out of the discussion. It is departure from the literature created on economic growth and development in Pakistan as it does not dilate upon the fiscal numbers, balance of payments, tax collection, public expenditure, et cetera. It reflects on the roots and long-term factors responsible for the creation of a vicious circle of underdevelopment. It is not confined to economic factors only. It highlights the significant role of non-economic factors such as culture, institutions, public sector, social capital, and governance in economic growth. The book is not about the short-term solutions and does not provide any magic wand for the economic woes of Pakistan in the short run. It rather takes a longer and broader view on economic growth and development. Its aim is to initiate a debate in the economic and policy circles for putting Pakistan on the track of sustainable long-term growth. The insights and empirics are predominantly derived from the discipline of economics and development literature. The book, however, adopts a multi-disciplinary approach and derives insights from political economy and political science besides relying on historical documents and reports pertaining to Pakistan.

The journey of the book starts with the claim that initially economic growth failed Pakistan by creating socio-economic dissensions and now socio-economic cleavages and low human development, outcome of inequitable distribution of endowments and growth, are failing the growth process. Economic growth has got many virtues. So argument is not against economic growth rather argument is that sustainable growth is required for a longer period of time, which would not be possible without prioritizing human resource development and pro-people policies. The human factor is important for productivity, socio-political stability, and innovation which are important inputs for economic growth. Growth and development go hand in hand. An equitable growth that is growth embedded in development would benefit all the citizens. In 1960s, economic growth was quite high but development indicators varied hugely between the two parts of the country. Huge regional and class differences also exist in present-day Pakistan. The best way to divide the dividends of growth among the people is to invest in human resource.

What are the major levers of human resource development? Certainly, quality education is at the top. A complete chapter is allocated to education. Difference between schooling and learning is discussed at length and it is argued that the quality and relevance of education matter the most for economic growth. Suggestions for improving access and learning are presented in the light of empirics. Public health care is another important dimension of human resource development. The inequities and insufficiencies of public health care system of Pakistan are discussed and suggestions are given to improve the system in a cost-effective manner. The challenge of poverty is recognized as multidimensional problem. The pros and cons of poverty alleviation strategies like microcredit, cash transfers, financial inclusion, distribution of productive assets, et cetera, are discussed. Untapped potential of the rural economy, misallocation of land, and inequalities of various kinds including those of gender and income are discussed as binding constraints to human resource development, socio-economic mobility, and economic growth.

The second broader theme covers long-term determinants of economic growth. After highlighting the importance of institutions, culture of growth, and geography (the deeper determinates of growth), working of public sector and judicial system are discussed in detail. An effective public sector is required for quality public service delivery and an efficient judicial system contributes to economic growth through better contract enforcement. Inefficiencies of public sector and judicial system negatively impact economic growth through several channels including reduction in investment. Negative implications of low social capital and weak fiscal capacities for long-term growth and development are analyzed. Low social capital increases transaction costs and reduces trust in the government. A weak state can neither raise taxes for provision of public services like education and health nor it can change dysfunctional and inefficient governance structures. In the paradigm of state–society relations, a weak state disempowers the poor and panders to the interests of the rent-seekers and in this way promotes exclusions in the society which erode the future prospects of long-term economic growth. Finally, the challenge of militancy, with focus on its structural causes and negative impact on economic growth and development, is discussed in a detail.

The journey of the book concludes with three case studies. First case study relates to misallocation of talent, a big constraint on economic growth generally ignored in development and public policy circles. This case study is based on employment and education data of 500 public sector employees. The second case study is on the pitfalls of reforms imposed by the multilateral institutions in developing countries without appreciating the local environment with the result that local expertise is crowded out and aid-dependent countries lose policy sovereignty having implications for long-term economic growth. This case study is based on the publicly available tax data of Pakistan. The third case study is on informal trade between Iran and Pakistan which highlights the neighborhood effects and scope of regional trade as a source of economic growth.

The book is not about the cyclical economic variables though they may find brief mention in some chapters. It is about the deeper malaise afflicting economic growth. The style of the book is formal, being a serious venture. The common thread running throughout the book is an emphasis on the vital role of human factor for economic growth and development. So the case is made out for investment in human resource (quality education, better health care, etc.,) and removing the constraints (not having access to credit and productive assets, etc.) which are not letting the people realize their potential. The book is not in the tradition of propaganda or strong opinions. Whatever is presented or claimed is based on empirics and evidence.

Pakistan has gathered a good amount of data on education, health, socio-economic conditions, nutrition, taxation, and agriculture. Pakistan social and living standards measurement (PSLM) surveys, Labor Force Survey, Household Integrated Economic Survey (HIES), Provincial Development statistics, Multiple Indicator Cluster Surveys (MICs) conducted by the Planning and Development departments of the provinces in collaboration with UNICEF, Agriculture Census Surveys, Pakistan Education Statistics, Pakistan National Nutrition Survey of the National Ministry of Health, Pakistan Maternal Mortality Survey, Economic Surveys of Pakistan, FBR Year Books, surveys and reports of PIDE, et cetera, are good sources of data. All these sources of data are publicly available. The World Development Indicators, World Inequality Database (WID), WHO data, Findex survey data, Worldwide Bureaucracy Indicators (WWBI), and WB data on intergenerational mobility and governance are some other sources of data. All the said data sources are also publicly accessible and this book has optimally availed of the data from the said sources.

Islamabad, Pakistan
30th June, 2024

Jamil Nasir

Contents

1	The Case for Equitable Growth	1
2	How Deep Are the Deeper Determinants?	27
3	Culture and Growth	53
4	The Question of Education	73
5	The Problem of Public Health Care	115
6	Multiple Inequalities	157
7	Misallocation of Land	209
8	Constraints on Rural Growth	235
9	The Challenge of Poverty	257
10	The Public Sector Performance Conundrum	289
11	A Noisy Legal System	321
12	Social Capital and Corruption Incorporated	347
13	Weak Fiscal and Trade Capacities	369
14	The Militancy Challenge	407
15	Conclusion	443

Case Study 1 453

Case Study 2 459

Case Study 3 467

Notes 473

Bibliography 559

Name Index 607

Subject Index 611

List of Figures

Fig. 1.1	Migration of highly qualified people	24
Fig. 2.1	Gross capital formation of selected countries (% of GDP)	45
Fig. 2.2	Beneficiaries of Federal Government spending, 2008–2022	47
Fig. 3.1	Two distinct demographic dividends	72
Fig. 4.1	Human Captial Index (South Asia)	96
Fig. 4.2	Human Captial Index (LMICs)	97
Fig. 5.1	Infant mortality rate (deaths per 1000 live births) by economic status (wealth quantile)	120
Fig. 5.2	Under-five mortality (per 1000 live births) by economic status (wealth quantile)	121
Fig. 5.3	Neonatal mortality (per 1000 live births) by economic status (wealth quantile)	122
Fig. 5.4	Underweight prevalence in children aged <5 years (%) by economic status (wealth quantile)	124
Fig. 5.5	Stunting prevalence in children aged <5 years (%) by economic status (wealth quantile)	125
Fig. 5.6	Wasting prevalence in children aged <5 years (%) by economic status (wealth quantile)	126
Fig. 5.7	Health expenditure (% of GDP)	140
Fig. 6.1	Lorenz Curve	197
Fig. 9.1	Growth in number of workers in SMEs (in million)	272
Fig. 11.1	Disposal, institution and pendency in the Supreme Court	326
Fig. 11.2	Disposal, institution and pendency in the High Courts	326
Fig. 13.1	Level of total Pakistan debt, public debt and government debt (% of GDP)	388

Fig. 14.1	Major incidents	409
Fig. 14.2	Yearly Fatalities	413
Fig. 14.3	UNHCR Refugees from 1979 to 2022	424
Fig. A.1	Growth in Revenue Collection (2014–2015 to 2017–2018)	462

List of Tables

Table 1.1	Boom-bust growth	12
Table 1.2	Growing at 7%	18
Table 2.1	Summary of natural hazards in Pakistan from 1900 to 2020	37
Table 3.1	Output per worker (GDP constant 2015 US$) of selected countries/regions	69
Table 4.1	Percentage of out of school children 5–16 years	76
Table 4.2	Percentage of out of school children 5–16 years in some selected districts of the provinces	76
Table 4.3	Physical infrastructure (% of schools)	78
Table 4.4	Number of schools, enrolment, and employment	88
Table 4.5	PTR, PSR, and TSR	90
Table 4.6	Mastery gap between the richest and poorest children at age 12	92
Table 4.7	Test Scores, HCI, and GDP per capita of some selected countries (2020)	95
Table 5.1	Life expectancy at birth, total (years) of selected countries	117
Table 5.2	Some key indicators (urban vs. rural)	123
Table 5.3	Percentage of children aged 12–23 months that have been fully immunized—by quintiles	127
Table 5.4	Maternal mortality ratios, maternal deaths for 100,000 live births for the 3-year period before the survey	128
Table 5.5	Nutrition status of children percentage of children under age five	134
Table 5.6	Trends in malnutrition for children under five	136

Table 5.7	Percentage of children aged 6–59 months having anemia and deficiencies of various food supplements	137
Table 5.8	Severe food insecurity	138
Table 5.9	Health expenditure per capita (current US$) of selected countries/regions 2000–2020	140
Table 5.10	Reason for not visiting Govt. Facility first for Diarrhea treatment—by region and province (percentage of responses)	153
Table 6.1	Ratio of female to male labor force participation rate of selected countries (%)	176
Table 6.2	Intergenerational mobility in selected countries (1980 Cohort) %	188
Table 6.3	Intergenerational mobility over time of selected countries	189
Table 6.4	Palma ratio 1 (Top 10% income share/bottom 40% income share) of some selected countries	198
Table 6.5	Palma Index (Top 1% income share/Bottom 40% income share) of some selected countries	199
Table 6.6	Distribution of state land	203
Table 7.1	Number and area of farms by size of farm (in thousand acres)	216
Table 7.2	Resumed and distributed lands under land reforms (in thousand acres)	222
Table 8.1	Competitive industrial performance by economy of some selected countries 2022	238
Table 8.2	The yield gap between wheat and rice	239
Table 8.3	Sources of credit in the Punjab	244
Table 8.4	Tenure classification of farms and farm area by size of farm (in thousand acres)	251
Table 9.1	Accounts holder in a financial institution	279
Table 9.2	Borrowed from a financial institution	279
Table 10.1	Public Sector Wage Premium (PSWP)	311
Table 11.1	Monetary and non-monetary costs of litigation	324
Table 12.1	Worldwide governance indicators of selected countries	356
Table 13.1	Overview of income tax and sales tax collection	381
Table 13.2	Incidence of Federal raxes, 2020–21% of the tax revenue	382
Table 13.3	Trend in exports, imports, and trade deficit (% of GDP)	390
Table 13.4	Exports 2018–2019 to 2022–2023	400
Table 13.5	Export promotion schemes (DTRE, EFS & EOU)	401
Table 14.1	Enrollment statistics	428
Table A.1	Analysis of educational background	455
Table A.2	Pakistan's Tax collection in an international context (in mid-1980s)	460

CHAPTER 1

The Case for Equitable Growth

In 1961, Rosenstein-Rodan wrote a paper[1] in which he predicted the growth rates of underdeveloped countries from all continents of the globe for the next 15 years. He categorized the countries into high growth, low growth, and stationary growth countries. Interestingly, he bracketed Pakistan in the high growth countries contrary to South Korea, Taiwan, Singapore, and Thailand which he categorized as low growth countries. However, his predictions failed to materialize. Over the next 15 years, South Korea, Taiwan, and Singapore achieved much faster and sustainable economic growth rates compared to Pakistan. Although Pakistan was able to initiate reasonable economic growth but it failed to sustain it.

The growth experience of Pakistan confirms the proposition that institutions and factors for 'acceleration of growth' and 'maintenance of growth' are different. Long-term growth would not be possible if its dividends are not widely shared. Economic growth deepened schisms along geographic and class lines in Pakistan. Despite very reasonable growth acceleration in 1960s, unrest and instability set in. In 1960s, Pakistan was being applauded as a model of development by the economists and international consultants. Gustav Papanek who served as an advisor to the Planning Commission and project Field Supervisor to the Harvard Advisory Group on Pakistan, in the opening chapter of his book on the development experience of Pakistan wrote:

J. Nasir, *Development Challenges of Pakistan*,
https://doi.org/10.1007/978-981-97-3064-3_1

> At independence, Pakistan-simultaneously created and disrupted by the partition of British India- was widely considered an economic monstrosity. The country was among the poorest in the world and had no industries to speak of, almost no industrial raw materials, and no significant industrial or commercial groups. It was difficult to see how Pakistan's economy could grow more rapidly than its population. Economic chaos and political disintegration seemed more likely. The 1950s were a period of apparent stagnation and mounting economic problems, when early dire predictions seemed to be fulfilled. Prophets of gloom and doom were disappointed by radical economic changes which began in the late 1950s. By the middle 1960s the rate of economic growth was more than double the rate of population growth; investment was approaching a healthy 20 percent, and savings exceeded 10 percent of domestic resources. Prices were stable, foreign exchange were being used with increasing effectiveness. Pakistan was widely regarded as one of the half dozen countries in the world with the greatest promise of steady development. In the face of its pitiable resource and capital endowment at independence, and in comparison with other countries, Pakistan's performance was outstanding.

While concluding the book Papanek wrote: "The economic performance of Pakistan in the last few years has been primarily the result of good economic management –sensible policies and plans. Most important has been Pakistan's pragmatic approach to the role of government and private enterprises".[2] Papanek's book, from which these extracts have been taken, was published in 1967, and only after four years of its publication, Pakistan was broken. Inequitable economic growth failed the country. Predictions of both Rosenstein-Rodan and Papanek proved wrong.

Undoubtedly, Pakistan enjoyed good economic indicators in 1960s to which Papanek has referred in his book. In real terms (1959–1960 prices), the value added in large-scale manufacturing grew 11-fold in 1967–1968 in comparison with 1949–1950. The national income figures indicate that during the said period, large-scale manufacturing grew in real terms by 172% or 13% per year.[3] Economic growth was, however, iniquitous and regional disparities gave rise to political instability and social unrest. The first edition of the 'Third Five year Plan', published in May 1965 but immediately withdrawn and suppressed, said: "There is no doubt that rapid industrial growth and capital formation, to some extent, has been based on squeezing the real wages of the laborers --the conflict between economic dynamism and social justice has become fairly sharp".[4]

There was a huge variation between per capita GDP in both Wings of the country. According to estimates, difference of per capita GDP in year 1969–1970 was over 60% at constant prices of 1959–1960. The disparity ratio in per capita GDP increased from 1.04 in 1949–1950 (Rs.324 against Rs. 310) to 1.61 (Rs.524 against Rs.314) in 1969–1970.[5] Not only the difference in per capita GDP between the two wings was huge, decline in real wages for both industrial and agricultural workers was also quite perceptible. The development strategy of 1960s, which aimed at high growth of national output, based on protected industrialization, financed through redistribution of resources away from agriculture, suppression of real wages, and in part financing through foreign aid, resulted in adverse income distribution effects.[6] Disparities were not restricted to regions alone. Interpersonal disparities also increased to dangerous proportions. Simply trickledown did not happen.

A detailed exposition, with separate concentration figures for 46 industrial economic power banks and insurance companies, is now fully documented.[7] The extremely uneven distribution of income and concentration of economic power resulting from economic growth of 1960s generated the 'problem of 22 families'. In an article published in Business Recorder in 1968, Dr. Mahbub Ul Haq wrote: "20 largest families controlled 66 percent of the total industrial effort of the country, 70 percent of the total insurance funds, and 80 percent of the total bank assets".[8]

In the late 1960s, there was a realization that a mere focus on economic growth was not sufficient and that the distribution aspect needed to be taken care of. The Planning Commission document, released in November 1968, with the title "The Socio-economic objectives of the Fourth Five Year Plan (1970–75)" confirms this assertion. The document said: "The present per capita income is still among the lowest in the world. It is estimated that about 75 percent of the total number of households receive an income less than Rs. 200 per month. The daily calorie intake is around 2100 per person compared to the minimum international standard of about 2600 calories. The average diet is quantitatively poor and qualitatively imbalanced. In a total population of 125 million, there are hardly 20 million who can read or write. There is still only one doctor to look after every 7000 persons. There are still 1.2 million families in urban areas who have no decent shelter over their heads".[9]

While highlighting the socio-economic objectives, the said document further emphasized that the Fourth Five Year Plan would, inter alia, be guided by the objective of reduction in inter-regional and intraregional disparities in per capita income by striking a viable synthesis between the claims of economic growth and social justice and by gearing the forces of economic and social change toward establishment of a just society. It was, however, very late to materialize such noble objective as severe disparities and economic exclusions had accelerated the movement of tectonic plates and the result was the separation of East Wing in 1971. Astonishingly, some 50 years later, according to an analysis conducted by PIDE, wealth in Karachi Stock Exchange (KSE), the biggest stock market of Pakistan, is largely owned and controlled by 31 families.[10]

A little caution! The argument here is not against economic growth. The argument rather is that economic growth has to be broad-based and inclusive. If divisions in the society become sharper as a result of growth, then it cannot be sustained for a longer period of time. It falters sooner or later and, with all probability, occurs in boom-bust cycles, as the experience of Pakistan amply vindicates. Before delineating the linkages among inclusiveness, stability, economic growth, et cetera, it would be appropriate to discuss as to why economic growth is required at all, so the message of the book is not misconstrued.

Dividends of Economic Growth

Growth phenomenon is not as old as Homo sapiens. For many centuries prior to the onset of Industrial Revolution, either there was no growth or it was very negligible. In the hunter-gatherer society or society characterized by the agricultural revolution, growth was a win-lose situation where one got rich at the expense of others as resources were almost fixed. The Malthusian doomsday scenario was predicted in the same context. The Industrial Revolution, which started in England around the year 1750, changed the entire landscape. Invention and application of new machines to the production process, development in communications and logistics, change in governance structures and management practices, and innovations altered the entire scene and in about two centuries, that is till 1950, average income in the countries now called developed economies had risen twenty times.[11]

One cannot directly see, smell, or touch economic growth. We, however, find it in the newspaper headlines and political debates. Economists and historians do research and publish books and papers on its determinants that is how economic growth can be enhanced. IMF and the World Bank forecast its short-term and long-term pace country-wise and for the globe. Despite its intangibility, it is omnipresent. It reflects itself in bricks and mortar, in schools, in hospitals, in kitchens, in health, in education, and in overall well-being of the people though it tells little about the rising inequality, that is distribution of said things in the society.[12] It is, however, now well-established that increasing the size of the GDP and creating wealth are important levers of prosperity. Sustained economic growth constitutes at least a necessary condition for poverty reduction and well-being. Economic growth is a type of 'god' worth worship in modern times.

Bhagwati and Panagariya, both believers in the primacy of the economic growth, raise some simple but interesting points, called myths, in *'Why Growth Matters'*. I have picked 'Myth 3' for highlighting the importance of economic growth. The proposition is: "Growth is not necessary for poverty alleviation; redistribution can do the job". On this point, rebuttal of Bhagwati and Panagariya is that the said proposition about growth may well have some relevance for developed countries as they have enjoyed the benefits of growth for more than a century. They, out of the riches generated by economic growth, were able to earn large revenues which they can use for anti-poverty programs. This proposition, however, does not hold for the developing countries whose overwhelming population is poor, they argue.

According to them even if it is assumed that politically it is feasible for the government of a developing country to massively redistribute, such redistribution shall have no tangible impact on poverty alleviation due to 'too many mouths' and 'too little' to redistribute. Poverty reduction is not one-shot affair, they emphasize. Governments need sustained efforts to attack poverty, as the salubrious effects of redistribution may vanish soon with a country's stagnant economic growth and rising population.[13] So, economic growth is important for poverty reduction and better living standards for the people. It works through multiple channels.

First, economic growth, that is increase in per capita income, gives an opportunity to the individuals to make their lives better by placing at their disposal more material resources and choices. They can improve their nutrition, can impart good education to their children, and can have access to health care. They can buy goods and services, and by consuming more, they boost aggregate demand which in turn contributes to economic growth. Second, growth in income of an individual enables him to impact the wider community. He can start a business and can hire services of others. He can provide loans to others for setting up businesses. Many small businesses in developing countries rely on individual investments because financial systems are not developed, or collateral requirements are high (which the new start-ups are unable to provide), or the procedures to obtain loans are cumbersome. He can even do charity.

An increase in income therefore has a multiplier effect, that is additional income earned by an individual will be transmitted in the economy in multiples of its original value. For example, if an individual gets additional income of $1 and he spends $0.8 out of it, the overall economy will get a boost of $5 through the multiplier effect. In this way, economic growth creates a 'virtuous cycle' for the overall economy.

Third, economic growth provides resources for the state through increase in taxes, which it can spend on public services like health care, education, and unemployment stipends. Fourth, economic growth enhances the quality of life by preserving democracy and transparent political structures. "Rights and freedoms can only exist if a society is able to hold government accountable. Growth allows society to sustain itself and to ensure accountability, but in the absence of growth, society weakens. In this way, economic stress creates the conditions for political upheaval, and at the extreme, the breakdown of liberal democratic institutions".[14]

Economic growth gives hope. It is like a social lubricant that helps ease tensions in the society. Societies with stagnant or low base growth cannot give hope to the younger generation of better economic future. Slow growth with widening inequality polarizes society and breeds distrust and hate. It was not an accident that the worst periods of intolerance in US history toward African Americans and immigrants in the post-Civil war period, the rise of Nazism in Germany following World War 1 (when the country was mired in both hyperinflation and stagnant growth), and rise of anti-immigrant sentiments in Continental Europe occurred when growth was stagnant and people were losing hope in future.[15]

Economic growth not only improves material well-being or living standards of the people, but it also shapes their social, political, and moral character. It fosters greater opportunity, tolerance for diversity, social mobility, commitment to fairness, and dedication to democracy. In this sense, economic growth is a positive externality due to the positive impact of rising living standards on the public character of the society.[16] And if it is a positive externality, then there is a clear role for the public policy in creating and sustaining economic growth which means that public interventions both for increasing the pie and its distribution shall be required.

Fifth, economic growth reduces poverty and hunger. A much-cited study in this regard is the one undertaken by Dollar & Kraay which finds that when average incomes increase that is growth takes place, average incomes of the poorest fifth quintile of the society also rise proportionately. According to this study, relationship between growth of mean income and growth of the income of the poor is one-to-one.[17] The results of this study provide some credence to trickle-down theory. The negative relation between economic growth and absolute poverty is consistent to some extent.

The growth elasticities of aggregate poverty, that is the proportional change in absolute poverty incidence with respect to the rate of growth of real GDP per capita, however, show huge variation among countries. For example, an investigation finds that elasticities of poverty incidence are −0.9, −3.8, −0.7, −2.1, −2.0, and −1.4, respectively, for India, China, Philippines, Malaysia, Thailand, and Indonesia.[18] It means that the strength of relationship between economic growth and poverty reduction shall depend on social, economic, and political structures of the society. There would be cases where the poor would benefit tremendously from economic growth, but there may be societies where economic growth may enrich only those who are already rich and may even impoverish people.

In the foreword to Karl Polyani's '*The Great Transformation*', Joseph Stiglitz pertinently points out that: "popular doctrines of trickle-down economics-that all, including the poor, benefit from growth—have little historical support. —There is also plenty of evidence from the modern era supporting historical evidence: growth may lead to an increase in poverty".[19] Conscious efforts and policies are needed to make growth work, especially for the poor, as markets left to themselves often do not lead to equitable and efficient outcomes.

Sixth, economic growth frees people from disease and drudgery. The ancestors of the people who are currently citizens of developed countries lived in miserable conditions when there was no growth or little growth. Refrigerators, washing machines, running water, and many other innovations, the result of economic prosperity, have reduced the drudgery of old times. The USA was not as prosperous and developed as it is today. According to some estimates, a typical North Carolina housewife had to carry water 8 to 10 times daily (like many in the far-flung rural areas of Pakistan today). Over the course of one year, she walked around 48 miles for bringing more than 36 tons of water.[20] Seventh, economic growth helps control population growth. "The typical rate of child mortality in the richest fifth of countries is 4 out of every 1000 births; in the poorest fifth of countries, it is 200 out of every 1000 births. Parents in the poorest countries are fifty times more likely to know grief rather than joy from the birth of a child. Researchers have found that a 10 percent decrease in income is associated with about a 6 percent higher infant mortality rates--At lower incomes disease is more dangerous because of lower medical knowledge, lower nutrition, and lower access of medical care".[21]

Economic development and not condoms are the best contraceptives in a country like Pakistan where population explosion is a big issue. "Suppose a country does not want to lower population growth, for whatever reason. There is one statistical regularity that everyone agrees on, and this is the negative relationship between per capita income and population growth. Parents in rich counties have fewer babies than parents in poor countries. The poorest fifth of countries have on average 6.5 births per woman, while the richest fifth of countries have on average 1.7 births per woman".[22] Economic growth reflects itself in the lives of the people if it is inclusive and broad-based.

Inclusiveness of Growth

The problem of growth in Pakistan can be attributed to number of factors like low inclusiveness, low productivity, lack of growth culture, narrow production structures (lack of economic complexity), a disconnect between growth and development, et cetera. One common point among these variables is low human development, which in fact is the binding constraint on economic growth. Low inclusiveness simply means that the majority has been left behind in the process of development. High illiteracy, a large number of out of school children, high learning poverty, poor health indicators, widespread poverty, sharp inequalities of all kinds, low intergenerational mobility, et cetera, are manifestations of low inclusiveness and neglect of human resource development.

Similarly, low productivity is also a correlate of low human resource development. Again, low economic complexity is indicative of low innovation and dearth of ideas. So the argument is that human resources, which are the ultimate source of economic growth, remain badly neglected in Pakistan. Sustainable economic growth is possible only through investment in human resource development. There is a need to understand the relationship between inclusion and growth. It is as simple as the story of a household. If all the members of a household are working and earning, the household's income will rise.

On the contrary, if one or two members of a family work whereas the rest are idle, the household's income will remain below the potential. If the earner gets ill or meets an accident, there would be a big shock to the household income, and the family may transit to poverty due to such a shock. Money brings economic power, that is choices to consume. If some household members are excluded, family decisions about spending and saving may not be democratic, and a lack of voice may yield resentment among the excluded members of the family.

A similar line of argumentation applies to nations. More dispersion of economic prosperity brings stability, both political and social, which in turn promotes long-term economic growth. Inclusionary policies promote economic growth, though the case of economic growth leading to inclusion is a bit tricky. Economic growth may not necessarily promote inclusion if it is not broad-based and inclusive. Focusing on 'growth alone strategy' creates economic and social disparities, resulting in stress and frustration among the people. People get disillusioned about the future of their children and think that all economic growth is unfair and serves only the rich.

Inclusiveness and fairness are deeply connected. We, as humans, care a lot about fairness. It is the sense of fairness ingrained in our psychological makeup that compels all Bollywood and Hollywood movie makers to invariably bring the villain of the movie to justice at the end as not doing so may hurt our sense of fairness and we may leave the cinema hall unhappy. After all, all entertainment is for enjoyment and not for unhappiness.

We make sacrifices if we are convinced from inside that our children and grandchildren will be better off as a result. We will, however, not do this if sacrifices are shared broadly but opportunities are not. The most important dimension of inclusiveness is the belief that no one will be left out of the growth process. Yuval Noah Harari, in his well-acclaimed book '*Sapiens*' postulates that it was trust in the future that triggered economic growth after remaining frozen for so long in history. The discovery of 'credit' and its use were basically a manifestation of trust in the future. "The problem in the previous eras was not that no one had the idea or knew how to use it (credit). It was that people seldom wanted to extend much credit because they did not trust that future would be better than the present. They generally believed that times past had been better than their own times and that the future would be worse, or at best much the same".[23]

Inclusion generally has four broad objectives, that is benefit sharing, opportunity, participation, and empowerment.[24] Benefit sharing means that incomes across all income groups, regions, and ethnic communities would witness an increase as a result of economic growth. The benefits of growth would spread widely among the society, and inequality shall be managed through public policies and redistribution. Individuals or groups would not be left out of the growth process to keep frustration and envy under check so they do not ruin the very cause of economic growth.

Albert Hirschman, a celebrated development economist, compared the process of growth to a two-lane traffic jam. If traffic in one lane starts moving, drivers in the other lane feel relieved and comfortable in the hope that their lane will also move soon. But if the drivers remain stuck in the traffic jam for too long, they will get frustrated. And the other lane thus becomes a provocation, not a consolation.[25] Both equity and equality of opportunity need to be taken care of, so no individual remains entrapped in poverty and low income due to his birth circumstances, like being born in poor family or in poor geographical region, or being born with some disability, or some other bad luck scenario. Historical experience shows that high economic growth on a sustainable basis generally occurred in countries that took care of inclusiveness by ensuring the equitable distribution of the cake through instruments of public service provision and human resource development besides reducing initial inequalities by way of the distribution of productive assets like land.

The second component is opportunity. Access to opportunity means that quality public services in health and education are available to all, even to those belonging to the poorest quintile of the population. And everybody would have full chances to cultivate his talent and acquire skills to lead a productive life. The third component, 'participation', means participation in economic life through gainful employment, access to credit, et cetera, for starting a business. Empowerment, the fourth component, goes beyond economic well-being. It emphasizes a strong system of governance and public sector accountability where people are free to voice their preferences.

Almost all countries have seen at one point or another acceleration of economic growth but accelerations are reversed after some time leaving countries rather worse in some cases than they were prior to the onset of acceleration. The explanation for such reversals lies in the fact that growth acceleration can occur even under extractive institutions, but it cannot be maintained without the inclusion of people in the process and the pie. Once growth starts, it can be maintained for a longer time only under inclusive political and economic institutions.[26] Pakistan's boom-bust cycle of growth is a case in point. If we assume that a growth rate >5% represents a boom while <5% a bust, we then had total 30 episodes (years) of boom and 29 episodes of bust during 1961–2021 (see Table 1.1).

Five episodes, three of consecutive booms and two of low growth, in particular, merit mention during the said period. During 1963–1970, 1980–1988, and 2003–2006, Pakistan had consecutive growth rates greater than 5% per annum, with respective average growth rates of 7.75%, 7.08%, and 6.44% for the said periods. Till 1989, pace of growth was above what is considered a good economic growth rate.[27] The ghosts of a low spiral started haunting Pakistan when a long-spell of IMF programs started in 1989. The decade of the 1990s was a 'lost decade' with an average growth rate of less than 4%. The story of growth in Pakistan is overall a wane and wax story but since the 1990s it is a story of just lows.

IMF policies since 1989, if not fully, are at least partly responsible for the low spiral of economic growth. IMF conditionality generates a trap that despite all the semantics of 'conditionality with a human face' proves detrimental to long-term growth. Austerity and micromanagement by the IMF tie the hands of the government. Sufficient Public investments do not flow toward health, education, and human development due to austerity with the result that growth itself decelerates. Inclusive growth is associated with human development, employment generation, productivity enhancement, and an equitable distribution of income and assets. It provides foundation for the social justice.

Ian Talbot, one of Europe's historians on South Asia, while emphasizing the need to recognize the deep nexus between social justice and sustainability of growth, very pertinently remarks: "Economic policy would recognize that past rapid growth, although giving Pakistan temporary advantage over its neighbors, had failed to raise it to middle-income status because it had neglected human development. Pakistan lacked in the long-term the human capital to take advantage of globalization. Requirements of international competitiveness as much as of justice and social cohesion should place the tackling of inequality at the heart of future growth models".[28]

Table 1.1 Boom-bust growth

Growth >5%												
Years	*1961*	*1963–1970*	*1973*	*1976*	*1978*	*1980–1988*	*1991–1992*	*2003–2006*	*2016*	*2018*	*2021*	*Total*
Episodes of growth (consecutive years)	1	8	1	1	1	9	2	4	1	1	1	30
Average growth (%)	5.99	7.75	7.06	5.16	8.05	7.08	6.39	6.44	5.53	6.15	6.49	2.40
Low growth <5%												
Years	*1962*	*1971–1972*	*1977*	*1979*	*1989–1990*	*1988–1902*	*2007–2017*	*2019–2020*	*Total*			
Episodes of growth (consecutive years)	1	2	1	1	2	9	11	2	29			
Average growth (%)	4.48	0.88	3.95	3.76	4.71	3.37	3.45	0.61	0.87			

Source Pakistan GDP growth (annual %) World Bank Data (data.worldbank.org)

The experience of other countries also does not vindicate the proposition that growth alone is sufficient for human development and poverty alleviation. India, which has shown rapid growth on a sustainable basis for a period of over three decades, is a case in point. The quality of life of hundreds of millions of Indians is far from satisfactory, as argued in detail by Sen and Dreze in '*Uncertain Glory*'. Half of Indian households do not have access to toilets and have to resort to open defecation. Undernourishment is common, and hundreds of millions lack good health care, decent work conditions, and warm clothes in the winter.[29] Similar account is presented by Ashoka Mody in '*India is Broken*'. According to Professor Mody, a vast majority of Indians live in a state of underemployment, and the provision of public goods such as health, education, clean air, water, et cetera, is woefully bad. He writes: "In the India of 2020, the Hindu-Muslim divide and egregious economic inequalities were reverberating echoes of Bengal in the 1940s. And disconcertingly, despite decades of economic progress, the echoes also sounded in the economic desperation of the reverse trek from the city to the village. The ongoing reverse trek revealed the continued risk of sudden income loss, health catastrophe, and even the loss of even woeful living spaces: it revealed an India that was broken for hundreds of millions of Indians".[30]

Interestingly, growth, as it is currently measured worldwide, does not take into account the aspect of inclusiveness. The very method of its measurement is not democratic. To make the point, consider an example (borrowing from an article by Kemal Dervis) of a hypothetical country inhabited by 10 citizens with a total income of $190, where 9 citizens have an income of $10 each and the tenth citizen enjoys an income of $100. And let us assume that there is no income from abroad and GDP is equal to national income, that is US$ 190. Now assume that all nine citizens experience no growth in income while the income of the 10th citizen increases by 10% in a given accounting period (say in a year).

What are the implications of the traditional method of growth accounting? The income of the country increases from $190 to $ 200, thus posting an annual growth of 5.26%, a reasonable economic growth for a country despite no change in the income or prosperity of 90% of the population. Let us change the calculation method of growth in GDP and assign equal weight to each individual in the country. The growth rate then would be weighted sum of nine 0% growth rates and one 10% growth rate, each weighted at one-tenth, which means the total growth rate is just 1% if measured democratically. The implicit practice in vogue for calculating growth rate involves the principle of 'one dollar, one vote' and not 'one man, one vote'.[31]

The existing method of calculating growth is thus inherently opposed to the concept of inclusiveness. The traditional yardstick that is average income or per capita income is, therefore, now under criticism as a measure of well-being. It is simply the size of the economy (created through growth) divided by the human population of the country. A simple trap of averages! Growth does not tell who is benefiting more and who is being left behind in the process. An industrialist may earn hundred times more than the people employed by him to run his enterprise. Those hired by him to maintain the accounts earn many times more than the security guards employed at the gates of his business or office premises. And a security guard definitely earns more than a casual laborer. But theoretically, all are earning US$ 1505 (approx.), average per capita income of Pakistan in the year 2021 according to the World Bank. If the rich are getting richer as a result of growth while the typical average person in the country is working harder and harder just to make both ends meet, then people shall question the very rationale of economic growth as to what growth is all about.

Widening inequalities do not make people happy. Happiness generally depends not on their absolute income (or wealth), but on their relative income compared to those around them. Human beings are psychologically hardwired to make comparisons. Empirics also confirm the wiring of human brains. In a research experiment, the employees of California University were given information about the salaries of their peers to study the effect of such information on job satisfaction and job search. The employees who discovered that they were being paid below the median became less satisfied, and the likelihood of their searching for a new job suddenly increased. No change was observed in the attitudes of those who were earning above the median.[32]

An experiment on monkeys also revealed similar results. Two capuchin monkeys, trained to do small chores in exchange for cucumber slices, were perfectly satisfied with their reward. But when one of them was given grapes instead of cucumber slices, the other became angry. "A capuchin might perform simple tasks for cucumber slices but if she sees a neighbor being rewarded with grapes for similar work, she will expect raise. Keep paying cucumbers and she will throw the gratuity in your face. Primatologists discovered the flame of justice flickering in simian hearts more than a decade ago, when many people still believed that the outsize fortunes of the rich mattered little as long as everyone else had enough".[33] Inclusiveness, democracy, and economic stability are linked. Participatory regimes deliver better for long-term economic growth and democracy produces greater stability, handles adverse shocks better, and delivers better on distributional outcomes.[34]

Socio-Political Stability

Economic policy in democracy is risk-avoiding relative to policies in non-democratic setups. The voters being risk-averse penalize an incumbent government for economic volatility, so in democracy, a government cannot politically afford to opt for policies likely to induce economic volatility.[35] Further, non-democracies generally have high barriers to entry of new firms and suffer from high industrial concentration. Growth swings are less in democratic countries. And democracy and industrial diversification are positively related. Empirics suggest that 10% increase in the index of democracy reduces the probability of experiencing a growth reversal by around 2%.[36]

Democracy has several virtues. For example, citizens have a voice in democracy. It acts as a safety valve against violence and frustration. All citizens can vote, so governments are motivated to invest in people at large rather than in small elite.[37] So theoretically speaking, democracy empowers people by giving them voice. It does not safeguard the interests of the elite alone rather it ensures collective good of the people. But some questions like the follows are often missed in the debate on democracy particularly in the countries like Pakistan. Is democracy just a political concept? Has it nothing to do with the economic and social lives of the people? Is the principle of 'one man, one vote' sufficient for the sustainability of democracy?

The remarks of Dr. B.R. Ambedkar, though in Indian context, are very apt regarding the answer to these questions even in our case. He said: "On the 26th of January, 1950, we are going to enter into a life of contradictions. In politics, we will be recognizing the principle of one man one vote, and one vote one value. In our social and economic life, we shall, by reason of our social and economic structure, continue to deny the principle of one man one value. How long shall we continue to deny equality in our social and economic life? If we continue it for long, we will do so only by putting our political democracy in peril. We must remove the contradiction at the earliest possible moment, or else those who suffer from inequality will blow up the structure of political democracy".[38]

Democracy is more than elections. Real and sustainable democracy is not possible without appreciating its economic and social aspects. One of the prime reasons for the failure of democracies is too much emphasis on elections and too little on its other essential features.[39] "When democracy fails to deliver economically and politically, perhaps it is to be expected that some people will look for authoritarian solutions. As long as the military remains the ultimate arbiter, these groups (political) focus their strategies on military rather than on one another", says Dani Rodrik.[40] The sustainability of democracy mainly depends on its capacity to incorporate more societal sectors and distribute public goods among the citizenry, meaning how inclusive the system makes itself with the passage of time is the real test of democracy. The history of the evolution of democracy testifies to this assertion.

For example, in the UK, not only the disenfranchised sections of society were given voting rights as the democracy evolved rather broad-based reforms were initiated side by side in the nineteenth century by Prime Ministers Disraeli and Gladstone (though belonging to different political parties) in the spheres of education, public health, and social security. Pakistan's situation is quite paradoxical. Rather than making the people stakeholders in the democratic system, the base of democracy has remained narrow due to an inequitable distribution of resources and low policy focus on human development. Economic development involving industrialization, urbanization, high education, and a steady increase in the economic well-being of the people, is a basic condition for democracy.

The democratic system also depends much on its effectiveness (actual performance of the political system as to what extent it satisfies the expectations of the people) and legitimacy (capacity of a political system to make people believe that existing institutions are the most appropriate).[41] Institutions also explain variations in the levels of instability across countries. According to this line of argumentation, extractive institutions inherited from the past with widespread corruption and weak rule of law are responsible for high volatility and distortionary macroeconomic policies.[42]

Empirics confirm that in countries and in time periods with a high propensity for government collapse, growth is significantly lower than otherwise.[43] Political instability is also connected to policy instability as political instability creates uncertainty with regard to policies and policy-makers. Firms and businesses adopt 'wait-and-watch' strategy and do not invest. The instability of 'polity and policy' thus has adverse consequences for economic growth. Empirics also confirm the proposition. For example, the results of an investigation based on data from 169 countries suggest that political instability reduces economic growth significantly.[44]

In order to address the problem of political instability its root causes need to be addressed which are the socio-economic exclusion of the people from the process of development and the fragility of institutions. And these two sets of factors are connected as in a society where the majority is excluded from socio-political and economic life, institutions would also be weak. "Social inclusion matters for itself. But it also matters because it is the foundation for shared prosperity and because social exclusion is simply too costly. There are substantial costs—social, political and economic—to not addressing the exclusion of entire groups of people".[45]

Social cohesion is a prerequisite for a politically stable society. A cohesive society is the one "which works towards the well-being of all its members, fights exclusion and marginalization, creates a sense of belonging, promotes trust, and offers its members the opportunity of upward social mobility".[46] Social inclusion (negatively correlated with income inequality), social capital (trust and civic engagement), and social mobility (the degree to which people can change their position in society) are three pillars of social cohesion. Social cohesion makes the competitiveness of a nation sustainable.[47] Cohesive societies are politically stable. Policies which allow everybody in society to share its prosperity are the basis of social cohesion. It is an important driver of long-term sustainable growth which Pakistan needs the most to meet the needs and aspirations of its rising population. Pakistan requires a growth rate of above 7% for about three to four decades to rise to the middle-level income country.

Magic of 7%

Seventy is a tricky number to predict the future income of a nation on the basis of economic growth rate of today. Divide 70 by growth rate (by the absolute number, for example, if the growth rate is 1% then divide by 1) and we will get the number of years required to double the income of a country. Suppose a country is growing at 1%, it will take 70 years to double the income. On the contrary if it sustains growth rate of 7%, the income will double in a decade. In 1970, Pakistan's per capita income was US$172.5 which in a period of over half a century grew to US$1505.[48] Had Pakistan grown at a sustainable growth rate of 7% since 1970, Pakistan's per capita income in 2020 would have been over US$5520 which means that by 2030 it would have entered the list of high middle-income countries ($10,000 per year).

Just one more doubling would have turned the economy into an advanced economy (with a per capita income of $20,000) once a country achieves high middle-income level.[49] Quite interestingly, it may take over half a century with sustainable growth of 7% to achieve a middle-income level but it takes just one decade after that to become an advanced economy if it sustains the speed. Overall, 50–60 years are required to transition from a poor to an advanced economy with a growth rate of 7%.

Pakistan's average growth rate for 2001–2010 hovered around 4.28%, and during 2011–2021, the average growth rate stood at 4.39%. If Pakistan continues to grow, say at 4%, it will take around 70 years to get to the per capita income of an advanced economy that is US$20,000 which simply means that at this speed of growth, none of us (who are alive today) or those who will be born in the next 4–5 years (the average life expectancy in Pakistan is 66 as per 2020 data of the World Bank) will see Pakistan as a developed economy.

In case Pakistan unlocks its potential by removing binding constraints to economic growth and starts growing at the rate of 7% and sustains this growth rate, then with a base per capita income of US$1505, Pakistan is expected to achieve the level of a high middle-income country in three decades and may vie to become an advanced economy by 2060 (see Table 1.2).

And how would it be possible to put the country on the trajectory of above 7% of growth? Perhaps at the top is human resource development. A synthesis of macro (economic growth, structural transformation)

Table 1.2 Growing at 7%

Year	*Per capita (US$)*
2021	1,505
2031	3,010
2041	6,020
2051	12,040
2060	>20,000

and micro (health, education, microcredit, asset transfers, etc.) factors is required to create opportunities, achieve improvements in the lives of the people, and make growth sustainable. The big push for poverty reduction will come from economic growth. Lant Pritchett, based on 633 observations for 141 countries, concludes that we may expect to high reduction in the number of people living below the poverty line when a country moves to higher levels of median income as no country reached the level where 75% of its households lived on more than $5.5 per day until its median income exceeded $1045 annually.[50] China is a pertinent example which pulled more than 850 million people out of poverty in a period of about four decades.

Growth is, however, not a sufficient condition as the impact of economic growth on the lives of the people depends on how the income generated by economic growth is distributed among the people (income distribution) and how public revenues raised by the government are spent (whether on guns or on schools). Both pace and pattern matter. Trickledown does not happen automatically particularly in countries where initial socio-economic inequalities are sharp. A rising tide may not necessarily lift all boats given the deep inequalities of income and wealth. The process of growth can be initiated even under extractive institutions but long-term sustainable growth would not be possible under such institutions. "Igniting economic growth and sustaining it are somewhat different enterprises. Ignoring the distinction between these two tasks leaves reformers saddled with impossibly ambitious, undifferentiated, and impractical policy agendas", argued Dani Rodrik in one of his papers.[51] If the majority of the people or sections of the society are left behind, economic growth policies how best they may be shall not sustained in the long run.

Growth and Development

Economists have treated economic growth and equity as a chicken and egg problem, that is first increase the size of the pie and then distribute it. It is simply an old trickledown mantra which the history, according to Stiglitz, does not support. Economic growth and equity go hand in hand. An equitable growth would not leave out or exclude people from the opportunities created by economic growth. Several interventions can be made for growth with equity. For example, the promotion of small business enterprises is one of the areas. Small businesses are considered growth engine of the economy as they provide jobs, foster entrepreneurship, and provide depth to the industrial base of the economy.[52] They, however, face difficulties in obtaining credit and accessing public services. Without access to finance and an enabling environment, it is hard for small businesses to execute their business plans, no matter how fancy and innovative those plans are. We can teach a fisherman some techniques for catching fish but it would be difficult for him to put the acquired technique to practice unless he has a net.

Picking winners would, in all probability, not prove to be a good public policy in Pakistan (and in other developing countries) due to weak state capacity. It is hard to tax the rents of the winners and make optimum use of such rents, if collected, for public service provision to the people. Some countries like South Korea picked up winners and put the country on the trajectory of development through that strategy. The strategy of picking up winners was successful in those countries due to host of factors and conditions such as low initial inequalities (for example due to land reforms), the capacity of the state to tax rents, and putting human resource development at the center—stage of all development. These conditions are lacking in Pakistan.

The argument that restricting competition in an industry or sector of the economy on the ground that having too many firms will fragment the industry and leave none big enough to be efficient for capitalizing on the economies of size has got economic logic theoretically, but this line of thinking may turn out to be fallacious when put into practice. Entry of new firms with new ideas, products, and technologies brings productivity gains that are greater than the potential static efficiency gains of restricting entry of firms. The monopoly rights impede the adoption of new technology and some empirics suggest that the elimination of such rights is expected to increase output three times without any increase in inputs.[53]

Unfortunately, Pakistan has not been able to make exports a major engine of economic growth. Its exports are substantially below the potential and the worrying part is that contribution of exports to GDP in terms of percentage has decreased.[54] Pakistan's potential, considering its characteristics like size, level of development, location, and factor endowments, is estimated at around US$88.1 billion worth of merchandize, almost four times its current level of exports.[55] The opportunity cost of missing exports of Pakistan is around 893,000 jobs and US$1.74 billion in foregone taxes. Besides factors (responsible for low exports) like anti-export bias, poor infrastructure, bad institutional quality, poor trade facilitation, et cetera, part of the problem, generally ignored, is the lack of policies to incentivize and support small exporters.

Pakistan adopted various policies like duty drawback and rebates, duty-free import of input goods and machinery, establishment of export processing zones, et cetera. The issue with all exemption schemes for importers and exporters is that they do not benefit all the firms. Their impact is highly skewed toward larger firms. "The top 100 firms in Pakistan accounted for roughly three quarters of duty-exempted value and only five firms accounted for about a third of that total".[56] An analysis of the profile of exporters in terms of export volume shows that around 50% of exporters in Pakistan just export 1% of merchandize.[57] Their contribution to exports is little but they have a comparative advantage over local traders in the sense that they are exposed to export documentation and dynamics of trading across borders. Since the number of small and medium-sized exporters is reasonably high compared to big exporting firms, policy focus on such exporters, through removal of constraints on credit, et cetera, shall help unlock their potential and help increase export growth. And such a growth would be comparatively more inclusive.

Similarly, policy focus on small agricultural farms and rural non-farm economy (shall be discussed in detail in Chapter 8), and effective land reforms (case made out in Chapter 7) are some areas for ensuring equitable growth and poverty alleviation in rural areas. The Southeast Asian experience of development suggests that land reforms were vital in the initial stages of development at least from three angles.[58] First, land reforms enhanced rural productivity and incomes of the rural people. Consequently, domestic savings increased. Second, higher incomes resulted in higher domestic demand for goods. Third, redistribution of income contributed to political stability, an important factor for economic growth. Empirics also suggest that land reforms have a significant and positive impact on income growth and the accumulation of human and physical capital. Land reforms introduced in India are a case in point.[59]

Skewed power structures also explain the wax and wane pattern of economic growth. Inclusive institutions (and institutions are one of the determinants of long-term growth) evolve and become strong in egalitarian societal arrangements. In Pakistan, at least four axes of exclusion can be identified visibly: regional exclusion, exclusion from access to land, exclusions from public services, and gender-based exclusions. In Punjab, the divide is very clear between the northern and southern parts due to uneven development. In Sindh, it is evident in the shape of rural–urban disparities. In KPK, there is a clear divide in development indicators and priorities between settled districts and tribal areas.

Due to concentration of power in a small minority, institutions have not become inclusive and pro-people, with the result that the majority of the people do not, in the true sense, consider them stakeholders in the affairs of the state. The path dependence (same civil service structure, same judicial structure, same land ownership structure, etc.) is visible in every walk of life. Several critical moments came in the history of Pakistan but all the 'critical junctures' were missed due to deeply entrenched power of the powerful elite.[60]

Education and health care systems are inequitable (shall be discussed in detail, respectively, in Chapters 4 and 5). The justice system is noisy and enforcement of contracts is weak. Enforcement of laws is differential as men are sometimes more powerful than the law. It is difficult to improve governance and ensure accountability in public sector institutions unless people are empowered economically, socially, and politically. Poor governance is a big source of instability, just like socio-economic exclusionary policies. "That governance in Pakistan is far from perfect is evident in many ways. Relations between the state and the people in Pakistan are weak. Service delivery to people is poor, if they exist at all, institutions are weak and law and order precarious. Various parts of the state cannot seem to work with one another. Poor governance increases frustration and reduces state legitimacy in the eyes of the people. It creates space for alternative ideologies. Many instances can be cited in Pakistan where weak governance results in frustration. There is some evidence to show that lack of governance is also a factor in the spread of extremism".[61]

A survey conducted by PIDE gives some startling results about the disillusionment of the people with the existing state of affairs. Overall, 37% of the population of Pakistan wants to leave the country if they get the opportunity. Around 40% in urban areas and 36% in rural Pakistan want to vote with their feet. The desire to leave is highest in Balochistan (42%), followed by KPK, Sindh, and Punjab.[62] Results of another survey[63] conducted by the International Organization for Migration (IOM) indicate that 39% of the sample population decided to migrate due to lack of jobs and livelihood opportunities whereas some 14% did so due to lack of quality education. The most worrying part of the migration story is that there has been a massive surge in the migration of highly qualified people from Pakistan since 2005. The unemployment rate for engineers is estimated at 23.5% and a similar situation prevails for other professional degree holders.[64]

Lack of opportunities, desire for respect, and poor quality of public services are three top factors that flicker the desire to leave the country. Opportunities come with economic growth. A nation needs to rise above the basic economic threshold to meet the basic needs of its people. Economic growth on a sustainable basis, as happened in the case of the Asian Tigers, is a necessary condition to improve the well-being of a nation. An empty stomach does not make one a patriot. People need environment and better environment to realize their potential. Employment provides not only income but also helps people realize their social needs through networking. A bad job is better than no job.

The distribution of material resources also matters. The happiest people in the world reside in societies with low Ginis and Palmas (for example Norway and Sweden). Variables like health and quality of governance having high correlation with the well-being of the people are also correlated with national income. 'Respect', as referred to in the PIDE survey, is reflective of the desire for an overall judicious environment in the country which we find lacking due to poor governance, weak rule of law, and elitist structures. "Good governance and sustainable development are indivisible. Without good governance- without rule of law, predictable administration, legitimate power and responsive regulation- no amount of funding, no amount of charity will set us on the path of prosperity"[65] (Fig. 1.1).

It would be hard for a state to acquire legitimacy, in a globalized world, without prioritizing quality public goods like education, public health, law and order, and justice. Practically, provision of public services is selective and class-based. The rich can buy their way out (through gated communities and private guards for ensuring the security of life and property, private schools, private hospitals, etc.), but the poor cannot. They have to suffer harassment and humiliation by the very state functionaries who are tasked with their security and well-being.[66] There are multiple factors for this state of affairs. But lack of political legitimacy of the state

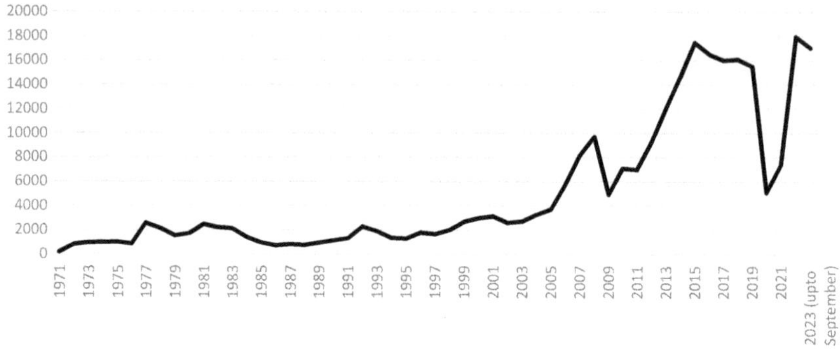

Fig. 1.1 Migration of highly qualified people (*Source* Bureau of Emigration & Overseas Employment, Pakistan)

is perhaps the prime reason. The governments generally seek legitimacy, from small but influential groups of people, through doling out favors and by providing them with opportunities of rent-seeking. The majority remains neglected. "The way people interrelate with one another, the way they perceive national issues and their role in affecting them, and the priority they assign to personal ties and group identification are all parts of the matrix of a society and indicators of its social cohesion. Until Pakistanis can come up with an inner commitment to a cause—which in Pakistan's history has been fairly rare outside of kinship circles—little can be done or will be done to serve the wider society impartially".[67]

The Scandinavian and East Asian countries (like South Korea) were able to provide universal access to basic public services when their per capita GDP was lower than that of Pakistan. The issue is more of will than wallet. The secret of the economic success of these countries lies in the prioritization of human development. By investing in people, a virtuous cycle is developed between economic growth and development where investment in human resources increases productivity, which in turn boosts economic growth. Further, it would not be possible to sustain the support of the people for the growth-enhancing policies, without making people stakeholders or beneficiaries of the growth. The goal of economic growth remains elusive if it is not integrated with development. Education (both quantity and quality), health, material well-being, livelihoods, the availability of employment opportunities, and decent living are important. For long-term sustainable growth, taking care of said dimensions of human resource development is highly significant. The binding constraints on economic growth imposed by deeper factors like institutions, geography, et cetera, (discussion in the ensuing chapter) can be overcome through focus on human resource development.

CHAPTER 2

How Deep Are the Deeper Determinants?

Debate on the role of institutions in economic growth and development, in modern times, started in 1990 when North wrote '*Institutions, Institutional Change, and Economic Performance*'. He defined institutions as "rules of the game", and "humanly devised constraints that shape human interaction".[1] Humanly devised constraints can be informal (sanctions, taboos, customs, traditions, and codes of conduct) as well as formal (constitutions, laws, property rights, etc.). The constraints can be in the form of prohibitions (that is what not to do) or conditional permissions (that is under what conditions certain activities can be undertaken by certain individuals). Institutions impact the performance of economies through their effect on the costs of exchange and production. They reduce uncertainty and create order by establishing a stable structure for human interaction, as North further emphasizes. Institutions are the creation of human beings. They evolve, change, and can be altered. Radical changes are rare and result from big historical events like conquest or revolution, North elaborates.

Later, economists tested the validity of the claim that institutions are the primary driver of economic development and growth. The key issue about the primacy of institutions as the ultimate source of long-term growth was how to empirically prove that institutions planted long ago, say 200 years ago, explain the economic prosperity or misery of today. Acemoglu and his colleagues came up with a novel empirical strategy to

J. Nasir, *Development Challenges of Pakistan*,
https://doi.org/10.1007/978-981-97-3064-3_2

prove the primacy of institutions for economic growth. They analyzed the colonizers' mortality rates for the Asian and African colonies and found out that in colonized countries where the settlers' mortality rates were high, institutions are poorer today, and these countries have lower per capita GDP. Why did a colonial power create different institutions in its colonies? Why did Britain create extractive institutions in the Indian subcontinent but inclusive institutions in the USA, Canada, and Australia?

The argument of Acemoglu and his colleagues is that in colonies where the environment, proxied by high mortality rates, for settling the colonizers on a permanent basis was not hospitable, the colonizers did not set up inclusive institutions. For example, in colonies where malaria was rampant (tropical regions), the heat was intense, or there were some other diseases against which the colonizers had no immunity, their only purpose was to "extract and leave". So in such colonies, extractive institutions emerged, which persist to this day. Besides many African countries, the Indian subcontinent is a case in point.

Based on soldier mortality rates from 1700 to 1900, Acemoglu et al. write: "The annual mortality rates of local troops serving with the British Army in Bengal and Madras were respectively 11 and 13 in 1,000. These numbers are quite comparable to, in fact lower than, the annual mortality rates of British troops serving in Britain, which were approximately 15 in 1000. In contrast, the mortality rates of British troops serving in these colonies were much higher because of their lack of immunity. For example, mortality rates in Bengal and Madras for British troops were between 70 and 170 in 1000".[2] There are several other investigations undertaken by the researchers that support the persistence of institutions implanted in the distant past by the colonizers.

The Fingerprints of Institutions

An analysis of colonial land revenue collection systems in India shows that areas where proprietary rights were given to the landlords (Zamindari System) have significantly lower agricultural productivity and investments in health and education even today compared to areas where other revenue collection systems that are *Raiyatwari* (cultivator-based) and *Mahalwari* (village-based)[3] were in place. The plausible channel through which the landlord system continues to have an impact is inequality. In areas with the Zamindari system, landlords enjoyed a great deal of economic and political power and were free to fix rates and collect revenue from one village or cluster of villages. These areas inherited an unequal land distribution in 1947.

The extractive nature of institutions, where political and economic power was concentrated in the landlords, continues to cast its shadows post-independence. Sokoloff and Engerman have also looked into the role of institutions in the persistence of inequality in Latin American nations.[4] Their thesis is that inequality in wealth, human capital, and political power in Latin American countries owes itself to the factor endowments of the respective colonies. The colonies in Central and South America had a high marginal product-to-labor ratio which is vindicated by the fact that a large number of migrants from Europe traveled to these colonies despite high transportation costs.

A large number of slaves were transported into these colonies from Africa from the year 1500 to the end of the eighteenth century. The transportation of a large number of slaves to these colonies shows that the said colonies were rich as slaves were moved to areas where they were more productive due to the competitive international market for slaves at that time. These slaves were employed mainly on sugar plantations. Large fortunes created by sugar plantations and an overwhelming population of 'black and slave' created huge disparities in human capital in Southern America. In contrast, in the Northern American region, progressive institutions evolved.

The result was that both regions took different trajectories of development which persist to this day. This thesis brings another point referred to as 'reversal of fortune' to the fore. The countries of the southern region were rich in the past, as evident from the rich factor endowments, but things changed as time went by. Now countries in the southern region have far less per capita income compared with the northern part that is the USA and Canada. Shashi Tharoor in '*Inglorious Empire*' makes out a similar case for the Indian subcontinent. He writes: "We have seen how what had once been one of the richest and most industrialized economies of the world, which together with China accounted for almost 75 percent of the world industrial output in 1750, was transformed by the process of imperial rule into one of the poorest, most backward, illiterate and diseased societies on earth by the time of our independence in 1947. In 1600, when the East India Company was established, Britain was producing just 1.8 percent of the world's GDP, while India was generating some 23 percent. By 1940, after nearly two centuries of the Raj, Britain accounted for nearly 10 percent of the GDP, while India had been reduced to a poor 'third-world' country, destitute and starving, a global poster child of poverty and famine".[5] The concept of the reversal of fortune weakens the case of those who believe in the primacy of geography as a determinant of long-term growth as well.

Numerous other accounts from other parts of the world also point to the long shadows of history on current-day institutions, economic performance, and inequality. For example, the negative impacts of an extensive forced mining system called mita, which was in vogue in Peru between 1573 and 1812 for over two centuries, are still lingering. In districts where the said system of forced mining was in vogue, household consumption is low, and stunted growth of children is high compared to non-mita districts. The mita influence has persisted through the land tenure system and public goods provision. In mita districts, landowners are few compared to non-mita districts. The presence of a large number of landowners in non-mita districts encouraged public goods provision compared to mita districts.[6]

Congo also offers a similar story of labor coercion. Between 1885 and 1908, the Congo witnessed the worst abuses of human rights in African colonial history. Before becoming the Democratic Republic of the Congo (DRC), it was the personal colony of King Leopold II of Belgium. The said king, who is known in history for greed and terror, granted private companies concessions to extract rubber in the upper Congo basin. "For Leopold, the rubber boom was a godsend. He had gone dangerously into debt with his Congo investments, but he now saw that the return would be more lucrative than he had ever imagined".[7] The concession companies forced people to collect rubber as a form of taxation, and those who failed to meet the targets were subjected to severe punishment, torture, and violence. They were made hostages by the concession companies until the required target was achieved. "Sometimes the hostages were women, sometimes children, sometimes elders or chiefs. Every state or company post in the rubber areas had a stockade for hostages. If you were a male villager, resisting the order to gather rubber could mean death for your wife. She might die anyway, for in the stockades, food was scarce and conditions were harsh".[8]

The ghost of King Leopard still haunts the former concession areas of the Congo. The concession areas have significantly worse health, wealth, and education outcomes relative to areas just outside the concessions. The individuals living in former concession areas on average have

1.5 years less education, are 20% less wealthy, and have lower height-to-age percentiles.[9] The rubber regime was for a very brief period, 15 to 20 years, but the negative impact of 'Red Rubber' still haunts the long-term development of Congo even after a period of over a century.

The majority of the studies undertaken on the impact of institutions planted during the colonial era point toward the adverse impact on the development indicators of today. There is not much evidence to prove the contrary. One study about the Dutch forced labor regime known as the Dutch cultivation system in Java, however, gives some different results. In the mid-nineteenth century the Dutch established sugar factories in Java and the areas where such factories were set up are now more industrialized, richer, have better infrastructure, and are more educated. Basically the economic structures established by the colonizers to facilitate production are continuing to promote economic activity.[10]

What does this deviation from standard results explain about the long-term negative impact of sugar plantations on inequality and prosperity? Some researchers, using data from 368 districts of Java, have provided a plausible explanation of the said puzzle.[11] They have found that sugar production in the nineteenth and early twentieth centuries encouraged expansion and persistence of communal landholdings with the result that the distribution of property became more equitable. The equitable distribution of productive assets (land) thus resolves the riddle. The immediate effects of the cultivation system on the Javanese population were, however, highly negative as evidenced by high rates of mortality.[12]

The conquest and colonization left a deep impact on the institutions and cultures of the colonized countries and areas. We may not see the impact on institutions as vividly (because we require some instrumental variables and techniques to delineate the impact on institutions) as we can see it on the culture. The US citizens speak English because their colonizer that is Britain spoke English. People in South America speak Spanish (Argentina is an exception) because their colonizer was Portugal. Similar impacts can be found in religion and sports. Now the key question is: which institutions matter for economic growth and development? An institution in economics is generally any recognized or accepted norm for interaction between the members of a society. For example, 'waiting' in a queue is an institution that is now well recognized for allocating goods and services. Security of property rights, contract enforcement, the rule of law, and the legal system of a country are generally the institutions economists are more interested in. All these institutions have been discussed in detail at various places of this book.

Besides institutions, geography is another determinant of long-term economic growth which attracted the attention of some leading economists and writers. For example, researchers like Jeffrey Sachs and Jared Diamond, respectively an economist and a geographer, have persistently argued in their writings about geography as the top single determinant that explains to a large extent variations in economic growth and development among countries and regions of the globe.

The Shadow of Geography

The discussion on geography as a determinant of development is not new. "Hot countries tend to be poorer", this observation dates back to the fourteenth-century '*Muqaddimah*' of Ibn Khaldun.[13] "Excess of heat made men slothful and dispirited", wrote Montesquieu in '*The Spirit of Laws*' back in 1750.[14] The arguments of the geography school of thought are briefly as follows: It is difficult for people to work hard in countries that are near the equator due to heat and exposure to disease. People living near water, rail links, and roads, on the other hand, benefit more from economic growth. Climate, rainfall, temperature, and quality of terrain do have an impact, and the uneven impact of economic growth across regions may be partly due to geographical factors. Natural resource endowments are also shaped by geography. Oil, minerals, diamonds, and copper can be important sources of income. Geography also determines to what extent a country can become integrated into the world market and what type of institutions will evolve.[15]

Jared Diamond in '*Guns, Germs, and Steel*' has argued at length how geography created haves and have-nots. His thesis is that it was the ability to produce food and domesticate animals which made all the difference. The people of the regions of the world which had a competitive advantage in food production, also gained an advantage over the trajectory which led to guns, germs, and steel.[16] Jaffrey Sachs in '*The End of Poverty—Economic Possibilities for Our Times*' also holds that physical geography is the main determinant of the prosperity or the poverty of the nations. He cites the advantages of geography enjoyed by the USA to support his contention. Prosperity of the American continent, according to Sachs, owes a lot to the abundance of natural resources, good quality of soil, sufficient amount of rainfall, and availability of large navigable rivers with long coastlines and sufficient number of natural sea-ports providing enormous opportunities of international trade via sea. Such opportunities are not available to many poor countries as they are either landlocked or they are located in the high mountain ranges. These countries are not endowed with navigable rivers, long coastlines, or natural sea-ports like the USA. Low agricultural productivity due to arid soil, exposure to droughts, and high disease burden are some other afflictions of the bad geography directly responsible for the poverty of many countries according to Sachs.[17]

Similar arguments echo in '*The Journey of Humanity*' where Oded Galor argues that around 86% of variation in the per capita income of the countries is explained by deep-rooted factors that is geography and culture. According to Galor dispersal of humans out of Africa, geo-climatic factors, disease ecology, and cultural factors, respectively, explain 17 to 26%, 27 to 38%, 9 to 14%, and 20 to 22% variation in development. He also argues that both institutions and culture are not manna from heaven rather they largely evolved and adapted to the environment.[18]

Some empirics are also brought in the aid of geography and at least two of them merit mention. First is a study by Gallup and Sachs who analyzed global data on malaria for the period 1965–1990 and found that the impact of malaria on per capita GDP is strongly negative. And geography (disease burden) explains a substantial amount of variation in the per capita GDP of the countries.[19] Another study empirically examined the historical relationship between temperature fluctuations and economic growth and found substantial effects of temperature shocks on economic growth. On average, one Celsius rise in temperature is said to reduce economic growth by 1.3 percentage points in poor countries.[20] Geography and development are connected from another angle. In an inhospitable geographical landscape comprising vast deserts or mountains, provision of public services becomes much costly in per capita terms. Balochistan and Federally Administered Tribal Areas (FATA) are some pertinent examples in Pakistan which are sparsely populated due to vagaries of geography. Low infrastructural development in said areas is at least attributable to high costs of public service provision compared to other geographical regions of Pakistan.

But despite all the empirics and theoretical work pointing toward the impact of geography on development, accepting the primacy of geography as a determinant of long-term growth creates a type of determinism or helplessness. If geography determines destiny, then you can do nothing to improve your lot. The only option available in such a scenario is that the countries endowed with better geography come forward for your rescue and dole out aid. Geographical determinism and foreign aid are thus connected, and the economists who believe in the primacy of geography as a long-term determinant of economic growth are at the same time staunch supporters of foreign aid for international development. Sachs is at the top.

Connected to geography is natural wealth like oil and diamonds. Abundance of natural resources does not necessarily guarantee economic success. Nigeria, an oil-rich country, fares worse than Pakistan on human development indicators. Several countries on the African continent like Sierra Leone are known for the 'blood diamonds' where control over diamonds played a large role in fermenting civil war and violence. Kenneth Kaunda, the President of Zambia, is said to have once said, "We are in part to blame, but this is the curse of being born with a copper spoon in our mouths". Juan Pablo Perez Alfonso, the founder of OPEC, expressed similar frustration when he said about oil: "It is the devil's excrement. We are drowning in the devil's excrement". The abundance of natural resources generates a phenomenon known in the literature as Dutch disease which implies a situation of artificial appreciation of the exchange rate. Resource endowments, rather than becoming a source of long-run prosperity, become a drag on the economy as exports in non-resource sectors get squeezed and lose competitiveness in the global market.

Further, human resource rather than investing its energies in the tradable sector shifts toward the resource sector during the boom thus causing misallocation of talent having all attendant negative socio-economic implications. It is not a coincidence that resource-rich countries like Nigeria, Zambia, Sierra Leone, Angola, Cameroon, Liberia, Congo, Mexico, and Venezuela lag far behind resource-poor countries like Japan, South Korea, Taiwan, Hong Kong, and Singapore in terms of economic growth and human development indicators. Generally, the richness of natural resources accentuates ethnic strife, thwarts nation building, undermines democracy, and promotes inequitable distribution of resources. Natural wealth contributes to prosperity only if it is managed well in a transparent manner through good governance and the rents are spent on the people.

For example, Norway, an oil-rich country, used its natural wealth for the prosperity of its people. Chile dedicated a portion of rents accruing from copper to a "competitive innovation fund" to finance a variety of technology and research projects in the public and private sectors. "If being at the equator is the economic kiss of death, how then does one explain the spectacular economic success of Singapore or the somewhat less stellar but still impressive performance of Thailand? If being land-locked condemns a country to backwardness, how does one explain the remarkable economic record of Switzerland, which is so landlocked by mountains on all sides that it has used its unique geography in the past as a symbol of neutrality?".[21]

Botswana, in Africa, is another example. It is endowed with diamonds. Rather than making diamonds a resource curse, it has shown miraculous economic growth. It is a positive outlier in Africa. On the other hand, Nigeria, despite having abundant natural and human resources, failed to put itself on the trajectory of development. Tim Marshall, a British journalist, in '*The Prisoners of Geography*' argues that 10 maps explain everything about the world.[22] Tim's account may be simplistic and too pessimistic but it is a fact that some countries are unable to put themselves on the trajectory of long-term growth despite having good soil and natural wealth. And historical baggage, peculiar geo-political conditions of the region, and neighborhood become constraints on their long-term economic growth and they fail to benefit out of the proximities of geography through the channel of international trade, et cetera. Paul Collier and Steve O'Connell, based on some statistical analysis, found that neighbors do matter for economic development. In '*Bottom Billion*', Collier writes about the results of the said analysis: "We found that in general all countries, landlocked or not, benefited from the growth of their neighbors: growth spills over. The global average was that if a country's neighbors grew by additional 1 percent, the country grew at an additional 0.4 percent. So nice neighborhoods, in the sense of fast growth, are pretty helpful for everyone".[23]

Similarly, neighbors can have negative externalities. For example, if a neighboring country is experiencing civil war, the negative impacts of such a conflict would spill over to the neighboring countries as well. Collier writes: "Civil war is a development in reverse. It damages both the country and its neighbors as well. Let us start with the country itself. Civil war tends to reduce growth by around 2.3 percent per year, so a typical seven year war leaves a country around 15 percent poorer than it would have been. -- Many of the costs are borne by neighboring countries. Diseases do not respect frontiers, and the economic collapse spreads.

Since most countries are bordered by several others, the overall cost to neighbors can easily exceed the cost to the country itself".[24] For Pakistan, the conflict with India over Kashmir issue, Iranian revolution in 1979, civil war in Afghanistan, Russian invasion, et cetera, contributed to the rise of militancy and terrorism in Pakistan, which in turn worked as a drain on economic development of Pakistan (detailed discussion in the chapter on militancy).

Pakistan is endowed with diverse topography, ecosystems, and climate zones. Its geostrategic position also confers certain advantages on it. Pakistan is not only endowed with fertile land, better irrigation system, and good seasons but it has also got good routes of access to the outside world. Its strategic location provides natural geographical connections with China and Russia through Central Asia. It is located at the fulcrum of huge market with increasing workforce, diverse resources, and huge potential for international trade. Ian Talbot writes: "Pakistan's geographical position does provide possibilities of its acting as hub for regional trade and a supply route to Central Asia and even to India for energy. The country is rich in natural resources. Sindh contains one of the world's largest coal reserves. Balochistan has one of the world's largest copper reserves".[25] Climate change is, however, fast becoming a daunting challenge due to adverse consequences for the environment, economic growth, and public health. Pakistan falls among the countries which have become highly vulnerable to the climate change. Altered weather patterns and devastating floods are some clear manifestations of the catastrophic climate changes in Pakistan.

Climate Change and Growth

On average, Pakistan has experienced 6 climate-related disasters during the year 2000 to 2022, an almost two-fold increase from the preceding two decades.[26] The number of events caused by a hydrological, as opposed to biological (insect infestations, epidemics, etc.), climatological (droughts, etc.), or meteorological (storms, landslides, etc.), increased the most. Historically, floods have caused the maximum damage. In 2010, around 10 million people were displaced due to floods which inundated around one-fifth of the country, killed 2000 people, and triggered mass migration toward the cities. And in the following year, floods struck again affecting 18 million people and destroying 1.7 million homes.[27] According to the World Bank estimates, total 106 flood disasters took

Table 2.1 Summary of natural hazards in Pakistan from 1900 to 2020

Disaster type	*Events count*	*Total deaths*	*Total affected*	*Total damage (1000 US$)*
Floods	106	18,105	80,944,904	22,581,178
Earthquakes	35	144,116	7,435,786	5,376,755
Storms	29	12,141	2,604,834	1,715,036
Landslide	23	805	34,154	18,000
Extreme temperature	18	2,954	80,574	18,000
Epidemic	11	403	72,812	0

Source Adapted from Table 5 of Climate Risk Country Profile of Pakistan by the World Bank Group (WBG), 2021

place between 1900 and 2020 in the area of Pakistan, causing horrendous loss of human lives and livelihoods (see Table 2.1).

The damage caused by 2022 floods was larger compared to the losses of earlier floods. It affected around 33 million (14% of the population) in half of Pakistan's 160 districts. Nearly 2.2 million houses were damaged, 45% of the crop area was inundated with water, and critical transport network (around 400 bridges and 13,000 kilometer roads) was disrupted and damaged. The total loss to the economy is estimated to the tune of 8.5% of the GDP.[28] Floods have negative impact on human capital due to damage to schools and hospitals. Furthermore, the impact of climate change is differential as floods and other climatic disasters have a tendency to disproportionately affect the poor and the marginalized. Climate change exacerbates existing vulnerabilities and inequalities by disrupting the local economies and sources of livelihoods of the people.

Rising temperature, in addition to floods, is a big cause of concern. Pakistani crops are highly sensitive to changes in temperature and water availability and a rise in temperature of 0.5 Celsius by 2040 could lead to 8–10% loss (around Rs. 30,000 per acre) in yield across all the crops.[29] Pakistan has witnessed rise in the maximum limit of temperatures in the districts lying in the heat surplus zones of Pakistan. It crossed almost 50 degree Celsius in districts like Larkana and Jacobabad.[30] "The impact of extreme climate events on the agriculture sector in Pakistan can be very significant, raising concerns regarding any increase in their frequency attributed to climate change. Floods inundate fertile land, kill livestock, destroy standing crops, and reduce or eliminate yields. This was demonstrated in the major flood of 2010, during which an estimated 2.4 million hectares of unharvested crops were lost, worth approximately US$5.1 billion. Droughts can be equally devastating to rural livelihoods. From 1999–2002, droughts in Sindh and Balochistan provinces killed two million livestock and necessitated emergency relief to provide drinking water and food aid to farming communities. Even minimal changes in precipitation patterns over prolonged periods can alter the country's food production by placing greater pressure on the water resources the country's irrigation system depends on".[31]

The issue of smog (smoke + fog), which has worsened in the last couple of years, is clear manifestation of deteriorating climate. Lahore, the metropolis of Punjab, with human population of 11.12 million (as per 2017 census), adjoining with Indian Punjab border, is a case in point. Every year smog returns to this city with increased intensity creating major health issues of lungs, eyes, skin, and heart. It features regularly in the list of most polluted cities of the globe. The situation has become so bad that the government resorts to a general lockdown during smog season on the pattern of the one done during Corona epidemic by closing schools, bazaars, restaurants, and shopping malls. Traffic pollution, industrialization, and stubble burning on both sides of the Pak–India border are the major contributing factors. Besides strict enforcement and monitoring of air quality and emission standards, meaningful regional and global cooperation would be required for coping with the challenge of climate challenge. The pollution arising out of the burning of stubble does not recognize borders! Similarly, global cooperation based on climate justice (which simply means that the most affected people and countries are not responsible for the climatic changes like global warming) would be needed.

In short, institutions and geography do matter and their relevance for long-term growth cannot be downplayed. The constraints imposed by them are not easy to overcome. We cannot change institutions overnight and geography is immutable to a large extent. A longer period is required to bring change in the said variables. We can, however, make good use of technology, can save to reinvest, and can elect honest and clean leaders. The ensuing discussion is about these determinants of long-term economic growth which are comparatively less rigid than institutions and geography.

Significance of Productivity

Economists mainly focus on two broad sources of growth: addition of more inputs (more capital and more labor) and total factor productivity (TFP). Baumol,[32] respectively, calls these sources 'growth by brute force' (which results from the addition of more inputs, that is labor and capital) and 'smart growth' (resulting from TFP). The story of modern growth starts with Robert Solow who won the Nobel Prize for showing that economic growth in the USA and few other industrialized countries could not be explained by capital and labor. There is 'something else' that is more important for economic growth. This 'something else' is given several names like total factor productivity, productivity, technology, or 'measure of ignorance' by the economists. Total factor productivity or productivity simply means how much we can produce with a given set of inputs that is capital and labor. In simple parlance, growth is a function of three key components: capital (which depends on how much money a country invests back domestically and how much investment it attracts from abroad), Labor (both quantity and quality, its education, its skill set, its work ethics, etc.), and TFP includes all factors (which can contribute to economic growth directly or indirectly) other than capital and labor like technology, laws, regulations, et cetera, that is some innovation of machine or method that can use inputs more efficiently to get more from the same amount of capital and labor.

Paul Krugman aptly remarks that "Productivity is not everything but in the long-run it is almost everything"[33] why? He explains: "A country's ability to improve its standards of living overtime depends entirely on its ability to raise its output per worker".[34] In Solow's model, productivity is something like manna from heaven which cannot be fully controlled by any government. It is at best a combination of good luck and some policy or process tinkering.

Roughly speaking, TFP accounts for more than half of the economic growth, meaning its contribution is greater than the combined contribution of capital and labor. Any talk on technology or productivity starts with machines and structures. We have to have some tool or machine to use. And in this sense, technology is embodied in fixed capital like tools, machines, and structures. But why does capital not flow to the poor and developing countries despite the fact that capital is scarce in countries like Pakistan where it can earn higher returns? In technical jargon, the marginal product of capital (MPK) is higher in capital-scarce countries compared to capital rich countries. Theory suggests that if returns in countries with little initial capital are high, then these countries would grow at a faster rate than developed countries. And capital would flow from the rich countries to the poor countries due to return differentials. This point was raised by Lucas in 1990 in one of his seminal articles on the subject.[35]

Lucas compared USA and India in 1988 and postulated that if the neoclassical model holds, then returns on capital, or simply MPK, in India would be 58 times higher than in USA. And capital, rather than residing in the USA, would fly to India but practically such is not the case. Capital does not flow to the poor countries, hence a paradox named Lucas Paradox. What is the plausible explanation for this paradox? One is technical and the argument is marshaled as follows.[36] In a cross-country comparison, the proper metric of returns on capital would be the capital-to-output ratio and not the capital-to-labor ratio. And if capital-to-output ratio is taken as the metric of return on capital, then capital would flow from countries with a high capital-to-output ratio to countries with a low capital-to-output ratio. And the countries with low capital-to-output ratios may not necessarily be the poorest countries. The comparison between China and the USA is a case in point. China has a lower capital-to-output ratio compared to USA, and that does explain capital flow to China. So, capital-to-output ratio (and not the capital-to-labor ratio) is a correct indicator of the marginal productivity of capital, the argument goes. A higher investment rate raises the capital-to-output ratio whereas a high rate of growth or a higher rate of depreciation lowers the capital-to-output ratio.

The second set of explanations relates to differences in fundamentals like factors of production, government policies, and institutions. Some empirics based on data of 50 countries show that institutional quality is the most important factor in determining the capital flow.[37] How are contracts enforced? What is the level of corruption? How many procedures are involved to obtain a certain permit or license? How many days does it take to obtain an electricity connection? How many business days are consumed to start a company? How much cost is involved? The said variables, all impinging on the ease of start-ups and continuation of business, shall determine whether the environment of a country is hospitable for capital or not. Judged against the indices of world competitiveness reports, constructed on such variables, Pakistan's position is not enviable. The barriers to entry (that is the number of days taken to register a new firm) are higher in Pakistan compared to regional comparators. The World Bank's Doing Business[38] and WEF's competitiveness reports have consistently ranked Pakistan very low on ease of investment and business.

Technology and best practices are not easy to diffuse and replicate in poor countries, partly due to a lack of complementarity between investments in new technology and human capital. Misallocations of inputs (capital, human, and land) are also responsible for low productivity. Reallocation of resources, which simply means where to put money, material, and people for enhancing and sustaining growth, can be an important policy priority area for long-term growth. It calls for policies to reduce distortions and misallocations of capital, labor, and talent. Results of a study by ADB,[39] based on firm-level data from 21,000 firms in 62 developing countries including Pakistan, suggest subject to the caveat of small sample size of 136 firms for Pakistan that the functioning of the courts and access to finance are two major determinants of misallocation within countries whereas political instability appears to be the top-most obstacle explaining misallocation between countries. The creation of distortions in the agriculture market through price control by the government is well-documented. Bates has given an interesting account of the politics of agricultural policy in Africa as to how the governments in various African states manipulate and create distortions in the markets through pricing (like Marketing Boards) and non-pricing strategies that determine the incomes of the farmers.[40] The prices of some crops are set by the government well below the market price and the rationale behind it is to provide cheap food to the industrial workers in the urban areas to avoid labor unrest. In some cases government purchases crops well above the market price and in this way the government's pricing policy benefits the big farmers.

Misallocation of talent, least appreciated in Pakistan, also impacts competitiveness and economic growth negatively. Whether educated people prefer to engage in productive entrepreneurial activities (activities that create wealth) or take up rent-seeking activities (involving the distribution of existing wealth created by others with the additional negative impact of distorting incentives) has important implications for long-term growth. The variations in productivity, capital accumulation, and output per worker are driven by differences in what Hall and Jones[41] call social infrastructure that is institutions and government policies that determine the economic environment within which individuals and firms operate. A good social infrastructure would encourage accumulation of skills and capital, innovation, and transfer of technology and would protect the output of the workers from diversions through theft and thuggery.

The share of productivity or smart growth in Pakistan's economic growth is noticeably low. An analysis[42] by PIDE for the period 1972–2019 shows that average growth rate of Pakistan for this period was 4.81% per annum. Labor, capital, and TFP, respectively, showed annual average growth of 2.21%, 4.11%, and 1.62% with an average investment ratio of 18.32%. What are the main factors contributing to low productivity in Pakistan? Insufficiency of inputs or capital is the part of the answer. There are issues of inefficiency in using the available inputs, and the potential benefits of improving allocative efficiency may be enormous. For example, better use of human resources, that is the right person for the right job may yield considerable growth in GDP per person. Developed countries like the USA have managed around 40% of their economic growth in the last five decades through better use of human resources. Reduction of resource misallocation accounted for about 40% of growth in manufacturing TFP between 1983 and 1996 in Chile due to reduction of subsidies on unproductive plants and banking reforms.[43]

Allocative inefficiencies and distortions are enormous in Pakistan. Misallocation of land is a huge area that needs reforms to unleash its productivity potential (discussed in chapter on misallocation of land). Similarly, misallocation of talent is a big source of allocative inefficiency. According to Labor Force Survey (LFS) conducted in 2021, only 15% of the migration happens due to economic reasons. Reasons for low mobility of labor are not difficult to guess. Lack of affordable housing, poor transportation network, reliance on social networks due to poor provision of public goods like health care, or lack of opportunities are some major factors responsible for the limited mobility of the labor workforce.

High effective rates of tariff protection are another area responsible for low productivity. Effective rates of protection are very high in Pakistan. For example, according to some World Bank estimates,[44] sugar, motor vehicles, dairy products, beverages, tobacco products, and wearing apparel, respectively, enjoy effective protection of 123%, 143%, 165%, 167%, and 185%. Excessive protection of traditional sectors of the economy shields Pakistani firms from international competition with a negative impact on consumer welfare (as these firms get a captive market) and productivity (firms are least incentivized to upgrade machinery and skills of their employees). An investigation into the productivity dynamics of publicly listed firms in Pakistan shows that foreign-owned or exporting firms were on average more productive than domestic-owned or domestic-oriented firms implying thereby that increased exposure of firms makes them more productive.[45] Further, protection is not based on some rigorous cost–benefit analysis. Some research work suggests that trade protection against international competition through tariff and non-tariff measures is linked to politically powerful special interest groups (SIGs), particularly during the period when trade policy became more complex.[46]

The complexity of tariffs besides high effective rates has negative consequences for productivity. Pakistan embarked on a liberalization program in 1990s. In 2000, the average MFN rate was 25%, which was reduced to around 12% in two decades registering reduction of over 100%. Before liberalization, both international trade and revenue collection were stagnant. Around 70% of the government's revenue was import-related. With the reduction of tariff rates both revenue and trade witnessed a quantum jump. The revenue imperative of the tariff, however, caused complexity despite liberalization. In addition to customs duty, additional customs duty (ACD) and regulatory duties (RD) were imposed on a number of imported items. For example, out of total of 7356 tariff lines, 5521 tariff lines, and 2075 tariff lines were, respectively, subjected to ACD and RD. In addition to said duties, sales tax, additional sales tax, and withholding tax are also charged against the majority of goods at the import stage. "High incidence of taxes at import stage motivates firms to underdeclare, misdeclare, misinvoice, and smuggle. Two perennial problems of Pakistan Customs that is under-invoicing and smuggling are largely due to high incidence of taxes on imports".[47]

Capital formation that is how much of its GDP a nation ploughs back as investment is also an important determinant of economic growth. Some nations are known for high savings rate. For example, Hindu rate of savings is considered one of the main factors for India's high growth rate. Patience matters for the prosperity of individuals as well as nations. What does patience mean in economics? Let me illustrate it first before highlighting the nexus between patience and prosperity. There is a Chinese fable of a monkey keeper from which proverb "three in the morning, four in the evening" originated. A monkey keeper proposed to his monkeys that they eat three chestnuts in the morning and four in the evening. The monkeys did not accept this proposal rather they accepted an alternative that is to eat four chestnuts in the morning and three in the evening. Is eating four chestnuts in the morning and three in the evening the same as eating three chestnuts in the morning and four in the evening? No, it is not like that. Monkeys in fact exercised what economists call intertemporal choice by not accepting the proposal of the monkey keeper. It is a sort of savings-consumption choice that every individual faces. Economists use subjective discount rate (simply called discount rate) to capture the relative weight one puts on present satisfaction.

Patience and Prosperity

A person with a high discount rate is impatient because he tends to value present gratification more than future gratification. A patient person, on the other hand, is willing to defer present gratification to the future. Attached to the very idea is hyperbolic discounting or present bias that is a tendency among people or policy-makers to discount the immediate rewards high compared to rewards in the distant future.[48] "The most serious influence of hyperbolic discounting on behavior is that it makes it difficult for people to carry out plans or decisions that were previously made with long-term benefits in mind. The reason is that as time passes, our degree of patience while we wait for future gratification becomes lower, so that previous plans or decisions that were made from the perspective of the long-term goal become suboptimal at the moment they are performed".[49]

Intertemporal choices and hyperbolic discounting concern not only individuals and households but nations as well. For example, Pakistan seems to behave like monkeys who insist on eating four chestnuts in the morning. It consumes more today and saves little for the future. Investment in fixed capital technically called Gross Fixed Capital Formation (GFCF) is an important variable of national productivity or competitiveness. That is why investment to GDP ratio (GFCF/GDP) is considered as one of the best indicators of economic growth potential due to empirical regularity of positive relationship between investment ratio and economic growth. The investment ratio gives us a fair idea of how a country is developing its productive capabilities. Hardly a country has achieved sustainable growth rate of over 6% for a long period of time without investing at least 25% of its GDP.

The investment ratio has traditionally remained low in Pakistan and more worrisome part of the investment story is that it is persistently on the decline. It is the lowest in the South Asian region. During the decade of 1960s, the investment ratio was above the South Asian region, but since 1970s, Pakistan's investment ratio is treading behind the South Asian average. Pakistan ploughs back around 15%, almost half of what is desirable, of its GDP for capital formation. A time series analysis shows that Pakistan's investment ratio has not witnessed any significant improvement over the last 60 years. In 1960, this ratio stood at 13.5%, which in 2021 was 14.6%. Other countries have improved over time. For example, Bangladesh (then the eastern part of Pakistan) in 1960s had a gross capital formation ratio of 6.9% and stands at 31% in 2021 (Fig. 2.1). Vietnam, a fast-emerging economy, has an investment ratio of 33.4% in 2021. Even the sub-Saharan region ploughs back 9% more of its GDP compared to Pakistan.[50]

What are the main factors responsible for low savings and investment in Pakistan? Low tax revenue is perhaps the major culprit. Pakistan's total revenue collection averaged to 12.8% of GDP in the last decade, substantially lower than the South Asian average of 19.6%. The worrying part is that total revenue collection in terms of GDP is on the decline. For example, total revenue collection averaged to 13.2% for the period 2013–2017, which was on average 12.5% for the period 2018–2022. During FY 2021–2022, Pakistan collected 12.4% of GDP in total while tax revenues constituted 11.2%. The revenues are persistently low and

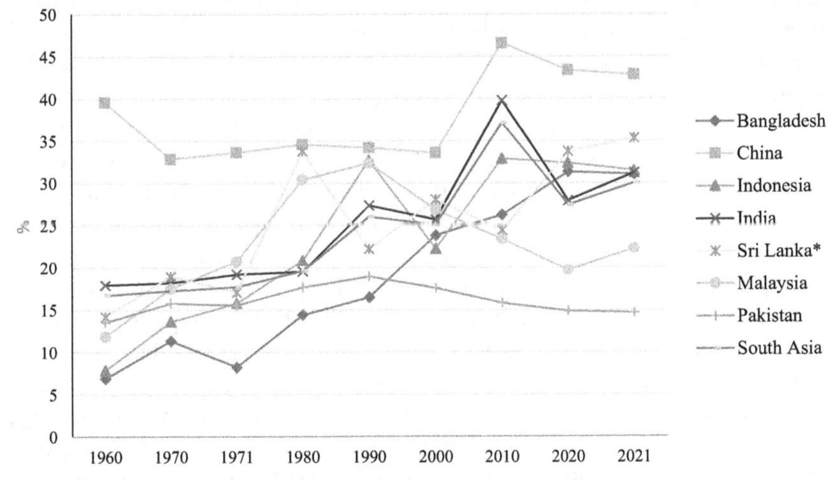

Fig. 2.1 Gross capital formation of selected countries (% of GDP) (*Source* World Development Indicator [databank.worldbank.org])

fall short of expenditures, resulting in large fiscal deficits. Tax exemptions, concessions, complexity of statutes, corruption in tax machinery, political economy considerations, low fiscal capacity, and hesitation by the government to take hard choices are some of the reasons due to which Pakistan is unable to realize the huge potential of tax. The large fiscal deficits contribute to the recurrent surges in the current account deficit.

An analysis conducted by the World Bank shows that Pakistan's fiscal deficit and current account deficit empirically tend to move together, meaning thereby that a strong correlation exists between the said two species of deficits. The financing of fiscal deficits generates other related but distinct macroeconomic challenges. The large fiscal deficits have led to accumulation of huge public and publicly guaranteed debt, which stood around 78% of the GDP at the end of FY 22. Moreover, extensive borrowing from the financial sector crowds out private sector from the credit market. The large public debts also crowd out development expenditure having negative implications for long-term growth. The debt servicing costs constitute a big share of the fiscal expenditures, which have now increased to the unsustainable level. During FY 2022, interest payments stood around 4.7% of GDP and accounted for 35% of the total federal expenditure. Large expenditure on interest payments and other pre-committed and largely rigid expenditure like government salaries, pensions, and government operating expenditures leave little for growth-enhancing expenditure and public investments. Subsidies to state-owned enterprises (SOEs), security, contingency expenditures, and salaries to the public sector crowd out public sector investment. In order to fill the savings-investment gap, Pakistan has to rely on foreign inflows. Foreign inflows have an in-built element of volatility. And pressure on reserves creates unsustainable current account deficits and macroeconomic instability.

Pakistan is not only consuming more today, it is also consuming on wrong things which have little to do with long-term growth and development. Due to low domestic revenue mobilization, it depends on loans from the IMF and other multilateral institutions. Dependence on the IMF which started in 1958 continues to this day with the result that it needs loans even to pay interest on past loans. Besides heavy borrowing, Pakistan artificially keeps its exchange rate overvalued to sustain imports with the danger of Calvo's sudden stop[51] persistently hovering over its head. Why Pakistan does behave like this? Some commentators argue that such behavior is due to political instability. Pakistan alternates back and forth between civilian rule and a military regime. Pakistani leaders being inherently insecure think myopically. "If the people get mad at civilian leader, they might let a military leader kick them out of office. And if they get mad at a military leader, they might kick them out and bring in a civilian".[52]

Perhaps this is the half-truth. The relationship between investment and economic growth rate is not that robust for Pakistan. Even when investment was high, growth rates were not necessarily high rather growth rate plummeted in some of those years. Pattern of economic growth is erratic. The issue is partly about the overall structure of investment in Pakistan. Are we investing in the right kind of heads? The component of public investment that contributes to long-term sustainable growth is very low. A negligible amount is spent by the Federal Government on the people (Fig. 2.2).

After the 18th Amendment in the Constitution, the overwhelming bulk of social spending has been devolved to the provincial governments. "Even, in provincial spending, however, which is beset by higher leakages due to great maladministration and corruption, the share of service providers tends to be greater than that of service recipients".[53] A major chunk of the earnings is eaten away by interest payments and

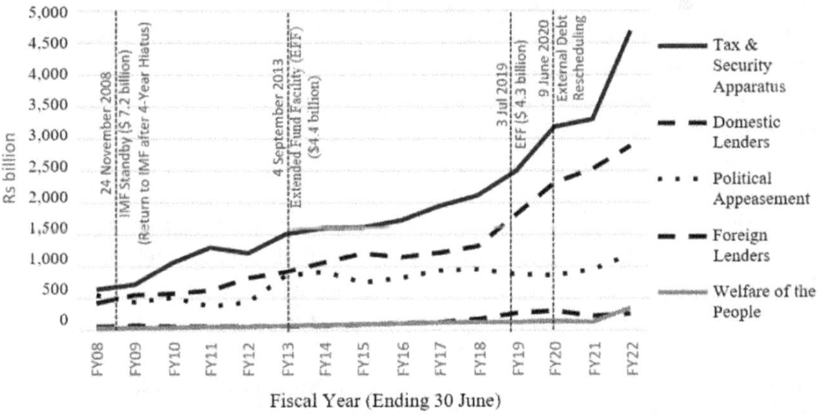

Fig. 2.2 Beneficiaries of Federal Government spending, 2008–2022 (*Source* Social Origins of Debt Crisis)

defense expenditures. This spending pattern is just like that of a hyperbolic individual who spends on cigarettes, drinks, and high carbs and in the end becomes victim of obesity and diabetes. If a hyperbolic individual had spent on a healthy diet and gym, his spending would have turned out to be beneficial in the long run in the form of better health.

Similarly, if a country spends more today on education, health, environment, and poverty alleviation such spending would help boost long-term economic growth. Certainly, temporal differences between the time of choice and the realization of effects would be longer for such investments. Just like self-destructive behaviors such as drinking and smoking, which are damaging for the growth of an individual, spending more on guns than on schools and hospitals is damaging for long-term economic growth at the national level. Patience pays. Alfred Marshall called it "a chief product and chief cause of civilization".[54] It is strongly correlated with per capita income, accumulation of physical and human capital, and productivity.[55]

How can impatient behavior be controlled? At the individual level, various banking instruments like fixed deposit accounts (lockboxes), compulsory deductions from salaries (compulsory savings for retired life), et cetera, are some ways to control impatience. The illiquid nature of the assets matters. We can spend income (which is comparatively liquid) with more ease than wealth (comparatively illiquid). One can be more impatient with spending cash than with land or stocks. This provides an important insight for poverty alleviation.

Although economists favor the provision of cash without strings as the recipients may use it according to their preferences but a better course of action would be to distribute productive assets of an illiquid nature like land or provide some skills or training as it is not easy to dispose of land or waste skills principally due to their illiquid nature. "And human capital can be the most illiquid assets of all. Once skills and knowledge gained through experience, training, and education are formed, they cannot be taken away, nor can the accumulated knowledge ever be reverted to zero. When parents educate their children instead of leaving "fertile field" properties this can be considered a type of commitment device that keeps children from reducing future assets by overspending, thus preserving the assets".[56]

Nations can also bind their hands to overcome impatient behaviors. For example, if human capital formation is the most illiquid asset, guarantees can be incorporated into the Constitution for social spending (like making it mandatory to spend 10% of GDP on education and health). Fiscal responsibility laws are also a case in point which many countries have enacted to ensure certainty, reliability, and transparency of fiscal policy. Pakistan also promulgated the Fiscal Responsibility and Debt Limitation Act in 2005 which provided for the elimination of revenue deficits and the reduction of public debt. It prescribed that the overall tax-to-GDP ratio shall not go beyond 60%, but violations happened (just like the fruit vendors in Hyderabad).[57] The debt burden has now become a big constraint on economic growth in Pakistan.

Impatience is connected to political instability as well. Political expediency does not allow political or military leadership to have a long view of economic development. "The political instability has made Pakistan's successive governments more like Mancur Olson's 'roving bandits' who loot only for today. The governments are not like Olson's 'stationary bandits' who invest in his victim's future prosperity so they can continue fleecing him".[58] Far-sighted growth-oriented policy shall require consensus among the elite to invest more for the future and to invest optimally. Binding the hands of the government through strengthening institutions of restraint and the socio-politico-economic inclusion of the people are important commitment devices at the national level.

Political stability is a prerequisite for investment. People in Pakistan get impatient with the government, irrespective of the political party in power, over a period of two to three years. This impatience causes instability. The solution to this impatience is reduction in the constitutional terms of the Assemblies, national and provincial, say from 5 to 4 years. Fixing the tenure of the Assemblies and local bodies at 4 years and holding elections for the said two broad types of representative bodies, with an interval of two years between them, would mean that the nation would go to election booths after every two years. Reduction in constitutional tenure and more frequent elections may help overcome the impatience of the people besides having some positive externalities for democracy. New leaders shall emerge, non-deliverers shall be weeded out, and people shall feel empowered.

The disillusionment of the people with the political system is also due to the unrepresentative nature of the Assemblies. In 1970 elections, 11% of the members hailed from peasant and working-class backgrounds[59] but the situation has now changed with increase in costs for contesting elections and betting of the political parties on winning horses. In the last few Assemblies, we cannot name even a single towering personality hailing from the peasant or working class who became a member of the National Assembly. 'First past the poll system' which declares the one who gets the highest votes among the candidates in a constituency leaves the majority unfranchised. A political party getting as few as 17% votes can even form a government. Patronage system also owes much to this system of elections.[60]

Achieving a high growth rate for a long period of time requires reforms in multiple areas including the political system with a view to reduce the cost of electioneering and induce competition. Doing so shall help in emergence of new leaders. The role of leaders is highly significant in sustaining high growth rates. The quality of leadership is an important determinant of economic growth which was generally ignored in growth literature. The role of leadership is, however, now being recognized in the emerging interdisciplinary growth literature. Dearth of quality leadership becomes a binding constraint particularly for some poor and developing countries.

Role of Leaders

The Commission on Growth and Development, set up by the World Bank in 2006 under the chairmanship of Michael Spence, identified thirteen countries that showed sustained high growth that is 7% or over 7% for twenty-five years post-World War II. These countries included South Korea, Hong Kong, China, Taiwan, Thailand, Japan, Malaysia, Indonesia, Singapore, Oman, Malta, Brazil, and Botswana. The leaders in these countries managed the transition from rural to urban, from relatively closed institutions in the beginning to more open institutions, and in several cases, from autocratic rule to more democratic governments. In 1960s, President Park set about industrializing South Korea and played an important role in catalyzing economic growth. The decision of Deng Xiaoping to allow farmers to grow crops beyond quota allocations boosted economic growth.[61] Leaders promote economic growth through various channels that are not included by economists in pure economic models and frameworks of growth.

For example, leaders build national unity as factionalism tends to reduce economic growth. To increase the pie, patience is required (you need to save). Leaders face the unrelenting challenge of "preventing the demands of the present from overwhelming the future. Leaders are inevitably hemmed in by constraints. They operate in scarcity, for every society faces limits to its capabilities and reach, dictated by demography and economy".[62]

"Courage and character are two vital attributes of a leader—courage to choose a direction among complex and difficult options, which requires the willingness to transcend the routine; and strength of character to sustain a course of action whose benefits and whose dangers can be only incompletely glimpsed at the moment of choice. Courage summons virtue in the moment of decision; character reinforces fidelity to values over an extended period".[63] "Launching a turnaround takes courage.—Turnarounds are rare because reformers are often suppressed and sometimes pay a high price for their efforts".[64] Leaders strive for political stability by promoting unity, cohesion, inclusiveness, and good governance. Nelson Mandela accelerated the creation of a shared sense of identity in South Africa. Lee Kwan Yew delivered on the promise of equality and inclusiveness through employment generation, public access to education, and public housing. Mahathir Mohammad improved governance by introducing corporate culture into the public sector.

Had it been possible for South Africa to emerge as a rainbow nation if Mandela was not there as their leader? Had Mahathir Mohammad not been the leader of Malaysia, would it have been possible for the country to manage ethnic divisions and emerge as a developed nation in a short span of two to three decades? Delineating the impact and role of leadership for economic growth is, however, not that easy, as we have neither 'counterfactuals' nor the luxury of scientists running experiments in controlled environments. Jones & Olken have attempted to lend empirical credence to the role of leaders in economic growth.[65] They used "deaths of leaders while in office" (an exogenous variable) as proxy for change in leadership. A leader, in their formulation, is a person with executive authority like the president, prime minister, or a dictator. Their results suggest that leaders matter for economic growth, especially in countries with weak democratic and accountability institutions.

Change in a political regime may not be that important in the USA for economic growth but the change certainly matters in a developing country. Leaders can affect economic growth in several ways. For example, in a country like Pakistan, where ideas generally do not flow from bottom to top, idea creation by the leaders is important. Leaders work as catalysts for change. They expedite the process of transformation by overcoming the collective action problem, unifying the interests of various ethnic and social groups, and providing stability. Leaders change the norms and rules society is organized around which may otherwise take centuries to change. Good leaders build institutions as it is the quality of the institutions that trumps everything else like geography and integration in economic development.[66] And from where does leadership come? Mahathir is said to have once said: "Although democracy is still the best form of government, there is no guarantee that it will throw up good leaders".[67]

If democracy is not inclusive, then the possibility of good leaders would be further diminished. Change of regime in such political setups may turn out just change of rent-seeking coalitions as change would not serve the cause of economic development.[68] For economic development, leadership has to be generous and inclusive, uncorrupted, and able to carve out consensus around a vision of what the future would look like and what sacrifices would be needed to get there.[69] "Leaders are visionary and diligent, selflessly devoted to national, not party or individual, interests. For credibility, leaders must have integrity, be incorruptible (or have the incentives to remain so), and be honest".[70] And successful growth policies require robust institutions (responsible legislature, independent judiciary, responsible press, effective civil service, and vibrant private sector), people consensus (through policies of inclusiveness, social cohesion and convergence), good leadership, and a culture of growth which encourages new ideas, learning, and innovation.

CHAPTER 3

Culture and Growth

History of the idea of culture as an explanatory factor of prosperity dates back to Adam Smith and Karl Marx. "The mode of production of material life conditions the social, political, and intellectual life processes in general", wrote Karl Marx.[1] According to Max Weber, shift in religious attitudes was responsible for the rise of capitalism in Europe. According to him, it was a change in the "psychological conditions" of the people that made the development of Western civilization possible as the pursuit of riches, which was once considered an enemy of the religion, became an ally.[2]

The protestant ethic of Calvinism became a powerful force behind the development of capitalism as attitudes toward the world and work changed fundamentally. A new kind of thinking emerged that emphasized rationality, order, diligence, and productivity. Stress on literacy for both girls and boys and the importance accorded to time were, in particular, two aspects of protestant teachings that facilitated the rise of capitalism.[3] The rise of capitalism in the West was thus closely connected to the rise of rationalism about the basic problems of life.

Similarly, Japan's Meiji Restoration of 1868 introduced social and political changes with far-reaching consequences. These changes are credited for Japan's emergence as a modern industrial nation in the twentieth century. A high level of literacy, work ethic, and self-discipline became

J. Nasir, *Development Challenges of Pakistan*,
https://doi.org/10.1007/978-981-97-3064-3_3

the basis of modernization. "No opportunity of learning was lost -- General schooling diffused knowledge; that is what schools are for. But it also instilled discipline, obedience, punctuality, and worshipful respect for (adoration of) the emperor. This was the key to the development of a we/ they national identity transcending parochial identities and status lines— The army (and navy) completed the job. Beneath the sameness of the uniform and the discipline, universal military service wiped out distinctions of class and place"[4] writes Landes. The prosperity or economic growth thus basically sprouted from the changes in work ethics, beliefs, education, and focus on people. The bricks and mortar structures were the outcome. Rationality in the West and patriotism in Japan provided the basis for changes in work habits and outlook.

The economy of a country is inextricably embedded in both economic and non-economic factors. The inclusion of non-economic factors like religion and government is as important as tools and machines for the structure and functioning of an economy.[5] Karl Polyani writes: "The formal economics of maximization and allocation principles–the theory of choice- represents only the portion of the subject matter of economics. Economics deals with the production and distribution of material goods and services. At one boundary of the subject it gets very close to the study of technology and processes of production. At the other limit it treats of attitudes and motivations, social classes and relationships, and the institutional framework within which production and distribution are carried on. Only a small part of the subject matter of economics is the theory of choice among alternatives- and even choices are constrained by technological possibilities and the social structure".[6]

Landes also echoes similar ideas when he talks about factors contributing to the economic backwardness of third-world countries. According to him, it is not the dearth of money that holds back the development of third-world countries; rather, the biggest impediments are social, cultural, and technological uneasiness, that is, a lack of knowledge and ability to use money.[7] Culture impacts economic behaviors like the propensity to save or innovate. Economic decisions like fertility choices, investment in the education of children, giving charity, labor supply, the role of women in the labor market, and willingness to contribute to public goods are culturally determined. Culture also impacts economic outcomes through several other channels including prior beliefs and preferences.[8]

Beliefs, norms, and outlooks on life matter for development. The history of economic growth and development amply vindicates the said proposition. Prosperity occurred in a growth-oriented culture. Joel Mokyr, a Netherlands-born American-Israeli economic historian, has propounded a forceful thesis about the origin of the modern economy from the perspective of cultural belief system.[9] His argument is that growth in the West was possible due to changes in cultural beliefs about the natural world and the diffusion of knowledge. According to Mokyr, cultures can be "backward" or "forward-looking". Cultures that hold knowledge and learning of previous generations in high esteem are backward-looking cultures, and in such cultures, new ideas are not encouraged whereas in forward-looking cultures everything new is welcomed as an improvement..[10] A future-oriented mindset basically fosters economic growth.

An important cultural belief that promotes economic growth and also complements the belief in the "virtuousness of technology", according to Mokyr, is the belief in economic progress, which has positive, normative, and prescriptive components. The positive component means acceptance of the point that material progress is possible and the upward trend of progress can be continued whereas the normative component postulates that economic progress is desirable, meaning accumulation of wealth or material goods is not sinful or bad.

Besides the possibility and desirability of economic progress, a clear agenda of policy measures and institutional change is required for long-term progress to take place, which Mokyr calls the "prescriptive component" of the said critical belief.[11] The role of the elite in promoting growth culture also matters. What values do they promote? What areas of knowledge and learning do they focus on? All matter. Highlighting this point, Mokyr writes: "In most slave societies, educated elites concerned themselves with philosophy, poetry, history, and such leisure activities as hunting and music. While they were usually interested in military technology, engineering, architecture, and large-scale hydraulic projects, more mundane subjects such as farming, ship building, iron working, food processing, and textiles were rarely on their agendas".[12]

As of today, education is perhaps the most obvious mechanism through which cultural values can impact economic growth. Cultural values determine how much time and money parents and the state decide to spend on the education of the children and what type of curriculum is taught in schools and colleges. Investment in human capital is widely regarded as important for economic growth and prosperity. The diffusion and absorption of technology depend on formal or informal education. Where does

Pakistan stand with respect to the norms of a culture of growth that Mokyr and Landes consider integral to economic development?

The results of a survey undertaken in 2006 in and around Rawalpindi revealed that around 41% of parents preferred religious education as opposed to secular education.[13] The results may not be very confidence-inspiring on grounds like the small size of sample (limited to only one city in Pakistan), the formulation of the question (leading questions), the socio-economic background of the respondents, and the low information of the parents about returns to education. Despite all possible shortcomings of the said survey, it is an irrefutable fact that themes like ideology, nation building, being a good Muslim, et cetera, dominate the minds of Pakistanis.

Interestingly, Pakistani immigrants belonging to less affluent sections who settled in developed countries like the UK also exhibit similar preferences when it comes to educating their children. Pakistani-origin British children on average have lower reading and numeracy skills than their white counterparts despite a better educational system, claims Hoodbhoy. According to him, the reason for choosing homeschooling for their children or sending them to faith-based schools is the fear among Pakistani parents that their children will lose their religious moorings if educated in secular schools.[14] It is jokingly said that Pakistanis prefer an American school for their children in Pakistan while choose a Pakistani school when settled in the USA.

Traditional Vs. Modern

A clear divide exists between the traditional and modern education. Traditional education is religious, immutable, and other-worldly. On the other hand, modern education is 100% secular and worldly. Its content is not fixed and changes with the demands of time and circumstances. Teaching methods and student–teacher relationships also differ between the two systems of education. The traditional teacher is an authoritarian who does not tolerate dissent, and obedience is taken as a big virtue. Memorization is all that is expected of a student.

Contrary to this, critical thinking is central to modern education where questioning and free thinking are encouraged. It requires a culture where curiosity, eagerness to explore, and tolerance of divergent opinions reign supreme. Some change is taking place. This change is, however, not about embracing outright modern education but a hybrid system taking care of traditional as well as modern education. This system is causing confusion. A Shakespearean "to be or not to be" situation emerges out of such a hybrid system. "Hybridization is often awkward. Old and new are put through a meat grinder; that which emerges is in mangled form".[15]

Scientific knowledge and religion belong to two different spheres. Scientific reality can be understood only through scientific knowledge. Temperature, structure of land, galaxies, composition of rocks, components of atoms, biological phenomena, human anatomy, and various ailments and their treatment are domains of scientific inquiry. The scope of the religion is metaphysical realities and teachings or commandments to enhance the quality of interactions between human beings in the society. Science and religion are two disciplines that do not meet due to their entirely different scopes. Regrettably, due to an overemphasis on religion and Muslim ideology, we embarked on the wrong path in Pakistan. The religious scholars started finding proofs of the divinity of religious scriptures in science and where apparently there was some conflict between scientific knowledge and religion, they altogether rejected science and scientific thinking.

A scientific reality cannot be rejected if it apparently conflicts with religious scriptures. The theories of science may change as research advances whereas religious scriptures are permanent, fixed, and eternal. Imam Ghazali, in the first chapter of his Ihaya Ulum-Ud-Din (The Revival of Religious Learning), writing around 1100 C.E., very pertinently pointed out: "A grievous crime indeed against religion has been committed by a man who imagines that Islam is defended by the denial of the mathematical sciences, seeing that there is nothing in the revealed truth opposed to these sciences by way either of negation or affirmation".[16]

Dogma, superstition, and intolerance are big stumbling blocks for the cultivation of a scientific mindset. Landes is right when he says that intolerance, superstition, and ignorance are easier to acquire and cultivate than to uproot.[17] It is perhaps not possible to make the mind of the entire nation a scientific mind. What is needed is a critical mass of people who have a scientific mindset to cultivate rationality and critical thinking in the society.

Technology, education, skills, and scientific knowledge are inseparable from each other. While highlighting the said linkages, the authors of '*Why Nations Fail*' write: "Intimately linked to technology are the education, skills, competencies, and know-how of the workforce, acquired in schools, at home, and on job. We are so much productive than a century ago not just because of better technology embodied in machines but because of the greater know-how that workers possess. All the technology of the world would be of little use without workers who knew how to operate it. But there is more to skills and competencies than just the ability to run machines. It is the education and skills of the workforce that generate the scientific knowledge upon which our progress is built and that enable the adaptation and adoption of these technologies in diverse lines of business".[18]

The Industrial Revolution in the West, harbinger of modern economic growth, owed much to the deep complementarities between groups of key industrial workers. There was relatively a small group of innovators who invented different things but a comparatively larger group of highly skilled craftsmen or technicians. These craftsmen possessed skills to carry out the instructions, new recipes, and blueprints inventors wrote. Technical competence was an integral part of the supply side as inventors would not have been able to carry out their ideas without trained technicians and skilled workers.[19]

The Pakistan Educational Conference held in Karachi in November 1947, convened immediately after the birth of Pakistan, highlighted one of the basic issues with the educational system of Pakistan that is its irrelevance to the changing realities of life. The conference emphasized that "Our educational system, as originally conceived by Macaulay, was intended to serve a narrow, utilitarian purpose and its growth has been largely a matter of artificial improvisation. It has rightly been condemned for its lack of realism and its inability to adjust itself to the needs of a rapidly changing environment, its over-literary bias and its utterly uninspiring, soulless character".[20]

We find a similar assessment in the Sharif Commission Report of 1959 which says: "The (Educational) system was designed to produce government servants who, under the superior services, operated the State. The range of educational opportunities was limited to those which contributed to the attainment of competence in some of the skills of the government".[21] A path dependence is clearly visible in the educational system. A type of ideological discomfort with science, technology, and vocational education can be seen in our policies, curriculum, and pedagogy. Still we see the dominance of the subjects (we may call them literary) that do not impart skills required for economic growth.

All types and disciplines of education are not alike from the perspective of contribution to economic growth. It is what Mokyr calls "the useful knowledge" that is the knowledge of science and technology which matters the most for economic prosperity. He writes: "Three general categories of human capital can be distinguished. Training- in which skills and useful knowledge are transmitted to the child. Education– in which the ability to consume certain goods and services–we can think of them as hobbies-is taught (for example, music, literature, and sports etc.) and in which certain values (moral codes, loyalty, respect for others, nationalism, and religion) are transmitted, and drilling in which child is taught such behaviors as politeness, table manners, hygiene, punctuality, and obedience. Decisions are made at two levels: how much to invest in children and what kind of education to provide. These clearly reflect cultural elements, that is, what society believes to be important".[22]

Knowledge, yes, useful knowledge, is important for which the society needs a technologically creative culture. A cadre of innovators who can think independently and are able to challenge the status quo and long-held superstitious beliefs is required as innovation cannot prosper in a "malnourished, superstitious, or extremely traditional society".[23] Social and economic institutions that provide the right set of incentives to innovators are needed for creativity and ideas. Actually a society that believes in tolerance, diversity, independent thinking, and logic is fertile ground for knowledge, technological creativity, and progress.

Useful Knowledge

Knowledge, ideas, and economic growth are inextricably connected. "Knowledge in the language of economics refers to any trick, technique, or insight that allows an economy to generate more out of its existing resources land, labor, and capital".[24] Knowledge is the key to economic growth and ideas are at the heart of the assumption that there is no limit to economic growth. Physical infrastructure decays. Capital depreciates. Humans age and then die. Ideas, however, remain. They remain embodied in technology. Ideas differ from physical capital from another angle. Physical capital is generally a private good with the properties of rivalry and excludability. If you consume it, less will be left for others.

On the other hand, ideas are like public goods. More and more people can use an idea as they are not depleted by use. It is technologically feasible for any number of people to use an idea simultaneously once it has been invented. Knowledge and ideas, being public goods, benefit everyone unless governments or monopolies restrict their dissemination or some people cannot use them due to their incapacity (for example, an illiterate person cannot use a computer program).

A book, a computer program, an instruction manual, a chemical formula, et cetera, are non-rival inputs in production, says Romer. Such goods have high costs for producing the first unit and very low or zero costs for producing subsequent goods. The non-rivalrous nature of ideas and innovation generate increasing returns to scale, thus relaxing the limits on economic growth.[25] Romer gives an illustration to make the point. Suppose one laborer builds one staircase in a day with one hammer. Now give another hammer to another person, and both people can now build two staircases by performing the same tasks. But if you are able to find an efficient way to combine nail and wood, then the two laborers can build more than two staircases in a day with the same inputs that is two hammers. Once invented, the method or recipe for combining nails and wood more efficiently can be passed on to other people at a much lower price than what it took to create the initial invention. Moreover, on constant returns to scale, in a competitive economy, factors of production that is labor and capital are paid their marginal product which means that the wage bill and capital rent combine to equal the entire value of output and nothing is left as profit.[26]

According to Romer, a nation that lacks physical objects like factories and roads suffers from "object gaps" whereas a nation that lacks ideas and knowledge to create value in the modern economy suffers from "idea gaps". And what the poor countries suffer the most from are the idea gaps.[27] In Pakistan (as well as other Muslim countries), theoretically, there is a lot of lip service about the significance of seeking knowledge. "Seek knowledge even if you have to go to China", you will find this saying, attributed to Prophet Muhammad, on the lips of common people as well as the elite. There is, however, no talk about the type of knowledge needed for development. What is needed is productive knowledge that is knowledge connected to economic growth and livelihoods.

Knowledge evolves. Knowledge that may be appropriate at one point in time may be dysfunctional or redundant at another point. All the erudition in the language and literature of Persian became irrelevant with the declaration of English as the official language in the Indian subcontinent by the British. There is a hierarchy of knowledge in terms of its importance for economic growth and human welfare. Knowledge of computing, calculating, organic chemistry, liquids and gases, macromolecular compounds, semi-conductors, image data, surgery, diagnosis, medical preparations, digital information, et cetera, is the knowledge that drives innovation and productivity. Knowledge of these areas is directly linked to economic growth, and the scientists and innovators who contribute to these fields are really contributing to the welfare of the people.

Productive knowledge persists, evolves, changes forms, and embraces improvements but does not vanish altogether as it is the result of a lot of research, hard work, and application of mind. An element of permanence is embedded in such knowledge. The knowledge with regard to the creation of electricity, light, surgery of the human brain, and diagnosis of cancer and AIDS is benefiting humanity and shall keep benefiting. Almost entire knowledge that contributed to economic growth and human well-being was created in the West. We cannot boast of the creation of such knowledge in Pakistan for multiple reasons.

First, we lack a culture of research and innovation. Second, we do not distinguish productive knowledge from other types of knowledge. Third, we write books on subjects that fall at the lower end of the hierarchy of knowledge with regard to economic growth. Travelogues, biographies, and religious books are the subjects where the majority of our writing or creativity is concentrated. Interestingly, these subjects are not productive knowledge in the true sense. At maximum, they are passing on some information to the readers. The writers of such stuff are not imparting any durable knowledge. For example, by writing a travelogue (which is very popular with Urdu writers), you are just conveying some information about some country or city. And it is very likely that Google will put most of the information contained in the travelogue at your disposal with the click of a button.

A clear positive bias would be required for the creation and dissemination of productive knowledge in developing countries like Pakistan. Public money need not be spent on stipends and subjects that do not promote productive knowledge. One may not require financial support to write poetry or conduct research on folklores. It would, however, be difficult to make a scientific invention or create an economic idea without teamwork and financial support. Economic ideas are not easy to find or create. They do not come out of thin air. They come from learning by doing, from coordination between different economic actors, from think tanks, and from quality research institutions having linkages with industry. Learning, not just schooling, is important for the generation of ideas.

The role of the universities as guardians of academic freedom and openness is vital where ideas for basic research germinate which are then put into practice by the firms. Ideas need a culture where 'connection' is valued more than protection and secrecy. "When one looks at innovation in nature and in culture, environments that build walls around good ideas tend to be less innovative in the long run than open ended environments. Good ideas may not want to be free, but they want to connect, fuse, and recombine. They want to reinvent themselves by crossing conceptual borders. Ideas are like selfish genes interested in their transmission and replication. They want to complete each other as much as they want to compete".[28] That is why meta-ideas that is ideas to support the production and transmission of other ideas are considered the most important ones. The emergence of 'economic societies' all across Europe in the eighteenth century and their role in the flow of economic ideas are well-documented.[29] These societies created an ecosystem for the generation, dissemination, and application of ideas for boosting manufacturing in the West.

The Power of Ideas

Knowledge resides in the brains of the people. It is embedded in the goods and services produced by a country. Economic Ideas crystallize into products. The product diversification and the production of more sophisticated goods depend upon the knowledge, learning, and technical know-how possessed by a nation. Rich countries, being rich in ideas and productive knowledge, not only produce more output per worker but they also produce different and more challenging products like chemicals and machinery (more complex products) while poor and developing countries produce rice, coca, textile goods, et cetera, (less complex products). Producing simple things has implications for the development trajectory of a country. Simple products bring low income to the global market as they are produced by many others. The economic phenomena of perfect competition and diminishing returns are associated with the goods generally produced by poor counties.[30] Further, the volatility of economic growth in poor and developing countries is also associated with their production structures. Empirics suggest that around 50% of the difference in volatility in growth is explained by the fact that poor countries specialize in more volatile sectors. As countries develop, their production structures move from more volatile to less volatile sectors, and the volatility of country-specific macroeconomic shocks also falls.[31]

When a country is producing agricultural commodities, textile goods, or minerals, it cannot influence the market price. It takes whatever the market offers. It is simply a price-taker. As production expands after a certain point, the addition of more and more input units will produce smaller and smaller amounts of new output that are diminishing returns to scale shall set in. After all, there is an upper achievable limit of agricultural yield in cotton, rice, wheat, et cetera. On the other hand, with the production of sophisticated goods like computer software, costs go down. The larger the volume of output, the lower the cost per unit produced once mechanized production starts. Moreover, production of cotton, maize, rice, potatoes, copper, et cetera, is dependent on immediate inputs like fields, mines, and underground wells, which are limited in quantity and quality, and thus the cost may increase with an increase in the volume of production. Their high dependence on the immediate inputs provided by nature also enhances the potential for volatility. Diversification and complexity of a country's production structure are thus important for managing volatility and accelerating economic growth.

A historical analysis of the product space of Pakistani goods simply shows that Pakistan has specialized in unsophisticated or less sophisticated goods typical of poor countries. Its exports are concentrated in textiles, clothing, rice, and food. An examination of the historical trends in the diversification of Pakistan's exports suggests that its export structure is fairly traditional.[32] In terms of economic complexity index (ECI), Pakistan scores very low compared to countries like China.[33] Contrary to Pakistan's experience, countries like South Korea and Malaysia have reduced their reliance on traditional sectors of the economy through an accelerated process of structural transformation. They have moved from the 'periphery' of the product space to the 'core' during this transformation.

For instance, the top ten items of export for South Korea in 1975 were footwear ($200 million), ships, boats, and other vessels ($111 million), articles of apparel ($127 million), crustaceans and molluscs ($107 million), refined sugar ($96.6 million), plywood ($94.9 million), wood-based panels ($94.9 million), silk yarn ($77.5 million), and cement ($667.2 million). In 2020, out of those 10 items, nine are no longer in the top 10. Only one item (ships, boats, and other vessels) is on the list at number 3 with exports of US$16.5 billion. Other items have been replaced by motor cars, machinery, electrical accumulators, perfumery, optical instruments, et cetera. On the other hand, out of the top 10 items exported by Pakistan, in 1975, eight related to cotton yarn and textile-related products, while the other two were rice and cement. In 2020, it has the same basket of exports.

Had South Korea gone by its natural comparative advantage, it at the maximum would have been producing better varieties of rice but it defied the traditional theory of comparative advantage by producing high-tech value-added goods. The mix of the goods a country produces has important implications for the subsequent growth patterns of its economy. Simply what you export matters.[34] We can notice a direct relationship between income growth and economic complexity. But the key question is: why does Pakistan not produce complex goods?

According to the *'Atlas of Economic Complexity'*, "countries simply do not make the products and services they need. They make the ones they can. To do so, they need people and organizations that possess relevant knowledge. Some goods, like medical imaging devices or jet engines, embed large amounts of knowledge and are the results of very large networks of people and organizations. By contrast, wood logs or coffee, embed much less knowledge, and the networks required to support these operations do not need to be large. Complex economies are those which can weave vast quantities of relevant knowledge together, across large networks of people, to generate a diverse mix of knowledge-intensive products. Simpler economies, in contrast, have a narrow base of productive knowledge and produce fewer and simpler products, which require smaller webs of interaction".[35]

The products a country produces are reflective of the useful knowledge, know-how, and imagination of that society. The goods like garments, cutlery, surgical instruments, et cetera, are all what Hidalgo calls "crystals of our imagination".[36] Hidalgo presents an interesting theory, which he calls personbyte theory, regarding the nature of goods produced by a country. According to said theory, human beings have limited ability to embody knowledge, know-how, and information, so there is a limit to what an individual can think of producing at his level. In order to overcome this constraint, you need networks to embody more knowledge and know-how that is more personbytes to produce complex goods. In this way, the theory postulates a positive relationship between the complexity of an economic activity and the size of professional and social networks.[37] Learning, productive knowledge, and the right type of education are needed to produce complex goods.

The importance of the right type of education was very clear to the founder of Pakistan. Just after three months of the creation of Pakistan, the Pakistan Educational Conference was held in Karachi on November 27, 1947, and Quaid-e-Azam, in his message to the conference, said: "There is no doubt that the future of our State will and must greatly depend on the type of education we give to our children and the way in which we bring them up as future citizens of Pakistan. Education does not merely mean academic education. There is immediate and urgent need for giving scientific and technical education to our people in order to build up our future economic life and to see that our people take to science, commerce, trade, and particularly well-planned industries".

The education policies of Pakistan, though invariably mentioning the importance of technical education, had high gaps of commitment and implementation. Confusions about the type of education remained unresolved. The Educational system failed to prepare a critical mass of individuals who could imagine the production of complex goods. Distorted reward structures (responsible for misallocation of talent), absence of networks (due to low trust in society), and above all, neglect of human resource development thwarted the development of an ecosystem for the generation of economic ideas and structural transformation of the economy. Pakistan, being a developing country, can still take advantage of its backwardness. It does not require big investments in R&D for cutting-edge innovations. Building capacity of its workforce to imitate ideas and instructions through technical education would be sufficient till it touches the Production Possibility Frontier (PPF).

Innovation vs. Imitation

Contrary to developing and poor countries, developed countries need to push the PPF outward to accelerate growth. Doing so requires some innovation, some new techniques, and some machines to substitute labor with capital. And in this context, even the assumption that growth will continue indefinitely comes under challenge as there may be limits to innovation. Robert Gordon, while dilating on the slowdown of economic growth in the USA, argues that there was no growth before 1750. It began in 1750s, witnessed the fastest rates in the middle of the twentieth century, and then began to plummet. And the falloff is continuing. Why did growth pick up in the 1750s and continue for almost 250 years?

According to Gordon, the pace of growth in this period is a sequence of three distinct revolutions.[38] The first Industrial Revolution owed itself to inventions like steam engine, cotton gin, and railroads. It took almost 150 years for the first Industrial Revolution to have its full impact. The second Industrial Revolution (1870–1900) influenced the lives of the people hugely. Electricity, internal combustion engine, telephone, phonograph, and motion pictures were all invented during this period. Although a lot of progress had been made until 1870 and machines had started replacing humans and animals, overall life was dull and tasteless, Gordon argues. Human living and productivity, however, increased dramatically as a result of the Second Industrial Revolution.

This revolution touched its peak around 1900 and then diminishing returns set in. The invention and emergence of computers, internet, and e-commerce (the third Industrial Revolution) then continued to bolster economic growth by augmenting the efficiency and productivity of human labor. However, the inventions made during the last two decades or so are more focused on entertainment and communication than labor saving. So their contribution to economic growth is not significant. Their impact on labor productivity is not as sharp as those of electric lights, motor cars, or indoor plumbing. Gordon is of the view that faltering innovation due to multiple reasons like exhaustion of demographic dividends (from female labor force participation), quality issues in education, rising inequality, et cetera, is the real culprit behind the slowdown of US growth.

Similar points were raised by Tyler Cowen. He wrote about US growth: "We are failing to understand why we are failing. All of these problems have a single, little noticed root cause: we have been living off low-hanging fruit for at least three hundred years—-yet during last forty years, that low hanging fruit started disappearing, and we started pretending it was still there. We have failed to recognize that we are at a technological plateau and the trees are more bare than we would like to think".[39] More investment in tertiary education and research, greater competition in the market as competition induces firms to innovate, and better regulation and organization of financial systems are the levers for stimulating economic growth in developed countries.[40]

Developing countries can capitalize on the advantage of operating inside PPF and can go for low-hanging fruit. Frontier technologies may not be that much needed to stimulate and sustain economic growth in developing countries. Even otherwise, frontier technologies are adapted to high-income and research-intensive countries and may even pose a threat in some cases to the productivity growth of low-income countries due to inappropriateness. Some estimates suggest that the inappropriateness of technology reduces global production by 58% and increases cross-country inequalities by 15%.[41] The theme of inappropriate technology in particular looms large in agriculture where technologies developed for pathogens and pests may not work effectively in different environments and climates. Despite the inappropriate technology argument, huge scope exists for imitation-driven growth in countries like Pakistan operating inside the PPF. Even a country like China worked in imitation mode and massively invested in primary and secondary education so its labor force could understand and access the knowledge embodied in cutting-edge Western technologies.[42]

What are the possible levers of catch up policies for such growth in Pakistan? First of all, the transfer of technology from developed countries requires improvement in the investment climate. Second, more focus is required on technical education to develop a skilled workforce to absorb the knowledge contained in technologies. Improvement in management skills is another lever of imitation-based growth. Management, both in the private and public sectors, matters. The World Management Survey (WMS) has found a strong correlation between scores on management practices and the performance of the organization on parameters like productivity, student achievement (management of schools), or mortality rates (management of hospitals).[43] The countries like USA, UK, Canada, and Germany are at the top on scores on management practices while African countries like Tanzania, Ethiopia, and Ghana are at the bottom. It simply means investment in improving management practices in the private sector and focusing on governance in the public sector can turn out to be important policy levers to enhance economic growth.

The endogenous growth theory postulates that economic growth is the result of the internal factors of the economy and accumulation of human capital (through education, training, fostering entrepreneurship, learning by doing, etc.) is at the heart of all economic development. An analysis of World Economic Forum (WEF) reports, which measure human capital dimensions of economic growth, makes it amply clear that low human development or an inadequately educated workforce is one of the top factors responsible for Pakistan's low national competitiveness.[44] Out of the 12 pillars of the WEF's reports, four are directly linked to skills. They are health and primary education, higher education and training, business sophistication, and innovation. Two pillars, that is technological readiness (the capacity of the workforce to use existing technologies to improve productivity) and labor market efficiency are indirectly related to human development. Three channels are quite obvious through which learning and education contribute to productivity and economic growth.

First, learning augments the skills of the workforce. Second, it increases the innovative capacity of the economy since knowledge of new technologies, products, and processes enhances productivity and promotes economic growth. Third, learning and education facilitate the diffusion and transmission of knowledge needed to understand and process new information and capitalize on new technologies developed by others.[45] It means human factor is the most important determinant of economic growth.

The Human Factor

According to ILO estimates, the output of a South Korean worker is over 1150% higher than a Pakistani worker while that of a Chinese worker is 345% higher. The output of a Malaysian worker is around 361% and the average output of a Sri Lankan worker is 115 higher compared to a Pakistani worker. On average, the output of a South Asian worker is 27% higher. The troubling part is that the pace of increase in output per worker is very slow. In 2011, the output of both Indian and Vietnamese workers was lower than a Pakistani worker. Both have surpassed Pakistan in a period of one decade that is in 2022. The gains made by Vietnamese workers are quite impressive. A Vietnamese worker is now 31% more productive than a Pakistani worker. Bangladesh is also fast-catching (see Table 3.1).

Skills and human resource development are missing from the debate on competitiveness and economic growth in Pakistan. Industry and businesses are stuck in the equilibrium of low competitiveness. They look for competitive advantage in exchange rate engineering, tariff structure, or low wages. Skills enhancement and innovation are not the priority. The infant industry argument, which has held sway in Pakistan since its inception, is still touted in various guises and stripes. Expectations and demands of business organization revolve around the old tools of competitiveness, which in fact are the sources of rent-seeking. Competitiveness is basically

Table 3.1 Output per worker (GDP constant 2015 US$) of selected countries/regions

Year	*2011*	*2012*	*2013*	*2014*	*2015*	*2016*	*2017*	*2018*	*2019*	*2020*	*2021*	*2022*
Bangladesh	2757	2894	3021	3144	3290	3458	3468	3636	3839	3967	4143	4311
China	11,040	11,901	12,822	13,757	14,712	15,706	16,823	17,982	19,128	20,277	21,008	21,715
India	3726	3896	4138	4440	4792	5187	5539	5905	5734	5621	5819	6001
Indonesia	6158	6335	6646	6873	7147	7420	7609	7838	7991	7886	8245	8479
Republic of Korea	52,917	53,047	53,687	53,912	54,712	55,749	56,823	58,307	59,023	59,184	61,015	60,980
Malaysia	19,292	19,541	19,535	20,107	20,672	21,269	22,022	22,510	22,937	21,706	21,881	22,464
Pakistan	3741	3807	3924	4032	4151	4357	4514	4739	4739	4721	4715	4876
Sri Lanka	8218	8921	9018	9489	9828	10,155	10,373	11,134	11,238	10,991	11,186	10,492
Viet Nam	3720	3877	4009	4213	4472	4756	5058	5359	5707	6022	6163	6456
South Asia	4254	4373	4558	4833	5099	5474	5744	6025	5897	5869	6042	6196
Sub-Saharan Africa	4240	4353	4482	4578	4568	4482	4466	4469	4457	4320	4368	4360

Source: International Labor Statistics (ilostat.ilo.org)

linked to people and their prosperity. Michael Porter writes: "When you start to look at location, I argue, and believe very strongly that the true metric of competitiveness is the productivity of the resources utilized in that location. Take for example a company making shoes in Massachusetts that is gaining market share, but it is paying its workers only 50 cents an hour wages. The low wage makes it competitive in selling shoes, but it is not boosting the prosperity of Massachusetts which would like to have high wages".[46]

Cutting nominal wages and engineering the exchange rate increase competitiveness only in the short term. The impact of such policies may even sometimes be counter-productive in the form of an increase in unemployment and inflation.[47] With the emergence of endogenous growth theories and the expansion of the scope of the definition of competitiveness, the fog surrounding the concept is becoming clearer. National competitiveness no longer oscillates around market share and cost advantages. It is not a zero-sum game. Improvement in the national competitiveness of one country is not at the expense of another country. In broader terms, the competitiveness of a country means more incomes, more growth, and economic development at a faster pace. Humans, the skills embodied in them, productive knowledge, innovations, and institutions (rules of the game) are the main determinants of competitiveness. "Improvements follow from science and from entrepreneurs such as Thomas Edison, who applied science to create profitable businesses. It should therefore be no surprise that it was US society, not Mexico or Peru, that produced Thomas Edison, and that it was South Korea, and not North Korea that today produces technologically innovative companies such as Samsung and Hyundai".[48]

Highlighting the importance of innovation for competitiveness and growth, Paul Romer points out that the ability to keep discovering new and better processes is of vital importance for growth. Merely educating existing knowledge does not spur economic growth, particularly in countries that are operating at the production possibility frontier. Romer writes while talking of a hypothetical situation in the Middle Ages that: "A farmer who educated his children and workers at the leading educational institutions of the day would not have been able to increase his output per acre by very much. It is not the dissemination of old information but steady arrival of new bits of software that makes education even more valuable and provides new opportunities for growth".[49] Pakistan is dependent on low-skill low-technology manufactured exports due to low development of human resources. Some daunting challenges like low complexity of the economy, low growth, low innovation, and low competitiveness are all connected to the human factor directly or indirectly.[50] Absence of sufficient skilled labor compels market adjustments which involve acceptance of less efficient methods and lower quality.[51]

The human factor is also important from the perspective of culture, the set of values and norms people hold or eulogize. Cultures encapsulating deep religious values are very persistent and the speed of evolution and adoption of new value systems is slow in such cultures.[52] Landes, talking of the culture of the Middle East, says that a culture having following characteristics is hardly conducive to economic development: "(i) does not produce an informed and capable workforce; (ii) continues to mistrust or reject new techniques and ideas; and (iii) does not respect such knowledge if its members are able to get it either by study abroad or by good fortune at home".[53] Culture also determines our attitudes toward work. Max Weber's thesis on the protestant ethic and the spirit of capitalism vindicates this point. What work ethics we have is also determined by the national and organizational cultures. Some cultures may not encourage female labor force participation, having negative implications for economic growth. For example, Mukesh Eshwaran et al.[54] have shown that in rural areas of India women may not participate in market work due to family status concerns in a culture that stigmatizes market work by married women.

Pakistan is the fifth most populous country in the world. The 2023 census puts the population at 241.499 million with growth rate of 2.55%. According to LFS 2020–21, working-age population is 159.8 million. More than one-third (40.0%) belongs to the age group of 0 to 14 years while the population of youth aged (15–24 years) is 41.8 million (18.8%) and as such constitutes the second biggest group after children. The population of old aged people that is aged 65 or older is just 3.4%. These statistics make it amply clear that Pakistan is a country with huge potential of demographic dividend. It can capitalize on the potential of the young population for accelerating economic growth but it is missing the opportunities offered by the demographic dividend due to, what a World Bank report on the status of human capital in Pakistan calls "confluence of low human capital, low labor force participation, low productivity, and low pace of job creation".[55] Pakistan can reap benefits from two distinct phases of demographic transition (Fig. 3.1).

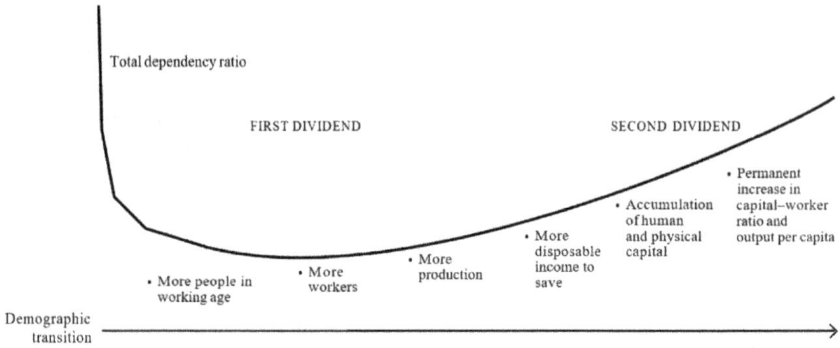

Fig. 3.1 Two distinct demographic dividends (*Source* World Bank elaboration)

In the first phase, dividends would accrue from decrease in dependency ratio and increase in the working-age group. The availability of more workers in the economy would boost production and disposable income of the people. The second phase would come later as a result of increase in savings and investment due to fewer dependent children, more disposable income, and increase in longevity.[56] For optimizing the demographic dividend, right set of priorities and investments in human capital would be required to make the youth more educated, more skilled, and more productive.

CHAPTER 4

The Question of Education

Alfred Marshall, in 1890s, highlighted the importance of education as a national investment. The most valuable capital of all is the one invested in human beings, Marshall held. "It (education) will be profitable as mere investment, to give the masses of the people much greater opportunities than they can generally avail themselves of. For by this means many, who would have died unknown, are enabled to get the start needed for bringing out their latent abilities. And the economic value of one great industrial genius is sufficient to cover the expenses of the education of a whole town".[1] Almost after one century, in 1995, Gary S. Becker delivering talk on 'Human Capital and poverty alleviation'[2] emphasized the role of human capital in economic development on the lines of Marshall's argument. He pointed out several channels through which education reduces poverty and enhances incomes.

For example, it helps control population growth, induces better health choices among the poor, and reduces mortality rates and gender discrimination. Becker said: "Education is the most effective way for able young people of poor backgrounds to rise in the economic hierarchy because human capital is the main asset of 90% of any population. That is why income inequality in a nation is greater when inequality in education is greater". Education is an expectation-builder. It creates expectations for social mobility, employment, and a better life. Sen and Dreze in *'An Uncertain Glory'*,[3] emphasizing the centrality of education

J. Nasir, *Development Challenges of Pakistan*,
https://doi.org/10.1007/978-981-97-3064-3_4

in socio-economic development, have listed around nine virtues of basic education. Those are briefly listed here to set the stage for the ensuing discussion on education in Pakistan.

According to them, first of all, education enhances the quality of life and freedoms through channels like living an informed life and communicating with fellow human beings. Two, education creates economic and employment opportunities by imparting skills. Three, it enhances people's voice and they become more empowered politically and socially as education gives them the ability to read newspapers and books and communicate with one another. Fourth, basic education helps in tackling health and public health care problems. Five, basic education makes people aware of their rights, and they become more demanding for the achievement of those rights. In this way, education is not just an intrinsic good; it is also an instrumental good that is it allows other goods to be achieved. Sixth, education sharpens understanding of legal rights as illiteracy limits the ability of the people to understand, invoke, and use their legal rights. Seventh, female schooling enhances their power in family decisions and reduces fertility and infant mortality rates.

Eighth, education helps reduce economic and social inequalities in society. "Education is the principal mechanism of convergence—the poor catch up with the rich to the extent that they achieve the same level of technological know-how, skill, and education.—All signs are that the Scandinavian countries, where wage inequality is more moderate than elsewhere, owe this result in large part to the fact that their education is relatively egalitarian and inclusive".[4] Nine, studying, learning, and the process of schooling bring joy and can add to the quality of life and well-being. Some researchers, based on a large-scale primary school construction programs, have found that an increase in schooling helps reduce armed civil conflict intensity.[5] This means that books work better than bullets for restoring peace and harmony in a conflict-ridden society. Education and democracy are also highly correlated as schooling teaches people to interact with others and enhances civic participation including voting and organizing.[6] So there is a compelling case, at the philosophical level, to make it obligatory for the state to ensure 100% education, at least at the basic level, to its citizens. And to fulfill this obligation, the first step would be to bring all the out-of-school children to schools.

Challenge of Out of School Children

Regrettably, 26.2 million children are still out of school in Pakistan.[7] Segregation of the out of school children on the basis of province shows that 11.73, 7.63, 3.36 and 3.13 million children are respectively out of school in Punjab, Sindh, KPK, and Balochistan. The population of the out of school children (OOSC) is bigger than the population of several European countries like the Netherlands, Belgium, or the entire population of the Scandinavian countries put together. Added to this, progress on bringing the out of school children (OOSC) is not very encouraging in the last two decades in all the provinces except Punjab which was able to reduce the number of OOSC. The situation is particularly disappointing in Sindh and Balochistan. Rural Sindh fares worse, in percentage terms, even compared to rural Balochistan. Variations exist in terms of gender as well in all provinces. More female children are out of school in all the provinces except Punjab. The province of Balochistan witnessed over 100% increase in OOSC (in absolute number) in a period of two decades (from 1.213 million in 1998 to 2.562 million in 2018–2019). The province of Sindh also registered an increase in OOSC during the last two decades.

At the national level, almost one-third of children (32%) are out of school (see Table 4.1). The pace of progress is also not enviable. We see a reduction of just around 0.5% per annum in OOSC. Further, no significant positive change is visible even after the 18th Amendment in the Constitution. The participation rate in schools constantly declined post-18th Amendment, particularly in Balochistan (from 53% in 2010 to 41% in 2018–2019). The rate of participation also declined in the province of Sindh (from 59% in 2010 to 58% in 2018–2019). The province of Punjab witnessed a respectable increase (from 73 to 79%) after the 18th Amendment. A modest increase in participation is also visible in KP (from 70 to 72%).[8]

Disaggregation of data at the district level shows severe deprivations in terms of school participation. The districts of Southern Punjab have more OOSC compared to other parts of Punjab. The figures for the top five districts of each province reveal that in some districts over two-thirds of the children are out of school (see Table 4.2). The situation is very alarming and Pakistan is not likely to achieve 100% literacy or basic education in the next four to five decades with such a large number of out of school children at the existing pace of progress.

Table 4.1 Percentage of out of school children 5–16 years

Sr. No		*Urban*			*Rural*			*Total*		
		Male	*Female*	*Total*	*Male*	*Female*	*Total*	*Male*	*Female*	*Total*
1	Pakistan	21	23	22	30	44	37	27	37	32
2	Punjab	17	15	16	25	31	28	22	26	24
3	Sindh	27	32	29	49	69	58	39	51	44
4	KP	15	25	20	23	48	34	22	44	32
5	Balochistan	29	42	35	41	65	51	38	59	47

Source District Level PSLM Survey 2019–2020

Table 4.2 Percentage of out of school children 5–16 years in some selected districts of the provinces

Sr. No	*Punjab*	*Male*	*Female*	*Total*	*Sr. No*	*Sindh*	*Male*	*Female*	*Total*
1	Rajanpur	43	55	48	11	Thatta	66	78	71
2	Muzaffargarh	37	49	43	12	Kashmore	60	76	67
3	Rahim Yar Khan	36	46	41	13	Tando Muhammad Khan	60	73	66
4	Lodhran	38	41	40	14	Sujawal	55	77	65
5	D.G. Khan	31	47	38	15	Badin	53	75	63
	KP	Male	Female	Total		Balochistan	Male	Female	Total
6	Kohistan	33	90	60	16	Shaheed Sikan-darabad	65	92	76
7	Mohmand	32	85	57	17	Sherani	50	97	70
8	Bajaur	36	77	56	18	Dera Bugti	63	76	68
9	Torghar	32	84	55	19	Nasirabad	64	76	68
10	South Waziristan	41	70	52	20	Harnai	60	74	66

Source District Level PSLM Survey 2019–2020

Why has Pakistan not been able to bring OOSC to schools? Several factors are responsible but at the top is the commitment gap reflected in low resource allocation to schools.[9] Financial constraints are certainly responsible for the deplorable state of affairs. After all, financial resources are required to build bricks and mortar structures. Building schools, even in corrupt regimes, tend to enhance schooling and school participation. Indonesia is a case in point where a massive program for building schools was initiated under President Suharto. Between 1973 and 1978, the Indonesian Government constructed over 61,000 primary schools throughout the country. Results of independent evaluations of this school building program confirm substantial improvements both in schooling and earnings.[10] The women exposed to the school construction program were more likely to have fewer children. Better living standards, better housing, and an increase in assets are also associated with the said program, confirming the long-term and intergenerational effects of education.[11] In a trade-off between guns and schools, schools got less priority in Pakistan. Low commitment to education is primarily responsible for the massive number of out of school children.

The commitment gap in education is also visible in the lack of physical infrastructure in public schools. Overall, 40% of primary schools in Pakistan are without electricity, 30% do not have drinking water, 28% do not have toilets, and 29% are without boundary walls. Disaggregation of data at the provincial level shows that in the province of Sindh, 49% of primary schools are without drinking water whereas in Balochistan this figure is as high as 75%. A similar pathetic situation can be seen for other infrastructural facilities such as availability of electricity, toilets, and boundary walls for public schools (see Table 4.3).

The commitment for bringing all children to schools has always existed on paper. All policy documents on education, issued since 1947, invariably mention this commitment. For example, Pakistan Educational Conference 1947, held in Karachi,[12] proceedings of which are considered the First Education Policy of Pakistan, constituted sub-committees on various categories of education and one sub-committee was on Primary and Secondary Education. In its report, the said sub-committee recommended to lay the basis of the national education system on strong foundations of free and compulsory primary education. To meet the expenses of free primary education, it recommended imposition of a special tax. Similarly, the report of the 'Commission on National Education (1959)', talking of the introduction of compulsory education, states that dropout rates are high and in this context "the first step to be taken is to compel all parents of children enrolling in primary schools to keep them in these schools until at the age of nine or ten plus or until the course has been satisfactorily completed".[13]

Table 4.3 Physical infrastructure (% of schools)

Sr. No	*Province/region*	*Primary*	*Middle*	*High*
Availability of electricity				
1	Pakistan	60	79	94
2	Punjab	99	100	100
3	Sindh	32	54	88
4	KP	81	87	95
5	Balochistan	16	33	67
Availability of drinking water				
1	Pakistan	70	84	94
2	Punjab	100	100	100
3	Sindh	51	67	90
4	KP	88	92	96
5	Balochistan	25	43	73
Availability of toilets for students				
1	Pakistan	72	89	96
2	Punjab	99	100	100
3	Sindh	53	73	93
4	KP	92	97	99
5	Balochistan	31	65	86
Availability of boundary wall				
1	Pakistan	71	87	94
2	Punjab	98	99	99
3	Sindh	51	74	92
4	KP	90	94	96
5	Balochistan	31	72	88

Source Pakistan Education Statistics 2020–2021 (NEMIS)

The Education Policy of 1970 talked about compulsory attendance up to the age of 10 years as a large number of children enrolled in primary classes did not attend classes regularly and many dropped out before finishing school. As an expression of determination for universal elementary education, the said policy also suggested that an element of compulsion needs to be introduced.[14] The Education Policy 1972–1980 described the eradication of illiteracy through universalization of elementary education and a massive adult education program as one of its eleven objectives.[15] The National Education Policy and Implementation Program 1979 in its policy statement about primary education said that universal enrolment for boys would be attained by 1986–1987 while for girls universalization would be achieved by 1992.[16] "5.5 million Children of the relevant age bracket are never enrolled in schools", the draft Education Policy 1998–2010 recognized.

The said draft policy also promised that every child of 6–12 years of age would be in school within 5 years and that universal literacy would be attained within 15 years. Other policy documents and action plans set similar targets and emphasized the importance of literacy and bringing all children to school. The noble goals and targets set in the educational policies and implementation documents were, however, not achieved due to low commitment and poor implementation, as rightly recognized by the National Education Policy 2009.

The 'paper commitment' rose to the highest level when amendment through Article 25-A was introduced in the Constitution of Pakistan making it obligatory for the state to impart basic education to all children in the age bracket of 5–16 years. All the provinces passed legislation in pursuance of Article 25-A for providing free and compulsory education to children. One interesting thing to note is that all the incentives laid down in the legislation are negative incentives. For example, Section 9(2) of the Punjab Free and Compulsory Education Act, 2014 provides that if a parent fails to admit and keep the child in a school he may not be entitled to any subsidy or poverty-targeted support from the Government. Section 6 of the KP Free Compulsory Primary and Secondary Education Act, 2017 stipulates that parents who fail to comply with the order passed by the School Attendance Authority shall be punishable with imprisonment and a fine. Section 8 of the Sindh Right of Children to Free and Compulsory Education Act, 2013 also contains similar provisions. The negative incentives to enforce attendance of the children are thus one of the defining features of the legislation promulgated by the provinces in pursuance of Article 25-A of the Constitution.

Incorporating such provisions shows our lack of understanding of the problem of OOSC which is purely an economic issue. The Balochistan Compulsory Education Act 2014 recognizes this aspect of the challenge. In the preamble, it lays down that economic limitations prevent the children from continuing education as they may contribute to household income. And here lies the essence of the issue. Sending children to school has an opportunity cost for poor parents. According to Annual Status of Education Report (ASER) 2019, children from lower wealth quartiles are more likely to be out of school than those hailing from upper quartiles. "When asked about the reason for a child not being enrolled in a school (never enrolled or dropped out), 57.3% of OOSC from wealth quartile 1 (the poorest) and 53.8% of OOSC from wealth quartile 2 were reported to be out of school due to poverty", the report says. Data from the Pakistan Demographic and Health Survey (DHS), 2018 (included in the World Inequalities Database in Education (WIDE), UNESCO) also confirms serious disparities based on wealth in OOSC. According to the said data, 51% of the OOSC belong to the poorest wealth quintile. For the richest quintile of population, this figure is 4%. As the level of schooling increases, population of OOSC also increases. The OOSC belonging to the poorest wealth quintile respectively constitute 55% and 75% of the OOSC population for lower secondary and upper secondary levels of schooling.

According to another study[17] by the Pak Alliance for Maths and Science on OOSC, 87% of the children who have not been to school reported it to be "too expensive". The said study further points out that among OOSC aged five years, 100% are those who have never attended school while among OOSC aged 16 years, the split between those enrolled and those who dropped out is virtually 50:50. The proportion of dropouts constituting OOSC is the highest between the ages of 10 and 11. In Balochistan, 64% of 16-year-old OOSC have never attended school while this figure is 63%, 53%, and 39% respectively for Sindh, KPK, and Punjab.

Poverty and Opportunity Cost

The children of poor families are engaged in some type of economic activity (which can be monetized) like garbage collection, working in homes as domestic servants, helping in auto workshops, grazing cattle, rendering babysitting services, or even begging on the streets. By doing such chores, they supplement the family's income. Their earnings may be small in absolute number but it matters for the family to keep the body and soul together. So the opportunity cost in the form of foregone earnings of sending the children to school for the poor is high. This aspect of the problem does not enter into the mental calculus of the elite and the policy-makers due to their poor understanding of the lives of the poor. The issue is not that the poor do not want to educate their children. They understand that education provides a window of opportunity for social mobility. The meanings of mobility are, however, structured along socio-economic and gender lines.

For the upper and middle classes schooling is a navigational tool to move in the society, visit foreign universities for higher education, enter the corporate world, or manage their family businesses. The entire perception of mobility is different for the poor. They engage in hard labor to earn a basic living. They need some source of stable income. Their expectations from education are thus to attain a stable source of income, a job, and some improvement in their livelihoods. So the design of policy prescriptions, for bringing OOSC to schools, would have to take into consideration the aspirations of the poor which are shaped by the material realities and socio-economic hierarchy of relationships in the society.[18]

In Pakistan, education is basically a story of expectations failure particularly for the poor. These failures are astounding in terms of reach, quality, and provision of livelihoods. It needs to be appreciated that for the families higher on the socio-economic hierarchy, education is a kind of consumption good. Better schooling for them is just like better food, better housing, or visiting a better health facility for treatment. On the other hand, it is an investment good for the poor. As is the case with all investments, the poor weigh the costs and benefits of sending their children to school. Education is a risky investment for them when compared with the guaranteed, though low, returns that their children get by engaging in low-income-generating activities particularly in rural areas. The constitutional amendment introduced through Article 25-A and legislation promulgated by all provinces pursuant to the said amendment would not ameliorate the situation unless the problem of OOSC is recognized and dealt with as an economic issue.

The right to education will just remain a paper commitment if its economic dimension is not taken care of. Declaring some right a fundamental right means that it becomes enforceable by the courts and even the state can be sued for the violation. Not a single case for the violation of the right to education has landed in the courts of law, despite grotesque violations found in every nook and corner of the country, confirming that the right to education is just a commitment on paper without any practical implications for the education of OOSC. Appropriate modalities and parameters, either by the Parliament or by the superior courts through the interpretation of Article 25-A of the Constitution, would be required for the enforcement of this right after taking into account the economic lives of the poor.

A significant number of children leave school before completing primary level of education. According to Pakistan Education Statistics,[19] out of 100 children enrolled in Grade 1, 63 make it to Grade-V. This number is 67 for male children and 59 for female children. Regional variations are also huge. The provinces of Sindh, KP, and Balochistan have low survival rates compared to the national average. Astonishingly, survival rates to Grade-V have decreased over last couple of years.[20] The overwhelming majority of the children who drop out of school belong to poor families. The problem is mainly connected to the opportunity cost of schooling, as discussed above. There are, however, some other reasons including the dungeon environment of the school, poor pedagogy, less focus by teachers on poor students, corporal punishment, et cetera. The Pakistan Social & Living Standard Measurement Survey (PSLM) survey 2018–2019 cites "child not willing" as the top reason for early dropout. A survey undertaken by the researchers of the Academy of Educational Planning and Management finds out that among various reasons, low socio-economic background that is poverty, is one of the major causes of dropout at the primary level.[21] The popular narrative that children drop out because they are not learning in school is not supported by data.[22] So bringing the out of school children to school is only one part of the challenge. Their retention in schools and making them economically productive are some other aspects of the challenge. So what can be done?

First of all, some kind of monetary benefit would be required to cover the opportunity cost of sending children to school. Such benefits may be in the form of stipends, cash transfers, et cetera. The amount of such incentives would have to be set at some level above the opportunity cost. Fixing it below the opportunity cost will not work. For designing workable monetary incentives, proper understanding of the economic lives of the poor and their aspirations would be highly important. Second, education has to be free in the real sense which means that books, food, uniforms, et cetera, are provided free of charge in public schools. A report of the Expert Group of Aid Studies (EBA),[23] a Swedish Government Committee mandated to analyze issues of development assistance, based on evaluations of 114 studies on education concludes that provision of conditional cash transfers, building new schools where local access is lacking, and provision of school meals are the most effective interventions to increase time in schools in communities where enrolment and attendance are sub-optimal. Further, education for poverty alleviation needs to be in sync with the demand for skills in the market.

Giving poor children education which is divorced from the skills required by the market reduces demand for schooling. Pritchett narrates an incident from India to show why poor people get frustrated with the entire system of schooling. He says that at a meeting, a man stood up, looked straight into the eyes of the school principal, and said: "You have betrayed us. I have worked like a brute my whole life because, without school, I had no skills other than those of a donkey. But you told us that if I sent my son to school, his life would be different from mine. For five years I have kept him from the fields and work and sent him to your school. Only now I find out that he is thirteen years old and does not know anything. His life won't be different. He will labor like a brute, just like me".[24] This incident is reflective of the significance of the right set of incentives for bringing and retaining children in schools as well as for their parents.

A clear-cut policy that attaches certain future opportunities to education, clearly visible to the poor parents, would be required. For example, an unemployment allowance can be provided to the educated youth during the period of unemployment to make them realize that education has clear-cut monetary benefits. "The low education level of poor countries is caused by economic institutions that fail to create incentives for parents to educate their children and by political institutions that fail to induce the government to build, finance, and support schools and the wishes of parents and children. The price these nations pay for low education of their population and lack of inclusive markets is high. They fail to mobilize their nascent talent. They have many potential Bill Gateses and perhaps one or two Albert Einstein who are now working as poor, uneducated farmers, being coerced to do what they don't do or being drafted into the army, because they never had the opportunity to realize their vocation in life".[25]

The incentive system needs to be designed in a way that some of the benefits of sending the children to school become obvious immediately when the children are still at school. For example, skills may be imparted in rural schools that make students better at agriculture-related work, like better use of soil through tunnel farming, enhancing the productivity of livestock, et cetera. Doing so shall require a curriculum with more emphasis on skills currently required in the households in a particular area, which means that an element of flexibility and 'local touch' would be needed even in the Single National Curriculum (SNC). Another important question is: whether education needs to be treated and provided as public good or its provision be tasked to the private sector?

Governments are the major providers of primary and secondary education throughout the world but privately funded institutions also exist. The degree of private involvement in the provision of education, however, greatly varies. For example, the share of private funding in Norway is just around 1.5%, while in Chile it goes to around 48.5%.[26] What are the implications of this huge variation in the footprint of the private sector in schooling? Some theorists have emphasized the deep nexus between inequality and private schooling. Countries like Norway, Sweden, Germany, Netherlands, Hungary, and the Czech Republic, where primary and secondary education are almost exclusively provided by public schools, are also characterized by low inequality. On the other hand, countries with the highest use of private schools by the rich like Austria, Australia, Brazil, Mexico, Spain, and the USA also are more unequal societies.

Private schooling has also got implications for the quality of public schools. The argument runs that when more and more parents send their children to private schools they no longer stand to gain from public schools. So they are not incentivized to lobby or vote for higher public spending on education.[27] There is another implication, not much discussed in the literature, and that is the negative impact on the quality of public schools when the children of those who are supposed to monitor the performance of public schools opt for private schools. It does not require much research to suggest that the elites of the society do not send their children to public schools in Pakistan. Even the members of the school bureaucracy and professors of public universities prefer to send their children to private schools.

Low-cost Private Schools

Pakistan has witnessed a peculiar phenomenon of the growth of low-cost private schools since the 1990s. The fee charged by an average rural private school is comparatively affordable for the lower middle class and households have emerged as significant investors in education. The students enrolled in these schools hail from the lower and lower middle classes.[28] The pay of teachers in the private sector is generally linked to performance. It is easy to hire and fire. So the question of absence of teachers in private schools is a rarity. On the other hand, public sector school teachers get a fixed salary that rewards length of service and nothing else. Marked differences are found in test scores not only between public and private schools but among public schools as well. A possible explanation for this variation among public schools in the same vicinity may lie in the intrinsic motivation of the teachers as some teachers may be intrinsically more motivated or altruistic so they put in more effort.[29] Overall, learning gaps are high. There is scarcely any correlation between pay and productivity in public schools. The absence of teachers is common in public schools, irrespective of gender.[30]

Private schools capitalize on the low salaries paid to the teachers and have also effectively employed less educated, low-paid young women to serve at the primary level. Even in urban elite schools, salaries paid to the teachers are lower compared to public sector schools. According to an impact evaluation[31] by the World Bank, private schools are proving successful in attracting students and teaching them for less money than it costs to run a public school. The said impact evaluation also suggests that the quality of education is better in low-cost private schools compared to public schools in the same area. In this context, an increase in the wages of public sector school teachers is not a well-founded proposition for increasing the quality of schooling unless pay is connected to productivity. Instead of increasing wages in a fixed manner, bonuses connected to performance may yield better outcomes in school enrollment and the level of student exam participation.[32]

The empirical evidence is scant to show that high salaries are helpful in raising teaching standards. Sen has raised an interesting point regarding the salaries of school teachers especially in rural areas. He writes with particular reference to India: "High salaries also increase the social distance between teachers and parents. In many Indian states today, the salary of primary school teacher is more than ten times what an agricultural laborer would earn, even if he or she were successful in finding employment every day at the statutory minimum wage. The social distance that has grown over the years, partly related to huge earning gaps, does not help to foster mutual cooperation between teachers and parents from most rural families, which could have been very important for the success of school education. The relatively high salaries of school teachers have also had the effect of making the expansion of school education immensely more expensive in a country with a large pool of people qualified to teach and eager to do so".[33]

Sen's observations, at least to the extent of public school teachers being overpaid, also apply to Pakistan. Teachers working in the public sector enjoy a high wage premium (PSWP) in Pakistan compared to private sector employees. Despite being paid more than private school teachers, learning outcomes, as mentioned earlier are low in government schools. The real issue is poor accountability and not low wages. "A major constraint to the delivery of quality education by the system is protection accorded to teachers by politicians owing to their role as poling agents during elections and the weak accountability systems that facilitate the blackmailing of government by powerful teachers' unions if they try to open proceedings against those guilty of rampant absenteeism".[34]

The provinces of Punjab and KP spend over Rs. 1600 per month per student (Punjab and KP respectively spend Rs. 19,743 and Rs. 19,407 per annum), while Sindh spends over Rs. 2300 per month (Rs. 28,301 annually). For Balochistan, the cost per student per month is around Rs. 3326 per month (Rs. 39,911 per annum). The national average is around Rs. 2000 per month (23,984 per annum) as per the latest available official figures.[35] Moreover, a government-run school generally occupies a far larger area on average than a private school. And the opportunity cost of the land occupied by public schools is not included in the per pupil cost as mentioned above which means that if cost–benefit analysis takes into account the cost of land (economic benefits accruing from some alternate use or amount of rent) occupied by a government-run school, the per pupil cost may turn out to be larger.

On the contrary, low-cost primary schools, especially in rural areas, charge fees in the range of Rs. 500–1000 per student (a lower per pupil cost compared to public schools). The case here is not for the privatization of education or doing away with government schools. Rather case is for strengthening accountability and improving governance in government-run schools. "It is fair to say that provincial education ministries—especially of Sindh and Balochistan—are not set up to educate kids. Their primary purpose seems to be to provide jobs to teachers and benefit administrators. Education is a mere byproduct",[36] wrote an ex-Finance Minister of Pakistan.

For enhancing accountability of public sector schools, both negative and positive incentives are needed and accountability of the entire schooling system is required. A robust system of regular school inspections, teacher selection through a meritocratic process, promotions based on the learning outcomes of students, parent-teacher associations, and grievance redressal facilities can make some difference.[37] Public sector schools are generally overcrowded. Pupil–teacher ratios (PTRs) are high. And schools especially in rural areas face acute shortage of teachers. Contract (for some tenure extendable subject to performance) appointments from the local population seem to be a good idea to ameliorate the situation. Doing so shall improve not only the accountability of teachers but also put less financial burden on the government exchequer. Contract recruitments, made in a transparent manner through school councils or public service commission to ward off political recruitments, would make the accountability of the system as well as teachers comparatively easy.

All the blame for the poor performance of government-run schools, however, cannot be attributed to the teachers. The teachers of public sector schools are required to perform several duties other than teaching such as election duties, BISP surveys, voter verification, census surveys, and polio vaccinations, with the result that the education of students suffers. Lack of accountability, overcrowding, poor access, and poor infrastructural facilities all contribute to the low quality of education in public schools. In this context, demand for private education is persistently on the rise. At the middle and high school levels, the number of private schools is higher than government-run schools. One interesting point: the number of female teachers is higher in private schools (see Table 4.4). This is perhaps one of the factors contributing to comparatively better educational outcomes in private schools.

What are some policy options? First, there is a need to create complementarities among private and public schools in such a way that the primary responsibility for the provision of education remains with the state. Some interventions or policy tinkerings in the public sector are of the nature that their impact does not remain confined to public schools. They rather create positive externalities for the private schools as well. For example, improving quality of public schools may positively impact the outcomes of private schools without any direct intervention by the government in the private sector schools. When the quality of public schools improves, private schools in that area will risk losing revenue as parents may opt for public schools. Results of an evaluation[38] of the public grants program, delivered through school councils in rural Pakistan, show that such grants had a large education multiplier from the public schools to the private schools. The size of the multiplier was comparatively large for the private schools which faced greater threat to

Table 4.4 Number of schools, enrolment, and employment

No of schools, enrolment, and employment (Public vs. Private sector)													
No. of schools			*Enrolment*			*Enrolment (gender-wise)*		*No. of teachers*			*No. of teachers (gender-wise)*		
Primary level													
Public	Private	Total	Public	Private	Total	Male	Female	Public	Private	Total	Male	Female	
119,202 (87%)	17,877 (13%)	137,079 (100%)	12.065 million (65%)	6.599 million (35%)	18.664 million (100%)	10.425 million (56%)	8.239 million (44%)	369,014 (76%)	117,248 (24%)	486,262 (100%)	227,661 (47%)	258,601 (53%)	
Middle level													
16,550 (35%)	30,115 (65%)	46,665 (100%)	4.238 million (66%)	2.184 million (34%)	6.422 million (100%)	3.600 million (56%)	2.822 million (44%)	140,946 (31%)	307,128 (69%)	448,074 (100%)	128,286 (29%)	319,788 (71%)	
High school level													
13,448 (43%)	17,944 (57%)	31,392 (100%)	2.353 million (70%)	0.996 million (30%)	3.349 million (100%)	1.925 million (57%)	1.424 million (43%)	247,447 (44%)	315,855 (56%)	563,302 (100%)	220,437 (39%)	342,865 (61%)	

Source Pakistan Education Statistics 2017–2018

their market power due to improvements in the quality of public schools (proxied by higher test scores).

In areas where public schools are not available, the government may work out some arrangements with private sector schools by either providing financial assistance to such schools or by providing school vouchers to the parents. The use of school premises and other infrastructural facilities can be optimized through a private–public partnership of schools for introducing more shifts or evening classes or for the provision of vocational and technical training. The Punjab Educational Foundation Model (PEF) has done some work on these lines, though on a limited scale. Its model is a private–public partnership model where the fees of the poor children are paid by the government but the management of the school remains in private hands. Similarly, some NGOs are working on the model of private–public partnership where the NGO adopts a school generally located in an underprivileged area to provide a comparatively better quality education to the children. In such an arrangement teachers are from the private sector but the building is owned by the government.

Second, private schools particularly in low-income and rural settings can be used to prepare a cohort of female teachers who would in all probability be more effective in bringing and retaining children into schools. The low cost of operation of private schools and better learning outcomes through the employment of female teachers have huge potential for increased delivery of school services to poor households by exploring various possibilities of providing subsidies to private schools, school vouchers, or public–private partnerships. Even in poor settings, students are sensitive to school fees, proximity, and quality.[39] The strong demand for private schooling in Pakistan is partly in response to better quality and learning opportunities in private schools. Empirics suggest that inputs particularly PTRs have significant effects on enrolment, on educational achievement, and on test scores of numeracy.[40] The pupil–teacher ratios are better in private schools (see Table 4.5).

It, however, needs to be kept in view that the business model of low-cost private schools works on high pupil–teacher ratios (to capitalize on the economies of scale) and low fees (competitive advantage based on costs). These schools generally employ uncertified teachers at very low salaries. Training uncertified private school teachers can be another area where complementarities can be explored between the public and private sectors. The teacher training institutions established in the public sector

Table 4.5 PTR, PSR, and TSR

Sr. No		*Pupil–Teacher Ratio (PTR)*		*Pupil–School Ratio (PSR)*		*Teacher–School Ratio (TSR)*	
		Public	*Private*	*Public*	*Private*	*Public*	*Private*
1	Pakistan	29	18	158	212	5	12
2	Punjab	30	16	236	178	8	11
3	Sindh	28	26	98	307	4	12
4	KP	32	21	170	286	5	14
5	Balochistan	20	29	67	266	3	9

Source Pakistan Education Statistics 2017–2018

can provide training to school teachers in private schools, or some subsidies or funds may be made available by the government for the training of private school teachers. There is a need to take care of both quantity and quality of education by creating complementarities among private and public schools. Pakistan is faced with serious issues of quantity (OOSC) and quality (poor learning outcomes) in education.

Learning Outcomes

Seventy-five percent of students cannot read and understand a simple text by age 10.[41] The level of learning poverty in Pakistan is higher compared to other countries with similar levels of development. For example, Vietnam performs exceptionally well compared to Pakistan on PISA scores.[42] Pakistan has certainly made some gains but the situation is not very encouraging. Forty-one percent in grade 5 and 82% in grade 3 cannot read a story with comprehension in national or regional languages. Sharp gender and geographical gaps also exist. According to ASER, 46% of boys aged 5–16 could read sentences in Urdu or regional language but only 38% of girls could. Similarly, 48% of boys could read at least some English words while 39% of girls could do the same. As regards numeracy skills, 43% of boys could do subtraction whereas only 36% of girls could do it.

Sharp divide exists between urban and rural areas as regards the above-mentioned three competencies. Children living in urban areas appear to perform better than their rural counterparts.[43] Internationally, Pakistani students' achievement in mathematics and science is the second lowest after the Philippines. In mathematics and science average scores of 4th-grade Pakistani students were respectively 329 and 290, almost half that of Singapore, the top scorer.[44] The World Development Report of 2018 correctly calls such learning outcome gaps "hidden exclusion". The learning inequalities are sharp not only in terms of gender and rurality but also in terms of socio-economic status (SES). Learning outcomes or grade attainments are substantially lower among children hailing from poor households.

The circumstances of birth determine a lot about the chances of the child getting ahead in life. The inequality begins at home. It develops from the myriad of differences in the ways parents of high and low SES interact with their children.[45] Early vocabulary development also differs with SES. Children belonging to low SES families build their vocabularies at slower rates compared to children of high SES families.[46] A longitudinal survey data from Punjab,[47] the largest province of Pakistan, confirms the above assertions. The cognitive skills are suggested to be lower among the children coming from households with lower SES. The results of a psychonueroendocrine study[48] show that children with low SES have significantly higher salivary cortisol levels than children with high SES. In simple words, salivary cortisol levels give a fair indication of brain function. A high salivary cortisol level is indicative of stress and impairment of cognitive abilities. The results of the said study also indicate that children's cortisol levels are highly correlated with their mothers' extent of depressive symptomatology. In short, socio-economic status is one of the main factors that impact the learning outcomes of children through channels like poor nutrition, parental education, support or attention, and stress.[49] The learning gaps in Pakistan, like those in other developing countries, are significantly high, almost touching 100% based on SES (see Table 4.6).

Sarah Gust and her colleagues[50] have estimated the share of children who do not reach basic skills levels in 159 countries including Pakistan (covering 98.1% of the world's population and 99.4% of the world's GDP). Their estimates suggest that at least two-thirds of the world's youth are not able to achieve even basic skill levels. The situation is more disappointing in Sub-Saharan African and South Asian countries where respectively 89% and 85% of children do not reach even basic skills. Pakistan fares among the worst. Over 90% of children do not reach the basic skills level in Pakistan. Other countries where the situation is as bad as in Pakistan (where over 90% of children are unable to acquire basic skills) are all African countries such as Ethiopia (91.8%), Gambia (91%),

Table 4.6 Mastery gap between the richest and poorest children at age 12

Variable	*Numeracy for richest 20% (%)*	*Numeracy for poorest 40% (%)*	*Rich–Poor mastery gap (% points)*	*Rich-Universal mastery gap (% points)*
Numeracy	60	35	25	40
Literacy (local language)	66	39	27	34
Literacy (English language)	65	36	29	35

Source Working paper 504, 2019, Centre for Global Development

Guinea (95.9%), Guinea-Bissau (90.9%), Lesotho (92.5%), Madagascar (92.3%), Malawi (94.9%), Mali (92.1%), Mauritania (93.8%), Mozambique (91.2%), Namibia (92.7%), Niger (96%), Nigeria (93.8%), Senegal (94.1%), Sudan (90%), Togo (91.5%), and Zambia (96%).

The said researchers have developed three scenarios and calculated, based on simulation exercises, economic gains of skill upgrades for different countries. The results of the simulation exercises suggest that if children who are currently in school are able to reach the basic skills (PISA Level 1), Pakistan is expected to gain US$10,360 billion (around 977% of its current GDP) by the close of this century that is 2100. In the event that all children (currently in school and OOSC) are able to reach the basic skills level, expected GDP gains would be US$68,626 billion (6472% of current GDP).

Some other papers also paint a grim picture of learning outcomes in developing countries. For example, Pritchett and Viarengo have analyzed[51] learning outcomes in 7 developing countries (Zambia, Senegal, Cambodia, Guatemala, Paraguay, Honduras, and Ecuador) and have found that for most of the countries and subjects the learning outcomes even for the advantaged and elite (95th percentile in PISA measured SES) students are below the Sustainable Development Goal (SDG) minimum learning level target of PISA level 2. And 80% of the children shall not be able to get to that minimum global level in the said 7 countries even if every child is fully included, meaning differences due to SES are abolished.

Are low incomes stopping these countries from achieving better learning outcomes? Perhaps this is not the case. The experience of Vietnam demonstrates that, even at current levels of income, these countries can show large improvements in learning outcomes.[52] School enrolment (in absolute numbers) and average years of schooling, in almost all developing countries including Pakistan, have increased but schooling has not delivered on the promise of economic growth due to poor learning outcomes.

Learning and Economic Growth

Several studies have explored the relationship between human capital (proxied by mean years of schooling), and economic growth. For example, Pritchett, in his paper '*Where has all the education gone*'[53] finds no relationship, based on cross-sectional data, between the increase in the rising educational attainment of the labor force and the rate of growth of output per worker. He writes: "In the decades since 1960, nearly all developing economies have seen educational attainment grow rapidly. The cross-national data show, however, that on average, education contributed much less than would have been expected in the standard augmented Solow model. Where did all the education go?"

Similarly, a meta-analysis spanning over 60 studies published during 1989–2011 suggests that around 20% of the studies found no (rather negative in some cases) correlation between human capital and economic outcomes.[54] Years of schooling as a measure of education implicitly assumes that one year of schooling, regardless of educational system and country, has a similar impact or outcome in terms of knowledge and skills. It implies that schooling, say for 10 years, both in a madrassa (religious seminary) and a vocational school will have the same impact. Similarly, 10 years of schooling in oriental studies or 10 years of schooling in science and technology will have the same outcome or economic value. It is very intuitive that 10 years of schooling in the USA and 10 years of schooling in Pakistan generally do not have similar outcome in terms of learning, knowledge, and skills. In the same way, education in various disciplines shall also differ with regards to impact on economic growth.

The difference between "knowledge and skills" and "schooling" needs to be appreciated. Education is not a univariate phenomenon. What goes into and comes out of the educational process is not the same across countries. Higher levels of education alone are not the deterministic factor of economic growth per se; rather skills acquired through education actually drive economic development.[55] Quality education with a focus on honing cognitive skills is considered important for economic growth. Education increases productivity of labor by increasing the human capital inherent in labor, enhances the innovative capacity of the economy, and facilitates the diffusion and transmission of knowledge required to understand and process new information and implement new technologies.

According to the World Bank[56] expansion of schooling is not a guarantee of improvement in economic conditions. It is the quality measured in terms of cognitive skills that matters for economic growth. Merely by focusing on school attainment, it would not be possible for the developing countries to improve their long-term growth.[57] This proposition is best illustrated by the Latin American experience. Historically, the Latin American region was significantly ahead of East Asia, Sub-Saharan Africa, and the Middle East and North African (MENA) region in terms of adult school attainment in 1960 but the growth performance of this region has persistently lagged behind East Asia and MENA. Low-quality education is rated as the main culprit for poor growth performance despite its high initial schooling level.[58]

One of the broader explanations for differences in economic growth across countries thus lies in the quality of education that is cognitive skills measured by achievement on international assessments of mathematics and science. Some researchers,[59] using a database of globally comparable learning outcomes from 164 countries, have shown that schooling and learning are two different things. Learning levels stayed low in many countries despite a significant increase in enrolment. Once learning is taken into account, human capital accounts for between one-fifth and around half of the cross-country differences in per capita GDP. The countries which generally have high scores on harmonized tests also score high on HCI and enjoy high per capita which means that a correlation exists between the said three variables but deviations do exist. Data of some selected countries points toward the said assertion (see Table 4.7).

The Harmonized Learning Outcomes (HLO) database[60] contains data of 175 countries. An analysis of this database shows that all the countries like Congo, Central African Republic, Chad, Liberia, Nigeria, Rwanda, et cetera, which score less than Pakistan belong to the African region. Only two countries, Afghanistan and Yemen, lie outside the African region which have low HCI (respectively 0.4 and 0.37) compared to Pakistan. Countries like Gambia, Namibia, Myanmar, Cambodia, Haiti,

Table 4.7 Test Scores, HCI, and GDP per capita of some selected countries (2020)

Countries	*Harmonized test scores*	*Human Capital Index (HCI) (scale 0–1)*	*GDP per capita, PPP (current international $)*
Singapore	575.27	0.88	100,226
Korea, Rep	537.21	0.80	44,695
Sweden	519.36	0.80	56,141
Vietnam	519.10	0.69	11,036
Norway	513.59	0.77	65,130
Malaysia	445.68	0.61	27,278
China	441.00	0.65	17,209
Sri Lanka	400.00	0.60	13,664
India	399.00	0.49	6,518
Central African Republic	368.73	0.29	895
Bangladesh	368.32	0.46	5,905
Pakistan	338.66	0.41	5,285
Chad	333.11	0.30	1,573
Nigeria	309.02	0.36	5,138

Source World Bank

and Nicaragua fare better than Pakistan on HCI score. Pakistan is sitting at the bottom in the South Asian region (Fig. 4.1). Pakistan scores low both on harmonized test scores (a measure of quality of education) and the HCI index[61] of the World Bank. And that does explain low contribution of human capital to long-term economic growth despite some gains made in schooling and literacy.

The income and human capital formation relationship is, however, not straight and one on one. For example, Botswana's per capita PPP-adjusted GDP is US$15,518 (current dollar terms) for the year 2022 whereas Malawi's per capita GDP is US$1467 which simply means that Botswana is more than 10 times richer than Malawi but both score 0.41 on HCI. Similarly, per capita income of Gambia is around US$2500 but it scores more than Botswana. Actually, priorities matter. For example, Senegal's per capita GDP in 2010 was US$1000 but 54% of its young people had no formal education and 85% had primary education or less. On the other hand, in Zimbabwe, another African country which is poorer than Senegal, 66% of the population gets secondary education or more.

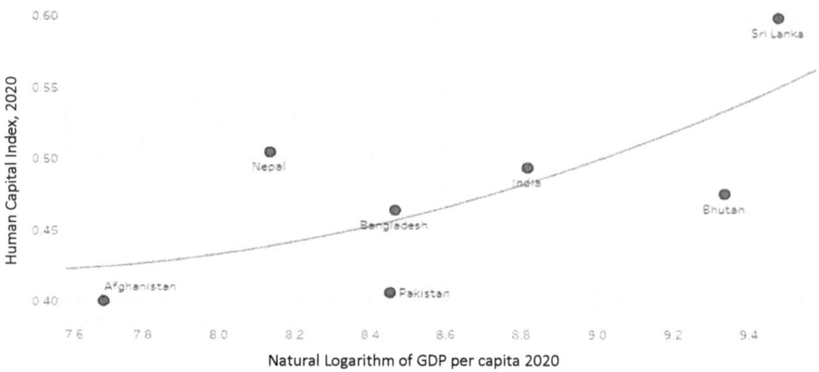

Fig. 4.1 Human Captial Index (South Asia)

In Tajikistan, which is poorer than even Zimbabwe, about 84% of the population receives secondary or tertiary education.[62] Deviations exist in the countries of the same income level. The low middle-income countries (LMICs) are a case in point. Zimbabwe and Kenya have greater HCI at lower per capita income compared to Pakistan. Similarly, Mongolia, Philippines, Tunisia, and Algeria, and Bhutan have higher per capita GDP but are lower on HCI compared to Vietnam with less income level (Fig. 4.2).

Public Policy priorities matter a lot for human capital formation. It is investment in human resource development which basically makes the difference. Some World Bank economists have examined the impact of investment in human capital on income and poverty.[63] Their results suggest that poor countries can reap huge gains by investing in human capital formation as investment in humans turns out to be more cost-effective compared to investment in physical capital for increasing GDP and reducing poverty.

A skilled workforce is needed to innovate as well as imitate. The developing countries operating inside the PPF can enhance growth through imitation for which capable workforce is needed to understand the codes and instructions to operate the machines. Besides skills enhancement and technical education, investment in managerial capital is needed as dearth of managerial capital is also responsible for low economic growth in developing countries.[64] Managerial and organizational practices have a direct impact on innovation and productivity. Managerial practices are

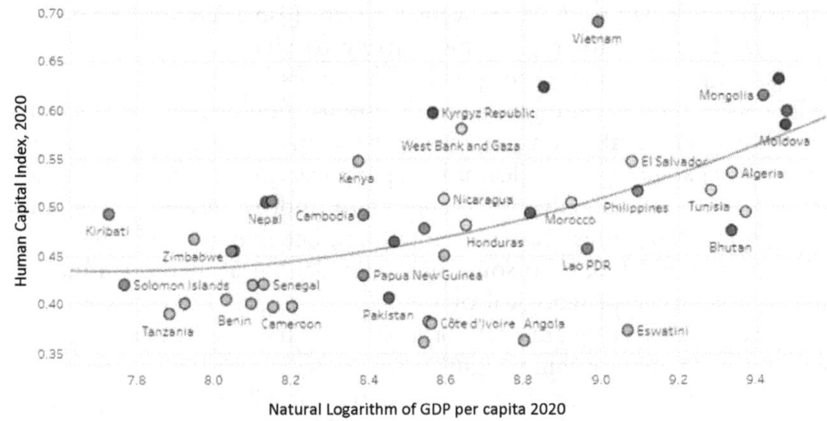

Fig. 4.2 Human Captial Index (LMICs)

key inputs for innovation and are in particular important for firms operating more distant from the technological frontier. The question now is how to improve learning outcomes to connect education with economic growth?

What Works for Improving Learning?

A vast body of knowledge is now available on what works and what does not work for quality education. Conventionally, much emphasis is laid on inputs but mere increase of inputs is not a guarantee for improving learning outcomes. "If your bicycle tire has a hole, pumping in more air won't do much good. This is not because you don't need air in the tire; it is because you have to fix the hole first, and then add the air. Pumping more books, more teachers or more training into existing systems is just a palliative measure", writes[65] Pritchett. Based on the analysis of a number of studies and evaluations, a RISE working paper[66] concludes that the usual approach of increasing spending on education is not going to have a tangible impact when it comes to learning outcomes. Instead, interventions that focus on improved and cost-effective pedagogy (especially providing foundational literacy and numeracy skills to the millions of first-generation learners who are falling behind the pace of curriculum) and on improved governance of the education system (especially teacher performance and accountability) are more likely to yield considerably better results compared to increased spending or inputs.

Evans and Popova also come up with similar findings on the basis of a review of several evaluations. According to them,[67] pedagogical interventions that change students' learning experiences and teacher training are some of the most effective interventions to improve learning outcomes in developing countries. Teacher training can become very effective when it is repeated and linked to some specific pedagogical method. Empirics suggest that some pedagogical or similar pedagogical interventions, like para-teachers delivering after-school supplementary classes, scripted lesson plans, and teacher coaching, significantly increase literacy and numeracy skills.[68] Two researchers from the Centre for Global Development[69] have reviewed 145 empirical studies from 2014 onward to find out how access and quality can be increased across the African continent. Their results suggest that structural pedagogy (like lesson plans and training of teachers), mother tongue instruction interventions, and school feeding deliver gains both in access and learning.

Teaching at the right level is important. Rather than teaching to the top in the classroom, children need to be taught at their current level. Clear learning goals need to be fixed to enable them to achieve those goals. Doing so may require changes in the curriculum and fixing of the misaligned pedagogy.[70] Banerjee et al. have documented results of two randomized evaluations of remedial education.[71] The first intervention targeted the weakest students, and a young lady called Balsakhi worked with children in grades three and four to hone their basic skills. These children were taken out of the class for two hours to work with the young lady, who was paid a meagre amount of $10 to $15 per month. The results of this remedial initiative were quite encouraging. It increased test scores of the target children significantly. The policy implication simply is that educational outcomes can be increased cost-effectively through the right set of interventions. The second intervention was addressed to all children but was adapted to each child's current level of achievement. It was a computer-assisted learning program where children in grade 4 were offered two hours of shared computer time per week. The children played games that involved solving math problems, the difficulty of which corresponded to their ability to solve them. This program increased math scores by 0.47 standard deviation.

Demand-side interventions are also needed to increase access and quality. The most important intervention, especially in poor settings, for increasing access is to impact household decisions about trade-off whether to send children to school or not. Such decisions are based on the perceived costs and benefits of schooling. School health programs, scholarships, and information about returns to education can cost-effectively improve access that is school participation. For poor households, sending children to school involves an opportunity cost, as discussed earlier in detail. Added to this perception (which is true to a large extent) that schools do not impart relevant skills needed for earning a livelihood also distorts the decisions of households. Improvement in basic schooling is undoubtedly important, but greater worker skills are necessary for fostering economic growth via innovation and diffusion of technology. In this regard, the differential impact of general, vocational, and science education needs to be recognized at the policy level.

Students even in developed countries, who adopt a vocational track, are expected to earn more with fewer chances of remaining unemployed.[72] The effects of vocational training on employment and wages are large and persistent.[73] Unfortunately, skills development has not remained a major focus of the education system in Pakistan. For example, an analysis of Punjab's curriculum and textbooks shows that the existing curriculum does not target skills explicitly and directly.[74] A low priority for skill development can be visualized from the fact that no comprehensive information about skill development is available. The policy document of the Ministry of Education and Professional Development recognizes that even information about publicly funded provision for skill development is not properly collated and analyzed.[75]

The development of professional skills for increasing lifetime earnings and social mobility need to be the prime goals of education in Pakistan but said goals do not seem to figure prominently in the eyes of education policy-makers. Development of cognitive skills gets low priority. Education in Pakistan is characterized by too much' prescription and 'telling'. Teachers act as either 'tellers' or information loaders and students are passive recipients of knowledge. Implementation of the policies is the hardest part and most of the time very ambitious and well-intentioned interventions to improve the management quality of public schools fail due to poor accountability or badly designed incentives.[76]

The existing assessment system also does not promote learning. It is on a one-time basis. Assessment is done by the regional examination boards generally at the end of the year. Regular and continuous assessment would be required to ameliorate the situation. A farmer who cultivates crops needs regular monitoring and care of the crop for a better yield. If, after sowing the seed, the farmer just visits the field at the time of harvest, he is least likely to raise a good crop. Similarly, one-time assessment at the end of a course or academic year may not help produce students with better understanding, training, and comprehension of the course material. Further, assessment is made by the teachers who teach the students in class. The roles of teaching and assessment need to be clearly separated. A separate cadre of assessors, trained rigorously in assessment techniques, would be required. Doing so will bring more professionalism to assessment besides strengthening the accountability of the teachers and the system.

There are other issues with the assessment as well. For example, there is a clear disconnect between the objectives of education and assessment tools. An assessment is made against some objectives. It is a determination as to whether the specified objectives were achieved or not. The objectives of education in Pakistan generally include character building, making students good citizens and Muslims, et cetera, but hardly any assessment tools are available to assess the students against such objectives. Solution would be to either redefine the objectives of education to make them quantifiable or develop new tools of assessment for the variables like character and integrity. Assessment tools and projective techniques for assessing performance against said variables can be developed with the assistance of psychologists. Personality and aptitude tests are important ingredients of an effective assessment system.

A shift in the pedagogical practices, through creative teaching and teaching for creative learning to abolish rote memorization, would be required. Encouraging activity-based learning in schools can be an option in this regard. Education policy needs to be embedded in innovation policy for which creativity in schools is a must. Regrettably, creativity as a curriculum goal is not part of Pakistan's education policy.[77] The current education system in Pakistan is inhibiting the creative potential of the children. The findings of a study based on the results of 154 children who took the Torrance Tests of Creative Thinking in some districts of the province of Punjab suggest that children have the ability to produce ideas that are at times original but generally find it hard to go beyond the ordinary in thinking because the designated books and teaching practices encourage rote memorization and regurgitation of information.[78]

Single-text books are the main culprit. According to K. K. Aziz, historian and academic, in Pakistan, text book is the only instrument to impart education at all levels. Teachers or lecturers do not teach or lecture but repeat what the text books contain and the students are simply encouraged or ordered to memorize the contents of the text books. "For the young student the text book is the most important book in his little world: he is forced to buy it, he carries it to the class room every day, he has it open before him when the teacher is teaching, he is asked to learn portions of it by rote, and he is graded by the quantity of its contents that he can regurgitate".[79] Prior to 1959, there was no monopoly over text books. Several text books written by different authors would be helpful in reducing several ills the education system is afflicted with. Broad outlines of the syllabus, from the Ministry of Education, for inclusion in the text books are sufficient. The provincial or district education departments can work out modalities for the purchase and provision of such books to public sector schools (books in public sector schools are provided at subsidized price). Competition among various publishers for capturing the market would not only incentivize publishers to produce quality books but would also discourage rote learning.

Besides serious issues with pedagogy and assessment, education system in Pakistan is characterized by deep inequities. The divide is not confined to medium of instruction rather it goes much deeper. "There are divisions on the basis of income of parents, gender, geography, caste, religion, culture, language, examination systems and books. What education a child gets, if she, indeed, gets any depends on many or all these factors. Is creating equity a goal for society and state? This question is much bigger than the single national curriculum issue".[80]

Is SNC Sufficient for Equity?

Multiple systems and streams of education, mainly depending on the socio-economic status (SES) of the parents, exist in Pakistan. For example, students in Urdu-medium public schools come from lower socio-economic strata and rural areas. Teachers in these schools also generally hail from the similar socio-economic class. The second category of schools consists of religious seminaries which predominantly enroll children of the poorest. These religious seminaries represent the continuation of the conflict that started in the subcontinent between the liberal education preached by Sir Syed Ahmed Khan and those who stuck to the guns of conservatism in reaction to the introduction of English language and education in the subcontinent. These religious seminaries have further divisions based on sects with the result that the students of the religious seminaries do not have a similar outlook on life and their worldview differs among themselves.

Hostility and intolerance are common among the graduates of one sect toward those who have graduated from the religious seminaries of other sects. One of the main reasons for the persistent increase in the number of religious seminaries in Pakistan, besides overemphasis on religious ideology, is the role of social security these seminaries play in the form of free meals and lodging for the students. After graduation from the seminaries, their students get employment as prayer leaders or become teachers of religious education. This creates an economic incentive system for establishing more religious seminaries.

According to the latest available official statistics[81] currently 34,010 religious institutions, called Deeni Madaris, are working in Pakistan. The total enrollment in these institutions is around 4.409 million out of which 2.588 million (59%) are male and 1.821 million (41% female). There are 145,603 (78%) male and 41,338 (22%) female teachers employed therein. All religious institutions work in the private sector. In comparison, the number of technical and vocational institutions is woefully low. Currently, 3740 technical and vocational institutions are operating in Pakistan, out of which 1627 (43.5%) are in the public sector and 2113 (56.5%) are in the private sector. This figure roughly constitutes 1.17% of the total educational institutions in the country. The provincial governments barely spend 1–2% of the education budget on technical and vocational institutions.

Elite schools are the third broad category of schools. Teaching methodology, syllabi (before the introduction of SNC), examination system, and the outlook these schools impart to their students is totally different from the schools of other streams. Students from elite classes are privileged. They use modern technology, speak English with their friends and parents, go to school in luxury vehicles, have the best tutors to assist them with homework, and are well-nourished. In the last two to three decades, the emergence of low-cost schools has been another category already discussed. Different streams of education in Pakistan create different classes, different mindsets, different worldviews, and different employment opportunities.

Students coming from various systems of education are denizens of alien worlds. Different streams of education intensify social stratification and education, rather than becoming an equalizing force or a great leveler, deepens socio-economic disparities it claims to end. Socio-economic class basically dictates educational success, intergenerational mobility, and prosperity. Children enrolled in public sector schools and low-fee private schools face the greatest disadvantages compared to their counterparts enrolled in elite schools. Different streams of education erode solidarity and embolden the elite to disassociate themselves from those less educated and less fortunate.

Theoretically, the idea of a National Single Curriculum (NSC) is an attempt to end educational apartheid and create a system where every child will receive the same kind of education and will thus have the same kind of opportunities for growth and employment. The goal is well-intentioned and laudable. Some serious concerns have, however, been raised by the educationists like about the inclusion of heavy content of Islamic studies in primary schools. Mastery of such content requires a large amount of memorization in Arabic and in some places Urdu. Further, if teachers come from the religious seminaries to teach religious stuff, serious implications will be involved for the overall academic environment of public sector schools.[82]

The issue with the religious content is that it does not remain confined to Islamic studies. It is spread in other text books as well and muzzles the spirit of inquiry, doubt, curiosity, and search among the students. One of the reasons for our backwardness in the spheres of science and research is the ideological discomfort with the world of creative science and technology. Professor Hoodbhoy reviewed some text books with regards to religious content and found serious discrepancies and distortions reflective of our distorted ideology and narratives. For example, a biology text book published in KPK declared that the theory of evolution as proposed by Charles Darwin is one of the most unbelievable and irrational claims in history while another text book declared that a person in a proper and stable state of mind cannot accept the wild theories of Western science.[83] Text books need to be reviewed to purge them of such distortions and value-loaded illogical statements. The religious content needs to be restricted only to Islamiyat books, as rightly proposed by the 'Suddle Commission on the Rights of Minorities'.[84] Efforts to tie faith and science together will not bear fruit; rather, doing so will add to the national confusion already available in abundance. Introducing religious content into text books of science and establishing universities with the hope of promoting the fusion of Sufism and modern sciences is a futile effort as the two shall never meet.

The SNC needs to incorporate an element of flexibility to take care of regional needs. The children of Gwadar (in Balochistan) may need skills in catching fish and exporting it while those of Okara district (in Punjab) may need skills and knowledge to increase productivity of cash crops like potatoes and maize. Theoretically speaking, SNC compromises on variety and aptitude which are two important aspects worth taking into consideration in any system of education. The psychologists have emphasized the cultivation and promotion of the real self of a person. 'Unconditional positive regard'[85] is what every person needs as it is only as a consequence of positive regard that a person feels free to try out things, grow, and self-actualize. SNC, by ignoring variety and aptitude, may restrict the freedom of the children to innovate and grow. Above all, 'uniform curriculum' and 'uniform education' are two distinct concepts but are often confused and used interchangeably.

SNC is basically about 'uniform curriculum'. Uniform education, on the other hand, implies much more. It essentially means provision of equal educational facilities to all, rich or poor, rural or urban, girl or boy. Only uniform education can ensure the abolition of educational inequities but it would require a high level of commitment. The introduction of a uniform curriculum is almost free but the introduction of a uniform education is not. Uniform curriculum is an easy part, but uniform education is the harder part as it requires financial resources to improve the infrastructure of public schools, train teachers for better pedagogy, bring OOSC to schools and retain them, and close learning gaps between the children of the poor and the rich.

SNC is a good step but not a recipe for an equitable system of education. Even equalization of inputs is not sufficient. Policy shift toward an emphasis on equity in outcomes, based on some minimum learning expectations at each grade and level, would be required.[86] Early interventions to improve literacy and numeracy have got huge dividends. Emphasis on learning outcomes, with more focus on children coming from the low SES, is highly significant to address the cognitive poverty. Equity simply means that more focus and resources should go into the well-being of the disadvantaged. Extensive evidence is available showing that a school feeding program can complement a good education program. School feeding not only influences education but can also work as one of the best social safety nets which helps promote human capital investments.[87]

Certainly, there is a need to reduce the negative impacts of home disadvantage, school quality, et cetera, but at the same time, it is also imperative to revisit the overambitious curriculum and discriminatory language of instruction, factors which are also responsible for poor performance of the students especially those of low socio-economic background.[88] The race for achieving A+ and As or 1100/1100[89] increases the stakes in exams and generates inducements for the teachers to teach to the top with the result that low-performing students keep on sliding downward on the performance ladder.

Rote memorization of text has played further havoc with the learning outcomes. Rote learning is all that determines the outcome of the grades and marks a child will get in the exams. "If you go to a madrassah you will see children memorizing and then regurgitating for their examination. If you go to a government school, you will see them memorizing then regurgitating for their examination. If you go to a low-fee private school, it will be the same. If you go to any private school, which is foreign, matric board, or federal board with state curriculum and state books, it will be the same".[90] SNC is just one baby step toward equity. It requires much more including improvements in pedagogy, upgrading infrastructure of schools, and improved focus on children of low SES through school feeding program (better nutrition), individualized attention (like Balsakhi), a better-customized curriculum that is close to the experiences of the children, and a better evaluation system with more emphasis on evaluating improvements in skills and not memorization of text.

The curriculum and education system need to be geared toward stimulating students' abilities to think, challenge themselves, apply logic, and be creative.[91] Quality needs to be the overarching priority of education, in schools, in colleges, and in universities, besides tying education and research to the livelihoods of the people. After the establishment of HEC in 2002, the number of universities has increased manifold, both in the public and private sectors. Now there are around 193 accredited universities with 45,000 faculty members. Over 1,600 scholars went abroad on HEC-funded scholarships. Expansion of research funding and linking the career progression of university faculty with the volume of research publications were put in place as principal instruments to promote research in the universities. Consequently, research output has increased manifold since 2002.[92]

Quality of Research

There are, however, serious issues with Pakistan's higher education institutions' research quality. Serious concerns are expressed time and again in the press and academic articles about the quality of research and graduates produced by the universities. Allegations of 'citation communities' or 'cartels', fake journals and websites, and 'junk production' by the universities have been expressed time and again. Cut and paste, invention of data, and plagiarism of ideas are rampant.[93]

The Retraction Watch, an online blog launched in August 2010, provides a list of retracted research papers related to science and allied topics. In simple words, retraction means the research papers that were published but afterwards withdrawn due to a variety of reasons like fabrication of data, non-adherence to ethical protocols, duplicate submissions, undisclosed conflicts of interest, plagiarism, et cetera. The retracted publications cannot be referred to or relied upon for further research. In this way, the Retraction Watch Database adds transparency about retracted publications by listing down papers and publications from each country along with reasons for retraction. An analysis of retractions from Pakistan shows that the number of retracted papers is significantly high and the majority of them were retracted due to plagiarism of thought or plagiarism of words (euphemisms for plagiarism). Similarly, a bibliometric analysis of 46,034 papers published in Pakistan-based journals shows that none of the journals fall under Scopus-defined quartile 1, and less than half (47%) of the publications received any citation.[94]

The incentive system connecting the career progression of university teachers with the number of publications has generated unintended consequences for the quality of research. Undoubtedly, the number of papers or publications provides an easy and verifiable indicator of the scholarship and hard work of a faculty member as does an academic degree for the consideration of an academic job at the initial level. But getting a degree does not necessarily make you a scholar. Similarly, the number of publications is not a reflection of the real contribution to knowledge.

The academic history shows that those who made original contributions to knowledge wrote very few papers in their entire academic careers but made a perceptible impact on the knowledge.[95] Pakistani academia needs to come out of the quantity game. More focus is needed on the quality and impact of publications. Original contributions to knowledge and creative research are what we actually need. Thematic research on problems confronting Pakistan needs to be promoted in universities with a view to connecting research with real-life issues and the livelihoods of the people.

Conducting research on university premises is now an outmoded concept. The institutions of higher education need to come out of the old paradigm. They need to reach out. For example, a researcher in agriculture working on seed development or enhancing crop yield needs to work in the area where seeds are to be sown and crops are to be cultivated. A researcher, working in the field of psychology, would produce better research if stationed in a fountain house or a prison where behavior modification or treatment of mental illness is more required. Researchers working in the field of chemistry are more likely to come up with research having functional value if they remain associated with the chemical industry or plant where the results of such research are intended to be put to practical use. The point being made here is that research needs to focus more on practical issues of Pakistan. Expending foreign exchange on earning PhDs from foreign universities in disciplines or areas, not directly connected to economic growth, is a big waste. In cases where expertise in some area is not available in the local market, the services of foreign faculty can be hired online.

Universities may also avail themselves of the services of people who have practical knowledge and expertise, even if they do not hold Ph.D. degrees. The law can be enacted to make it mandatory for the university to hire a certain number of 'Professors of Practice' as faculty to bring their practical experience to the academic institutions. Out of box solutions would be required by the universities to come out of the utopia and conservatism for which they are widely known. A strong liaison between universities and the private sector and government is essentially required for the creation of ideas and the cultivation of research culture. "The rot starts at the top, where overambitious and unrealistic schemes to produce a flood of PhDs, who would presumably strengthen the overall education and research capacity of Pakistan, were promulgated. Those schemes ran against the political culture of Pakistan, which is decidedly not sympathetic to research except in few areas pertaining to national security, nor to mass education".[96]

In the existing educational system, more emphasis is placed on the bricks and mortar structures that is concrete buildings for schools and universities. There is no doubt that the construction of new schools and institutions is important (school building program in Indonesia delivered even in a corrupt environment). However, changes in curriculum and pedagogy, though highly cost-effective, are a harder part of the problem and fail to grab the attention of teachers, policy-makers, and educationists. There are many success stories and models to follow. Khan Academy, Coursera, Edx, et cetera, provide good digital platforms where students and teachers can enhance their skills. If some support is provided, like remedial education programs discussed in the Indian context, the quality of education can be improved even within existing resources. If education is the transfer of information from teacher to student, the digital age has made it cost-effective. Education can be customized and individualized through the use of technology.

Promise of Educational Technology

Mainstreaming technology in education allows greater flexibility in the delivery of education. Pedagogical innovations like technology-assisted instruction and tracking by achievement can raise learning at low costs.[97] Some researchers have examined the effect of computer-assisted learning on students' long-term development in a Chinese context. China implemented the largest ed-tech intervention in the world which connected the best teachers in China to more than 100 million rural students through satellite intervention. The impact evaluation of this program indicates that education technology can have long-lasting positive effects on students' academic achievement, labor performance, and computer usage.[98]

Results of a randomized controlled trial[99] of an intervention in middle schools in the Punjab province of Pakistan also indicate that delivery of content through technology has great potential to improve students' achievement. In order to implement the randomized controlled trial, an intervention was made to provide classrooms with LED screens, math and science multimedia content, teacher tablets, teacher in-service training, and SMS review questions via mobile phones as homework. The results suggest that the intervention increased scores on standardized math and science tests just after four months of exposure. The intervention had some other positive results like it increased the attendance of both students and teachers. There was a clear indication of improved effort both by teachers and students.

Underfunding of education is a perennial issue in Pakistan. After the 18th Amendment, sufficient funds became available to the provinces and each province allocated out of its budget between 21 and 26% on education but statistics show that education spending (in percentage terms) is on the decline.[100] The underfunding of education is one part but it is not the whole story. It is not fair to shift all blame of the lethargy, indifference, and incompetence of the teachers, weak accountability of the schooling system, and sub-optimal policies and options in education to underfunding. Undoubtedly, financial resources matter but through the use of technology, better pedagogy, and optimal use of space in existing schools, costs can be substantially reduced. The digital world has brought about a transformation and there is a need to think beyond bricks and mortar structures in education. Most of the knowledge is now available on a mobile phone or on a tablet costing a few thousand rupees. Moreover, concrete structures of schools can be used in a more optimal way by adding more shifts and changing the current 5-day, 8–3 routine.

According to some estimates,[101] families in Pakistan are expending respectively about Rs. 750 billion, Rs. 350 billion, and Rs. 300 billion, on school fees, tuition after school, and transport. Reducing school attendance from 5–6 days to 3 days can save a significant amount of money. Similarly, the delivery of education through technology can substantially reduce the costs involved in pedagogy. Tech entrepreneurs can develop content for delivery through technology.

The point is that the issues of both quality and quantity can be addressed without even a substantial increase in education spending. Better use of current concrete schools, the use of technology in delivering information, and using digital technology for customizing and individualizing education have huge potential for improving educational standards within given resources. New education models are needed. The present model of direct learning is largely influenced by the needs of the First and Second Industrial Revolutions where uniform talent for mass production through repetitive and process-oriented manufacturing was required. The drivers of economic growth are changing fast.

The emergence of production automation and increased globalization require a massive shift in skills for contributing to the economy. "There is an urgent need to update education systems to equip children with the skills to navigate the future of work and the future of societies—This transformation calls for shifts in learning content to include both the technical and human-centric skills needed to build growing and inclusive economies and societies and shifts in learning experiences that more clearly mirror the future of work".[102] Skilled workplace is needed for enhancing and sustaining economic growth. The question of education remains unanswered, with reference to the relevance of education and human capital to long-term economic growth, without discussion on its product. What kind of graduates an educational system is producing? Is it producing wealth creators and entrepreneurs? Or it is predominantly producing graduates who are more interested to become rent-seekers? And why the individuals prefer to become rent-seekers instead of wealth creators? The ensuing discussion is an attempt to answer these questions.

Wealth Creators vs. Rent-Seekers

Some 260,000 engineers are registered with Pakistan Engineering Council (PEC) out of whom 30% are working abroad and 50,000 are jobless.[103] As regards the number of lawyers, the Punjab Bar Council alone claims over 100,000 members.[104] The preferences of a society and its education system have implications for economic growth just like physical and financial capital that is machines and money. A society that prefers engineering education is likely to witness faster economic growth compared to a society that produces more lawyers. Murphy et al.[105] wrote a seminal paper in 1991 on the implications of talent allocation for economic growth. They used UNESCO data on college enrollments in different fields for a large cross-section of countries. Their thesis simply is that when a country's talented people typically organize production and innovate they foster growth. And when they indulge in rent-seeking, they just redistribute wealth and reduce growth. For example, an engineer, who sets up a construction firm, invents a machine, or reinvents a manufacturing process, creates value for the society. On the contrary, a lawyer who just charges fees from his client is not adding to the wealth of the country. Money changes hands as a result of an exchange or redistribution of already-created wealth, argument runs. On the same analogy, it can be argued that the employees in the public sector, members of the military, and civil servants who receive compensation from wealth and income generated by others are not wealth creators.

Murphy and his colleagues empirically found that countries with a higher proportion of engineering college majors grow faster whereas countries with a higher proportion of law concentrators grow slower. They write: "The positive effect of engineers (on growth), and the negative direct effect of lawyers are consistent with our theory, which says that the rate of technological progress is determined by the allocation of talent. If engineering is an attractive major, the quality of talent in engineering is higher, therefore entrepreneurs are of higher quality, the rate of technological progress is greater, and the growth of GDP per capita is higher. This argument of course assumes a positive correlation between the fraction of college majors in engineering and the rate of technological progress that they will generate and does not deal with the abilities of engineers. Similarly, if law is an attractive major, the quality of rent-seekers is high, and hence, indirectly, the quality of entrepreneurs is lower and technological progress and income growth are smaller". Their findings also suggested that countries that have more engineering majors also invest more in human and physical capital.

Some researchers[106] have linked present-day variations in economic growth to engineering population density in 1900. These researchers suggest that countries which in 1900 had very similar levels of income but had widely different engineering densities show different trajectories of development today. Chile, Argentina, Denmark, Sweden, and the American South had similar levels of income in 1900, but engineering density differed. The Nordic countries had densities of 100, the American South had 60, and Chile, Argentina, and the rest of Latin America had densities of less than 20. Interestingly, these engineering differentials predict the subsequent divergence in incomes between these countries. Why is engineering more important in developing countries like Pakistan? Engineering basically captures a different kind of human capital than inventors or innovators. Engineering has more to do with absorptive capacity as the diffusion of scientific knowledge and technology is assumed to be a big driver of economic growth.

The argument about lawyers as rent-seekers, however, should not be misconstrued. An optimal number of lawyers, civil servants, and army is respectively needed to enforce the rule of law, coordinate business activities, and safeguard the prosperity from foreign predators. According to Mancur Olson: "An ideal legal system with a socially optimal number of lawyers will reduce the uncertainty and conflict in a society, and it will make an overwhelming contribution to economic progress. In an ideal legal system an optimal number of lawyers will be profoundly useful to society—they will be "conflict-reducing" and "uncertainty- reducing" engineers".[107] Special interest legislation, cartelization, and collusion are harmful to economic efficiency and growth and it is here where the role of the lawyers and the courts of law become crucial for rectifying distortions created by such harmful economic activities. But employing excessive lawyers' services means more costs to the firms and as a result low production and higher commodity prices for the consumers. Similarly, the role of bureaucracy is crucial in coordinating business activities as the experience of Japan, South Korea, Taiwan, and in very recent past that of China confirms (detailed discussion on Developmental Bureaucracy in chapter "Public Sector Performance Conundrum"). The question basically is about the allocation of talent in various fields and occupations out of the pool of entrepreneurs. Every society is faced with a limited supply of talent or entrepreneurs and has to strike trade-offs while allocating talent among competing sectors, occupations, and tasks.

Moreover, all entrepreneurship is not growth-enhancing as theorized by Baumol.[108] Entrepreneurship may be productive, unproductive, and even destructive. According to Baumol, entrepreneurship is an input like other inputs and can be reallocated to different tasks depending on the relative prospects of profit offered by available tasks and sectors. "Entrepreneurs are not suddenly created in profusion by spontaneous generation and their ranks are not suddenly decimated by some undescribed plague– Baldly put, the activities that promise the greatest monetary (or other) returns lead to a reallocation of entrepreneurs from one sector of the economy to another, and this reallocation can take forms that give the appearance of vanishing or emergence of entrepreneurs as a group".[109] North has very beautifully explained the phenomenon of talent allocation in a society with the metaphor of a pirate and a chemical manufacturer. His argument is that to become a successful pirate one needs a lot of knowledge and skills about naval warfare, the trade routes of commercial shipping, et cetera. So a pirate has to be an entrepreneur in some sense.

Similarly, to be a successful chemical manufacturer, one requires a great deal of knowledge of chemistry, chemicals, and their potential use in industry. But the outcomes of both types of knowledge and skills are different for a nation and what profession an individual adopts, piracy or chemical manufacturing will depend on the rules of the game in that society. If the basic institutional framework in a society makes rent-seeking (symbolized by piracy) the preferred economic opportunity, then a different set of knowledge and skills will develop in that society and individuals shall prefer to join rent-seeking professions (for appreciation of this point in Pakistani context, see *Case Study No.1*). Conversely, if the rules of the game are such that productivity-increasing skills (symbolized by chemical manufacturers) are valued by the institutional framework of a society, then people will gain skills that help generate wealth. The argument further runs that the incentives that are built into the institutional framework play a vital role in promoting the kinds of skills and knowledge that pay off.[110] Individuals align their preferences and choices for the type of education and skills according to the signals of the market and society. The traditional model of utility maximization, however, does not fully explain their choices. An engineer or doctor joining the civil service in Pakistan at a lower salary (compared to the private sector) takes into account the non-monetary factors such as social status and potential of rent-seeking in his utility function. Besides education (quality education), health is an important component of human capital. Health leads to economic growth through a number of mechanisms.

CHAPTER 5

The Problem of Public Health Care

In January 2000, the World Health Organization (WHO) established a Commission, chaired by Jeffery Sachs, on Macroeconomics and Health (CMH) to evaluate the role of health in economic development. The focus of the CMH was mainly on the poor of low-income and middle-income countries. The commission, in its report 'Macroeconomics and Health: Investing in Health for Economic Development', affirmed that it was highly essential to improve the health of the poor to reduce poverty and achieve economic development, as returns to investment in health are astoundingly high for the developing countries.[1] Improvements in health influence economic growth through several channels. One of the channels which can be directly observed is through its impact on labor productivity.[2] There are indirect channels as well.

For example, better health and greater life expectancy generate incentives to invest in education, lead to lower population growth, help develop human capital, and increase per capita income.[3] Better health particularly of women reduces fertility and accelerates transition from economic stagnation to sustained economic growth.[4] Both micro-based and macro-based evidence show that public health measures are an important lever for fostering economic development.[5] Health is human capital itself as well as an input for producing other types of capital.[6] A healthy mother is more likely to give birth to healthy children besides being more productive in the labor market. Substantial experimental evidence suggests that

J. Nasir, *Development Challenges of Pakistan*,
https://doi.org/10.1007/978-981-97-3064-3_5

improvements in health and productivity can be made at a relatively low cost. For example, deworming of school students has enormous benefits.

A cost–benefit analysis of the deworming program in the Kenyan context confirms that deworming increases school participation. The benefit of additional schooling is estimated to the tune of $30 over the life of the child at a cost of $0.49,[7] just the price of a soda bottle or a few cigarettes in Pakistan. All studies and papers rate health either as the top or second-top factor after income upon which the happiness of a person depends.[8] Despite high promise, health particularly for the poor is not accorded the level of national priority it deserves as is very evident from low life expectancy and other health indicators.

Gaps in Life Expectancy

The wisdom contained in the old saying that health is wealth is now well recognized by economists and public policy-makers. It is not just a coincidence that poor countries tend to be unhealthy and unhealthy countries tend to be poor. Wealthier people are healthier, wrote Pritchett and summers in 1993. They argued that poor economic performance in developing countries is responsible for high infant and child mortality and low life expectancy[9] Countries with better general health have higher GDP than countries with poor general health, a relationship formally stated by economists through the Preston curve which postulates that longevity increases with income. The relationship between population health and income is upward sloping, especially at low income levels, but improvements in health also occurred even if income remained fixed. More than 75% of gains in health are attributed to the upward movement of the income-health curve, whereas around 25% come from movements along the curve as countries get rich. It means that improvements in health are possible without prior improvements in GDP.[10]

Interestingly, China had a low life expectancy in 1960 compared to Pakistan. India and Pakistan had almost the same life expectancy at birth in 1960. The life expectancy in East Pakistan (now Bangladesh) was almost the same as that of West Pakistan (now Pakistan) in 1950. The eastern part of Pakistan, however, witnessed a reduction in life expectancy in 1960. It was 42.59 years in 1970 when it separated from Pakistan. In 1970, life expectancy in the Western part of the country was 54.76 years, a gap of over 12 years between the two Wings of the country. In 2020, on average Pakistan has five and a half years less life expectancy than

Table 5.1 Life expectancy at birth, total (years) of selected countries

Country name	*1960*	*1970*	*1980*	*1990*	*2000*	*2010*	*2020*
Bangladesh	44.74	42.59	51.85	55.99	65.78	68.64	71.97
Bhutan	33.47	39.95	48.22	55.97	62.01	68.43	71.61
China	33.28	56.61	64.42	68.01	71.88	75.60	78.08
Indonesia	46.45	52.99	58.75	63.18	66.43	68.68	68.81
India	45.22	48.24	53.61	58.65	62.67	66.91	70.15
Korea, Rep	54.32	62.16	66.05	71.60	75.91	80.12	83.43
Sri Lanka	60.70	65.27	68.66	71.93	70.36	73.22	76.39
Malaysia	56.50	63.11	68.25	71.31	72.78	74.44	75.94
Nepal	38.56	42.83	47.89	54.83	62.61	66.81	69.25
Pakistan	**44.93**	**54.76**	**57.61**	**60.07**	**62.10**	**64.44**	**66.27**
Vietnam	59.66	56.22	66.20	69.21	72.46	73.51	75.38
South Asia	45.10	48.28	53.76	58.56	62.89	66.75	69.75
Sub-Saharan Africa	41.42	44.37	48.57	49.82	51.26	56.85	60.85

Source World Bank Data (data.worldbank.org)

Bangladesh. Pakistan is now at the bottom of the South Asian region[11] (see Table 5.1).

A time series analysis of some selected countries confirms that both income and priorities matter. In 1950s, South Korea and China were poor countries, so they had a lower life expectancy. They grew rich and now have a far greater life expectancy[12] Bangladesh is not a rich country and had a lower life expectancy than Pakistan in 1970 but it has witnessed greater gains in life expectancy than Pakistan, perhaps due to better use of women's agency, in the last two decades.

Life expectancy is an important indicator of lifetime education and earnings. According to a World Bank Paper,[13] gains in life expectancy at birth increase both investments in human capital and lifetime earnings. An addition of one year to life expectancy at birth is estimated to add 0.12 years of schooling and 1.7% to the lifetime earnings of an individual. The relationship between health and economic growth is not one-way. The gains from economic growth also flow into gains in health. An increase in income leads to expenditure, both private and public, on goods like food, safe drinking water, better sanitation, and better shelter, which improve health. It is a historical fact that with increasing incomes, life expectancy has increased and infant mortality has gone down worldwide.

Mortality inequality or a difference in life expectancy is also important from another angle.

The inequality of mortality captures the length of time over which an income or consumption is enjoyed which typical income inequality measures do not take into account.[14] Suppose two persons, namely Khan Baba and Allah Ditta, are born into families belonging to the richest and the poorest quintiles respectively. Allah Ditta by some stroke of luck or by dint of his hard work amasses as much wealth as the lucky Khan Baba has, but due to low nutrition or other factors whatsoever, Allah Ditta lives 60 years while Khan Baba is able to celebrate his 80th birthday before his death. So due to mortality inequality, Khan Baba enjoyed his income or wealth for 20 years more than the unfortunate Allah Ditta.

In all probability, the poor die younger compared to the rich, both in developed and developing countries. Empirics also confirm this proposition. For example, in Canada, some researchers using fifty years of administrative data have found that men in the top ventile of earnings live 8 years (11%) longer than those in the bottom ventile. Interestingly, for women, this difference is 3.6 years.[15] The gap in life expectancy in the USA between the richest 1% and the poorest 1% is 14.8 years for men and 10.6 years for women and that gap is more pronounced between women and men at low income levels. Overall, in the USA, life expectancy increased for men and women in the top 5% of the income distribution during the period 2001–2014 but remained stagnant for the poorest 5% of men and decreased for the poorest 5% of women.[16] Another study finds that life expectancy is more than 10 years higher in the top one percent of a country compared to the bottom one percent.[17]

Besides the income effect, life expectancy also varies substantially across local regions of a country. The geographic variation in life expectancy is particularly large among the poorest.[18] So the Policy focus on health inequality or mortality inequality is as important as taming the Gini and Palma ratios, the measures of income inequality. Gini and Palma give a snapshot that is inequality in a country at a particular point in time but how long you enjoy that income depends on longevity. Any policy measure for improving health or increasing life expectancy shall essentially require taking care of income and making health amenities better, especially in low-income settings.

Health, despite all its positive externalities for economic growth and development, is badly neglected as a national priority in Pakistan. Despite voluminous data available from the World Bank and WHO and detailed surveys undertaken by the Planning and Development Departments of the provinces with the collaboration of UNICEF, we hardly see any informed debate on health in mainstream media and public policy circles. There are no potent narratives about the public health care system for children, women, and the poor, the majority of whom live in rural areas. The Pakistan Social and Living Standards Measurement (PSLM) Survey, Integrated Household Surveys, Multiple Indicator Cluster Surveys (MICS), and surveys and data compiled by international organizations, which are all publicly available, provide a wealth of information for analysis, debate, research and narrative building on the public health care system but unfortunately such data is rarely used for informed debate and discussion.

The absence or low visibility of health care for the poor, children, women, rural dwellers, and those suffering from mental illnesses is partly due to their voicelessness. Health was never deliberated as a political priority.[19] Health lacks political ownership despite the fact that there are serious issues with regard to equity, coverage, and public investment in the sector. The worrying part of the story is that when a comparison is drawn among the poorest 20% of the population of the counties of the same income level, Pakistan fares the worst.

Health of the Poor

According to WHO' Health Equity Monitoring'[20] among low middle-income countries (LMICs), the infant mortality rate of the lowest quintile of population in Pakistan, that is poorest 20% is the highest. Countries like Afghanistan, Yemen, and Sudan fare better than Pakistan on this indicator (Figs. 5.1 and 5.2).

The death rate of newly born babies (neonatal mortality rate) among the poorest people of Pakistan (lowest quintile) is the second highest when compared to the poorest people of LMICs. Pakistan fares the worst not only in comparison to regional countries like Bangladesh, Nepal, and India but it is worse on the said indicator compared to African countries like Morocco, Somalia, Sudan, Tunisia, and Yemen (Fig. 5.3).

According to a review published in the Journal of Perinatology in 2016, about 99% of neonatal deaths occur in low- and middle-income countries, and about two-third of deaths occur on the first day of birth.[21] It means that three interventions that are prenatal consultation, presence of skilled birth attendant at delivery, and postnatal consultations are

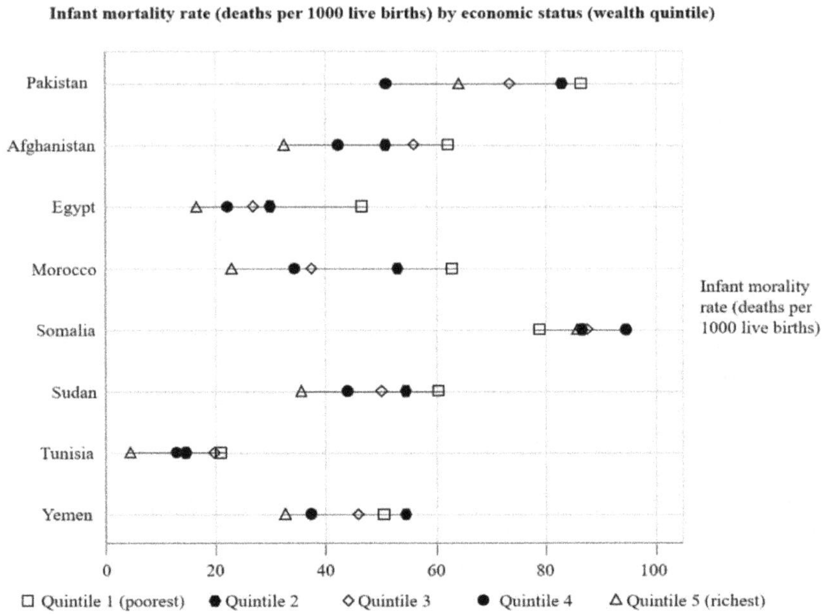

Fig. 5.1 Infant mortality rate (deaths per 1000 live births) by economic status (wealth quantile) (*Source* WHO inequality monitors [https://www.who.int/data/inequality-monitor])

important for reducing neonatal mortality. According to PSLM 2019–2020, prenatal consultation has witnessed an increase in the last couple of years. In the urban areas of Pakistan, the rate of prenatal consultation is 86% whereas in rural areas, it is reported at 72%. In the province of Punjab, which has developed a better health care system in the last two decades or so, prenatal consultation is the highest among all provinces that is above national average. Balochistan fares the worst. The same applies to the availability of skilled birth attendants. Over half of the births still take place in Balochistan without skilled birth attendants. The national average is even worse as regards postnatal consultation. Around three-fifth of births do not receive postnatal consultation at national level. The situation is worse than the national averages in Balochistan and KP provinces for this variable (Table 5.2).[22]

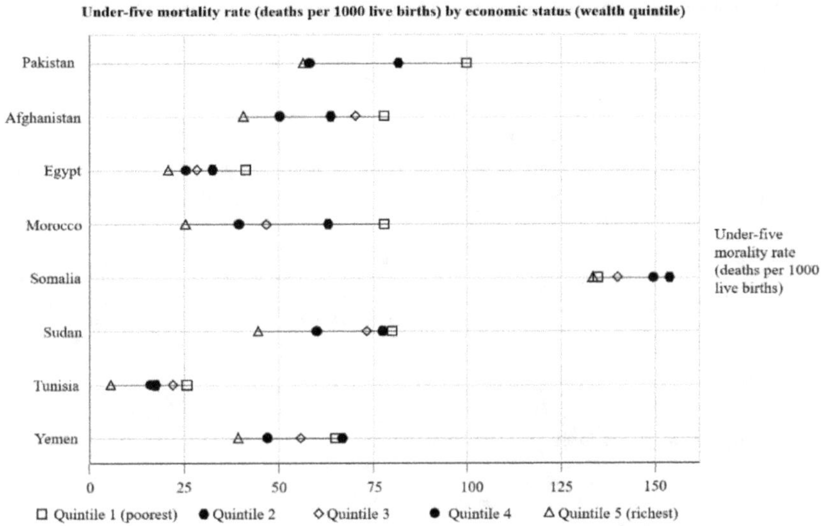

Fig. 5.2 Under-five mortality (per 1000 live births) by economic status (wealth quintile) (*Source* WHO inequality monitors [https://www.who.int/data/inequality-monitor])

Underweight prevalence is overall high in Pakistan but the babies born in the poorest 20% of families fare among the worst when a comparison is made among lower middle-income countries. A similar situation prevails against indicators of stunting and wasting for the children of the poorest segment of society (Fig. 5.4, 5.5 and 5.6).

Sharp Health Inequities

The poorest 20% of Pakistan are poorer than the 20% poorest of countries of the same income level that is low- and middle-income level countries, in terms of basic health facilities like immunization coverage, nutrition, infant mortality rates, and other health indicators, though national averages have improved consistently over the years against indicators like immunization. According to PSLM Survey 2019–2020, full immunization rates, based on the record, increased to 70% in 2019–2020 from 60% in 2014–2015 which means about two-third children of Pakistan are now fully immunized. This number further improves if we include

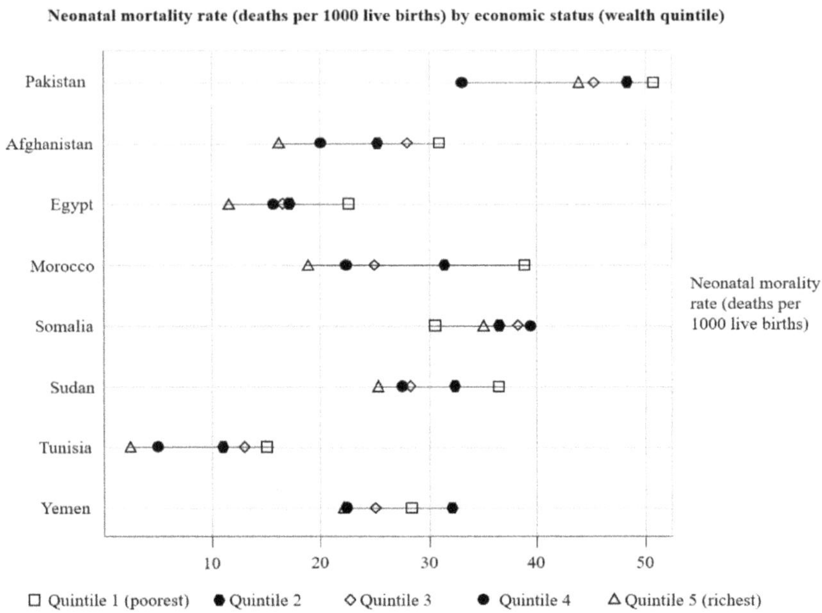

Fig. 5.3 Neonatal mortality (per 1000 live births) by economic status (wealth quintile) (*Source* WHO inequality monitors [https://www.who.int/data/inequality-monitor])

the number of children who were reported as immunized on the basis of recall by their parents as record keeping in Pakistan like other developing countries is poor.

All provinces have witnessed an increase overtime in the number of children who got immunization though comparison at province-level reveals huge variations. Based on the record, 81% of children were fully immunized in the province of Punjab whereas in case of Sindh and Balochistan number of children in terms of percentage is respectively 52 and 35, much lower compared to Punjab.[23] The variations become starker if the analysis is extended to the district-level. Even the best-performing province of Punjab unmasks severe variations. Some districts in particular of Southern Punjab like Multan (69% immunized), Muzaffargarh (68% immunized), and Rahim Yar Khan (65% immunized) have less immunization rates than provincial average.

Table 5.2 Some key indicators (urban vs. rural)

	Urban	*Rural*	*Total*
Pre natal consultation			
Pakistan	**86**	**72**	77
Punjab	89	80	83
Sindh	84	63	73
Khyber Pakhtunkhwa	82	66	69
Balochistan	75	59	63
Skilled birth attendant			
Pakistan	**82**	**62**	**68**
Punjab	82	64	70
Sindh	83	60	70
Khyber Pakhtunkhwa	84	63	66
Balochistan	71	46	52
Post natal consultation			
Pakistan	**48**	**34**	**39**
Punjab	48	39	42
Sindh	48	32	40
Khyber Pakhtunkhwa	45	28	30
Balochistan	36	25	28

Source PSLM 2019–2020

In the province of Sindh immunization status of some districts is pathetically bad where over 70% of children are still not fully immunized as per record. Districts of Jacobabad (only17% immunized), Tando Muhammad Khan (only 21% immunized), Tharparkar (25% immunized), Kishmore (26% immunized), and Shikarpur (29% immunized) are some examples to make the point. Similar situation can be observed in several districts of KPK province (for example, Kohistan 21% immunized, North Waziristan 21% immunized, and South Waziristan 7% immunized). At district-level, situation in Balochistan is the worst. Majority of its districts have very low rates of immunization (for example, Killa Abdullah 6%, Shaheed Sikanderabad 8%, Khuzdar 10%, Sheerani 19%, Lasbela 20%, Nasirabad 21%, Sibbi 21%, Washuk 23%, Duki 23%, Awaran 25%, and Harnai 29%).

Besides variations of location, inequities in immunization coverage are severe based on the income status of households. PSLM 2019–2020 does not give quintile-wise rates of immunization which earlier surveys contained. Non-inclusion of this information is a departure from earlier

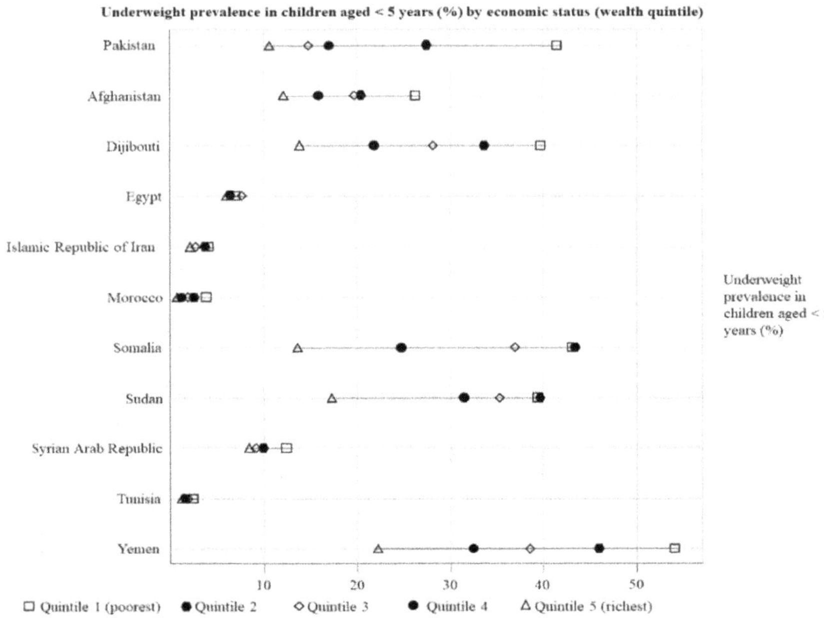

Fig. 5.4 Underweight prevalence in children aged <5 years (%) by economic status (wealth quintile) (*Source* WHO inequality monitors [https://www.who.int/data/inequality-monitor])

surveys. The said information is vital for monitoring inequities between the affluent and the indigent sections of the society. PSLM 2018–2019, however, provides this information. According to PSLM survey 2018–2019, the percentage of children aged 12–23 months who were fully immunized differ dramatically among the poorest (see Table 5.3).

Huge variations are also found in terms of access to other health services like prenatal care, postnatal care, and skilled assistance during the delivery of a baby based on location, education, and income. According to the Pakistan Maternal Mortality Survey (PMMS), 2019, only 36% of the poorest households had access to postnatal care, while 82% of households in the richest quintile had access to postnatal care. Similarly, 43% of illiterate mothers had skilled assistance during antenatal delivery and postnatal care, whereas 83% of mothers with higher education had said assistance. So there is an interplay of income, education, and location with

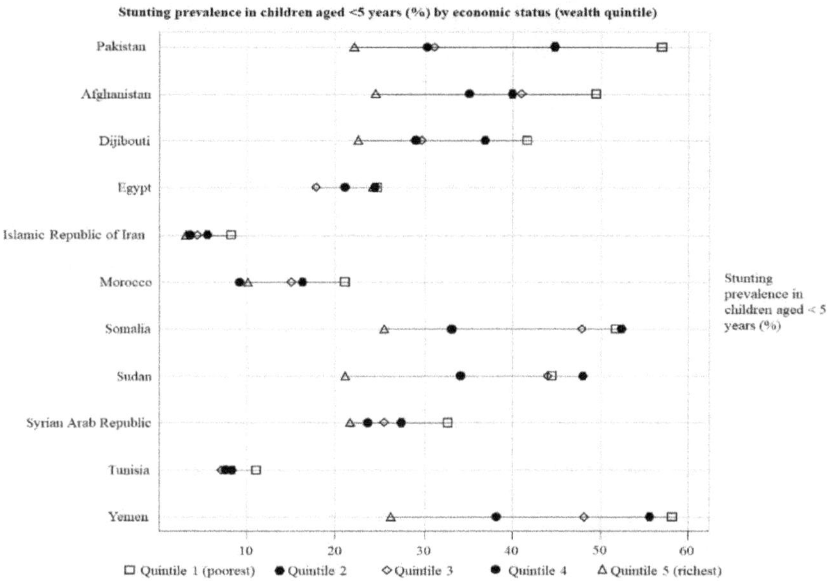

Fig. 5.5 Stunting prevalence in children aged <5 years (%) by economic status (wealth quintile) (*Source* WHO inequality monitors [https://www.who.int/data/inequality-monitor])

regards to accessibility to health care services in Pakistan. How much is the probability of a child surviving at the time of birth or a certain time after birth (infant mortality rate) and how many years is he expected to live (life expectancy) are two important variables reflecting on the accessibility and quality of health services in a country. Infant mortality measures the temperature of the entire population. There are many things that can kill a baby as they are very fragile. This variable provides a glimpse into the nature, riches, status of women, and quality of life enjoyed by the people of a country. A host of factors like income, distribution of income, food security, sewage system, availability of clean drinking water, and education of women are captured by the said indicator.

The provision of government services is, however, a metric that has gained precedence over other factors. If the provision of services like prenatal care, postnatal care, and birth by a skilled attendant exists and is of better quality, the probability of a child's survival is high. That is why

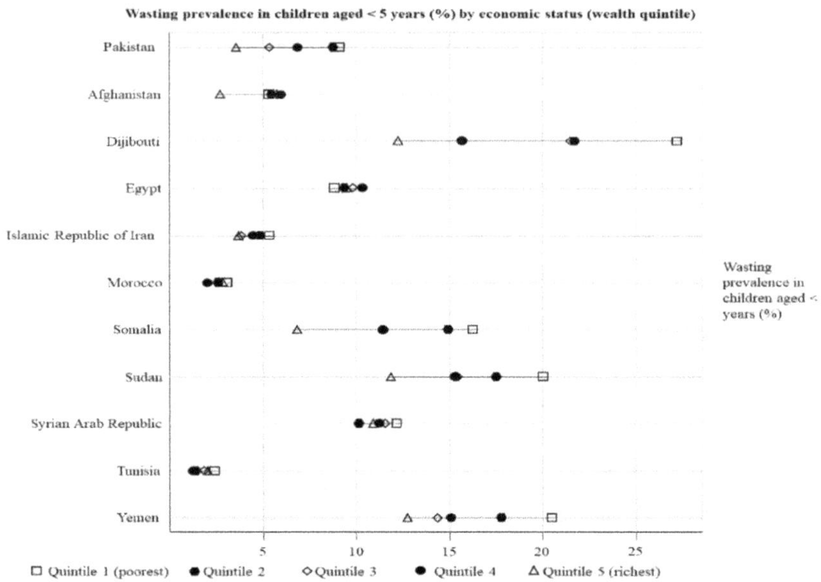

Fig. 5.6 Wasting prevalence in children aged <5 years (%) by economic status (wealth quintile) (*Source* WHO inequality monitors [https://www.who.int/data/inequality-monitor])

this is taken as an important variable of health and the quality of health service provision in a country. According to WDI, in 1990, the infant mortality rate in Pakistan was 106.7 which decreased to 55.9 in 2019. This is still a big number and the worst in the world when compared to countries in the region and even African countries except Nigeria, an oil-rich country, where the infant mortality rate is higher than Pakistan. The national average infant mortality rate masks huge variations of location and class. The number of deaths among children born to poor families or in rural areas is higher than among children born to rich families and in metropolitan areas of Pakistan. This point is best illustrated by the disaggregated data from Punjab, the biggest province of Pakistan in terms of population, which has better health facilities compared to other provinces.

The data collected by the Planning and Development Department of Punjab in collaboration with UNICEF provides some interesting insights about health inequities in spatial terms. Lahore, the second-largest city in

Table 5.3 Percentage of children aged 12–23 months that have been fully immunized—by quintiles

	Urban			*Rural*			*Total*		
	Male	*Female*	*Both*	*Male*	*Female*	*Both*	*Male*	*Female*	*Both*
Pakistan									
1st quintile	68	45	57	58	52	55	59	51	56
2nd quintile	70	75	73	62	60	61	64	63	63
3rd quintile	65	71	68	67	65	66	67	67	67
4th quintile	81	81	81	68	79	73	74	80	77
5th quintile	86	87	86	81	82	81	85	85	85
Punjab									
1st quintile	87	61	74	76	67	72	78	67	73
2nd quintile	90	88	89	78	75	77	81	78	79
3rd quintile	68	81	74	82	79	81	78	80	79
4th quintile	88	89	89	75	87	81	81	88	84
5th quintile	88	90	89	88	89	89	88	90	89
Sindh									
1st quintile	58	20	42	38	36	37	42	33	38
2nd quintile	51	47	49	35	27	31	40	33	37
3rd quintile	57	62	60	35	29	31	47	47	47
4th quintile	71	70	71	46	64	54	65	69	67
5th quintile	81	73	78	27	68	49	79	73	76
KP excluding merged areas									
1st quintile	65	53	60	54	52	53	55	53	54
2nd quintile	79	78	78	61	62	62	63	64	64
3rd quintile	80	64	72	63	59	61	65	60	63
4th quintile	83	79	81	64	59	62	67	65	66
5th quintile	96	100	98	71	64	67	79	72	76
Balochistan									
1st quintile	28	30	29	16	25	20	18	25	22
2nd quintile	49	68	57	32	19	26	38	31	34
3rd quintile	50	51	51	23	13	19	30	27	29
4th quintile	71	75	73	50	48	49	58	56	57
5th quintile	81	85	84	39	73	66	68	79	76

Source PSLM 2018–2019

Pakistan after Karachi, is the metropolis of the province, where some of the best health facilities in the country both in the public and private sectors are concentrated. According to Punjab Development Statistics 2020, there is a 0.038% (38 out of 1000 live births) chance that an infant born in the metropolis may die between birth and his first birthday. The

Table 5.4 Maternal mortality ratios, maternal deaths for 100,000 live births for the 3-year period before the survey

S. No	*Country/province*	*No. of deaths*
1.	**Pakistan**	**186**
2.	Punjab	157
3.	Sindh	224
4.	KP	165
5.	Balochistan	298

Source Pakistan Maternal Mortality Survey (PMMS), 2019

probability almost doubles for Nankana Sahib (76 out of 1000), a district of Punjab named after the first guru of Sikhs, Baba Guru Nanak, which is just around 50 kilometers away from the metropolis. In the case of Kasur, the city of Sufi poet Baba Bulleh Shah, Hafiz Abad, and Okara, all located mostly in the circumference of 100 kilometers of the metropolis, the probability of infant mortality is 0.073, 0.097, and 0.072, much higher than the metropolis number. Almost all the districts of South Punjab have substantially high infant mortality rates compared to North Punjab.

A similar pattern can be observed in other provinces. Urban areas have lower infant mortality compared to rural areas. For rural areas, the figure is 67 compared to 49 for urban Pakistan. The same pattern of variation based on location and socio-economic factors is visible for maternal mortality rates. According to the Maternal Mortality Survey 2019, the maternal mortality ratio is 186, but again, there are huge variations between rural and urban areas and provinces. The MMR rate is 158 in urban areas compared to 199 in rural Pakistan, with the highest in Balochistan standing at 298, almost twice the national average (Table 5.4).

Life Before Birth

The story of 'health capital' begins with fetal development. Life before birth, that is 9 months in utero, is one of the most critical periods that shape the future of a baby. What will her future abilities be? What will be her health trajectories? And what will be her path to earnings? These important dimensions of life are determined to a large extent in utero. This is called the "fetal origin hypothesis". One of the important implications of said hypothesis is that the best way to help children is by helping their mothers.[24] It means that pregnant women and women of childbearing age need to become the focus of public health policy interventions. Low nutrition during pregnancy affects both maternal and fetal health. The researchers have analyzed the impact of fasting to prove the validity of the hypothesis.

Empirics[25] in this regard confirm that as a result of fasting during pregnancy, babies are likely to be born underweight with a persistent negative impact on cognitive ability and learning. Some researchers[26] have shown, with particular reference to Pakistan using parent–child data from the Demographic and Health Survey (DHS) and income data from the income tax returns of the period 2007–2009, that in-utero exposure to Ramadan fasting has a significant negative impact on earnings later in life through two possible channels: the skills channel and the health channel. These researchers suggest that lower earnings are mainly due to lower skills, which means that the children exposed to fasting are born with low capacities to produce cognitive and non-cognitive skills, which in turn are responsible for their less education, joining low-skilled professions, and earning less.

Similarly, exposure to other shocks like natural disasters, pandemics, famines, military conflicts, et cetera, during pregnancy may have short-term, medium-term, and long-term negative effects. For example, prenatal exposure to famine is empirically found to be more harmful than postnatal exposure based on an analysis of the Dutch famine of 1944–1945.[27] The negative impact of prenatal exposure to the 1957 Asian flu is well-documented on birth weight and future test scores.[28] Newborns exposed to homicide or violence during pregnancy have low birth weight and socio-economic factors like the mothers' low level of education amplify the adverse consequences of violence on birth outcomes which simply means that violence aggravates the disadvantages that the newborns already suffer due to low socio-economic status.[29] Literature on life before birth simply implies that effective public health interventions would start before the birth of newborns. Enhancing women's agency for better rearing and caring for children is highly significant in this regard.

Health and Women's Agency

Infant mortality and mother's education are positively correlated. The PSLM Survey 2018–2019, on the basis of data for the period 2014–2016, estimates that infant mortality was 69 for babies born to women with no education whereas in the case of women with 10 years of schooling and above, the number falls to 32 that is a decrease of over 100% pointing toward the significant impact of women's agency on child health. According to the MMR survey, over half (52%) of the ever-married women of age 15–49 had no education or just received primary-level education. The economic status of women is highly correlated with education. Experience of Sri Lanka, Costa Rica, and the Indian state of Kerala shows that the status of women raises child health for a given level of income.[30] The relationship between education and health holds both for developed and developing countries. An important empirical confirmation of this connection comes from Sweden where some researchers, using data of children raised with their biological parents and those of adoptive children, found a positive relationship between adult health and parental education.[31]

According to these researchers, children coming from households whose parents were educated at the level of university were on average six percentiles better on health indicators as adults compared to children from households with parents having only primary education. These results are based on data of about 3 million individuals. These researchers further investigated a large sample of 11,000 Swedish-born adoptees for whom they observed the educational attainments of both biological and adopting parents to delineate the impact of pre-birth and post-birth factors on the long-term health status of children. Results suggested that both pre-birth and post-birth factors matter. The association between adopting parents' education and the educational attainments of the adoptees was found to be mainly due to more investment in human capital by the parents with good education.

According to PSLM 2018–2019, the infant mortality rate among male infants is 62 whereas it is 58 for female infants. The overall mortality rate for women in the age bracket 15–49 years is 1.72 per 1000 persons compared to a male mortality rate of 2.48 per 1000 persons as per the MMR survey. These two numbers lend credence to the fact that biologically women are stronger than their male counterparts, a vindication of Amartya Sen's 'missing women' hypothesis. The child survival rate is perhaps the best proxy variable used in empirical research for investment in a child's human capital. If the infant mortality rate is high, then investment in child health is low. A reduction in infant mortality rate is thus an indication that investment in child health has increased with time, but variations in mortality rates in terms of socio-economic class and location still demand strong affirmative action for the poor families and residents of poor locations to improve their incomes, education, and access to quality health services. Investment in women's health increases their participation in the labor market and increases opportunity cost of having children. Consequently, investments in women's health lead to a substitution away from having many children toward having fewer healthy well-nourished children.

Sex ratios have tended toward normalization in Pakistan if we go by national averages. Sex selection in Pakistan is not a problem like that of India and China, thanks to religious factors. In India, sex selection has become a big issue. Some researchers[32] claim, in an Indian context, that technological growth in villages increases returns from investing in boys' health while technological growth outside the village, potentially in the marriage market, increases returns from investing in girls. It means that the gap in male and female mortality rates increases with technological change in the village while the gap decreases with technological change in the labor market. So child survival is affected by the expected returns from having girls. Sometimes skewed sex ratios have some unintended but important economic consequences.[33] The high savings rate in China is partly attributable to skewed sex ratios. Due to the imbalance in the marriage market created by the one-child policy (fewer females compared to males), parents of the groom are required to save for the marriage of their son, thus boosting the savings of households.

Several studies suggest that the boy-girl mortality gap is negatively correlated with women's wages. In 2003, Nancy Qian conducted a natural experiment using the liberalization of tea plantations in China.[34] In the regions where tea production was liberalized, the ratio of boys to girls diminished considerably after the liberalization of tea production. Why? Because girls are better at picking tea leaves than boys, so in such areas girls had better prospects of earnings. This motivated parents to invest more in girls. Implication simply is that investment by parents in education and health is motivated by the earning potential of the boys and girls and if girls have more opportunity or equal opportunity to earn, the female child mortality rate shall fall.

Another experiment in the Indian context[35] also confirms that making employment opportunities more salient for women increases investment in the health and education of girls. Some researchers conducted a randomized intervention by providing three years of business processing and recruiting services to women in randomly selected villages. Consequently, girls in the age bracket of 5–15 years experienced an increase in Body Mass index (BMI) reflecting better nutrition and medical care. So education and market labor force participation are two important factors for enhancing women's agency. Women's empowerment, in turn, has important positive externalities for the health and nutrition of children.

The Challenge of Undernutrition

Child undernutrition is a big challenge Pakistan is faced with. It falls among the worst countries in terms of low birth weight, stunting, wasting, and underweight children, some important variables determining the nutritional status of children. The economic losses from undernutrition are estimated around US$7.6 billion annually for Pakistan corresponding nearly to 3% of GDP.[36] According to Pakistan National Nutrition Survey (PNNS), the prevalence of low birth weight is estimated to be 20.1%, with a higher proportion among rural dwellers (26.2%) than urban dwellers (16%). Considerable differences exist with regard to levels of poverty and education. The uneducated mothers gave birth to 23.5% low-weight babies which means that out of four babies, one has a low birth weight.

Similarly, a baby born to parents belonging to the poorest quintile has a higher probability of being born with a low weight compared to a baby born to rich parents. The results of the Nutrition survey are based on weights recorded at the time of birth. In the majority of cases particularly among the poor and illiterate families weight at the time of birth is not recorded which means that the number of low birth weight babies has a strong probability of being underestimated. The stunting prevalence is 40.2% when compared to the average child height-for-age (HFA) Z-score which is among the highest in the world. The situation is more glaring in terms of rurality and socio-economic status (SES). In rural areas, stunting is 8.4% higher compared to urban areas at the national level, and for the provinces of Balochistan and Sindh, it is respectively 6.4% and 5.3% higher than the national average.

Over half of the children (51.4%) of the poorest 20% of families are stunted, and 46% of the children of illiterate mothers are stunted. These figures of stunting are similar to those of India which stands out in the world for stunting. There are some socio-cultural explanations for the severity of stunting in India. Based on an analysis[37] of 168,000 children, Seema Jayachandran and Rohini Pande have shown that India's height disadvantage increases sharply with birth order due to unequal allocation of resources among siblings. The height of the eldest son is normally greater than that of his younger siblings due to patrilocal and patrilineal Hindu kinship system as parents typically live with the eldest son when they grow old and bequeath property to him. The eldest son is also supposed to perform post-death rituals. The said researchers further confirm that such a steep birth order gradient is not found among Muslims in India or in low-eldest son preference states like Kerala and the Northeast. And that one-third of the India-Africa height gap is well explained by son preference in India. What does explain the high prevalence of stunting in Pakistan? It may not be due to son preference but it is simply due to low coverage of health, weak women agency, illiteracy, and poverty. A similar picture emerges with regards to wasting and underweight prevalence.

At the national level wasting prevalence is 17.7% but when disaggregated quintile-wise, wasting is highest (23%) among the children of the poorest 20% of families, whereas for the richest 20% of families, it is 14.6%. A comparison among provinces shows that the province of Sindh has the highest wasting prevalence (23.2%) followed by Balochistan (18.9%). The situation becomes more troubling when a child is the victim of both stunting and wasting. This number is also quite high. For example, in the province of Sindh, 10% of children have stunting and wasting concurrently. The underweight prevalence in Pakistan is as high as 28.9% at the national level with all variations of location and socio-economic status. 43% of children born to the poorest quintile are underweight compared to 17.8% of those belonging to the richest quintile. A similar relationship holds for the mother's education as underweight prevalence is the highest (34.6%) among the children born to mothers with no education (see Table 5.5).

Data gathered through the Multiple Indicator Cluster Surveys (MICS) by the respective Planning and Development Departments of the provincial governments of Punjab, Sindh, and KP in collaboration with UNICEF also presents a similar picture. If both moderate and severe underweight prevalence are taken into account, over one-fifth of children in Punjab and KPK provinces are underweight. In the case of Sindh province, the proportion of underweight children is over two-fifths, that is almost twice that of Punjab and KP. District-level disaggregation of data

Table 5.5 Nutrition status of children percentage of children under age five

		Stunted	*Wasted*	*Underweight*	*Both stunted & wasted*
Pakistan		40.2	17.7	28.9	5.9
Urban		34.8	16.2	24.0	4.4
Rural		43.2	18.6	31.6	6.8
Province					
Punjab	Urban	33.0	13.5	19.9	3.2
	Rural	38.5	16.3	25.7	4.9
	Total	36.4	15.3	23.5	4.3
Sindh	Urban	36.4	20.7	30.9	6.4
	Rural	53.2	25.4	50.0	13.0
	Total	45.5	23.3	41.3	10.0
KP	Urban	34.7	13.2	18.6	2.4
	Rural	41.4	15.5	24.3	4.0
	Total	40.0	15.0	23.1	3.7
Balochistan	Urban	44.0	19.7	29.8	6.2
	Rural	47.7	18.5	31.5	6.7
	Total	46.6	18.9	31.0	6.5
Sex					
Male		40.9	18.4	29.3	6.5
Female		39.4	17.0	28.4	5.4
Mother's education					
None		46.0	19.4	34.6	7.7
Primary		37.6	16.5	25.8	4.7
Middle		35.2	15.6	21.9	4.1
Secondary		30.8	15.7	20.7	3.3
Higher		27.4	14.3	17.2	2.8
Wealth index quintile					
Poorest		**51.4**	**23.0**	**43.0**	**10.7**
Second		45.1	18.1	32.1	6.2
Middle		39.1	16.5	26.5	5.4
Fourth		32.6	15.1	20.9	3.7
Richest		**29.2**	**14.6**	**17.8**	**2.7**

Source Pakistan National Nutrition Survey (PNNS), 2018

presents a bleaker picture. There are districts, particularly in the provinces of Sindh and Balochistan where stunting and underweight prevalence are over 60%. Out of the 10 top districts with the highest prevalence of underweight, seven are in Sindh province.

A similar pattern emerges for wasting. In some districts, over one-third of the population suffers from wasting. Disaggregation of data at the provincial and district levels unmasks the severity of the challenge that national averages hide. Malnutrition is rampant throughout with a higher incidence in South Punjab, Sindh, Balochistan, and KPK. Information on underweight prevalence among children under age 5 is available for the majority of countries and regions through the World Bank. A comparison of Pakistan with other countries and regions of the world gives a very dismal picture. According to WDI,[38] the proportion of underweight children in Pakistan is much higher than in Sub-Saharan Africa (19.1%), lower and middle-income countries (15.8%), low-income countries (20%) and the world average (14.2%).

The story of malnutrition does not end here. The disturbing part is that the pace of coping with this challenge is very slow which reflects some fundamental flaws in assumptions. An assumption is that children are the responsibility of the parents and if the state is doing something for the nutrition of the children it is just an act of benevolence on its part. This assumption may not be publicly declared by the state but it is clearly reflected in its spending priorities and policies. It is quite puzzling that both stunting and wasting have registered an increase over time. Underweight prevalence registered some decline during the last two decades but at a very slow pace (see Table 5.6).

The poor nutritional status of children in Pakistan is enigmatic and cannot be explained by income alone as regions like Sub-Saharan Africa and low-income countries fare better than Pakistan on child nutrition. An analysis of various quantitative and qualitative studies undertaken by the World Bank[39] shows that multiple factors are responsible for child undernutrition. These factors broadly include child-level factors (breastfeeding, gender, birth at a health facility, number of children in the household, birth intervals, etc.), mother-level factors (education, age, mental and physical health), and household level factors (economic status, availability of flushed toilets, access to piped water, etc.). Another analysis[40] of 28 articles published on child malnutrition between 2000 and 2016 identify early marriages, large family size, high fertility rates with a lack of birth spacing, and low income as causes of undernutrition in Pakistan. A study,[41] conducted in 2018, found that only 15% of Pakistani boys and girls aged 6–23 months received the minimum acceptable diet for effective growth and development (see Table 5.7).

According to 2016 study[42] 'Minimum Cost of the Diet' around 68% of the country's households faced food insecurity which means that two

Table 5.6 Trends in malnutrition for children under five

	2001	*2011*	*2018*
Pakistan			
Stunting	36.8	43.7	40.2
Underweight	38.0	31.5	28.9
Wasting	13.1	15.1	17.7
Stunting			
Punjab	32.5	39.2	36.4
Sindh	44.2	49.8	45.5
KP	43.5	47.8	40.0
Balochistan	39.1	52.2	46.6
Wasting			
Punjab	12.1	13.6	15.3
Sindh	18.2	17.5	23.3
KP	10.9	17.2	15.0
Balochistan	13.9	16.1	18.9
Underweight			
Punjab	35.1	29.8	23.5
Sindh	49.4	40.5	41.3
KP	36.6	24.1	23.1
Balochistan	35.3	39.6	31.0

Source Pakistan National Nutrition Survey (PNNS), 2018

out of every three households experienced severe hunger due to unaffordability and unavailability of food. Another survey[43] undertaken in 2017 revealed that 42 districts, out of which 32 were in the provinces of Balochistan and Sindh, were highly vulnerable to food insecurity. According to PNNS, 2018, over half of the children in the age bracket of 6–59 months face childhood anemia. This figure is higher for the poorest households and rural areas of Sindh, KP, and Balochistan. Same pattern prevails for deficiencies of Vitamin A, zinc, and Vitamin D.

Poor parental education (in particular the education of the mother), poor availability and quality of food, lack of access to water and sanitation, and inadequate health care are other associated factors with malnutrition. Out of multiple factors, three stand out which are poverty, food insecurity, and the well-being of the mother. About 18.3% of households face severe food insecurity at the national level whereas over 42% of the households in the poorest quintile suffer from severe food insecurity (Table 5.8).

The National Food Security Policy 2018[44] talks of policy measures like school feeding programs, nutrition programs for children under age

Table 5.7 Percentage of children aged 6–59 months having anemia and deficiencies of various food supplements

		**Childhood anemia*	*Iron deficiency anemia (anemia and low ferritin)*	*Vitamin A deficiency*	*Zinc deficiency (60 ug/dl)*	*Vitamin D deficiency*
Pakistan		53.7	28.6	51.5	18.6	62.7
Urban		48.9	28.1	51.2	17.1	65.6
Rural		56.5	28.9	51.7	19.5	61.0
Province						
Punjab	Urban	52.7	31.2	49.5	17.3	75.7
	Rural	51.9	28.9	48.8	18.4	67.9
	Total	52.1	29.7	49.1	18.0	70.7
Sindh	Urban	42.3	26.3	54.5	17.4	48.8
	Rural	61.2	39.7	61.6	21.3	23.9
	Total	51.1	32.4	57.8	19.2	37.0
KP	Urban	54.7	19.4	44.9	11.9	77.8
	Rural	62.3	20.5	47.1	20.2	76.7
	Total	60.8	20.3	46.7	18.6	77.0
Balochistan	Urban	60.7	22.9	57.8	21.7	75.2
	Rural	74.3	23.2	58.7	21.9	69.3
	Total	70.5	15.3	58.5	21.8	70.9
Sex						
Male		54.2	29.1	51.6	18.8	62.3
Female		53.3	28.0	51.3	18.4	63.0
Mother's education						
None		55.8	29.0	53.7	19.2	57.8
Primary		55.0	31.1	49.4	19.3	67.1
Middle		51.9	28.0	50.5	16.4	70.0
Secondary		49.3	26.6	49.1	16.8	67.2
Higher		47.5	25.4	46.2	17.9	71.6
Wealth index quintile						
Poorest		**60.3**	**32.4**	**56.4**	**22.1**	**47.5**
Second		56.6	29.7	52.6	19.0	61.6
Middle		53.8	27.2	51.1	17.9	63.9
Fourth		49.3	26.4	48.0	17.5	69.1
Richest		**48.1**	**27.1**	**49.5**	**16.2**	**72.1**

Source Pakistan National Nutrition Survey (PNNS), 2018

*It includes both severe and moderate

Table 5.8 Severe food insecurity

		Households (%)
Pakistan		18.3
Urban		13.9
Rural		20.9
Province		
Punjab	Urban	15.2
	Rural	37.9
	Total	26.0
Sindh	Urban	11.8
	Rural	11.8
	Total	11.8
KP	Urban	26.9
	Rural	38.5
	Total	35.3
Balochistan	Urban	13.0
	Rural	12.0
	Total	12.5
Wealth index quintile		
Poorest		**42.1**
Second		21.4
Middle		14.4
Fourth		9.0
Richest		**4.8**

Source Pakistan National Nutrition Survey (PNNS), 2018

5, and zero-hour shops in low-income areas of major cities but we rarely see implementation of these policy commitments. The provision of mid-day meals to children studying in public schools became mandatory in India as a result of a judgment of the Supreme Court which held that the right to dignity includes the right to food. Pakistan has not yet come up with a comprehensive initiative on the right to food and child nutrition. It needs to be appreciated that maternal nutritional status is closely linked to the growth of a child. Some researchers investigated economic returns to parental health in Indonesian context[45] and found that returns to parental health are very high and that maternal health not only significantly affects her children's health but is also linked to child schooling outcomes.

The results further suggested that children of parents with poor health have long-term effects in the form of a lower probability of high school completion, fewer years of schooling, and poorer adult health. In this context, nutrition-specific interventions to avert maternal and child undernutrition and micronutrient deficiencies, especially for the poorest segments of society, can make a big difference.[46] Better nutrition has paid dividends both at the individual and national levels. For example, being taller does not just mean being attractive and beautiful. Rather taller adults are expected to earn more than other workers and do better on cognitive tests. They generally enter occupations that have higher cognitive skill requirements.[47] They are also expected to live longer. In case of Pakistan, some researchers at the World Bank have found that height is an independent determinant of earnings and not merely through the channels of other cognitive and socio-emotional skills.[48] Health demands high priority. Empirics[49] suggest that one percentage increase in health expenditure can potentially increase GDP per capita by 0.38%.

Sub-Saharan Africa Spends 100% More Than Pakistan

Pakistan spends the least on health in per capita terms in the region. It spends around 100% less in comparison with Sub-Saharan Africa. According to WDI data for the year 2020 (latest available data), the per capita expenditure of Pakistan on health is US$38.18, lower than regional comparators countries such as India, Sri Lanka, and Bangladesh. Moreover, countries like Vietnam and Bangladesh registered an impressive increase in per capita health expenditure in the last two decades compared to Pakistan. Moreover, per capita health expenditure is much below compared to averages of sub-Saharan Africa, lower middle-income countries, and South Asian region (see Table 5.9).

Pakistan's spending on health in terms of GDP is also quite low. It spends less than three percent of GDP on health which is less than the average spending of low-income countries, low middle-income countries, and Sub-Saharan African region (excluding high-income countries), reflecting low priority of health care in the national scheme of things.

A point of caution! Per capita spending on health and spending in terms of GDP are important variables but may not necessarily be direct determinants of health outcomes. They are indicative of a county's capacity to finance its health care system. GDP per capita fails to reflect the degree of universal health coverage and inclusiveness of income in a society. So the link between income and health is not mechanical.[50] Institutional capacity matters for building a strong health care system. Deaton is right when he says that a marked improvement can be made in

Table 5.9 Health expenditure per capita (current US$) of selected countries/regions 2000–2020

Country name	*2000*	*2005*	*2010*	*2015*	*2020*
Bangladesh	8.56	11.61	20.80	32.85	50.66
India	18.50	27.67	45.13	58.92	56.63
Pakistan	**15.58**	**19.88**	**25.26**	**35.98**	**38.18**
Sri Lanka	43.72	57.30	108.28	149.96	151.06
Vietnam	18.92	35.04	78.64	117.86	166.23
South Asia	17.46	25.48	41.28	54.97	55.73
Sub-Saharan Africa (excluding high income)	33.83	58.70	86.87	85.57	73.74
Low- and middle-income countries	60.57	91.22	177.86	230.11	274.30

Source World Bank Development indicators (WDI)

the health care provision only if the "Rajasthan attitudes" can be moved closer to the "Kerala attitudes". In Kerala, absenteeism is rare and people expect public clinics to serve them.[51] It simply means that accountability is important, and to ensure accountability, people need to be educated and empowered to demand their health rights (Fig. 5.7).

An extensive debate on the health care system needs to be initiated with a focus on the residents of rural areas and the poorer segments of society whose voices are missing from the mainstream media on issues

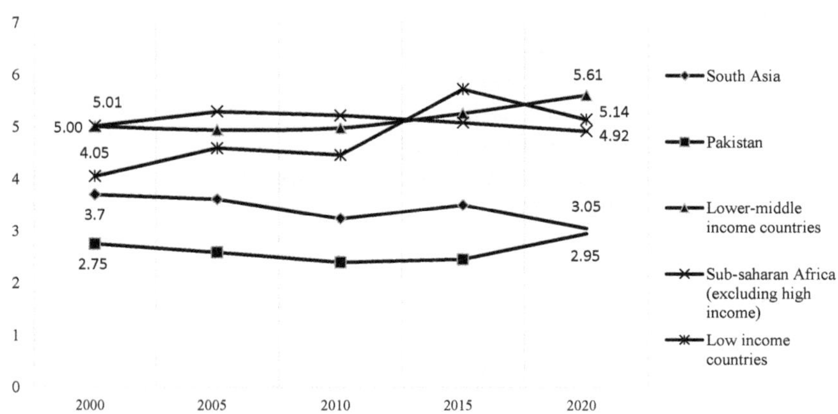

Fig. 5.7 Health expenditure (% of GDP) (*Source* World Bank Development indicators [WDI])

concerning their lives and well-being. In Pakistan, where huge differences in income, education, and access to public services exist, child care cannot be left to poor parents and illiterate mothers. The state needs to assume the total responsibility for child care, in particular their nutrition, health care, and education. Given the deep disparities in health outcomes based on location and socio-economic status, there is a need for the state to ensure comprehensive universal health coverage (UHC) focusing both on body (physical health) and mind (mental health).

Mental Health

Mental health is badly neglected in Pakistan. The Sindh Mental Health Authority conducted a five-year study of registered cases of suicide in the province of Sindh.[52] According to the said study, seventy-nine and sixty-four cases were respectively registered in Tharparkar and Umerkot, two districts with the highest number of suicide cases, in the year 2020. This number may be underestimated as the report itself recognizes this limitation. The research was limited to information from only registered cases at District Health offices and District Police offices and did not include cases reported in the media, private hospitals, or cases not registered by the families of the victims. WHO estimates the suicide rate in Pakistan at 8.9 per 100,000 people, slightly below the global average of nine. SMHA got another study on psychological autopsies of suicide cases in Tharparkar. Chronic mental illness, financial burden, and unemployment were found to be the top triggers for suicide according to the said report.[53] Unfortunately, we have little appreciation of the cost mental illnesses like depression, anxiety, and other mental disorders impose on individuals and on the national level. The poor segments of society in particular perceive mental illness as a result of some supernatural influence. The greater part of the community seems to be in a denial mode regarding mental health. They approach spiritual or traditional healers for treatment.

Political will and priorities are more limited for mental health. There are also issues of disgrace, stigma, and prejudice against patients and families that prevent individuals from seeking psychological help and mental health care.[54] "Those who suffer from mental illness are doubly unfortunate. They have the condition in the first place, but in addition, they are discriminated against and written off as hopeless cases. It is time for every society to become much more open about mental illness just as with other illnesses. If we want a happier world, we need a completely new deal on mental health".[55] Mental health is a neglected area. Few hospitals and centers exist in the country for the treatment of mental diseases. The mental diseases are very common but hardly enter into our planning and budget allocations. Severe anger, domestic violence, torture, et cetera, are all manifestations of mental disorders.

At least two policy steps would be required to ameliorate the situation. First, separate budget allocations may be earmarked for the treatment of mental ailments. Second, all the individuals tasked with the responsibilities of public service delivery need to be identified and treated for mental disorders on a priority basis. It would be beneficial for them not only at an individual level but its impact would also help improve the quality of public service delivery. Moreover, mental health care needs to be incorporated as an integral component of primary health care.

Some steps like decriminalization of attempted self-harm (repealing or suitable amendment in Section 325 of the Pakistan Penal Code), setting up an effective mechanism for suicide death registration (for analysis and research purposes), school-based interventions (suicide prevention strategies like crisis management and self-esteem enhancement), and mental health awareness programs at the community level can be initiated. These steps do not involve any additional financial costs. The suicides are what Case and Deaton call "deaths of despair"[56] as the driving factor for such suicides is despair due to bad economic and social conditions. Such deaths of despair are more prevalent among the poor and less educated (even in developed countries like the USA), so targeted interventions are needed to improve the underlying economic and social conditions of the people. Inequality, poverty, and low social capital are in fact the factors behind the deaths of despair.

There is some awakening about the health of the poor. Pakistan launched Waseela-e-Sehat (WS) under the auspices of BISP with the aim of providing health insurance to the poor and improving their access to health services with a pilot project in Faisalabad district in 2012. The government of Pakistan and the World Bank were the main financiers of the WS Health Initiative. The program was limited in its scope and coverage. The lack of awareness also undermined its utility.[57]

Sehat Sahulat Program

By the end of 2015, Pakistan had initiated the Sehat Sahulat Program (SSP) for households living below the poverty line (BPL) based on national socio-economic registry data. The BPL households can get indoor hospitalization services from the panel hospitals on the basis of health cards provided by the government. It is fully subsidized and has been administered by the State Life Insurance Corporation (SLIC). The government pays a fixed premium per eligible family to SLIC, which in turn manages members' health care expenditures. Ninety percent of the unspent net premium is refunded back to the government at the end of the three-year contract period as per arrangement.

This program has undoubtedly provided relief to the poor and vulnerable households. It is certainly an improvement over the out-of-pocket health expenditure system. The question, however, is: what type of health system is going to emerge in the long run out of SSP? Arguments are being made that salvage lies in this system as it would eventually bring private insurance players into the market where the government would pay premiums for the poor households while those who could afford them would buy premiums from the private insurance companies. The people shall get health services from hospitals on panels, private or public, and the costs shall be reimbursed by the private insurance companies. The scheme on the face of it seems attractive but how this model would evolve and mature leaves room for many concerns.

The very idea that the government will pay for insurance premiums for households living below the poverty line has serious targeting issues when it comes to health. For example, in the current scenario in Pakistan, out-of-pocket (OOP) expenditures are very high, and costs of treatment like cancer, et cetera, may push households, which may be above the poverty line today, to below the poverty line tomorrow. Besides health contingencies, other economic shocks like natural calamities, bad harvests, and joblessness due to low growth may render households at least temporarily poor. In such a scenario, BPL targeting issues may get complicated as revisions to the BPL list may take years due to the rigidity attached to such lists.

The poverty lists for eligibility for social support, et cetera, are generally based on per capita income or consumption. The multidimensional nature of poverty is not taken into account for such purposes. There may be a scenario where a person who is physically challenged is above the poverty line. He may be in dire need of health insurance because of costs and disabilities but may fail to qualify for the BPL list. In this context, the route taken for UHC through health insurance may not turn out to be an adequate and optimal public policy option. The equity issue is also not adequately taken care of through targeted insurance subsidies mainly due to exclusion errors and the obstacles that poor people face in using the health insurance system due to illiteracy or low education.

The SSP, despite all its attractiveness, is marked by poor utilization. A report on the actuarial review of the program undertaken in April 2019 found that admission rates were low compared to other countries.[58] The private health insurance model, which may eventually emerge if the focus is not shifted to primary health and preventive care, is fraught with not only standard market failures like adverse selection[59] and moral hazard,[60] but private insurers may also emerge as a big lobby difficult to reckon with. The USA is a case in point. It spends more in terms of GDP than European countries but the life expectancy is lower and infant mortality and maternal mortality rates are high compared to European countries and Japan.[61]

Further, the system of health insurance based on commercial considerations is inherently biased in favor of hospitalized care. This is true in all countries where the health system is based on private insurance, but the problem in Pakistan may be more severe due to the least importance accorded to preventive care. A holistic approach to public health care that takes care of both curative and preventive aspects is important. There is a need to go back to the basics for the provision of universal health coverage and reducing health inequities. Basic health care units and rural health centers needs to be the epicenters of the public health care system. Big hospitals are concentrated in cities and the governments are more focused on building and upgrading hospitals in urban centers due to visibility and voice factors.

Primary and Preventive Health Care

On the contrary, BHUs and RHCs lack political visibility as rural areas are almost missing from the print and electronic media. Urban dwellers can better organize, protest, and articulate their demands. On the other hand, rural people lack voice due to collective action problem. Further, big hospitals and gigantic health projects have the potential to generate rents and opportunities for corruption. The result of all these factors is that BHUs and RHCs are badly neglected.

The problem with Pakistan like other poor countries is that the public health budget is not only low but most of it is consumed by big hospitals. The remarks of Deon Filmer et al. in this regard are very pertinent. They write[62]: "The public budget for health is principally absorbed by public hospitals staffed by doctors expensively trained at public expense who use costly medical technology to treat conditions of the urban elite, while in those same countries children die from diseases that could have been treated for a few cents or avoided altogether with basic hygiene practices".

According to a WHO study[63] on the primary health care system of Pakistan, the disadvantaged areas particularly remote rural areas have witnessed slow or little change in access to key elements of health coverage. "Poorly functioning health facilities, formidable distances (especially in Balochistan, KP and Sindh), and low awareness of preventive services are the main barriers reported by different studies. Private sector establishments, while reported to be more functional than government health centers, involve expense, hence use is limited mainly due to acute conditions in both low-income urban and rural populations. In rural areas the scarcity of health centers involves the additional expense of transport to reach private clinics located in district centers, or transiting to more affluent districts that have health providers. The transportation barrier has generally been overlooked in health sector planning. Clients in remote districts prefer child birth at home due to high transport costs and inconvenience of travel. The transportation cost is highly variable across districts with a range of 3000–6000 Pakistani rupees for obtaining obstetric care in Sindh's more disadvantaged districts", the report says.

Out-of-pocket (OOP) health expenditures are a huge burden on the household's resources especially for poor families. The OOP spending is the payment made directly to the providers for obtaining health services and products. These are basically private transactions made to private doctors and pharmacies and also include informal payments. The size of OOP spending shows that it is still the largest source of health care financing in Pakistan which is over 56%. OOP is the most inefficient and regressive forms of health care financing. Private expenditures constitute 48.5% of total health expenditures in Pakistan out of which 88% are households' OOP health expenditures.[64]

Preventive health care needs to be prioritized to reduce public as well as private health expenditures. A focus on preventive health care means public involvement in a range of activities like sanitation, public hygiene, health education, safe drinking water, et cetera. The historical experience of the developed world bears testimony to the fact that investment in the provision of clean water was one of the major factors in reducing mortality rates and improving health outcomes. For example, mortality rates fell more rapidly in the USA during the nineteenth and early twentieth centuries than in any other period. Clean water was responsible for nearly half of the total mortality reduction, three-quarters of the infant mortality reduction, and two-thirds of the child mortality reduction.[65] For preventive care, health profiling of the entire population is required. It seems a daunting task but with a robust health information management system, it is doable.

Information technology, in particular mobile phones, can come to the aid of documenting the particulars and health profiles of the citizenry. Detailed surveys of the communities can be conducted to take down the medical histories of each and every person. Trained health workers can conduct workshops on nutrition and preventive medicine. Preventive medicine can head off ailments before they turn more serious and require medical intervention. Education, information, and incentives have the potential to increase the sustained adoption of preventive behavior. Baby steps like awareness campaigns about the harmful effects of the use of sweets, beverages, soft drinks, candies, junk foods, et cetera, can help decrease lifestyle diseases like high blood pressure and diabetes. Activities promoting optimal health and a healthy lifestyle can be promoted in schools and colleges. The coverage of health-related topics can be enhanced in text books, and physical activity sessions can be encouraged in educational institutions.

The role of education and information is undoubtedly very important for preventive health care but incentives also matter a lot. Experiments in the Indian context have shown that a small bag of lentils may incentivize parents to get their children immunized.[66] Conditional cash transfers can help improve the uptake of health interventions in low-income and poor settings. It is better to strive for low-hanging fruit in the health sector and this would be partly possible by shifting emphasis from cure to prevention. Banerjee and Duflo talk of many preventive-type interventions and cheap technologies that can help improve public health with a low amount of public money. Provision of ORS, access to safe drinking or chlorinated water, promotion of breastfeeding (which practically costs nothing), piping water to homes along with sewage, et cetera, are some such interventions. If the emphasis shifts from cure to prevention then multiple interventions with very low costs can be made. Local communities can be mobilized to pay for such interventions if the government is unable to provide resources. "The issue is not how much the poor spend on health, but what the money is spent on, which is often expensive cures rather than cheap prevention", write Banerjee and Duflo in '*Poor Economics*'.

The problem of poor public health care is also connected to poor accountability and bad governance. Absenteeism among health workers and doctors especially in rural areas is common in the poor and developing countries. Deaton says that absenteeism is a big problem in the health and education sectors of developing countries. He writes[67]: "A great deal of government health care in many countries is that medical workers - nurses and doctors- are frequently absent from work. In Rajasthan, only about half of the small clinics were open at all when we made random checks, and while the larger ones were open, many of the health workers were not there. The World Bank has carried out surveys on absenteeism, and it turns out that in many countries---although certainly not all--absenteeism is a huge problem in both health care and education".

Bad governance and weak accountability, broadly reflected in huge absenteeism, are endemic in the health sector, and sometimes very well-intentioned initiatives for improvement flounder badly due to poor governance. An NGO, namely Seva Mandir, and the Government of Rajasthan in India introduced an incentive program to ensure the attendance of nurses in the local health centers of Udaipur District, where nurses simply did not show up for duty. The NGO used time clocks to monitor the attendance of the nurses in health centers and passed on this information to the government, which used the attendance data with a specific schedule of fines and punishments to determine the nurses' wages. Initially, the system worked, which showed that the nurses responded to the incentives. But after a few months, the health administration colluded with the nurses to undermine the program, and after a period of 18 months, the program had become totally ineffective.[68]

A similar situation prevails in Pakistan. A team of researchers conducted a survey of 850 out of roughly 2500 BHUs in the province of Punjab in 2011. The surveyors visited each facility unannounced in the guise of walk-in citizens. What these surveyors found was startling. Out of 850 BHUs, 61 were found closed during working hours, while in those that were found open, on average 52.4% of the essential staff assigned to each BHU was unavailable to attend to patients.[69] The facilities of BHUs and RHCs are unevenly distributed in geographical terms besides issues of poor governance and poor accountability. Additionally, shortages of staff at government facilities, confinement of government clinics to daytime hours, and permission of private practice to doctors with the result that doctors employed in government centers transfer patients to private clinics contribute to sub-optimal use of public sector health facilities.

Poor use of primary health care facilities, especially for preventive care is a big challenge. The majority of poor live in rural areas. In the majority of villages, either rural health centers do not exist or lack the necessary infrastructure. Doctors are not willing to serve in rural areas. The reasons for the reluctance of doctors to serve in rural areas are multiple like fewer opportunities for professional growth, delays in post-graduation, poor living conditions, et cetera.

One of the reasons is the non-exposure of doctors to rural life and the lack of community orientation in the curriculum taught at the graduation level in medical colleges.[70] Several incentives and disincentives can be used to make doctors work in rural areas. For example, a special rural allowance may be provided; working in rural areas may be considered a prerequisite for promotion and post-graduation. Such incentives and disincentives were, however, used in the past as well for the retention of doctors in rural areas, but no marked improvement in the efficiency of the health services delivery was witnessed. Results of a study[71] undertaken to evaluate efficiency based on a sample of 29 RHCs in the province of Punjab showed that only 11 RHCs (38%) were working efficiently.

The governments of Punjab and Sindh established respectively Public Health Facilities Management Company (PHMFC)[72] and People's Primary Health Care Initiative (PPHI),[73] companies under the Companies Act for managing basic health facilities. These companies have taken over a number of BHUs and RHCs in rural areas to improve the provision of basic health services. This is a type of outsourcing of governance to companies, though these are managed for all practical purposes by civil servants. No evaluation or impact study is, however, available to comment on the performance and prospects of these companies, though they make tall claims of performance. For example, PPHI Sindh claims that their journey started in District Kishmore in 2007 and gradually expanded to 22 districts. If health indicators are the yardstick of performance, District Kishmore is one of the worst performers among the districts of Sindh on all health indicators.[74] The government's abdication of responsibility or the outsourcing of RHC governance to businesses will not solve the issue of public health care, particularly in rural areas and low-income settings.

Two stylized facts about health spending in developing countries merit mention. One, households with low incomes spend a significant portion of their budget on cures, and second, they spend very little on preventive care.[75] Pakistan is among the countries with the highest utilization of the private sector, and interestingly, people mostly approach the private sector for primary and secondary health care. Those belonging to the poorest segment of the society resort to quacks and spiritual healers due to unavailability and unaffordability of care by the public health care system. Such quacks, pirs, and spiritual healers now advertise their 'spiritual power of healing' on social media without any fear of the law. They are available to provide every sort of service, including treatment of deadly diseases like cancer, diabetes, heart issues, and gynecology-related treatments.

Even the regulation of trained doctors is lax. Over-prescription, exploitative pricing, and unnecessary surgeries are quite common in the private health sector. The average number of medications prescribed in Pakistan is higher compared to many low and middle-income countries. It is an open secret that pharmaceutical companies give incentives to doctors for prescribing medicines manufactured by them. The problem here is that a patient does not purchase medicine like a customer who purchases other goods from the market as per his preferences. It is the doctor who determines which medicines are to be purchased from the medical store for the treatment of certain ailments. Even where substitutes for a certain medicine are available in the market, it is the doctor who determines which particular brand or substitute a patient is required to use. In this context, the affordability of medicines has become a big challenge, particularly for the poor.

Generic Drugs

The problem of high prices cannot be resolved merely by price controls or monitoring of prices by the government. Over-prescription and exploitative pricing shall continue and no ethical sermon is going to resolve them unless some out-of-the-box solution is devised. The citizens of Pakistan have raised their concerns about said issues on various forums, including the Prime Minister's Performance Delivery Unit (PMDU) and the Drug Regulatory Authority of Pakistan (DRAP). Some instructions are also issued by the DRAP to the provincial health authorities to allay the concerns of the citizens but finally, such instructions turn out to be the 'bureaucratic disposal' of such complaints without any tangible improvement.

One such letter issued to the provincial health departments by the DRAP, however, captures the essence of the problem. The letter reads as follows: "Several complaints have been received through PMDU wherein the citizens have raised concerns over company influenced brand-based prescription of medicines by doctors in government and private sectors. This practice adds to the economic burden of the country and also puts financial load on patients due to purchase of pricier brands. Such practice is also against Code of Ethics for medical and dental practitioners".[76] The letter then asks for taking necessary measures to promote generic prescriptions by doctors and discourage the practice of incentivized prescription. Such instructions just show that instead of initiating an informed debate for concrete policy steps and necessary legislation, et cetera, to tackle the issue of unaffordable prices of medicines and drugs, a post office bureaucracy treatment has been meted out to such an important issue.

Unfortunately, Pakistan, instead of moving forward, has regressed on this issue. Pakistan was perhaps the first country in the developing world to legislate in 1972 to effectively fix the problem of exploitive pricing. The Drugs (Generic Names) Act, 1972, forbade the prescribing, sale, or distribution of any drug included in the National Formulary[77] under any brand, patent, or proprietary name. This piece of legislation was, however, not put into practice due to pressure from multinational pharmaceutical companies. The law was repealed in 1976 on the pretext that the quality of drugs and medicines was compromised due to said piece of legislation. Perhaps the issue was not the quality. The real issue was the vested interests of the pharmaceutical companies and the doctors who could not make fat profits under the generic regime of medicines and drugs.

In developing countries like Pakistan, medicines and drugs are an issue of life and death, and the poor cannot afford anything branded including medicines and drugs. The issue has an international dimension as well. It is an issue for the entire Third World and for those who cannot afford medical insurance in developed countries like the USA. The patent system is itself regressive as it restricts the use of knowledge by granting monopoly rights. The pharmaceutical companies make huge profits and spend more on advertising and marketing drugs than on research. So efforts are needed at the international level as well. Pakistan can play an active role in raising the concerns of the poor in the Third World.

At the domestic level, there is a need to reintroduce legislation similar to the Drugs Act of 1972 with appropriate changes where so required in the light of international obligations arising out of being a signatory of the TRIPs agreement. The use of generic prescriptions and medicines can make a big difference in alleviating the problems of over-prescription and exploitative pricing. The impact can be best visualized through AIDS medicine. The price of drugs for first-line AIDS defenses has been reduced almost by 99% since 2000 that is from US$10,000 to US$130 with the introduction of generic medicine.[78] Besides prescription of generic medicines, the establishment of village community dispensaries is another idea to work on. Doing so shall ensure at least basic health services at the doorsteps of the common man.

Village Community Dispensaries

It seems unlikely to make BHUs and RHCs efficient with the existing incentive system and resources. The idea of community dispensaries at the village level, to be managed by the representatives of local communities, can be explored to alleviate the situation. The local committees, a combination of elected and selected individuals (with good educational backgrounds or social service standing), may oversee the working of such dispensaries. Instead of reluctant doctors, the idea is that properly trained health technicians would be tasked with managing such community dispensaries. A new cadre of health professionals trained in preventive and basic care can be created to man the dispensaries. It is important to keep in mind that cheap and workable solutions are the answer to public health care in a developing country like Pakistan. Huge amounts of money will neither be available in the short run nor guarantee better health outcomes unless a paradigm shift takes place in our policies and priorities regarding the public health care system.

Blindly following or copying the health care system of the developed world like that of the USA would not work in a developing country like Pakistan. "Why do the poor countries reject inexpensive effective sanitation—the cheap and easy way to dramatically improve people's health—in favor of spending a lot of money on things that do not help and might actually hurt? Part of the answer is that a lot of the cheap gains are in prevention, and prevention has traditionally been the area where the government is the main player. The trouble is that governments have a way of making things much less easy than they should be. The high absenteeism rates and low motivation among government health providers are certainly two reasons we do not see more preventive care being delivered", write Banerjee and Duflo in '*Poor Economics*'.

The community dispensaries model envisages that they would become the foundation of the public health care system where basic services like immunization, prenatal and postnatal consultation, vaccination, and prevention and cure of illness would be available to all residents of the village. Major transformations in existing health and social policies are needed. Besides enhanced emphasis and policy focus on health care, accountability, and governance mechanisms also need change. The PSLM surveys with regard to Diarrhea treatment provide some insights. Three factors almost account for two-thirds of the reasons for not visiting a government facility for Diarrhea treatment that is (1) the facility is too far away; (2) No government facility is available; and (3) the staff is not courteous (see Table 5.10). The said factors provide a rationale for setting up a network of community dispensaries at the village level, as doing so shall eliminate the above-mentioned reasons for not utilizing health facilities and pave the way for ensuring universal health coverage.

The village community dispensaries can become the starting point for all investigations including serious diseases. Technology can come in handy in this regard. The village dispensaries can be connected to big hospitals. The preliminary investigation can be shared online with the specialists and consultants employed in big hospitals. The consultants and specialists may be administratively tasked with dedicating, say 2 hours daily, to attend online the patients visiting such dispensaries and may prescribe medicines, et cetera, to them after diagnosis with the assistance of preliminary reports and medical histories prepared at the dispensary. In cases where some detailed investigations are required, patients may be referred to big hospitals. Doing so shall reduce not only the burden on the big hospitals but also save resources (expended in transportation etc.) for the patients. Health is a public good, and being a public good, the state is required to provide quality health care to all its citizens without any discrimination. The public good character of health also emphasizes that health care cannot be abdicated to private hospitals and health insurance companies.

Table 5.10 Reason for not visiting Govt. Facility first for Diarrhea treatment—by region and province (percentage of responses)

	Pakistan	*Punjab*	*Sindh*	*KP excluding merged areas*	*KP including merged areas*	*Balochistan*
Pakistan						
Too far away	25	33	11	27	28	7
Not enough medicines	2	3	1	0	0	8
Doctor not available	7	4	11	7	8	15
Staff not courteous	11	13	11	9	10	2
No Govt. Facility	22	18	29	23	23	18
Doctor never available	5	4	5	7	7	4
Other reasons	28	25	32	26	25	45
Total	100	100	100	100	100	100
Urban						
Too far away	27	33	18	25	37	14
Not enough medicines	4	5	1	0	0	10
Doctor not available	3	0	5	11	10	11
Staff not courteous	13	16	9	24	21	0
No Govt. Facility	14	11	23	9	7	5
Doctor never available	3	2	5	2	2	3
Other reasons	35	33	38	29	23	56
Total	100	100	100	100	100	100
Rural						
Too far away	25	34	8	27	27	4
Not enough medicines	1	2	1	0	0	6
Doctor not available	8	5	14	7	7	17
Staff not courteous	11	12	12	7	8	3
No Govt. Facility	25	21	32	25	25	25

(continued)

Table 5.10 (continued)

	Pakistan	*Punjab*	*Sindh*	*KP excluding merged areas*	*KP including merged areas*	*Balochistan*
Doctor never available	5	5	5	7	7	5
Other reasons	25	21	28	26	25	40
Total	100	100	100	100	100	100

Source PSLM 2018–2019, Pakistan Bureau of Statistics

Public Good Character and Right to Health

At least three points make health a public good. First, the provision of universal health care has benefits for the entire community. Take the example of immunization, which, like quality water and quality air, involves spillover effects as the utility of each household depends directly on the actions of other households. The Corona epidemic has made the public good character of health more understandable. Selective vaccination on the basis of capacity to pay could not safeguard the entire community against the Corona epidemic unless all of the population was vaccinated. Second, due to information asymmetries, poor and illiterate parents do not have perfect information about the dividends of immunization and nutrition. They may not be able to make efficient decisions, particularly about the health of their children. In this context, the government has an important role in disseminating information about diseases, sanitation, nutrition, et cetera. Third, sharp socio-economic inequities also make a valid case for universal health coverage and for more policy focus on the poor segments of society to build at least some threshold level of health capital.

The provision of free health services is like transfer payments. It redistributes resources to the poor. An effective system of universal coverage of health care would essentially include immunization, vaccination, prenatal consultation, postnatal consultation, birth attendance by skilled health personnel, vitamin A and D supplementations, and mid-day meals in schools. The UHC and achievement of a reasonable level of health among the population shall not be possible with much reliance on the private health care system. It does not mean the abolition of the private health care system altogether, as doing so is neither desirable nor practically feasible. The public good character of health care means that all Pakistanis are entitled to health care irrespective of their ability to pay. The well-being and health care of a child, in particular, cannot be left by the state to the parents alone, who, with all probability, may not raise taller and smarter citizens due to illiteracy and poverty. Once it is settled that health is a public good, the question of the excludability of anybody does not arise, which means that health would become a fundamental right.

The Constitution of Pakistan does not explicitly recognize the right to health. The preamble of the Constitution and its Principles of Policy refer to socio-economic rights but these rights are not enforceable by the courts. The majority of countries in the world recognize the right to health as a fundamental right. Brazil is a case in point to emphasize the importance of declaring the right to health an enforceable right by the courts. With the return of democracy in 1980, Brazil embarked upon pro-development reforms through substantial investments in the social sector to alleviate poverty and improve the quality of life of poor families, which included overhauling the public health care system. The 1988 Constitution of Brazil established universal and egalitarian access to health care as a right of the citizen, enforceable by the courts of law. It created a unified health care system to resolve the issues of the 1980s health care system (characterized by fragmentation and inequities) with more focus on curative cure, coverage, and care. The system of health care is now much improved on these three points.[79] With the introduction of the right to health as a constitutional right enforceable by courts, Brazil achieved significant improvements in life expectancy and infant mortality. Geographic inequalities in health outcomes and disparities across socio-economic groups also declined.[80]

Declaring the right to health a constitutional right, enforceable by courts, on the pattern of Brazil would be required as toothless constitutional promises (in the form of principles of policy) do not deliver. There may, however, be concerns about the capacity of the courts and the way justice is administered in Pakistan. The courts are very slow and getting justice is costly in terms of money and time. The poor segments of society for whom the provision of public health care matters may find it difficult to bear the cost of right-to-health litigation. Access to courts is generally skewed toward those who already have access to the social determinants of health like education, housing, and nutrition due to their better socio-economic conditions. Most of the right-to-health litigation is likely to be preventive healthcare-related, requiring drugs and expensive medicines, with all probability that the people who are already financially better off and who can hire the services of a lawyer will move the courts to enforce the said right.

Some mechanisms shall be needed to ensure swift and cost-free enforcement of the right to health so that the poor segments of society are benefited. A regulatory authority may be created (like the office of the ombudsman) where any aggrieved citizen may approach without hiring the services of the legal counsel, and decisions are announced within a reasonable time. An appeal against the orders of such authorities may be filed in the High Court of the province. Such a mechanism would make health a justiciable right and delays in enforcement would also be avoided. The sharp inequalities of health and health care services are just one part of the story. Pakistan is in the grip of multiple inequalities of all types. And the case against inequalities, in the ensuing section, is not on moral or ethical grounds. Rather reduction of inequalities has an economic case as acute inequalities become binding constraints on long-term economic growth.

CHAPTER 6

Multiple Inequalities

According to traditional economic thinking, inequality is the handmaiden of economic development. For over half a century, the inverted U was the dominant discourse on the development-inequality relationship. This relationship known as Kuznets curve simply means that during the early stages of development, inequality rises, reaches a peak, and then declines. Two lines of argumentation can be deduced from the inverted U relationship. The first line of argument would be: there is a natural tendency for inequality to increase in the early stages of development, so policy interventions would be required to mitigate its negative consequences. The second line of argument, more popular with the capitalists, emphasizes that since inequality would eventually decrease, it is worth waiting out the initial increase as policy tinkering to hold back the initial inequality increase via redistribution can dampen economic growth. So it would be better to postpone the turning point of the inverted U.[1]

Development is fundamentally inequitable according to said line of argumentation. For example, Arthur Lewis wrote about the inegalitarian nature of development back in 1976 as follows. "Development must be inegalitarian because it does not start in every part of the economy at the same time. --- There may be one such enclave in an economy, or several; but at the start development enclaves include only a small minority of the population".[2] According to the dualistic model of the economy of Lewis, the narrowing of the gap between incomes in agriculture and

J. Nasir, *Development Challenges of Pakistan*,
https://doi.org/10.1007/978-981-97-3064-3_6

non-agriculture sectors, as a result of structural transformation, mitigates inequality at the developed stages of the economy. The gap between the agriculture and non-agriculture sectors would occur mainly due to two reasons, argument goes.[3]

First, through policy interventions like investments in physical, human, and social capital, the incomes of the lagging sector can be increased. Second, the movement of labor from agriculture to industry, through phenomenon of structural transformation, would create shortage of labor in agriculture. Consequently, wages would increase in that sector simply due to the forces of demand and supply or the scarcity of labor in the agriculture sector. When a society undergoes structural transformation from the agrarian to the industrial economy, the process creates both losers and gainers. Industrialists and the middle classes gain while, in a world of mechanization and desperation, the laborers work only for subsistence wages in the initial stages of industrialization. They live in pitiable conditions and the harvest of their sweat and blood is reaped by the owners of the capital, as depicted vividly by Charles Dickens in his novel '*Hard Times*'. At one place Dickens writes: "Any capitalist----who had sixty thousand pounds out of sixpence, always professed to wonder why the sixty thousand nearest Hands didn't each make sixty thousand pounds out of sixpence, or more or less reproached them every one for not accomplishing the little feat. What I did you can do. Why don't you go and do it?".[4]

Once industrialization becomes the dominant mode of economic activity, pressure mounts for an increase in wages as laborers start organizing them. Literature on inequality recognizes at least three channels through which inequality can impact political outcomes.[5] First, inequality leads to a desire for redistribution. Second, higher inequality might reduce redistribution and the provision of public goods as economic resources not only determine preferences but also have the ability to influence political outcomes. Third, economic inequality can influence the entire structure of political institutions. The evidence for Kuznets hypothesis is, however, mixed. It is not necessarily always an inverse U relationship. Inequality does not necessarily decline even at the most advanced stages of development. For example, according to a study,[6] based on longitudinal data from 26 countries covering the period 1900–2010, the inequality-development relationship even turns positive at higher levels of economic development. A decrease in inequality is not automatic. It depends on the power structures and socio-political arrangements of a society.

The elite (the one percent) are interested in perpetuating their hegemony over authority and resources. Political reforms for the wider sharing of power become possible only if there is a threat of revolution or a change in the status quo[7] (as argued by Acemoglu and his colleagues) and people are least polarized on ethnic, linguistic, clannish, or geographical lines. The political parties would feel more incentivized to articulate the demands of the people in terms of class and public service delivery if they are not much polarized in terms of said divisions. Moreover, if people do not feel empowered to change their destiny either through the ballot (democracy) or through the threat of bullet (constant pressure on the elite for reforms to avert a bloody revolution), such a society, in all probability, would experience high inequality due to weak redistribution of resources.

Merely structural transformation of the economy does not guarantee that inequality will eventually decline at the advanced stages of development. "The historical and contemporary evidence suggests that the downward segment of the curve is driven by political reforms and their subsequent impact. In turn, these political changes are induced by the rising social tension and political instability that arises from the increased inequality on the upward segment of the curve. Nevertheless, as the empirical evidence has established, such a curve does not characterize all development paths", write Acemoglu and Robinson.[8]

There are limitations regarding the analytical power of the Kuznets curve as well. This curve is at its most descriptive and not an analytical tool, even if there are situations or cases where Kuznets relationship holds. It does not tell what causes what. For uncovering the causality, an analysis of social and political factors is required, as solely economic factors would not suffice to provide a satisfactory explanation. Kuznets actually observed the phenomenon of the decline of inequality in the USA from the First World War onward. The decline was not an automatic result of economic growth. Rather, it was mainly due to social unrest and political reforms resulting in the rise of state redistribution.[9]

Inequality and Growth

The conventional economic narrative on the inequality-growth relationship was as follows: the marginal propensity of the rich to save (MPS) is higher, and more savings mean availability of more money and resources for investment and more investment means increase in economic growth. So income inequality was necessary for the generation of savings and inequality was thus the key to capital accumulation and economic growth.[10] And inequality is not a problem worth worrying about, according to this line of argument, as it creates a virtuous loop of savings, investment, and growth.

The sole concern regarding high inequality in a society could be that if it becomes severe, then there would be a threat of massive redistribution, and redistribution being a puncture in the virtuous loop of savings, investment, and growth could be detrimental to economic growth. And the investors could feel uneasy about a nation's future due to fear of redistribution, expropriation, or confiscatory taxes, the traditional argument goes. This reasoning is, however, now under challenge. It is being argued that extreme inequalities dampen growth by reducing aggregate demand (line of argument taken by Stiglitz in his writings). If income and wealth are concentrated in the tiny minority at the top (say among the 1%), spending or aggregate demand will be low as the rich tend to spend a smaller fraction of their income compared to the middle class and lower middle class. Consequently, economic growth would be low implying closure of the factories and businesses giving rise to unemployment. On the other hand, if income is widely distributed in the society, aggregate demand would be high due to high spending, which in turn would boost economic growth.

Besides quantum (how much of your wealth or income you spend), composition of spending (where you spend) is also relevant to understand the contribution of aggregate demand to economic growth. Insights from economic literature confirm that the middle class spends major portion of its earnings on goods and services like food, schooling, health care, and household effects. Spending on the said goods and services stimulates aggregate demand. On the contrary, the rich people spend most of their earnings and profits to build palatial houses and to accumulate diamonds, jewelry, and other luxury items. Once a house is built or diamond is purchased, it becomes a dead capital as it does not create a stream of aggregate demand like other goods and services. The implication is that distribution of resources toward the poor and the middle class increases consumption. A reverse process happens if resources move from the poor and middle class to the higher-income individuals. In such a case total demand in the economy would remain less than its potential of supplying goods and services. It simply means that there would be unemployment in the economy which would persist unless either investment increases or exports are enhanced.[11]

Historical evidence suggests that societies with comparatively low Ginis showed high growth rates compared to those with high Ginis. For instance, in the 1960s, South Korea and the Philippines were similar with respect to major economic and development indicators like per capita income, urbanization, and primary and secondary school enrollment, except for the size of Gini. Disparities in wealth, income, and land distribution were higher in the Philippines compared to South Korea. The ratio of the share of the top 20% to the bottom 20% or even the bottom 40% was about two times larger in the Philippines. Similar disparities existed with regard to land ownership as the Gini coefficient was 0.387 for South Korea in 1961 in contrast to 0.534 for the Philippines in the same year.[12] And perhaps it was the difference in Ginis that put the two countries on different paths of development.

Similarly, results of another investigation, based on cross-country data on income and land distribution, suggest a strong negative relationship between initial inequality in land distribution and long-term economic growth.[13] The negative impact of high-income inequality on economic growth, especially in poor countries, is even confirmed by the investigations which overall suggest a weak relationship between inequality and economic growth.[14] The problem with many poor and developing countries, including Pakistan, is the sustainability of growth. Many poor countries were able to initiate growth but failed to sustain it for longer periods, as we saw in our discussion on the growth experience of Pakistan. Sustainability of growth or longer spells of growth are deeply associated with equality in income distribution.[15]

The massive land reforms in Japan and South Korea changed the distribution of initial endowments whereas Latin American, African, and South Asian countries failed to change the initial endowment structures and that difference led to divergence in the development trajectories of East Asian countries and other regions. There is little evidence for the growth-destroying effects of redistribution, both of initial endowments (like land reforms) and distribution along the way (like investment in human resource and transfer payments, etc.). Rather, empirics confirm that inequality in land and income ownership has a negative correlation with subsequent economic growth.[16]

It is a mistake to focus on growth without taking care of inequality simultaneously. If we do not take care of inequality, the resulting growth will be low and unsustainable.[17] Very small changes in distribution can have large effects. For example, according to some estimates, if the share of income of the lowest quintile is increased, say, from 6% to 6.25%, this would represent a 4% increase in their total income, similar to the effect of doubling the annual growth of national income from 4 to 8%.[18] Inequality is not a virtue to be eulogized. It is bad not only for economic growth but has also got many other negative externalities.

Some More Negative Externalities

Economic and social outcomes are hugely influenced by the level and extent of inequality in the society. Inequality diminishes the effectiveness of the state institutions. In a highly unequal society, it is easy for the wealthy to use political, regulatory, and justice systems in their favor. For instance, in a scenario where a rich person is pitted against a poor person and judicial system is soaked in corruption, it is more likely that the judicial system would favor the rich and not necessarily the poor. Similarly, if political and regulatory institutions are susceptible to influence and wealth, they would be inclined to support the established and not necessarily the efficient.[19] Inequality also negatively impacts the democratic governance. The rich can buy political influence or can manage formulation and interpretation of rules and policies, comparatively with ease, in their favor in an unequal society. Political power and economic power are inextricably linked. The political consequences of the highly skewed distribution of economic power in a society are quite disastrous. The entire rationale behind the concept of the rule of the law is protection of the weak against the powerful and the privileged. In an unequal society, the wealthy and the privileged would use the political power to shape the rule of law in such a way that the legal and economic frameworks favor them and can be used to exploit the others in the society. All political power in an unequal society is geared toward perpetuation of existing inequalities and not for the attainment of egalitarianism and justice. Furthermore, political capture of the system eventually leads to an economic capture.[20]

Inequality reduces the ability of the people to stand up and work for some collective cause. It decimates what the Indian economist Raghuram Rajan[21] calls the '*Third Pillar*' of the society that is the community. It impacts institution building and resource distribution. Allocation of public goods is a case in point. The rich and the resourceful, by virtue of enjoying more power, get more allocation of resources for the public goods they value. At the same time, high levels of inequality make it tempting for them to opt out of the public services for which they have some alternative. Out of the two options that is to get more allocation for a public good or altogether opt out of it would depend on whether opting out is a viable option for the rich or not.[22] For instance, if the rich can buy education and health services from the private sector, they would have no stakes in the public sector education and health care systems. A phenomenal increase in the number of private schools in Pakistan bears testimony to the said proposition. Moreover, when the rich no longer use a public service, they also lose incentives to pay taxes. Consequently, it becomes difficult to sustain the provision, at least quality provision, of the public services due to financial constraints.[23]

It is quite expected that the crime ratios would be high in unequal societies. Decision to commit a crime is a rational decision as postulated by the economic theory of crimes. For instance, a thief or burglar while contemplating commission of crime would be, broadly speaking, faced with a trade-off and that is whether to allocate his time for some lawful work or for stealing the property of others. The rise in inequality increases returns to the crime for the poor because opportunity cost of committing a crime decreases as rich are getting richer and the poor are becoming poorer. Moreover, inequality negatively affects policing and deterrent impact of legal sanctions as in some situations life for a poor person is likely to be better in the prison than outside.[24] Some estimates show that homicide rates are around four times higher in extremely unequal societies in comparison with the societies characterized with egalitarianism and low inequality. Latin America, considered to be the most unequal and insecure region, is a case in point. Out of 50 dangerous cities of the world, 41 are situated in this region and it is estimated that around one million murders were committed in the cities of this region during the period 2000 and 2010, simply implying that highly unequal societies are dangerous places to reside.[25]

The survival of a child also depends to a large extent on the pattern of income distribution in the society. Bangladesh and Nigeria, countries with almost similar per capita income, are two pertinent examples to make the point. The distribution of income is more skewed in Nigeria compared to Bangladesh and so are the life chances. For a child born in Nigeria, the probability of dying before his fifth birthday is three times higher compared to a Bangladeshi child.[26] Extreme inequalities are a big hindrance in poverty alleviation. Empirics,[27] based on micro-census data of US states for the period 1960–2010, confirm that high levels of inequality worsen income growth of the poor while impact for the rich is opposite. Their incomes increase with rise in inequality. Generally riches at the top holds back the growth at the bottom. What does explain this proposition? One ready explanation lies in the fact that the rich lobby for the policies which benefit them but reduce growth opportunities for the people sitting at the bottom of the socio-economic ladder.

Inequalities are also reflective of the social separatism in the society. And social separatism has implications for economic growth. It reduces people's capacity to grow as argued eloquently by Ravi Kanbur, an Indian-born American economist, in his writings. Think of a society characterized by high levels of socio-economic stratification. In such a society, the poor or disadvantaged lack the capacity to aspire. On the other hand, think of a society where socio-economic gaps are not that large among different segments of the population or where society offers opportunities for social mobility. In such a society, people shall set some milestones in their cognitive window which they shall aspire and try to achieve. The people belonging to segment A (say, with the lowest income or wealth) shall be trying to join the people of segment B (having more income or wealth than A), and those of segment B shall try to catch up with segment C, and so on. Aspirations will induce increased efforts and investment, thus contributing to economic growth.

On the other hand, if there exists a big socio-economic chasm between various segments of the society that is if socio-economic inequality is high, people shall either resign to their fate by not setting goal posts and by not aspiring, or they shall become instrumental in aggravating social tensions in the society out of frustration and deprivations. "If aspirations are largely socially determined, considerations of inequality become paramount. Ensuring that all individuals retain a basic claim on some minimal share of national prosperity, rather than a minimal amount, becomes the deeper policy question that we need to put on center-stage".[28]

Acute inequalities reduce the well-being of people. Traditionally, economists thought that inequality was the very basis of diversification in society. It incentivized people to work hard, and achievement gave a sense of satisfaction and success; hence, it was happiness-enhancing. Thinking is changing thanks to emerging interdisciplinary research on the subject.

Happiness levels in society depend not only on the absolute income but on relative income as well.

"We constantly compare our lot with that of others, feeling either superior or inferior, whatever our income level; well-being depends more on how the fruits of growth are distributed than on their absolute amount. Put another way, what matters for life satisfaction is the growth not of mean income but of median income----the income of the typical person".[29] Many economists argue that the real issue is poverty alleviation, and if the income of everybody is increasing, it does not matter much if inequality is also increasing. The claim that need to focus only on poverty alleviation and not on inequality is internally inconsistent.[30] Let us illustrate this point with an example (borrowed, with slight changes, from Brank Milanovic, a Serbian-American economist).

Suppose a group of economists gathers at a conference or contributes to an economic journal. And each participant or contributor is given, say, Rs. 50,000 in honoraria for attending the conference or contributing to the journal. The well-being of everybody goes up, and nobody will be worse off. So what is wrong? Apparently, nothing seems wrong to this extent. Let us now modify this illustration a bit. Suppose one of the participants or contributors is given Rs. 200,000 while others are paid differentially, say, between Rs. 100 and Rs. 500. Even in this scenario, the welfare of everybody increases as everybody has more money than he originally had. The outcome or effects would, however, be different. Some would refuse to receive it, while others would throw the money away in disgust. Some would gossip and conjecture various explanations about the one who received Rs. 200,000.

Those receiving less will feel worse off, not better off. Why? Because we always compare our lot with our peers, and the income of others enters into our utility function. And what implications does this illustration have for the group? There would be gossip. There would be speculations of nepotism and favoritism regarding the one who received the highest amount of honoraria. And there would be distrust and feelings of envy, injustice, and unfair treatment among those who received less. This illustration brings us to the point that inequality is a big social divider. We generally use differences in living standards as markers of status differences. "We tend to choose our friends from our near equals and have little to do with those much richer or much poorer. And when we have less to do with other kinds of people, it's harder for us to trust them---Imagine living somewhere where 90% of the population mistrusts one another and what that must mean for the quality of everyday life—the interactions between the people at work, on the street, in shops, in schools".[31]

Human beings are equipped with mirror neurons, which trigger feelings of empathy when they see another body inflicted with pain. They enjoy friendship, cooperation, and trust, as these are embedded in their neurons. Social structures based on inequality, inferiority, and social exclusion inflicts a lot of social pain and perhaps that is why more unequal societies are socially more dysfunctional.[32] High inequalities or increasing inequalities are associated with a rise in anxiety, low self-esteem, social insecurity, low women's status, low trust, poor physical and mental illness, low life expectancy, low educational performance, more crimes, and low social mobility.[33]

The creation of a happy society requires reduction in the gulf between the rich and the poor. A big palatial house standing out among many small houses scattered around undermines the happiness of those who live in the small houses. Ostentatious living, the display of wealth (often result of rent-seeking and corruption), and the perverted values that employ such behaviors as measures of status and prestige further deteriorate the happiness of the people in a society. Extravagant spending on marriages, palatial houses, big cars, et cetera are some of the demonstrations of the ostentatious display of wealth in a society which create negative externalities in the form of unhappiness for the majority. So we have a valid case for high taxation of such externalities. Before analyzing various species and manifestations of inequality, let us first try to find an answer to the following question of critical nature: why has inequality persisted almost throughout the human history despite huge negative externalities of all nature that is economic, social, political, et cetera?

Legitimation of Inequality and Identity

Joyce Marcus and Kent Flannery, two American archaeologists, while highlighting the creation of inequality, argue that human beings as well as chimpanzees, the closest primate relatives of human beings, both have ranks but there is an important difference between the two. They write: "It is not predestined from the moment of birth that a given chimpanzee will become an alpha or beta. Having an alpha parent may increase the likelihood but in the end an individual's position in the hierarchy is the result of his or her interactions with other individuals. And any chimp's position can rise or fall over time. Human rank societies differently. The child of a great Ang parents is born to be a great Ang, no matter how short of talent he or she may be. The child of commoner parents will never become a great Ang, no matter how clever he or she is. The ability to negotiate one's position in rank society is much more limited than in a chimpanzee troop".[34]

So according to Marcus and Flannery, the societies of human beings are more stratified and unequal even compared to those of animals considered genetically closer to human beings. Why is it so? It is because humans create ideologies for their ranks and hierarchical dominance which champs cannot. They create ideologies for racial supremacy, colonialism, gender-based discrimination, and what not, to create and perpetuate inequalities. And then they bring different categories of tools to enforce such ideologies. "The fact that highly unequal societies have endured for such long periods of time is significantly due to the ideology that justified extremely unequal division of wealth and privilege—With the exception of periods of extreme crises, inequality has always been adequately legitimated such that most people found it acceptable, even when it meant their lives were filled with extreme hardship and misery".[35]

Historically, the elite have maintained inequality by using different tools. Initially, the most obvious tool was physical force and violence. Until a few hundred years ago, slaves were considered like other commodities who could be openly traded in the market. So the ideology of that time was that slaves were just property like land, buildings, merchandise, and machines over which all rights of ownership could be exercised by other human beings (their owners). They could be used for personal benefits and to maximize wealth. They could be sold in the market. They could be transported to other countries and regions of the world where the marginal productivity of their labor was high (case of South American countries and sugar plantations). There were no qualms, no pricks of conscience, as the ideology of that time justified the ownership of humans by other humans. Ironically, before abolition of slavery in the USA, slaves were not only owned like other goods, they were even used as collateral to secure loans.[36]

Traces of such ideology can still be found in the workings of, what sociologists call total institutions, and in dictatorial regimes where people are not their own masters and their opinions and choices do not matter. Bonded labor is another trace of said ideology which persists to this date in various regions and areas of the world. For example, according to the report, prepared by the Australian consultants for the government of Sindh and ADB under the Sindh Rural Development Project, around 1.7 million landless agricultural workers (haris) and sharecroppers live in Thatta, Dadu, Badin, Mirpurkhas, and Umerkot, five districts of the Sindh province. Majority of them are the victim of debt bondage. Though debt bondage is prevalent in entire rural Sindh the conditions of the labor in the said districts are highly pitiable. Most of these bonded laborers in these districts hail from Tharparkar region, a drought-prone region of the province. They had to accept cash advances from the landlords due to extreme poverty and starvation. They work from dawn to dusk. They are detained or guarded by the landlords so they do not escape. The landlords have a type of total ownership of their bodies and incidents like rape of the women in such an environment of subjugation cannot be ruled out. The report further highlights that many of the bonded laborers do not get wages for their work. The food and clothing given to them is added in the loan amount. The bonded laborers can be transferred to another landlord usually at a price higher than the debt they owe to the previous landlord and in this way bonded labor's debt keeps on mounting.[37]

There is, however, a problem with brute force. It is relatively inefficient due to policing costs and the constant threat of revolt by the suppressed and caged as physical force generates resentment. A long-term and sustainable strategy for the elite to perpetuate inequality, therefore, is to devise an ideology that convinces at least the majority of the moral and functional appropriateness of the existing moral and economic order in a make-believe way. Even the victims of such an ideology of inequality become subconsciously convinced of their lower status in terms of wealth, income, and privilege. Religion is one such ideology that has invariably been used historically to legitimize inequality. "This life is not worth worrying about. Real life is the life hereafter. It is God who has given preference to some persons over others", these sermons are very common which we hear from the pulpits of mosques. Religion, thus, even in modern times, is playing an ideological role in legitimating inequality.

There are justifications for inequality on the grounds of economic growth and wealth creation as well. The argument runs that those who take risks create wealth for society, so society owes such persons a debt which it can pay by keeping low rates of taxes, by ensuring security of property rights without challenging the nature and allocation of such rights, and by not challenging their socio-political influence which they get by virtue of riches. Sometimes the stability argument is brought up in the aid of extreme inequalities. Drastic changes in ownership structures or the status quo would trigger a self-reinforcing process which may ultimately affect even the poor, argument is advanced. The stability argument, according to Piketty, is reminiscent of the justification for slave societies when such an argument was advanced to justify slavery in the name of stability. He writes: "Human beings have demonstrated great creativity in devising ways to justify and organize social inequality, and it would not be wrong to view the resulting ideological and political constructs as mere veils intended only to conceal the perpetual domination of ruling elites".[38] Contrary to whatever justifications economists gave for the sanctification of property, stability, and inequality, an interdisciplinary approach gives an entirely different conclusion that is economic development and human progress owe much to the struggle for equality and education.[39]

The elite of Pakistan have excessively used ideology to perpetuate inequality and to divert the attention from the real issues of life like health, education, speedy justice, poverty alleviation, et cetera. Rushbrook Williams, a civil servant by profession, wrote in 1966 that the Pakistani elite were more obsessed with political and ideological issues and that matters that were equally important for the welfare of the country were not their priorities. He further wrote that they (the elite) were more concerned about the division of power between the center and the Provinces, between East and West Pakistan, and among different competing interests that is landlords, religious leaders, businessmen, and industrialists. He laments: "(Pakistan's leaders) came to live in a kind of artificial gold fish bowl of their own creation, which distorted their sense of values and fixed their attention not upon the needs of the country but on competition for power, influence and spoils of office".[40]

This situation persists to date. The elite are more concerned about their monopoly over power and influence to the exclusion of real issues like poverty, inequality, poor service delivery, low human resource development, and slow economic growth. Rosita Armytage, an anthropologist by profession, has peeped into the lives of the elites of Pakistan in her book '*Big Capital in an Unequal World*'.[41] Based on field work in some big cities of Pakistan, she has given a sociological account of how the elites of Pakistan (1%) were able to gain and perpetuate economic and political advantage since the very inception of Pakistan through strategies of collaboration and alliance making (elite networks, matrimonial alliances, and social practices, etc.). They use the governance, legal, and regulatory infrastructure of the state to the fullest extent to thwart competition and maintain their market dominance. She argues that the state of Pakistan is now in the hands of landlords, industrialists, the military establishment, bureaucrats, and Navay Raje (nouveau riches) like commercial bankers and urban real estate developers. Physical demonstrations of the riches and closeness of elite networks can be best visualized at social gatherings when land cruisers, Mercedes, and BMWs clog the nearby streets where such social gatherings are taking place.

Why did the elite not feel any threat of revolution from the common and disadvantaged people (99%) of Pakistan?[42] Overemphasis on religious identity is at least partly responsible for keeping people engaged in the issues which have nothing to do with the improvement in their material well-being. "Pakistan's emphasis on religion is primarily a function of the desire to erase identities derived from ethnicity, culture, and language".[43] Moreover, the dictates of 'Two-Nation Theory' (an ideological basis for the creation of Pakistan) required a separate national identity based on religion. The decision to forge religious identity was, however, fraught with serious inherent pitfalls to which saner voices alluded even in the very formative phase of such nationalism.

For example, British historian Arnold Toynbee wrote in 1955 that Pakistani leaders saw religion as a force that binds the majority of the people of Pakistan together but Islam could become a disruptive force compared to racial and linguistic forces as Pakistan, contrary to some other Muslim countries, could not be identified with a particular sect.[44] Religious nationalism and narrow identities along sectarian and caste lines worked as an ideological instrument for the elite who strategically exploited these divisions, to acquire and perpetuate their power, without addressing socio-economic and public service delivery issues.

Religious nationalism was touted with such fanfare that it became a genie that is hard to put back in the bottle. "Any discussion of poor performance in the economic or social sphere, or about differences among Pakistan's ethnic groups is often described as questioning the country's very right to exist, which it is not".[45] There are issues which cannot even be approached for discussion with hands on gloves. Salman Taseer, Punjab's Governor, was shot dead in Islamabad by his bodyguard in January 2011, as the slain politician was a critic of blasphemous laws and supported liberal reforms. Mishal Khan, a Pashtun and Muslim student at the Abdul Wali Khan University in Mardan, was lynched by the angry mob on the university premises on April 13, 2017 over allegations of posting blasphemous content online. On February 26th, 2024, an angry mob in Lahore accused a lady wearing dress containing word 'Halwa' (literally meaning sweet or beautiful) in Arabic letters as the mob took the words and script as the verses of the Quran. The "Halwa lady" was rescued from the mob by the Police and she had to render public apology to pacify the mob.[46]

Emphasis on religion-based identity has unintended consequences as well. Intolerance and violence are the logical offshoots. Intolerance diminishes space for discussion, dissent, and debate. Little knowledge and superficial ideas (without research) are the perfect recipe for inflated egos and big disasters. Culture with an emphasis on not questioning the authority imbued with religious fervor creates an environment where productive knowledge and ideas neither germinate nor are welcomed. And nonsense gains ascendancy. The absurdities like creation of electricity from jinns[47] and invention of water-fueled cars[48] are the outcome in a society which abandons science and logic. Division of the people along sectarian lines facilitates the ideology of control. As people are divided along imaginary distinctions having little to do with their economic lives, the elites manipulate such identities to perpetuate their control. This is what happened in Pakistan.

No human being can have a single identity. A person can have multiple identities as argued by Sen in his writings. It is neither easy nor even required to submerge all identities into a single identity. Religious identity is one of the identities one can have. For example, a typical Pakistani would have multiple identities like gender-based (male, female, or transgender), residence-based (Pakistani, Sindhi, urban or rural, mohajir or local), profession-based (teacher, a civil servant, businessman, laborer, etc.), based on matrimonial status (married, unmarried, widow, etc.), religion-based (Muslim, Sunni, Shia, etc.), country and continent based (Pakistani, Asian), and several others can be thought of and listed. Nothing is good or bad about any identity per se. The problem arises when an individual assigns weights to her multiple identities and those identities are manipulated for vested interests.

For example, a person may assign very huge weight to his identity as a person or to some profession he belongs to (for example, I am superior to others because I am a Rajput or a Syed, or I am, by virtue of belonging to the civil service or the Army, more important than the people belonging to other professions) and the result will be an inflated ego. Then there are some people who transcend all narrow identities and emphasize just their identity as human beings. Martin Luther King, Nelson Mandela, Mother Teresa, and Abdul Sattar Edhi are some examples. Their identities transcended religion, creed, race, caste, et cetera.

Religious identity is one of the identity among multiple identities an individual can have. "A person's religion need not be his or her all-encompassing and exclusive identity. In particular, Islam, as a religion, does not obliterate responsible choices for Muslims in many spheres of life. Indeed, it is possible for a Muslim to take a confrontational view and another to be thoroughly tolerant of heterodoxy without either of them ceasing to be a Muslim for that reason alone",[49] writes Sen. The route taken by Pakistan is quite contrary to the one taken by some other multiethnic nations, which preferred state-building through provision of quality public services and economic development. Belgium and Singapore are two pertinent examples to make the point. Belgium has three ethnic groups, namely Flemish, Walloons, and German, and is surrounded by neighbors with overlapping ethno-linguistic groups. It did not feed its nationality or survival on either ethno-lingual differences or religious divisions (Protestants versus Catholics).

"By the time it was seventy years old, in 1900, Belgium had become a highly industrialized country that took advantage of its position at the crossroads of European commerce and diplomacy. Since then, it has survived German occupation during two world wars to occupy a central position in the European Union and NATO. The inflated national ego of Pakistanis might balk at comparison with Belgium, which is much smaller than Pakistan. But Belgium's relatively brief history, its multi-ethnicity, its historic and ethnic overlap with neighboring countries, and its size relative to possible regional rivals offers a model for an alternative imagining of Pakistan".[50] Similarly, Singapore was carved out of Malaysia in 1965 in an atmosphere of vulnerability and ethnic conflict. Chinese, Malays, and Indians—three different ethnic communities now live in perfect harmony, each trying to live up to the ideals and standards of behavior decreed by the state. The lessons Belgium and Singapore provide are simple and straight: increase the size of the cake, distribute it among all, and improve public services.

The inequality problem is multidimensional. Multiple facets and factors are involved. Both vertical and horizontal inequalities matter. And when we talk of horizontal inequalities, gender-based inequality would be at the top particularly in the South Asian region. A baby girl born in this region starts her journey of life with acute disadvantages. "When I was born, people in our village commiserated with my mother and nobody congratulated my father—I was a girl in a land where rifles are fired in celebration of a son, while daughters are hidden away behind a curtain, their role in life simply to prepare food and give birth to children", writes Pakistani Nobel laureate Malala.[51]

Gender Inequality

Similar description of the trials and tribulations based on gender can be found in other fiction and non-fiction literature created by Pakistani writers. Bapsi Sidhwa, in her well-acclaimed novel '*The Pakistani Bride*',[52] discusses the dilemmas females face in a patriarchal culture. Zaitoon, the central character of this novel, goes through a series of problems in her struggle for emancipation from the authoritative code of conduct developed by the males until she breathes her last. Such depiction of the suppression of women's agency is not confined to tribal and rural cultures. Tehmina Durrani's '*My Feudal Lord*'[53] is another well-rendered description of the dire consequences a woman, even with brain and beauty hailing from a privileged background, can face when she challenges the restrictions and norms imposed by a feudal society. Gender inequalities in terms of human development indicators, access to public services, and ownership of productive assets like land are huge in Pakistan. For example, female enrollment ratios are lower in comparison to boys at all levels of school education that is pre-primary, primary, middle, and secondary. When the number of out of school children is decomposed in terms of gender, the female number is quite high.[54]

During the past couple of decades, women have gained de jure rights owing to legal reforms but the prevalence of customary law creates a gap between the law on the books and the actual practice. The gains in legal rights for women have not resulted in comparable benefits in economic and social life due to prevalence of the customary justice system.[55] For example, women's control over the land through inheritance is still restricted despite legal and policy initiatives taken by the government, mainly due to patriarchal practices, lack of education, and swap marriages. The agricultural censuses or economic surveys in Pakistan do not give a gender-based breakdown of the land distribution. Pakistan Health and Demographic Survey 2017–18, however, provides some information. According to the findings of the said survey, 3% women and 72%

men own a house while 2% women and 27% men own land.[56] Even otherwise, it is quite obvious a fact that women's ownership of land is highly restricted. And even if they own land, they are not de facto owners.

Bina Agarwal has very pertinently argued that granting women their legitimate share in landed property can turn out to be the single most critical factor for the empowerment of women in South Asia. And to do so, gender ideologies need to be revisited critically. She writes: "Gender ideologies can obstruct women from getting property rights. For instance, ideological assumptions about women' needs, work roles, capabilities, and so on, impinge on the framing and implementation of public policies and laws relating to property. Again, ideas about gender underlie practices such as female seclusion, control of women's mobility and sexual freedom, and so on. These ideologies and associated practices restrict women's mobility both to exercise their existing claims and to successfully challenge persisting gender-inequalities in law, policy, and practice in relation to such claims".[57]

Women have comparatively longer life expectancy. Biologically, it is an undisputable fact. But this advantage is not that large for the South Asian women. Besides inequalities in health, education, and possession of productive assets, huge gaps can be observed in time poverty, labor force participation, bargaining power, and autonomy. Females suffer doubly as regards labor force participation. The work of housewives remains unrecognized in the national accounts for want of a price tag on their domestic work. If a woman is carrying out tasks like babysitting, preparing children for school, helping them do their homework, cooking food, cleaning the house, taking care of the elderly, et cetera at home, in economic terms she is contributing nothing to the GDP. Household chores, how important they may be, fall under unpaid work.

So one of the issues rarely mentioned in the debates on the work of women is the non-monetization of the household tasks and chores performed by them. Further, women spend more time on 'committed activities', whether formally employed or working at home, like household maintenance, cooking food, and taking care of children and the elderly. They have little time for leisure and personal care compared to men. Time poverty among unpaid family helpers in Pakistan is estimated to be five times greater than time poverty among their male counterparts.[58] The committed activities have got important implications for the welfare and long-term well-being of women. As women work more hours at home compared to men, the opportunity cost of getting enrolment in schools is thus high having far-reaching negative consequences for female literacy.

Women suffer from huge underrepresentation in the labor force in Pakistan. ILO estimates of the selected countries show that FLFP in Pakistan is far below compared to the Sub-Saharan African region, China, Vietnam, South Korea, Malaysia, Indonesia, Sri Lanka, and Bangladesh. The pace of FLFP in Pakistan has remained very slow compared to other countries where FLFP comparatively increased at a much faster pace (see Table 6.1).

Overall, labor force participation rate (LFPR) is an important indicator of economic growth as it provides information about the relative size of the labor supply currently available for the production of goods and services. The experience of the developed countries shows that enhancing FLFP dramatically spurred economic growth in these countries. The home production services were marketized, the share of agriculture shrank, and women took up jobs outside homes. Women's participation in the labor market also enhanced their status at home and in the social hierarchy due to economic power they gained. The shift of women from unpaid work to paid work in the market was thus a major feature of high-income economies.[59] One point needs to be emphasized here: empowerment means wider participation of women in the labor force as happened in the USA and European countries in the nineteenth century. The presence of a small number of women in the labor market or in some important roles by virtue of nepotism or family background does not mean that women are empowered in that society. We can find prominent names in some societies in ancient history, but women's empowerment or emancipation happened when women's participation in the labor force became wider.

Arash Nekoei and Fabian Sinn, both of Stockholm University, have documented the evolution of women's status across the globe over the last 5,000 years of human recorded history.[60] They constructed the Human Biographical Record (HBR) of over 7 million individuals which contains information about date and place of birth and death, gender, occupation, education, and family background. The analysis gave startling results. The women's share throughout recorded history has always remained low averaging around 10%. And interestingly, the share of self-made women was just 3%. The probability that a prominent woman was self-made was just 30%, whereas for a male, this probability was 80%, according to said researchers. Ancient Egypt, in the third millennium

Table 6.1 Ratio of female to male labor force participation rate of selected countries (%)

Country	*1990*	*2000*	*2010*	*2020*	*2021*
Bangladesh	29.32	32.28	36.58	45.52	46.29
China	85.88	85.09	81.54	83.59	84.22
Indonesia	61.05	61.41	61.91	65.15	65.30
India	35.15	37.06	36.29	31.39	31.62
Korea, Rep	63.48	66.26	68.39	73.10	73.82
Sri Lanka	58.16	48.22	45.77	46.96	47.34
Malaysia	54.58	55.81	57.01	65.95	66.68
Pakistan	13.32	19.55	28.01	29.46	30.41
Vietnam	93.38	90.41	88.30	85.97	87.66
Low income	80.64	81.66	81.00	81.40	83.93
South Asia	33.07	35.09	35.52	33.08	33.57
Sub-Saharan Africa	82.53	84.89	84.99	83.82	84.23

Source ILOSTATS (ilostats.ilo.org)

BCE, appears to have been a positive outlier where women were said to have equal rights to men. Women could own and transfer property, initiate divorce, and receive an equal inheritance in those times. Impliedly, women's emancipation or empowerment is not necessarily a modern-age phenomenon. Perhaps there was equality between the genders at some point in ancient history before it regressed.

In modern times, we find prominent female political leaders like Indira Gandhi, Benazir Bhutto, and Bandaranaike et cetera in the South Asian Region. Likewise, we can find several ladies of prominence in the recorded history of humans like Sappho, Joan of Arc, Cleopatra VII, Razia Sultana, Queen Elizabeth, and Queen Christina, but scattered examples do not imply that women in general had more status and empowerment during the times of prominence of these ladies. Nekoei and Sinn, based on analysis of individual-level data, postulate that women's status was a side effect of nepotism as the women who became part of the elite were either born in influential families or were married into such families. The isolated rise of some women to the top echelons of political power (like entry into Parliament on reserved seats) due to family connections is not reflective of the rise in the status and empowerment of the typical woman. The general emancipation of women comes when women massively participate in the labor workforce and move out of their homes.

Interestingly, bicycle is a big symbol of women's mobility. Susan B. Anthony, the American Women's rights activist is said to have said in 1896 about bicycling by women: "Let me tell you what I think of bicycling. I think it has done more to emancipate women than anything else in the world".[61] We see a large number of women bicycling in countries where women enjoy better socio-economic status. And coincidentally, their socio-economic status improved as the frequency of bicycle use increased. A bicycle symbolizes not only cheap transport but also a sense of freedom to move without fear of harassment or eve-teasing. The negative impacts of sexual harassment are horrendous in countries like India and Pakistan where eve-teasing is a big impediment to women's freedom of mobility. Such incidents may discourage parents to send their daughters to schools and women to join labor force. Incidents of harassment even in public places are many though all may not be reported due to cultural and social barriers. According to the report of the Federal Ombudsman for Protection against Harassment,[62] 5008 cases were registered with the ombudsman from 2019 to 2022. This number is a big jump compared to the periods prior to 2019 (84 cases from 2010 to 2013, and 398 cases from 2013 to 2018) suggesting that cases were underreported in the past.

In the USA and Europe, real revolution came with economic power when women moved out of homes to participate in the labor market. These countries started granting economic rights to married women in the second half of the nineteenth century. Prior to that, the husband enjoyed unlimited power within the household. The common saying regarding the power of the husband was that "man and wife are one, but the man is the one".[63] Extension of economic rights to women increased her bargaining power 'causing a household revolution of decreased fertility and more education'.[64] The technological change in the nineteenth century which increased demand for human capital also facilitated the expansion of women's rights. Demand for human capital simply meant more investment and more focus on female education. "When the return to education increases, finding well-educated spouses for one's children becomes a bigger concern. Similarly, a rising return to education increases fathers' concern about the rights of their daughters because the daughters' marital bargaining power matters for the grandchildren's education".[65]

Physical mobility of the women is restricted in the name of chastity, purity, and security. The women are not bicycling in India, Afghanistan, or Pakistan. Restrictions on physical mobility are also responsible for low schooling and less participation in the labor market. The policy implication is that in countries like India, Pakistan, Afghanistan, et cetera distance to school needs to be factored in as one of the important elements of any initiative or strategy aimed at maximizing girls' school enrolment. The results of an evaluation of village-based schools, using a sample of 31 villages in Afghanistan, confirm that the effect of reducing distance to schools was larger for girls compared to boys in terms of test scores and enrolment.[66] An evaluation from Pakistan also confirms similar results where creation of private girls' schools in poor neighborhoods of Quetta increased girls' enrollment significantly compared to similar neighborhoods (people of similar socio-economic profiles) where private schools were not established for girls.[67]

Cultural factors like patrilocality are also at play. In South Asian region, a girl shifts to the house of the husband's parents (patrilocality) on marriage. It means more investment in the health and education of a daughter would not financially benefit the family she is born into. Investment in the education and health of boys is more important as they will stay with the family, earn for the family and take care of the parents in old age. The financial mindset about investment in daughters is best captured in the local sayings.[68] An Indian saying goes, "Raising a daughter is like watering your neighbor's garden" while a Chinese proverb, with little modification, says that raising a daughter is like "ploughing someone else's field".

It is in this context that parents, particularly poor parents faced with liquidity constraints, are more likely to get medical care for a sick son than a sick daughter. For example, some researchers undertook a study on the utilization of corrective surgery for congenital heart disease in Indian context.[69] The sample of the study comprised 405 children of both sexes whose parents and guardians had been told by the doctors that their child needed surgery to save his or her life. After one year of the advice, over two-thirds (70%) of boys had been operated whereas less than half (44%) of girls had undergone surgery. How the situation can be ameliorated?

A single-minded focus on eliminating gender inequality would not be helpful. At the root of all inequalities is the inequality of income and wealth. Sometimes focusing on horizontal inequalities distracts us from the real issue. Has quota allocation for women in the National Assembly and civil services reduced gender inequalities in Pakistan? Perhaps not much. The women who enter the Parliament belong to political families (not representative of the typical Pakistani woman). And women in the civil service generally come from the middle class of urban areas. An average Pakistani woman is as unrepresented as she was prior to said affirmative actions. The better course of action would be to push for the reduction of income inequality even if our primary objective is to reduce horizontal inequalities like those of gender.

Branko Milanovic finds three basic problems with an exclusive focus on horizontal inequalities. First, focusing on group differences quickly turns into identity politics and the joint front against inequality crumbles. For example, women's organizations and advocacy groups working in Pakistan to abolish discrimination against women are many but divided. Second, focusing on horizontal inequality leaves the real issue unresolved because the way problem is posed is not correct. The real issue lies somewhere else. For instance, since last one decade or so, some women activists celebrate Women's Day every year with huge fanfare, and the slogan 'mera jism meri marzi' (I am the owner of my body) has emerged as a divisive line between the so-called right-wingers and a tiny group of women generally based in the posh areas of big cities in Pakistan. Is it the core issue of gender inequality or discrimination? Perhaps not. Third, an emphasis on horizontal inequalities is politically easy as just sloganeering is required. Semantics take precedence over the core and the entire issue gets confused.

Further, equalities in the statutes are not sufficient which generally exist in all societies in this modern age. "Formal equality is a necessary condition for overall betterment. But it is not sufficient. A movement towards more generalized equalization of the human conditions requires not only legal equality between different groups that humans are divided into, but also substantively greater income and wealth inequality---- Those who care exclusively about identities aim to place everybody on the same starting line with Ferraris and others with bicycles. Their job is done once everybody is on the same starting line. Case closed: just when the real issues begin".[70]

The real issue is the economic disempowerment of women. If the prospects of girls for earning are high, the number of missing women reduces (as empirically confirmed by Nancy Qian in her study on tea plantations in China), their bargaining power at home increases (experience of the USA and Europe vindicates this), and their educational attainments improve. For example, bride price that is the amount or payment (which may not necessarily be in cash) the parents receive when their daughter is married has been found to be an important determinant of female education in societies where this custom is prevalent.[71] Educational attainment is higher among bride price groups and more educated brides command a higher bride price in marriage.

Some work by Nava Ashraf and her colleagues[72] on bride price or bride wealth shows that completing primary education on average enhances bride price by 58% in Indonesia while completing junior secondary and attending college are respectively associated with a 67% and 86% increase in bride price payment. They estimate that returns for respectively completing their daughter's primary, secondary, and college education are 14%, 22%, and 38% of per capita consumption of one year. The Middle East and North Africa (MENA) region presents an important paradox with regard to the enrollment of women in tertiary education and their participation in the labor force. The enrollment of females in tertiary education is higher than that of males, but FLFP is the lowest in the world. This applies to the South Asian region as well. And this paradox is hard to explain by the standard book models like labor supply[73] or the feminization U hypothesis.[74] The phenomenon of the bride's price does explain this paradox. For example, returns to bride price are sometimes much higher than returns to education which does explain improvement in female education despite stagnation in FLFP.[75]

Cultural norms matter and have unintended consequences, in some cases positive and in some cases negative. Bride price, though seemingly a negative norm (at least it does not sound good to ears), has positive consequences for female education as it incentivizes parents to educate their daughters. Such customs, however, do not help promote economic growth if female talent is not tapped and put to its best use. The growth experience of the developed countries confirms (as argued by Professor Gordon for the US growth experience) that tapping the talent of women is highly significant for achieving fast and sustained economic growth. Female labor force participation (FLFP) in Pakistan is far lower compared to countries with a similar level of economic development like Bangladesh. One of the top secrets for Bangladesh's rise on the economic trajectory since last decade or so is the use of women's agency, which has impacted the economy through various channels like contribution to economic growth via labor participation and its reduced fertility rate (2 compared to 3.6 in Pakistan).

On the contrary, Pakistan did not adequately capitalize on women's agency. Some empirical work on intra-household decision-making (which is a good proxy variable for empowerment) in Pakistan confirms that women's influence on household decisions is low and strangely women have little pent-up demand for agency, possibly due to a combination of factors like fear of retaliation, internalized social norms, and failure of aspirations.[76] According to World Bank estimates,[77] closing the female employment gap relative to Bangladesh is expected to create around 7.3 million new jobs and could boost GDP by 5 to 10%. And if Pakistan is able to close the female employment gap relative to the LMIC average, employment effects are estimated at 19.3 million jobs and GDP gains would be in the range of 8.86% and 22.6%.

Socio-cultural attitudes, as pointed out earlier, are also responsible for low FLFP. For example, caste plays a vital role in time allocation and the autonomy of women in India and Pakistan. Some evidence[78] in the context of rural India suggests that the ratio of women's market work to men's declines as we move up the caste hierarchy. Similarly, social norms about female work, restrictions on physical mobility, fear and threat of sexual harassment, lack of adequate transport, limited access to digital connectivity, low expectations of returns to female education, and domestic responsibilities like childcare are considered the main factors responsible for low FLFP in Pakistan.[79] What can be done?

Better access to infrastructure and public services like electricity, gas, et cetera are some important areas for bringing about change in women's time allocation. For example, in poverty-stricken settings, women spend hours in fetching water and firewood, and in performing other household chores. Home production activities constrain their abilities to invest in their health, in the health of their children, and to engage in market work. Changes in women's time allocation may impact economic growth, directly (better access to infrastructure would enable them to devote more time to market activity, thus promoting growth) and indirectly (like through human development for example, more time for one's health and improved childcare practices).[80] Reducing the gender-based inequalities of opportunity would help females realize their potential. The concept of equality of opportunity is, however, not restricted to FLFP. It is a wider concept involving multiple complexities.

The Inequality of Opportunity

One of the chief justifications for income inequality and capitalism, as elaborated earlier, was that more savings could be accumulated from capital compared to wages. And with the ratio of profits from capital to wages being high, only savings by the capitalists could promote economic growth. Capital was thus at the heart of all development discourse and inequality was a logical by-product. The entire line of argumentation would, however, change if we substitute the centrality of capital with humans. Focus on human capital accumulation as the prime source of economic growth would qualitatively change the impact of inequality on the growth process.

The recognition of the centrality of human capital for economic growth would require that income and wealth are widely distributed or dispersed among all the segments of the society and do not get concentrated among the rich or just 1%. Human capital is embodied in humans and human capital accumulation would be large if more humans acquire skills, education, and training. And what happens with the increase and spread of human capital in the society? Simply, individuals become more productive, their wages increase, credit constraints become less binding, and differences in marginal propensity to save become less pronounced.[81]

Implication is that the process of economic growth would accelerate if the individuals have equality of opportunity.

The genesis of the inequality of opportunity lies in the circumstances which are beyond one's control like parental education (we have seen in our discussion on health care how deep nexus mother's education has got with the health outcomes of her children). Similarly, the place or country of birth also matters. A child born in a rural area faces discrimination in terms of health, quality of education, longevity, and employment opportunities, even within the same country. If we talk of inequality at the global level, citizens of developed countries enjoy huge 'citizenship rents'. "Just being born in the United States rather than in Congo, a person would multiply her income by 93 times--The very existence of a large citizenship premium indicates that there is currently no such thing as global equality of opportunity: a lot of our income depends on accident of birth",[82] writes Milanovic. And roughly half of the income variance worldwide is explained just by two variables that is country of residence and income distribution within that country.[83]

Equality of opportunity, at least theoretically, seeks to provide a level playing field to dilute the adverse influence of circumstances and factors, which are beyond the control of an individual, like gender, birthplace, ethnicity, family background, et cetera. The concept of the equality of opportunity emphasizes that success or rise should depend on an individual's choices and effort, and not on his circumstances at birth. And inequality of opportunity is bad for economic growth. Policies that equalize opportunity not only promote equity but also boost economic growth.[84] The concept of a level playing field can be better operationalized by providing the children access to services that are critical for their full development. The children cannot be held responsible for their family circumstances on the day of their birth. Moreover, evidence shows that early interventions to equalize opportunity are more cost-effective and successful than interventions at the later stages of life.[85] What are the policy choices to equalize opportunity in childhood? Public services like immunization, food supplements, free quality schooling, et cetera are some interventions that immediately come to mind in this regard. The majority of the governments are focused on these public services, though coverage and quality leaves much to be desired.

Moreover, opportunities need to be equalized before the competition starts which means that even life before birth matters (as discussed in the public health care chapter of this book). Besides health, education is another important input for a better life. And equality of opportunity in education requires that all children have access to better quality schools. If one child is studying in a low-quality public school while another is enrolled in a high-quality private school, it cannot be called equality of opportunity even if both are allowed to compete for a job without any discrimination on the basis of caste, creed, gender, age, domicile, et cetera. Early family advantage, brilliantly emphasized by Malcolm Gladwell in '*Outliers*', explains to large extent individual differences in success. While highlighting this point, Gladwell writes about Bill Gates that his father was a wealthy lawyer in Seattle and his mother was the daughter of a well-to-do banker. They sent him to Lakeside, a private school for the elite. Bill Gates was in 8th grade when this school started a computer club. And in this way, Bill got an extraordinary early opportunity to learn programming as an 8th grader, and a series of other opportunities connected with enrollment in Lakeside made the real difference in the future success of Bill Gates.[86] Simply, the point is that early opportunities matter. But the hard part of the question is: how to equalize opportunities?

One option would be to equalize per capita financing of education for children in all schools. But equalizing per pupil expenditure may not necessarily equalize equality of opportunity. "Guaranteeing equal per capita financing of educational facilities is, however, not sufficient to provide equal educational achievement since different children are able to use educational resources (teachers, books, school buildings) with different degrees of effectiveness and efficiency – mentally retarded children will require more resources. Equalizing opportunity for educational achievement requires distributing educational resources in such a way that different abilities of children to turn resources into educational achievement are compensated for, where those abilities are determined by circumstances beyond the control of the individual", Roemer writes.[87]

Generating employment opportunities or making it obligatory on the state to provide employment to every citizen would be another important plank of any equal opportunity policy. The state is required to provide equal opportunity unemployment insurance, but certainly such insurance cannot be a perfect substitute for employment. While on job, an individual uses his skills which enhance his self-esteem which means that it would be always better to earn income through application of skills that is through employment rather than through receiving welfare payments or grants. According to Roemer: "Self-esteem, unlike income, is not transferable; moreover, income can substitute for self-esteem as an input in a person's production of welfare, but only to a limited extent".[88]

The equality of opportunity, though an appealing concept, is fraught with formidable difficulties when put to policy as beautifully explained by Ravi Kanbur, through a simple illustration, of soup distribution to the indigent.[89] Imagine, he writes, that you are serving on a soup line for the indigent, and imagine that doling out soup is conditional on the assessment as to whether it was circumstance or effort that led the individual to stand in the indigent soup line. Would it not be morally repugnant to make such an assessment or deny a cup of soup to anybody in the soup line if he does not meet the condition? Similarly, if children's health is outside their control, then entire inequality in their health would be a legitimate policy objective, and you cannot just focus on the part that is attributable to parental circumstances. Even in adults, if bad luck leads to ill-health, it would be morally offensive not to make it a serious policy concern, even if such ill-health is not purely a result of circumstance. Equality of outcomes remains relevant even if we are able to provide a level playing field. People may exert effort, but they may fail. Would it be a desirable act to leave an athlete, who falls due to some sudden injury on competition day, to himself?

The inequality of outcomes also directly impacts equality of opportunity for the next generation. "Today's ex- post outcomes shape tomorrow's ex ante playing field: the beneficiaries of inequality of outcome today can transmit an unfair advantage to their children tomorrow. ----Inequality of outcome among today's generation is the source of unfair advantage received by the next generation. If we are concerned about equality of opportunity tomorrow, we need to be concerned about inequality of outcome today".[90] Inequality is intergenerational which is interpreted in two distinct but related terms that is absolute IGM and relative IGM.

Intergenerational Mobility (IGM)

The absolute IGM refers to the improvement in living standards of a generation compared to their parents. This is closely linked to income growth and a rise in shared prosperity or income growth of the bottom 40% with sustained improvements over an extended period of time.[91] The relative IGM is, however, the extent to which an individual's economic position is independent of his parents' position and depends much on equality of opportunity.[92] Lower IGM dampens aspirations (which are critical to mobility). The aspirations window of children and parents belonging to low socio-economic status is likely to be narrow with all negative consequences for human resource development. Low mobility misallocates resources and may lead to unrealized human potential. Even talented individuals from low socio-economic backgrounds are excluded from opportunities while those born into greater privilege with less potential and talent may get opportunities. So, low mobility induces inefficiencies that have negative implications for economic growth.

On the other hand, empirics[93] show that high mobility is associated with higher tax revenues, higher government expenditure on public education, and better quality schools (lower school dropouts and high teacher-pupil ratios). And countries with high IGM show better child health indicators (like less stunting and lower infant mortality rates). The intergenerational mobility is very low in Pakistan. According to a report[94] on inequality, children born in income-poor families in Pakistan in the years 2010–2011 are less likely than those born in the years 1994–1995 to break the poverty trap and move to the middle-class category. About 40% of the sons born to fathers belonging to the bottom quintile remain in the bottom quintile; only 9% make it to the top quintile, while 52% of the sons born to the rich remain rich. The report identifies four peculiarities of the inequality trap in Pakistan.

First, the majority of the sons of poor fathers remain poor, and the majority of the sons of rich fathers stay rich. Second, the educational gap between the rich and the poor is increasing. Third, sons follow fathers in the choice of occupations, and fourth, girls are discriminated against in terms of educational expenditure and choice of occupation. Based on 24 years of panel data, another study[95] has explored the impact of village-level inequality in land ownership on the intragenerational and economic mobility of poor households. Results of this study suggest that the poor living in more unequal villages are less likely to have escaped poverty and that upward educational mobility is significantly lower in villages with a higher concentration of land. The results of the study also show that the quality of public school teachers is low in villages with higher land inequality.

Education is considered a ticket to social mobility and perhaps that is why education is used as the sole indicator of social mobility by the World Bank on intergenerational mobility, both absolute and relative. The

World Bank data maps mobility on the educational ladder since 1950. An analysis of the data of some selected countries like China, India, Indonesia, Malaysia, Sri Lanka, Thailand, and Vietnam, in comparison with Pakistan, shows that social mobility, both absolute and relative, is the lowest in Pakistan. For example, against 60.64% of parents with less than primary education, 42.39% of children had the same education as their parents for the 1980 cohort. For the 1950 cohort, parents with less than primary education constituted 85.04% while children with less than primary education for that cohort were around 70.85%.

Countries like Indonesia, Malaysia, and Sri Lanka started with some advantage and showed high mobility on the educational ladder. China has made big strides. For the 1950 cohort, parents with less than primary education in China were 64.51%, with 43.25% of their children at the same education level. For the 1980 cohort, the number for the parents was 14.93% while for the children with less than primary education it was just 6.54%. The share of children with tertiary education in China, Thailand, Malaysia, and Vietnam for 1980 cohort is respectively 25.35%, 35.4%, 55.23%, and 47.02%. It is 22.29% for Pakistan (see Table 6.2).

The mobility on the educational ladder can also be estimated from another variable that is the mean years of schooling of parents and children for various cohorts. For the 1950 cohort, Pakistan had mean years of schooling, respectively for parents and children, of 0.8 and 2.65 years. For the 1980 cohort, it is 3.47 and 7.7 years. Other countries like China, Indonesia, Malaysia, and Vietnam, were better in 1950 in terms of said variable and continued with more mobility for later cohorts. The case of India is, however, bit curious. For the 1950 cohort, India had 1.69 and 5.27 mean years of schooling, respectively, for parents and children, meaning that things were better compared to Pakistan. For the 1980 cohort, said figures are, respectively, 3.35 years and 7.64 years, little worse than Pakistan (see Table 6.3).

What does low intergenerational mobility imply? It simply means that disparities in Pakistan are structural in nature. Highly unequal societies tend to have low social mobility—a relationship popularized by Alan Krueger as the 'Great Gatsby Curve'. In countries like Finland, Norway, and Denmark, the link between parental economic status and adult earnings of children is the weakest. Less than one-fifth of any economic advantage is passed on to a son in adulthood.[96] Contrary to this, Pakistani society is highly stratified. Generally, a civil servant's child becomes a civil servant. A doctor's child becomes a doctor, and a lawyer's child,

Table 6.2 Intergenerational mobility in selected countries (1980 Cohort) %

Country	*Share of parents with (less than primary)* P1	*Share of parents with (primary)* P2	*Share of parents with (lower secondary)* P3	*Share of parents with (upper secondary)* P4	*Share of parents with (tertiary)* P5	*Share of children with (less than primary)* C1	*Share of children with (primary)* C2	*Share of children with (lower secondary)* C3	*Share of children with (upper secondary)* C4	*Share of children with (tertiary)* C5
Bangladesh	51.68	22.73	16.03	8.25	1.31	23.86	14.78	34.99	3.95	2.42
China	14.93	33.09	35.7	14.39	1.89	6.54	16.77	34.09	17.25	25.35
India	49.9	22.81	16.23	6.84	4.22	26.17	16.38	19.37	12.84	25.25
Indonesia	22.1	48.4	16.31	9.09	4.1	6.73	19.64	23.97	33.42	16.24
Malaysia	10.92	22.34	20.69	31.73	14.33	0.27	1.59	4.26	38.65	55.23
Pakistan	60.64	21.48	11.62	4.22	2.03	42.39	10.3	16.55	8.48	22.29
Sri Lanka	5.78	25.24	44.26	23.61	1.1	3.19	6.97	31.68	47.39	10.77
Vietnam	8.9	20.44	30.31	27.69	12.65	1.68	9.36	13.45	28.49	47.02

Source Global Database on Intergenerational Mobility (data.worldbank.org)

Table 6.3 Intergenerational mobility over time of selected countries

Country	*Cohort*	*Mean of parents' years of schooling*	*Mean of children's years of schooling*
Bangladesh	1980	3.42	7.69
	1950	1.59	5.20
China	1970	4.26	7.85
	1980	6.27	10.05
	1950	1.69	5.27
India	1970	2.45	6.03
	1980	3.35	7.64
	1950	2.80	5.89
Indonesia	1970	4.72	9.15
	1980	5.39	10.04
Malaysia	1970	6.78	12.62
	1980	8.76	14.09
	1950	0.80	2.65
Pakistan	1970	1.93	5.26
	1980	3.47	7.70
	1950	5.85	8.28
Sri Lanka	1970	7.62	9.43
	1980	7.92	9.94
Thailand	1980	6.56	11.91
	1950	3.89	11.15
Vietnam	1970	6.82	11.56
	1980	7.73	12.50

Source Global Data base on Intergenerational Mobility (data.worldbank.org)

in all probability, joins the legal profession to build on the goodwill and clientele of his father. "There are business, political, army and bureaucrat families where several generations have produced seths, politicians, generals, and high ranking officers. In such a society, a driver's son is constrained to become a driver, a jamadar's son is destined to become a jamadar, and a maid's daughter ends up becoming a maid".[97]

The institutional overhang is very much visible in the power asymmetries in Pakistan. The British Empire promoted a landed aristocracy and a bureaucratic structure to rule its vast areas. The historical configuration of access to power, privilege, and economic resources gave a competitive advantage to the tiny elite, which is passed on to the next generations with all the inefficiencies that society has to bear. The scions of the elite families enter politics and other areas of life due to a stratified socio-economic structure, no matter how rotten they may be.

Pakistanis do miracles in the fields where entry is not restricted for the common people. Cricket is a case in point. Had the Pakistani cricket team just included players from rich families, it would not have been possible for Pakistan to compete at the international level and produce world-class cricketers like Waseem Akram, Shoaib Akhtar, Mushtaq Ahmed, or Muhammad Yousaf. On the other hand, fields which are dominated by the elite and where parentage and class determine entry are the ones beset with most of the rot. Politics is a pertinent example, which is dominated by a few dozen families, and that is perhaps the main reason that we see no imaginative or innovative ideas being debated in politics. Majority of those who get to the parliament do not participate in the debates taking place for legislation. For example, during the 15th National Assembly of Pakistan, out of 342 members of the National Assembly, 174 (50.88%) did not speak for a single minute in the Assembly.[98]

The Majority of the representatives fail to make effective and meaningful contributions even in the most crucial assembly budget sessions and just rubber stamp this most important annual legislation. "There are not 342 members in the assembly; they are 204 families. The families that had big names at pre-partition time are ruling over and over again. This system makes inexperienced people leaders because of their family background".[99] Competition is the essence of efficiency. The cricket team produced world-class cricketers because entry was open even to those from humble backgrounds. The political system is rotten because it is monopolized by a few families, with all the attendant inefficiencies induced by them in the system. Generally, less attention is given to the mirror image of income inequality in the political sphere that is political dynasties. Political inequality has a deep nexus with poverty. Some researchers have studied patterns of political dynasties in the 15th Philippine House of Representatives (2003–2007). Their results suggest that about 80% of dynastic legislators witnessed an increase in their net worth. Political dynasties in the Philippine Congress, like those in Pakistan, tend to dominate the major political parties. The troubling part of the findings was that the incidence of poverty was found to be high in the regions where political dynasties were located.[100] This finding is otherwise very intuitive. Political competition compels politicians to deliver public services and good governance. And in the dynastic constituencies, political competition is low, so the politicians are not compelled to deliver good governance et cetera. Empirics also confirm this intuition. For example, evidence from Italian elections confirms that Italian politicians shirk less when they are from a closely contested district.[101]

A few dozens of families dominate the political landscape of Pakistan with all attendant adverse consequences in the form of fragile democracy, weak rule of law, short-sightedness in politics, and disempowerment of the common man. The so-called 'electables' belonging to these families use political power for rent-seeking and to perpetuate their socio-economic stranglehold. One of the UNDP's report laments the unholy alliance between political power and money in Pakistan as follows: "The economic elites often use their wealth and power to influence government policies, political decisions, and public debates in ways that lead to a greater concentration of wealth. Money buys political clout, which the richest and the most powerful use to further entrench their influence and advantage. Many of the Pakistan's wealthiest people today have made their fortunes thanks to exclusive government concessions, tax exemptions, sweat heart contracts, land concessions, subsidies, privatization (even in the education and health systems), corruption, and the monopoly of power. Powerful elites also use their money, power, and influence to capture the media and other spaces to shape narratives and public debate. They use their influence to promote ideas and norms that support economic and political interests of the privileged. As a result, there is considerable misperception about the scope and scale of inequality, as well as its causes".[102] The role of mainstream media is also questionable with regard to building informed narratives on issues like inequality and poverty which concern the common people. The media like land and power in Pakistan is dominated by few groups. Inequalities of media are as high as the inequalities of other species and stripes.

Inequalities of Media

Media throughout the world is owned by the government or by private families. The ownership of media by the government is explained predominantly through two theories that is public interest theory and the public choice theory. The public interest (Pigouvian) theory is postulated on the assumption that governments maximize the welfare of consumers from three angles. First, information is a public good, and once it is supplied to some consumers, it would be highly costly to withhold it from others. Second, the provision and dissemination of information are subject to increasing returns to scale. Significant fixed costs are involved for gathering and distribution facilities, but once those fixed costs are recouped, marginal costs for making the information available to consumers are drastically reduced. Third, private media outlets may serve the interests of the elite only and may keep the consumers ignorant and in this context, state media is supposed to give the consumers less biased and more complete information. The public choice theory, on the other hand, postulates that the state media may manipulate and distort information in favor of the incumbent politicians and may prevent voters and consumers from making more informed decisions. Some researchers[103] tested the above theories by examining media ownership in ninety-seven countries and concluded that the data supports the public choice theory, which means that government ownership of the media undermines political and economic freedoms.

Electronic media in Pakistan, until its deregulation in 2002, remained state-dominated and was used for agenda advancement by the governments, civil as well as military, and for identity construction and narrative formulation. Since 2002, deregulation of the media has resulted in the proliferation of private cable and satellite TV channels. Pakistan now has around 112 Satellite TV channels, 4060 cable operators, and 43 landing TV channels from abroad like BBC, CNN, et cetera. Many print media houses expanded to include TV news platforms after deregulation. Viewership is quite high, and at least 30 channels exclusively broadcast news and current affairs programs.[104] The biases associated with the mainstream media are, however, huge. Some of the inequalities and biases are easy to detect while others are bit hidden. For example, issues and the lives of rural people find very little coverage in both print and electronic media. It is tilted in favor of the rich and the powerful, a bias easy to detect and understand.

All media houses are owned by the rich who are more interested in furthering their commercial interests through the media. There are issues of ownership concentration in media as well. The Reporters Sans Frontiers (RSF)[105] used the Media Ownership Monitor (MOM) to map media pluralism in several countries including Pakistan. They mapped the top 40 in print, television, radio, and digital media (top 10 in each category). The majority share of the top four in each medium (television, radio, newspapers, and online) is in the control of four owners or less. And seven cross-media groups, owning titles in each of the four categories, control nearly 70% of the audience share. Ownership concentration has implications. Both the state and the elite can easily manipulate the media in such a scenario. Those who control the state apparatus can use it to propagate peculiar versions of national interest and ideology to further their vested interests, which would not necessarily be in the interest of the common people.

Similarly, it becomes easy for the elite to build narratives to perpetuate hegemony over power and resources. For example, leftist narratives and discourse are completely absent from the mainstream media. Serious issues of inequality, poverty, social mobility, et cetera rarely find any meaningful debate in both print and electronic media. The media research wing of Gallup & Gillani conducts a monthly content analysis of newspapers published in Pakistan. According to their research, political issues occupy the majority of the space, while issues like health, education, and science and technology only occupy a fraction of the space compared to politics.[106] Discussions are mostly generalized, and subject specialists seldom find a place in the TV debates. An analysis of selected prime-time confirms that 73% of guests were politicians, 22% were analysts, and just 5% were experts.

The media is dependent on advertisements with the result that a special focus is created on potential consumers which means that the rich matter more than the poor for the media. The corporate sponsorship of advertisements promotes corporate culture and the interests of the powerful. For example, underreporting, transfer pricing, or tax evasion by the big conglomerates or corporates hardly find any mention in the narrative on tax collection in Pakistan. There is no space for the poor in the media. Issues like undernourishment, poverty, and the bad quality of public education do not enter the mainstream. Even if some discussion takes place that is not forceful due to being generalized. A huge amount of data in the form of household surveys, et cetera is publicly available but hardly would you find a debate on the conditions of the people in the light of such data.

There are clear dividing lines between the Urdu press and the English Press. As it is difficult to coin easy and immediate expressions for the fast-evolving vocabulary of economics, psychology, sociology, and philosophy in Urdu, the Urdu press, rather than giving some informed opinion, generally indulges in generalized and non-expert views on issues like inflation or economic growth. On the other hand, English-language newspapers comparatively give more informed, balanced, and liberal views about issues confronting Pakistan. “These (English) papers’ focus is on the big cities in terms of coverage. Owing to the lack of reporters, the smaller cities receive virtually no coverage and the districts not at all. This is the biggest drawback for English-language journalism in Pakistan. Owing to the fact that its coverage is restricted to the big cities, it is unable to establish links with civil society and respond to the requirements of the masses”.[107]

The emergence of social media, however, holds some promise for democratizing people’s access to media. Two important features distinguish social media from traditional media: low barriers to entry and reliance on user-generated content. Low entry barriers give a platform to the marginalized and disadvantaged sections to express their opinions and views. The role of social media in the Arab Spring is well-documented. The number of Twitter posts with key words related to Tahrir Square was predictive of the number of participants in the protests on the next day in the plaza.[108]

Evidence is also available confirming the role of social media in non-political protests. For instance, in 2011, there was a sharp rise in the price of cheese in Israel. Some consumers created a Facebook page introducing 30 users boycotting cottage cheese as they viewed the rise in price as unjustified. Just one day after the creation of the page, 30,000 consumers joined, and the number of followers increased to 100,000 in just two weeks. Sales of cheese plummeted substantially, particularly in places with high Facebook penetration. The boycott was effective, and prices stabilized.[109]

The omnipresence of social media has huge implications for politics and governance. “As communication technologies such as social media and the internet can be used to convey different kinds of messages, it is therefore not surprising that they may facilitate pro-democratic changes in some cases and steer societies away from democracy in others. In places where the main public grievances are related to corruption, subversion of power, and control of traditional media by autocrats, free Internet and social media do improve accountability by informing the public and facilitating the organization of protests”.[110]

Social media in Pakistan has great promise to metamorphose the landscape of politics and has all potential to decrease the fixed costs of entry into politics. There are, however, huge challenges to reckon with. First of all, low entry barriers and the unprecedented speed with which users can share content on social media have the potential to spread misinformation and fake news. As immediate reactions are often based on emotions rather than reason, lies that evoke anger, fear, or sensation generally spread faster than real news. Three MIT scholars have found, based on data from 126,000 stories tweeted by 3 million people more than 4.5 million times, that false news or lies "diffused significantly farther, faster, deeper, and more broadly than the truth". Their findings further confirm that false stories evoked fear, disgust, and surprise whereas true stories inspired anticipation, sadness, joy, and trust.[111]

Humans form perceptions or misperceptions generally on the basis of stories and anecdotes and not on the basis of evidence and statistics. The nature of human memory is such that misperceptions once formed persist and anecdotal information in the form of stories (even if concocted) comes to mind more easily than statistical information.[112] And if fake and unverified content becomes common, then an environment of distrust and disbelief is created. Hannah Arendt, a German political theorist, in an interview with the French writer Roger Errera, made very pertinent remarks about lies. She said "If everybody always lies to you, the consequence is not that you believe the lies, but rather that nobody believes anything any longer".

Another challenge connected to misinformation on social media is the erosion of the very foundations of human communication and social cohesion. What distinguishes us from the animals is our communication, our learning ability from other community members, and our reason. "Our skills and our general knowledge owe less to individual experience than to social transmission. In most of our daily undertakings, in family life, in work, in love, or in leisure, we rely extensively on what we have learned from others".[113]

The community still plays a vital role in our lives. Raghuram Rajan very pertinently writes about the community that: "It anchors the individual in real human networks and gives them a sense of identity; our presence in the world is verified by our impact on people around us---our community gives us a sense of self-determination, a sense of direct-control over our lives, even while making local public services work better for us".[114] And virtual interactions cannot substitute for real interactions in communities. Despite some obvious downsides, the fact remains that social media is powerful and omnipresent. It is going to provide a platform to the common man. Its proliferation in Pakistan in the last few years has started to show a profound impact on politics and social lives.

And now the crucial question: armed with so much wealth of information and insights on various aspects of inequality, what can be done to fix the problem? All the species and stripes of inequality generally germinate from income inequality. So first of all, we need to have knowledge in which segments of the population most of the income inequality resides as once we are able to tame income inequality, process of reduction in other forms of inequality shall automatically start.

Sting in the Tails

Traditionally, the Gini index is used to determine how unequal a society is. Its value ranges between 0 and 1. A value of zero means that income is uniformly distributed among all the citizens of a country. If the value of Gini is one, it means that one person in that society owns all the income. But no nation has ever had either absolute income equality or absolute income concentration. Countries end up with some number between 0.3 (Scandinavian countries) and somewhere around 0.7 (some African countries).

If the Gini of country A is 0.45 and country B's Gini is 0.5, it means that country B is more unequal compared to country A. Moreover, say in year 1, the Gini is 0.45, which increases to 0.47 in year 2. What does it tell? It says that the distribution of income has become more unequal in year 2 but it does not offer any clues about the drivers of such change. Are the rich getting more, the poor losing ground or are income changes taking place in middle-income households? The Gini index is represented through the Lorenz curve which is a graphical representation to show the variability of the distribution of income and wealth (Fig. 6.1).

There are other measures of inequality as well but the Palma ratio has emerged as a more policy-relevant measure of inequality.[115] Given the stability of the middle class, it is very clear what needs to be changed. Based on data analysis from a number of countries, Gabriel Palma, a Chilean economist, observed that in almost every country half of the gross national income of a country is captured by the middle class while the remaining half is distributed among the top 10% (the rich) and the bottom 40% (the poor). The whole of the distributional politics is how the 50% is divided between the rich (top 10%) and the extremely poor (bottom 40%), while the share of the middle class remains stable (deciles 5–9).[116]

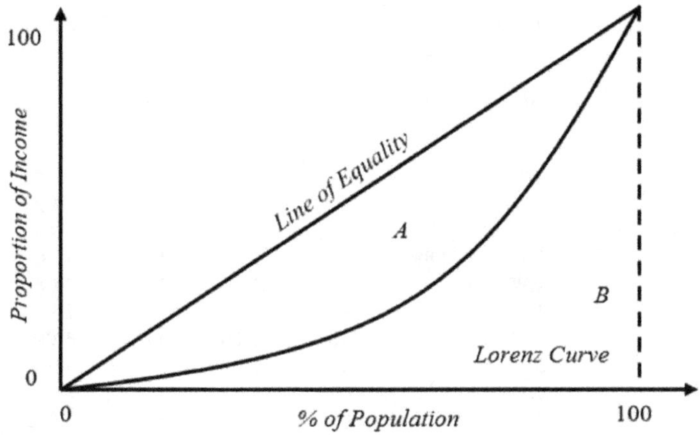

Fig. 6.1 Lorenz Curve

The beauty of the Palma ratio is that it captures the two extremes of inequality, being ratio of the incomes of the top 10% to those of the bottom 40%. Thus, extreme inequality resides in the tails. "It is Palma's simplicity which is its greatest strength. A Gini coefficient of 0.5 implies serious inequality but yields no intuitive statement for a non-technical audience. In contrast, the equivalent Palma of 5.0 can be directly translated that the richest 10% have five times more income compared to the poorest 40% of the nation".[117] Traditional indicators of inequality are less sensitive to changes at the extremes of the income distribution.[118]

Pakistan had a Palma ratio of 3.2 in 1980. It remained above 3.00 till 2006, except in 1993, 1994, and 1995, when it was below 3. Since 2007 to 2014, it again remained below 3, went above 3 since 2014, and has been on the same trajectory since then as evident from Table 6.4.

Overall, it simply means that the share of the top 10% in the income is more than three times the income of the poorest 40% of the population of Pakistan. The years 1993–1995 and 2007–2014 show bit improvement in income distribution. It means that either the income of the top 10% decreased or the income of the bottom 40% increased. The decrease in income of the top 10% may possibly occur due to high taxation on their incomes which does not seem to be the case. Agricultural income enjoyed exemption from taxation during the said period as it does now. Taxation rates almost remained the same for the higher brackets of income. It

Table 6.4 Palma ratio 1 (Top 10% income share/bottom 40% income share) of some selected countries

	1980	*1990*	*2000*	*2010*	*2019*	*2020*	*2021*
Afghanistan	3.06	3.06	3.06	2.84	2.88	2.88	2.88
Bangladesh	2.29	2.63	3.51	3.19	3.10	3.10	3.10
China	1.40	1.80	2.58	3.83	3.85	3.92	3.94
India	1.91	2.12	2.76	5.07	5.44	5.44	5.44
Indonesia	3.13	3.89	2.70	4.31	4.70	4.70	4.70
Korea	1.93	1.93	1.93	2.10	2.08	2.08	2.04
Malaysia	4.29	4.03	4.03	3.17	2.91	2.91	2.91
Pakistan	**3.38**	**3.30**	**3.37**	**3.10**	**3.09**	**3.09**	**3.09**
Sri Lanka	3.17	3.41	4.62	4.21	4.33	4.33	4.33
Viet Nam	4.12	4.12	4.43	4.12	3.74	3.74	3.74
South Asia	3.56	3.22	3.68	5.14	5.15	5.13	5.24
Sub-Saharan Africa	9.62	9.28	8.92	7.90	7.62	7.55	7.55

Source World Inequality Database (WID)

means that decrease in income sitting above the line (in the denominator) is not a plausible explanation for improvements in Palma ratios. So what did happen?

The poor have two broad sources of income: receipts from their labor and receipts from income support programs. Interestingly, in the said years, Pakistan Peoples Party (PPP), a leftist political party, was ruling the country, which, through an increase in minimum wages and by initiating income support program, helped reduce income inequality a bit. "The PPP was formed on the socialist promise of food, clothing, and housing for every citizen. It was famously successful in West Pakistan in the 1970 elections, where the party pitted its socialist workers against large landowners and feudal politicians—even if there were many of the latter in the party's ranks and Bhutto himself was a feudal lord. Following the end of General Zia-ul-Haq's martial law, however, Benazir Bhutto's government that came to power was relatively more market-oriented and did not re-nationalize the industries but started a large transfer program, the Benazir Income Support Program".[119]

Similar observation also holds for India as well. The Palma ratio for India in 1980 was 1.9 (much less than Pakistan). Till the 1980s, predominantly Indian Congress Party was in power in India. It was the party of the left believing in a socialist model of development. And then came the neoliberal policies of the 1990s. The Palma ratio rose to above 3.0 in 2003. It kept on increasing and almost touched 5.0 in 2011. And Since Modi's coming to power in 2014, it has hovered around 5.4 as Table 6.4 shows.

Overall, South Asian region is characterized by high levels of inequalities like Latin American and African regions. For example, in Pakistan, top 1% had around 1.2 times more income than the income of entire bottom 40% population in 2021. Interestingly it was same in 1980. In India, income of top 1% is more than double the income of the poorest two quintiles (bottom 40%) (see Table 6.5). It can be argued that she has consistently witnessed high growth rates and inequality is an inevitable outcome of economic development. Before giving some verdict on this proposition, let us examine development experience of some other countries besides South Korea, Taiwan, Hong Kong, et cetera which find mention at several places in this book.

Let us analyze Malaysia and Vietnam. Inequality decreased in Malaysia as it continued treading on the trajectory of development. Palma ratio in Malaysia in 1980 was 4.29 (higher than Pakistan) which was 2.9 in 2021. In 1980, top 1% had over 1.8 times more income than bottom

Table 6.5 Palma Index (Top 1% income share/Bottom 40% income share) of some selected countries

Country/Region	*1980*	*1990*	*2000*	*2010*	*2019*	*2020*	*2021*
Afghanistan	1.18	1.18	1.18	1.06	1.06	1.06	1.06
Bangladesh	0.73	0.88	1.28	1.20	1.18	1.18	1.18
Bhutan	1.84	1.84	1.84	1.41	1.16	1.16	1.16
China	0.33	0.48	0.75	1.36	1.33	1.41	1.43
India	0.44	0.66	1.05	2.06	2.07	2.07	2.07
Indonesia	1.12	1.30	0.95	1.64	1.79	1.79	1.79
Korea	0.51	0.51	0.51	0.62	0.71	0.71	0.69
Malaysia	1.82	1.67	1.69	1.27	1.07	1.07	1.07
Maldives	3.91	3.91	3.91	1.25	0.90	0.90	0.90
Pakistan	1.21	1.16	1.34	1.19	1.20	1.20	1.20
Sri Lanka	1.11	1.35	1.84	1.73	1.81	1.81	1.81
Thailand	2.97	3.07	2.68	2.04	1.60	1.60	1.60
Viet Nam	1.48	1.48	1.60	1.68	1.34	1.34	1.34
South Asia	1.60	1.32	1.46	1.98	1.94	1.94	1.97
Sub-Saharan Africa	3.43	3.21	3.24	2.96	2.83	2.78	2.79

Source World Inequality Database (WID)

40% which has decreased to 1.07 times—a substantial decrease. Vietnam is another country which set off on the path of fast structural transformation and growth in last few decades. In 1980, Palma ratio was 4.12 which decreased to 3.34 in 2021 (see Table 6.5). It is not a dramatic change but lends credence to the proposition that economic development does not necessarily deepen inequality if pubic policies for human resource development and redistribution are simultaneously put in place for taming the inequality.

The verdict of the jury simply is that inequality is not inevitable. It is a choice like all other choices of a society. Inequality is mainly due to structural factors like inequitable ownership structures of productive assets. For example, distribution of land in Pakistan is characterized by a notable disparity, with the greatest concentration found in Punjab, trailed by KP, Sindh, and Balochistan. A highly skewed distribution of land has serious implications for egalitarianism in society. Empirical evidence[120] suggests a deep nexus between land and power. Skewed ownership of land results in strong patron-client relationships where the employers that is landlords concede some rents to the landless, and the threat of withdrawal of such rents influences political preferences. Land thus creates not only economic inequality but also inequalities of power. So equitable distribution of land is undoubtedly a big leveler of inequality. What are the other levelers of inequality? Let us first discuss the set of factors which we may call a revolutionary or thorny road to inequality reduction.

Thorny Road

Walter Scheidel, an Austrian historian who teaches at Stanford University, has postulated in '*The Great Leveler*' that death and destruction are the biggest levelers of inequality. The causes of death or destruction may be external in the form of wars (fighting across borders) or internal (fighting within the country that is revolution). According to his argument, what happens is that when tensions heighten among the countries, high taxes are imposed to mobilize resources to meet the expenses of war. It happened in Japan and it happened in Europe due to World War II. Even when the war was over, taxes and spending remained high, which in turn kept inequality levels low for quite a long time. Scheidel writes: "We can thank Piketty for an answer to the question of why inequality did not quickly recover after 1945 that is elegant in its simplicity. Capital accumulation is a process that takes time, and the nineteenth century, largely peaceful in much of the West had offered favorable conditions. Once capital was destroyed on a large scale in the periods of world wars, it proved much more difficult to rebuild as long as wartime measures such as progressive taxes on income and estates remained in place".[121] The establishment of a communist (conflict within states) regime in Russia, the French Revolution ("we should cut the heads of the rich men"), and Mao's cultural revolution in China all reduced inequalities.[122]

The state's failures and system collapses also level off inequality. The terminal phase of the Tang dynasty in China and the state collapse in Somalia are both documented to have reduced inequality.[123] Similarly, death and destruction caused by pandemics, famine, and microbes whenever they wrought havoc in human history also leveled off inequalities. These all levelers are, however, either the corrections of nature (pandemics, etc.) or the result of some of the biggest follies of humans (wars) or some of the biggest ideas and collective struggles (the French Revolution or Cultural Revolution). So revolution can be one of the most potent ways to level off inequality, according to this line of argumentation.

Destruction, death, and disruption (3Ds), which a revolution unleashes certainly level off inequalities in society. There are at least two big impediments to such a big change. First, a major section of society belonging to the upper and middle classes will never support such a change. The elite capture of politics and institutions is so entrenched that they will not let the power slip from their hands. Second, the poor are unable to articulate a narrative for revolutionary change and forge such a change due to what the economists call the 'collective action problem'.

Massive land reforms, which Scheidel discusses in his book, can be another big leveler, Interestingly, most of the land reforms in the recorded history of human beings were the result of war. For example, after World War II, land reforms were undertaken in Japan while the country was under American occupation. The reforms entailed uncompensated confiscation and the wholesale restructuring of land ownership across the country. At the end of World War II, land inequality in South Korea was high, but land reforms took place under the threat of North Korean communism, where all land had been confiscated by the state. In the early 1950s, private land in South Korea was capped at three hectares of good cropland, and the rest was distributed among the peasants. "A little more than half of the land changed hands. The redistributive effect was huge:

landlords lost 80% of their income whereas bottom 80% of rural households gained 20% to 30%. By 1956, the richest 6% of landowners held merely 18% of all land, and the share of tenants had fallen from 49 to 7%. The Gini coefficient of land ownership, which had been as high as 0.72 or 0.73 in 1945, fell to the 0.30s by the 1960s".[124]

The most redistributive reforms just came in the wake of war, civil war, revolution, or threat of revolution, like in Revolutionary France, Mexico, Russia, China, Vietnam, Bolivia, Cuba, Cambodia, Nicaragua, Ethiopia, and Zimbabwe. About 87% of all major land reforms undertaken outside Latin America between 1900 and 2010 were the result of a world war, decolonization, a communist takeover, or the threat of a communist regime.[125] In countries where threat of war or revolution was absent, land reforms had a very modest impact, like in Pakistan as the reforms were half-hearted. The judiciary (religious bench) practically rendered the 1977 Land Reforms Act ineffective (which could bring some tangible change), as discussed in detail elsewhere in the book, by holding that uncompensated confiscation of land was not in line with the injunctions of Islam.

Pakistan still has some room for peaceful leveling through land reforms. Amendments can be introduced in the Land Reforms Act in light of the observations of the Sharia Bench of the Supreme Court of Pakistan. The ownership of land can be capped (say, 12.5 acres per family) and excess holdings can be confiscated by the state against compensation on a sliding scale, with compensation shrinking with increase in size, though the case for confiscation of land without compensation is quite strong and convincing (to be discussed in detail in next chapter). Besides confiscatory land reforms, available state land can be distributed among the landless in a transparent manner strictly on the principle of equity. The state had 8.4 million acres of land, out of which 5.7 million were allotted among 0.484 million beneficiaries (around 12 acres per beneficiary if distribution was equitable) (see Table 6.6).

The details about the beneficiaries and criteria for allotment are, however, not publicly available. According to available statistics, 2.7 million acres of state land are still available as per Table 6.6. If it is distributed among the landless households (for example, five acres per family), over 500,000 households can be lifted out of extreme poverty and inequality. There are, however, some options to reduce inequality through peaceful methods as well. For example, restructuring the tax system can be another potent leveler.

Table 6.6 Distribution of state land

Province	*Available land for disposal*	*Land distributed*	*No. of beneficiaries*	*Balance (in acres)*
Punjab	75,585	53,813	4,717	21,772
Sindh	6,305,450	5,573,667	470,973	731,783
Balochistan	1,499,402	82,641	5,586	1,416,761
N.W.F.P*	553,710	26,780	2,994	526,930
Total	8,434,147	5,736,901	484,270	2,697,246

Source The Year Book of Cabinet Division 2007–2008

Peaceful Choices

Existing taxation system of Pakistan is not progressive. It is riddled with many exemptions and all sources of income are not subject to taxation. It is predominantly focused on revenue generation from indirect taxes which are regressive in nature. Taxation system is the best reflection of the nature of social contract Pakistani state has struck with the citizenry. It also best illustrates the political economy of the country. For example, agriculture contributes 20% to the GDP but a miniscule of one percent to the taxes. Similarly, service sector contributes 50% to the GDP but only 30% to taxes. The contribution of the wholesale and retail sub-sectors is also pitiably low. Both the said sub-sectors collectively contribute around 19% to GDP of Pakistan but only 0.5% to taxes.[126]

Taxation system intensifies inequality in Pakistan at least via three channels as follows. First, government does not collect sufficient amount of money to invest massively in health and education sectors which can go a long way in reducing inequality. Second, government is constrained to borrow from the multilateral institutions to fill the gap between revenue and expenditure. Money from multilateral institutions comes with stringent strings attached. Austerity is invariably one of the strings hammer of which generally falls on the social spending due to inflexible nature of public expenditure structure. Third, tax evaders are persistently witnessing rise in their incomes and wealth due to huge opportunities of tax evasion as it is very easy to find ways and means to evade taxes in a corrupt system. The proposition about the rampancy of corruption is not a hard science to prove. It is very much visible from the lifestyle of the rich. In majority of the cases, it would be hard to establish a correlation between their luxurious life style and the peanuts they pay into the government exchequer as taxes.

In this context, introduction of a progressive wealth tax is an idea to work on, which can be levied in addition to income tax. It is easier to hide and manipulate income than wealth. Additionally, income tax only accounts for a small portion of rich men's wealth. Wealth is, per se, an indicator of the capacity to pay. It is also an irrefutable fact that the majority of the assets accumulated by the rich in Pakistan are the result of rent-seeking activities. So it provides an additional ground to tax wealth and that too heavily. The wealth of the elite and the rich is not the result of merely their own efforts. They benefited from the physical and social infrastructure as well as a favorable policy environment for accumulating huge fortunes.

A confiscatory wealth tax can also be imposed to liquidate public debt. The debt, foreign as well as domestic, that Pakistan has accumulated over the years was not used for health, education, or the welfare of the poor. It was mainly on the projects used by the elite or embezzled by the elite along the way, even if some of that was meant for the poor. So the primary responsibility to pay back the debt rests with the elite, and confiscatory wealth taxes can be an option to make them discharge their said responsibility. The proceeds accruing from the sale of properties and buildings that are under exclusive use by the elite can also be used to pay off the debt. Moreover, introduction of wealth tax, with payment mechanism like that of progressive income tax, is an idea worth serious consideration. According to this idea, paying wealth tax would not be one-time activity rather it would be paid annually, like income tax.

Other forms of wealth tax, like inheritance tax, can also be introduced to directly address the transmission of monetary advantage from one generation to the next. "If a large bequest from my parents leads to my being better off than you, then it leads to an advantage that is in need of justification".[127] Inheritance tax is likely to be opposed on the ground that taxing inheritance amounts to double taxation as bequests are accumulated out of net earnings after payment of taxes. This proposition does not hold, at least for Pakistan, on several grounds. For example, tax evasion is rampant, and the majority of the assets are the result of untaxed money. Second, capital gains tax has never remained a major source of revenue in Pakistan. The real estate sector has traditionally remained a lucrative sector for black money investors. The prices of the land multiplied in a short span of time, and gains were either not taxed at all or taxed at very modest rates.

Third, the double taxation argument is also misplaced, even otherwise. If we go by this argument, then sales tax also amounts to double taxation. Simply put, you go to a restaurant and pay sales tax on your bill out of the salary upon which you have already paid income tax. Fourth, inheritance tax is also desirable from an efficiency perspective. Taxing inheritance will discourage investments in bricks and mortar, which often turn into dead capital in developing countries. This step will boost spending and aggregate demand. Inter vivos transfers or gifts between living people also need to be taxed to make the inheritance tax effective, as the rich may avoid such taxes by making gifts in their lifetime.

Control of rent-seeking is also important to level off inequality. Rents can be collected thorough several modes. Getting a subsidy on production of particular goods, reduction or elimination of tariff for goods imported by a particular group of importers or industry, creation of a special regulation to perpetuate monopoly and hamper competition, and getting special and differential treatment by virtue of belonging to an elite group or club are some examples of rent-seeking.[128] Societies characterized with ubiquity of rent-seeking suffer economically at least on two accounts.[129] First, rent-seeking activities generally have a natural tendency of increasing returns which simply means that high levels of rent-seeking are self-sustaining but economically inefficient and damaging for the overall economy. Second, public rent-seeking kills innovation and as a result, economic growth suffers. Rent instruments like permits, quotas, licenses, special regulatory orders (SROs), and outright bribery create a coalition of rent-seekers in the society through symbiotic relationship between economic interests and political power.

According to the UNDP report,[130] a total of eight groups can be visibly identified as having captured the state apparatus, which appropriate state resources largely for their personal gains. These groups include state-owned enterprises, the military establishment, high-net-worth individuals (top 1% of earners nationwide), large traders, exporters, banks, industry, and the feudal class. Overall, these groups are estimated to devour a staggering amount of 8% of GDP through privileged access (to land, capital, infrastructure, and services), lower taxation (exemptions, concessions, lower rates, and outright evasions), and favorable prices (favorable pricing formulas, high effective protection, ease of forming cartels and monopolies, access to cheaper inputs like duty-free raw materials, etc.).

Duty and tax exemption schemes like the import of machinery and raw materials free of duty under export-oriented units (EOUs), the duty and tax remission scheme for exports (DTRE), and manufacturing bond schemes are generally availed of by big businesses. The tax expenditure is estimated at 3.36% of the GDP, which constitutes 36.43% of the total revenue collected by FBR.[131] All tax expenditures are not necessarily bad. It is not even high when compared with the global average, which ranges between 3.4 and 4.4% of GDP. The real issue is that the majority of the tax concessions and exemptions are not based on the principles of equity and efficiency; rather, they are the result of political economy considerations and promote rent-seeking.

Moreover, monopolies and cartels in businesses like sugar are well known and show lax enforcement of anti-trust laws.[132] For instance, the report of a commission,[133] set up by the government of Pakistan to probe into the increase in sugar prices, came up with startling revelations like the following. First, the sugar market is manipulated by few large players, sugar mills, and brokers who earn huge profits through cartelization, hoarding, forward selling, speculation, and satta (imaginary/virtual advance sales). Second, only six groups control about 51% of the production of sugar. Third, the sugar sector is the 2nd largest manufacturing borrower, after textile in Pakistan. Fourth, the default rate is over 16% (much higher than the national average of around 9%) and in case of loans from public banks, default ratio crosses a whopping figure of 59%. Regrettably, the entire concept of conflict of interest is still alien to the governance structure of Pakistan. It would not come as a surprise in Pakistan if the Ministry of Production or the Ministry of Commerce is headed by an industrialist having direct stakes in the policies of these Ministries.

Education is considered one of the keys to socio-economic mobility. That is why one of the stated goals in all countries is to provide access to education regardless of the social origins of the children. The Constitution of the Islamic Republic of Pakistan promises education as a fundamental right to all children up to 16 years of age. Despite constitutional guarantees, around 24 million children are out of school while 22 million are enrolled in low-quality public schools.[134] The public education system is beset with serious problems of coverage, access, and quality. Just inclusion of the right to education in the Constitution does not affect quality or educational outcomes.[135] "There are around 400,000 schools in Pakistan. Yet in some years, half of the Supreme Court judges and members of the federal cabinet come from just one school: Aitchison College in Lahore. Karachi Grammar School provides an inordinate number of top professionals and the richest businessmen. If we add three American schools, Cadet College Hasanabdal, and a few expensive schools, which may be graduating 10,000 kids in total, we can be sure that these few kids will be at the top of most fields in Pakistan in the future, just as their fathers are at the very top today".[136]

Some empirics[137] on educational attainment over three generations in rural Punjab, the largest province of Pakistan, show that the class differences institutionalized at the time of colonial village settlement led to sustained divergence in the rate of intergenerational educational mobility, with little mobility for nonproprietary and marginalized groups compared to proprietary groups. The inter-class differences in educational attainment are so sharp that the current generation of marginalized households seems to have fallen a generation behind in terms of educational attainment despite being residents of the villages where proprietary households also reside. Education and health care services are strong weapons against inequality. According to a report by Oxfam, these public services reduce the impact of skewed income distribution and put "virtual incomes" in the pockets of the poorest of the poor in society. Estimates[138] suggest that for the poorest 20% of families in Pakistan, sending all children to a low-cost private school would cost approximately 17% of their household incomes. The quality of such services is also crucial to reduce the effects of unfair income distribution. For example, if the public schools lag behind the privately run schools in quality, children with low-quality education would be unable to compete in the labor market. And in this way, public services, even if free, would fail to make the desired impact on inequality.

"Inequality is neither economic nor technological; it is ideological and political. --- These choices are shaped by each society's conception of social justice and economic fairness and by the relative political and ideological power of contending groups and discourses. Importantly, this relative power is not exclusively material; it is also intellectual and ideological",[139] writes Piketty. Moreover, inequality is not inevitable. It is not predetermined. It is a result of policies, preferences, choices, and power interplay within a society and, hence, can be tackled by altering social and economic structures of the society like through allocation of land and productive assets.

CHAPTER 7

Misallocation of Land

Zekiye Eglar, a Georgian anthropologist, wrote her dissertation on "*Vartan Bhanji: Institutionalized Reciprocity in a Changing Punjabi Village*" in 1958 to earn a Ph.D. degree from Columbia University. This dissertation was published by Columbia University. Later on, Eglar worked on the sequel, "*The Economic Life of a Punjabi Village*," at Harvard. Her dissertation as well as her work at Harvard was posthumously published in 2010 in the form of a book by Oxford University Press. Elgar's research is a field study on socio-economic relations in rural Pakistan. Her analysis, particularly with regard to the power of land, still holds.

She wrote: "Land is the central point around which the life of the village is organized. For the villagers, land is of both economic and social importance. It is both a source of income and the basis on which village society is divided into two distinct groups: owners and non-owners. Owners as a group enjoy a higher social status than non-owners".[1] In another place, she writes, while commenting on the nexus of land and prestige, that exclusive ownership of land has given the landowners as a group a superior social position compared to non-owners. And among the landowners themselves, the size of their landholdings is the basis of their relative position on the ladder of social prestige. A large landowner enjoys more power, prestige, and influence than a small landowner.[2]

J. Nasir, *Development Challenges of Pakistan*,
https://doi.org/10.1007/978-981-97-3064-3_7

After about 35 years of above assessment of the socio-economic power of the land, Bina Agarwal wrote: "Land has been and continues to be the most significant form of property in rural South Asia. It is a critical determinant of economic well-being, social status, and political power".[3] Empirics show that initial inequality in land distribution is strongly but negatively correlated with long-run economic growth.[4] Land inequality is also deeply associated with political and social inequality.[5] It means that a big dent in poverty and inequality is possible by altering existing structures of land distribution and ownership. The narrative that parceling out land into small farms through redistribution or land reforms will reduce productivity due to diseconomies of scale is hotly disputed in the light of empirical research. The ensuing discussion on the relationship between the size of farm and productivity shall clarify the point.

Size-Efficiency Relation

Small is efficient. This assertion was first forcefully made by Amartya Sen in 1962 when, based on data on Indian agriculture, he found out that the relationship between size of farm and productivity had an inverse relationship. He raised the following points[6]: (a) On average, productivity per acre decreases with the size of the landholding that is there is an inverse relationship between the size of landholding and productivity; (b) The total amount of family labor used per acre goes up remarkably as the size falls that is the total amount of labor is inversely correlated with the size of the farm. The assumption of Sen was that the marginal product of labor (MPL) was below the market wage rate on small farms due to relative abundance of family labor, so impliedly variations in labor input explained the inverse relationship between the size of the farm and productivity.

The small farms used family labor whereas the large farms employed relatively greater proportion of wage-paid labor. Cultivation on small farms is done to the point where MPL is zero or at least below the prevalent wage rate while on large farms cultivation is done to the point where marginal product is equal to the wage rate. "The practice of imputing the market wage rate to family labor in peasant farming used in Indian official publications, which show a considerable part of Indian peasant agriculture having losses seems to be based on confusion of concepts", Sen wrote.[7]

Some other explanations were also put forward with regard to the determinants of farm size and efficiency. One explanation is based on agency problem. The agricultural work generally resists supervision. In agriculture, laborers are not working on industrial machines in a factory. People in agriculture work at a distance from one another which makes supervision of agricultural labor difficult. On the contrary, small farms do not use hired labor; rather, family members work in the fields.

Another explanation lies in the variation in the quality of the land. It is argued that the proportion of irrigated land or better quality land decreases as the size of the landholding increases and that labor and other inputs also decrease as farm size increases.[8] Similar thoughts resonate in other investigations as well. For example, G. R. Saini has argued that Indian agriculture is characterized by constant returns to scale and variations in productivity per acre as farm size changes are due to the level of inputs associated with farm size and that the higher output of smaller farms is a function of higher inputs of labor.[9] With a slight variation of assumptions, it has been argued somewhere else that even if there is no variation in the quality of land cultivated by small and big farmers, it is still more optimal for a small farmer to use more inputs per hectare and get more yield under a situation of uncertainty relating to yield per hectare due to the vagaries of weather.[10]

Even if there are some disadvantages of being small, those are due to the non-availability of better technology, quality inputs, and credit to smallholders. A minimum amount of land is at least required to make optimum use of tractors, harvesters, et cetera. Some of the disadvantages that may enter the world of small farms compared to big farms are at the post-harvest and marketing stages. And these all are disadvantages of the scale effect in the case of small farms that can be mitigated through pro-small farm public policies and institutional interventions.

The farm size-efficiency relationship has also been investigated in Pakistan. Results are not consistent. The results of a study[11] undertaken in 1979 suggest a positive relationship between farm size and productivity. According to the findings of the said study, large farms (over 25 acres) were 9% more productive than small farms. This study suggests that the explanation of the positive relationship lies in the more efficient use of hired labor and tractors (a greater use of non-traditional inputs) on large farms. The positive relationship across farm sizes also implies that Pakistani agriculture appears to have higher capital and labor substitution possibilities. The sample of this study consisted of 732 farms, all irrigated, which, by virtue of just being irrigated are more likely to have made intensive use of capital like seeds and fertilizer as water facilitates use of such inputs. So an element of bias cannot be ruled out as regards the findings of this study.

Another study[12] was conducted in 1981 based on sample from 19 districts of the Punjab province. The results of this investigation suggested U-shaped relationship between farm size and productivity. The agricultural productivity was high on small farms due to intensive use of labor and irrigated water and on bigger farms it was due to capital-intensive inputs. The middle-level farms were relatively inefficient due to sub-optimal use of inputs as per findings of this investigation. Interestingly, some researchers[13] also came up with similar findings in the case of farms in the center-west of Brazil and concluded that the relationship between farm size and productivity is non-linear and that access to institutions, credit, and modern inputs are important determinants of variation in productivity.

Another investigation[14] undertaken in Pakistan in the 1970s to test the inverse farm size productivity hypothesis in the wake of the 'Green Revolution' precludes the possibility of a positive relationship. According to this study, the explanation for the validity of the inverse relationship lies in higher labor input, more intensive land use, a higher rate of adoption of HYVs, and a greater irrigated area for small farmers compared to large ones. The study posits that green revolution technology in Pakistan was scale-neutral in its effects on various classes of farmers. The results of another study[15] undertaken in 2012 based on a sample of 302 farms from six districts of central Punjab also confirmed the validity of the inverse farm size and productivity relationship.

There is a valid economic case for pro-small farm policy as analysis of various investigations, which cover almost all the phases of the Green Revolution that is prior to its onset, during its currency, and related to the period of its aftermath, on farm size and productivity relationships suggests. Further, experience of small farming, on a philosophical level, can be more rewarding in terms of job satisfaction compared to monotonous assembly-line repetitive tasks in big manufacturing industries. "The basic aim of modern industrialism is not to make work satisfying but to raise productivity; its proudest achievement is laborsaving whereby labor is stamped with the mark of undesirability. But what is undesirable cannot offer dignity so the working life of a laborer is a life without dignity", wrote economist E. F. Schumacher.[16]

Moreover, small farms require few economic incentives for expanding production as they have a great capacity for self-exploitation. On the contrary, big farms require costly investments and incentives to achieve the same results. Besides the efficiency argument, focusing on small farms is also desirable from the considerations of poverty alleviation and equity given the rampancy of poverty and inequality in rural areas.

Countries that introduced agrarian reforms on time had two clear advantages. First, they were able to put the country on a trajectory of equitable growth and second, they pushed through reforms for fundamental changes in the socio-economic structures comparatively easily due to lack of resistance from landowners (who are considered the protectors of the status quo). And both of these factors created a loop of positive change in society for rapid economic development. For example, the rise of South Korea and Taiwan as Asian Tigers was made possible, among other factors, due to agrarian reforms with a greater focus on 'peasant farming', which helped stimulate sustainable economic growth. Compared to other regions like Latin America, East Asian countries undertook agrarian reforms that helped them industrialize, ensure political stability, introduce reforms without much resistance from landowners, accelerate the structural transformation process, and promote equitable economic growth.[17]

In Pakistan, big landowners remained the focus instead of 'peasants' and small farmers. The landowners blocked or delayed any sort of reform, not only with regard to the redistribution of land ownership and the land tenure system but also in other socio-economic reforms for changing the old-age power-oriented structures of the society. Changes in agriculture under the Green Revolution increased per acre yield and a substantial amount of land was brought under cultivation but these changes mainly strengthened the politico-economic power of the big landholders. The small farmers did not benefit much. The 'Green Revolution' created both gainers and losers.

Gainers and Losers

The agricultural performance of Pakistan in the 1960s was hailed loud and clear. "The government and the people of Pakistan should be saluted for the results which are unprecedented among the developing countries of the world----now the battle for manifold production is over---West Pakistan has provided a model for the hungry nations of the world".[18] Performance was impressive. There's no doubt about it. The gains, however, mostly accrued to the large farms and were concentrated in the provinces of Punjab and Sindh. Growth was not inclusive. The rising tide did not lift all the boats. The majority was left out. After all, it was not the 'French Revolution'; it was not the 'Glorious Revolution' either. It was not even an all-embracing strategy or scheme formulated after due deliberations by the policy-makers. The Green Revolution was simply the cumulative result of a number of independent developments in the agriculture sector, to which big landlords who possessed resources responded favorably due to the opportunities these developments offered for an increase in their income.[19]

If it was a strategy at all, it was an elite farmer strategy, which increased income and wealth disparities between different strata of the rural population and created regional disparities. Increase in the incomes of the big farmers boosted demand which in turn generated inflationary pressures, resulting in the erosion of the real incomes of the small farmers, landless people, and rural labor.

The 'Green Revolution' thus 'increased prosperity for the few, but impoverished the most'. "If such complex secondary effects (that is inflation) of the 'Green Revolution' are taken into account, it is not surprising that it was in 1968, the year in which the biggest harvests had ever been reaped, that the entire country and countryside erupted with popular discontent on a scale that was unknown",[20] writes Hamza Alvi.

The uneven impact of the Green Revolution was due to underlying differences in the socio-economic structures of society. Agricultural productivity differed among various regions depending on factors like availability of water and natural conditions. The areas with a good amount of water availability benefited more from the Green Revolution than the rain-fed areas. The Green Revolution not only deepened inter-regional or inter-district disparities of wealth and income, but it also sharpened disparities among the people living in the same region or district due to eviction of sharecroppers and tenants.

In many instances, small farmers were pushed into 'indebtedness' due to diminished incomes and had to sell their land. The policies adopted for agricultural development in the 1960s for subsidizing tractors, tube wells, fertilizers, pesticides, and seeds practically benefited the big farmers, though in theory these benefits were available to all farmers.[21] The small farmers, the tenant farmers, and the landless labor force, which constituted the majority of the rural population, were left out of the blessings of the Green Revolution.[22]

Production increased but poverty remained widespread. A correlation between agricultural production and poverty reduction in rural areas did not emerge mainly due to the skewed distribution of land and earnings from land. If one does not possess land or an agriculture farm, how could he directly benefit from growth in the crop sector?[23] Rural non-farm economies could have become vehicles for poverty alleviation for small and landless rural dwellers but that failed to grab policy attention. No strategy for the small farmers or those evicted due to mechanization was put in place. The policy vacuum is still persisting. A comparative data analysis of the Agricultural Census of 1972 and that of 2010 reveals several interesting results as follows.

(a) The number of small (less than 12.5 acres) farms has substantially increased. In 1972, 68% farms (2.6 million) fell in the category of small farms and as per census of 2010 around 89% (7.4 million) farms are small farms, though there is substantial increase in the cultivated area of the small farms which increased from around 13.87 million acres to 23.49 million acres; (b) The medium-sized farms (12.5 to less than 50 acres and 25 acres to less than 50 acres) have reduced both in terms of number and cultivated area; (c) The farms having size of 50 acres to less than 150 acres have witnessed decrease both in number, farm area, and cultivated area; (d) There is decrease in number of farms and cultivated area in case of large farms (150 acres and above) but farm area has increased in this category of farms contrary to all other categories (except small farms); (e) The cultivated area as percentage of farm area shows an inverse relationship that is cultivated area in percentage terms decreases as the size of farm increases. For example, in the case of small farms, around 92% to 93% of the farm area is under cultivation whereas it decreases to just 26% in the case of large farms with a size of 150 acres and above (see Table 7.1).

The small farmers are cultivating above 90% of the farm area whereas medium-sized landholders (25 to 50 acres) and those above medium-sized (50 to 150 acres) are respectively cultivating above 80% and 70% of the farm area. The large landholders (above 150 acres of land) are cultivating just 26% of the farm area and as such around three-fourths of the area is not under cultivation. An analysis of large farms (150 acres and above) along time lines reveals some other interesting trends as well.

In 1972, the farm area of the large farms was 4.48 million acres while the cultivated area was 2.07 million acres (46% of the farm area). As per the Agricultural Census of 1980, the farm area of large farms was

Table 7.1 Number and area of farms by size of farm (in thousand acres)

Size of farm		*Number of farms*		*Farm area*		*Cultivated area*		*Cultivated area as percentage of farm area*
		Number	*Percent*	*Number*	*Percent*	*Number*	*Percent*	
Less than 12.5 acres	1,972	2,560	68	14,900	30	13,867	34	93
	2,010	7,400	89	25,426	48	23,492	55	92
12.5 to under 25 acres	1,972	794	21	13,061	27	11,784	29	90
	2,010	561	7	9,361	18	8,270	19	88
25 to under 50 acres	1,972	289	8	9,215	19	7,736	19	84
	2,010	211	3	6,726	13	5,388	13	80
50 acres to under 150 acres	1,972	103	3	7,402	15	5,240	13	71
	2,010	79	1	5,548	10	3,940	9	71
150 acres and above	1,972	16	0	4,482	9	2,069	5	46
	2,010	13	0	5,850	11	1,534	4	26
Total	1,972	3,762	100	49,061	100	40,696	100	
	2,010	8,265	100	52,910	100	42,622	100	

Source Agriculture Census 1972 and 2010

4 million acres, out of which 2.28 million acres (57% of farm area) were under cultivation and in 1990, farm area and cultivated area increased to 4.77 million acres and 2.57 million acres (54% of farm area).

Both farm area and cultivated area of large farms decreased to 4.15 million acres and 2.17 million acres (52% of farm area) in 2000. In 2010, large farms witnessed dramatic changes. The farm area increased to 5.85 million acres whereas the cultivated area fell to 1.53 million acres (26% of the farm area), which means that there is an increase of 1.7 million acres but the cultivated area has decreased. So the decade of 2000–2010 was the period when more land was added to the large farms without a concomitant increase in cultivated area as amply clear from Table 7.1.

There may be several reasons for the huge difference between farm area and cultivated area in the case of large landholdings. The simplest explanation is that the entire land owned by large landowners may not be cultivable. Or the phenomenon of absentee landlordism is still persisting. And the large landowners have diversified their sources of income and do not care much to cultivate all the farm land. Further, economic factors alone may not explain the motivation behind the purchase and retention of large landholdings due to the close nexus of power and land. Socio-political power attached to land is thus one of the major factors for retention of large tracts of land. The British heavily relied on the landed elite for maintenance of order and effective economic accumulation in exchange for state patronage of such landlords. This unholy alliance of the landlords and the state has persisted in Pakistan (particularly Punjab and Sindh) even after independence due to path dependence. The critical junctures for abolishing landlordism and putting society on the trajectory of an equitable and progressive trajectory were missed due to the deep nexus between the ruling elite and big landholders.[24]

Inefficient use of large landholdings is also confirmed by many investigations pointing toward an inverse relationship between productivity and farm size; hence, we have a valid case for redistribution of land on efficiency grounds in Pakistan. Redistribution is also desirable from the perspective of equity as the ownership of land opens up several channels for the poor to participate in economic activities. They can use land as collateral for better financial services like credit and insurance. The redistribution of land enables the beneficiaries to educate their children and thus escape poverty. Successful land reforms facilitate the transition of a society from an "agriculture-based state of poverty" to a "human-capital-based developed economy".[25] Efforts at land reforms in Pakistan remained ineffective in bringing about some transformative change in the agrarian landscape of the country.

Half-Hearted Land Reforms

The All India Muslim League committed for agrarian reforms before the creation of Pakistan. The "Memorandum on Economic Development"[26] of 1944 of the All India Muslim League outlined a commitment to a more equitable rural economy. The Tenancy Legislation Committee, formed by the Sindh Provincial Assembly in 1943 in response to pressure exerted by the Sindh Hari Committee (formed in 1930) to examine the problems and grievances of the haris, gave its report in 1945. It recommended that permanent heritable tenancy rights be given to the haris with certain conditions. It also recommended for encouragement of cash rents instead of batai share.[27] No action was, however, taken on the recommendations of the committee.

The Sindh Hari Committee kept on mounting pressure, compelling the Sindh Government to appoint the Hari Enquiry Committee in March 1947 with the mandate to 'examine all the alleged grievances of haris, whether express or implicit'. This committee gave a report that was retrogressive in nature. It proposed for the continuation of the batai system, a recommendation contrary to what the earlier committee had emphasized. It also recommended that haris need not be granted permanent tenure rights. This report, in a sense, held to a large extent the haris responsible for their woes.

Masud Khaddarposh, a bureaucrat having leftist leanings, however, gave his famous 'Minute of Dissent'[28] to the majority report. He dwelt at length on the deplorable conditions of the haris and the injustices committed by the landlords. He wrote about haris and zamindars as "two extremes of mankind: one lives in the height of depravity and misery, the other in the height of luxury and extravagance". Mr. Masud deplored that the present system of Zamindari was incompatible with the very concept of freedom and created poverty and pauperism.

The solution to the hari problem, according to Mr. Masud, was a complete switch-over from the existing land tenure system to a system of peasant proprietorship. He gave the following specific recommendations: (1) abolition of existing land tenure system, particularly the batai practices; (2) expropriation of land from the landlords and its distribution among the tenants to establish a system of peasant proprietorship; (3) The possession of land should depend on its use or cultivation. The ultimate ownership of the land should be vested in the state. Mr. Masud's note of dissent was a voice of sanity when the majority of the committee members had badly failed to appreciate the Hari problem. The proposals were also put on the backburner by the Sindh government like the recommendations of the earlier committee.

From the above-mentioned reports and the memorandum of the All India Muslim League, it becomes very clear that thinking for land reforms existed very much before the creation of Pakistan but nothing tangible was done. Pakistan inherited an inequitable and unproductive land tenure system. It was not only unjust given the asymmetry of relations between the landlord and the tenant but was also economically inefficient as it hardly offered incentives to the tenants and the landlord to enhance the productivity of the agricultural land. The creation of Pakistan increased the power of the landlords but, at the same time, the elite felt pressure for land reforms to gain political legitimacy in the new state as they could no longer shift the blame for landlessness and misery among the common people to the British or Hindu money-lenders.

So, immediately after partition, the 'Agrarian Committee of the Muslim League' prepared a report on land reforms in 1949 which, inter alia recommended[29]: (a) immediate abolition and cessation of all Jagirs and Inams (rewards) without compensation. (b) resumption of all grants of land made by the British Government in lieu of services, irrespective of the point in time when such grants were made. (c) grant of full proprietary rights to the occupancy tenants. (d) Security of tenure to the tenants-at-will who formed the majority of the tillers of the soil and the producers of the agricultural wealth. (e) limitation of area for self-cultivation (*khudkashat*) to 25 acres for a certain period of time.

The recommendations of the committee were really 'revolutionary' in nature. No action was, however, taken to implement its recommendations. Had those been adopted, the socio-economic and political landscape of Pakistan would have been, in all probability, entirely different. On October 31, 1958, the Chief Martial Law Administrator appointed a Land Reforms Commission, composed of seven members (all civil servants), to 'consider problems relating to the ownership and tenancy of agricultural land and to recommend measures for ensuring better production and social justice as well as security of tenure for those engaged in cultivation'.

The commission recommended a ceiling on individual holdings equivalent to 500 acres of irrigated land, 1000 acres of unirrigated land, or an aggregate area worth 36,000 PIUs, whichever was greater. The ceiling was too liberal and a retrogression from the report of the Agrarian Committee which had recommended a ceiling of 150 acres of average irrigated land, 300 acres of semi-irrigated land, and 450 acres of barani land as the maximum ceiling for private ownership.

Ghulam Ishaque Khan, one of the members, disagreed with the ceiling of 500 acres of irrigated land recommended by the commission. He was of the view that concentration of land in a few hands meant denial of opportunity to the majority for social mobility with the result that economic growth stagnates, social progress is hampered, and society remains 'indefinitely stratified'. "In a situation where there is no part of the soil which the 'have-nots' can or even hope to call as their own at some future date, they tend to lose their sense of citizenship as 'Sons of the soil' and as useful partners in national struggle for growth and progress",[30] he wrote.

Besides high ceilings on land, some other liberal exemptions were also recommended like exemption of 10 acres to orchards. The majority of the recommendations of the commission were adopted in 1959. The land reforms of 1959, however, failed to make a tangible impact on the agrarian structure. A large proportion of the declared area of the affected landlords was retained by them, thanks to the allowances and exemptions on intra-family transfers. Around 66% of the resumed land was retained at the national level. The retained area for Punjab and Sindh was respectively 76% and 56%. The result was that only 1.9 million acres were resumed by the government, of which 55% were in the Punjab and 35% in Sind. The total resumed area in the country represented only 25% of 7.5 million acres reportedly owned by 6061 landowners with individual holdings of over 500 acres.[31]

The land reforms were such that at the end of the day, the landowners actually gained. Most of the landlords surrendered the uncultivable land. Up to 1967, the government had paid the landlords about Rs. 89.2 million to a few landowners for nearly two million acres of land surrendered by them. Besides the very liberal provisions of the Regulation favoring landlords, there were implementation issues as well. The landlords had always enjoyed much influence in the traditional revenue system (the system revolves around the patwari), but there was no organization to protect the interests of the landless, tenants, and small landholders.

The Report of the Land Reform Commission published in 1968 acknowledged the wrongs of the implementation of the 1959 Regulation. According to the said report, instances came to light during the sale of land to landless tenants where the sale of land to existing tenants was subsequently cancelled on the ground that tenants were not willing to purchase the land. The inquiries into such instances, however, revealed that the tenants had not in fact refused to purchase the land, but the interested landlords got such sales cancelled through the local revenue officers.[32]

Ayesha Jalal in '*The State of Martial Rule*' even doubts the very motivation and intention behind the Land Reforms of 1959. She writes: "The land reforms of 1959 were, on the face of it, intended to break the hold of the landed gentry in West Pakistan. But in actual fact they were aimed at ingratiating the regime with middle-sized landlords, many of whom were ex-military and civil officials. A large part of the resumed land was handed over to military and civil officials at throwaway prices. Hundreds of thousands of acres of newly irrigated land in Sindh and sizeable plots of land in the urban areas were parcelled out to both military and civil officials-Punjabis in the main. Since there was nothing to prevent them reselling the land at fantastic prices in the open market".[33] The Land Reforms of 1959, in short, failed to reduce the feudal stranglehold over the agrarian landscape of Pakistan.

The second reform law of 1972, which repealed an earlier law, lowered the ceiling of individual landholding to 150 acres of irrigated or 300 acres of unirrigated land or an aggregate area worth 12,000 PIUs, whichever was greater, with an additional allowance of 2000 PIUs for a tube well or a tractor. The limits on individual landholdings were further reduced to 100 acres of irrigated or 200 acres of unirrigated land or an aggregate area equivalent to 8000 PIUs of land, whichever was greater with a compensation of Rs. 30 per PIU to the owners of the resumed land.

The Land Reforms of 1972 too failed to make a dent in the agrarian structure of Pakistan. Landlords surrendered waste land as the law provided that they had the option to retain the best land. The tenants felt insecure, and evictions were high. The tenants were unable to make the waste land allotted to them cultivable due to a lack of accessibility to inputs like seeds, fertilizer, tractors, et cetera.

The Land Reforms Act, 1977 (Act II of 1977) was promulgated on January 9, 1977. According to said piece of legislation, the ceiling was fixed at 8000 PIUs or 100 acres of irrigated land or 200 acres of unirrigated land that is two-thirds of the ceiling allowed in the 1972 Land Reforms Act. The land owners were to be paid compensation at the rate of Rs. 30 per PIU in bonds, heritable and transferable. This Act was just an act on paper.

In brief, Pakistan introduced three land redistribution reforms since 1947[34] viz., the West Pakistan Land Reforms Regulation, 59/64, the Land Reforms Regulation, 1972, and the Land Reforms Act, 1977. "The end result of these land reforms is that they did not succeed in significantly changing the status quo in rural Pakistan. The unfinished agenda of land reforms still remains large and challenging".[35] As a result of the Land Reforms of 1972 and 1977, just 1.76% of the farm area was distributed. Overall, just 6.10% of the farm area was distributed as a result of all land reforms undertaken in Pakistan since its creation (see Table 7.2).

Table 7.2 Resumed and distributed lands under land reforms (in thousand acres)

Province	*Reforms*	*Land resumed*	*Land distributed*	*No. of beneficiaries*	*Land under litigation*	*Un-allotable land*	*Balance*
	1959	1286.79	1167.16	89.90	32.60	20.43	66.60
Punjab	1972	262.39	213.31	33.99	27.62	3.84	17.62
	1977	118.94	87.83	14.14	12.68	1.58	16.86
Total		1668.12	1468.30	138.02	72.90	25.85	101.07
	1959	835.48	819.21	42.72	4.41	10.83	1.03
Sindh	1972	265.40	231.36	15.40	8.88	24.63	0.54
	1977	31.46	26.84	2.61	4.11	0.08	0.44
Total		1132.34	1077.41	60.73	17.39	35.54	2.00
	1959	131.63	131.45	6.22		0.18	
Balochistan	1972	404.27	212.71	8.88	45.20	0.11	146.26
	1977	19.75	14.10	1.43		0.06	5.60
Total		555.66	358.25	16.54	45.20	0.34	151.86
	1959	231.39	176.70	25.88	36.62	7.86	10.21
NWFP*	1972	157.41	133.60	14.49	10.53	9.47	3.81
	1977	22.26	16.19	3.23		4.54	1.53
Total		411.05	326.48	43.60	47.16	21.87	15.54
Grand Total		3767.16	3230.44	258.88	182.65	83.60	270.48
Distributed land (percentage of farm area)						1959	4.33
						1972	1.49
						1977	**0.27**
Total distributed land (percentage of farm area)						6.10	

Note Land farm area as per Agriculture Census 2010 is 52,910,408 acres while total allotted area is 3,230,441 under all three reforms which constitutes 6.10% of the total farm area. *Khyber Pakhtunkhwa (KPK)
Source Year Book of Cabinet Division 2007–2008, Government of Pakistan

But the question is: what went wrong? There were multiple factors responsible for the failure of land reforms to introduce some fundamental change in the agrarian structure of rural Pakistan. First, the ceilings imposed on individual landholdings were many times larger than the average landholdings in Pakistan or the official subsistence level of 12 acres per household. Further, many caveats and loopholes were included in the regulations in the form of exemptions (for example for orchards in the 1959 reforms) and provisions for gift transfers to family members.

Second, there was a strong nexus between the landlords and the revenue officials. The landlords managed to minimize the impact of reforms through the exploitation of loopholes in the regulations and 'outright falsification of documents and measurements'. Third, a significant amount of land resumed through reforms was barren and uncultivable. For example, 67% of the land resumed under the 1959 reforms in the province of Punjab was just from two districts, Dera Ghazi Khan and Mianwalli, both least developed in agriculture.[36]

Despite all failures, some action and thinking existed that land reforms were required to change the agrarian landscape of Pakistan but the forces of the status quo then reacted with full vengeance. A number of provisions of both the Land Reforms Regulation 1972 and the Land Reforms Act, 1977 were challenged in the Federal Shariat Court which held the provisions of law inconsistent with the injunctions of Islam. The Shariat Appellate Bench of the Supreme Court also upheld the decision of the Federal Shariat Court. Briefly speaking, both the said fora, in a nutshell, decided that[37]: (1) religious *waqaf* land[38] cannot be resumed by the state; (2) Inherited land[39] cannot be resumed; (3) compensation of the resumed land be paid at market price[40]; (4) resumption of land cannot be made retrospectively. The said judgments for all practical purposes rendered the initiatives of the land redistribution into nullity.

Some half-hearted attempts have been made since 1990 by the Federal Land Commission (FLC)[41] to bring a new piece of legislation in the light of the judgments of the Shariat Court and Shariat Appellate Bench but the same did not materialize due to the influence of the landed elite in the Parliament. None of the governments, democratic or military, showed the courage to introduce fresh legislation for land redistribution due to fear of losing the political support of the landlords, who mainly make their way to Parliament from rural areas. The empirics[42] suggest otherwise. The political dividends of land redistribution are massive and the political party introducing such reforms enjoys voters' gratitude for a long time.

For instance, the Italian land reforms of 1951 are a case in point. In the aftermath of World War II, the Christian Democratic Party of Italy initiated massive land expropriation from landowners and redistributed it among rural workers. The electoral benefits of said land redistribution persisted for a long time and are still persisting, as the voters in the town where reforms were introduced favor the Christian Democratic Party agenda and its candidates. Another area connected to land reforms is the sub-optimal use of state land. The state land was allocated in Pakistan to those who are already privileged without considering the principles of efficiency and equity.

Land Conferrals

The policy of allotment of state land to the elite shows a path of dependence. The British used allotment of lands to their loyalists in lieu of 'services rendered'. The allotment of agricultural land to serving and retired army personnel is also rooted in the legacy of the British Raj. They granted agricultural land to military men in the Province of Punjab to induce them to join the army. Land was allotted to the non-military men as well for helping the British in army recruitment. Large land-owning families like the Noons, Tiwanas, Daultanas, and Mamdots who had allied with the British in the 1857 war or in the Sikh uprisings were granted big tracts of land and private canals in the canal colonies of Punjab.

The allotment of land by the British was not based on the principles of efficiency or equity. Despite enormous potential, the political and economic interests of the British did not let the agrarian structure of Punjab transform into a structure more conducive to technical change. A large proportion of land was allocated for military horse breeding. In a sense, the British government privatized the promotion of technical change as it rather than investing in and demonstrating new inputs and techniques, gave land grants conditional on the introduction of new seeds, inputs, et cetera to private farms and this policy failed due to a lack of clear direction for change.[43] After independence, the same practice has persisted.

Allotment of state land is considered a reward for the 'services rendered'. It was on this premise that state land was allotted to ex-Army men in different parts of the country. In response to a question, the provincial Assembly of Punjab was informed in January 1988 that the Punjab Government allotted about 450,000 acres of land to 5538 military personnel in a span of 8 years that is from 1977 to 1985.[44] Interestingly, the land distributed in pursuance of the Land Reforms Act, 1972, which remained in the field till almost 1990, was 142,226 acres, less than one-third of the state land allotted to ex-Army men.

Professor Rizvi, highlighting the context of land conferrals to Army officers in Pakistan, writes in '*Military, State, and Society in Pakistan*' as follows. "Land in the Thal desert under the colonization scheme of the Punjab government was given to the military for settling ex-servicemen families. Similarly, land was given to service personnel in various schemes in different barrage areas in Sindh and Punjab that is Ghulam Mohammad, Gudu, and Taunsa. The government gave land in Campbellpur, Jhelum, Kohat, Rawalpindi and Hazara districts to local ex-servicemen who developed this with the help of the Army. Land was also allotted to them along India-Pakistan border in the Punjab. Agricultural land was also awarded for gallantry".[45] Professor Rizvi further writes that plots of land for the construction of houses in cantonments and urban centers and commercial plots were among some other material rewards given to the Army officers during the Zia period. "A large number of officers got more than one plot at cheap rates, which they sold to civilians at exorbitant rates. In June 1982, the Armed Forces Housing Scheme was launched to provide houses for retiring officers at a cost to be paid in easy instalments. The first project was completed in early 1984".[46]

The data on the allotment of state land to Army men is not publicly available but one thing is certain that distribution of the state land in Pakistan does not meet the touchstone of equity. Allocation of land on the principle of equity has got several advantages. At least three are very obvious. First, it will help alleviate poverty in rural areas. Second, doing so will spur economic growth. Third, it shall contribute in the evolution of an equitable society. Giving away state land to those who are already well placed in society makes resource distribution more skewed and deepens inequality. On the other hand, distribution of land to the landless shall give voice and power to them as "greater wealth increases the ability of the poor to directly participate in the political process".[47]

The allotment of plots and agricultural land is a big source of rent-seeking. Ironically, such allotments have no legal or constitutional backing, besides having no case on equity and economic efficiency grounds as well. The Supreme Court of Pakistan in its judgment of 2021, dealt with the legal and constitutional aspects of allotment of plots and land to the members of the Armed Forces, senior Judges, and civil servants at great length. The Supreme Court of Pakistan, while dilating upon the precedents on land conferrals, observed the following.[48]

> The judiciary and the armed forces of Pakistan are patterned on the British model. Land is not given away to judges and to the members of the armed forces in Britain, in the United States of America nor in any commonwealth country, with the singular exception of Pakistan. At the time when subcontinent was captured and ruled by the East India Company, and later when it came under the direct rule of the British Crown, British officers, soldiers and judges, whether deployed in the subcontinent or serving at home, were not conferred land. Sometimes a portion of captured property was distributed amongst officers and soldiers as prizes, but it was made clear that this was not by way of entitlement. ----------- When a portion of captured property was distributed amongst officers and soldiers it was done pursuant to a legal enactment. The land distributed amongst the officers of the armed forces of Pakistan is not captured land nor did Parliament authorize its distribution. Those who serve the judiciary and in the armed

> forces of Pakistan receive a salary for their services and receive a pension on their retirement; they do not serve in the expectation of receiving land from the state.

The apex court has also observed that land conferrals are pertinent manifestations of elite capture. Had the land been sold at market price, Pakistan would have escaped the indebtedness, and the way land is distributed 'impoverishes and marginalizes the poor further'.[49] The judges and officers of the armed forces who receive land in prized urban areas invariably do not build a house for themselves to live in and those who get agricultural land do not cultivate it. They sell it in the open market and become absentee landlords.[50]

The apex court has also warned about the grave consequences of granting land or benefits to those holding official positions. Doing so creates a 'prebendal order' where the strong exploit and abuse the weak and once prebendalism is set in motion, it becomes difficult to determine the true extent of public corruption.[51] Misallocation of land is not just restricted to agricultural land. Huge tracts of land are lying as dead capital in urban areas, which if put to productive use can unleash huge opportunities for economic growth and employment generation.

Huge Dead Capital

A huge growth potential is lying dormant in the government-owned buildings located in the centers of the cities due to sub-optimal use of the land covered by these buildings. According to Nadeem Ul Haque,[52] who has worked as the Deputy Chairman of the Planning Commission of Pakistan, the public sector in Lahore (capital of the Punjab province) alone holds more than 10,000 acres of prime commercial land, out of which five government officer residences (GORs) occupy 4000 acres. Thirty-five high-rise mixed-use buildings, with huge possibilities for economic growth and employment (estimated at 350,000–500,000 during construction), can be carved out of this land. Governor Houses (around 10 in number that occupy city center space), if put to commercial use, are expected to generate one billion dollars and around 3000 jobs. Similarly, public sector training institutions like NSPP, Civil Services Academy, and NIPA located at the Mall Road of Lahore occupy very precious land and can be put to commercial use with enormous possibilities for investment and employment. Similarly huge dead capital is lying in other big cities of Pakistan.

Land is a big source of rent-seeking. "Much of the rent-seeking that occurred in Pakistan is tied to the regime of land ownership and land management. The elite operate like a mafia and resist change in land management. Cumbersome zoning laws help them continue to accumulate wealth".[53] Housing stock on average lasts 20–30 years, and zoning needs renewal every generation. The areas that were suburbs, say, two decades ago, have now become commercial hubs, generating large valuation gains. New zoning laws, the sale of government buildings like GORs Governor Houses, et cetera, and the construction of high-rise buildings in their place can unlock the dormant potential of these places through the process of creative destruction.

There are cases where state land was leased out for the benefit of the elite at the throwaway prices. Two instances will illustrate the point. According to the report of the Auditor General of Pakistan for the year 2019–2020,[54] Karachi Port Trust (KPT), in Karachi, allotted land on lease to the Defence Housing Authority (DHA), KPT Housing Society, and KPT Officers Cooperative Housing Society Limited for 99 years at the nominal price ranging between 0.10 and 0.18 rupees per square feet. The second example is from Lahore, where the government of Punjab leased land measuring over 1030 kanals for 50 years (from 2000 to 2050) to the gymkhana club at a token rent of Rs. 5000 (for just US$15).

Both examples, besides pointing toward gross misallocation of land, also vindicate the point that, due to elite capture, the state is subsidizing the rich. And preferential allocation of land at subsidized rates is an important mechanism for rent-seeking by the elite in Pakistan. The irony is that these clubs are meant for the tiny rich and elite to play polo and golf. Dr. Ishrat Husain echoes similar views as those of Mr. Haque while writing about the elitist nature of the economy of Pakistan.

He writes: "The most common source of the origin of wealth of all classes of elites in Pakistan is through acquisition of state land by military officers, bureaucrats, business tycoons, feudal landlords, and real estate speculators below market prices, and getting these housing societies and estates developed through the public exchequer, securing all public utilities on priority basis as they themselves are dispensers of these scarce allocations, and then disposing them off at prevailing market prices. The multiples between the acquisition cost and sale proceeds runs into

1:100 depending upon the city, location, and years the plot or property is held".[55]

In short, there is no case for distribution of the state land for 'services rendered' on efficiency, equity, or legal grounds. And the use of prime land for government officers' residences or offices is an egregious waste of productive resources. Privileged access to land by the civil or military bureaucracies and the practice of doling out state land as gift need to be abolished. Such land can be put to the best alternative uses for enhancing economic growth and creation of wealth. Besides optimum allocation of land, security of property rights is another area which is said to have deep nexus with economic growth. The literature on development guides us that property rights affect economic activity or growth through various channels. The simple rationale behind the security of property rights is that property embodies the fruit of hard work and if your earnings are not secure (expropriation risk), you are not incentivized to work. The expropriation risk generally refers to the vertical view of the security of property rights, thereby meaning that danger of expropriation of property is from the state. The horizontal view on property rights often escapes the debate by the economists.

Security of Property Rights

The horizontal view simply means protection of property from fellow individuals. Your property may be grabbed by your neighbor (all neighbors may not be gentlemen!). Property may be insecure from private citizens, land mafias, and robbers. For example, one of the reports of the Transparency International mentions violations of property rights in Pakistan as follows[56]: "Land grabbing by the so-called land mafia is reportedly prolific in Pakistan, particularly in and around Islamabad, Lahore, and Karachi. In some cases, housing authorities have allegedly colluded with property developers, who employ private militias to secure the land". The report further described an incident of land grabbing by a builder with the connivance of a local politician. The land had been purchased by an individual in a government-run auction. When the individual visited the allotted land, he was greeted by a wall constructed around his plot by the land grabbers.

The institution of property rights is deeply connected to the quality of governance and legal system. If governance is weak and the state is unable to protect property rights, alternative private arrangements like private guards and gated communities emerge for the protection of property rights. The private protection of property rights, however, has some very harmful effects, as unlike state protection, protection by private agents is selective. You have to buy this protection and the probability that unprotected properties will be hit by land grabbers or bandits increases. It creates a negative externality. Demand of the mafia increases and it is in a position to extract a high price for its services.[57]

Secure and well-defined land rights that is rights to use, sell, rent, mortgage, pledge, or gift boost agricultural investment.[58] Individuals who have more secure property rights invest more in land fertility and as a consequence have substantially higher agricultural output.[59] Strengthening property rights even in slums significantly increases residential investment as slum dwellers invest more in housing renovation even if they are credit-constrained.[60] Granting property rights also alters people's beliefs. In the context of Buenos Aires, Argentina, some researchers have found that the allocation of titles to the squatter dwellers makes them more individualistic and materialist, and they are more likely to hold beliefs consistent with social capital accumulation.[61]

One important aspect of property rights is clear title. Hernando De Soto argues in detail in '*The Mystery of Capital*' that the developing countries have a lot of bricks and mortar just like developed countries, but this is dead capital as clear titles are lacking. According to De Soto, the worth of such dead capital (due to a lack of titles or clear titles) is unimaginatively high. For example, in the Philippines, 57% of city dwellers and 67% of rural dwellers live in housing, which is a dead capital. In Peru, Egypt, and Haiti, the value of dead capital is even higher.

"The poor inhabitants of these nations do have things, but they lack the process to represent their property and create capital. They have houses but not titles; crops but not deeds, businesses but not statutes of incorporation", he writes. Trillions of dollars, if not "acres of diamonds", are ready to be put to use if the mystery of transforming them from dead capital to live capital is resolved in these countries.[62] The link between land titling and economic development is much emphasized in the literature of development. Empirics[63] suggest that the allocation of clear land titles promotes investment and makes the land more productive. Clear titles not only confer transfer rights that is rights to sell, rent, mortgage, pledge, or gift, but collateralization also becomes easier.[64]

The administrative institutions tasked with deed registration or mutations in records regarding transfer of property, et cetera also matter.

Rights related to possession of title and how easily property can be transferred mainly depend on such administrative institutions. The quality of such institutions differs across countries and a great promise of improvement lies in the use of information technology.[65] The issue of land titling in Pakistan is complex. The state, in the true sense, does not guarantee the title. A buyer is required to himself investigate the seller's title, and if later on the title turns out to be defective, the buyer has to bear the responsibility himself. The state shall not compensate the buyer for the eventuality. The matter shall be settled only through litigation.[66] Land titles need to be recorded openly.

The security of property rights, however, has got a big caveat. Strong security of property rights, without questioning the allocation, may not be a justifiable proposition in all situations and at all times. The remarks of Ha-Joon Chang seem to be very pertinent in this regard. He writes: "While it is probably true that a very weak protection of property rights is bad, too strong a protection may not be good either, as it can protect obsolete technologies and outmoded organizational forms".[67]

Allocation of Property Rights

The relationship between development and the security of property rights is not necessarily linear. Land reforms in Japan, South Korea, and Taiwan violated the existing property rights of that time, but such reforms paved the way for the subsequent economic development in these countries. For example, in Taiwan, the government of the Nationalist Party expropriated tenanted-out land above a low ceiling and the low ceiling so fixed on agricultural land ownership has remained in force since then. The result was that landlords did not remain a powerful group and could not thwart efforts by the state toward modernization, development, and industrialization. The reallocation of land ownership helped keep inequality in check and induced socio-economic stability, a must for long-term economic growth.

It also had some unintended positive consequences for development. People did not invest in land to build assets; rather, investments were made in industries, businesses, and the service sector for jobs and wealth creation. A low ceiling on agricultural land ownership has remained in force ever since, ruling out or at least greatly restricting investment in land as a means of accumulating wealth.[68] Contrary to East Asian countries, agricultural land ownership is highly skewed in Pakistan. In the 1950s, the Gini coefficient of land was 0.64 which decreased to 0.55 in 1976 that is after land redistribution as a result of the land reforms of 1959 and 1972 but it is still very high.[69]

No ceiling exists on agricultural or commercial land ownership. Investment in land is the most preferred investment. A vicious circle of black money, dead capital, rent-seeking, and ever-increasing inequality is very much evident in the land market of Pakistan. The existing land ownership structures are neither efficient nor equitable. There is a valid case for revisiting these structures and confiscating land from the big landowners without compensation on several grounds. First of all, the land owned by the big landlords is not the fruit of their hard work. Rather, it was bestowed on them for the 'services' they rendered to the imperial masters. So expropriation of such land in the name of the state without compensation does not violate the principle of the security of property rights.

The argument is simple. The rationale behind all security of property rights is to protect the fruit of hard work, so people are incentivized to work and invest. The land, which is not the fruit of hard work but rather where the claim of ownership rests upon the favors of the colonial power, does not violate the rationality of the security of property rights. We know that inequality and underdevelopment are rooted in institutional structures (like sugar plantations in South America) implanted by the colonial powers, so these structures need to be revisited. The land ownership and institutional structures as they emerged from colonial times have created what Samuel Bowles calls "institutional poverty traps"[70] in Pakistan and feudal stranglehold has persisted since colonial times.

Second, appreciation in the value of land owned by big landowners was either made by the tenants or through investments by society from state revenues. The landlords were generally absentee landlords and did not work themselves to improve the land. As the income from agriculture is exempt from taxation, whatever infrastructure was developed in the form of roads, electrification, or digging of canals was either from foreign loans or from the tax money of the people of Pakistan (landlords did not contribute to taxes due to the exemption of agricultural income).

Third, uncultivated or waste land is a type of dead capital that the big landlords are holding just due to the socio-political power attached to the land. Such waste land is not contributing to economic growth, and if it is confiscated from the landlords and distributed among the landless or tenants, it can be turned into productive land with huge potential for rural economic growth. Fourth, the purchase of land from the landlords at market price as per the judgment of the Appellate Shariat Bench of the Supreme Court requires huge amounts of finances, which would not be possible for the state to pay to the landlords given the fiscal constraints. Further, funds will also be needed for making waste land productive after the confiscated land is distributed among the beneficiaries of such reforms.

Allocation of property rights (pre-redistribution stage) and security of property rights (post-redistribution stage) are two separate notions which need not be confused. The allocation of property rights is as important as security. But redetermination of the allocation of property is the hardest part of the problem. Why would those, who are beneficiaries of the existing allocation of property, disturb the status quo? And why would they amend the rules if rule-making power rests with them? For example, suppose there is a basketball match between team A and team B. And suppose players in team A are seven feet tall (the elite, the landlords, the legislators), while players of team B (the poor, the disadvantaged, the masses) hardly exceed five feet. The umpire (the state) is impartial (assumes that the existing allocation is fair), and the rules of the game are universal that is the same for the two teams and treat each player equally. What result can we expect? Certainly, the outcome of the match is predetermined. Team A shall win as the outcome is dependent on the resources they bring to the match.

So how do we remedy this situation? Simply change the rules (like lowering the height of one of the baskets to equalize the chances). But if those who are taller have to decide what the rules would be, they will not change the rules.[71] It is an undisputable fact that the principles of economic efficiency and equity, especially in developing countries, are not always overriding considerations when it comes to public policies. For example, despite all empirics that economies of scale are insignificant in agricultural production and small family-unit farms are generally more efficient production units, efficient reallocation of land is resisted by vested interests.

Socio-politico-economic power in a society determines what the rules are. The people of property and privilege set the rules of the political and economic game generally to further accumulate more property and privilege. The basic guiding principle here is that the property, which was not secured through hard work but was given as a favor by the colonial powers, may be reallocated on the principles of equity and efficiency. Similarly, reallocation of property accumulated out of rent-seeking, corruption, or embezzlement of public money does not violate the principle of the security of property rights.

Objections can be raised on the said proposition. Ideology, politics, law, and even religion is used to defend the status quo and existing property rights. After all, inequality in society is justified on the basis of said factors, which are formulated, shaped, propagated, and justified by the people of property and privilege that is the elite. "Choices are shaped by each society's conception of social justice and economic fairness and by the relative political and ideological power of contending groups and discourses. Importantly, this relative power is not exclusively material; it is also intellectual and ideological. In other words, ideas and ideologies count in history. They enable us to imagine new worlds and different types of society. Many paths are possible".[72]

What ideological justification do the owners of the land or the state have for not reallocating the land which is not the fruit of hard work? No convincing justification can perhaps be offered except the point that those who possess such property not only have political and social power but also control intellectual and ideological narratives. Optimum allocation of agricultural land through effective reforms is highly significant for unlocking the huge growth potential of the rural areas of Pakistan for prosperity and poverty alleviation.

CHAPTER 8

Constraints on Rural Growth

Over three-fifths of Pakistanis live in rural areas, out of which two-thirds live below the poverty line. The agriculture sector, the main pillar of the rural economy, contributes around one-fifth of GDP that is more than industry, and employs two-fifths of the overall labor force. Around 67% of rural women are associated with agriculture.[1] The livestock sector contributes around 58%, while the crop sector contributes 38% toward agricultural GDP. Agriculture has historically shown reasonable but erratic growth with the usual boom and bust pattern of overall economic growth in Pakistan.

The role of agriculture in poverty reduction and economic growth is well-established. Several investigations provide massive evidence of the close relationship between said variables. For instance, a study, based on cross-country data, estimates that 1% increase in agricultural yield reduced the number of poor people by 0.72% in Africa and 0.48% in Asia.[2] Another study in Indian context finds that the impact of 1% increase in agricultural yield increases the incomes of the farms by 0.4% in the short run, whereas in the long run impact is almost double when the indirect impacts like reduction in food prices and increase in wage earnings are taken into account.[3]

According to an investigation, economic growth explains around 37% of poverty reduction, while a massive 63% is explained by other factors.[4] It means that not only economic growth per se but its sources and structure

J. Nasir, *Development Challenges of Pakistan*,
https://doi.org/10.1007/978-981-97-3064-3_8

are also important for poverty reduction. Some investigations[5] do show, though a very bold assertion, that industrial growth has much less or even no effect on poverty reduction. It is quite intuitive that economic growth that enhances employment opportunities is more poverty-reducing than economic growth resulting from consumption, more capital-intensive industries, or financial services like insurance.

The poor have little capital or land, so poverty reduction is mainly to come from the use of their labor (the only capital they have!). And in this sense, poverty and employment are two sides of the same coin, which means that agriculture demands more policy focus due to its more favorable impact on poverty reduction and comparatively less unfavorable distributional impact. At least two effects of increase in agricultural productivity are easily observable with regards to poverty reduction. First, an increase in agricultural productivity is associated with higher wage rates.[6] Second, higher agricultural productivity reduces food prices through a simple demand and supply phenomenon. Increase in food prices impacts the poor the worst as a major chunk of their domestic budget is spent on food items. As a crude estimate, 50% increase in food prices induces 40% decline in the real income of the poor and roughly some level (40%) decrease in food consumption.[7]

The relationship between agriculture growth and poverty reduction is not one-to-one, thereby meaning that 1% growth in agriculture may induce more than 1% reduction in poverty. "A one percent increase in agricultural GDP per capita leads to a 1.6% increase in per capita incomes of bottom quartiles of the population."[8] Moreover, the impact of agricultural growth is not restricted to rural poverty reduction alone. Based on Chinese data for the period 1985–1996, it has been found that higher growth in agriculture reduced both rural and urban poverty, though the pro-poor effect was stronger in rural areas.[9]

Empirics also suggest that an increase in agricultural productivity is also linked to an increase in non-agricultural output. For instance, as a result of reforms in the agriculture sector in China, higher agricultural output led to quantitatively higher growth in the non-agriculture sector. One percent increase in agriculture output was associated with 1.2% increase in non-agriculture output between 1978 and 1995.[10] The effect of agricultural productivity on the non-agriculture sector generally comes through the channels of rural savings and increased spending on goods and services. An increase in agricultural productivity reduces poverty through its impact on real household incomes (via employment generation), rural non-farm multiplier effects, and food price effects.

Focus on agriculture is also important from the gender perspective. In Pakistan and India respectively 64% and 53.6% of female workforce is employed in agriculture whereas South Korea and Malaysia respectively employ 4.5% and 6%. It means that focus on agriculture in a country like Pakistan means improvements in the livelihoods of rural women. Historically, structural transformation in Pakistan has remained relatively slow. The industrial sector has not been able to absorb an increasing labor force. The industrial competitive performance of Pakistan is very low against variables like manufactured value added (MVA) per capita, share of MVA in GDP, share of manufactured exports in total exports et cetera compared to regional comparators. (see Table 8.1).

There is a strong case for more focus on agriculture productivity from a structural transformation perspective as well. Structural transformation accelerates economic growth, enhances productivity, and reduces poverty through the channels of production, consumption, and more revenue generation for the government.[11] For instance, production route of structural transformation results in employment generation, growth in wages, and higher agricultural productivity. And the prices of goods and services go down as a result of more production by the manufacturing and services sectors, and poor consumers also benefit.

Now the question is: how do we make agriculture a pathway for poverty alleviation and economic growth? The first step in this regard is to concentrate on increasing productivity, particularly of small farms, to achieve huge untapped potential as agriculture dominated by small commercial farms boosts spending in the local economy, drives economic growth, alleviates poverty, and enhances food security.[12]

Low Agricultural Productivity

Two Indian agricultural economists wrote a paper[13] in 2005 comparing two Punjabs that is Indian Punjab and Pakistani Punjab. Both Punjabs, by and large, have similar resource endowments and agro-ecological potential but the growth performance and per acre yield production of various crops substantially vary. Two Punjabs thus provide a natural experiment for comparing factors or public policy differences responsible for variation in agriculture productivity. The researchers who conducted comparison between two Punjabs observed huge differences in the per acre yield of

Table 8.1 Competitive industrial performance by economy of some selected countries 2022

Country	*Manufacturing value added per capita*	*Manufactured exports per capita*	*Manufacturing value added share in total GDP (%)*	*Medium- and high-tech MVA share in total MVA (%)*	*Manufactured exports share in total exports (%)*	*Medium- and high-tech manufactured exports share in total manufactured exports (%)*	*Impact of a country on world MVA (%)*
China	2844	1727	27.98	41.45	95.93	61.36	30.08
Republic of Korea	8357	9665	26.38	63.83	96.65	77.70	3.15
Malaysia	2437	6474	22.95	43.32	89.53	65.17	0.58
Viet Nam	463	2598	17.44	38.25	89.86	57.46	0.33
Indonesia	755	436	20.08	35	73.03	31.57	1.52
India	307	171	16.61	44.58	85.86	40.04	3.11
Bangladesh	337	198	20.21	7.81	97.54	1.87	0.41
Sri Lanka	666	357	16.06	8.28	77.14	9.09	0.10
Pakistan	168	77	11.60	22.90	77.72	11.13	0.27

Source UNIDO Report (2022)

major crops like wheat, rice, sugar cane, and maize. Pakistani Punjab fared better just in cotton.[14]

According to the latest estimates, yield gaps in various crops persist to date, except in cotton, where Indian Punjab has been able to catch up with Pakistani Punjab, contrary to earlier estimates from 2005. The yield gap between wheat and rice, two main staple crops of the region, is respectively estimated at around 75% and 28% between the two Punjabs. (see Table 8.2).

More use of fertilizers and pesticides, favorable agriculture policies, easy and better access to institutional credit[15] (both in terms of availability per unit area and growth over time) and liberal subsidies[16] to farmers in the Indian Punjab are the main factors that explain the variation in agricultural productivity between the two Punjabs. The results of a World Bank study[17] also confirm that Indian Punjab's rapid growth in yields owes itself to a rapid increase in agricultural inputs through a strategy of massive subsidization of fertilizer, credit, power, and irrigation.

Contrary to Indian Punjab, subsidies to the agriculture sector in Pakistan were low and directed toward big farmers. The majority of the farmers who were small landholders did not benefit. Overall yield per acre for almost all crops witnessed a substantial increase on both sides of the border in the 1960s. Agricultural research, better extension services, and technological breakthrough in the form of high-yielding crop varieties (HYVs) of rice and wheat gave agricultural productivity a big jump. In Pakistan, total factor productivity (TFP) is estimated to grow at an average rate of 0.28%, which explains more than 7% of the value added to agriculture.[18] Undoubtedly, huge productivity gains were achieved in all

Table 8.2 The yield gap between wheat and rice

Yield Gap			*(maunds per acre)*
Crop	*Pakistan Average*	*Indian Punjab Average*	*Pakistan: Progressive Farmer Average*
Wheat	29	51	45
Rice	50	64	80
Maize	57	42	80
Cotton	18	18	35
Sugarcane	656	796	950

Source Ministry of National Food Security & Research Government of Pakistan

the countries that embraced the changes introduced under the umbrella of the 'Green Revolution'. Estimates, based on data from 86 countries, suggest that delaying the Green Revolution for 10 years would have reduced GDP per capita by 17% in 2010.[19]

Stagnation, however, set in. Now yields on average farms in Pakistan are lower by 31–75% compared to progressive farms while the productivity of progressive farms is 25–57% less than the technology potential realized at the research stations. The unachieved potential is even higher in livestock production. For example, milk productivity per animal is estimated to be less in the range of 61%–78% than the maximum achievable production.

The problem of low agricultural productivity is not wholly just of the scarcity of inputs. The insatiable appetite of land developers and housing authorities has serious implications for agriculture. In this context, enforceable zoning regulations for protecting good farmland from its less agreeable alternate uses need to be put in place and implemented religiously. Extensive land surveys and quick disposal of civil cases by the courts (speedy contract enforcement and better judicial dispensation) can also ameliorate the situation in resolving the competing claims of titles of land for unlocking its potential for growth. Digitization of the land record, enhancing the quality of land (through zero tillage, green manuring, and crop rotation), protecting good farmland from sub-optimal uses, and better planning and management of land are some important elements of the productivity story of agriculture. The said elements, however, do not complete the story. The other part starts once the crops are harvested. The post-harvest inefficiencies are high especially for small farmers who fail to get the optimal price of their produce.

From Farm to the Fork

The agricultural produce markets do not operate in favor of the farmers in general and small and medium-sized farmers in particular due to distortions in the produce market. The farmers basically do not get a fair price for their produce due to an outmoded system of agents, middlemen, and market committees where fees are charged at every stage. The gap between farm gate and retail prices is generally huge. For instance, for perishables, the difference can be as much as 100% and there is a tremendous amount of waste and inefficiency as well. The capacity of farmers, particularly small farmers, for post-harvest management is low.

Post-harvest losses range from 25 to 40%, which simply means that if post-harvest losses are controlled, farmers' incomes can increase substantially even with existing levels of yield per acre. In this context, the 'yield per acre', though an important variable, may not fully capture the growth potential of small farms. Production or harvest is one part. Post-harvest management is equally important.

New models and mechanisms to remove inefficiencies and to make the produce markets work for farmers need to be evolved at the policy level. One such model is of modern retailing. Connecting agriculture to world markets through modern retailing holds a big promise. With the emergence of supermarkets in developing countries, the primitive system which is fragmented and monopolistic in nature, can be fixed. Farmers' access to competitive but well-regulated markets for buying farm inputs and services and selling their products can be facilitated by the government. Integration of small farmers and livestock holders into a growing commercial environment would boost their incomes.

Supermarkets have both backward and forward linkages. Backward linkages include the development of a modern procurement system with wholesalers and associated infrastructure such as warehouses, cold storage chains, and logistics. As regards forward linkages, supermarkets, as part of the global supply chains, can procure on behalf of their sister stores in other countries. Once Pakistan is able to meet international quality and domestic quantity requirements, such stores may begin to supply some agricultural products to stores in other countries. Facilitating the growth of modern retailing through appropriate public policies and investment in infrastructure can turn out to be big step in the right direction for boosting rural economic growth and agricultural incomes.

Small farmers need to be facilitated and encouraged to form 'marketing cooperatives' to fully benefit from the higher prices and to expand the market for high-value agriculture products. Halal markets have emerged rapidly almost in the entire world in the last decade or so, which can be explored for the export of agriculture-related products. In this regard, programs to increase livestock production, especially milk and meat production are vital. Promotion of small dairy farms in Punjab and Sindh and sheep and goat farms in KPK and Balochistan can have a significant impact on the incomes of the rural poor. The production gains from small dairy farmers are feasible through the use of improved feeds, better veterinary services, and more efficient marketing channels.

Agriculture is, however, susceptible to natural calamities. Productivity risk is endemic in agriculture. Risks like losses from natural calamities such as floods and droughts, virus and bacterial attacks on crops, and huge fluctuations in commodity prices always loom large.

Insurance Against Bad Luck

The productivity shocks hit subsistence-level farmers and agricultural labor the most. Seema Jayachandran has provided some empirical evidence to confirm the said proposition. She analyzed data from 257 districts in India for the period 1956–1987. Using rainfall as an instrument variable for agricultural productivity, she found that districts with 'fewer banks' and 'high migration costs' were more affected by the fluctuations in agricultural productivity.[20] The implication is that quality banking services are important in the rural areas to mitigate the impact of productivity shocks. Besides deepening financial inclusion in rural areas, some mechanisms for crop insurance are also needed. Insurance shall not only protect the farmers against weather shocks but also incentivize them to increase their use of inputs. Some empirics in the Kenyan context suggest that Weather Index Insurance (WII) uptake contributes to higher use of chemical fertilizer, improved seeds, and higher yields.[21]

The introduction of agriculture insurance in Pakistan will broadly involve three categories of issues. The first category pertains to issues common in all types of insurance like 'moral hazard' (insured farmers may increase risk-taking, or farmers may have less incentive to work hard at protecting their crops from damages if the crops are insured, or may engage in false declarations of losses that are hard to objectively verify) and 'adverse selection' (only riskier farmers may be insured due to asymmetric information). The second category of issues relates to costs associated with the preparation and processing of insurance claims, and the third category is about reluctance among farmers to take up insurance due to socio-religious factors.

Traditional indemnity-based crop insurance does not exist in developing countries due to high transaction costs. The weather insurance index (WII), mainly intended for small farmers and rural dwellers, is different from traditional indemnity-based insurance. Unlike indemnity-based insurance, under the WII insurance, payments to the farmers are not made according to actual crop damage but on the basis of objectively measurable climatic data like rainfall, temperature, wind, and hail et cetera, collected at meteorological stations. The average outcome can be measured over a small area of crop yield or mortality of livestock et cetera and farm-level verifications are not required.

The novelty of WII insurance thus takes care of high costs and long delays in claim verification, moral hazard, and adverse selection. As regards demand for WII insurance among farmers, at full actuarial price, there would be no demand and farmers would be reluctant to take up insurance. At least in the beginning, only publicly provided insurance or subsidized insurance provided by the market will work. Further, a full-fledged campaign for educating farmers and rural dwellers on the benefits of WII insurance would be required. The poor are generally more vulnerable to shocks, which have a long-term impact on their well-being. The WII insurance holds a huge promise to manage shocks and prevent small farmers and rural dwellers from sliding into abject poverty. The limited access of the small farmers to formal credit is another big constraint in realizing the potential of rural economic growth.

Chronic Credit Crunch

The Agricultural Inquiry Report 1951[22] is a good starting point for the contextual appreciation of the issue of credit to rural dwellers The said report raised some important points about rural finance and rural life in the 1950s, which are summarized as follows: First, agricultural indebtedness is very high, as only in the province of Punjab 34% of the families were in debt and on average every indebted family had to pay a debt of Rs. 414, substantially more than Shambhu Maheto's family pictured in Bismal Roy's "*Do Bigha Zamin*",[23] a 1953 Hindi movie made on the theme of agricultural indebtedness, had to be pay. Second, most of the loans are taken to pay off old debts or to incur expenditures on marriage, litigation, or some household needs, implying that most of the loans are taken for non-productive purposes.

Third, one important factor in the large part of the infructuous expenditure incurred by rural people is party affiliation. Fourth, small agriculturists get loans from money-lenders and traders as banks and cooperative societies are at a distance while money-lenders are close at hand. Payment of loans by money-lenders is prompt and does not require intricate and complicated rules. Fifth, interest rates charged by the money-lenders range from 30 to 300% and the traders advance loans on the condition that the grower will not sell his crop to any other body, which obviously compels the farmer to sell his produce to the trader at a lower price. Sixth, agriculturists require short-term (at the time of sowing, harvesting, and marketing of the crop), medium-term (purchase of live-stock and implements), and long-term credit (for improvements and developments like construction of embankments etc.). Seventh, 'friends and relatives' are the major source of credit accounting for over 63% of overall credit obtained by various classes of people in rural areas. Other sources of credit are cooperative societies, proprietors, shopkeepers, and money-lenders. (see Table 8.3).

What has changed since 1950s? We observe both elements of continuity and change. 'Friends and relatives' are no longer the main source of credit. Formal financial institutions have emerged for financial intermediation but rural areas in general and poor rural dwellers in particular are not their main targets. They are biased toward large farmers. According to some estimates,[24] big landholders, who constitute 4% of rural households, get 42% of formal loans whereas landless and subsistence farmers who represent more than 69% of rural households, receive only 23% of formal loans. The data of SBP[25] shows that formal agricultural credit disbursement has skewed further with the passage of time.

If we analyze disbursements to the farm sector, 46% of formal farm credit was disbursed among just 0.18% borrowers in FY 2020–21. The

Table 8.3 Sources of credit in the Punjab

Class of People	*Co-operative societies*	*Relatives and friends*	*Proprietors*	*Shopkeeper*	*Taccavi*	*Money-lenders*	*Total*
Land proprietor	19.1	63.3	9.5	2.8	4.9	0.4	100
Owner-tenant	11.1	53.8	14.9	1.7	0.9	17.6	100
Occupancy-tenant	11.2	51.5	19.1	NA	18.2	NA	100
Non-occupancy tenant	5.7	65.4	24.1	2.2	25.2	0.1	100
Laborer	9.9	56.6	30.9	1.5	2.5	0.2	100
Artisan	7.5	70.8	18.5	2.5	0.9	0.6	100
Shopkeeper	3.7	69.3	22.9	4.1	0.1	NA	100
In service	14.6	67.4	37.8	0.2	NA	NA	100
Miscellaneous	13.6	63.1	20.2	3.1	NA	NA	100
Average	13.2	63.2	16.9	2.5	2.9	1.3	100

Source The Agricultural Inquiry Report (1951)

same is true for non-farm credit as out of total non-farm credit, over 46% was distributed among 0.68% borrowers. A highly skewed distribution of formal credit has severe negative implications for agricultural growth and poverty alleviation. Small farmers and landless people are left with no option except to resort to informal sources of credit. Results of a survey conducted by PIDE[26] revealed that around 38% of total borrowers, who obtained loans from informal lenders, were small farmers. They got loans at exploitative interest rates ranging from 48 to 120% per year. The results of the survey estimated markups for fertilizers and pesticides, respectively, at 29% and 35%.

The SBP's 'report of the Committee on Rural Finance'[27] depicts a similar picture about the prevalent situation regarding credit to the agriculture sector in particular to the small farmers. According to the report, the rural sector suffers from policy neglect, poor design, and weak implementation of the delivery system for financial services. The volume of loans in terms of agricultural needs does not exceed 30% and the time lag in disbursement of loans is high with the result that the loans are not often put to optimum use. Subsidized agricultural loans generally go to big farmers who have a comparative advantage in terms of clout, collateral, and connections. The cost of borrowing even from formal sources is higher for small farmers. Based on survey data from two villages in Peshawar district in the KPK province, some researchers have found that the cost of formal borrowing has a negative correlation with the size of landholdings. The cost of borrowing is high for small landholdings, but it falls as the size of the holding increases.[28]

Moreover, small landholders also have a higher dependence on informal loans, and rates of borrowing are much higher. The World Development Report 2006 quotes about exorbitant rates of informal lending prevalent in some areas of Pakistan as follows: "Chambhar is a market town in Sindh (Pakistan) on the east bank of the Indus. In 1980–81, farmers from the area around Chambhar got most of their credit from about 60 professional money-lenders. Based on detailed data from 14 of the lenders and 60 of their clients, Aleem (1990) calculated the average borrowing interest rate charged as 78.5%. But if these farmers wanted to lend their money, the banking system would pay them only 10%".

According to a study conducted by the Punjab Economic Research Institute (PERI) in June 2006, the cost of a tied loan in the case of cotton is 45%, and in case of wheat the cost of borrowing from a commission agent is around 47%. This study further suggests that the cost of urea credit purchase is 76% and that of DAP is 68%. In the case of weedicides and pesticides, the cost of credit purchases is about 83%.[29] Even in today's rural Pakistan, middlemen (arthis and dhodis) finance over 90% of the input costs and household needs of the small farmers on the condition of selling 75% to 100% of their produce to the middlemen, who provide them with finances.

Small farmers are thus tied to an exploitative arrangement as the credit market is not working for them. International surveys also confirm this assertion. For instance, Banerjee and Duflo's 2006 survey of 13 nations, including Pakistan, revealed that the poor borrowed no more than 6% of the funds from formal sources. According to the said survey,[30] the credit markets were characterized by the following five facts in the countries surveyed. First, lending rates in the informal markets were high relative to deposit rates in the same area. Second, lending rates differed even in the same local credit market as different rates were charged to different borrowers. Third, richer people borrowed more but paid low interest rates. Fourth, the divergences in the interest rates were not due to defaults in payments as defaults were very rare. Fifth, the monopoly power of the lenders over particular borrowers was not the reason for high interest rates.

Why do formal lending institutions hesitate to go to rural areas and lend to small agriculturists, landless people, and rural labor? The dilemma a formal institution is faced with is: how to screen potential creditors and how to monitor borrowers so they do not renege on their promise to return the loan on negotiated terms and time? If a creditor is living in a village, his creditworthiness and reputation are known to the lender, generally an informal lender, who resides in the same community or area. The lender can easily screen and monitor the creditor. No documentation or big procedural formalities are needed.

For the banks, such is not the case due to asymmetries of information.[31] The banks therefore rely on collateral, generally in the form of land, to overcome the difficulties of screening and monitoring potential creditors. Those who do not own land or other tangible assets or have disputed titles to land are not welcome creditors in the formal credit market. The credit markets have unfortunately not developed alternative guarantees based on 'intangibles' in Pakistan. Such guarantees have worked in other areas of the world. Grameen Bank of Bangladesh is an example which developed a guarantee in the form of group responsibility and it worked fairly well.

What can be done to ameliorate the situation of credit for small farmers in rural areas? One option is to restrict the domain of the federal agriculture bank that is ZTBL to the provision of credit to small farmers and rural entrepreneurs who require a small amount of credit. In this way, the subsidy (the difference between the interest rate charged by the federal agricultural bank and the market interest rate) provided by the government shall benefit the small farmers who in actuality are the deserving target of the credit subsidies. Currently, a major chunk of the subsidized credit by the federal agricultural bank is provided to the big farmers who can easily manage loans from other banks in the credit market due to their comparative advantage over poor rural dwellers in terms of collateral and connections.

Another option is the creation of a Small Farmers Development Corporation (SFDC), registered as a public limited company. The dividends earned from SFDC can be used as loans to small farmers. The SFDC, with the primary objective of providing credit to small farmers and entrepreneurs working in rural areas, can also provide extension services for marketing and diversification of small farm crops into export-based products like fruits, vegetables, milk products, meat, and fisheries. The said corporation may also be mandated to provide integrated support services to the small farm sector through land development, drip irrigation, soil testing, the provision of fertilizers, and high-quality seeds.

Incentivizing financial institutions to provide financial services can be another option. Tax breaks like reduction in the rate of corporate tax for financial institutions supplying financial services to small farmers can also be effective in inducing financial institutions to work for rural dwellers. Further, innovative credit instruments can be designed using savings or membership of a small farmers' organization (SFO) as collateral to overcome the difficulties of screening and monitoring arising out of asymmetries of information.

Small Farms as Engine of Rural Growth

Small farmers need sharp policy focus to boost economic growth and alleviate poverty in rural areas. Small farm-holders have a strong case not only on the ground of equity but also on economic efficiency (due to inverse farm size–productivity relationship). Around 7.4 million farms (89% of total farms) in Pakistan are small farms[32] (less than 12.5 acres of land) with 48% farm area. And if small farms become the focus of public policy and constraints like access to credit and quality inputs are removed, millions can be lifted out of poverty. The Agricultural Census gives disaggregated data on smallholders having land less than one acre (15%), one acre to less than 2.5 acres (28%), 2.5 to less than 5 acres (21%), 5 to less than 7.5 acres (14%), and 7.5 to less than 12.5 acres (11%). There is no universal definition of a small farm. Generally, smallholders are characterized by low production, limited access to capital and inputs, lack of effective participation in markets, production for home consumption, reliance on family labor, and low skills and education. A lot of heterogeneity exists with regards to smallholders.

In order to improve the productivity of small farms and make them a vehicle of economic growth, investment in education and skills of the small farm-holders is highly significant so they can effectively participate in high-value agriculture and modern markets. Storage, packing, and processing facilities are essential for exploiting modern market opportunities. Small farm-holders need to be facilitated to switch from traditional crops of wheat and rice to the production of labor-intensive products like vegetables (which require transplanting and multiple harvests by hand), and similar other products requiring attention to details.

The quality and scope of extension services need to be expanded for enhancing agricultural productivity. The extension services provided by the government mainly focus on production issues. At what time and in how much quantity fertilizer is needed for a particular crop? What seeds to sow and how much pesticide to spray? What feed is more appropriate for the animals to enhance milk and meat production? Marketing issues get little priority with the result that, despite good output, small farmers in particular do not receive fair price of their produce.

There are some other important factors responsible for low productivity. The capacities to embrace new technologies and to connect effectively with markets are two key factors besides access to credit and control of post-harvest losses. Small farmers are often credit-constrained, do not get quality inputs and produce market is pitted against them. It would be difficult for them to break out of the vicious circle of exploitation and apathy unless they organize themselves. The SFOs can turn out to be an effective model to break the vicious circle. They can perform a number of functions such as maintaining digital data of the loans, produce, and sale et cetera, can negotiate prices for outputs, can collectively purchase inputs for further distribution among farmers as per their requirements, and can develop storage infrastructure. The SFOs can take aggregated payments from processing companies, contract farmers, and traders, and can make collective payments for the purchase of quality inputs on behalf of member farmers.

A digital platform can be established where SFO can act as a clearing house financial aggregator. In this way, the model of SFO can be helpful in eliminating the role of the middleman and can capitalize on the productivity gains arising out of the rise of agribusinesses. Empirics[33] suggest that small farmers are not benefiting much from agribusinesses. Generally, big farmers sell to agribusinesses, and that is why the distributional impacts of agribusinesses are skewed against small farmers. The SFO model can alleviate the negative distributional consequences for small farmers by helping them overcome the diseconomies of scale in marketing and technology adoption et cetera. So theoretically speaking, the benefits of the SFO model are huge. "When communities have well-established organizations where the poor are sufficiently empowered, the participatory approach is on safe grounds. The problem arises when local organizations do not exist or when they are dominated by strong elites driven by their peculiar interests."[34]

The role of the government is highly significant in facilitating small farmers in realizing their 'cooperative potential'. Deliberative forums like 'stakeholder workshops' and 'value chain roundtables', can be used to bring stakeholders to joint action where the government can play the role of a facilitator. The government can also provide necessary capacity-building training and support in establishing digital platforms for such organizations. The SFOs will have several other positive externalities as well. The rural people shall feel more empowered and confident to effectively engage with the local public institutions. Eventually, SFOs would be helpful in building social capital in rural areas. Besides organizing small farmers, there is a need to focus on the rural landless to realize the potential of rural areas. The rural landless have suffered policy neglect due to two main factors. First, they lack voice for being landless as it is mainly the land, as emphasized earlier, which determines socio-economic and political power in the rural areas. Second factor is the wrong assumption at the policy level that rural development is synonymous with agriculture which is certainly not the case, particularly in the aftermath of the Green Revolution.

The Landless Rural Poor

The 'Green Revolution' set in motion changes in the methods of production, which in turn induced changes in the socio-economic relationships between various classes and segments of the rural society. A comparison of the Agricultural Census of 1972, conducted in the aftermath of the Green Revolution', and the latest available survey of 2010 gives interesting insights about the transformation. These changes can be best visualized by the following facts: (a) around 55% of small farms (less than 12.5 acres of land) were operated by owner-tenants and tenants. This number went down to 17% as per the Agricultural Census of 2010. In terms of farm area, only 36% was cultivated by the farm owners which increased to 78% as per the latest survey. (b) 69% of farms of size 12.5 acres to 25 acres were cultivated by owner-tenants and tenants in 1972 compared to 29% in 1972. The farm area under cultivation by owner-tenants and tenants also fell with the same ratio.

A similar pattern is visible for other farm size holdings except for the category of landholdings of 150 acres and above where the majority of farms and farm areas were self-cultivated by the owners in 1972. There is, though, a decrease in the number of farms and farm area cultivated by owner-tenants and tenants in this category but the change is not as drastic as in other categories and sizes of landholdings (see Table 8.4).

What does a change in numbers imply? Simply put, the changes that the Green Revolution induced resulted in large-scale eviction of sharecropping tenants. With the introduction of agricultural machinery, a small number of full-time wage laborers and sharecroppers were required. Peasants who owned very small holdings but could make both ends meet, by leasing in some additional land, also could no longer sustain and were forced to sell even their small landholdings. "There was a general pauperization of large sections of the rural population in the midst of an enormous increase in the prosperity of a few big landholders. Large numbers of sharecropping tenants and full-time laborers were displaced; the amount of full-time employment declined very considerably."[35] Before the advent of mechanization of farming, the majority of the people living in rural areas were, directly or indirectly, associated with agriculture. Those who did not own land either worked as agricultural laborers on the farms or rendered services to the agriculturists.

At the time of sowing and harvesting of seasonal crops almost all family members of the agriculture laborers worked on the farm. Landowners and

Table 8.4 Tenure classification of farms and farm area by size of farm (in thousand acres)

Size of Farm	*Year*	*Number of Farms*				*Farm Area*			
		Total	*Owner*	*Owner-cum-Tenant*	*Tenant*	*Total*	*Owner*	*Owner-cum-Tenant*	*Tenant*
Less than 12.5 acres	1972	2560	1,149	506	904	14,900	5,348	3,603	5,949
	%	100	45	20	35	100	36	24	40
	2010	7400	6125	455	820	25,426	19,765	2,433	3,229
	%	100	83	6	11	100	78	10	13
12.5 to under 25 acres	1972	794	248	250	296	13,061	4,085	4,268	4,708
	%	100	45	20	35	100	36	24	40
	2010	561	399	94	68	9,361	6,680	1,575	1,106
	%	100	45	20	35	100	36	24	40
25 to under 50 acres	1972	289	111	99	79	9,215	3,516	3,299	2,400
	%	100	45	20	35	100	36	24	40
	2010	211	152	38	21	6,726	4,818	1,236	672
	%	100	45	20	35	100	36	24	40
50 acres to under 150 acres	1972	103	50	36	16	7,402	3,652	2,665	1,085
	%	100	45	20	35	100	36	24	40
	2010	79	58	15	6	5,548	4,019	1,142	387
	%	100	73	19	7	100	72	21	7
150 acres and above	1972	16	10	5	1	4,482	2,798	1,325	359
	%	100	63	28	9	100	62	30	8
	2010	13	10	3	1	5,850	4,151	1,198	501
	%	100	72	22	6	100	71	20	9
Total	1972	**3,762**	**1,569**	**897**	**1,296**	**49,061**	**19,400**	**15,160**	**14,500**
	%	100	42	24	34	100	40	31	30
	2010	**8,265**	**6,744**	**604**	**916**	**52,910**	**39,432**	**7,584**	**5,894**
	%	100	82	7	11	100	75	14	11
* Total as per Agriculture Census 2010		8,264	6739	604	916	52,910	39,432	7,584	5,894

Source Agriculture Census 1972 and 2010

agriculturists paid them in kind. In this way, they were able to secure their basic food necessities at least for the next six months. 'Seypis', generally skilled artisans like barbers, cobblers, carpenters, weavers, tailors, washer-men, butchers, potters, and blacksmiths, gave their services to the agriculturists around the year. Out of these, the services of several categories of artisans were directly linked to agricultural production. For example, carpenters and blacksmiths provided services such as mending hand tools and implements while potters made earthen pots. They were also paid in kind at the end of the year or crop season.

"In medieval Indian societies, even though the seypi system was not egalitarian, it traditionally allowed all categories of villagers to make a living. Each group had its specific responsibilities and obligations towards the others within a subsistence economy based on an archaic technology. Irrespective of the attitude of superiority exhibited by the landowners towards landless people, both classes shared the feeling of belonging to self-sufficient productive units. Socially, the 'Zamindari/kammi' relations were based on centuries-old co-existence principles. Exploitation was camouflaged under a paternalistic ideology. With the subsequent transformation of the village economy and its integration into a market economy, many traditional relations of production became unnecessary and vanished. Those which still remained through being indispensable have changed in nature. From being interpersonal, relations between economic categories of villages have become more impersonal and can be replaced by wage-labor instead of payment in kind. In other words, the progress of the productive forces through the Green Revolution has been accompanied by a concomitant change in the relations of production."[36]

In case agriculture was hit by some natural calamity, surplus agricultural labor temporarily migrated to the cities to work in industries or as construction workers. And when the industrial sector was down due to an adverse business cycle, they returned to rural areas to work on farms. In the wake of the Green Revolution, a process of structural change started in response to technological and institutional changes. These changes impacted household labor allocation. Sowing, harvesting, threshing, et cetera are now mostly done by machines. Tractor mechanization led to the displacement of labor and an increase in the landless labor force which was not absorbed by the non-agricultural sector. Estimates suggest that 20,000 tractors replaced 198,000 rural workers[37] meaning that one tractor displaced almost 10 agriculture workers.

Now two profound changes are very much visible even to the naked eye in rural areas. First, agriculture is no longer able to absorb agricultural labor due to the replacement of human tasks by machines and increasing population pressure. Second, agriculturists no longer pay the agriculture laborers in kind which means that the price of labor (due to the phenomenon economists call stickiness of wages) has not kept pace with the price of agricultural commodities having implications for rural poverty and food security.

The economy of Pakistan, like other developing countries, is characterized by 'dualism', where growth is driven by structural change. In developed countries, the process of structural change is driven by technological changes and innovations whereas in developing countries it is the capacity to absorb such technical changes, though with a lag, that drives economic growth. But unfortunately, the industrial sector of Pakistan neither upgraded nor diversified itself with the changing technology. Partly, it happened due to protectionist policies pursued by the state. The process of moving from low-productivity to high-productivity sectors that drive economic growth remained slow with the result that the country remains stuck in manufacturing and exports of low-value-added goods. Due to the low diversification of the industrial sector, it was unable to absorb the surplus agricultural labor.

The policy thinking remained static with regard to rural growth and development. At the policy level, rural growth remained synonymous with agriculture especially the agriculture of large farmers. The agrarian changes created policy voids that still exist as no concrete policy measures were taken to create opportunities for those abandoned by the 'Green Revolution'. Rural non-farm economies (RNFE), which could absorb the evicted sharecroppers, landless labor, and village artisans, failed to attract policy priority from the successive governments. Industry is concentrated in urban areas. Around 92% of villages have no industries of any category. Small-scale and cottage industries, which do not require much infrastructure and can be established with comparative ease in rural areas, are also concentrated in urban centers. Only 3.64% and 3.43% of villages reported, respectively, during the Mouza census, the existence of small-scale and cottage industries in the rural area.[38]

The neglect of rural areas can be best explained through the prism of political economy. The rural poor suffer from collective action problem and lack of voice. So neither policymakers nor mainstream media nor even the intelligentsia are constrained to dive into their lives and articulate their interests. The policy neglect is still continuing. RNFE is absent from the manifestos of the political parties and the priorities of the governments.[39]

Rural Non-Farm Economy

An Increase in agricultural productivity promotes non-farm economy by creating backward and forward linkages. For instance, agriculture production creates a need for further processing of agricultural produce and as a result economic activities like rice husking, wheat milling, oil extraction, cotton ginning et cetera evolve through forward linkages with agriculture. Similarly, agriculture inputs like auto parts for tractors and harvesters, fertilizers, pesticides, repair shops, et cetera create backward production linkages. Consumption linkages are also associated with agricultural productivity as an increase in agricultural productivity boosts the incomes of rural people and consequently demand for goods and services increases. The growth of RNFE stimulates agricultural productivity via lower input costs, investment of profits back into agriculture, and technological change.

So there is a valid case for the pro-active role of the government in promoting RNFE. What Public interventions are broadly needed to promote RNFE? First of all, there is a need to create missing markets or fix imperfections in existing markets. The poorly functioning rural credit market is a case in point. Micro and small-scale enterprises are credit-constrained and the start-up funding for most enterprises in rural areas comes from savings or informal loans rather than from formal financial institutions. Credit programs targeted exclusively at small-scale enterprises are almost non-existent. The private sector banks have a clear bias toward industries and businesses established in urban areas. Moreover, due to the lack of low-cost savings institutions, pooling local resources is costly.

Contrary to general belief, some evidence suggests that households engaged in agricultural activities save more (in terms of percentage of savings) compared to urban households but a small percentage of rural people have access to banking facilities.[40] Consequently they hold their savings in the form of currency notes, jewelry, or some other form. They, in a sense, put their savings under the pillow to avoid the risk of theft. If rural savings can be pooled, perhaps a major chunk of the credit requirement for small farmers and rural businesses can be met out of such savings.

The second broad area for public intervention is the development of rural infrastructure to support the expansion of the non-farm economy. Rural households are less served than urban households in developing countries in terms of infrastructural services. Part of the explanation of this imbalance lies in the higher per capita cost of infrastructure provision in rural areas. Weaker political influence (due to the collective action problem) and an inherent urban bias in public policies are some other factors responsible for the infrastructural imbalance. It is a proven fact that farm-to-market roads play an important role in creating business and employment activities in rural areas. Farm-to-market roads, village electrification, et cetera are some development strategies that are not only helpful in promoting rural non-farm activities but also improve the overall welfare of rural areas.[41]

Besides physical infrastructure, investment in social infrastructure is also important for rural development. Investments in rural education, health, and skills development are highly significant and provide essential building blocks for the high productivity of the non-farm rural economy. Returns to education are generally high in rural areas for non-farm activities. Education levels are important in determining the type of non-farm activity people are engaged in. The poor are typically less educated and in this context, efforts to improve the education levels of rural people would definitely be a pro-poor policy. The contribution of education tends to be higher in the non-farm economy than in agriculture.

Based on FAO data for 15 developing countries, some researchers have suggested that division of landholdings into small agricultural operations and education are poverty alleviation tools in rural areas.[42] An investigation, based on data from four districts of Pakistan as to how human capital affects productivity and labor allocation in rural households, shows that education increases off-farm productivity and induces rural households to shift labor resources from farm to non-farm activities. Estimates show that one additional year of schooling for male adults enhances household income by 8.9%, of which one-fifth comes from the reallocation of labor resources from farm to non-farm activities.[43]

Though no correct estimates of the size of the rural non-farm economy are available. The size of RNFE varies hugely (from 20 to 50%) in developing countries. The RNFE is undoubtedly a vehicle for poverty alleviation. The impact on inequality reduction is, however, not straightforward. A comparative study of Egypt and Jordan regarding the impact of RNFE on inequality provides some insights for Pakistan. According to the said study,[44] the impact of RNFE on inequality depends on the availability and distribution of agricultural land in a country. In Egypt, cultivable land is generally productive but highly skewed. People belonging to the lowest quintile of the population (the poorest) get 60% of their per capita income from non-farm activities in Egypt. Perhaps on-farm income reduces inequality as inadequate access to land pushes poor households out of agriculture. On the contrary, only 30% of the land in Jordan is cultivable, and yields are very low. The poor in Jordan receive less than 20% of their income from non-farm sources. The study thus concludes that in Egypt RNFE is inequality-reducing whereas in Jordan it is inequality-enhancing.

Generally, better-off rural households earn more from non-farm activities. An investigation into the nexus between non-farm activity and rural households' incomes, based on microdata from the Philippines, confirms the above proposition.[45] According to said investigation, all non-farm activities may not necessarily increase the incomes of poor households. The non-farm activities which require minimal capital tend to increase the incomes of the poor more equitably. Geographical segmentation of rural areas is important to treat richer and poorer zones differently. More subsidization is required for poorer zones whereas in richer zones, reduction of transaction costs would be a prudent public policy.

Even substantial agricultural growth alone is not sufficient to reduce poverty in rural areas due to its differential distributional impact as the majority of people living in rural areas are neither tenant farmers nor farm owners.[46] Agriculture incomes accrue to those who have access to key factors of production like land and water. Due to the highly skewed distribution of these resources, landless rural agricultural labor and the rural non-farm poor, who collectively constitute over 60% of the rural population, do not benefit directly from growth in the crop sector. So more policy focus is needed for the expansion of the rural non-farm economy for poverty reduction in rural areas.[47]

Off-farm and non-farm sources of income are relatively more important for small farmers and landless rural dwellers. For example, some estimates[48] show that farmers cultivating less than four acres of land earn around 24% of their income from off-farm and non-farm sources whereas farmers with over 20 acres of land merely earn less than 7% of their income from non-farm sources. Simply put, a multi-pronged strategy is required to meet the challenges of economic growth and poverty reduction.

CHAPTER 9

The Challenge of Poverty

Poverty has many faces and dimensions. Poverty is about hunger and lack of adequate food and shelter. It is about lack of education and health. It is about deprivations, both income and non-income, and lack of freedom of choices and capabilities. And last but not least, it is about being voiceless and powerless. The World Development Report 2000–2001,[1] the central theme of which is poverty, mentions some voices expressing their feelings about poverty: "(a) Do not ask me what poverty is because you have met it outside my house. Look at the house and count the number of holes. Look at the utensils and clothes I am wearing" (Poor man, Kenya). (b) "Certainly our farming is little; all the products, things bought from stores, are expensive; it is hard to live; we work and earn little money; we buy few things or products; products are scarce; there is no money, and we feel poor" (from a discussion group of poor men and women in Ecuador). (c) "We face a calamity when my husband falls ill. Our lives come to a halt until he recovers and goes back to work" (A poor woman of Egypt). (d) "Poverty is humiliation, the sense of being dependent on them and of being forced to accept rudeness, insults, and indifference when we seek help (poor woman, Latvia)".

The poverty may simply be lower food intake and resulting depression and low energy, as we see in Pak Sohlin's story in '*Poor Economics.*'[2] The voices of the poor in the World Development Report and Banerjee's Pak Sohlin point toward multiple dimensions of poverty. Before dilating on

J. Nasir, *Development Challenges of Pakistan*,
https://doi.org/10.1007/978-981-97-3064-3_9

the multidimensionality of poverty further, let us have a look at poverty incidence in Pakistan. Poverty, measured against traditional yardsticks, has declined at the national level as well as in provinces. According to the cost of basic needs (CBN) methodology,[3] poverty incidence was 50.4% in 2005–06, which declined to 21.5% in 2018–19. An analysis at the provincial level shows that Punjab is the least poor province (16.3%) while Balochistan is the poorest province with a poverty incidence of 40.7%. Sindh and KPK respectively have 24.6% and 27% poverty incidence. In rural areas, the situation is worse compared with urban Pakistan.

In urban areas, 10.7% while in rural areas 27.6% of the population lives below the poverty line. In rural Sindh, 40% of the population is poor, while in Balochistan around 47% of the population is mired in poverty. The poverty profile in terms of poverty bands shows that almost 5.5% of the population falls into the categories of extreme poor and ultra-poor. About 37.2% of the population is quasi-poor and 21.4% can, in the true sense, be called non-poor as per CBN methodology.

The way the policy definition of the poverty line has been constructed involves an arbitrariness. It uses a basic adult equivalence scale by assigning 0.8 to each individual below the age of 18 and a weight of 1 to each individual of age 18 and above while calculating welfare aggregates. The assumption of assigning lower weights to children in determining equivalent adults is per se questionable. The nutritional requirements of children may be different than those of the adults and may be even higher in some cases. They need more milk, more protein, and more calcium for healthy growth. "Because of variations in family size, economies of scale in family consumption, and age-specificity of needs, the problem of converting families into "equivalent adult" involves serious difficulties--frequently used "policy definition" of poverty is fundamentally flawed. The exercise of describing the predicament of the poor in terms of prevailing standards of "necessities" does, of course, involve ambiguities, which are inherent in the concept of poverty, but ambiguous description is not the same thing as prescription."[4]

Poverty lines do not capture the true severity of the challenge of poverty. The commonly used yardstick for identification and measurement of poverty in terms of some dollars a day only captures the income dimension. Defining poverty in this way gives us a simplistic division of the people of a country into two mutually exclusive segments and distracts attention from the real issue. Division of households and individuals on the basis of monetary criteria such as income or consumption of $1 a day or \$2 a day, an absolute way of defining poverty, does not help in proper conceptualization of the issue.

The absolute definition is based on the assumption that with a certain amount of money, an individual or household is able to purchase a bundle of goods necessary to meet their caloric requirements. It is typically static. It is constant over time and just takes inflation into account. It has been termed 'asocial', as it does not take into account gender, age, health status, or the special needs of an individual. It is 'atheoretical', as it fixes the absolute poverty level arbitrarily with no choices involved. It focuses on passive variables like expenditure, and altogether ignores the income generation process.

Multidimensionality of Poverty

Some other measures, more comprehensive in nature, have now been developed. For example, the Oxford Poverty and Human Development Initiative (OPHD) reflects on multiple deprivations faced by a poor person with regards to education (years of schooling; child enrollment), health (child mortality; nutrition), and standards of living (availability of electricity, drinking water, sanitation, flooring of the house, assets like TV, bike or motorbike or car or tractor). This multidimensional poverty index better guides us as to what public policy interventions are required to alleviate poverty. The 'basic needs approach'[5] and the 'capabilities approach' are some other alternatives to the income approach to poverty measurement and alleviation. The concept of basic needs is, in a sense, an extension of the subsistence concept. Broadly speaking, it embodies two elements. First, the minimum consumption needs of a family including adequate food, shelter, clothing, and certain household furniture and equipment and second, essential services such as safe water, sanitation, public transport, and health care for the community at large.

The capabilities approach, advocated by Amartya Sen, postulates that human beings are active agents in their lives. The essence of development is not just economic growth or accumulation of wealth. Rather development needs to be assessed on the basis of improvements in the lives of the people. Capabilities are the means to achieve a good life, to escape from deprivations, and to realize one's potential. The capabilities approach provides important insights for poverty analysis. For instance, this approach emphasizes that lack of resources is not the only constraint of interest for poverty analysis and that poverty alleviation needs to be approached from multiple angles.[6]

Why an individual stays poor? Certainly, a person is not poor by the divine will or due to some personality defect.[7] People do not stay poor as God wills or due to some predetermined '*qismat*' (luck) or some inherent flaw in their moral character or physical makeup. They stay poor due to the socio-economic structures of the society which create and perpetuate what we call poverty traps. Just two centuries ago, priests preached that poverty is preordained. For example, Robert Moss is said to have instructed the poor in the early eighteenth century to "rest contented with that state or condition in which it hath pleased God to rank him".[8] So poverty was seen as a manifestation of some natural order.

It is interesting to note that, in the twenty-first century, when we place a lot of emphasis on differences in talent, ability, and motivation as causes of poverty, we may unwittingly be falling prey to the ideas that Robert Moss held in the eighteenth century. The line of thinking that poverty is caused by 'bad behaviors is patently wrong'. The behaviors that have historically been seen as causes of poverty may instead be the outcomes of poverty. A person is poor because he is denied opportunities which are available to his rich counterparts. For instance, a poor person is excluded from the endowments and ownership of land and other productive assets. Similarly, exclusion from quality education, poor nutrition, bad health, and denial of access to finance and employment opportunities are some other factors responsible for the poverty of an individual.

These social denials and deprivations can only be addressed through multidimensional approach to poverty. There are even scenarios where some of the most vulnerable members of society may experience circumstances which are not due to a lack of just material resources. The physically challenged, functional illiterates, or those who have suffered physical or mental abuse are some instances to make the point. The multidimensional approach to poverty requires an informed idea, based on empirical research and studies, of the lives, constraints, and preferences of the poor for poverty alleviation. "People who are rich find it hard to understand the behavior of poor people. Economists are no exception, for they do find it difficult to comprehend the preferences and scarcity constraints that determine the choice that poor people make", said Theodore W. Schultz delivering his Nobel Prize talk in 1979.[9] How do the poor earn their living? What are their consumption and saving patterns? Do they lack entrepreneurship or something else? What are the economic choices they are confronted with while making their decisions? Why do they not send their children to school? Why do they have comparatively large families? These are some very pertinent questions that beg for satisfactory and evidence-based answers for informed public policy-making.

The Empirics of Poverty

In the last two decades or so, the technique of randomized control trials (RCTs) has emerged as a full-fledged science. RCTs are now being widely used for evidence-based answers to what works and what does not work for poverty alleviation. This technique of investigation was primarily introduced by Banerjee and his colleagues, who won the Nobel Prize in 2019 for the introduction of RCTs in development economics. In 2007, Banerjee and Duflo documented the economic lives of the extremely poor in 13 different countries including Pakistan.[10] Based on household surveys, they discussed in detail the consumption, savings, and earning patterns of the poor. *'Poor Economics'* also contains evidence-based insights into the economic choices and lives of the poor in the light of RCTs. The ensuing discussion in this section is mainly based on research undertaken by the said economists and some other researchers (generally through RCTs) into the lives and economic choices of the poor.

The majority of the poor reside in rural areas. And contrary to popular perception, most of them are not linked to agriculture. They have comparatively large families. For instance, according to the Household Integrated Economic Survey (HIES), the average members of a household in the poorest quintile in Pakistan are 8.11 compared to 4.72 in the richest quintile. Around half of the total expenditure of the poor is on food.[11] They spend a disproportionately high percentage of their earnings on weddings or festivals. The poor find it difficult to resist the temptation of spending the cash in hand on items that do not have long-term payoffs (the behavioral poverty trap!). They may spend more on tobacco, cigarettes, and festivals than on the education of the children. For instance, per capita expenditure of the poorest quintile on education in Pakistan is Rs. 24.24 compared to Rs. 41.91 on cigarettes and tobacco as per HIES.

The poor have their own concerns and experiences about schooling. They are less incentivized to educate their children as the public schools are either dysfunctional or do not impart relevant skills that is skills required to get gainful employment. Further, teaching methodology does not help the students coming from poor backgrounds who do not have support for their homework et cetera. The governments in developing countries increase inputs like textbooks with a view to increase quality, but the same does not often work for the poor. For instance, results of a randomized control trial[12] undertaken to determine the impact of textbook distribution to randomly selected primary schools in Kenya, confirmed that only the best students benefitted. The average student got no benefit confirming two points as follows. First, there is a big mismatch between the official curriculum and the needs of the students in developing countries and second, merely increasing educational inputs shall not deliver unless pedagogy, the needs of individual students, and the quality of teaching become the main focus of educational reforms.

Contrary to popular perception, the poor do not lack entrepreneurship. Both observation and empirical evidence confirm that it is not the lack of entrepreneurship that is responsible for their poverty. Their engagement in multiple occupations is a clear vindication of their entrepreneurial spirit. For instance, a poor individual in the rural area may work as an agriculture laborer. In the morning, he may collect milk from the farmers and sell it in the nearby town. At the same time, he may also rear a goat or buffalo. If he does not have money to buy a goat or buffalo, he may setup a tea stall or become street vendor to add to his income. Risk is always looming in the lives of the poor. The real issue, Banerjee emphasizes, is that the poor are engaged in small businesses which are generally not profitable. Medium-sized businesses may be profitable and may provide employment but formal medium-sized businesses are almost absent in developing countries.

Some researchers studied the economic lives of the poor by constructing a technique they named 'financial diaries'. The researchers interviewed a sample of the poor people in Bangladesh, India, and South Africa, at least twice a month, for a full year and used the data to construct the diaries of incomes and spending of the poor, and to search out commonalities. "Of all the commonalities, the most fundamental is that the households are coping with incomes that are not just low, but also irregular and unpredictable, and that too few financial instruments are available to effectively manage these uneven flows. It is "triple whammy": low income; irregularity and unpredictability and a lack of tools. In the villages, farmers earn the bulk of their income during two or three peak harvest months, earning nothing during troughs. Farm laborers get a daily wage when there's work to do; at other times they sit around idle, migrate to towns, or scratch living from other sources. In the cities and urban townships, self-employed folk have good and bad days. Women's paid work in the towns, such as maidserving, is often part-time, occasional, or temporary. Unless they are very fortunate, even full-time, permanently employed poor people suffer at the hands of employers who pay irregularly."[13]

The poor do multiple chores. What they lack is specialization. For example, they are engaged in agriculture but not in a way that it provides them profits to lead a reasonable living. If financial pressure mounts and earning becomes difficult in the rural areas, they migrate to the cities in search of livelihood. They go to cities to work as laborers but in most cases they do not move permanently to cities. "There is paradox of the poor and their businesses. They are energetic and resourceful and manage to make a lot out of little. But most of their energy is spent on businesses that are too small and utterly undifferentiated from the many others around them. As a result, their operators have no chance to earn a reasonable living———. The very small scale of many of these businesses explains why their overall returns are often so low, despite the high marginal returns. One part of the answer we already know--most of these businesses cannot borrow very much and what they borrow is very expensive."[14]

Engaging in multiple chores and migration from the native village are two major indicators of the entrepreneurial spirit of the poor. So the assumption that the poor are not entrepreneurs does not hold in reality. The reason they fail to setup proper businesses is that the financial sector neither supports nor trusts them. Whatever the poor save, they keep that cash at home. They rarely have bank accounts. Resultantly, the value of their savings not only decreases due to inflation but they also cannot resist the temptation of spending money on expenditures which do not have pay off in the long-term. They tend to value present gratification more than future gratification (technically speaking, they behave impatiently showing high discount rates).

Some researchers[15] conducted three experiments with small fruit and vegetable vendors, one in India and two in the Philippines to understand why the poor do not save their way out of poverty. The vendors' production function is simple and almost the same in all poor countries. They purchase fruit and vegetables early in the morning and sell them throughout the day. They rely on money-lenders for working capital borrowing on a daily or weekly basis at exorbitant interest rates. The researchers paid cash grants and provided financial training to the vendors to pull them out of the vicious circle of debt and high interest rates.

Strangely, most of the vendors fell back into the debt within six weeks and after one to two years all were borrowing as they had been doing previously. There may be several explanations for their reversion to the earlier position. The poor vendors may not be aware of the high interest rate (say 10% per day) they are paying. If so, then public policy needs to focus on financial literacy and planning for the poor. Public policies requiring disclosure of the cost of debt for various horizons may work to change behavior. If the poor are paying a 10% interest rate daily or on a weekly basis, it runs into a horrendous amount if calculated on per annum basis.[16]

There are problems of self-control as well. Some researchers[17] conducted an experiment among the poor of the Philippines by providing lock-boxes (commitment devices) to them where the subjects of the experiment could put money and could commit to restrict their access to the savings deposited in the lock-boxes for a certain period of time. The results of this experiment suggest that commitment devices can help with self-control, spousal control, and social pressure issue to share part of income with relatives (a type of kin tax in village economies). Results further suggested an increase in the power of women in the household who could purchase more female-oriented durable goods. The public policy implication is to facilitate the establishment of financial institutions and introduce commitment features in credit and savings schemes to ameliorate the problems of self-control, spousal control, and rotten kin.[18]

The presence of financial institutions is generally in the posh areas of big cities and towns. There are multiple schemes like savings accounts, pension accounts, and home equity loans for the rich and middle classes but hardly some dedicated scheme exists for the poor to take care of self-control issues et cetera. Banerjee and Duflo pertinently point out in '*Poor Economics*' that: "Decisions about how much should be saved are difficult decisions for anyone, rich or poor alike. These decisions require thinking about the future (a future probably unpleasant to contemplate, for many of the poor), carefully laying out a number of contingencies, negotiating with a spouse or child. The richer we are, the more these decisions are made for us. Salaried workers contribute to social security, and their employers often contribute something more to a provident fund or a pension plan. If they want to save more, they have to just decide once, and the money is then automatically deducted from their bank accounts. The poor have access to none of these props".[19] The introduction of attractive schemes of compulsory savings can be helpful in adding value to the money earned by the poor.

The poor people generally tend to have large families. The proposition that large families are bad is, however, a contentious proposition in the light of empirical research. Historically, all population control public policies worldwide were premised on two assumptions: (a) large families are bad and (b) poor people are unable to control their fertility. The sterilization policy of India, the one-child policy of China, and contraception programs in several countries are manifestations of this thinking. Some ideas, even if they are fallacious, are so powerful that they keep haunting human minds for centuries. Malthusian prediction of doom and gloom was such an idea.

In 'An Essay on the Principle of Population', written in 1798, Malthus postulated that when there are more people on earth, there is less for everybody, and nature eventually puts the population back in check through high mortality, as happened during the Black Death in the UK. History, however, proved that Malthus was wrong. The population of the world has grown multiple times since Malthusian times. And technological advancements have made people more productive with the same resources as fixed land but Malthusian doomsday still haunts our minds. The influence of Malthus can be discerned easily in public policies and writings on population control.

In 1970s, economists produced a model of the quality–quantity trade-off regarding the procreation of children. The model was primarily based on the assumption that siblings compete for resources like parental attention and money so more children means that each gets fewer. "An increase in parental income would lead to a relatively large increase in parental expenditures on children if their endowments were fixed because all the desired increase in the quality of children would have to come from an increase in these expenditures. The large increase in expenditures would reduce the demand for children because the cost of each child is directly related to the expenditure on each."[20]

Empirical evidence does not lend credence to the model of quality–quantity trade-off. For example, Angrist et al.[21] tested this model by exploiting exogenous variation in family size due to twin births and preferences for a mixed sibling-sex composition. The data included Israeli

Arabs who were quite poor. The results did not support the quality–quantity trade-off empirically. Similarly, relaxation of the one-child policy in China also refutes the claim that increasing the quantity of children reduces quality as having two children proved better than having one child in terms of the welfare and human development of the children.[22]

Researchers have also studied the mental lives of the poor. We distinguish the poor from the non-poor on the basis of material possessions, amount of money, nature of work (irregular vs. regular, white-collar vs. blue-collar work), or lack of productive assets (landlord vs. landless). This distinction fails to capture the true intensity of the deprivations and distress that poverty creates. Resource scarcity imposes an additional burden on the minds of the poor and creates cognitive overload. Sendhil Mullainathan and Eldar Shafir in '*Scarcity: Why Having Too Little Means So Much*'[23] argue that scarcity limits or distorts skills and imposes a bandwidth tax on the cognitive skills of the poor. According to them, failures of the poor are part and parcel of the misfortune of being poor in the first place but it is not due to some inherent flaw in the poor that they have less bandwidth; rather, all people, if they were poor, would have less effective bandwidth.

A study,[24] based on several field experiments found that thoughts about cost are easily triggered in the daily experiences of the poor. Such thoughts come to their minds spontaneously even when money has not been mentioned. One study very relevant to our own environment, conducted in the Indian context, begs for some details to make the point. A sample of 464 sugarcane farmers living in 54 villages in the sugarcane-growing areas was selected by the researchers. The selected farmers were small farmers who owned land between 1.5 and 3 acres. They earned 60% of their income from sugarcane farming. The researchers found that the farmers were more stressed in the pre-harvest period (due to financial worries) compared to the post-harvest period. "A potential explanation of these findings is stress. Financial concerns could reasonably induce stress in pre-harvest farmers. — Being poor means coping with not just a shortfall of money, but also with a concurrent shortfall of cognitive resources. The poor, in their view, are less capable not because of inherent traits, but because the very context of poverty imposes load and impedes cognitive capacity".[25]

A review[26] of interdisciplinary evidence of a relationship between poverty and mental illness confirms that mere anticipation of economic shocks may cause mental illness as poor people face a lot of uncertainty and income volatility in their lives. Further, they are more exposed to environmental irritants like pollution, extreme temperatures, and challenging sleep environments. Lower-income impacts physical health as poverty implies limited access to health care and a greater burden of chronic and acute health conditions. Exposure to poverty in early life can profoundly impact brain development and cognitive abilities. The poor are generally more vulnerable to trauma, violence, and crime. All these channels negatively impact the mental health of the poor. The causality also runs from poor mental health to poverty. Mental health reduces people's ability to work by impacting cognitive faculties. It may distort beliefs about oneself, circumstances, and the external world. Mental illness may affect economic preferences like deferment of gratification, tolerance of risk, and reduction in motivation to supply labor and stay productive.

The point is that a deeper understanding of not only the economic lives of the poor is required but a true appreciation of the mental lives of the poor is also equally important to make poverty alleviation strategies more effective. Evidence-based research can affect public policy by changing the beliefs of those who matter for policy-making. In developing countries, policies generally flow from the top without rigorous evidence-based analysis. All the blame, however, cannot be heaped on the politicians and policy formulators for the sub-optimal policies. Part of the malaise lies in the fact that the developing countries lack quality research institutions and think tanks to guide policymakers. Hardly meaningful research is produced by universities and research institutions for impacting public policy. There is a need to bridge the gap between public policymakers and research institutions. This would be possible if meaningful research is produced by academia and research institutions. Politicians respond like other human beings to ideas and incentives. Empirics confirm this assertion. For example, some researchers[27] worked with 2150 municipalities and mayors in Brazil who controlled these municipalities to investigate whether the mayors were interested in research findings and whether their beliefs and policies changed in the light of the research outcome. Findings suggested that mayors and other municipal officials were ready to update their beliefs when informed about the findings.

Now the key question is: What are the pathways for poverty alleviation? The World Development Report 2008 talks of three broad routes to poverty alleviation: agriculture, labor, and migration. The literature on poverty also talks of some other pathways, like focusing on the non-farm rural economy, human resource development, financial inclusion, and good governance et cetera, as important planks of the poverty alleviation strategy. The ensuing discussion is about some pathways like microcredit, cash transfers, and financial inclusion not discussed elsewhere in this book. Let us start with microcredit, which has received a significant amount of attention as a pathway for poverty alleviation in developing countries since 1970s.

Neither Miracle nor Mirage

The claim of microcredit is that it fills in the void left by the formal financial sector by providing credit to the poorest of the poor. "The time has come to recognize microcredit as a powerful tool in the struggle to end poverty and economic dependence", declared the Microcredit Summit.[28] Microcredit is generally provided without the requirement of collateral, in small amounts, and for shorter periods of time. The big lending institutions generally require tangibles as collateral that is goods, property, or land. The poor neither have land, nor possess cash, nor have rich relatives, nor they have secured flow of income in the form of salaries. The poor are poor because they are poor in tangibles.

Microcredit replaces the requirement of tangibles as collateral with intangibles. It originated in Bangladesh where Dr. Muhammad Yunus built on earlier models of micro-lending (such as the Comilla Model) and established a network of lending institutions, which were formalized in the shape of Grameen Bank in the 1980s. The euphoria about micro-lending emanated from the fact that it allowed entry of formal institutions into forms of lending dominated by informal money-lenders and into areas where big financial institutions dared not enter due to problems of high transaction costs, adverse selection, and moral hazard. These problems were tackled by the micro-lending institutions through 'peer monitoring'. The credit is extended to a group of individuals who collectively guarantee as group and as members of the group, have a direct interest in ensuring that no individual member defaults. So nobody shall choose to be in a group with potential defaulters.

What do the empirics say about the impact of microcredit on consumption, business creation, and human development outcomes such as education, health, and women's empowerment? Banerjee et al.[29] used a randomized design to evaluate the impact of a group-lending microcredit program in 52 randomly selected neighborhoods of Hyderabad in 2015. Their results suggest that microcredit did not appear to fuel an escape from poverty for small business owners. Only those borrowers who already had businesses witnessed an increase in profits. Consumption also did not significantly increase though its composition changed as expenditure on durable goods increased.

They also explored relationships across different groups of borrowers that is established business owners, new entrepreneurs, and those who did not go into business. Results suggested that established businesses witnessed increase in both investment and profits; household consumption of new entrepreneurs decreased; and those who did not go into business increased their non-durable spending. No improvements in health, education, or women's empowerment occurred as a result of microcredit. The results also suggested that households that had access to microcredit seemed to work harder on their businesses which means microcredit affected labor supply.

The data on households, collected and reported in 2015 by Banerjee and his colleagues, was examined again after a few years to conclusively confirm the impact of microcredit on households. These results[30] were reported in 2019 which confirmed that households that were already running a business (called gung-ho entrepreneurs) before the entry of microcredit showed a persistent increase in profits over time. They built more assets and generated more revenue. However, no effect was observed on non-gung-ho households that is those who started new businesses or who never started a business. The results thus point toward heterogeneity in entrepreneurial ability as an important variable in determining whether microcredit can unlock the poverty trap for some entrepreneurs.

The policy implication is simple: identify the right kind of beneficiaries to make microcredit an effective path of poverty alleviation. There is some evidence[31] that microcredit can even worsen poverty among a section of borrowers (generally the poorest of the poor) under certain scenarios like delayed return on investment, suffering losses in the initial stages of business, using loans for emergency purposes or for household expenditure. It implies that a contingency fund that can be used as a safety net for failed cases, besides active guidance and technical support for setting up and running small businesses, would be an important ingredient of the poverty alleviation strategy via microcredit.

The debate on the efficacy of microcredit as a poverty alleviation tool is, however, not conclusive. The results[32] of an analysis of the Pakistan Poverty Alleviation Fund (PPAF), which works through a network of partner organizations, suggest that the impact of microcredit on the extreme poor is very little, though for those who were not in the category of the extreme poor, it helped reduce poverty. Another survey[33] was conducted to analyze the impact of microcredit on poverty alleviation and well-being in Dera Ghazi Khan and Layyah districts of Punjab province. Based on a sample of 400 clients of Khushhali Bank, a microfinance institution, results suggested that microcredit positively impacted the income generation and consumption levels of the poor.

Results of another study[34] based on a sample size of 2070 respondents, however, suggest that microcredit programs are not equally beneficial to all segments of the poor and show weak evidence of benefiting lower-quartile community members. This study further informs that the MFIs in Pakistan do not focus on the extreme poor and marginalized segments as less than 25% of the total credit is allocated for the poor, ultra-poor, and extreme poor while more than 75% is disbursed among the vulnerable poor, quasi-poor, and non-poor.

Another analysis based on the fieldwork conducted during 2010–2012 shows that the microcredit sector has experienced 'mission drift' and is no longer serving the poorest.[35] What impact does microcredit have on human development outcomes in the context of Pakistan? The results of surveys and studies conducted in this regard are also not consistent. The results of a study,[36] based on a sample of 3,400 households, suggest that microcredit helped in consumption smoothing and the enrollment of the children of the borrowers in schools increased.

A study[37] regarding the impact of credit on health and education spending in rural Pakistan, based on data from the Pakistan Panel Household Survey 2010, shows that the impact of borrowing on education was insignificant whereas the impact on health care spending was positive and significant. As regards the impact of microcredit on women's empowerment, a study[38] conducted in 2011 in Gujrat district of Punjab province shows positive results through the channels of enhanced self-awareness about themselves, about child education, and about health care utilization.

Microcredit, considered a silver bullet for poverty alleviation in the 1970s, is, however, now under serious debate with regards to its role in poverty alleviation. It is now even being described as a "poster child of exploitation of the vulnerable."[39] In the words of Jayati Ghosh, microcredit has gone from 'hero' to 'zero' in the development discourse in relatively short span of time.[40] The opinion and empirics are divided on the effects of microcredit on various aspects of poverty alleviation and development outcomes.

Banerjee et al.[41] conducted six randomized evaluations of microcredit programs introduced in six countries that is Bosnia and Herzegovina, Ethiopia, India, Mexico, Mongolia, and Morocco. The evaluations covered both urban and rural areas. The evaluated microcredit programs included programs of both individual liability and joint liability (group lending), and some of the lending institutions were for-profit organizations while others were non-profit. The nominal interest rates varied between 12% (Ethiopia) and 110% (Mexico). The results of all evaluations suggested a consistent pattern of modestly positive but not transformative effects of microcredit on the lives of the borrowers. Across all evaluations, microcredit did not help lift poor households out of poverty, both in the short-run (a period of 18 months) and the long run (three to six years). The results of all six studies also showed that access to microcredit did not increase children's schooling. Microcredit, however, helped in consumption smoothing.

Some policy tinkering in the product design of microcredit may improve its efficacy. Designing more flexible repayment schedules is one such area that has some promise. Microcredit practitioners generally argue that frequent repayment is critical for fiscal discipline and to reduce loan defaults. Empirical evidence, however, suggests the contrary. For example, results of a study,[42] in Indian setting, suggest that a more flexible schedule can reduce transaction costs without increasing default and delinquency.

The loan contracts requiring early repayment discourage illiquid and risky investments and, in this way, limit the potential impact of microfinance on microenterprise growth and household poverty. While redesigning repayment schedules, seasonal aspects need to be kept in view, as schedules that better reflect borrowers' income flows can help borrowers make better use of their loans. For example, agricultural lending tailored to the farmers' seasonal cash flow is likely to be more effective in increasing investments in agriculture and improving yields.[43] Besides tinkering with repayment schedules, segmentation of the borrower market can also help in increasing the efficacy of microcredit.

For example, existing small businesses can be one segment. They may be offered credit for transition to SMEs, as existing businesses have more potential to grow and earn profits. SMEs are considered the growth engines of the economy as they provide jobs, foster entrepreneurship, and provide depth to the industrial base of the economy. But SMEs get a disproportionately small share of credit relative to their contribution to the overall economy of the country. According to some estimates, there are around three million SMEs in Pakistan which, according to the Labour Force Survey 2020–21 employ 14.9 million labor force. They get only 6% share in the private credit despite having contribution of over 35% to the non-agricultural employment in the country. Moreover, the contribution of SMEs to employment as well as GDP has persistently increased (Fig. 9.1).

Segmentation of markets can be done on the lines of demographic characteristics (age, education, and gender etc.) and severity of poverty (poor, ultra-poor, transient poor, and vulnerable etc.). The segmentation shall induce the development of new product designs for microcredit in addition to focused and evidence-based interventions. The overall verdict of the jury on microcredit is that it may help some households and entrepreneurs in moving out of poverty but its role is not transformative. Empirical studies and evaluations have shown that it is not a miraculous cure for poverty alleviation. And the lofty claims of its proponents regarding its impact on poverty involve a lot of subjectivity and rhetoric. Besides microcredit, cash transfers to the poor have also emerged as an important policy tool for poverty alleviation.

Fig. 9.1 Growth in number of workers in SMEs (in million) (*Source Labor Force Survey (LFS), Pakistan Bureau of Statistics (PBS)*)

Cash Transfers

Results of several studies and evaluations point toward a positive impact of cash transfers on household consumption, food security, and other variables of economic and social well-being. For example, experimental evidence from Kenya suggests that unconditional cash transfers (UCTs) induced a substantial increase in household consumption and psychological well-being of the recipients.[44] Unconditional cash transfers give flexibility to the poor to choose the best opportunities to use the cash themselves rather than others choosing opportunities that may not accord with their preferences. The critics of UCTs, however, argue that the poor may waste much of such money on uses that may even be harmful for their health and long-term welfare.[45]

Contrary to UCTs, well-targeted conditional cash transfers (CCTs) are said to have a more positive impact on improving the lives of the poor. Evidence suggests that CCTs have raised household consumption levels, redistributed income toward the poor, and reduced poverty. Moreover, taxpayers are more likely to support transfers to the poor if such transfers are linked to efforts by the poor to overcome long-term poverty, particularly through actions to improve the welfare of children.[46] Cash transfer programs are also said to have multiplier effect on the local economy. For example, evidence from Brazil suggests that the expansion of Bosla Familia, a large-scale cash transfer program, increased local formal employment.[47] It means criticism that cash transfers to the poor may create a dependency culture is not well-founded.

An evaluation of Progresa, the cash transfer program of Mexico, suggests substantial intergenerational benefits of CCTs via their impact on education, work, earnings, household economic status, and the closing of gender gaps.[48] Empirics show that cash transfer programs significantly impact women's power by enhancing their say in household decisions like expenditures on various goods and investments in children.[49] The cash transfer programs are justified not only due to their appeal for poverty alleviation but also on the grounds of productivity and economic growth. It is argued that the CCTs would help build human capital as investment in education and health is required to produce healthier and well qualified workforce which in turn would boost economic growth. The influence of clientelism in the distribution of all social transfer programs including cash transfers particularly in developing countries cannot be ruled out. "The motivation for adopting and expanding these programs is not purely benign. Rather, program expansion has been shaped by a range of political interests and ideological influences, with politicians often seeking to utilize programs as a means of securing political advantage by winning votes or appeasing opponents; maintaining social order and projecting political authority; or placating the demands of social movements."[50]

Making cash transfers conditional involves a philosophical issue that is whether to let humans exercise their free will and preferences or to constrain their free choices. "Conditioning transfers is often based on the assumption that illiteracy, child health or poor health outcomes are the result of irrational behavior engaged in by the poor or of their incapacity to understand their own best interests- a moot assumption which can be challenged on many grounds. This becomes tantamount to blaming the victims of their conditions, is demeaning to the poor, and hence is likely to be resented".[51] Cash transfer programs are also likely to compromise on the dignity of the recipients. Respecting people's dignity while delivering well-being is important as rightly argued by Banerjee and Duflo in '*Good Economics for Hard Times*'.[52] Moreover, errors of exclusion cannot be ruled out as People may be ill-informed. They may have distorted beliefs about the program due to the prevalence of corruption et cetera. The process may be unnecessarily complicated and the poor and illiterate people may find it difficult to meet procedural requirements or conditions attached with the program.

For example, Tara Patricia Cookson in '*Unjust Conditions*' has documented the hurdles women face in rural areas of Peru in meeting the conditions of 'Juntos' (together), a conditional cash transfer program. She argues that imposing conditions is unjust and CCTs are efficient only if the cost of time, hassle, and labor to access them is not included in the model. She writes: "One of the appeals of conditional aid is its alleged efficiency, but in practice CCTs are efficient only if women's time and unpaid labor is worth nothing. Women labor is taken into account. When we account for all of the work that rural women are required to do to implement a CCT program, we inevitably uncover a number of hidden costs. CCTs are often rolled out in places where poor people have a difficult time accessing quality services. In Peru, rural mothers do a lot walking and waiting."[53] Additionally, all cash transfer schemes generally require disclosure of private information by the program recipients to access the program which people would not like to disclose in the normal course of things and the poor may opt out of the program due to the social stigma attached with such programs and the hurdles in complying with the conditions. These factors do explain, at least partly, the poor take up of such programs.

Going by the zeitgeist, Pakistan also initiated Benazir Income Support Programme (BISP) in 2008 which was a big jump from earlier anti-poverty alleviation frameworks in Pakistan. The objectives of this program were consumption smoothing, poverty alleviation, and women's empowerment. BISP was mainly an unconditional cash transfer program.[54] With increasing coverage, BISP included a conditional cash transfer component as well, requiring the enrollment of children in school under the Waseela-e-Taleem initiative. The conditional cash transfer component serves children aged 4–12 years by providing a stipend for primary education.

Despite changes in political regimes, budgetary allocations for BISP have increased. In FY 2022, the federal government spent 0.36% of GDP on the BISP. Empirical evidence on the outcomes of the BISP, however, is not consistent. An analysis undertaken by some researchers of the World Bank for the FY 2019 suggests that BISP reduced poverty by 1.45 percentage points and inequality by 0.48 Gini points.[55] On the contrary, another evaluation of BISP for the period 2011–2019, conducted by the PIDE, to measure the welfare impact of this program does not give encouraging results.[56] PIDE analysis shows no impact of the cash transfer on various welfare indicators related to consumption expenditures at the national level. Small positive impact is observed in the poorer provinces of Balochistan and Sindh for food expenses. No progress on expenditures on health, education, clothing, and transport was observed rather expenditure on children was found to be Rs. 74 less compared to the non-beneficiary households.

The decline of cash value in real terms, disruptions in payment frequencies, and the insufficiency of the amount may be some of the factors. After all, a paltry amount of US $10–15 per month is not likely to pull a poor household out of poverty. The contribution of the amount that beneficiaries actually receive is just 5.3% of the total consumption or 7.5% if they receive the full amount. The PIDE evaluation found no impact of cash transfers on the labor supply of the households. Perhaps the amount of cash received is so paltry that it does not impact the work-leisure trade-off. Positive impacts are more likely to happen if the amount of cash transferred is substantial as in that case poor people may work more to supplement income to break out of the poverty trap or build some assets to improve their livelihoods in the long run.

In 2019, the Ehsas program was launched under BISP with a holistic approach to poverty alleviation with social safety nets, education, human capital formation, livelihoods, and health. The Ehsas program, through its multi-pronged strategy, holds much promise for poverty alleviation. Moreover, the use of data, digitization, and technology is expected to have some other unintended positive consequences like weakening of patronage networks, building institutional capacities, and improving governance. But the program will face at least two big challenges as it grows in age and scope. The first is its fiscal sustainability.

High debt and fiscal deficit can bring the program under pressure at any time and further scaling of the program or its operations may not be possible due to fiscal constraints. "There is no foolproof measure against it. Only a focus on economic growth can provide the certainty of a greater base from which to fund Ehsas. As such, the sustainability of Ehsas is critically linked to the government's overall ability to grow the economy and tax base. Growth underlies the anti-poverty agenda in several ways, most crucially by providing 'graduation' opportunities from poverty through employment opportunities and various other benefits."[57]

The second challenge is to evolve and implement a robust strategy to facilitate the ultra-poor graduate out of poverty which would require a long-term implementation plan and overhauling of training and vocational institutions besides improving business and investment climate for creation of employment opportunities by the private sector. A well-thought-out national poverty graduation plan needs to be embedded in the Ehsas program to make it sustainable and more meaningful. The demographic profile of BISP beneficiaries shows that recipient households have a fair share of a young population. Vocational and skills training for such youth can be an important component of the graduation plan through self-employment. Cash transfers, along with some complementary interventions, can prove to be an important strategy for poverty alleviation.[58]

For example, one-off transfer of a productive asset like some land, a dairy cow, or some lump-sum cash grant, small regular transfers (that is cash transfers) to protect beneficiaries from liquidating the productive asset in case of some negative shock, and training to acquire skills required to succeed in the chosen income-generating field can turn out to be an important package for poverty alleviation. Succinctly put, the success of any cash transfer program depends on the following points: How is cash transferred that is with some strings or without strings? Generally, CCTs are more successful. To whom is cash being given? Empirics do not confirm the unitary model of household decision-making. If women's empowerment is one of the goals, then cash transfers to women are expected to produce better results. Shifting income within a household from man to woman is more likely to benefit the mother and the children.[59] How much cash is given? Small handouts just serve the purpose of some consumption smoothing and do not have some tangible impact on poverty reduction. And whether the cash transfer program is embedded in the overall graduation from poverty strategy?

Cash transfers alone are not going to lift the poor out of poverty. The programs for cash transfers existed even prior to BISP and Ehsas. For example, the distribution of Zakat funds among the poor is, for all purposes, unconditional cash transfer program, but it did not help the poor move out of poverty.[60] Cash transfers can be one of the ingredients of a poverty alleviation strategy, but they alone are not sufficient to pull the poor out of poverty traps. John Weiss and his colleagues analyzed, in 2005, the poverty targeting programs of five Asian countries (India, Indonesia, China, Thailand, and the Philippines) in detail, and their finding was that while some poverty alleviation schemes or programs had a modest positive effect on the poor, trends in poverty reduction were mainly driven by economic growth rather than by targeted interventions.[61]

The poverty alleviation strategy has to be broad-based, essentially incorporating equitable economic growth, financial inclusion, asset transfer, and better public service delivery as its main ingredients. Exclusion is the word that perhaps best differentiates the poor from the non-poor. The poor are excluded from ownership of productive assets. They are excluded from better education and health facilities. They are excluded from better public services and they are excluded from the banking system. They are socially excluded from elite spaces and from doing small businesses in elite areas in Pakistan. So exclusion is basically the name of poverty.

Financial Exclusion

When we talk about the financial system, the majority of the poor lack access to bank accounts and have to use either informal channels of savings or put their savings under the pillow, with all attendant negative consequences like fear of theft and decrease in the value of money. "Stashing money in mattresses puts it at the risk of being stolen and means it neither accrues interest nor gets used more productively through lending, as it would be if it were in a bank."[62] Based on financial diaries of 250 poor households of Bangladesh, India, and South Africa, some researchers show that the poor households fully understand the significance of the savings and also have some room in their budgets to save for the future as vindicated by their use of informal saving mechanisms and use of saving clubs. The saving clubs have limited life-spans, so the poor have fewer opportunities to build up savings into large sums over the long-term and due to this limitation, they are unable to deal with "expensive life-cycle events, with purchase of big assets, and with emergencies."[63]

The World Bank has published financial inclusion data regularly since 2011 covering aspects like worldwide account ownership and gaps on the basis of gender, education, income, and residence (urban versus rural) with regards to access to financial services. According to Findex data, Pakistan is the least inclusive country in the South Asian region in terms of access to financial services. Discussion on two main variables that is ownership of bank accounts and borrowing from banks shall prove the point. According to Findex, only 13.5% of females have bank accounts in Pakistan whereas in Sri Lanka and India over 89% and 77% of females respectively have accounts in financial institutions. Out of the poorest 40%, only 17.6% have accounts in banks whereas for Sri Lanka and India this figure is respectively 87.1% and 78.3%. Similarly, yawning gaps exist in terms of education and residence. (see Table 9.1).

Having a bank account means opening up of vistas for saving and borrowing. Second variable which merits particular mention is borrowing from the banks. Hardly 3% Pakistanis borrow from the financial institutions. Borrowing from formal financial institutions is over 14% in Bangladesh, around 12% in India, and over 21% in Sri Lanka. Again gaps in terms of education, income (rich versus poor), gender, and residence (rural versus urban) are very sharp in Pakistan compared to other regional countries. (see Table 9.2).

Table 9.1 Accounts holder in a financial institution

Country/ Region	*All (% age 15 +)*	*Male (% age 15 +)*	*Female (% age 15 +)*	*Primary education or less (% age 15 +)*	*Secondary education or more (age 15 +)*	*poorest 40% (age 15 +)*	*richest 60% (% age 15 +)*	*Rural (% age 15 +)*	*Urban (age 15 +) %*
Bangladesh	52.8	62.9	43.5	46.6	56.6	48.7	55.6	50	53.7
India	77.5	77.5	77.6	75.3	84.9	78.3	77.1	77.3	77.8
Nepal	54	58.6	49.9	51	63.3	44.6	60.3	51.6	61.5
Pakistan	**21**	**28.2**	**13.5**	**15.3**	**35.3**	**17.6**	**23.2**	**15.6**	**24.5**
Sri Lanka	89.3	89.3	89.3	76.9	93	87.1	90.7	NA	NA
South Asia	67.9	69.9	65.8	65.4	72.8	67.5	68.2	NA	NA
World	76.2	78.4	74	66	84.6	71.9	79.1	NA	NA

Source Global Findex Database (2021)

Table 9.2 Borrowed from a financial institution

Country/ Region	*All (% age 15 +)*	*Male (% age 15 +)*	*Female (% age 15 +)*	*Primary education or less (% age 15 +)*	*Secondary education or more (% age 15 +)*	*poorest 40% (% age 15 +)*	*richest 60% (% age 15 +)*	*Rural (% age 15 +)*	*Urban (%age 15 +)*
Bangladesh	14.2	12.5	15.8	12.2	6.9	16.5	-14.0	11.8	15.0
India	11.8	13.3	10.2	10.0	15.5	10.7	12.5	10.6	13.2
Nepal	14.1	15.5	12.8	13.6	15.8	13.3	14.7	14.6	12.6
Pakistan	3.5	3.7	3.3	3.6	3.3	3.9	3.3	3.8	3.3
Sri Lanka	21.3	21.2	21.4	11.7	24.1	20.5	21.8	NA	NA
South Asia	6.6	12.2	10.0	9.5	14.1	10.3	11.6	NA	NA
World	28.4	29.6	27.2	17.8	37.0	23.0	32.0	NA	NA

Source Global Findex Database (2021)

Financial inclusion promotes inclusive economic growth by facilitating access of the poor to economic opportunities. Some evidence based on microdata suggests that financial development disproportionately boosts the incomes of the poorest quintile and reduces income inequality.[64] An inclusive financial system that provides financial services to the poor households is a key ingredient of any strategy for inclusive growth. Exclusions of various types are all connected. For example, a financially excluded person has every probability of being socially excluded.

Results of a study,[65] based on data from Pakistan panel household survey, suggest that deep social exclusion drops from 81% to 34.5% if people are financially included. The study also revealed that none of the women who had access to the financial system were socially excluded. Empirics from other countries also confirm that expansion of the banking sector to poor areas helps reduce poverty. For example, India between 1977 and 1990 adopted a 1:4 licensing policy aimed at forcing banks (wishing to expand branches in already banked locations) to open branches in locations in unbanked areas. The results of an evaluation of this social banking experiment suggest that rural branch expansion increased access for the unbanked rural population to credit and saving facilities. And consequently, poverty decreased in those rural areas.[66]

Results of another investigation utilizing state-level data for the period 1983–2005 on financial depth, branch penetration, and rural poverty from 15 Indian states found that financial deepening reduces rural poverty through fostering entrepreneurship, migration of the poorest toward more financially developed states, and structural reallocation.[67] Similarly, an analysis of Jan Dhan Yojna (JDY), the largest financial inclusion program in India (which was launched in August 2014 and led to 255 million new bank account openings), suggests that regions more exposed to the program experienced an increase in lending as the banks created more demand for formal credit by previously unbanked households. The analysis also suggests that regions more exposed to the program witnessed increased borrowing and spending for health-related reasons.[68]

Similar results emerge from the analysis of the Umurenge Program of Rwanda, a large-scale government-supported, subsidized microfinance expansion program. The said program aimed to expand financial inclusion through the creation of an extensive network of community-focused savings and credit cooperatives (Umurenge SACCOs). Based on an analysis of the administrative dataset of the loans granted by the financial institutions between 2008 and 2016, the results show that the program raised the likelihood of access to bank loans for previously unbanked individuals.[69] Results of another experiment in the context of rural Kenya suggest that around 40% of women market vendors, who took up savings accounts even at negative real interest rates, were able to save more and increase their productive investment and private expenditure.[70]

Similar results were observed in Nepal where, in a setting with low penetration of bank accounts, access was provided to simple bank accounts with no fees at local bank branches to a large sample of female household heads. The zero fees and physical proximity of the bank branches led to high take-up and usage rates of bank accounts. Access to the savings accounts increased monetary assets of the households and their total assets without crowding out other kinds of assets. The results also suggested that financial access increased households' investments in education and their ability to cope with shocks.[71]

Providing individuals with simple informal savings technologies can substantially increase investment in human resources like preventive health. For example, in Kenya, provision of just safe boxes for keeping money was found to increase health savings by 66%.[72] Evidence from the Chhattisgarh province of India also suggests that switching from cash to account-based transfers promotes savings among the poor. Some researchers sampled 442 villagers in 17 villages in Chhattisgarh and collaborated with an NGO providing banking services to the villagers on behalf of a bank. They selected and trained one shop owner per village to become the local banker. The villagers sampled for analysis either already had an account or were assisted in opening new ones.

The researchers gathered detailed information on the evolution of earnings and expenditures among the households included in the sample. The interviewees were paid for each interview and randomly allocated to be paid on the account or in cash. Those paid on account were free to deposit or withdraw the amount they wanted. The transaction costs were negligible, and the bank was located at their doorstep. The results suggested that a simple change from cash payments to payments in accounts had a tremendous impact on the savings patterns of the villagers. Being paid on the account instead of cash increased the account balance on average by 110% and the effects were long-lasting.[73]

Despite all empirics pointing toward the crucial role of financial institutions for poverty alleviation, formal financial institutions consider the poor to be risky customers with little potential for revenue and profit generation. Financial resilience and the ability to save money for future expenses, make payments, and transfer money to friends and family are some of the basic necessities of the poor. Both supply and demand-side factors matter. Better enabling environment to access financial services like lower banking costs, greater proximity to banking branches, and fewer requirements for documentation for opening accounts, promote financial inclusion.

For example, a team of researchers collected data on 148 economies through the Gallup World Poll (GWP) in 2011. The survey gathered data from 1000 individuals (at the minimum) from each country. The target population was the entire civilian population aged 15 and older. Finally, data from 123 countries including Pakistan was used which included over 124,000 individuals. Results[74] confirmed that policies like requiring banks to provide low-fee accounts, exempting financially excluded households from onerous documentation requirements, allowing correspondent banking, and using bank accounts to make government payments are some effective policy tools for financial inclusion. Besides socio-economic variables like employment, education, and gender et cetera, cognitive resources like attitudes, values, and socialized experiential learning that is mental models also determine access to financial services.[75]

An inclusive financial system would incorporate both supply and demand-side factors. On top is the presence of banks in areas where the poor reside. Some researchers have studied the impact of the Brazilian program 'Banks for All' (Banca para Todos) launched by the federal government of Brazil in 2004. This program targeted underbanked cities that were not being served by the government-owned banks. The results showed a strong positive effect on the overall amount of credit and deposits and as a result of the program the number of firms, wages, and demand for labor increased in the said areas.[76]

Besides banking penetration in underbanked areas (generally rural and low-income areas) and relaxation in documentation requirements, introduction of new forms of collateral is also important to promote financial inclusion. The role of the government is highly crucial as private banks may not venture into rural and poor areas due to high transaction costs and moral hazard issues. It means that government-led pushes would be needed and in this regard establishment of a champion institution dedicated to financial inclusion would be a step in the right direction. Revisiting regulations requiring banks to provide services to the poor at low fees, launching agent banking model to increase the outreach of financial institutions in remote areas, encouraging digital payments, and investing in financial literacy can be some public policy measures for a financial inclusion strategy to boost economic growth and reduce poverty.

Initial Endowments and Productive Assets

Actually, it is the poverty which causes poverty.[77] And in order to pull out of the poverty trap, a poor person needs a basic threshold level of capital or initial endowments. The minimum level of capital or endowments is a type of fixed cost, a threshold limit which a poor household needs to cross to break out of the vicious circle. Initial endowments determine the trajectories of growth of the households. For instance, if at point A, a household is endowed with productive assets above the threshold level, it shall accumulate more assets and, in all probability, shall make positive bequests to the next generation in the form of physical assets, good education, and better health et cetera as assets help build more assets. On the other hand, a poor household with no productive assets or having endowments below a threshold limit at point A shall find it difficult to break the poverty trap and, in all probability, it shall make negative bequests to the next generation in the form of poor health, illiteracy, and child labor as with lower initial levels of wealth or assets, future wealth or income will be even lower (that is threshold effect).

The majority of the targeted interventions for poverty alleviation miss the threshold effect. A large exogenous income push is required to attain a sustainable trajectory of higher income. It is similar to our physiology. Around 65–70% of the energy intake goes for maintaining human life while 30–35% is spent on discretionary activities like work or leisure.[78] The maintenance requirements are like fixed costs—a threshold one must meet before one can do some physical work. Similarly, one day of schooling will not give you a bump in your earnings. Some critical minimums, like attaining a certificate level of education, will be required to get an earnings bump.

The major part of the poverty story is basically the story of productive assets required to overcome the threshold effects. Tools like microcredit and cash transfers help smooth consumption or give temporary relief. They alone are insufficient to lift the poor out of the poverty on a permanent basis. They are food supplements, not the food. An integrated approach entailing the transfer of productive assets on one-time basis, with some cash transfer or credit on a regular basis until a household graduates from poverty by creating a stream of regular income from the productive assets, is required. For example, transfer of ownership of some land through land reforms, along with financial assistance to purchase seed and fertilizers would be a strategy that may pull households out of the poverty trap. Similarly, providing some cattle and financial assistance on a regular basis for some time with a clear graduation strategy would be a good policy option for poverty alleviation. This integrated approach to poverty alleviation is premised on the assumption that giving people fishing nets (some productive asset) is better than giving them fish (cash or a handout). What the poor need is a tract of land, a net to fish with, or simply an opportunity for gainful employment. Moreover, transfer of productive assets and provision of gainful employment do not rob the poor of their dignity and agency. On the contrary, deep disregard for the human dignity of the poor is endemic in the social protection system.[79]

The productive assets enable the poor to create a stream of regular income after some time, if the productive assets are put to use and are not disposed of or liquidated to meet the adverse economic shocks. Some regular financial assistance to avert the chances of liquidation of such a productive asset is required till the time such productive asset starts giving a stream of income. Transfers of productive assets increase opportunity for the people in contrast to traditional policies of cash transfers or welfare support which are in essence consumption-focused. The traditional programs generally do not help break the poverty traps. The transfer of one-time large productive assets does. Researchers have empirically tested the said hypothesis.

For instance, a program in Bangladesh targeted the ultra-poor and offered one-off transfers of productive assets (cows in most cases and mostly to women) and training, thus relaxing both credit and skills constraints to create a regular flow of income by productively utilizing the asset. The program, exploiting variation in the initial endowments of 6,000 extremely poor households in 1309 villages, found that one-time transfers of productive assets help break the poverty trap by expanding opportunity to the poor and eliminating misallocation of labor.[80] Similar results have been found in the Indian context where asset transfers (livestock) are found to have a positive impact on the lives of the ultra-poor through increased consumption and income and better health, even after a period of 10 years, and thus appear to have durably lifted them out of extreme poverty.[81]

In the Pakistani context as well, results of a field experiment confirm that asset-based microfinance for microenterprises can yield significant and persistent effects in the form of higher profits, an increase in household consumption of food, and children's education.[82] Results of evaluations from six different countries including Pakistan suggest that an integrated approach combining productive asset transfer with consumption support (cash transfers etc.), training (like vocational training for skills enhancement), savings encouragement (through financial inclusion), and health education and services can make sustainable improvements in the lives of the poor in a relatively short period of time.[83]

According to some estimates[84] about rural Pakistan if a household possesses physical assets like land and livestock, the incidence of poverty tends to fall by 55%. Interestingly, results of some simulation exercises show that gains from increases in the production of livestock are more evenly distributed compared with increases in the production of crops.[85] A 10% increase in the output of major crops overall increased income by 2.5%. The large and medium farm owners' incomes respectively increased by 6.2% and 4.3% in contrast to the incomes of small farmers and tenants who witnessed a rise of 3.3% and 3.7% respectively. The incomes of the non-farm rural poor just witnessed an increase of 2.7% through the multiplier effect. Compared to this, gains from a 10% increase in livestock production are more evenly spread out given the distribution of ownership of animals. A 10% increase in livestock production in Punjab is estimated to increase the income of small farm owners, small farm renters, and landless agricultural households by 6.4%, 10%, and 7.1%, respectively. The transfer of livestock as a productive asset for poverty alleviation also involves an important gender dimension, as women generally play a major role in the rearing and caring of animals.[86]

When we talk of the transfer of productive assets, giving ownership of some animals (cows, buffalo, sheep, goats etc.) is an important area but perhaps the most important area is giving ownership of some land through redistribution. It is not a coincidence that Japan, South Korea, and Taiwan, the countries that showed fast economic growth, did land reforms as their first step toward economic development "When Korea was an overwhelmingly an agrarian country, land reforms undoubtedly contributed to greater equity in the size distribution of income. In the late 1930s, 3% of all farm households had owned over two-thirds of all land, whereas ten years later, fewer than 7% of all households were landless."[87] More than three thousand acres changed hands in Taiwan contributing to the evolution of an equitable and socially stable society.[88]

In modern times, Chinese agrarian reforms are perhaps the most pertinent example of how equitable allocation of land can reduce poverty within a short span of time. China established the household responsibility system in 1978 and introduced a series of agrarian reforms. The collectives were dismantled and almost all the farmland was allocated to the farmers. The equitable allocation of land among farmers and the incentive system associated with said redistribution became one of the chief reasons for the dramatic reduction of rural poverty in China in the 1980s.[89]

Despite strong evidence pointing toward huge efficiency gains and an impact on poverty, redistributive land reforms are now out of the development narrative in Pakistan principally due to the vested interests of those who wield power in society. “The structure of rural society, in areas where landownership is highly unequal, tends to be strongly hierarchical, with large landowners or tribal chiefs exercising considerable control over the decisions, personal or otherwise, of people living in the area under their influence, as well as over their access to social infrastructure facilities.”[90]

Transfer of land has multiple advantages compared to transfer of livestock (cows, buffalo, sheep etc.). It is comparatively difficult to liquidate land compared to livestock. A buffalo can be sold, stolen, or slaughtered. Further, land can increase the poor's income in at least five ways.[91] First, small farms use much more labor per acre than big farms so an equal distribution of land by creating smaller farm units raises demand for the labor. Second, if landless or lower-income people get ownership of some land, they get at least some addition to their income whether they cultivate it themselves or rent it. Third, if the poor control the farmland, they start enjoying income from farm enterprises as they plan, manage, and supervise the farm activities. Fourth, land reform tends to increase non-farm income as well. Small landholders are more likely to use their income in the local area for the purchase of farm inputs which are mostly labor-intensive. Consequently, rural incomes rise due to the multiplier effect whereas in the case of big landowners rural incomes generally shift to urban areas. Fifth, poor people gain from the country-wide effects of land redistribution as extreme inequalities of assets and income slow down economic growth. Inequalities in assets further skew growth away from the poor and poverty reduction becomes harder.

Quality and rule-based public service delivery is another important route for poverty alleviation. Poor public service delivery and poverty are connected. In the last two to three decades, copious amounts of literature have emerged to gage the quality and determinants of public services. The researchers have devised very ingenious methods to empirically assess the quality of governance and service delivery.

Poor Public Services

Some researchers[92] mailed letters to non-existent business addresses in 159 countries and measured how long it took to return the letter. They observed huge variation across countries in terms of the number of letters returned and the time of return (how long it took the letters to return with a report of being undelivered by postal authorities). Interestingly, the rate of return was high in countries like Canada, Norway, Germany, and Japan (countries known for better public service delivery) while the return rate from 16 countries, mostly located in the African region, was zero. The countries known for quality public service are generally the rich countries having higher per capita incomes while those where return was zero are the poor countries. So, a direct relationship between the quality of public service delivery (governance) and prosperity can be easily discerned. The causality runs both ways that is from good governance to prosperity and from prosperity to good governance.

One thing is, however, quite conspicuous. The poor face exclusions and denials of basic public services as we have seen in our discussions on health and education. In rural Pakistan, 16% do not have electricity. Only 33% have brick houses. 26% defecate in the open.[93] The poor are constrained to visit private health facilities due to non-availability of public health care or due to the fear lurking in their minds that they may be served with expired drugs and dangerous diagnoses besides facing long delays in obtaining consultation due to absenteeism of doctors. "Studies suggest that the poor more frequently remark on the impact of a brutalizing police force and a corrupt judiciary than is apparent from official accounts of indicators and causes of poverty. -- Dysfunctional institutions do not just fail to deliver services; they disempower and even silence the poor through humiliation, exclusion, and corruption. The persistent inability of the government to rectify these conditions is arguably the most important constraint on long-term growth prospects and inequality".[94]

"Come tomorrow as Sahib is not in office". "Your file is not traceable". "Sahib is not in the chair". "The time for public dealing is over". "Sahib is in the meeting". It is common to hear such responses when you happen to visit a public office to obtain a public service. Improving the quality of service is important for poverty alleviation and economic growth. Poor quality of services creates disincentives for obtaining them. For example, poor health facilities in public sector dispensaries and rural health centers may create disincentives for the poor and they may not use these facilities. An education system with the least focus on skills required for gainful employment may discourage parents from sending their children to school. Long delays in getting justice may disillusion them with the formal judicial system.

Non-market and non-deferential access to public goods and services should be the broad principle for ensuring equality among citizens. It would be possible if the men on street feel empowered to hold the government accountable. "Governance-related impediments have historically muted the ability of the poor, women, and marginalized citizens to hold governments and government functionaries accountable. This has, in turn, set an incentive for governments and government functionaries to be unresponsive to the poor, women, and socially excluded and marginalized groups. This suggests that a viable poverty reduction strategy needs to analyze and overcome governance-related impediments to poverty."[95] And to remove such impediments to good governance, the most important initiative would be to introduce reforms in the public sector, particularly civil service, with a view to make it more productive, development- oriented, and pro-people.

CHAPTER 10

The Public Sector Performance Conundrum

Peter Evans starts *'Embedded Autonomy'*,[1] a book on state's economic role, by quoting a Brazilian joke on the working of public sector. Two lions escape from the zoo and take two different paths. One goes to a wooded park. He is captured as soon as he becomes hungry and eats a passerby. The second lion is captured, sleek and fat, after remaining at large for months. His companions ask the second lion when he is brought to the zoo, "where did you find such a great place to hide"? "In one of the ministries", says the lion. "Every three days I ate a bureaucrat and none noticed". On it, his companions further inquire, "then how did you get caught?" "I ate the man who served coffee in the morning break", replied the lion.

This joke typifies the general image of the public sector employees in the developing countries like Pakistan. Perception is deeply entrenched that the bureaucrats do nothing. They are bothered about their coffee (impliedly they are a burden on the exchequer and care more about their benefits and privileges), and are not missed even by their colleagues (inference is that there is a lack of coordination among sections and departments they are working). It is an extreme view about the performance of the civil servants brandied by some economists even in Pakistan. Their argument is that public sector, being inefficient, lazy, and rigid, creates hindrances for the entrepreneurs. Therefore, solution is to reduce the role of the public sector to the minimum. Reduce its footprint on the

J. Nasir, *Development Challenges of Pakistan*,
https://doi.org/10.1007/978-981-97-3064-3_10

economy, privatize most of its functions, and let the market forces decide the outcomes to induce efficiency in the economy, they advise.

The debate about the footprint of the public sector is fundamentally flawed. For instance, 22% of Singapore's GDP is derived from state-owned enterprises (SOEs) (which are persistently incurring losses in Pakistan) and around 89% land is managed by the state. Similarly, in Scandinavian countries, public sector is simultaneously big-sized and efficient. Even otherwise, there is hardly any counterfactual or empirical evidence to prove that public sector enterprises are always inefficient compared to private sector. We can find many instances of public sector organizations which have demonstrated miraculous performance. Singapore Airlines, Pohang Steel Company (POSCO) of South Korea, and Empresas Publicas de Medellin (EPM) of Colombia are a few pertinent instances to make the point. And privatization is not the only alternative to make the public sector organizations efficient. Increasing competition and administrative reforms can be some other alternatives to outright privatization.

The size of the Leviathan has kept on increasing in the twentieth century even in developed countries like USA. Robert Higgs in *'Crisis and Leviathan'*[2] gives a comprehensive and critical account of the outgrowth of government in USA. His thesis is that whenever there is a crisis, there is a demand from the government to 'do something'. Even after the crisis is over, the government does not return to its pre-crisis position, as it is hard to disband the bureaucracy created to tackle the crisis. Crises help grow the size of the government. And crises are more frequent in developing countries due to poverty, low income, fragility of state, and poor governance, so the debate on the size of the public sector in such countries becomes even less relevant. For example, in response to earthquake disaster, National Disaster Management Authority (NDMA) and Provincial Disaster Management Authorities (PDMAs) were set up in Pakistan. Similarly, Dengue control units were established for handling dengue. Can a government afford not to respond to a disaster, a natural calamity, or an epidemic? It cannot. It has to do something and once the government does something additional, which it was not previously doing, its footprint increases.

Is Public Sector the Problem?

Public sector differs from the private sector in terms of tasks, objectives, and sources of motivation. The overriding motive of the private sector is profit maximization whereas objectives of public bureaucracies are less clear-cut than of private firms.[3] Private sector shall not produce things where it can either not earn profit at the end of the day or where it cannot prevent others from using or benefitting out of the product. "The problem is that there is no substitute for a lot of things the government does. When a tornado strikes, when an indigent needs healthcare, or when an industry shuts down, there is usually no market solution. The government exists in parts to solve problems no other institution can realistically tackle".[4] So, there are certain goods and services that only government can produce due to the problems of free riding and non-excludability. The economists call them public goods. Pertinent examples are defense, public health care system, public safety, and a legal system et cetera.

Then there are some goods produced by the private sector having benefit or harm for others. For instance, if you plant trees in your house, the benefit would also be for the neighbors as trees would have a salubrious effect on the environment or if you get yourself vaccinated against Covid, others interacting with you shall also be saved. Similarly, if a government adopts pro-growth policies, the society shall be benefitted out of economic growth (if it is inclusive). These are examples of positive externalities. Contrary to this, throwing of waste by a factory in the stream shall have negative impact on the people living the downstream. The negative impact of effluent of the leather tanneries on the health of the people and ground water in the cities of Karachi, Kasur, and Sialkot are well-documented. The government is required to regulate such externalities by imposing taxes, called Pigouvian Taxes.

Economic transactions involving asymmetries of information also need to be regulated by the government. For instance, a drug supplier or manufacturer, based on clinical trials or studies, is aware that the drug produced by him is harmful. The patients may, however, be ignorant about the clinical results or harmfulness of the drugs, hence the asymmetry of information and need for regulation. Some degree of social control and redistribution are two other categories of functions which a government is supposed to perform.[5] Governments may want their citizens to be law-abiding (police stations, courts, traffic signals etc.). They would like their citizens to be educated (establishment of public schools and universities), and healthy (public health care system, establishment of sports centers and stadiums, high taxes on cigarettes to discourage their use, control of drug use, ban on use, transportation and smuggling of heroin, provision of meals and food supplements in public schools, and vaccination etc.). The government may also like their citizens to be patriotic (paying taxes honestly, voting in elections, volunteering for community service, serving in army and civil service, and being proud as citizen of the country).

Then there are some 'dos and don'ts' in the society, depending upon its value system, for which market solutions are not morally desirable. In '*What Money Can't Buy*[6]', Michael Sandel, a Harvard political philosopher and a Nobel laureate, discusses in detail the moral limits of the market. According to Sandel, market choices are not always free choices because some people are so poor that they have virtually no choice except to participate in the market. They may be coerced to sell their kidney, or to have sex, or other kinds of labor they would otherwise reject. So market values work for the advantage of the wealthy and powerful at the expense of the poor and the vulnerable, and can thus promote economic injustice. They also crowd out other values like moral equality, civic duty, norms of cooperation and respect, and altruism et cetera, Sandel argues.

Redistribution of resources (taxing the rich and transfer payments to the poor, provision of targeted subsidies to the poor, better public services, and provision of credit to small businesses and farmers free of interest or at low interest rates) is another important function of the government to correct the distortions of the market. Taxing the rich and transferring part of the tax money to the poor is also a mechanism for ensuring stability. The poor are in majority, above 50% in any case, and through redistribution, government provides security to the businesses and the riches of the elite. Suppose no mechanism of redistribution is in place and only factors like market, luck, talent, or merit determine the outcomes, the first causalities would then be the law and order and stability in the society. Even the elite may not keep enjoying prosperity in such a scenario. Redistribution of resources is, for all practical purposes, a tax for maintaining harmony in the society.

Transfer payments are not necessarily motivated out of the benevolence or some grand ethical considerations. They are simply pure self-interest or realpolitik or bargain between the elite and the non-elite. What would be the bargain between the elite and the poor shall depend on the potency of the voice of the poor, level of their cohesiveness (how much united they are), education or awareness, ability of collective bargaining, capacity to overcome the collective action problem, and type of government (repressive or democratic).

Non-rivalry and non-excludability are two essential ingredients of a pure public good. The character of public good is, however, not divinely defined or rigidly fixed. A society or a system expresses its preferences by declaring various goods and services as public depending on the ideals it holds and power sharing arrangements in the contending groups. A communist regime is an extreme where everything would be a public good whereas in capitalism emphasis is on leaving the majority of goods and services to the private sector and restricting the role of government to the provision of fewer public goods.

Preferences differ. The rich may prefer to treat education and health as private goods and not to be burdened with taxes for public health care and education. On the other hand, the poor and disadvantaged sections would like to keep said areas in the domain of the public sector. So how to resolve this riddle? Certainly, this riddle would be resolved through the aggregation of preferences and the best way designed so far by the human ingenuity for the aggregation of preferences is democracy based on the principle of one man one vote. Another point, relevant for the resolution of the riddle, is that the society has to agree on at least some basic goods, services, and requirements of life to which every citizen shall be entitled, irrespective of his social status, income level, gender, ethnicity, and other such variables. Such a consensus is needed in the society, partly due to a sense of justice lurking in human conscience and partly to live better lives.

Need to Renegotiate the Common Good

Psychologically "a central concern in human lives is maintaining the belief that they live in a just world and a variety of acts which we appropriately label as cruel or indifferent stem directly from their attempt to protect this belief, it is also true that this commitment remains a powerful untapped source for generating constructive social change."[7] Our belief in a just world demands a society which is free from misery, poverty, injustice, and oppression. A sense of justice is deeply ingrained in the human psyche. That is why we would remain uneasy after watching a movie where the villain gets away with his evil deeds (and no Hollywood or Bollywood producer can afford to produce a movie with an unjust ending).

The question now is how this sense of justice can be brought out of the minds and hearts of the people for devising a criterion for a just society. The concept of 'veil of ignorance' of John Rawls seems quite appealing in this regard. The said concept assumes a situation when we are still not born. We do not know about our gender. We do not know whether we would be endowed with good health or bad health. We do not know to which parents, circumstances, and place we would be born. "–no one knows his place in society, his class position or social status; nor does he know his fortune in the distribution of natural assets and abilities, his intelligence and strength, and the like".[8]

Through the reasoning from behind the veil of ignorance, we have to arrive at some principles or touchstones of justice and common good. The thought experiment of reasoning may not be an ideal one as we are conditioned by the place and status we already occupy in the society. There are certainly limitations of reasoning regarding the veil of ignorance or 'original position'. For instance, 'the closed impartiality' may exclude the voice of those who are not part of the focal group doing this reasoning, inconsistencies may arise with the change in size and composition of the group, and shared prejudices and biases of the group may not be ruled out in the final decisions.[9]

The virtual absence of laborers, small farmers, illiterates, and wage earners from any decision-making group, say Parliament, shall certainly not take care of their preferences and interests. One of the myths of the modern age is that we need well-groomed, well-educated, and gold medalists for better governance. "Governing well requires practical wisdom and civic virtue-an ability to deliberate about the common good and to pursue it effectively".[10] The capacity for political judgment to define common good requires character, insight, and a sense of judgment. Despite limitations of the 'veil of ignorance' reasoning, at least one benefit is very much obvious in this way of reasoning and that is rights do not remain just a 'sloganeering' rather acquire a 'rationale'. For example, right to health can provide an insurance against the misfortune of having bad genes. The right to education insures us against the disparities from the situation in which we are born or we grow up.[11]

We may visualize the bad luck scenarios in Pakistan and allocate resources to compensate for those bad luck scenarios. Bad health is one such scenario. Failure in the provision of health care to ailing persons means that they cannot fully participate in life. Can a civilized society afford its members not to live a full life just due to the reason that they are debilitated by illness? It means that health care needs to be treated as a pure public good universally provided by the state out of the tax money. Same argumentation applies to education. Health and education are the areas that need not be abdicated to the private sector.

Similarly, some guaranteed income in case of unemployment, disability, and old age needs to be provided without any strings attached. A roof on head and ownership of some productive resource like land to earn income are some other areas warranting public policy interventions on the principles of equity and reasoning from behind the veil of ignorance. Unfortunately, majority of the economic gurus in Pakistan fail to understand that economics does not end on just taxation, balance of payments debate, debt issue, less regulation, or less footprint of the government on economy.

Economics is about well-being of the community and society. It is not just about the creation of wealth but also about the distribution of that wealth among the members of a society for equity and for making the lives of the people better. Unfortunately, all welfare and redistributive economics has gone missing from the debate among Pakistani economists, intellectuals, and media. When we say that economics needs to embrace the interest and welfare of the poor, all debate distills down to the management of the common good.

How land and other productive assets would be distributed? How natural capital would be preserved and for what purposes its rents be used? These are important questions worthy of debate by the economists. Jean Tirole, a French professor of Economics and Nobel Laureate, pertinently emphasizes that: "Economics is not in the service of private property and individual interest, nor it serves those who would like to use the state to impose their values or to ensure that their own interests prevail--its goal is to make the world a better place. To this end, its task is to identify the institutions and policies that will promote the common good. In pursuit of the well-being of the community it incorporates both individual and collective dimensions".[12]

Social well-being hugely depends on cohesion and solidarity in the society. Existence of high level of general culture and a strong sense of common interest are required to be able to lead a life of dignity and culture.[13] The equality of condition is direly lacking in Pakistan and socio-economic disparities are such that people hardly have common grounds to interact. Those with means rarely encounter with the poor on equal grounds. Their interaction is always hierarchical that is master and subordinate positions. They live and work in different conditions and environments. Their children go to different schools. Their health facilities differ in terms of access and quality. The inter-class marriages are rare.

For negotiating the common good, not only Parliament needs to be made more representative in terms of socio-economic classes but common places and spaces are required where people from all classes and walks of life can interact with one another. It is only through the encouragement of speech between people of different socio-economic classes that new narratives for the common good can be developed, cohesion and solidarity can be forged, and intolerance in the society can be minimized. We, in Pakistan, have a potent case for renegotiating the common good as distribution of resources is very uneven. Everything cannot be left to the market as the market can neither provide all the goods, nor does it generally favor the poor and the marginalized. But at the same time some pertinent questions are as follows. Is the public sector working particularly for the poor and the underprivileged if market is not working for them? And why is the public sector unable to deliver public goods effectively?

Scarcity and Clientelism

Elite capture, entrenched political interests, and domination of the ideology and preferences of the rich, and weak implementation are some possible factors for the poor provision of public goods. Who are the elite? In the broader sense, the elite are the individuals or sections of the population who are endowed with power, economic and political. They are "a distinct group within a society which enjoys privileged status and exercises distinctive control over the organization of the society."[14] Due to asymmetric distribution of economic and political power, they influence developmental outcomes through control over resources, institutions, and media. They build narratives in the society and their impact, both positive and negative, is disproportionately high due to public policy capture.

For instance, big farms are preferred over small farms despite all sub-optimality. Big hospitals in metropolitan areas are preferred over village dispensaries in rural areas. Palatial houses are preferred for the Ministers and the bureaucrats over small apartments in high-rise buildings. The elites generally do not favor high taxes and provision of public goods. In addition, political economy literature guides us that inefficient structures, responsible for poor provision of public goods, are not accidental but are by design.[15] The political elite is, however, faced with a dilemma. Even in the weakest form of democracy, they need votes in elections. They resolve this dilemma through clientelism or patronage politics.

The question why the poor vote under conditions of extreme socio-economic structural inequality in Pakistan has been investigated. There may be several explanations. First, divisions based on caste and kinship are sharp. People vote on these lines particularly in the rural areas without consideration of the provision of public goods by the politicians. Second, the landed elite have perpetuated their influence, over the lives of the people, by establishing oligarchies across villages and forming vote blocs when their control loosened in the village. And the voters do not want to be left out of such vote blocs.[16] These factors are just manifestations and not the underlying causes of such a voting behavior.

The real issue is the poor and differentiated delivery of public goods. The public goods in the rural areas are not delivered by rule and as a matter of right to the citizens. The culture of clientelism and patronage is so enmeshed and insensitivity of the public service delivery institutions is so high that you need some connections for getting services from the local public service departments. Moreover, provision of public goods like health, education, and transfer payments is insufficient and resultantly, rationing has to be done to manage the scarcity. There may be several methods for managing scarcity.

For instance, scarcity of food and other essential items can be managed through queues. Another method is drawing lots (the principle of randomness). Suppose there are 1000 candidates who have applied for the lower cadre jobs of peons and security guards against 50 vacancies and all meet the laid down criterion. In such a case, decision of allocating such jobs can be taken by drawing lots on random basis. Scarcity in Pakistan is, however, generally managed through corruption and favoritism. Managing scarcity in this way promotes a culture of patronage. Poverty and powerlessness further deepen such a culture as low-income groups whose marginal utility of income is higher are more prone to patronage and every politician or political party favors its own support group.[17]

"In many settings, the economic elite can exploit their social connections and economic power to provide poor voters with individual incentives to vote in a particular way. The result is widespread political buying and perverse use of clientelistic policies– As a consequence, far too often the poor elect politicians and administrators who do not share their interests."[18] With the socio-economic changes in the wake of the Green Revolution and political awakening of 1970s, some change is visible in the rural areas but largely, rural political landscape is still dominated by the landowners.

The public goods and services can be obtained in rural areas not by rule but are doled out as a matter of privilege and discretion. And once there is discretion and that too without accountability, it is an invitation to a number of ailments including reinforcement of the system of patronage and clientelism. In such a scenario voters particularly the landless in rural areas "strategize, bargain, and negotiate their way to better livelihoods and services within this system."[19] In a society having asymmetric power relationships, clientelism also suits the politicians. It reduces the time lag between votes and benefits but the adverse consequences are that provision of goods remains confined to small constituencies instead of the society and often entails corruption.[20] Clientelism also has negative implications for the state capacity. It comes about when political contestation moves from the extraction of private benefits form public resources to provision of widely shared public goods.

The remarks of Maleeha Lodhi, a journalist turned diplomat, are apt about the pitfalls of political clientelism in Pakistan. She writes: "Political clientelism has a patronage not policy focus, encourages rentier behavior as well as corrupt practices. This form of politics places the accent on the local and hobbles thinking about larger, national interests. It is not geared to resolving issues of modern governance or structural economic problems that warrant urgent policy attention. Clientelist politics are in fact dysfunctional to the needs of a modernizing society, however uneven that process. Moreover, clientelism operates in an environment of scarcity – in resources and opportunity- makes for uncompromising politics and bitter conflict that serves to reinforce instability and contributes to making the country more ungovernable."[21] Therefore, besides investing more in the provision of public goods to reduce scarcity, effective distribution is also important. Efficient and rule-based delivery of public goods makes the debate on the nature and quality of bureaucracy more relevant. A well-functioning and motivated bureaucracy, which can deliver public services efficiently, is highly important. If bureaucracy is weak, inefficient, or corrupt, the performance of the public sector shall remain low.

Bureaucracy is criticized for a host of failings associated with it. It is overweight. It is non-responsive. It is overpaid. It is lazy. It is arrogant. And in developing countries, it is corrupt as well. An article[22] on bureaucracy lists down not less than 182 common 'bureaupathologies' including red tape, lack of commitment, lack of initiative, lack of credibility, lack of performance indicators, favoritism, arbitrariness, mediocrity, highhandedness, inability to learn, indecision, tokenism, unprofessional conduct, insensitivity, and overstaffing et cetera. There is no doubt that waste in governments in the majority of the countries particularly developing countries like Pakistan is enormous. It would, however, not be possible to run a modern state without bureaucracy despite all its failings and pathologies. After all, bureaucracy implements laws and policies. It is responsible for public service delivery, and above all an effective bureaucracy matters for development[23].

Developmental Bureaucracy

A vivid account of Robert Wade in '*Governing the Market*' on the role of economic bureaucracy in the industrialization of Taiwan speaks volumes about the contribution an effective bureaucracy can make toward economic development of a country. The Council for Economic Planning and Development[24] (CEPD), an advisory body to the cabinet consisting of economists, engineers, and experts of finance, accounting, and statistics played vital role in the development of Taiwan. Its responsibilities included overall planning, sectoral planning, economic research, urban development, performance evaluation, financial administration, and personnel administration. The CEPD staff was paid more than the civil servants working in other organizations and thus CEPD could attract higher-quality talent. The entrant to this organization was not required to take the usual civil service examination.

Japan's Ministry of International Trade and Industry (MITI) is another classic example of the role professional bureaucracy can play in development. "The particular speed, form, and consequences of Japanese economic growth are not intelligible without reference to the contributions of MITI."[25] The key characteristics of MITI's success story were its small size, think tank functions, high capacity for implementation of industrial policy, and internal democracy. Discussion groups were set up on different industries like petrochemicals, paper pulp, ferroalloys industry, and synthetic textiles et cetera. These discussion groups provided a forum for interaction with the businesses for investment and coordination.

MITI issued administrative guidance to businesses and other ministries on policy statements. "Administrative guidance differs from orders issued in accordance with, for example, the Foreign Exchange and Foreign Trade Control Law in that it is not legally enforceable. Its power comes from government-business relationships established since 1930s, respect for the bureaucracy, the ministries' claim that they speak for the national interest, and various informal pressures that ministries can bring to bear."[26] Similarly, Economic Planning Board (EPB) played vital role in economic planning and development of South Korea. It prepared guidelines for budget, evaluated the feasibility of proposals submitted by other ministries, and overall monitored instruments of industrial policy like rationing of preferential credit.[27]

Now the question is what did make the said organizations a success? First, these organizations had a strong sense of ownership from the top leadership and the input, proposals, plans, and development frameworks et cetera did not pass through the routine bureaucratic labyrinthine process. Second, the civil servants employed in these organizations were either pure professionals or more professional than their counterparts managing other affairs of the state. Recruits were generally graduates of the top universities trained in disciplines like engineering and economics and were not generalists. Third, the salaries of the professionals working in these organizations were higher compared to their counterparts working in other line ministries. The structures of the organizations like CPED were constructed such that they were not part of the formal bureaucratic structure. And such a structure allowed the government to bypass civil service laws with regards to pay et cetera.

The role of bureaucracy for development and poverty alleviation in China is also well-documented. For instance, a forceful account by Yang in '*How China Escaped Poverty Trap*,'[28] in contrast to competing narratives like 'inclusive institutions first' and 'good governance', emphasizes the role of state capacity (reflected through bureaucracy) in poverty escape. Her argument is that China leveraged its local level public functionaries named 'street level bureaucrats' for investment promotion and market development. This leveraging triggered a co-evolutionary process of institutional change across time and space for the escape of China from poverty. "Governance or state capacity has multiple dimensions. --- It is the bureaucracy which implements the decisions made by the power holders. Whether the bureaucracy has the incentives or ability to perform its assigned tasks, as well as how it interprets its tasks, is thus central to state capacity."[29]

According to Yang, the local officials were incentivized to innovate constantly (she calls the process franchised decentralization) to implement the policies of the center, meaning it was due to the combination of the incentive system and capacity of the local bureaucrats that the center was able to implement its policies and programs in the vast areas of China. On the contrary, despite multiple policies to promote regional development in Southern regions of Italy, development programs remained ineffective mainly due to low-quality local institutions[30].

The developmental role of bureaucracy was also conceived in Pakistan. The creation of 'Economist Group' and organizations like Planning Commission of Pakistan point toward this role but the essentials like top ownership and attracting top talent to such organizations remained lacking. Generally, economic, planning, and financial issues were left in the hands of bureaucrats or civil servants who are generalists. The civil service structure, which Pakistan inherited form the British, remained intact even after independence. The civil servants who replaced erstwhile CSP became financial wizards, economic gurus, planners, and eyes and ears of the ruling elite in independent Pakistan. They blocked any change conceived for reforming the civil service to safeguard their hegemony and self-interests.

It promoted a type of caste system in the civil service of Pakistan. In a caste system, your birth determines your place or status in the social hierarchy. A person born to a Syed or Rajput family shall remain socially supreme to a person born to some lower-caste family. Simply your social status is determined at birth and accompanies you to the grave. During the entire life-from birth to death- your caste is fixed. No hard work, no virtuosity, and no training can change your caste. The civil service structure of Pakistan hinges on similar caste system. You take competitive examination, are allocated to some service group (your birth into civil service), and remain in the same until superannuation (your death in service). During the intervening period, there is no effective mechanism in place to reward or punish you for your performance and each service group is isolated from outside competition with all attendant inefficacies and lack of incentives to innovate, improve, or change.

The structure of civil service is based on some fallacious assumptions which need to be challenged for any meaningful reform. For example, one assumption is that productivity is static (it is not declared but the entire structure and working of the bureaucracy confirms this). Determination of productivity based on one-time evaluation is not an optimal decision. Productivity is dynamic. It may go up. It may go down. It may remain static for certain period. Determination of career prospects on one-time evaluation or performance is not an optimal policy choice. Doing so reduces competition and distorts incentives. Once you have no competition from outside, you are least incentivized or pushed to improve your skill-set or make public service delivery better.

Competition from inside is not sufficient as entire organization or service group can become victim of a culture of lethargy and self-interest. Dr. Ishrat, who himself started his career from civil service and remained associated with the government for civil service reforms, proposed the creation of an executive group at the mid-career level to prepare a corps of professional civil servants. The proposal, however, did not materialize due to politics of civil service in Pakistan. Why civil service needs to be shielded from outside competition and why the public sector not be opened for other professionals? Talent hunt from within the civil service as well as from outside is necessary to create a pool of professional personnel like the one created in Taiwan, Japan, and South Korea which can work as think tank of the government. Idea creation for development and identification of ways for implementing such ideas in an optimum manner would be the prime responsibility of such a think tank.

Lack of competition is not the only factor. Weak accountability (not punishing indecision) is another big factor for turning Pakistan's Max Weberian bureaucracy into Kafkaesque bureaucracy. For example, the current structure does not put any premium on timely action or service delivery. It does not punish deferrals or procrastination in decision-making. This has promoted a casual attitude among the public sector employees. The accountability mechanisms are weak. "In the Punjab, for instance, only 102 government functionaries were charged for any irregularity during the period 1985–2000 and even among them conviction rate was below 20%, while the proceedings lasted a number of years. The system protects government servants. It is difficult to proceed against those not turning up for duty let alone those who attend office but do not provide any service."[31]

Multiple visits to officialdom are generally required for obtaining a simple public service. Unnecessary documentation is very common despite the point that many regulations and standard operating procedures for conducting business (still on the statutes books) have become redundant and outdated in view of new emerging realities and fast-changing technology. Huge amount of papers, stamps, and time is wasted in the transportation of official correspondence among public offices which can be transferred through WhatsApp without wasting time and money. Similarly, biometric system is well in place for verification of the antecedents but in all probability you would be required copies of some other documents like CNIC, domicile certificate, and undertaking on stamp paper that the particulars given by you are true.

The cost of complying with various administrative regulations is substantially high having implications for investment, entry into business, and economic growth. GDP in crude form is just sum and size of commercial transactions. If commercial transactions reduce or slow down due to overregulation, the quantum of GDP shall be reduced. Similarly if the entrepreneurs are not able to establish businesses due to high entry requirements, GDP shall remain below its potential. Various reports of the WEF on competitiveness and Doing Business Report of the World Bank clearly point out how the complexity of bureaucratic procedures reduces national competitiveness of Pakistan.[32] PIDE has published a number of research reports[33] under the name of sludge audit to determine costs of complicated application forms, paper work, waiting in queues, time consumed in seeking registrations, licenses, certificates and permits, and securing attestations and verifications. The results are worrisome as the costs of compliance of such administrative regulations are estimated to be as high as 39% of the GDP.

Obtaining permission for high-rise building takes 4 years, involves 104 steps or procedures and cost of sludge is estimated 77% of the project cost. Setting up a pharmaceutical unit consumes 2 years and involves 114 procedures, and the cost of sludge[34] is estimated 10.3% of the project value. Ayn Rand's following remarks are perhaps bit apt about the state of affairs prevalent in developing countries like Pakistan. "When you see that in order to produce, you need to obtain permission from men who produce nothing- When you see that money is flowing to those who deal not in goods, but in favours-when you see that men get richer by graft and by pull than by work, and your laws don't protect you against them, but protect them against them- When you see corruption being rewarded and honesty becoming a self-sacrifice- You may see that your society is doomed."[35]

A developmental bureaucracy, which instead of creating hurdles for the entrepreneurs through indecisions or delayed decisions becomes a partner in the process of economic growth, is needed. A shift in the attitude of the bureaucracy in a way that it considers the idea of wealth creation an enviable pursuit and does not look at wealth creators and entrepreneurs just as tax thieves and fraudsters is highly crucial. The present-day bureaucracy is faced with at least two issues when it comes to taking decisions particularly involving huge economic implications. First, majority of the bureaucrats, being generalists, are not trained for taking such decisions. Second, due to rampancy of perception of corruption in the bureaucracy, even honest and very fine civil servants avoid taking decisions due to fear of being dragged into politically motivated inquiries by the NAB even in the cases where decisions were taken in good faith and in national interest. And ironically such inquiries are conducted by the investigating officers who do not have specialized training to conduct inquiries in such matters.

Indecisions and delayed decisions have serious negative consequences for investment and economic growth. Frequent transfers and postings of the civil servants on political considerations also have some unintended consequences as the civil servants are incentivized to delay certain decisions to evade responsibility in such an environment of quick transfer and postings. A simple test shall prove the point. Just visit the office of a federal secretary and see the incumbency board. The average tenure would be not more than few months and during such short tenure a civil servant has all the incentives and bureaucratic techniques to delay the decisions (which can take him to NAB inquiry) and leave it to his successors. In this way he can save him from any uncalled for investigation or inquiry. And as regards penalty for the indecision, no mechanism is practically in place to penalize a civil servant for not taking timely decision. In this way inefficiency creeps into the public sector and reduces productivity of the firms, thus having negative consequences for economic growth. Pakistan can realize significant productivity gains if it is able to increase public sector efficiency.

What are the options to ameliorate this situation? Two broad categories of options can be explored for public policy interventions in this regard. First, changes can be introduced in the incentive structure in a way that civil servants become direct stakeholders in the process and dividends of economic growth as done by China (argued in detail by Ang in her book). Second, criterion and process of induction into civil service can be modified. Currently, cognitive skills are practically the sole criterion for induction into the civil service. The candidates need to be screened and tested for variables like intrinsic motivation, prosociality, and integrity besides intelligence. So the individuals imbued with the zeal of public service, who are motivated from inside, join the civil service. Once the overall perception develops that civil servants are in general not corrupt, confidence in their decisions shall also increase. So prioritizing the variables of prosociality and integrity in the recruitment process of public sector employees may bring a fundamental change in the quality of service delivery, public sector decision-making, and perceptions about the bureaucracy, though in the long-run.

Integrity and Prosociality

Suppose an interviewer asks a candidate the following question. Why do you want to join public sector? The expected responses would be recognition (path-dependent factors - prestige and power), job security (risk-aversion), low potential of private sector to provide decent jobs (limited opportunities), and passion for public service (prosociality). No individual shall reply that he is joining the public sector for corruption and rent-seeking. And if the candidates are hiding their real motivation for joining the public sector, how to get into their minds is a big challenge. Some researchers attempted to read the minds of those who prefer public sector jobs in Indian context. They conducted a series of experiments with 669 students in their final year of college at seven different universities.[36] The results were startling. Students who cheated on a simple laboratory task were more likely to join the public sector. On the contrary, students who demonstrated prosocial preferences were less likely to prefer government jobs. So a big dilemma- how to attract men of character and integrity to the public service.

Currently, recruitment and screening into civil service is generally done on the sole criterion of cognitive ability or merit. Character, competence, and credibility are equally important. Integrity and character are as important for a public functionary as his cognitive ability. The screening process for the public sector recruitment hardly considers said variables and if it does, process is damn faulty. Widespread corruption and poor work ethic among the public sector employees are the testimony to the said assertion. The word meritocracy is also very fascinating in theory but when it comes to operationalization, it has serious drawbacks. For instance, according to Federal Public Service Commission (FPSC)'s annual report,[37] majority of the candidates who are finally allocated to civil service come from private, Forces/Garrison, and missionary schools. Over 60% candidates who finally get the job are those whose father hold graduate or higher qualification degrees. From said statistics, it is evident that the huge benefit of education and income is passed on to the next generation.

"The institution of the family complicates the project of giving everyone an equal chance. It is not easy to offset the advantages that affluent parents confer on their children---Even the best, most inclusive educational system would be hard pressed to equip students from poor backgrounds to compete on equal terms with children from families that bestow copious amounts of attention, resources, and connections."[38] Allocation of opportunities on pure merit, as it is understood and operationalized, also entails other consequences.

Merit is attached with hubris. One may look down upon those who are left behind. They are not as smart or intelligent as I am. They are dumb. If they had been intelligent, they would also have risen by effort, talent, and hard work, those who succeed think. "Sir, I assure you that it is not possible to find anyone more capable (than these under training officers). They are the Aristotles and Platos (of today). They are the best rather best of the best. They are the cream of the nation Sir,"[39] one of the Heads of the Civil Services Academy, while inviting the attention of the then Prime Minister of Pakistan, said in his address on the eve of passing out ceremony of the officers trained in the Civil Services Academy. This line of thinking inculcates arrogance in the civil servants. Hubris is antithetical to the very concept of public service delivery. Public service delivery does not require heroes, Aristotles, Platos, or Socrates. It requires humility. It requires people of small egos who are empathetic toward the common people, who can build teams, and who can innovate to make public service delivery cost-effective.

What can be the additional criterion for recruitment and screening of public officials? If we were to identify a single variable that can make the difference it would be the prosocial[40] behavior of the candidates. Not all individuals are motivated to do public service. The desire of doing public service may be strong in some individuals. Some studies show that motivated public servants perform on the job even for the sake of service.[41] The individuals demonstrating more prosocial behavior are intrinsically motivated, are less likely to shirk even in an environment of low incentives, and perform better in public sector[42]

A field experiment even confirms that non-financial rewards are more effective than financial rewards for eliciting efforts for prosocial tasks.[43] Samuel Bowles in '*The Moral Economy*' mentions in detail how financial incentives may not work in many situations. He writes: "Incentives work. They often affect behaviour almost exactly as conventional economic theory predicts, that is, by assuming that the target of the incentive cares only about his material gain. --- But whiteboard economics sometimes fails. In an unusual natural experiment, the imposition of fines as a way to shorten hospital stays in Norway had the opposite effect. In contrast, hospital stays in England were greatly reduced by a policy designed to evoke shame and pride in hospital managers rather than to rely on the calculus of profit and loss"[44].

Bowles further writes that incentives some times and in several situations crowd out what he calls 'social preferences' which are "motives such as altruism, reciprocity, intrinsic pleasure in helping others, aversion to inequity, ethical commitments, and other motives that induce people to help others more than is consistent with maximizing their own wealth or material payoff."[45] "Being honest need not be motivated by the harm that the lie would do to others; it may be an end in itself."[46] The point is that what type of persons we are recruiting for the public services matters for the quality of the service.

A significant amount of literature has emerged which confirms that personality traits like prosociality can be measured and they have predictive power similar to that of IQ. Further, standard measures of cognition are hugely influenced by personality traits.[47] The question is whether psychological tests conducted for screening of candidates joining the public sector assign due weightage to prosociality. There are serious doubts. Corruption, low productivity, sub-optimal public service delivery, and poor work ethic among civil servants are reflective of the point that our civil service tests poorly screen for honesty, prosociality, and passion for public service delivery. According to a survey,[48] almost 93% of civil servants perceive that performance of the civil servants have deteriorated over the years and majority of them believes that bribes make things work in the public offices. "-demotivation, demoralization, and despondency among majority of civil servants is reflected in the poor service delivery, indifference, inaction, and apathy toward clients, and a mind-set resistant to change becoming ingrained in their psyche."[49]

The role of training is also important. There is a need to re-evaluate the basic objectives of training. Whether we want the civil servants to rule the people (as was the objective with the British civil service) or the civil servants are required to be real servants of the people, is the most important point of determination. If the objective is to rule and suppress, then the civil servants have to be aloof, indifferent, and masters. The language they speak, the dress they wear, and the way they eat would be different from the people they are supposed to rule. And perhaps that objective still pervades the training of the civil service in Pakistan. In the bureaucracy of Pakistan, the British Raj still lives on and the fresh recruits are still taught Victorian table manners.[50] Z. A. Bhutto was perhaps right to some extent in castigating the civil service when he said: "No institution in the country has so lowered the quality of our national life as to what is called Naukar-shahi (bureaucratic rule). It has done so by imposing a caste system on our society. It has created a class of Brahmins or mandarins, unrivalled in its snobbery and arrogance, insulated from life of people and incapable of identifying itself with them."[51]

A civil servant would be more effective and productive if he knows the manners and the milieu of the people he is supposed to serve. Instead of training them in table manners, it would be better to sensitize them about the trials and tribulations of the common people. The institutionalized aloofness created through GORs and clubs needs to be abolished. All training content and strategies need to be revisited with a view to make them professional in their outlook who are capable enough to use the evidence, produced by researchers, on the ground in their organizations for better public service delivery. This is the area where civil servants of Pakistan badly lack. Some researchers conducted a survey of total 1509 civil servants (a reasonable sample) where civil servants were asked to interpret simple numerical information which they failed to correctly interpret.[52] Data analysis, evaluation of evidence, and its application for better decision-making are the neglected areas of their training.

Accountability based on an objective criterion of performance evaluation is also highly significant to improve the productivity of the public sector. The nature of goods produced by the public sector and its objectives, however, make it difficult to measure the productivity objectively. In the private sector, profit maximization is the overriding objective, so all metrics of private sector delivery are connected to the said objective. How much sale did you make? How many items did you produce? How much profit did you bring to the company? These are the metrics of the private sector. On the other hand, measuring the output of the public administration is highly complicated as market prices do not exist for many outputs of public sector such as those of regulations. Further, broad externalities, both positive and negative, are associated with goods produced by the public sector such as Covid immunization (positive externality) and pollution by a factory (negative externality).

The gap between the inputs and the outputs in the public sector is undeniably very wide. An objective measurement of government activity would essentially include a relationship between the money spent (inputs), the quality of government processes (throughput), the quality and quantity of government outputs, and the outcomes. Measurement of these dimensions at the national as well as at international level has either been missing altogether or remained very crude. Ideally, increase in public expenditure is supposed to reflect itself in better public service delivery. In this context, some objective and measurable parameters would essentially require the determination of some correlation between inputs, throughputs, and outputs for establishing a linkage between the public money and outcomes in the shape of improvement in public sector governance.

Gaps of Pay and Performance

An optimal public sector remuneration system is important where public sector wages have some relationship and comparability with the private sector wages to attract, retain, and motivate the staff. Some empirics[53] suggest that higher wages induce more able applicants (measured against IQ, personality, and proclivity toward public sector work) to join public sector. Higher wages may constitute a necessary condition to attract good candidates but they are not the sufficient condition for motivation and performance.

A good pay system has to be internally equitable (that is the people are paid in proportion of the relative value of their job), and externally competitive (that is the people are paid in proportion to the market price for their job). Modern-day public sector has to compete with the private sector in the labor market of the country to attract people from the given pool of talent, which is generally scarce in developing countries. Though it is not conclusively settled as to what constitutes optimal remuneration in public sector, but competitive salary undeniably constitutes an important ingredient of effective civil service.

At the same time rising wage bills in public sector have been one of the major concerns. Reforms in the name of retrenchment, rightsizing, or downsizing of public sector are primarily motivated by fiscal consideration. Fiscal sustainability is one of the primary principles for setting public sector pay. As the public sector jobs are generally guaranteed, pension has also to be paid to the retired employees. Pakistan follows a legacy pension system where pensioners are paid directly from the revenues a part of current expenditures. According to PIDE estimates,[54] pension burden is doubling every four-years and federal superannuation and pension expenditures are estimated to be over 80% of the value of PSDP expenditures.

Contribution of the compensation system to better performance inter alia depends on the composition of the remuneration paid to the public sector employees. If "in-kind or deferred benefits" constitute a major chunk of the compensation or such benefits are linked to the seniority element, then it is more likely that in-kind benefits will fail to improve performance in the organization. Furthermore, execution of such benefits may result in horizontal inequities among the civil servants. One of the common mistakes in the design of "other monetary benefits" is that increase in these benefits per se contribute toward better performance. If these benefits are poorly targeted, are badly designed, and are not connected to measurable objective outputs, then they will hardly contribute toward organizational goals.

Another implication is that the wage bill constantly increases if these benefits are linked to position and seniority. If in-kind and deferred benefits are properly accounted for, then public sector wages can turn out to be much higher in some cases compared with the private sector for the workers of similar characteristics and skill sets. General perception is that public sector employees are underpaid. Data does not support the said perception and public sector wage premium (PSWP) is larger in poor and developing countries compared to developed countries.[55] For instance, PSWP for Bangladesh, Kenya, Ethiopia, Colombia, and Chile respectively is 0.121 (2015), 0.495 (2015), 0.279 (2016), 0.68 (2017), and 0.161 (2015). On the contrary, PSWP for the developed countries is in the negative. PSWP for Norway and UK (both developed countries), for instance, is respectively −0.173 (2017) and −0.047 (2016).

Interestingly, higher wage premium is also not associated with low corruption. The WWBI data suggests that there is no relationship between corruption (indicated by lower control of corruption scores) and PSWP.[56] Earlier empirical findings also at best suggest weak and ambiguous link between bureaucratic pay and corruption. In order to have impact on corruption, relative wage (compared with the manufacturing/private sector) of the public sector has to be 3 to 7 times along with strong internal and external accountability controls.[57] Like other poor and developing countries, public sector employees in Pakistan also enjoy considerable PSWP. Overall, it is 0.63 (2014) approximately equal to that of Colombia and is larger compared to other countries of Africa and Latin American region like Nigeria (0.2), Zimbabwe (0.5), Uganda, Somalia, and Mozambique (all three having PSWP of 0.4), Paraguay (0.3) and Uruguay (0.2). The point is that Pakistan is among the very few countries with very high PSWP (Table 10.1).

Other studies on the subject also confirm existence of large PSWP. For instance, according to a report of PIDE,[58] total compensation of the civil servants including monetary wage, allowances, and quantified in-kind and intangible rewards shows that civil servants are not underpaid as large chunk is not visible from the pay slips. The said report estimates that the total cost of a senior officer[59] is 15% more compared to a Pakistani national working in the UN officer cadre. Special allowances, official residence, cost of utilities borne by the government, free of cost petrol, services provided by peons and drivers, cost of medical treatment, and subsidized social clubs et cetera are major components of the compensation of the senior level public employees, the report says. The findings of the PIDE report may not be perfect but undeniably issue of low performance has little to do with public sector wages in Pakistan.

The real issues are "disconnect between pay and performance" and "inequities" in compensation structure due to in-kind benefits. Pay is not linked to measurable targets and "in-kind benefits" create inequities among the employees of same level and category. For instance, "other monetary compensation" forms the major portion of the compensation

Table 10.1 Public Sector Wage Premium (PSWP)

Occupational Group	*PSWP*
Teachers (compared to)	1.418
i. Formal wage employees	1.843
ii. All private employees	2.055
iii. Paid wage employees*	
Other Professions (compared to formal wage employees)	0.201
1. Clerks	0.500
2. Professionals	0.112
3. Managers	

Source Worldwide Bureaucracy Indicators (WWBI) (data.worldbank.org)
*This is for female teachers

structure if a civil servant is able to get an official house allocated. All employees even in senior positions do not get official accommodation. Those who do not get official accommodation are paid house rent in lieu thereof. House rent is generally lower than the rent value of official accommodation. The difference is not small and may be higher in the range of 10 to 20 times.

Such perquisites (official accommodation, cars, and other facilities not reflected on pay slip) are not related to performance and by inducing inequities among officials of same grade and level rather have a negative impact on overall productivity of the employees. After all, human beings do comparisons and do not like unfairness. There are two options to rectify the situation. First, ensure that all government officials of the same level and grade get same in-kind benefits (accommodation etc.) and for doing so, the government rather than providing big palatial houses needs to construct high-rise apartments by demolishing existing GORs. Doing so shall provide enough number of apartments to accommodate all public sector employees.

The second option is to abolish all perks, sell GORs (which are practically dead capital) in the open market, and make all payments to the public employees in cash. This option seems more feasible, cost-effective and may have far-reaching consequences. It would help utilize the dead capital for economic growth and shall abolish 'institutionalized aloofness' of civil servants created through GORs. They will be more sensitized to the problems faced by common people by living in the communities.

Besides inequities, no correlation between compensation and public service delivery seems to exist. There is a clear disconnect between pay, performance, and service delivery. There is practically no incentive for the public sector employees to upgrade the skills. One-time evaluation determines your career path. "Once the officers join the civil service, there is no compulsion to upgrade their skills or knowledge. The promotion and placement policies are not aimed at rewarding those who perform well and capable of taking higher responsibilities. According to the NCGR (2008), a fair and equitable compensation system cannot work well unless accompanied by an objective performance appraisal system."[60]

Disconnect between performance appraisal and service delivery is vindicated by the fact that current PER system categorizes 80% of the civil servants as outstanding.[61] It is ironic that 80% of the officers are outstanding but public service delivery in Pakistan is rated among the worst performers. Basically performance appraisal system is flawed. Performance evaluation report is a tool of control and not an objective measure of performance. It has outlived its utility. "ACRs have long ceased to give a true picture of the performance of a civil servant because reporting officers did not dare to make adverse entries in the ACRs of their subordinates for fear of harassment. Therefore, all attempts to improve the method of promotion will have little effect until our values change-the most important qualities required in a civil service are integrity and character, and as the assessment of these qualities by another officer can only be subjective--ACR system has broken down because officers are reluctant to pass adverse remarks against their subordinates."[62] This has created a culture of low performance in the civil service of Pakistan.

The performance measurement needs to be objectively operationalized in the public sector. There can be some indicators which can be quantified to measure the productivity. For instance, speed is one such indicator. How fast a project or task is completed? How much time it takes to decide a case? How much time is taken in clearing a consignment from the port? "Measuring the productivity of the bureaucracy is difficult given the dearth of quantifiable outputs but the speed and quality of task completion can provide a useful proxy measure. In Ghana, there is a considerable variation across organizations in the rates of completion of tasks that organizations committed to in their performance agreements. The speed and quality of responsiveness of ministries to requests from the centre of government can be another measure of productivity, and there is also substantial variation in these across Ghanaian organizations."[63]

Another measure, proxy for efficiency, may be the amount of reduction in administrative costs involved. Quantitative measures and KPIs would be required for productivity assessment. Clear linkages between salaries (inputs) and public service delivery (outputs) need to be established. Current career progression is dependent on the length of service (performance factor not involved), PERs (not written objectively), and management courses which are generally ineffective.[64] Subjectivity in performance evaluation, promotions and placements on factors other than performance reduce overall productivity of the public sector.

The public sector employees are on average more educated than their counterparts in the private sector. According to WWBI, 45% of public servants on average have a tertiary-level education in contrast to the private sector where 17% have tertiary education.[65] There is no dearth of fine minds in the civil service of Pakistan. There are many who voluntarily, out of their love for learning, upgraded their skills and knowledge. They have degrees from top universities of the world but due to patronage-based system of placements and postings, even available expertise in the public sector remains underutilized.[66]

Patronage vs. Professionalism

Contrary to popular perception that all the civil servants are generalists, factual position is that many of them are trained in disciplines like economics, finance, economic policy management, international development, and international trade et cetera but they are scattered in different service groups and cadres. There is no mechanism to pool the expertise of this human resource and utilize the domain knowledge acquired by them. Moreover, politicians in developing countries often hold a simplistic view of policy problems and are more critical of the bureaucracy as it sells at least in the short run.[67] They prefer loyalty to professionalism and bear in mind that professionalism is at odds with loyalty. A professional or expert shows loyalty to his work, organization, and the state and not to a person or a faction. What happens is that politicians replace professional bureaucrats with loyal bureaucrats who are ready to implement the sub-optimal policies of the politicians.[68] Expulsion of professional and expert bureaucrats from the process of policy-making involves long-term costs for the country.[69]

Bureaucracy is supposed to implement the laws passed by the legislature. The long horizon and bureaucratic efficiency jointly determine the success of the reforms (certainly reforms would be introduced through laws). For having long horizon, political stability is a must as political instability shortens political horizon and increases pressure for reforms and delivery. Political instability also impacts the quality of legislation. Low-quality legislation is passed hurriedly without much debate in the parliament and press. Over-production of laws negatively affects the bureaucratic efficiency and shifts the economy toward Kafkaesque economy that is an over-regulated economy.[70]

Over-production of laws and overregulation of the economy promote corruption and reduce economic growth. The implementers may implement the law selectively. The distinction between "professional bureaucrats" (competent and loyal to their work, organization, and state) and "bureaucrats showing personal loyalties" does explain not only the difference in the level of their professional competence but also reflects on the sources of their motivation. The professional bureaucrats generally derive their motivation form inside (intrinsic motivation) while non-professional bureaucrats derive their motivation from power, pelf, and rent-seeking. The non-professional bureaucrats are generally sycophant and toe the line of their political masters. They rely more on manipulation and lobbying for remaining on posts where they can further their personal agendas at some cost to the country in the form of bad governance and poor public service delivery. They network, and not work.

The civil servants recruited in various groups and cadres of civil service in Pakistan come through competitive exam. Hardly one to two percent candidates applying for said services get allocated to some service group,[71] implying that civil servants are recruited through a highly competitive process like that of South Korea. But public service delivery is poor. Inefficient civil bureaucracy is identified as one of the top problematic areas every year by the international competitiveness reports.[72] There are issues with the criteria of recruitment, screening, and performance evaluation et cetera but the politicization of the civil service is also a major factor for low performance. Politicization of the civil service crowds out integrity and non-partisan character of the civil service, two basic pillars upon which edifice of a professional bureaucracy rests. An alignment between the political and bureaucratic values would be required for better service delivery and effective implementation of public policies.

Over the years, an unholy alliance has developed between the politicians and the civil servants particularly those belonging to administrative services. This deep nexus has crowded out integrity, neutrality, and professionalism from the civil service. A study on the performance management in public sector of Pakistan concludes: "Lack of merit-based transfers and postings make officials unconditionally loyal to their political masters and this fear factor heavily influences performance of the civil servants. In essence, the servants of the state, reduced to the conditions of personal servants of the politically powerful, have become miniature reflections of their masters. It means that all too often, the officers with integrity do not get sufficient opportunity to gain experience in important positions while those subservient to the rulers are placed in the key positions where they can effectively promote the personal interests of their masters. Thus, on the one hand Pakistan has many honest but inexperienced bureaucrats while on the other hand it has a greater number of dishonest ones who invest their time not in performing their statutory functions but in pleasing the boss."[73]

Empirics confirm that costs of patronage-based appointments and placements of civil servants entail high negative costs to the state. Guo Xu of California University examined digitized personnel and public finance data from the British colonial administrations for the period 1854–1966 to study the patronage effects and found that patronage-based appointed governors in British colonies provided more tax exemptions and raised less revenue. The patronage system distorts the allocation of public sector positions and reduces incentives to perform.[74]

Career incentives like reaching to the top is a powerful determinant of bureaucratic performance. Based on nationwide stakeholder survey and administrative data of Indian Civil servants, some researchers have found that officers who cannot reach the senior-most positions in the organizations before retirement are less effective.[75] If reaching to the top is based on professional competence and integrity, then a career civil servant shall endeavor throughout his career to remain competent and clean. Contrary to this, if political patronage determines the rise to the top, then a civil servant shall pander to the politicians instead of performing his job professionally.

There is another implication. The civil servants who enter into the civil service at higher age than the average age of entry into civil service or get suspended or are not promoted with their fellow colleagues of the same batch or have less chances of rising to the top due to some other factors shall not remain professional and productive. If they are not retired or weeded out or expelled, they shall negatively influence the overall professional character of the organization. The proposition that a civil servant would stay in the public sector employment until the age of retirement, even if he is no more productive, needs to be re-examined. Exits at each level and grade on the pattern of Pakistan Army, where every commissioned officer is not expected to become a General and majority gets retired at the mid-career level, would be required to improve productivity and accountability of the civil servants.

The patronage culture is much entrenched when it comes to frontline workers.[76] The jobs to frontline workers were generally doled out in the past on political considerations. The mess of misgovernance, corruption, and incompetence we see today in the organizations like Police, revenue, Customs, public health, and public schools are at least partly due to political recruitments of frontline workers in such organizations. The successive governments in the past rather than creating employment played the role of employment bureaus. An argument can be made that a political party, which ascends to the power, is entitled to hire the party ideologues who can provide public service efficiently to further its public service provision and welfare agenda. After all, USA doles out different positions under the well-known spoils system.

But the public sector jobs so provided in developing countries like Pakistan are not on ideological considerations. Empirics suggest that public sector jobs are not necessarily provided to individuals who remain loyal to the party for long rather are provided mainly to those who switch loyalty in elections, meaning thereby that the amount of support and not the degree of ideological alignment is the primary driver of such favoritism.[77] Patronage-based recruitments lead to the selection of less competent individuals.[78] Using public sector employment and placement as patronage has serious implications for public service delivery. Even basic requirement of showing up on the job may not be met in a culture of political patronage. For instance, the results of an intervention[79] in the province of Punjab in Pakistan show that in constituencies where politicians won with huge margins (lack of political competition) absenteeism of doctors was much higher compared to highly contested constituencies. Interestingly intervention of monitoring attendance through smart phones worked better in politically competitive districts compared to less competitive districts pointing toward the deadly effects of patronage on the public service delivery.

Besides patronage and politicization, public sector organizations kill professionalism by discouraging innovation. "Form" takes precedence over "functions" as the goals and objectives of the organization are missed somewhere along the way. More emphasis on form means that the possibility of functional evaluation of an organization is closed. Space for innovation squeezes when form becomes the yardstick of the performance of the organization. When an organization is unable to conduct its functional evaluation or secure legitimacy through demonstrated performance the organization adopts what Lant Pritchett calls "isomorphic mimicry"[80] that is more emphasis over form than on function. Doing so changes the form and may sometimes lead to a brief localized success but fails to bring some fundamental change in the performance of the organization, Lant argues.

It is easier to build the "forms" like recruitment of civil servants through Public Service Commission, creating new cadre out of Police force, establishing some model courts, introducing uniforms for the personnel, providing inputs having visibility like vehicles, buildings, modern equipment, and weapons et cetera. Developing countries generally resort to such tactics to give an impression of productive and capable government. For instance, the Ministry of Education of Peru in 2005, in a bid to ensure conditions of optimal learning especially in the poorest areas provided laptops in the schools. The provision of laptops improved accessibility to computers significantly but did not have much impact on learning outcomes of Maths or language for which laptops were intended as local context was not taken into account. Teachers were not proficient in new technology, internet access was poor in rural areas, and financial resources to integrate the software and for training et cetera were meager. Budget focus was just on the attainment of laptops. Thus, the program focused more on form than function pertinently qualifying for Lant's isomorphic mimicry.[81]

What happens is that when more focus is on form, little room is left for innovation, research, and professionalism in the organization. A camouflage of a capable organization through tinkering at the margins does not bring cultural change in the organization. For instance, Pakistan established large taxpayer units and improved physical infrastructure like office buildings et cetera under the auspices of World Bank assistance program, supposedly to buttress its Inland Revenue organization. Similarly, Pakistan Customs metamorphosed itself into uniform service. As a result no substantial change is, however, visible with regard to broadening of tax base,[82] control of tax evasion, reduction in smuggling or increase in collection efficiency ratio (CEF).[83]

Improving physical infrastructure or wearing uniforms without focus on professionalism and performance is not a guarantee for success of an organization. A clean, competent, and professional bureaucracy, which can provide public services efficiently, is the linchpin and provides legitimacy to the state. Some empirics[84] even confirm that public goods demonstrate a stronger and more consistent impact on state capacity compared to other determinants like wars and economic shocks. Results of another study[85] of legal reforms in German cities in 1500s show that the origins of the state capacity mainly owe to welfare improvement reforms and public goods provision had a positive impact on institutions, human capital, and growth.

The policy implementation failures (for which bureaucracy is mainly responsible) reduce trust as well as demand for public services. Empirical evidence of the said claim comes from Peru. The authoritarian regime of President Alberto Fujimori launched a large-scale family planning program to cut down fertility and poverty rates. The program included consensual male and female sterilizations. The allegations surfaced that in many cases sterilizations were performed without consent and severe violations of ethical and medical guidelines were committed. After public disclosure of forced sterilizations, the municipalities with more victims witnessed sharp decline in demand and utilization of public services such as contraceptive methods, prenatal care, and birth delivery services.[86] Impliedly message is that efficient provision of public goods like health, education, and justice et cetera is necessary for augmenting state capacity and gaining trust of the people. A well performing public sector can be an important market signal as well for future employment if the public sector is recognized to be credibly efficient.[87]

Lack of knowledge as what needs to be done for reforming the public sector is not the issue. Many reports and studies on civil service reforms were prepared since the inception of Pakistan, which are shelved in the dustbin of civil service reform history. No Serious effort was, however, made to change the culture of public service to make it people-centered. "Civil service reform is reduced to a technical exercise—problems are reduced to boxes and then solutions are found to fit into boxes. The political and cultural contexts are lost in these exercises", one bureaucrat once said.[88] People-centered reforms in the civil service are not possible unless a broader constituency for such reforms is created. Media (both electronic and print), academia, think tanks, and civil servants (majority of whom believes in professionalism and not politicization) can play an important role in creating such a constituency. No doubt improving the quality and performance of civil service is important for efficient provision of public goods and economic growth but the story of public service delivery shall remain incomplete unless legal capacities are also improved simultaneously for provision of justice to the people. Investment and economic growth are difficult to enhance without proper enforcement of contracts by the legal system which is presently very noisy and requires some out of box solutions for improvement.

CHAPTER 11

A Noisy Legal System

Katharina Pistor, Professor of Columbia Law School, in *'The Code of Capital'* gives an interesting account of the deep connection between law and capital. Capital is coded in the institutions of private law including property, collateral, trust, corporate law, and contract law et cetera. "There is no capital without law, because only law can bestow priority, durability, convertibility, and universality on assets, and thereby privileges its holders."[1] Capital is one of the three major inputs (labor, capital, technology) of economic growth, which means that in case the judicial system is unable to enforce the codes and contracts efficiently, it can become a big constraint on economic growth by negatively impacting the firms' ability to invest, innovate, and reallocate resources toward more productive uses. The judicial system affects economic growth and governance through the channels of the rule of law, contract enforcement, and security of property and person et cetera. The countries having efficient judicial systems generally have more developed credit markets and enjoy high per capita income.[2] A strong judiciary also tends to promote rapid growth of small firms.[3]

Theoretically, justice is a public good. It means that the principle of non-excludability squarely applies to justice. A quality justice system creates positive externalities in the form of increased trust in state institutions besides promoting economic growth through a better business climate and attracting foreign direct investment. Justice, being a public

J. Nasir, *Development Challenges of Pakistan*,
https://doi.org/10.1007/978-981-97-3064-3_11

good, is a fundamental right of every citizen of Pakistan. The Constitution of Pakistan guarantees access to justice to all its citizens without discrimination of any sort. Reality is, however, different. Getting justice is quite costly in terms of money and time. The disputants have to pay various costs, formal and informal. Lawyer's fees and documentation costs et cetera constitute two major components of the expenses. Informal costs vary and are hard to quantify (being secret deals).

Justice is like an economic commodity responsive to the forces of demand and supply where price plays the key role. On the demand side are the disputants who are willing to pay a price in pursuance of justice, whereas on the supply side are the lawyers who are eager to supply their services against some price that is not advertised or displayed but generally determined by the legal services market depending on the willingness of the disputant to pay. Asymmetries of information are huge. Due to restrictions on the market structure, lawyers enjoy a type of monopoly in the justice market. The monopoly problem in reality is not that individual lawyers and law firms do not have competitors. They do have competitors. According to an estimate, Pakistan has a total of 137 law colleges affiliated with 22 universities.[4] Competition exists but it is within the members of the same clan without any outside pressure for improvement of the quality of legal services or justice system.

System Lacks Competition

The problem of monopoly, in essence, is that the system lacks competitors. Individual lawyers may lose clients but the legal profession does not lose customers. When a system is not facing competition, it would not be under pressure to innovate or produce a better product. It applies to every field including the legal profession. Gillian Hadfield in '*Rules for a Flat World*' writes about the nature of the monopoly of lawyers: "The legal profession is not unlike a tribe living on Tropical Island thousands of miles from other people. They might be a violent tribe, fighting each other on daily basis for access to the fruits of their profession. But so long as they are collectively able to produce, whatever dysfunctions they might exhibit-- strange beliefs or rules written into their biological or cultural DNA that keep them from getting healthier, smarter, and better able to harvest their crops--will persist so long as they are the only types around. This is particularly the case of upstarts among them with strange ideas are voted off the island. As a group, they would not face any pressure to adapt their ways until and unless the boats pull up and unload a horde of folks with different beliefs and rules to compete for access to the food supply."[5]

The existing rulebook of the formal justice system and legal profession is, however, not being challenged by the horde of folks from other islands. The legal services market is characterized by a restricted market structure and high economic rents. Governments worldwide are wary of regulating the legal services market structure due to the difficulties peculiar to the nature of this market and resistance from the legal clan. The fee charged by the lawyers depends on several factors like explicit and implicit contracts with the clients, reputations, and relationships which are hard to detect, monitor and quantify. The lawyers, particularly senior lawyers who charge exorbitant fees for the so-called 'face value', would resist the regulation even if government intends to do so.

Moreover, the lawyers and courts have managed to maintain the law and court proceedings so mysterious, complex, and boring that even well-read and intelligent people feel safe in staying off the topic. The result of the monopoly of lawyers over the legal profession is that the lawyers have become part rather than the solution of the justice problem due to vested interests in maintaining business as usual strategy. The professors of law and judges may resist changes in the substantive or procedural features of the existing legal system as change entails costs. Change in the existing legal procedures, language, and curriculum means depreciation or redundancy of the existing human capital of lawyers, law professors, and judges and would require investments in new human capital. Lawyers who are trained in or who operate in a socially dysfunctional legal system, and have made investments in the existing human capital, in learning to work in such a system, are often resistant to change.[6] There are other groups to lose from reforms such as individuals who make money by speeding up judicial processes in a corruption-ridden environment, and firms and private agents who benefit of dysfunctional judicial system (by delaying payments of taxes, etc.). The current system is designed in a way that it satisfies the producers of justice and not the consumers of justice. The problem with the reform of the judicial system is that while losses to the producers of justice are 'immediate, clear, and concentrated' the benefits for the consumers are thinly spread among the population at large.[7]

Further, the complexity of the legal system adds to the costs which are not small. According to an estimate,[8] the average cost of the lowest court amounts to Rs. 11,7000 (see Table 11.1) whereas the average income

Table 11.1 Monetary and non-monetary costs of litigation

Types of court	*Average fee charged by a lawyer (PKR)*	*Other costs per case (PKR)*	*Average duration of case in years*	*Average number of hearings per case*	*Average number of postponement of hearings per case*	*Total life of case (in years)*
Civil/ Magisterial Court	65,000	52,000	4.0	40	15	7
District Court/ Session Court	70,000	62,000	3.0	30	28	7
High Court	120,000	140,000	2	10	6	8
Supreme Court	260,000	295,000	2	4	6	8
Tribunal/ Services Court	70,000	55,000	2	15	5	3

Source PIDE Knowledge Brief No 2022:59

and expenditures of a typical Pakistani are respectively Rs. 35,662 and Rs. 32,578.

Weak Contract Enforcement

There are other costs as well, particularly delays, in the form of loss of daily wages, transportation costs, mental agony, neglect of children (especially for poor people who are not left with many resources), loss of productivity (due to disincentives for investing on land involving title disputes), and costs incurred for personal security (in case of criminal litigation). The courts are generally perceived ineffective and untrustworthy. "The verdict on the prevalent Pakistani legal and judicial system is uncontroverted-- it does not work well, and to the extent that it does, its benefits are differentially distributed, with a clear tilt to those with better access due to class, capital and social networks--not many would disagree that it is slow, expensive, vulnerable to exploitation and misuse, coercive, unintelligible to the majority due to its complexity."[9]

Efforts were made from time to time to reform the judicial system. Projects were initiated, with the help of donors like ADB and the World Bank, for increasing access, decreasing delays, and training of judicial officers. Salaries of the judges increased substantially and some improvement has also been made in the infrastructure of the courts. The situation on the ground, however, is that people are disillusioned with the workings of the judicial system. This disgust often translates into support for informal dispensation of justice through non-state actors. The establishment of a parallel judicial and administrative system in some parts of KP province of Pakistan, particularly the Swat region in 2009, is a case in point. Recourse to the informal justice system through panchayats, comprising of village elders and influential locals, may also be partly due to the disillusionment of the people with the formal justice system. Reduction of delays in the dispensation of justice is highly likely to change the negative perceptions of the people about the formal system.[10]

The reports of international institutions and research bodies also strengthen the perceptions of the citizens that the state judicial system is not optimally delivering. The World Justice Project ranks Pakistan at the bottom with regard to access to justice.[11] The World Bank's Ease of Doing Business Surveys place it among the lowest scorers on the variable of the enforcement of contracts.[12] The judges themselves are also cognizant of the inordinate delays in the dispensation of justice but perhaps the system is such that even the finest and good-hearted judges find themselves helpless in breaking the vicious circle of delays and sub-optimality. Jawwad S. Khawaja, an ex-judge of the apex court of Pakistan, referring to long delays, once said that "a hundred years ago, the average time taken to conclude a case was one year. During this period, a case would go all the way from a trial court to the court of last resort. Today, this very process takes 25 years."[13]

A simple analysis of opening balance (as on 1st day of the calendar year), number of cases instituted and disposed of during the year, and closing balance (pendency as on last day of the calendar year) since year 2007 shows that all three variables that is number of cases disposed of during the year, number of cases added, and the number of pending cases at the end of the year have consistently registered an increase at all levels that is district judiciary, High Courts, and Supreme Court. According to judicial statistics, the increase in backlog of cases has increased by around 300% during the period between 2007 and 2020, both in the High Courts and Supreme Court of Pakistan. At the end of 2020, over

1.8 million cases were pending disposal with the judiciary. This high pendency is despite the point that there is a significant increase in the number of cases disposed of by the Supreme Court as well as the High Courts (Figs. 11.1 and 11.2).

Due to delays, a large number of under-trial prisoners are languishing in overcrowded prisons in hellish conditions. The appeals against convictions are not taken up for years by the High Courts and the Supreme Courts and in the majority of cases, the convicts (mostly convicted by the trial courts on weak evidence or oral evidence by interested witnesses)

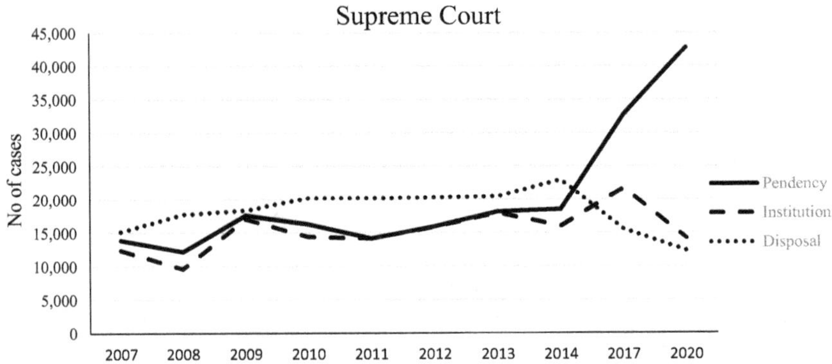

Fig. 11.1 Disposal, institution and pendency in the Supreme Court (*Source* Judicial Statistics of Pakistan, Annual Reports 2017 and 2020)

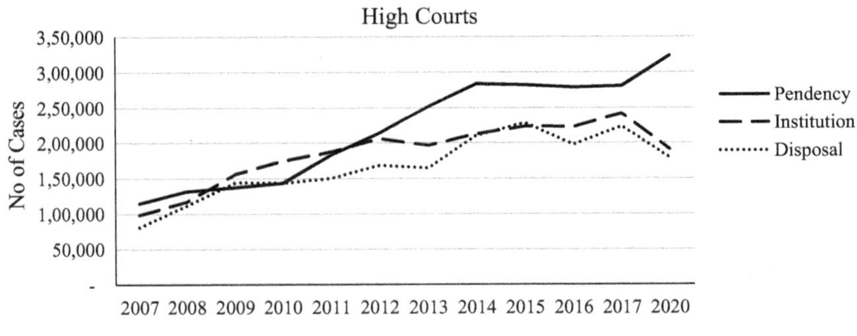

Fig. 11.2 Disposal, institution and pendency in the High Courts (*Source* Judicial Statistics of Pakistan, Annual Reports 2017 and 2020)

complete their sentence before their appeals are taken up by the superior courts. Delays in decisions by the courts generally do not create deterrence against frivolous litigation and future violations of law. Incentives to cooperate in a contractual agreement weaken as delays in decisions by the courts lower the discounted value of punishment from deviation.[14] Long delays create incentives for the wrong party to file lawsuits in the court of law with the result that the judicial system gets clogged with frivolous litigation. At the same time, such a system may work as a disincentive, particularly for those who have a valid legal dispute and want its speedy resolution. Access, speed, and quality of the judicial system not only matter for increasing deterrence to reduce future litigation but also for the development of a modern economy. A firm-level analysis shows that judicial efficiency and firm productivity are positively related and judicial reforms targeting all the above characteristics (access, speed, and quality) increase firm productivity.[15]

A study on the judicial efficiency of lower courts finds that the average shelf life of a civil case in the province of Punjab is over three years and, on average, the case requires 58 hearings from its institution in the civil court to the passing of decree.[16] The disputes of titles are many and a large chunk of land cannot be used as collateral for getting credit from the financial institutions, due to joint ownership or ambiguity in titles. The only evidence of title in Pakistan is the registry system which can be challenged on the basis of oral transactions and earnest money. According to an estimation, 60–70% of civil litigation in Pakistan is land-related. The land-related civil litigation turns into criminal litigation in 40–50% of cases.[17] Empirics suggest that speedy disposal of civil cases impacts the firms' contracting behavior and economic performance through the channels of decrease in breach of contracts, more investment, and better access to finance.[18]

It must also be recognized that delays just do not happen in all cases as a matter of coincidence. They are sometimes by design. In every case, at every stage, some party is benefitting out of the delay. Delays can be prevented by enforcing penalties on those instituting false cases and employing dilatory tactics. The most important tool to avert false litigation is the imposition of the costs of litigation. The law of costs is generally ignored by the courts of law. Non-enforcement of anti-perjury laws is another area. The courts generally do not prosecute or penalize people for perjury despite the rampancy of the phenomenon of false evidence in the courts of law. Laws exist but the courts have abdicated their duty to enforce anti-perjury laws. According to an estimate, out of 48,000 cases decided by the Lahore High Court, not even a single case of perjury was detected and prosecuted.[19]

Another reason for delays is the lack of an effective case-flow management system. Every case invariably culminates at all costs, after a long trial, into a judgment by the court. Pre-trial communication between the parties, to explore the possibility of resolution of the case before the start of the trial, is non-existent. Once a case is filed, there is no sacrosanct time frame to complete the adjudication proceedings. The judicial discretion for granting unnecessary adjournments is very wide and exercised quite frequently. Mechanism can be put in place for curtailing this discretion by making it mandatory that, say, not more than two adjournments shall be granted to each party by the court and the party seeking an adjournment shall be liable to pay the cost incurred by the other party. Mandatory time limits imposed on plaintiffs and defendants at each stage of the litigation can also be useful in reducing delays. Optimum litigation is partially the answer to the woes of the judicial system. Increasing litigation is reflective of the poor quality of the judiciary. A judicial system that leads to a lot of litigation is inefficient at least on four counts. First, it is consuming too many resources, both private and public. Second, it indicates that the system is encouraging frivolous litigation. Third, it is reflective of the point that the laws and the judgments of the courts are not well-defined and people do not respect them. Fourth, the system has lost its deterrence. Similarly, too little litigation means that the individuals and firms do not trust that the judiciary would protect their rights or the costs of resorting to the judiciary are too high. The optimality of litigation would depend on a host of factors like the nature of the legal system (common law or civil law), the complexity of the economy, the availability of alternative mechanisms of dispute resolution, and fiat of the administrative law et cetera. Delays, costs, and sub-optimality of litigation make the justice dispensation system inherently anti-poor as evident from the stories of miscarriage of justice appearing in the press from time to time.

Inherently Anti-poor

On October 24, 2016, for example, the newspapers of Pakistan reported an incident of macabre miscarriage of justice.[20] Two brothers were acquitted by the Supreme Court of Pakistan deciding their review petition filed from the prison. The trial court had handed down capital punishment in the said case in the year 2005 (the case was registered in year 2002) as per reported facts. After the verdict of the Supreme Court on their review petition, it transpired that they had already been hung on the gallows. On May 19, 2019, the newspapers reported another incident of miscarriage of justice. A small vendor, jailed for 5 days was freed from the prison after 06 years. Reportedly, the appeal was filed by the poor chap against his imprisonment by a magistrate for selling betel leaves and cigarettes as a vendor during Ramzan, the holy month of fasting, immediately after his conviction but the decision on his appeal consumed 06 years.[21] These two incidents basically point toward the popular perception that the courts are for the rich while jails are for the poor.

The perception of the differential dispensation of justice in Pakistan is perhaps not misplaced. When it comes to the interpretation and implementation of the constitutional provisions aiming at equity in society, record of the superior judiciary of Pakistan leaves much to be desired compared with its counterpart in India. Several instances can be quoted. For example, courts both in India as well as Pakistan have held that the 'Right to life' enshrined in the constitution means the right to live with dignity which includes the right to food. As food is essential for survival, the right to food, by implication, is an essential ingredient of "right to life". To implement the right to food, the Supreme Court of India ordered the state governments, in 2001, to provide free of cost mid-day meals in government-run primary schools. The Supreme Court orders led to campaigns for mid-day meals all over India and it is estimated that 120 million children are now getting free mid-day meals in schools. The better nutrition of the children coming from humble socio-economic backgrounds induced substantial increases in primary school enrolment.[22] The mid-day meals program triggered by the orders of the Supreme Court on a petition of public interest has made it the largest school feeding program in the world. The program is mainly aimed at encouraging the poor, downtrodden, disadvantaged, and vulnerable children to attend school regularly and retain them at school.

The Supreme Court of Pakistan has also held in a few judgments[23] that the right to life includes the right to food but not in a forceful way like the Supreme Court of India. Hamid Khan, one of senior advocates of the Supreme Court of Pakistan writes in this regard in '*A History of the Judiciary of Pakistan*' as follows: "It is noticeable that there is little innovation on the part of the judges in developing fundamental rights. Although the Constitution provides for a wide variety of fundamental rights yet the judiciary has done little to develop them jurisprudentially. --There are very few judgments on the Right to Life under Article 9 of the Constitution and little effort has been made to develop this area of jurisprudence--. Similarly, there are few judgments on important fundamental rights like Human Dignity, Fair Trial, Due Process, Right to Information, Freedom of Movement, Freedom of Occupation and Profession et cetera. Even where the Supreme Court has been innovative in respect of fundamental rights, it has shown clear reluctance to invoke its jurisdiction in respect of armed forces or intelligence agencies".[24]

Article 38(a) of the Constitution of the Islamic Republic of Pakistan provides that the state of Pakistan shall secure the well-being of the people by raising their standard of living, by preventing the concentration of wealth and means of production and distribution in the hands of a few to the detriment of general interest and by ensuring equitable adjustment of rights between employers and employees, and landlords and tenants. The said provision is contained in the Principles of Policy about which the apex court has held that they are the conscience of the Constitution.[25] The court, however, missed the opportunity to set some direction whenever any opportunity came its way. For example, the declaration of legislation with regard to land reforms repugnant to the injunctions of Islam by the Shariat Appellate Bench of the Supreme Court frustrated all efforts to make the distribution of productive assets equitable in society. The review of the Government of Pakistan against said judgment was also rejected by the Supreme Court on technical grounds that is petition being time-barred by 144 days, though the court held that the petition was not tenable on merits as well. Declaration of land reforms law repugnant to injunctions of Islam simply meant that the court rather than adjudicating the matter in the spirit of the constitution for an equitable distribution of land and means of production facilitated the concentration of resources and wealth in the hands of the landlords. Maulana Abdul Kalam Azad was perhaps right in saying that the authority of the courts is a force that can be used both for justice and injustice. "Next to the battlefields, it is in the court-rooms that some of the greatest acts of injustice in the history of the world have taken place."[26]

Another example is the judgment of the Supreme Court regarding the demolition of squatter dwellings in Karachi. The Supreme Court ordered demolition on the grounds that lease documents may be fake. The possibility of regularizing the squatter dwellings was not considered by the court nor was the government asked to evolve some mechanism to regularize these poor dwellings. The poor have neither voice nor money to hire the services of smart lawyers who can plead their case effectively in court, so many angles of the debate that may favor the poor go unappreciated by the court due to not being pleaded at all or ineffective pleading. "There are also different criteria for judgments related to the poor and those related to the rich. For example, Baharia Town was fined Rs. 460 billion, and the land that it illegally occupied was regularized at a fraction of its market value".[27]

Under the Constitution, all citizens of Pakistan are equal in the eyes of law but in reality, huge disparities of all kinds exist. "All animals are equal but some animals are more equal than others" was the proclamation made by the pigs in George Orwell's *Animal Farm*. This proclamation perhaps squarely applies to justice system of Pakistan. "Defendants with financial and political capital often evade punishment, while those without remain in jail, most often without being convicted or convicted on half-baked and concocted evidence."[28] Most of the time, the attention of our superior courts is focused on the meta-constitutional and high-profile political cases and there is hardly any conversation or time left for the cases of the common people.[29] And when it comes to the adjustment of rights between the employer and the employee, the interpretation made by the superior courts seems tilted toward the employer. The fixation of minimum wages is a pertinent example. In 2021, the government of Sindh increased minimum wages in the province. The said notification landed in the Supreme Court of Pakistan mainly on the ground that the Minimum Wage Board had not recommended the increase in wages and that the recommendations of the Minimum Wage Board could not be ignored by the government.[30] The fixation and increase in the minimum wage is politics all over the world. The right-wingers oppose both fixation and increase in minimum wage whereas left-wingers and labor unions support increase in minimum wages. The empirical research, however, does not support the long-held view of the right-wingers that minimum wage has negative implications for employment and that minimum wage is an inefficient transfer program.

The results of a case study[31] by David Card and Alan Krueger to ascertain the effect of an increase in the legal minimum wages on employment in the fast-food industry in New Jersey and Pennsylvania did not confirm the validity of the textbook model that an increase in minimum wages causes unemployment. Contrary to the popular view, an increase in minimum wages induced employment in some cases. The unskilled wage-earner generally belongs to the poorest quintile of the population and an increase in minimum wage is a type of transfer payment without burdening the government. In a budget-constrained country like Pakistan, increasing the minimum wage at least provides some attraction to the government to alleviate the sufferings of the poor people. The problem with the standard text model and economic thinking is that the minimum wage issue is approached from the demand side. The supply side is generally not analyzed. "An increase in the minimum wage clearly affects the value of work for a sizeable fraction of less-skilled workers in the economy. Relative to some other transfer programs, the minimum wage has the feature of "making work pay", rather than discouraging labour market participation."[32] Besides an inherent anti-poor bias and delays, noise—unwarranted variability in the judgments is another area that reduces the credibility of the formal judicial system in the eyes of the people.

Noise and Bias

Face-to-face interviews of the lawyers,[33] conducted by this author, suggest that there is too much noise in the system. Judges hugely differ in their approach and outlook toward bail decisions and the quantum of punishment for similar nature of crimes. And such variability is not small. Lawyers in their interviews on the condition of non-attribution said that judge A holds a favorable view on a particular nature of issue, for example, grant and confirmation of bail in cases of burglary, while judge B holds quite the opposite view on the same issue. Judge D is pro-prosecution while judge E is pro-accused. There is a high probability that judge F shall not decide a civil case conclusively but shall remand it back to the original adjudicating authority while judge K shall dispose of the case but, in most probability, shall not intervene in the decision of the lower court. About the attitude and inclination of the judges, Hamid Khan writes: "Lawyers, who practice before various High Courts, find a marked difference in the environment of each High Court with the varying attitudes of their judges. For example, the environment of the Peshawar High Court has always been quite relaxed and its judges' attitudes have been informal. The judges and the lawyers at times talk to one another in Pashto during the court proceedings. The Lahore High Court judges have been more formal than other High Courts. Formality of the court proceedings is an essential requirement but sometimes it is taken too far to the point that tension hangs heavy in the environment of the court. Generally, the Lahore High Court and its judges have been known to be pro-establishment. It is generally perceived that judges of the Lahore High Court are less inclined to grant relief against the government. On the other hand, other High Courts are regarded as less pro-establishment and more liberal in granting relief against the government in power. However, even this differs from judge to judge within a High Court."[34]

This noise (unwanted variability in judgments) is also prevalent even in the judicial systems of developed countries like the USA. Daniel Kahneman and his colleagues have dealt with this subject at length in *'Noise- A Flaw in Human Judgment'*. According to them, the first step is recognition of the fact that noise is an issue worth our attention. Once recognition of the problem is there, several steps can be taken to minimize the noise in judgments. For example, a noise audit of judgments can be conducted. "In noise audit, multiple individuals judge the same problems. Noise is the variability of these judgments. There will be cases in which this variability can be attributed to incompetence: some judges know what they are talking about, other do not. When there is such a skill gap (either in general or on certain types of cases), the priority should of course be to improve the deficient skills", they write.[35]

Noise in judgments is not a small issue. For instance, a noise audit of sentencing by US federal judges was conducted in 1981. The researchers of the said study developed 16 hypothetical cases where the defendant was found guilty and was to be sentenced for his crime. The crimes included robberies or cases of fraud and the defendant differed on some other variables like a criminal record (whether first offense or repeated offender), nature of involvement (principal accused or accomplice), and use of weapon in the commission of the crime (in case of robberies). The researchers organized structured interviews with a national sample of 208 active federal judges who were presented with all 16 cases to set a sentence. The result was a huge amount of noise within the judgments in each case. The obvious interpretation of noise is the variation of disposition among judges to set severe sentences, according to Kahneman and his colleagues. Some judges are known as "hanging judges" while some have got a reputation of "bleeding-heart judges" who are more lenient in sentencing than average judges. The study showed that the judges vary widely on this dimension. The average level of sentencing is just like a personality trait determined on a scale of 1–10 and the severity of sentencing by a judge depends on genetic factors, life experiences, and other aspects of the personality. This variability has nothing to do with justice.[36]

There is then "occasion noise" in judgments arising out of the mood of a judge when a judge can disagree even with himself due to mood fluctuations. "You are not the same person all the times. As your mood varies (something you are, of course, aware of), some features of your cognitive machinery vary with it (something you are not fully aware of)."[37] Weather, stress, fatigue, and the order in which cases are examined are some other sources of occasion noise. It is true that you are not the same person all the time but occasion noise is not the largest source of system noise.[38] If a group of judges, instead of a single judge, hears, examines and decides a case, the level of noise would be less. In the High Court and Supreme Court, cases are generally heard by more than one judge. In the lower courts, cases, both civil and criminal, are heard and decided by a single judge.

Discretion is another source of noise. Rules decrease discretion and noise in judgments. A lot of scope exists for reducing noise through rules in areas such as granting of bail in criminal cases and restraining orders against recovery in fiscal matters et cetera. Rules serve better in regulating human behavior compared to standards. "Rules are meant to eliminate discretion by those who apply them; standards are meant to grant such discretion."[39] Standards are open-ended whereas rules are specific. Standards involve all judgment whereas rules reduce the role of judgment. A standard may be that a judge shall decide a matter without causing unreasonable delay. The word "unreasonable" involves an element of subjectivity and discretion. On the other hand, a rule may prescribe that a judge shall decide a case within three months of the initiation of trial. A legal counsel shall submit a reply in writing to a suit within the minimum possible time (a standard) whereas the rule may say that reply shall be submitted within 15 days of the filing of the suit. Several provisions of criminal, civil, and fiscal statutes provide time limits for completing certain tasks. Enforcement of such timelines would improve if penal provisions for non-adherence were introduced in the law.

Various statutes provide for doing certain things as "prescribed" (meaning as provided under the rules) but rules are, sometimes, not framed partly due to the reluctance of the implementers to reduce their discretion. Furthermore, rules do reduce noise but replacing all standards with rules would entail difficulties of implementation in situations not envisaged at the time of framing of the rules. The new situation shall require either enactment of a new rule or amending the earlier one. Amending a rule is not that easy, so an element of rigidity is built into the rules. The standards, on the other hand, give flexibility and discretion. In case, it is not possible to enact rules in certain situations, prescribing details of the standards can work. The goal of a judgment is accuracy and not subjective expression of an individual's personal values, views, or personality traits even if broad standards, and not rules, are in place to regulate the conduct of the judges. Competence (knowing one's job), better cognitive skills, and professionalism are some important parameters impinging upon the quality of judges and their judgments.

Judgments are better when made by better judges which means the quality of judges is highly important for an effective judicial system. According to Hamid Khan, the standards of competence and integrity among judges have declined over time. He writes: "It is generally believed that the judges of the Superior Courts at the time of independence were competent and honest with few exceptions. This was partly due to strict standards that were maintained in respect of selection of judges of the Superior Courts during colonial times and early days of Pakistan. There were exceptions such as Chief Justice Young of the Lahore High Court, who was known to be corrupt, but such exceptions were rare. The selection process was seriously impaired during the regime of Ayub Khan, when appointment of judges was made for political or other considerations and not on merit. Regardless of whether the appointments are made during military or civilian governments, the standards have been constantly declining. Every government is keen on making appointment of persons who would cooperate with it rather than dispense justice evenly to all."[40]

Fundamental changes in the recruitment process of the judges would be required to enhance the quality. Transparency and merit are the keys. Unfortunately, perception prevails that currently connections play a role in the induction of judges in the superior judiciary. Considerations like affiliation with particular law chambers or blessings of the leaders of the Bar Councils are perceived to influence the process. These perceptions may be misplaced but need to be dispelled and managed for the credibility of the judicial system and the judges. This is very much possible through a transparent induction process on the pattern of competitive exams for civil services. Minimum qualifications for consideration as a judge should be advertised and as a first step, a rigorous exam should be conducted for screening. The names of the successful candidates then should be made available for public scrutiny before final selection. Those who pass the initial test and emerge successful out of the public scrutiny process should be considered for appointing as judges in the High Courts by the judicial commission.

Selection of judges through a merit-based and transparent process would not only improve the quality of judgments but would also enhance the prestige of the judiciary in the eyes of the public. The judgments would be less noisy and less biased if made by competent, well-trained, honest, and intelligent judges having the right cognitive style. "Highly skilled people are less noisy, and they also show less bias."[41] As a general principle, good intelligence is likely to be associated with good judgments as it is associated with academic achievement and high job performance. A judge is different from a worker performing repetitive tasks on the assembly line who does not engage himself in a serious thought process. A judge should not tend to trust his first impulse. A judge would, therefore, be required to have a reasonable understanding of the complexities and traps of the mind. The authors of the '*Nudge*' quote about Beethoven that he wrote his incredible 9th symphony when he was deaf but it was also normal for him to misplace his house keys, pointing toward the complexity of the working of the human mind.

Psychologists and neuroscientists make a distinction between two kinds of thinking. One is intuitive and automatic (Automatic System or System 1) while the other is reflective and rational (Reflective System or System 2). The Automatic System is instinctive and fast. It is rather not a thinking system in the true sense of the word. It is a reflex action. For example, when somebody throws a stone at you unexpectedly, you will duck or when your airplane faces turbulence due to bad weather, you would get nervous or when you see an innocent cute baby, you would smile. All these actions are automatic and no thinking is as such involved.

The brain scientists say that the activities of the Automatic system are associated with the oldest part of the brain, the parts we share with lizards or puppies.[42] On the other hand, the Reflective System involves conscious thought and not gut feeling. A judge is supposed not to go by heuristics that is rules of thumb or shortcuts to answer a question or legal proposition. Heuristics can mislead and channel our emotions. An awareness of the biases and structured ways of thinking for a judge would improve the quality of his judgments.

Better Self-Regulation

The concept of independence of the judiciary in simple understanding implies that the courts are independent in making judgments and interpreting the law. No other organ of the state or organization can interfere in the domain of the judiciary. Some empirical evidence[43] suggests that judicial independence and the quality of decisions have improved since April 2010 after the enactment of the 18th Amendment in the Constitution of the Islamic Republic of Pakistan due to a change in the procedure of appointment of judges of the superior judiciary from presidential appointments to appointments by the peer group that is through Judicial Commission. The said change in the selection process is estimated to have prevented land expropriations amounting to about 0.14% of GDP or US$ 390 million per year.

Are there any confines or limits on the judiciary? And who will judge the judges? These are some simple but important questions. As a matter of principle, every state functionary or public office holder is responsible to the people of Pakistan by virtue of being paid out of public money. The quality of judgments and decisions can be monitored by the hierarchy of the judiciary itself as the majority of the judgments and orders of subordinate judiciary land in the superior courts through the process of appeal and revision. One of the possible areas where the performance of the judges can be monitored by the public, without jeopardizing the independence of the judiciary, is the disposal of cases to avoid delays.

Delays partly occur due to a lack of accountability of the judges who can easily get away with it due to non-disclosure of their performance for public scrutiny. Even vital judicial statistics are not collected and published for the consumption of the public. The most vital judicial statistic is "shelf life data" which is average time taken by various levels of courts to decide different categories of cases like obtaining a decree, an order, or a judgment. Regular collection and publication of vital statistics can work as a performance check on the courts.

The introduction of changes in the assistance process of the courts or outsourcing of some of the judicial functions can also help ameliorate the situation. A "model of a busy doctor" can provide some insights in this regard. When a patient goes to the doctor for diagnosis, his assistant does some preliminary tests like checking blood pressure and pulse rate et cetera. He lists down the history of the patient. The patient is then examined by the doctor who gives a prescription to the patient considering the preliminary report of his assistant and after undertaking further investigation if required. In this way, the doctor saves time and can diagnose more patients in less time.

On the same analogy, assistance can be provided to the judges by employing junior lawyers to prepare synopses of the cases, getting necessary verifications done where so required, and recording statements-in-chief et cetera before placing the case before the judge for hearing of arguments of the parties to the dispute. And why not outsource some parts of the judicial functions or certain categories of disputes if state courts are not delivering? The opposition to outsourcing may be on the sole ground that justice is a public good, so dispensation of justice cannot be left to the private sector. If this is the argument, then education, health, and security are also public goods. But we send our children to private schools. We go to private doctors for treatment. And hire services of private guards for our security.

The character of public goods is not rigidly fixed. It varies over time, and with respect to place and ideology. For instance, street lighting was once a private good purchased by wealthy pedestrians from lamp carriers which is now a pure public good (variation over time). Health care is a public good in the UK but it is a private good in the USA (variation by place). Most economists favor a strong system of patents and intellectual property rights but Joseph Stiglitz does not agree as he thinks that knowledge (books, inventions, new techniques, etc.) is a global public good to be made available freely without barriers to all in developed as well as developing countries (variation due to ideology). Compartmentalization of private and public goods is not that watertight and outsourcing some judicial functions to the adjudicators, duly licensed, is an idea worth experimenting.

Many developed countries have well-established jury systems for the participation of citizens in the adjudication or trial process. And some countries have adopted such a system of citizen participation lately. South Korea is an example that implemented the Citizen Participation Criminal Trial Act in 2008.[44] The said piece of legislation is a mixture of a citizen jury and a lay judge system. The citizen juries comprise approximately ten persons and include professors, lawyers, experts, local assembly members, and vocational representatives. The point, in a nutshell, is that out-of-the-box solutions would be needed to ensure speedy and quality dispensation of justice through better self-regulation by the judges of the formal system, and by creating linkages between the formal and informal systems of justice.[45]

While contemplating any legal or judicial reforms, the interconnectedness of relevant institutions shall have to be taken into account. What happens in the courtroom is connected to a series of events that precede and succeed in court room proceedings. An operational framework for the legal empowerment of the poor focusing on the capacity and sensitization of the judiciary and state institutions would make the law work for the poor. "Reforming the law on paper is often not enough to change the reality on the ground. The poor also need a legal and judicial system that is accessible to them and that can make their legal entitlements practical, enforceable and meaningful. -- Legal empowerment must be firmly anchored in the realities of poverty and exclusion. It requires changes in the relations between the state and the poor and their relative powers."[46]

Pakistan, after independence in 1947, like many other developing countries, adopted the laws of the British. Even after 75 years of its independence, Pakistan continues to practice the British formal system without bringing any reform to it.[47] The judicial superstructure is based on the code of Civil Procedure (CPC) 1908 and the code of Criminal Procedure (CrPC) 1898. The said statutes form the bedrock of civil and criminal law in Pakistan. The colonization thus left deep imprint on the legal system. A substantial amount of scholarship has emerged in the last few decades empirically confirming the impact of institutions, transplanted by the colonizers, on the divergence of long-term growth trajectories between the countries. One of the channels explaining the divergence, which has received scholarly attention from economists in the last two to three decades, is the legal system bequeathed by colonizers.

The Debate of Legal Origins

Out of two broad categories of the families of law that are common law and civil law, common law is associated with better security of property rights and contract enforcement[48]. In the common law tradition, appellate judges establish precedents while solving specific legal disputes. Dispute resolution tends to be adversarial and judicial independence, both from the executive and legislature, is central. A study[49] based on data from 71 countries finds that judicial independence and constitutional review are good predictors of economic and political freedoms which do at least partly explain better economic performance of common law origin countries. "English common law developed because landed aristocrats and merchants wanted a system of law that would provide strong protections for property and contract rights, and limit the crown's ability to interfere in the markets."[50] Contrary to the common law tradition, civil law is associated with a higher expected duration of judicial proceedings, less consistency, less honesty, less fairness in decisions, and more corruption.[51]

There are, however, some big holes in the scholarship on legal origin. It revolves just around common and civil law implanted in the colonies by the West and neglects non-European legal traditions which still prevail in a large part of the developing world. For instance, Islamic law still operates in many Middle Eastern countries. Then there are informal systems of legal dispensation which, for example, were operational in large parts of the subcontinent before the advent of British rule. "The domination of formal dispute resolution systems in post-colonial developing countries has been such that any mention of informal dispute resolution systems invariably generates a reaction and critique that categorizes any reliance on and continuation of a role for the informal- especially traditional mechanisms for dispute resolution- as regressive and inequitable."[52]

The formal justice system is advocated on the following three grounds.[53] First, the absence of a potent formal system may accentuate violence in society, especially in countries that lack central authority with a monopoly over violence. Second, the formal justice system provides a level playing field to all, creates equal opportunities for justice, and safeguards the poor and vulnerable against the influential and the powerful who can obtain unfair settlement of disputes through exploitation of power and money. Third, it helps achieve the goal of right and wrong established by the state. The formal justice system creates deterrence at the national level by punishing and penalizing wrongdoers which the informal justice system may not. And that justice is a public good and its provision cannot be left to the private or non-state actors.

In theory, all above objectives of the state judicial system are very noble and appealing. But what about the practice? A rich and powerful litigant enjoys a competitive advantage in litigation over the poor or less powerful by hiring expert lawyers, increasing the cost of the other side by filing suits that have little merit, and using his social connections. The judicial system hardly provides a level playing field as, leaving all other variables aside, the probability of receiving incorrect assistance from poorly trained lawyers is much higher for uneducated and low-income households.[54] A smart lawyer matters due to the huge noise in the judicial system. After all, 'face matters' in a power-oriented culture and society.

Results of a survey conducted in 2010–11 in Lahore District courts revealed that two-thirds of the rural litigants had experienced threats of violence or actual use of violence from their legal opponents[55]. More than half of the litigants were unable to understand court language, proceedings of the court, and legal texts as court proceedings are largely in English and almost half of the litigants were even unable to understand technical Urdu used in court proceedings.[56] About one-third of litigants expressed doubts about the impartiality and integrity of the judicial officers and many litigants expressed preference for alternate dispute resolution fora.[57] A sample of households spanning over entire Punjab province to elicit the perception of the people about the criminal justice system revealed a general sense of insecurity and lack of faith in state institutions for security. The respondents rather expressed more faith in "personal influence", "influential relatives, not falling foul with criminals or local powerful people" and "on having male children"[58]. The judicial system, inherited by Pakistan like many other developing countries from the colonists, has deepened poverty despite many well-intentioned initiatives of the national governments and the global community as it fails to serve the poor and save them from violence and injustice.

Haugen and Boutros in '*The Locust Effect*' pertinently point out why dysfunctional systems of justice are continuing in developing countries. They write: "After the colonial powers went home, the colonial system of policing and law enforcement never transformed to serve a new purpose. Constitutions were changed and over the decades many laws were changed—but the actual machinery of law enforcement was generally never re-purposed for a post-independence mission of serving the (overwhelmingly poor) common public. Authoritarian regimes and political elites came to power in the post-colonial developing world and seemed to find the colonial law enforcement system as useful for their purposes as the imperial power did."[59] 'Plumbing' of the public justice system remained neglected because the politicians and economic elites figured out to thrive in lawlessness and the rule of the law could threaten their interests.[60]

Why are the police not trained to investigate a crime? Why does the legal system use the foreign language (not spoken and understood by almost 99%)? Why is there no transcript of the proceedings of the court? Why are the police rude, abusive, and unhelpful to the people they are supposed to serve? According to Haugen and Boutros, these anomalies and drawbacks of the justice system of developing countries are deliberate. "Of course the legal system is conducted in a foreign language. That's the language of the colonial power (and now of the political and economic elite). Of course there are an absurdly low number of public prosecutors. A colonial criminal justice system has no incentive for allocating expensive resources to provide the general public with excellent criminal justice services. Of course there is no transcript of the proceedings in court. A colonial administration will not be interested in having its magistrates subject to public scrutiny in protecting colonial interests or restricted their discretion in administering state power through public exposure."[61]

Many of the grotesque dysfunctions of the current-day justice system are rooted in the colonial character under which the justice system was designed and instituted. Unfortunately, even after independence, the dysfunctions of the systems planted by the colonists are lingering due to the vested interests of the elite. "One of the more obvious dysfunctions involves the most fundamental ingredient of the justice process --and that is words. Laws are written in words, evidence is gathered and presented in words, arguments are made in words, reasoning is exchanged in words, facts are described in words, and judgments are issued in words. But in much of the of the developing world, almost the entire legal process is conducted in a foreign language that most poor people do not speak or understand."[62]

When the formal justice system fails to deliver, people approach informal adjudicators like Bonasera, a character in Mario Puzo's 1969 novel *'The Godfather'*, who fails to obtain justice from the formal court for her daughter who was raped. He then goes to Don Corleone (Godfather) of the Sicilian mafia for justice. Don Corleone says to Bonasera about the formal justice system of Sicily: "You go to the law courts and wait for months. You spend money on lawyers who know full well you are to be made a fool of. You accept a judgment from a judge who sells himself like the worst whores in the street". Don Corleone's distrust of the formal justice system is mainly due to corruption in the justice market. His distrust perhaps reflects the perceptions of Pakistani citizens, about today's justice system of Pakistan where corruption and bribery are endemic in the subordinate judiciary and the superior judiciary has failed to control them. There were certain chief justices of the High Courts and even the Supreme Court who had a stinking reputation for corruption.[63] Delays, high costs, low quality, and corruption are big question marks for the efficacy and effectiveness of the formal justice system. And despite all claims of modernity, Weberian legal authority, and personalization, disillusionment with the formal justice system is quite visible, particularly among the poor people.

Informal Justice System

The results of a survey[64] confirm high distrust of people in police and the courts. Around 90% of the respondents of the survey who approached police felt that the police was not trustworthy and 65.7% showed their distrust in the courts. The survey results also confirmed the high level of corruption in police and the court system, implying that deep pockets are needed to get justice. Long delays, high costs, huge noise, and failure in emotional closure are some of the defining characteristics of the formal justice system. Despite all said serious issues with the formal justice system, the informal justice system is looked at with much disdain, especially by the elite and the intelligentsia. The majority of the disputes resolved by the informal justice system do not catch the eyes of the press as judgments by the informal justice institutions are not in writing and no mechanism is in place for compiling and maintaining statistics of such judgments.

Contrary to what the elite think, the results of some independent surveys show that an overwhelming majority of the people of Pakistan repose their strong trust in the informal justice system. Pashtun Jirga is highly trusted as an informal dispute resolution system in KPK and Pashtun areas of Balochistan. Even the majority of the respondents of such surveys did not know about several of the formal institutions and held negative perceptions about the formal justice system.[65] Many people are ill-informed of the fact that informal mechanisms like alternate dispute resolution (ADR), court-assisted as well as non-court-assisted, still play a major role in the judicial system of even developed countries.

Vast possibilities exist for speedy and cost-effective dispensation of justice. Lawyers, judges, civil servants, and others trained in formal law, however, do not want to lose their institutional turf. The lawyers in particular have become part of the problem due to the financial benefits attached to delay. The judicial system in Pakistan is perceived in a narrow perspective that is civil and criminal cases and does not take into account the socio-economic and political dynamics of the society. The legal culture is dominated by the English-speaking class. The lawyer argues the case in English. The judge writes judgment in English. The charge sheet is served in English. An appeal against the judgment of the lower court is filed in English. The lawyer and the judge wear the dress of the English. The English language would be incomprehensible in most probability only to the disputants for whom all English is being spoken and written in the court. The disputants or accused most often find them in the situation of Franz Kafka's Joseph K. in '*The Trial*' who did not know why he was being tried.

The informal justice system is unintelligible to the post-colonial mind-set which takes it culturally inferior.[66] Perceptions of the common men are not in accord with the English-speaking elite of the formal justice system. According to surveys, the general perception is that the informal justice system is effective and efficient when dealing with both civil and criminal matters though it may be more effective in the resolution of civil disputes.[67] It is believed to be quick and less expensive compared to the formal justice system and due to said two factors informal system is perhaps the only viable option of justice for the extremely poor despite the availability of formal remedies.[68]

All is, however, not rosy about the informal justice system. The cases of human rights violations in the form of practices like Swara, Karo Kari, and Vani have been reported in the press from time to time. The world of informal justice is generally a man's world with no or very little participation of women in the bodies of informal decision-making and the proceedings. The fact, however, is that legal pluralism is a reality in Pakistan. It is not easy to abolish the informal justice system just by declaring it illegal. It has got certain definitive comparative advantage over the formal system in terms of speed and cost.

So the appropriate course of policy action would be to reform the formal justice system and explore possibilities for creating linkages between the formal and the informal system. Amendments in laws and procedures to encourage ADR or out-of-court settlement of disputes may be introduced. The courts may refer cases to alternate dispute resolution methods like arbitration, conciliation, and mediation. The informal justice system can be brought under the regulatory discipline to ensure fair play, adherence to the basic norms of justice, and take care of human rights aspect.

The informal adjudicators may be required to issue the judgments in writing with copies to the judicial officer of the district for judicial oversight with regard to the propriety of the decisions in terms of fair play and human rights. Undoubtedly, there exists a lot of room for integration of formal and informal justice systems and mechanisms can be explored for creating synergies between the two. There are, however, serious stumbling blocks hindering full integration. "The first is obviously the economic interests of judges, lawyers and policemen, all of whom would stand to see their incomes from bribes and fees greatly diminished."[69] Then there are ideological and intellectual blocks requiring change in the narrow narratives of justice. New narratives are needed based on data, research, ground realities, and the socio-economic dynamics of the society.

Contrary to the formal justice system, the informal justice system generally helps achieve emotional closure between the disputants due to its emphasis on dialogue, negotiation, and reconciliation. It takes care of the interests of the community by restoring harmony and disputants generally walk away claiming satisfaction. The dispute between two individuals in Pakistan generally does not remain confined to them rather its negative impacts spread to families and communities of the litigants. This does not happen in Western societies where the predominant structure of families is nuclear. Emotional closure is secondary or irrelevant in the formal system of adjudication of the USA and Western countries, says Jared Diamond.[70]

This is not the case in a society like that of Pakistan which is dominantly collectivist. People live in extended families, tribes, or clans. In individualistic societies (as in USA and the Western Europe) everybody is responsible for his actions, good or bad (epitome of human freedom and personal responsibility). On the contrary, a feud in Pakistani society is practically not between two individuals. It is between two families or clans. The litigants generally come from the same community, area or socio-cultural setup.

Even after the closure of a dispute by the courts, enmity or bad blood remains. "Far from helping to resolve feelings, court proceedings often make feelings worse than they were before. All of us know disputants whose relationship became poisoned for the rest of their lives by their court experience."[71] And resultantly if the aspects of emotional closure and reconciliation are not taken care of, the damage is far huge. A spiral of unending litigation is generated which not only increases the burden on the courts but also impacts community relations badly. The informal justice system adequately takes care of the emotional closure, having positive implications for harmony and social capital in the society.

CHAPTER 12

Social Capital and Corruption Incorporated

Edward Banefield, an American political scientist, conducted his landmark study on social capital in a village of Southern Italy namely Montenegro (not real name) in 1958 to highlight the pitfalls of low trust for a society. He observed that the people of the village had strong ties within the families but did not trust strangers that is people outside families or kin groups. He named this phenomenon 'amoral familism'. The word familism simply means putting the values and demands of the family above individual needs. Familism very closely, though not perfectly, corresponds to individualism and the nuclear family system. Banefield wrote: "In some underdeveloped lands, economic development can take place only when bonds of custom and tradition which prevent the individual from acting rationally in his self-interest are loosened or broken".[1]

Familism turns bad when it becomes 'amoral' and regressive. Cognizant of its ill effects, Banefield suggested that 'amoral familism' must be modified (to make it moral!) at least in three respects as follows, so it can positively contribute toward economic and political development. "(1) The individual must define self or family interest less narrowly than material, short-term advantage. He need not cease to be a family-minded or even selfish, but some of the time, at least he must pursue a larger self-interest. (2) A few persons, at least, must have the moral capacity to act as leaders. (3) Voters and others must not destroy organization gratuitously out of spite or envy".[2] What were the main factors

J. Nasir, *Development Challenges of Pakistan*,
https://doi.org/10.1007/978-981-97-3064-3_12

behind low trust and lack of cooperation in Montenegro? According to Banefield, six broad factors namely poverty, illiteracy or ignorance, vested interests by the upper class (we may call them the elite of today), clinging to the status quo, pathological distrust of authority and government due to centuries of oppression, and resignation to fate (hopelessness; nothing is going to change syndrome) were responsible for low trust and lack of cooperation in Montenegro.[3]

Interestingly, Banfield's recount of Montenegro seems familiar in majority of the developing countries including Pakistan. According to the World Values Survey,[4] 77.6% of Pakistanis completely trust their families, 34.3% completely trust their neighborhoods, and 42.2% completely trust the people they personally know but only 8.9% trust people from outside groups (not members of family or neighborhood) that is strangers while 6.9% trust people from other nationalities. On average, 75.9% of Pakistanis think that one needs to be very careful when dealing with other people, meaning that over three-fourths are distrustful of people in general. Colombians (95.5%), Peruvians (95.6%), Serbians (80.1%), Nigerians (86.4%), Mongolians (73.7%) and many other poor and developing countries also express a high level of trust deficit when dealing with strangers.

On the contrary, level of trust is high in developed countries like Finland, Norway, Sweden, Netherlands, and Switzerland where respectively 68.4%, 72.1%, 62.8%, 57%, and 57.1% people think that most people can be trusted. The relationship between level of trust and per capita income is certainly not one-to-one but trust is an important explanatory variable for the prosperity of a nation. Knack and Kafeer,[5] using indicators of trust and civic norms from World Values Surveys for a sample of 29 economies, find that trust is high in nations with comparatively more equal incomes, better education, and better institutions of restraint. Why trust in society is so important? What nexus has it got with economic growth?

Transaction Costs and Growth

Social capital or simply trust is an important source of competitive advantage for economic growth. It contributes to economic growth through multiple channels. Economic transactions require exchanges between people. Terms and conditions are invariably attached to every transaction and need to be complied by the parties to the exchange. "Virtually every commercial transaction has within itself an element of trust, certainly any transaction conducted over period of time. It can be plausibly argued that much of the economic backwardness in the world can be explained by the lack of mutual confidence", wrote Kenneth Arrow.[6]

In high-trust societies transaction costs are low, which provide comparative advantage to such societies over low-trust societies. You do not need to go to the bank for signatures and verification. A telephone call or email is sufficient to complete a transaction. You do not require a formal contract (paper, witnesses, hassle and time for completing formalities, and a long battle in terms of time and money for enforcement) rather your words are your contract. And you do not need security guards, big locks, or big public expenditure on police and courts in a high-trust society. "By contrast, people who do not trust one another will end up cooperating only under a system of formal rules and regulations, which have to be negotiated, agreed to, litigated, and enforced, sometimes by coercive means. This legal apparatus, serving as a substitute for trust, entails what economists call "transaction costs". Widespread distrust in a society, in other words, imposes a kind of tax on all forms of economic activity, a tax which high-trust societies have not to pay".[7]

Low transaction costs simply mean that more time and resources become available for spending on physical capital, business, and innovation. Trust promotes growth and expansion of complex industries. What happens is that complexity of economy leads to higher verification costs, but trust works as substitute for such verifications and thus leads high-trust locations to specialize in complex industries.[8] Trust can make access to credit easier by replacing the requirement of collateral. In social, economic, and institutional environments in which trust is low, the rate of investment will also be low.[9] An environment of distrust imposes costs on businesses. Tarun Khanna of Harvard Business School, quoting Sarah Lockwood, a Zimbabwean researcher, writes: "Even an ordinary trip to KFC to Soweto, a township of Johannesburg famous for uprisings against apartheid and now a tourist destination, requires extreme security measures. The counter where you order is completely barricaded by metal bars and bullet-proof glass, with just a few small gaps for you to put your money in and get your food out. The entire system there is weighed down by an extreme lack of trust. Such distrust imposes a tremendous cognitive burden, like sand in society's wheels, which slows things down and consumes extra energy".[10]

Robert Putman, in '*Bowling Alone*', highlighting the significance of social capital for economic growth, argues that the success story of Silicon Valley owes a lot to horizontal networks of informal and formal cooperation among companies in the area as the leaders of these companies have high social capital, shared information, and problem-solving techniques despite being competitors. "At the local and regional level, there is mounting evidence that social capital among economic actors can produce aggregate economic growth".[11] Trust or social capital (embodied in social relations) not only helps in accumulation of physical capital (tools, machines, equipment, and structures of bricks and mortar) and boosting of investment (through access to credit and low burden of regulation) but it also helps in creation of human capital (skills and knowledge).

For example, according to Coleman, social capital both within and outside the family matters for creation of human capital. "Ordinarily, in the examination of the effects of various factors on achievement in school, "family background" is considered a single entity, distinguished from schooling in its effects. But there is not merely a single "family background"; family background is analytically separable into at least three different components: financial capital, human capital, and social capital. Financial capital is approximately measured by the family's wealth or income. It provides physical resources that can aid achievement: a fixed place in the home for studying, materials to aid learning, and financial resources that smooth family problems. Human capital is approximately measured by parents' education and provides the potential for a cognitive environment for the child that aids learning. Social capital within the family is different from either of these. Of course, the human capital that parents possess has a significant impact on their children. But this human capital may be irrelevant to outcomes for children if parents' are not an important part of their children's lives or if their human capital is employed exclusively at work or elsewhere outside the home".[12] The child–parent relationship is also important for fostering entrepreneurship. Results of a research study[13] show that the majority of male entrepreneurs start a business firm in an industry closely related to the one their father was employed in. "Dinner table human capital" that is industry knowledge learned by the children through their parents is an important determinant of entrepreneurship.

People are happier in societies with higher social capital as trust and subjective well-being are strongly linked.[14] High social capital (more trust) can lead to higher accountability of public functionaries, a point also made by Banefield, as it is easy to overcome the collective action problem in high-trust societies and make governments responsive to the needs of the people. More civic citizens are better at holding politicians accountable. "They demand more effective public service, and they are prepared to act collectively to achieve their shared goals. Their counterparts in less civic regions more commonly assume the role of alienated and cynical supplicants".[15]

According to a survey,[16] only 3% Pakistanis are members of any club or organization (are socially engaged), 4% in urban areas and 2.5% in rural Pakistan. As regards provinces, Balochistan has the largest proportion (6.5%), while Punjab has the lowest (2.4%). Overall 5% male share any club or organizational membership while only 1.1% of females have any form of membership. Those lower on the education and income ladder have comparatively lower club or organization membership pointing toward lack of social connections. The results of the survey further suggest that 9.2% of the people do some voluntary work and that civic engagement increases with increases in education and income levels.

An important distinction about trust needs to be kept in view. When we talk about the crucial role of social capital or trust, we are basically referring to what we call generalized trust. We may trust our families, clans, or people from the same occupation whom we know through our social interactions, whereas generalized level of trust is the trust extended to people about whom we do not have direct information. It is generalized trust that nurtures a culture of civicness and accountability. We may have clean houses from inside but not clean streets outside due to low social culture required to promote cooperation in cleaning the streets or hold the relevant officials tasked with cleanliness accountable. All social capital may not be good. After all, mafias and gangsters are also closely knit but such social capital is damaging for the society. For making social capital work for development, it is the degree of generalized trust that matters. And when the radius of social capital starts increasing, the impact of damaging social capital decreases.

The generalized degree of trust in Pakistan is low as confirmed by the results of the World Values Survey. Additional evidence in support of this assertion is provided by the types of businesses in Pakistan. According to Fukuyama's line of argumentation, societies which have strong family ties but weak bonds of trust among unrelated persons tend to be dominated by small family-owned and managed businesses. This assertion squarely applies to Pakistan. The majority of the businesses are sole proprietorships. The number of companies or joint firms is low and even in such companies, majority shares are owned by family members. Key management positions in the firms are filled on the basis of kinship and not professional competence. And if placement and promotion decisions are not tied to performance, employees would not exert effort and their turnover would be high. Nepotism has thus got adverse spillover effects on productivity.

In modern times, president Suharto's rule in Indonesia provides a glaring example of the pitfalls of nepotism. Indonesia's automobile sector is a case in point. Tommy, Suharto's son had grandiose dreams to make Indonesia a world leader in car manufacturing. Many gurus of the automobile industry did not subscribe to his idea as it did not make an economic case. Suharto, however, made Tommy head of a family firm so he could pursue his dream of producing domestic cars. Tommy started production of a car with the name of Timor but the project did not materialize into success. Despite failure of the Timor project, Tommy persisted with his fascination of car manufacturing. Suharto facilitated him in becoming a majority stakeholder in Maserati, a car manufacturing company engaged in producing Lamborghini, a luxury car. This project also proved to be a perfect disaster.[17] So narrow social capital, reflected in nepotism, can turn out to be destructive for economic growth. It is the generalized trust which would create positive externalities for the society at large. A pertinent question, therefore, would be: how can we promote generalized trust in the society if it is of such an immense significance for economic development?

How to Improve Social Capital?

Income inequality, poverty, corruption, weak rule of law, and lack of credible commitments are some factors. Divisions, inequalities and injustice promote values, norms, and beliefs of mistrust which individuals internalize. For example, communities in Africa whose ancestors were heavily affected by the slave trade are found to be less trusting today.[18] Similarly, individuals and communities that feel historically discriminated against or live in a community with a high degree of income disparity are less trusting.[19] High economic growth which lifts all boats would help induce trust in society as economically better-off individuals feel more secure and are less averse to risk. The level of trust can change in response to economic shocks. Some researchers[20] studied the effect of the 2008 financial crisis on trust. Based on a panel dataset on Russia, which experienced an 8% decline in GDP in 2009, they found that 10% decrease in income is associated with 5% decrease in social trust. The results of the study also suggested that post-crisis economic recovery did not fully restore trust to its pre-crisis level. It means that once trust level deteriorates, it is hard to restore it.

Corruption and bad governance are big obstacles to the cultivation of generalized trust. Corruption or bribery particularly harassment bribery means that you are being taken advantage of. How do citizens experience feelings of protection and security? How do they draw inferences from the system and public officials about the treatment meted out to other citizens? How do they experience discrimination against themselves or those close to them? These questions are very pertinent from the perspective of generalized trust. The impartiality of institutions and procedural fairness are important determinants of trust in institutions.[21] The proportion of the citizenry approaching a public sector institution for obtaining public services, given some alternative, is a vital indicator for gauging the level of trust in the fairness and impartiality of institutions.

For example, only 5% of the litigants in Kenya approach the formal justice system for adjudication of their cases.[22] The majority prefers private adjudication mainly for two reasons. First, the judicial and governance systems are corrupt and do not deliver. Second, people are divided along ethnic and linguistic lines and courts do not have the legitimacy to adjudicate political cases. The situation in Pakistan is not much different. Trust in the judicial and governance systems is not that high due to long delays, high costs and corruption as pointed out in our discussion on the judicial system of Pakistan.

Low social capital is mainly caused by dysfunctional public institutions. Consistent evidence that effective democracy fosters generalized trust is a powerful indication that good governance not only reduces transaction costs in the economic sphere but also produces social capital.[23] The elected local body system is a tried-and-tested form of local governance worldwide. After all, local public services like health care, education, transfer of land title, sanitation, and police protection are needs of every individual and can be cost-effectively rendered at the local level. The devolution of powers to the local governments in 2001 could promote broader participation of the people in governance. The system was, however, not fully implemented in its true spirit. And as soon as the regime changed, it was dismantled.

The irony is that whenever a military regime is in power local governments are installed, whereas democratic regimes are averse to the very idea of local governments. Provincial ministers and legislators vociferously demand autonomy from the Federal Government but fiercely oppose devolution of power to local governments despite the fact that local governments are the real essence of democracy. And strengthening local bodies and village councils can empower the people and enhance social and civic engagement. What are the reasons for opposing an effective local government system by the politicians? Three factors stand out.

First, democratic regimes are not democratic in the true sense of the word. They can at best be called competitive authoritarian regimes.[24] Second, politicians at the provincial and national levels win elections through clientelism and devolving powers to the local government means that client-patron cliques will erode. And it would become difficult for them to get reelected. Third, devolving power to the local governments means reduction in the potential for kickbacks by the provincial and national level politicians associated with infrastructural projects.

The role of politicians is important in promoting generalized trust in society. By making promises in elections they make a commitment to the people and if commitments are not credible, as has been the case in Pakistan, the generalized level of trust in society will remain low. False promises inflate expectations of the people and failure to keep promises erodes their trust. Rather than making commitments that are not credible, politicians need to understand the complexities of the problems and manage expectations. The role of schools and colleges is also important in fostering social trust. Educational programs that teach about social dilemmas and the potential gains of cooperation can create an improved environment for building trust. Focusing on a "life-skills curriculum" in schools would be a good step in this regard. Moreover, universal access to quality education can promote social capital through several channels like raising awareness of the social dilemmas, reducing social and economic inequalities, fostering a better understanding of the public policy debates, and creating an educated citizenry.

Improving quality of public service delivery is another important variable for enhancing trust level in the society. The issue of the public sector is not that of its footprint, as discussed while highlighting its rationale at some other place in this book. The real issues are the low performance and weak accountability of public sector organizations. The state-owned enterprises in Pakistan are persistently running on losses and the government has to inject large amounts of tax money to keep them going. Theft of electricity is widespread and "undisciplined power consumers" are a big hindrance to any possible revival of the power sector.[25] Infrastructure like roads, schools, and college buildings decay fast due to low-quality inputs and the inattention of those who are tasked with the maintenance of the infrastructure. Absenteeism among teachers and doctors is common in public schools and hospitals. Regrettably, Pakistan persistently comes up short on the governance indicators.

Persistently Low

According to the World Governance Indicators (WGI), Pakistan scores very low on the governance rankings. Its estimates on the variables of control of corruption, government effectiveness, political stability and absence of violence, regulatory quality, rule of law, and voice and accountability are all in the negative.[26] The low percentile rankings of Pakistan on governance indicators have stubbornly persisted. A comparative analysis of some of the countries, like India, Indonesia, Malaysia, South Korea, China, Vietnam, et cetera shows that Pakistan fares badly on the majority of the indicators of governance indicators compared to said countries (see Table 12.1).

Other global indices depict a similar picture. For example, the Fragile States Index ranks Pakistan consistently among the countries that are at the tail. Other reports like the World Competitiveness Report of the WEF, Doing Business Report of the World Bank (now disbanded), and the Corruption Perception Index (CPI) of Transparency International, all confirm poor governance in Pakistan. The problem of poor governance is connected to corruption (a good proxy for governance). Corruption undermines economic development and the rule of law. This thinking about the devastating impact of corruption on development and institutions, however, was disputed in the past at least to the extent of developing countries.

"*Economic development through Bureaucratic Corruption*",[27] a representative paper by Leff reflecting economic thought of the 1960s on the problem of corruption in developing countries, argued that the government and bureaucracy in a developing country may be simply indifferent

Table 12.1 Worldwide governance indicators of selected countries

Variable	*Bangladesh*	*China*	*Indonesia*	*India*	*Korea, Rep*	*Malaysia*	*Pakistan*	*Sri Lanka*	*Vietnam*
Control of Corruption: Percentile Rank	18.27	58.17	38.46	46.63	77.40	61.06	23.56	44.23	47.12
Government Effectiveness: Percentile Rank	28.85	76.44	65.38	62.50	90.87	81.25	37.50	50.48	62.02
Political Stability and Absence of Violence/ Terrorism: Percentile Rank	16.04	29.25	27.83	24.53	67.45	50.94	6.60	34.91	44.81
Regulatory Quality: Percentile Rank	20.67	41.35	62.50	49.52	83.65	72.60	25.96	39.42	37.98
Rule of Law: Percentile Rank	28.85	53.85	46.63	51.92	84.62	70.19	27.88	54.33	48.56
Voice and Account-ability: Percentile Rank	28.02	5.31	52.66	51.69	77.78	39.13	25.12	44.44	13.04
Government Effectiveness: Estimate	−0.63	0.84	0.38	0.28	1.41	0.99	−0.40	−0.08	0.28
Control of Corruption: Estimate	−0.96	0.05	−0.43	−0.29	0.76	0.17	−0.79	−0.33	−0.29
Political Stability and Absence of Violence/ Terrorism: Estimate	−0.97	−0.48	−0.51	−0.62	0.66	0.14	−1.67	−0.32	−0.11
Regulatory Quality: Estimate	−0.85	−0.31	0.30	−0.08	1.10	0.72	−0.73	−0.37	−0.40

(continued)

Table 12.1 (continued)

Variable	*Bangladesh*	*China*	*Indonesia*	*India*	*Korea, Rep*	*Malaysia*	*Pakistan*	*Sri Lanka*	*Vietnam*
Rule of Law: Estimate	−0.61	0.04	−0.22	−0.08	1.13	0.56	−0.64	0.04	−0.15
Voice and Accountability: Estimate	−0.77	−1.64	0.16	0.11	0.93	−0.15	−0.84	−0.07	−1.30

Source Worldwide Governance Indicators World Bank (data.worldbank.org)

to the needs of entrepreneurs who want to undertake business activities. As businessmen do not have effective participation in the public policy-making process, the bureaucracy of a developing country is least pushed to become a partner in the process of economic development. Governments in developing countries have other priorities and goals, like increasing military power or expanding control over society and promotion of economic development hardly becomes a priority, Leff argues. In such an environment of indifference toward economic development, graft provides a direct incentive to the bureaucracy to help entrepreneurs and in this way corruption works as a hedge against bad economic policy. This is called "greasing the wheel hypothesis" of corruption.

This hypothesis assumes that laws, procedures, and regulations in developing countries are opaque, lengthy, and cumbersome, so in order to circumvent such tedious regulations, which may not be required at all, corruption works as lubricant. Corruption saves resources as it helps reduce time spent in queues. It helps attract better talent to the civil service despite low salaries. And corruption may help improve efficiency and promote economic growth by removing distortions induced by growth-retarding regulations and policies. The argument further runs that allocative efficiency is ensured through corruption as public goods would be provided to the firms that can give the maximum amount of bribe, which means to the firms that are in greater need of goods and are more efficient. Another efficiency argument in favor of corruption is with respect to speed money which helps reduce red tape in government offices. Two models that is the queue model and the auction model formally developed in the 1980s by economists are advanced to show that corruption improves allocative efficiency.

In the queue model,[28] a bureaucrat is tasked with allocating, for example, licenses to industrial firms or importers who queue up to obtain such licenses. The patience level of those standing in the queue varies from person to person. Generally, people do not like waiting in line but the patience levels of different individuals cannot be observed by a bureaucrat. So how can he get an idea as to who is more efficient and wants to get the license first? Bribery in such a situation provides a mechanism for screening among the firms based on their willingness and capacity to pay bribes and those with more willingness to pay are served first.

The queue model further postulates that the bureaucrat is not expected to slow down the speed of the queue as doing so would reduce the number of individuals entering the queue with the result that bribe income would be negatively impacted. This line of argument has been further fine-tuned in the auction model where an analogy is drawn between bribery and the competitive open auctions. It is argued that corrupt officials perform covert auctions and allocate public goods like licenses to the entrepreneurs who offer the highest bribe.[29] The only difference between the two arrangements is that in case of bribery money goes to the pockets of corrupt official while in competitive auction government gets the revenue. There are, however, serious issues with the idea of efficient corruption.

Corruption and Economic Growth

Bribery cannot be equivalent to a competitive auction model as at least some resources are wasted in search of partners for the secret deal. There is also the issue of enforcement of such secret deals as corrupt contracts cannot be enforced by the courts if the bribee reneges on his understanding or comes back and demands more bribes. Issues of asymmetric information and uncertainty further weaken the assumptions of the queue and auction models of efficient corruption. The greasing-the-wheel hypothesis remained in fashion until the 1980s. The dominant view now, however, is that corruption is bad for economic growth and development. The argument that corruption helps surmount tedious bureaucratic procedures does not hold ground in the light of empirics. At the maximum bribery can work as a trouble-saving device for an individual in a society where corruption is rampant but a nation cannot grow out of corruption.

An argument is sometimes made, even in intellectual circles, that it is not corruption that is hindering the economic growth of Pakistan. After all, East Asian countries and China grew economically despite corruption, argument runs. This thinking about corruption is fundamentally fallacious. The level of harm to economic growth and production also depends on the corrupt structures of a society. If the bribe-collecting monopolist is one like a centralized political party (as in Communist Parties) or a corrupt dictator like Marcos, then the impact of corruption is comparatively less distortionary compared to structures where there are multiple independent agencies or bureaucrats collecting bribes. The economic growth in South Korea and China despite the prevalence of corruption may be best explained by the centralization of bribery (the argument of Pranab Pradhan).

According to the argument of centralization of bribery, businesses were required to pay lump-sum contributions to the ruling party without bureaucratic interference. In response to such contributions, the ruling party credibly committed to keep the promises made to the businesses, and as such issues of coordination and credible commitment were taken care of. "The independent monopolist model which shows that under free entry of bribe takers supplying complementary inputs the total bribe rises to infinity and productive output falls to zero, may help explain why the most corrupt countries are so poor. In the case of an economy-wide bribe-collecting monopolist such as Marcos, corruption is similar to revenue-maximizing taxation. Taxes are the markup that goes into the treasury and bribes are the markup that goes into the pocket of the monopolist. When the treasury and the pocket are one and the same, as in the case of kings and Marcos, taxes and bribes are the same. Despite similarities, bribes differ from taxes in one crucial way, namely, unlike taxation, corruption is usually illegal and must be kept secret. Efforts to avoid detection and punishment cause corruption to be more distortionary than taxation".[30]

Contrary to the mechanism of the centralization of bribery, there are multiple veto powers in countries like Pakistan and India due to the hierarchical order of the bureaucracy. "If you want me to move a file faster, I am not sure if I can help you, but if you want me to stop a file, I can do it immediately", wrote Pranab Bardhan while quoting a public servant of India in one of his papers.[31] By highlighting the ability of a public servant to stop a file, Professor Pranab has actually emphasized that in bureaucratic organizations, bribery does not necessarily speed up the pace of the file as bribery is not centralized. Similar arguments are advanced by some other academics and commentators. For example, Ang, a Singaporean-American Professor of Political Science, has argued in "*The Gilded Age of China*"[32] that all types of corruption do not cause the same kind of harm to economic growth.

According to Ang, corruption can be broadly of four varieties that is petty theft (acts of stealing, misuse of public funds, or extortion by street-level bureaucrats like asking money by the Police from tourists for small violations), grand theft (embezzlement or misappropriation of large sums of public monies by the political elite like transferring money received from kickbacks and commissions to Swiss accounts or the money received by Army Generals in arms deals and buying islands outside the country), speed money (petty bribes citizens pay to bureaucrats to get around hurdles or speed up things like some amount received by income tax or customs officials to process refund claims or clearance of goods) and access money (high stakes rewards to powerful officials to access exclusive privileges). Petty theft, grand theft, and speed money are illegal while access money may also involve partly legal exchanges like cultivating political connections, campaign finance, influence peddling et cetera.

Petty theft and grand theft are like toxic drugs and are economically more damaging as they drain private and public wealth, subvert law and order, and deter investors and tourists. Speed money is like a pain killer, which may lessen pain temporarily but does not give health benefits on a permanent basis. Access money, on the other hand, is like the steroids of capitalism, according to Ang. They are growth-enhancing drugs but have serious side effects like misallocation of resources, exacerbation of systemic risks, and deepening of inequality. The argument of Ang is that out of said four varieties of corruption, petty theft, grand theft, and speed money are detrimental to growth without any shadow of a doubt while access money cuts both ways. It stimulates investment and growth while creating serious risks in the form of systemic risks for the political system and the economy. Since China opened its markets, corruption evolved toward access money which explains its economic rise amid vast corruption. The argument of Ang is very close to that of the centralization of bribery argument.

Corruption of other types like speed money contains an element of uncertainty as a bureaucrat cannot advertise his price whereas tax rates are known to everybody. The element of uncertainty thus makes corruption more distortionary than taxation. Results[33] of an investigation in the context of Ugandan firms suggest that the impact of an increase in bribes is more regressive compared to an increase in tax rates. One percentage point increase in bribes reduces annual firm growth by three percentage points whereas one percentage point increase in taxes reduces firm growth by one percentage point, results of said investigation suggest. It means that the negative impact of bribery is three times greater than that of taxes on the performance of firms.

Another empirical study[34] about corruption at ports, based on a sample of 1300 shipments cleared from two customs ports (Durban in South Africa and Maputo in Mozambique), directly calculates bribe payments and resulting efficiency losses. Results suggest that average bribes at Maputo and Durban respectively were 14% and 4% of a shipping container cleared through these ports. The differential informal payments at these ports induce about 46% of South African firms located in the region (from where overland costs to the Maputo port are about 57% lower) go a long way to get clearances from Durban port to avoid higher bribe payments reflective of real efficiency losses to the firms.

Bates in '*Markets and States in Tropical Africa*'[35] while analyzing the genesis of poor economic growth in Africa pointed out inefficiency losses created through the production decisions of farmers as one of the main factors behind the growth tragedy of African countries. In many African countries, peasants resorted to subsistence production as crops beyond certain limits were taken away by the government. The result was a simple decline in agricultural productivity and living standards in Africa. De Soto in '*The Other Path*'[36] also raises a similar point. He says that high start-up costs in Peru due to regulatory constraints and corruption discourage the development of formal firms. The entrepreneurs preferred to establish new small firms in the informal sector with negative implications for economic growth. The costs of inefficiencies induced by corruption have also been estimated by economists from different angles. For example, results of an analysis of a large Indonesian anti-poverty program, whereby subsidized rice was distributed among poor households, suggest that 18% of the rice was lost from the program through corruption and the redistributive program was not cost-effective due to huge welfare losses.[37]

There are other channels as well through which corruption impedes economic development. Empirics confirm that child mortality rates, the probability of low-birth-weight babies, and dropout rates from schools are significantly high in corrupt countries.[38] Such negative consequences of corruption on human resource development are confirmed by several other studies. For example, audit results of Brazilian municipalities revealed that the test scores of the students were low in corrupt municipalities compared to those where corruption was not detected as a result of the audit. Dropout rates were also higher in corrupt municipalities.[39]

Estimates by Khawaja Asim and Atif Mian suggest that politically connected firms in Pakistan receive 45% larger loans in spite of 50% default rates on such loans with efficiency losses in the range of 0.15% to 0.3% of GDP due to such corrupt lending.[40] Corruption diminishes the efficiency of public sector expenditure by creating distortions in the structure of public spending. An analysis[41] of data from 64 countries for the period 1996–2001 shows that corruption distorts the composition of public spending by reducing the share of social expenditures like health, education, and social protection and by increasing the share of spending on defense and the military. A study based on data from 120 countries for the period 1985–1998 empirically confirms association between corruption and higher military allocations, both in terms of share of GDP and total government spending.

Overall verdict of the jury is that corruption is bad for economic growth. Further, corruption is an economic phenomenon and insights from dismal science would be required to tackle this problem. One very basic and standard argument, we are taught in Econ 101, is that competition induces efficiency and monopolies create inefficiencies or deadweight losses. Let us analyze what insights the said argument provides for tackling the problem of corruption.

Theory of Competition

A bureaucrat enjoys a monopoly over the provision of public goods. A driving license can only be obtained from the police. A passport can be issued by the passport office. An FIR can be registered only at the police station. An investigation of the case can only be conducted by the police and only a formal court of law can decide the case. It is the monopoly over publicly produced goods where the genesis of corruption can be traced, at least partly. It implies that the reduction of monopolies over production and provision of public goods can be an important step toward controlling corruption.

Accordingly, the policy implication is to give the power to produce public goods to more individuals or organizations to foster competition. There is, however, a catch in this piece of advice. The said mechanism shall work only if multiple officials or firms are competent to produce the public good. On the contrary, if all officials are required to put their signatures, each with veto power, corruption or bribery amount shall increase as pointed out earlier. Starting from a section officer to the level of Minister each public functionary has to sign the file in the existing scheme of things, causing a lot of wastage through red tape. Changes in the existing decision-making process or rules of business to reduce the number of steps or signatures to the minimum possible level can be an important area of reform in public administration.

Another option to induce competition and reduce monopolies is to hire integrity from the private sector, either by outsourcing the entire production of public goods or part of it. For example, customs clearance at ports involves several tasks like the examination of goods, valuation, and assessment of import duty and taxes by applying the rates given in the tariff code. A number of developing countries hired the services of private international firms to conduct pre-shipment inspections of imports. This pre-shipment inspection was, in a sense, a substitute for the physical inspection of goods at the destination ports. The rationale behind outsourcing the function of pre-shipment inspection was to reduce corruption and delays at the customs ports.

The inspection by PSIs could reduce corruption by decreasing the power of inspectors to negotiate informal payments at the ports as PSIs generate independent information on the description of imported goods. Pre-shipment inspections are said to be associated with a growth rate of import duties in the range of 6–8% per annum.[42] On similar lines, outsourcing of various publicly produced goods can be considered. Interestingly, outsourcing is already being done for a number of public goods like the provision of security for the lives and property of the citizenry. The privately hired security guards by banks and other private institutions are basically providing the services that the police are supposed to provide, as the protection of the lives and property of the citizenry is a public good.

On the same lines, private investigation firms can be licensed to conduct investigations into cases to reduce complaints of corruption and extraneous influence. The endemic issues of capacity and corruption in the judiciary also demand some out-of-the-box thinking. Private adjudicators can be licensed so that private parties may approach them for the resolution of their disputes. Alternate dispute resolution (ADR) mechanisms can be developed for speedy and cost-free dispensation of justice.

Similarly, instead of getting a copy of the land record from a specific revenue official, making it available electronically to the farmers and lending banks would help reduce corruption. So, there are many possibilities worth exploring about the publicly produced goods to change the way they are currently produced and provided. Developed countries have already done such experiments. For example, we are required in Pakistan to go to the passport office for the issuance of a passport whereas in the US you can get a passport from any post office.

Political corruption can also be reduced by maximizing competition. Presently, the cost of entry into politics is formidably high. Young and promising citizens with a passion for public service do not enter politics due to high costs of electioneering. Bans on student and labor unions and the indifference rather than hostility of the ruling elite to the local government system have also acted as barriers to entry into national politics. As a result, dynastic politics reigns supreme and due to monopoly, the politics of Pakistan suffers both from low quality and corruption. In order to reduce political corruption, easing of barriers to the entry into politics would be needed.

Enhancing accountability and transparency is another broad area warranting focus for controlling corruption. Corruption prospers in informational darkness which means that by making the systems, processes, and decisions transparent, corruption can be tackled to a large extent. Transparency and corruption are opposite to each other. Corruption is supposed to be secret while transparency means openness. Publicizing information, rules, regulations, and procedures promotes transparency and reduces informational darkness.

Transparency and Accountability

The heavy tradition of secrecy and confidentiality in the working of the government compromises the cause of transparency. Transparency in government decision-making can be encouraged through open government, and increased public oversight via Parliament, independent media, and the strengthening of civil society watchdogs. Hearings of Parliamentary committees, question hours in the National and Provincial assemblies, and investigative reporting by responsible and well-trained journalists are some tools for ensuring transparency in the actions and decisions of the government. "Most of these measures exist but more in form rather than in substance".[43]

The accountability system is weak in Pakistan. Dr. Ishrat, in this regard, writes: "A number of laws and institutions exist in the name of accountability in Pakistan. Starting from the Public Accounts Committees at the Federal and Provincial Assembly level there is plethora of committees, bureaus and task forces, charged with this responsibility. The National Accountability Bureau made a very promising start and instilled some fear and induced a deterrence effect but this was only for a short period of the initial three years of the Musharraf government. Soon after, political compulsions gave way to a pragmatic approach whereby the impartiality and neutrality of the NAB came under serious questioning. Accountability has lost its true sense and meaning in the vocabulary of governance and instead become associated with retribution, settling political scores and tool for winning over opponents and witch hunting the recalcitrant".[44]

Corruption, being an economic phenomenon, responds to the standard economic theory of incentives, both positive and negative.[45] Several cross-country studies show that higher wages in the public sector are associated with lower corruption. The results of a study,[46] covering 31 low-income countries, suggest that public sector wages compared to wages in the private sector are negatively connected to corruption in the country. The multi-fold increase in public sector wages is, however, not a viable fiscal proposition due to the bloated public sector structure. The idea is workable with a lean structure, which would not be possible, without reforms of a fundamental nature, given its dynamics as bureaucracy tends to increase its size as predicted by Wagner's law.[47] In order to get promotions and perks, bureaucracy creates positions and subordinate organizations, the existence of which can hardly be justified on a cost-benefit criterion. Unless restructuring of such organizations is done, with a view to making the bureaucracy lean, a substantial increase in monetary incentives is not possible given the budgetary constraints.[48]

Accountability not only of employees but of the entire public sector departments and organizations is required regarding their performance and raison d'être. A small incremental increase in wages would not reduce corruption. Large increases that are 5–10 times would be required to have some tangible impact. Further, higher wages in the public sector are, at best, a necessary condition for performance. They do not constitute sufficient condition. Even higher wages will not reduce corruption without putting in place a strong accountability system. Empirics[49] suggest that performance pay can reduce absenteeism among school teachers, and can improve test scores of the students if monitoring mechanisms are effective. But if service providers collude with their monitors, then performance pay or higher wages would not deliver on the promise of corruption reduction.

Technology has some promise. Things have changed fast in the last two to three decades. We are not living in the 1990s. Improvements in technology and communication have provided effective tools in our hands to expose corrupt activities and improve governance. For example, corruption of public officials through the theft of official time can be monitored through electronic attendance and CCTV cameras. Technology can also be used for better tax collection by decreasing interaction between the tax payer and the tax collector. An analysis of customs revenue collection at ports in Pakistan for the period 1997–1998 to 2018–2019 shows that with the introduction of a computerized risk assessment system collection efficiency increased significantly.[50] Technology can also help reduce tax evasion by matching taxpayer declarations with information on electronic sales and purchases. Electronic procurements by governments and electronic auctions by public sector departments can also be instrumental in reducing corruption. Online procurements and e-auctions increase competition and undermine the collusive power of the bidding rings. Argentina is a case in point where the introduction of e-procurement reduced prices, shortened the procurement process and increased the number of bidders.[51]

Banerjee and his colleagues tested the efficacy of e-governance as an anti-corruption tool. They analyzed a large field experiment of a nationwide scale-up of a social protection reform program. The results suggested that reform reduced the number of intermediaries involved in the disbursement of funds. Advance payments were replaced with just-in-time payments (that is expenditure-based) through e-invoicing which made the detection of misreporting easier. As a result, leakages went down and program expenditure dropped by 24%. There were fewer fake households in the official database and program officials' wealth went down by 10%.[52] Similarly, the results of another study suggest that equipping health inspectors with smartphone apps for channeling data on rural clinics improved the governance of rural health centers even in low-capacity settings.[53] Banerjee and Duflo perhaps rightly argue[54] that rather than resorting to simplistic formulae like privatization (which is not a panacea) for reducing wastage in government, a better course would be to find an alternative way of organizing the government activity that works better. Waste may also be substantially higher than we perceive inside private firms as management of resources is harder both in the private as well as public sector.

It also turns out that controlling corruption in institutions, where it has become endemic over the years, is very difficult. An increase in the salaries of judicial officers is a case in point. Despite a significant increase in the salary of the lower judiciary, corruption among the judicial officers is still perceived to be very high.[55] An increase in wages may not bring a change in the culture of the organization. According to standard economic thinking, corrupt officials like criminals are rational human beings. They evaluate the costs and benefits involved in the commission of a crime. It means that both the quantum of the penalty and its enforcement play an important role in determining whether a person will commit an illegal act or not.

Whistle-blowing can play a significant role in reducing corruption. The first person who notices the act of corruption, mismanagement, or patronage is generally the individual who either works inside the organization or comes into contact with such an organization. Employees of an organization are better placed to raise their concerns against corruption, but at the same time, they are the worst losers by disclosing such an act if they do not have legal protection. In a society where corruption is endemic and people think that 'everybody does it', costs to the accuser, in terms of social capital like loss of friends et cetera are very high. The fear of retribution becomes a hurdle in their disclosure of a corrupt act. If the law gives the whistleblowers confidence and security, corruption can be tackled by the organization itself, and essentially, such an approach shall be proactive, as an alarm bell may ring before a corrupt act is actually committed.

Traditionally, civil servants and politicians have remained targets of all blame and criticism for promoting, perpetuating, and tolerating the culture of corruption. Things are now changing. Trust in the institutions is so low that none is now sacred in the eyes of the public. Allegations are not restricted to civil servants and politicians. Farzana Sheikh, in '*Making Sense of Pakistan*', has alluded to this change. She is of the view that the issue of corruption came under renewed focus with the ouster of President Musharraf in 2008. Traditionally all the blame by the critics as well as the people was heaped on the politicians even for the corruption and bad governance of the hybrid regimes having deep civil–military alliances. Critics have now started to challenge the claim that only elected politicians are responsible for all corruption and rot in the country. She has further argued that due to the supremacy enjoyed by the military regimes in Pakistan for a long time, the armed forces have become a political class with high economic stakes.[56]

Corruption and bad governance are symptomatic of the weak state capacity. The literature on state capacity approaches this concept from various angles. A state would be weak if the legitimacy gap is high or if it does not enjoy a monopoly over violence. Similarly, a state would be weak if it is unable to provide public services to its citizens. The ensuing discussion on state capacity shall, however, mainly revolve around weak fiscal capacity. A state with weak fiscal capacities is unable to raise due taxes. Consequently, it does not have money to provide quality public services to its citizens and to alleviate poverty. Its dependence increases on foreign aid and loans. Consequently, it is caught in the cobweb of debts.

CHAPTER 13

Weak Fiscal and Trade Capacities

Adam Smith, about two and half centuries ago, wrote: "Little else is required to carry a state to the highest degree of opulence from the lowest barbarism, but peace, easy taxes, and a tolerable administration of justice; all the rest being brought about by the natural course of things".[1] Simply, the recipe for prosperity, according to Smith, has three important ingredients that are peace or stability, capacity to raise taxes, and good administration of justice. Peace in society or socio-economic stability is a big prerequisite for long-term sustainable economic growth. In view of the significance of socio-economic stability, we discussed it at the very beginning of the book (Chapter 1). Contract enforcement, which is at the heart of all growth and development, depends on the quality of the judicial system and that is why, a separate chapter was allocated to discuss various aspects of the administration of justice in Pakistan (Chapter 11).

The administration of justice and collection of taxes require a strong judiciary and a capable tax machinery. Besley and Persson write in '*Pillars of Prosperity*' as follows. "For state capacity, we can distinguish two broad type of capabilities that allow the state to take action. One concerns the extractive role of the state. We call this capability fiscal capacity. Does the government have the necessary infrastructure- in terms of administration, monitoring, and enforcement-to raise revenue from broad tax bases such as income and consumption, revenue that can be spent on income support or services to its citizens? The other type of capacity concerns the

J. Nasir, *Development Challenges of Pakistan*,
https://doi.org/10.1007/978-981-97-3064-3_13

productive role of the state. Is it capable of raising private-sector productivity via services such as road transport or the provision of power? Or does it have the necessary infrastructure- in terms of courts, educated judges, or registers-to raise private incomes by providing regulation and legal services such as protection of the property right or the enforcement of contracts (legal capacity)".[2]

In simple words, state capacity is the ability of the state to collect taxes, dispense justice, and provide public goods. An effective state instead of pandering to the vested interests, invests in public goods like health and education, collects taxes from the rich, and ensures peace through its monopoly over violence. The development of fiscal capacity that is building institutions for tax compliance is an important feature of economic development. Any country with regards to fiscal capacity at any particular time can be broadly bracketed into any of the three categories namely common-interest state, redistributive state, or weak state.[3]

According to Besley and Persson, in a common-interest state, future government revenue is expected to be used for common interests like defense and development, and the ruler makes considerable investments in developing the fiscal capacity to maximize revenue. The common-interest states have strong institutional constraints on the government. In the redistributive state, a single group captures the state which runs the state affairs like a fiefdom. The institutional constraints on the ruling group or elite are weak. Dictatorships, countries with one party rule, or ruling monarchies generally fall under this category. In such a state, the state money is just an extension of the personal wealth of the rulers and citizens rely in a sense on the benevolence of the ruling monarchs. The pertinent examples are the monarchies of the Middle East and communist rule in North Korea. These states, however, also build state capacities capitalizing on the political stability in such countries. The weak states have neither cohesive institutions nor are they controlled by a single group. Due to political instability, incentives to build state capacities are weak. State capacity depends on the political culture of a country. It is not exogenous to the power structures and political economy of a country. Patronage and politicization of bureaucracy, tolerance for corruption and rent-seeking, and structural adjustment programs undermine state capacity.[4]

Successful societies, from the earlier civilizations to modern states, had the dual ability to produce surplus (prosperity) and to secure surplus (security). Thus, civilization was just a function of two elements that is prosperity and security. The efforts of a state to create wealth could undermine its sovereignty if it attracted predatory attacks from within the country or outside the country and it did not have the force to counter such attacks. So, historically most societies were trapped between two alternatives[5] that is "self-defeating prosperity" (investment and economic growth efforts that would induce predatory attacks) or "backwardness by design" (keeping the economic activity low or close to subsistence level). The wars were basically for capturing the surplus, the argument goes. The societies where relatively enormous wealth was created as a result of the Agricultural Revolution became potential objects of attack by armed outsiders.[6]

The modern state emerged out of prolonged wars and military competition for capturing surplus. The rulers, however, needed money to bear the expenses of war. "Military struggle created incentive to tax populations, to create administrative hierarchies to provision armies and to establish merit and competence rather than personal ties as the basis for recruitment and promotion".[7] The wars also paved way for the modern democracy. The monarchs required money to fight wars and people (generally rich people of that time) demanded concessions and share in authority in return. In the UK, the major concessions extracted from the Crown were the outcome of new taxes. "War made the state and the state made war".[8]

Historical evidence[9] confirms that inheritance taxes were systematically higher during periods of mass mobilization of conflicts during the period 1816 and 2000. Whenever the Crown introduced new taxes or increased tax rates, the elite (or society of that time in the words of Acemoglu and Robinson) came up with a new charter of demand to curtail the powers of the Crown. "No taxation without representation" was the slogan of the American Revolution which well explains the grievances of the British colonists who were required to pay taxes without their representation in the British parliament. Stasavage in '*The Decline and Rise of democracy*' also presents a similar thesis. According to him, rulers lacked information about what people were producing having implications for taxation. The information asymmetry between the state and the people gave rulers an incentive to share power with the elite through councils to determine what sorts of taxes could be levied.[10]

The state that emerged out of taxation is not just a descriptive story told by historians. Empirics and data also support the hypothesis that the functions of the state (monopoly over violence and taxation) were created by the armed actors to extract revenue. A pertinent vindication comes from the Democratic Republic of Congo (DRC).

Taxation and State-Building

Research[11] based on a dataset of 650 locations in DRC shows that the armed actors introduced sophisticated fiscal and legal administrations to extract revenue when the output of a village was valuable and could not be easily taxed. The research story goes like this. The villages in eastern DRC have natural resources which differ both in value and physical properties. Some villages are linked to columbite-tantalite deposits that is Coltan (which is a bulky mineral). Its output is easy to tax. Contrary to this, some villages are linked to gold deposits, a mineral hard to find and hard to tax as it can be concealed by the miners. Exploiting the said variation in mineral endowments and demand shocks, the research showed that coltan shock gave rise to essential state functions like taxation, protection, and monopoly over violence. The armed forces provided security (that is physical monitoring) on coltan mines located near airports as coltan was traded to the international markets from these mines.

In contrast to that, the armed forces instead of increasing security on gold production sites used sophisticated techniques to tax the gold. They imposed taxes on transit, consumption, and head taxes, and developed legal and fiscal administrations to manage tax evasion and enforce contracts.

This research points toward an important distinction about the nature of taxes and their impact on democracy and governance. Taxes imposed on coltan mines were a type of trade tax, easy to monitor by manning the borders. The collection of such taxes was optimized by beefing up just security on the mines from where coltan could be traded abroad. On the other hand, the optimum taxation of gold required the introduction of some novel techniques and the development of legal and administrative structures.

Collecting trade taxes requires only observing trade flows at borders while collecting income taxes requires a much more elaborate system of monitoring, enforcement and compliance. One way to illustrate this is to look at the shares of revenue coming from trade and income taxes whatever the level of taxation. High-income countries depend more on income taxes and many of them do not use trade taxes at all. On the other hand, middle-income countries and especially low income countries use trade taxes more. Broadening the tax base rather than tax rates shall be the key to increasing tax revenues in many low -income countries.[12]

Improving fiscal and legal capacities is perhaps the best strategy for state-building. Taxes put more revenue at the disposal of the government, which it can spend on productivity-enhancing public goods. Taxation also increases civic engagement of the citizens who hold the government accountable for public service delivery whereas better legal capacity, reflected through the speedy and cost-effective dispensation of justice, increases the trust of the people in the state institutions. Quality provision of public goods eventually stimulates economic growth. Empirics confirm this assertion. For example, in the aftermath of the French Revolution, one of history's biggest state-building experiments, administrative reforms were initiated in city centers or capitals of the local administrations. The local governments or administrations invested in the enforcement capacities of the capital cities which facilitated the local governments to deliver public goods, which in turn stimulated long-term economic growth.[13]

State-building through developing fiscal capacities is generally with the participation of the members of the society. Contrary to this, military strategy to eliminate non-state armed actors to ensure the monopoly of the state over violence does not involve the consent of the people. The top-down approach of "state first" or "security first" creates significant negative consequences. Such an approach is usually unidimensional and prioritizes military objectives ahead of all other objectives. This approach not only fails to develop other crucial aspects of the state capacity but leads to deterioration in the existing capacities. In the recent past, vindication of said assertion comes from Colombia.

In a classic case of state-building, the Colombian government empowered army personnel to combat left-wing guerillas. The size of the army was expanded and huge incentives were given to the military personnel. The high-powered incentives like promotions, medals, training courses, vacation time, and appreciation from the seniors induced gross violations of human rights. The army officials killed civilians and portrayed them as guerillas to earn rewards. At the end of the day, the military strategy for state-building turned out to be counter-productive and worsened even existing judicial institutions.[14] In modern history, several other examples can be found where the top-down state-building approach has backfired. In Peru and Guatemala, the post-conflict truth and reconciliation commissions documented widespread killings of civilians and the weakening of the judicial systems. In Vietnam where General William

DePuy argued that "solution in Vietnam is more bombs, more shells, more napalm" and "get the people by the balls and their hearts and minds will follow"[15] but evidence points to the contrary.

The bottom-up approaches (gaining the support of the people through civic engagement etc.) are more successful in nation building than violent top-down interventions.[16] '*Nation building: Big Lessons from Successes and Failures*', published by Centre for Economic Policy Research, on "what works" and "what does not work" for nation building, concludes that military intervention and military aid generally backfire as regards nation building. Instead, democracy, promotion of inter-group interaction, and fostering a positive common identity (like through education) are some better strategies for nation building.[17] The failure of the US top-down attempt to recreate the monopoly of state over violence in countries such as Afghanistan and Iraq is a big testimony to the failure of the military strategy (even if the military is as powerful as that of the US). Simply, the top-down military strategy of state-building does not work. The best approach would be to build state institutions in multiple dimensions by appreciating state–society interactions with a view to make both the state and society stronger simultaneously.

State–Society Synergy

This brings us to the important point of state–society relationship. The literature looking at state formation through the prism of taxation gives the impression that if state and society are in competition with each other. And there is win-lose relationship between the two. The King was the state and the elites at the time of the Glorious Revolution in England were the society of that time. Shifting some powers from the Crown in favor of the Parliament was a win for the society and a loss for the king (state of that time). The state was therefore viewed with suspicion and more power to it meant sacrifice of the freedom of the individuals (society).

For instance, Friedrich Hayek was apprehensive of the emergence of a strong state with taxes and a generous welfare system that could curtail the freedom of the people. And therefore strong checks on the unbridled powers of the state were required. He wrote in '*The Road to Serfdom*': "We can rely on the voluntary agreement to guide the action of the state only so long as it is confined to spheres where agreement exists. But not only when the state undertakes direct control in fields where there is no such agreement it is bound to suppress individual freedom once the communal sector, in which state controls all the means exceeds a certain proportion of the whole, the effects of its actions dominate the whole system. Although the state controls directly the use of only a large part of the available resources, the effects of its decisions on the remaining part of the economic system become so great that indirectly it controls almost everything".[18]

The concerns of Hayek, basically in the context of state control through central planning in communist countries, did not prove true, particularly in the West where democracy triumphed. The footprint of the state, however, kept on increasing due to the state turning itself into the main provider of public services and welfare in the majority of the countries. The role of the state, democracy, and vibrancy of the civil society increased simultaneously. Both state and society gained. It was a type of win-win situation.

The 'State-in-Society approach' to the interaction also postulates that there is always a conflict between the state and other organizations for social control. The power of an organization depends on the number of people who follow the rules of a certain organization (that is compliance) and their motivation to follow such rules (that is legitimation). Like other social organizations, the state plays by the same rules but on a grander scale. According to said approach, state and social organizations compete continually for social control, hence a conflict. Joel Migdal, in '*Strong Societies Weak States*', gives an interesting example of this conflict from Turkey. He writes: "Mustafa Kemal of Turkey locked horns with religious organizations over whether men should wear hats with brims or without. As with so many skirmishes, the issue was not as inconsequential as it may first appear; over 70 people were hanged for wearing the wrong hats. In reality, the conflict was over who had the right and ability to make rules in that society".[19]

Migdal goes further and says that state capabilities include capacities to penetrate society, regulate social relationships, extract resources, or appropriate or use resources in determined ways. A strong state is one that is high at said capabilities. In the Third World countries, Migdal theorizes, societies are mostly made up of local organizations with local constituencies. Such organizations are headed by strongmen like chiefs, landlords, clan leaders, and rich peasants et cetera. The state struggles both at the macro and micro level for social control but there is a dilemma.

At the macro level, strengthening state agencies or a few institutions can create autonomous power centers within the state structure which can turn up against the state leadership. A state leader, in a bid to survive, uses tactics to control centrifugal forces in such institutions by making non-merit-based appointments along familial, ethnic, or patrimonial lines, a regular reshuffle at the top and middle-level officials, and blackmail and other dirty tricks (perhaps that is the reason that people who have skeletons in their cupboards are more fit for top official positions in the Third World countries).

At the micro level, local state officials (called implementers by Migdal) are tasked with the implementation of state policies. These officials are caught in a web of pressure and demands from various sources like superiors, strongmen, and local politicians et cetera. Hardly such implementers are motivated to resist local pressure. They avoid open conflict with these power centers as doing so may jeopardize their career prospects. So state and society become inseparable despite being in conflict over social control. Both influence and reshape each other. Strongmen exert a strong influence over the outcome of public policies. Even well-intentioned policies may not be implemented due to the influence of such strong men. And the state is left only with two options, either to dilute their influence or to appease them by doling out favors and concessions. If the state finds that dilution of the influence of such strongmen is difficult or doing so may create problems, it indulges in clientelistic politics, Midgal argues.

Acemoglu and Robinson in their book '*The Narrow Corridor*' also dilate upon the tussle between 'society' and 'state' and their overarching theme is that state and society complement each other though there is a continuous struggle between them. The strongest states have the strongest societies, they postulate. A strong state is required to solve the collective action problem of maintaining order—"control violence, enforce laws, and provide public services".[20] At the same time, strong society is required to "control and shackle the strong state",[21] so the state does not indulge in repression. They name such a state a 'shackled state'. There are two other extremes of state that is 'Absent Leviathan' (a stateless society that can degenerate into total disorder and chaos), and 'Despotic Leviathan' (oppressive to serve its interests through levy of exorbitant taxes, and imposing restrictions on freedom of thought, etc.). The 'Shackled State' falls within said two extremes where the powers of the state and society are balanced. And such a balance is required to yield optimum outcomes, the argument proceeds.

If we analyze Pakistan in the framework of Acemoglu and Robinson (AR) in the said book, the state of Pakistan is not an absent Leviathan as we have a strong army. We have bureaucracy recruited through competitive and merit-based processes. We have a written constitution. And we have a central authority. Nor Pakistan is a despotic Leviathan as we have a parliament. We have an election commission. And we have a judiciary to adjudicate disputes. But at the same time, the Pakistani state is not a shackled state as the quality of public goods like justice, education, and health care et cetera leaves much to be desired. Rule of the law is weak and monopoly over violence is also challenged by non-state actors from time to time. In the AR framework, we may classify it among the states categorized as 'Paper Leviathan'. Such a state is generally unresponsive to its citizens across the board (poor public service delivery), seeks little input from its citizens (weak democracy, sham elections, and flow of policy from the people at the top), and does not have scruples to be oppressive to its citizens (picking up citizens without due process of law, and subjecting them to torture and unfair treatment to suppress dissenting opinions). So a 'paper Levitation' can be both oppressive and ineffective at the same time. This type of state survives, Acemoglu and Robinson argue, due to two factors.

First, those in power (the elites of the time) do not want the state to mobilize the people and second, they exploit clientelist relations. It means that a paper Leviathan is neither neutral nor effective. It is partial and ineffective while dealing with its citizens. Such a state is characterized by low trust, high inequalities, and rent-seeking. Even morality gets confused in such states. The "moral" and "immoral" and "legal" and "illegal" are perceived by the elite as well as the broader population as synonymous. Rosita Armitage, commenting on the culture of exemptions enjoyed by the Pakistani elite, writes: "There is a tacit pact established between the members of the elite, which provides a high degree of impunity for illegality and extra-legality. This ability to manoeuvre around the laws and regulations of the State enables elites to constantly shore up and reconstitute their power in alignment with shifting political and economic conditions".[22]

The tax structure of a state with weak capabilities is generally regressive in nature as it is difficult to collect taxes from the elite. For example, no correlation exists between the tax paid and the life standards of the affluent in Pakistan. Suppose an alien descends to Pakistan who does not know the numbers of GDP, debt, poverty et cetera. He stands by the motorway. And suppose only physical objects like vehicles can enter into the mental calculus of the alien. It would never enter into the imagination of our alien guest, after seeing shiny vehicles plying on the roads, that Pakistan is a poor country.

Tax Structure

Pakistani elite is very fond of luxury vehicles like SUVs and their thirst is so high that the automobile assemblers take months to deliver the vehicles and charge additional money than is own money. According to some estimates, Rs. 30–40 billion are paid annually as 'own money' per annum to auto assemblers. When it comes to taxes, the SUV elites pay nothing or pay very little as either their income is from agriculture (which is exempt from income tax) or they are able to evade taxes due to the weak and corruption-soaked tax system of the country. Reasons for the weak tax culture in Pakistan are many. For example, no clear social contract exists between the elite and the state for revenue generation. People hardly pay taxes out of love for the sake of patriotism. "Tax compliance seems more about our reactions to government performance and honesty than a sense of solidarity with our fellow citizens".[23] Tax money is not returned to the public with better value as corruption in public institutions is high.

Institutions are inefficient and are inefficient with purpose. The thesis of Daron Acemoglu and his colleagues seems very pertinent in the case of Pakistan. In their paper "*Emergence and Persistence of Inefficient states*",[24] they postulate that inefficient state structures are by design. Their argument is that in less-developed countries where the democratic system has not yet matured, the elite who hold the power are opposed to high taxes and public investments. The bureaucrats hired to collect taxes also facilitate tax evasion by the rich elite as rents of evasion also accrue to them in an inefficient tax structure. And that the elite fear that in a real democracy, the poor who are in the majority in such countries will come to power and may embark on revolutionary reforms in tax structure and tax bureaucracy to generate more taxes with additional levies. If that happens then both the elite and the tax bureaucracy will lose. At the same time, the elite face a dilemma. They need to perpetuate inefficient structures to remain beneficiaries of such a system and for doing so they need to remain in power. So, they rely on patronage to win elections and not on redistribution or public service delivery, the argument runs.

Empirical studies[25] also confirm the negative impact of corruption on tax revenues and compliance. Based on a comprehensive dataset of 147 countries spanning over the period 1995–2014, compiled by the IMF, some researchers confirm the negative impact of corruption on all kinds of taxes like Sales Tax (VAT), import taxes, and income tax. Particularly in developing countries tax structures are more amenable to corruption due to the complexity involved. "Some tax structures provide less opportunity for corruption than others. Some bases of taxation are easier to observe and verify. Consider, for instance, the window tax imposed in medieval England. The tax was distortionary-it led to dark homes. But it had one advantage. It was easy to count the numbers of windows. It would be easy to check on the collection efforts of any tax official: a random check would quickly ascertain whether he had by and large counted the number of windows correctly. If a tax official tried to charge a taxpayer for having too many windows, the aggrieved taxpayer could appeal to a court, which could, in turn, verify the number of windows. In today's world, there are other bases of taxation which can similarly be (relatively) easily verified-the number and size of cars, the square meters of a house. It may be easier to design institutional arrangements for the collection of such taxes without corruption".[26]

Optimal tax policy and tax structures in developing countries, characterized by low tax revenue and high evasion, may significantly diverge from what is prescribed in standard textbook models. For example, turnover tax is known to distort production decisions but it is more difficult to evade than profit tax.[27] If tax design and tax statute are understandable by the common tax payers, tax compliance increases. Simplifying communication by the tax administration consistently improves tax compliance, so making compliance easy is highly a significant policy tool of an effective tax administration for optimizing revenue collection.[28]

The taxation system of Pakistan is unfair due to horizontal inequities arising from exemptions and the informal economy. "One of the most salient features of Pakistan's tax system is the special favorable treatment given to particular sectors, and sources and uses of income. This causes serious distortions in investments and other decisions by taxpayers, imposing inefficiency losses on the economy and slowing economic growth".[29] Equity demands that 'like' households would be treated 'like' for tax purposes which means that all sources of income are liable to be taxation. If our neighbor pays no tax or pays less tax having almost the same income, we shall also be induced to pay less taxes. Similarly, if preferential treatment is available to the income earned from capital (such as capital gains) compared to labor income (wages), wage-earners will feel pinched.

Inequality is also connected to tax evasion and corruption. There is a limit to hiding assets and wealth inside the national boundaries. You can purchase a palatial house, accumulate gold and pearls, gift money and property to your sons and daughters, get an SUV of the latest model, spend on the education of your children in a foreign university, and do a bit of social money laundering. Wealth, however, multiplies perhaps in geometric progression in a fertile environment of rent-seeking and tax evasion. All wealth or income may not be spent and hidden inside the national boundaries. So the super-rich indulge in shifting of income and wealth to tax havens outside the national boundaries. And money laundering may not be that difficult for them. "There is an industry that sells wealth concealment services, and this industry primarily targets very wealthy customers. Think of a representative Swiss bank. It derives revenue by levying fees on the wealth it helps concealing".[30]

Besides huge tax evasion, low compliance, and corruption, the tax structure of Pakistan is beset with many distortions, anomalies, and imbalances. For example, the contribution of agriculture, industry, and services sector to GDP is 23%, 19%, and 58% whereas the contribution to revenue is 2%, 53%, and 45% respectively. Some statistics of tax collection shall give credence to the said assertion. (1). Around 50% of tax revenue is collected by the Federal Government at the import stage as Custom duty, sales tax, Federal Excise duty (in sales tax mode), and withholding tax; (2) Sales tax is collected against imports as well as domestic supplies. On average collection of sales tax on imports is higher than collection from domestic supplies. (3) Income tax is collected under three major heads: withholding tax, voluntary payments, and tax out of demand. Around 65% is collected as withholding, 28% as voluntary payments, and just 7% out of demand. (4) An analysis of tax collection for the period 1990–2020 shows that out-of-demand payments have decreased in percentage terms (in 1990–2000 14% was collected out of demand which reduced to 7% in 2010–2020). Voluntary payments were 34% in 2000–2010 which reduced to 28% in 2010–2020. (5) Withholding tax continues to be the major mode of collection of income tax (see Table 13.1). The tool of withholding tax in Pakistan as a source of revenue is "too large in scale, size, scope, and intensity" and is negatively impacting the entire economic system as withholding taxes "get stuck into the pricing structure of the final goods and services produced in the country rendering them price-incompetitive in the international market".[31]

Table 13.1 Overview of income tax and sales tax collection

Decade			Income Tax				Collection (%)
	Total Collection	Out of Demand	Voluntary Payments	Withholding Tax	Out of Demand	Voluntary payments	Withholding tax
1991–2000	811,938	112,265	178,420	521,253	14	22	64
2001–2010	3,327,566	404,797	1,147,350	1,775,418	12	34	53
2011–2020	12,721,670	942,689	3,547,657	8,231,325	7	28	65
Decade			Sales Tax				Collection (%)
	Total	Domestic	On Imports		Domestic		Import stage
1991–2000	620,105	269,006	351,099		43		57
2001–2010	3,402,477	1,630,376	1,772,101		48		52
2011–2020	12,892,639	5,976,340	6,916,299		46		54

Source Pakistan Year Books, FBR

These statistics make it amply clear that the tax structure of Pakistan is highly regressive. More reliance is on indirect taxes, the incidence of which is finally passed on to the consumers. It is typical with indirect taxes. A fiscal incidence analysis[32] conducted by the World Bank shows that sales tax is neither progressive nor regressive but the Kakwani index[33] of the Sales tax is just 0.02, which means that sales tax imposes a substantial burden on the poor due to its neutral redistributive properties. Estimates suggest that poverty in Pakistan would be four percentage points lower in the absence of sales tax all else being equal.[34] The quintile-wise analysis of tax incidence further confirms the regressivity of the tax regime (see Table 13.2).

The impact of income tax which is being collected as withholding tax is also like that of indirect taxes, which speaks of the low capacity of tax machinery. More emphasis is on 'easy to collect taxes' like taxes at the import stage. The amount of income tax collected through efforts that is through demand constitutes a small portion of the overall composition of taxes collected by FBR. Moreover, due to the regressive nature of

Table 13.2 Incidence of Federal raxes, 2020–21% of the tax revenue

	Bottom Quintile	*2nd, 3rd and 4th Quintile*	*Top Quintile*	*Palma Ratio**
Income Tax	5.6	30.4	64.0	11.42
Import Sales Tax	9.4	49.0	41.6	4.42
Domestic Sales Tax	8.3	49.5	42.2	5.08
Customs Duty	7.8	46.7	45.5	5.83
Excise Duty	9.0	50.9	40.1	4.45
Total Tax Revenue	**7.6**	**42.5**	**49.9**	**6.56**
Total Income	**6.3**	**42.2**	**51.5**	**8.17**
Ratio	1.206	1.007	0.968	

*Ratio of share of top quintile to bottom quintile
Source Leading Issues in the Economy of Pakistan (Table 16.4)

the tax structure burden of taxes is disproportionately higher on wage-earners and low-income groups. The tax–to–GDP hovers around 10%, much lower than the potential.

Tax collection requires high fiscal capacity and will by the state. Tax evasion by a citizen is a rational decision like other decisions. A tax payer rationally trades off the benefits of tax evasion and risks of costs of being caught and punished. If the probability of investigation or being caught is low (due to low capacity of tax machinery), there is a high chance that tax shall be evaded through underreporting.[35] Taxes are not like gifts or alms. Taxes in the practical world are not connected to some visible exchange or reward. The economists guide us that human beings think on margins which simply means that while striking a trade-off human beings give away something only to get something of equal or greater utility in return.

A gift is given in expectation of reciprocity. An act of philanthropy is done for social money laundering or validation from society to become respectable in the eyes of friends and relatives or to earn some reward in the life hereafter. Such is, however, not the case with paying taxes. The beneficiaries of tax payments and those paying taxes are two different sets of people. In the real world majority would not like to pay taxes just due to patriotism.

The problem in Pakistan is that the rich (top 1%) are evading taxes through rent-seeking, exemptions, money laundering, and transfer pricing due to elite capture, lack of political will, and capacity issues of tax machinery (hardly we have taxmen who can unearth tax evasions of multinationals through transfer pricing, etc.). Due to low tax collection, Pakistan is persistently faced with huge deficits and to finance such deficits, it relies on 'seigniorage' that is government revenues from monopoly control over the creation of money, and on foreign aid. Some estimates, based on panel data of about 100 countries for the period 1960–1999 show that greater political instability leads to higher seigniorage, especially in developing, less democratic, and socially polarized countries.[36] And seigniorage comes with inflation which acts like a tax but its hammer falls more heavily on the poor. It makes the poor worse off, lowers the share of the bottom quintile in the income, reduces real minimum wages, and tends to increase poverty.[37]

And foreign aid has got many ills. Fiscal capacity inter alia depends on the availability of aid and debt. If a country is getting easy money through rents from natural resources or foreign aid, incentives to invest in fiscal capacity would be low. The availability of alternative sources of finance hampers state-building.[38] Dependence on debt and foreign aid lowers subsequent growth in real tax revenues and becomes a daunting barrier to the development of fiscal capacity and state-building.[39]

Aid and Growth

Revenue from VAT and income tax (direct taxes) shall be lower in case of access to alternate sources of revenue. Empirics confirm that low taxes and high dependence on aid are the recipes for disengaged citizenship. Two experiments in the neighborhood of Kampala, Uganda, were conducted to ascertain the impact of tax and aid money on civic engagement.[40] In the first experiment, two players, a leader and a citizen, divided 1500 Ugandan shillings. The leader received 1000 Shillings as aid and the citizen 500 shillings as wages. In the second experiment, the citizen was given 1000 shillings out of which 500 shillings were taxed. The tax was supplemented with 500 shillings of state money and given to the leader. Now the leader had to decide how much of the 1000 shillings was to be allocated to the citizen and whether citizens accepted that division. The disgruntled citizens could punish the leader with a fine of 400 shillings if they considered the division unfair. However, exacting the punishment was not free and citizens had to pay 100 shillings to exact the punishment on the leader.

The result was that the citizens in the tax game punished the leaders when they received on average less than 460 shillings. This figure was 13% higher than the threshold for the aid group and in the case of wage-earners, this threshold was 30% higher. Simply speaking, besides proving loss aversion theory, embezzlement of tax money provoked greater wrath from the citizens than the money stolen from aid, empirically proving a strong link between taxation and accountability. There are several channels through which aid, rather than promoting growth and development, kills growth and accentuates poverty. Dambisa Moyo in '*Dead Aid*' has argued at length with particular reference to African countries that aid is detrimental to long-term sustainable growth and poverty alleviation.

Aid fuels inflation, reduces investment and savings, weakens social capital, ferments conflict, negatively impacts export sector, creates dependency and is a "silent killer of growth".[41] Moyo writes: "In fact, across the globe recipients of aid are worse off; much worse off. Aid has helped make the poor poorer, and growth slower. The notion that aid can alleviate systemic poverty and has done so is a myth. Millions in African are poorer today because of aid; misery and poverty have not ended but have increased. Aid has been, and continues to be, an unmitigated political, economic, and humanitarian disaster for most parts of the developing world".[42]

Aid promotes a culture of corruption. It undermines the rule of law and thwarts the establishment of transparent civil institutions simply implying that aid acts as a drag on economic growth and state capacity. Along with aid come ideas and foreign consultants. The imposed reforms most often do more harm to the aid-recipient country by eroding local capacities and expertise (*Case Study 2*). Moreover, aid makes the governments lazy with little incentive to develop fiscal capacity. Why displease the rich and the elite by taxing, those who may be fund providers and supporters of the ruling regime, when easy money is available with more potential for embezzlement? It is now well documented that aid disbursements to aid-dependent countries coincide with sharp increases in offshore bank financial centers known for opacity and private wealth management.

The leakage is estimated as high as 7.5% of aid disbursements.[43] In the case of petroleum rents the figure of leakage is almost 100% higher. The windfall gains due to exogenous shocks that as an increase in the price of oil are associated with a 15% increase in hidden wealth (proxied by an increase in offshore accounts) of petroleum-producing countries ruled by autocratic rulers.[44] Emmanuel Saez and Gabriel Zucman in '*The Triumph of Injustice*'[45] have documented in detail how the amount of dark money circulating in tax havens has multiplied and how this dirty wealth is becoming a danger to liberal democracy even in countries like the US and the West. "Wealth is power. An extreme concentration of wealth means an extreme concentration of power", they write.

According to some estimates,[46] 10% of global GDP is parked in tax havens but there is a lot of heterogeneity. Scandinavian countries have the lowest while it is as high as 60% in the case of Gulf countries and some Latin American countries. Revelations by Panama Papers,[47] Pandora Papers,[48] and Paradise Papers[49] have demonstrated that the issue of corruption and tax evasion by rich individuals and multinationals is much graver than earlier thought. The tax havens providing easy opportunities to launder wealth have grave implications for democracy (by depositing money offshore through tax evasion, people opt out of their obligation toward their fellow citizens), equality, and poverty reduction efforts of the states.

Aid encourages the misallocation of talent by increasing the likelihood that most entrepreneurial and talented shall engage in what Bhagwati calls directly unproductive profit-seeking (DUP) activities.[50] DUP are basically the activities that generate profit through rent-seeking without producing directly or indirectly goods or wealth for the society. Disillusionment with the entire phenomenon of aid is now increasing both among the donors and the recipients. The foreign aid era is coming to a close as multilateral institutions are fast becoming irrelevant due to the external political and internal organizational dynamics of these institutions.[51] Unfortunately Pakistan often looks to these institutions particularly IMF for help. It is one of the few countries which are permanent clients of the IMF.

Stabilization and Growth

According to an estimate, Pakistan accumulated US$53.3778 billion in loans through IMF programs.[52] There is a dilemma. The aid amount is quite substantial but long-term growth is declining over time confirming Mayo's thesis that aid is a silent killer of economic growth. A rudimentary analysis of IMF programs for the period 1988–2008 shows that instead of bringing improvement in macroeconomic and human development indicators, things worsened under IMF stabilization programs.[53] Similar results hold for the stabilization programs introduced after 2008. For example, Dr. Ashfaq Hassan Khan, analyzing Pakistan's experience with the IMF, writes that IMF dictated stabilization policy slowed economic growth, created unemployment, and increased the size of the public debt and cost of deficit financing.[54] Dr. Arshad Zaman also holds neoliberal policies pursued under IMF conditionality responsible for the deceleration of economic growth (discussed in Chapter 1).

The biggest argument for the failure of all IMF loan strategies and conditionality is that a country that once approached the IMF for loans has resorted to it again and again. All aid and loans including those of IMF have got a political angle. Much depends on the political relations of the country with the USA. In 2000–2021, when Pakistan was negotiating three three-year Poverty Reduction and Growth Facility (PRGF) with IMF, one English daily of Pakistan reported: "Pakistan is under considerable pressure from the United States to accept certain political conditions in return for an IMF bail-out package—The biggest issue is Pakistan's Afghan policy. One of the biggest economies of the world, the US holds majority shares in the IMF and greatly influences the Fund's decisions through the Federal Treasury to fulfil Washington's political agenda. The unofficial set of political conditions include a change in Pakistan's policy on Taliban government—acceptance of UNSC monitors on Afghanistan, reining in of Jihadi (militant) organizations, freezing of the nuclear and missile programs, and relationships with India—Despite the implementation of a painful reform program dictated by the IMF, any deviation by Pakistan on political conditions will make it difficult for Islamabad to get the PRGF".[55]

Another English daily wrote just after one week of 9/11: "The United States being one of the key stakeholders in international financial institutions IMF and the World Bank, is expected to be much favorable than in the past—Pakistan's recent pledge to work with the international community against terrorism is expected to win a lot of support from the financial institutions".[56] The report of the Independent Evaluation office of IMF itself admits that there is no shortage of anecdotal evidence that non-economic considerations played a predominant role in IMF decisions to grant loans to Pakistan.[57]

Pakistan has borrowed from the IMF continuously with only two breaks that is around 20 months in 1992–1993 and nearly four years during 2004–2008. The neoliberal policies of the IMF were a drag on the economic growth and development in Pakistan. IMF acknowledged it in one of its evaluations as follows: "From 1970 to the late 1980s, Pakistan enjoyed an impressive growth (6–7% a year on average). Fiscal and external imbalances were large during most of the period, but unlike in many other developing countries, they did not lead to hyperinflation or to a debt crisis, which led Pakistan to be sometimes referred to as a 'development puzzle'. However, the picture deteriorated markedly from the late 1980s onward, as growth faltered and continued failure to rein in the fiscal and current account deficits. Pakistan made an intensive use of IMF resources during both periods (1970–1988 and 1988–2002) but became continuously dependent upon IMF-supported programs only in the second one".[58]

The share of foreign creditors in debt and debt service payments has been persistently on the rise. According to Arshad Zaman, who worked as Chief Economist to the government of Pakistan, neoliberalism guised in the IMF conditionality has basically failed Pakistan. According to his guesstimates, the loss to GDP during 1990–2020 due to the slowdown of economic growth under a long spell of IMF policies is around US$75.6 billion which is roughly two-thirds of Pakistan's total external debt and liabilities as of June 2020.[59] "The surrender of economic sovereignty to the IMF led to persistence in the pursuit of neo-liberal dogma, despite accumulating evidence that it was not working. This resulted in multiple system-failures, which caused the secular decline in long-term growth".[60]

IMF could neither bring political stability nor economic growth. Rather its austerity-driven anti-Keynesian programs block the economies from riding on the trajectory of long-term sustainable economic growth. Michael Hudson in '*The Bubble and Beyond*' writes very candidly about the havoc IMF program brings with it. "The situation becomes worse as the government borrows from the International Monetary Fund. IMF imposes austerity on debtor economies, shrinking their investment and production. This causes unemployment and a domestic fiscal crisis, while making them more dependent on foreign suppliers. A widening trade deficit ensues financed by further borrowing whose interest charges aggravate the overall payments deficit in a deteriorating spiral".[61] This is what happened with Pakistan.

The Debt Problem

Debt-servicing expenditure on interest payments has become a big drain on current expenditure which is the largest spending category of Pakistan and is rigid and non-discretionary in nature.[62] The issue with the foreign bilateral and commercial loans is that they were primarily mobilized to support foreign currency reserves. The foreign exchange reserves and the exchange rate generally remain under pressure due to liberal capital account regulations, increasing payments for imports, and stagnant exports. "Both the stock of external public debt and debt service payment flows are within tolerable levels of export receipts. From a low of over just 2% in FY 2014, debt service rose sharply to about 7% of export of goods and non-factor services in FY2020. With the rescheduling of 2020, it has fallen to just over 2% again in FY 21 and FY 22. Similarly the stock of debt has hovered between one to two years of exports of goods and non-factor services. The pressure on reserves, therefore, comes not from debt service payments but from structural economic weaknesses". Over 40% of export earnings are spent just on debt-servicing. The share of foreign debt and debt service payments has been rising since 2014 which has increased the level of currency risk (Fig. 13.1).

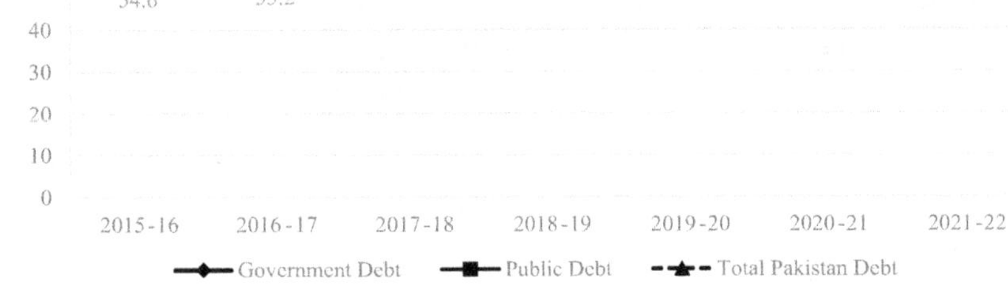

Fig. 13.1 Level of total Pakistan debt, public debt and government debt (% of GDP) (*Source* Economic Survey of Pakistan)

Public debt may be unavoidable as governments use it to finance their expenditures for protecting and investing in their people but it turns out to be a drain on economic development if it grows "too much or too fast".[63] Interest payments crowd out development expenditures. According to some estimates[64] of the World Bank, one rupee increase in interest payments reduces development spending by about 0.5 rupee while current expenditure, due to its rigidity, is not affected by interest payment shocks. Other IMF loan recipient countries show similar results where costs of cuts and austerity have blocked long-term economic growth and increased debt burden. For example, in one of the IMF's own studies,[65] average debt ratios in Sub-Saharan Africa increased from 30% of GDP at the end of 2013 to almost 60% of GDP by the end of 2022.

The study also finds that the debt has become highly costlier as the ratio of interest payments to revenue has more than doubled since early 2010. It means that debt distress would increase worldwide, as time goes by, in debt-ridden countries having implications for global peace and solidarity. What are the options? Stephanie Kelton in '*The Deficit Myth*'[66] advises that a better course of action for poor and developing countries (debt-ridden countries) would be to cut them from international commerce, improve their own food production systems, and implement stricter capital controls to decrease deficits and debts. Kelton's arguments are a bit fascinating to the extent of the USA and UK which can print dollars and pounds. But developing countries like Pakistan do not enjoy such a luxury. They have to import from other countries and are required to pay for imported goods in foreign currencies. So, the country needs dollars which can be earned by selling merchandise and services abroad that is by enhancing exports and remittances from abroad.

Low Exports

Contrary to general perception, the challenge of trade deficit is not of the import bill, rather it is the problem of low export receipts. Major imports of Pakistan are POL products, edible oil, kits of vehicles imported by OEMs, machinery, and industrial raw materials. The said goods constitute an inflexible basket and it is hard to bring some fundamental change through import substitution in their composition. Moreover, Pakistan collects around 50% of its revenue from imports and any import compression policy for improving the balance of payments position hits revenue collection, increases smuggling, and creates anti-export bias. Ironically,

Table 13.3 Trend in exports, imports, and trade deficit (% of GDP)

Years	*Exports*	*Imports*	*Trade Deficit*	*Home Remittances*	*Current Account Deficit*
2000–01	12.9	15.1	−2.1	1.5	−0.7
2005–06	12.0	22.5	−9.5	2.9	−4.5
2010–11	11.6	18.9	−7.3	5.2	+0.1
2015–16	6.6	14.2	−7.6	6.3	−1.6
2016–17	6.0	15.6	−9.6	5.7	−3.6
2017–18	6.5	17.0	−10.5	5.6	−5.4
2018–19	7.1	17.0	−9.9	6.8	−4.2
2019–20	7.1	14.8	−7.7	7.7	−1.5
2020–21	7.3	16.2	−8.9	8.5	−0.8
2021–22	9.9	22.0	−12.1	8.0	−4.6

Source Pakistan Economic Survey

exports have witnessed a continuous decline in terms of percentage of GDP and resultantly current account deficit has increased with adverse implications for other economic variables (see Table 13.3).

Exports are an important stimulator of economic growth and development. They not only bring dollars but also make the exporting firms more productive through learning by exporting. Export-led growth was an important development strategy for the Asian Tigers. South Korea, Singapore, and Hong Kong adopted export-led growth policies and achieved the status of developed nations. They put them on the trajectory of sustainable economic growth by integrating themselves into the global economy. Malaysia and Thailand also started the journey of export-led growth in the 1970s and substantially diversified their exports. Both the said countries decreased their export concentration in the last four to five decades. They moved into manufacturing exports like clothing and electronics but also developed resourced-based sectors. For example, Malaysia capitalized on its comparative advantage in palm oil and rubber while Thailand developed its agriculture and fish sectors into high-value-added products. China and Vietnam are two other pertinent examples whose high economic growth owes much to export diversification and structural transformation. Chile and Costa Rica in Latin America, and Tunisia and Botswana in the African continent are the developing countries that have made exports an engine of growth for their economies. Most of these economies transitioned from exports of primary products to value-added and high-tech exports.

Compared to said countries, Pakistan has not been able to make exports an engine of economic growth. Its exports are substantially below the potential and the worrying part is that the contribution of exports to GDP in terms of percentage has decreased with the passage of time. For example, the contribution of exports to GDP fell from 16% in 1999 to 10% in 2020. In 1990, Pakistan exported 0.19% of the global exports which fell to 0.12% by 2019. Pakistani exports are substantially below the potential. Results of an empirical analysis suggest that Pakistan should be exporting merchandise worth US$88.1 billion, around 4 times its current level, considering the characteristics like size, level of development, location, and factor endowments.[67] Such a big gap between the actual exports and the potential puts Pakistan among the countries known for huge missing exports. The opportunity cost of missing exports of Pakistan is estimated at around 893,000 jobs and US$1.74 billion in foregone taxes. The export market share of Pakistani firms had decreased since 2000 as out of US$10,000, goods and services of worth US$13 originated in Pakistan which fell to US$11 in 2020. Vietnam in the same period increased its export market share from US$21 to US$127. In 2005, Pakistan's per capita exports were US$117 which increased to US$188 in 2020 while for Bangladesh and Vietnam, the increase was respectively from US$192 to 353 and UD$660 to 4288.[68]

Export diversification not only leads to higher growth but also helps overcome export instability or the negative shocks of the terms of trade.[69] Trade diversification promotes economic growth through structural transformation. Regrettably, export diversification in Pakistan has remained low, in terms of both products and destinations. Textile and apparel products account for almost 60% share in the total exports and even in the textile sector lack of sophistication is very much evident from its tilt toward cotton-based production and not toward synthetic fibers. The index of export diversification, the value of which ranges between 0 and 1, has shown minor improvement from 0.535 in 2005–2006 to 0.581 in 2021–2022. The share of high-tech exports hovers around 2%. Pakistan's exports are concentrated in low complexity items like textiles and agriculture. An analysis of the export mix shows that the majority of export items belong to low complexity items like textile, cotton, apparel, clothing, cereals, leather, minerals, fish, fruit, nuts, plastics et cetera. The share of high-tech exports hovers around 2%. On the contrary, high-tech exports from India, Vietnam, and Malaysia respectively hover around 10%, 40%, and 50%. In 1986, the sophistication of its export basket was higher than that of Vietnam but in the last three decades or so, its export basket has not shown any improvement while Vietnam has moved upwards on the ladder of sophistication. During the period 2002–2017, Pakistan added 33 new products to its basket with export value of just US$1.2 billion with a per capita income increase of US$6. Generally, countries whose exports are more complex than expected for their income level comparatively grow faster, research from the Growth Lab of Harvard suggests.[70] A mix of a country's products is a predictor of not only subsequent pattern of diversification and economic growth but also a good predictor of economic inequality as the ability of an economy to both generate and distribute income has a strong correlation with the mix of products a country is able to produce and export.[71] Countries that produce high-productivity goods grow faster compared to countries that produce low-productivity goods.[72] Let us now critically analyze the policy levers adopted by Pakistan to boost exports.

Contractionary Devaluation

A standard prescription for boosting exports is through exchange rate engineering. A depreciation of real exchange rate or devaluation makes the exports more price-competitive in the international market while an appreciation triggers the opposite. The magnitude and the speed of taking place these effects would, however, vary from country to country depending upon several other economic variables. Devaluation can turn out even to be contractionary depending on the existing trade deficit.[73] If a country is having current account deficit, devaluation is likely to be contractionary as increase in price of tradable will increase real income abroad and reduce it at home. The larger the trade deficit, the bigger will be the contractionary effect. The contractionary effect will also depend on the sensitivity of imports to devaluation. The price of raw materials and intermediate goods will increase, which will have an impact on the exports as well. In the case of Pakistan, some empirical evidence suggests that the long-run elasticity of exports with respect to imports is about 37 percent. The effect, however, appears with a lag.[74]

Pakistani economists hold that primarily over-valued exchange rate is responsible for Pakistan's poor competitiveness in the export sector. Some analysts have, however, ruled out that the overvaluation of

Pakistani currency is responsible for the low competitiveness of exports in Pakistan.[75] Even otherwise, the controversy over the efficacy of competitive exchange rates in enhancing export competitiveness is not conclusively settled.[76] An analysis by the World Bank, based on 2003–2017 disaggregated export product-level data, suggests that export responses to real exchange rate (RER) depreciations in Pakistan are asymmetric. "Every 10 percent bilateral real appreciation leads to a decline in exports to the destination by a 0.68 percent while every 10 percent bilateral real depreciation leads to an increase in exports of 0.51 percent".[77] The impact of the deprecation of the exchange rate also depends on the export basket of a country. The exports of Pakistan are heavily concentrated in the low end of textiles and garments. Devaluation is helpful in enhancing exports when the constraints are on the demand side.

Devaluation of currency in case of Pakistan might also turn out to be contractionary given the high dependence on imported raw material and huge trade balance. For example, as a result of the downward spiral of the rupee which started in Pakistan around May 2021, the price of the dollar doubled in a period of less than thirty months (from Rs.150 to around Rs.300) whereas it had taken almost one decade to double the dollar from Rs.75 to 150. The devaluation of currency increased inflation and uncertainty but hardly we see any appreciable impact on the exports. The problem of exports in Pakistan is not that of tax incentives or overvalued exchange rate. The problem is basically connected to the political economy of the country. Exports are hugely concentrated in the hands of a few large exporters. This dominance of few exporters has increased overtime and is associated with low rates of product innovation and experimentation, and the low ability of the Pakistan export sector to enter into new high growth sectors. Large export firms are less likely to change their export strategies and primarily rely on intensive margins (increasing existing products in already established markets) and not on extensive margins (product diversification, the introduction of new products in new markets, or introducing existing products in new markets). Contrary to this, small firms rely primarily on extensive margins reflected in the higher turnover among the firms with lower export volumes. Each year 16–37% of firms exit and 19–37% enter the export market.[78] The establishment of export processing zones is another policy lever used to achieve the objectives of industrialization and export promotion.

Export Processing Zones

Multiple approaches may be adopted to implement the Export Processing Zone (EPZ) scheme. Sometimes EPZ may comprise the entire city. Sometimes entire or part of a port or Airport area is declared as an EPZ. They can be developed as an industrial or technology park or they can be an individual factory. Whatever the form, they have a commonality in that they have a secure perimeter around the zone that is under Customs control. In this sense, these zones are treated as separate countries from a Customs perspective. They are, however, not a first-best solution, overall improvement of the investment climate is first-best. They work best in countries with developed infrastructure. Further, EPZs may encourage exporters to import from abroad but they tend to disappoint those who expect EPZs to bring development via backward linkages rather EPZs divide the economy between exporters and import-substituting firms, with little connection between them.[79]

A close coordination between the government and the private enterprises is required for the success of EPZs. Merely attracting foreign firms due to advantageous tax treatment may not turn out to be a successful experience unless firms operating under EPZs are integrated with the local economy by creating backward linkages. Firms which get located in EPZs get favorable treatment in several ways. They are allowed unlimited access to duty-free raw material, receive tax holidays on corporate and income taxes and they are generally sheltered from bureaucratic regulations which other firms located outside EPZs have to comply with.[80] In Pakistan, the Export Processing Zone Authority was established in 1980 with the mandate to plan, develop, and operate EPZs in Pakistan. A number of incentives like duty-free import of machinery, equipment and input goods, 100% repatriation of capital and profits, no sales tax on input goods including electricity and gas, and relaxation in national import restrictions and foreign exchange regulations of Pakistan et cetera are available to the units set up in EPZs. Several EPZs were established in the country. The export share of EPZs is stuck up just between US$250 to 300 million per annum. They have been unable to trigger a structural transformation of the export sector and create backward linkages with the local economy.

In 2012, the government of Pakistan promulgated the Special Economic Zone (SEZ) Act to facilitate new enterprises. Under the said Act, seven SEZs were notified. The SEZs are to be set up by the Federal and Provincial Governments alone, in partnership with the private sector, or entirely through the private sector. Huge tax incentives have been provided to the SEZ developers like duty-free import of machinery, equipment, and material, exemption from all taxes on income for 10 years, and exemption of all imported capital goods from customs duties and taxes. Factors like substantial investment, inadequate clustering of industries, weak institutions, unskilled human resources due to limited vocational education, poor receptivity to modern technology, high business costs, and lack of hard and soft infrastructure have historically remained big challenges restricting Pakistan's industrial development.[81] The competitive advantage only on the basis of tax and duty exemptions is not sufficient for the success of a SEZ or EPZ. Improving the business environment and the upgradation of skills of the labor are equally important. Another important area that needs focus is to avoid real estate activities at SEZs. Industrial zones are very vulnerable to real estate activities. The difficulties usually arise when the developers fail to provide the promised facilities in time. Resultantly unwarranted real estate activities start when investors purchase and occupy plots without starting production.[82]

Duty Drawback

The first lever, which the countries have used to boost exports, relates to duty and tax incentives. The scheme of duty drawback has historically remained the most prominent scheme used by the governments to boost exports. Under this scheme, duties and taxes paid on importation of goods used for manufacturing of output goods meant for export are repaid as a drawback once goods have been exported. Duty drawback is available for a number of products like textile products, leather, sports goods, footwear, engineering, and metal products et cetera under various special regulatory orders (SROs). Duty drawback scheme differs from exemption schemes in the sense that under such schemes duty and taxes are charged at the time of import and are refunded subsequently. The governments normally prefer duty drawback schemes over exemption schemes due to the possibility of diversion of non-duty paid material into the local market. The exporters on the other hand prefer the exemption scheme due to cash-flow advantage. Generally, both schemes prevail concurrently. The drawback scheme which is administratively simple is applied in case of new or occasional exporters who do not have a track record of their business practices. The exemption scheme on the other hand is considered a better option for reputed manufacturers who regularly export a specified minimum percentage of their production. However, in both the schemes, technical calculations, called rate of yield, are required for determining the ratio of imported material used per unit of output.

The duty drawback scheme has, however, not delivered for export promotion in Pakistan and at best these schemes are a source of rent-seeking for the established exporters. For example, the results of an analysis conducted by Haque and Kemal suggest that export financing schemes and rebates or duty drawbacks have an insignificant impact on export promotion in the long run.[83] The removal of tariffs is considered a superior policy to export subsidies in the form of duty drawbacks and rebates as export subsidies due to their little impact on exports (case of India) and being costly instruments of export diversification (experience of Brazil and Mexico).[84] It is generally perceived that the duty drawback scheme was highly instrumental in promoting exports of China. Empirics,[85] however, do not confirm the said proposition. The duty drawback system in China is revealed to be not significant in export promotion. There may be multiple reasons for the ineffectiveness of the duty drawback system like inefficiencies in administering the system, incentives for over-reporting of imported inputs, uncertainties of payments, and delays in reimbursements of import duties.

Why the duty drawback scheme has not been delivered particularly for Pakistan? According to a World Bank report, the lackluster impact of export incentive schemes is due to the fact that such schemes tend to focus on established firms. About the duty drawback scheme, the report says: "By design, these duty drawback mechanisms reward less dynamic, less sophisticated, and incumbent firms, preserving the current export structure rather than transforming it. First, products eligible for rebates or entitled to higher rebate rates face less dynamic global demands than non-eligible ones. Second, eligible products tend to have low sophistication or complexity. Third, the schemes have a marked anti-new, pro-incumbent bias".[86] Besides duty drawback scheme, temporary importation, manufacturing bond (MB), exported-oriented units (EOUs), and DTRE are some other schemes that come under the broad category "duty and tax incentives" for boosting exports. These schemes can broadly be called suspensive regimes of duty and taxes.

Suspensive Regime

The scheme of temporary importation entails suspension or exemption of duty and taxes against securities on the import of accessories used in the production of output goods meant for export. The utilization period is 18 months which is extendable in exceptional circumstances. No license or pre-authorization is required to operate under this scheme. It is perhaps the easiest scheme of duty suspension to be availed of by the importers. The amount of duty and taxes is secured through a post-dated cheque and as such no cost is involved. The inputs imported under the temporary importation scheme should be identifiable at the time of export.

Under the manufacturing bond scheme, a manufacturer operates within a specific bonded factory which is licensed as manufacturing bond by the customs and the importer deposits a financial security with the Customs Department for securing the liability of duty and taxes against imported goods. This scheme is appropriate for big manufacturers -cum-exporters who have a high proportion of imported dutiable inputs. The manufacturers licensed under this scheme are required to maintain a record that document which has been imported and details of the final products. There is also a technical calculation called input-out ratio or rate of yield. It is the ratio of the imported materials used per unit of output agreed between the licensee and Customs Department and is monitored through an audit. The monitoring or audit is designed to verify the percentage of the total production exported, sold in the local market and wastage occurred during the process and its disposal. The manufacturers availing of this scheme are required to apply to the Customs Department before they begin importation (pre-authorization).

Before granting a license, the Customs Department undertakes physical verification of the factory premises to check the manufacturing process. The manufacturer is required to maintain records of imports and exports and file periodic returns wherein he gives an account of the transactions taking place under this scheme. The manufacturer is required to maintain and retain records of imported inputs, materials used in production, inventory, output goods produced, goods exported, contracts of sale, goods sold into the domestic market, details of waste, and anything relevant to the rate of yield. In Pakistan, operations of manufacturing bonds are governed by Warehousing Rules 2001. A manufacturer-cum-exporter having an export order or contract for the supply of goods to a foreign country can establish a manufacturing bond initially for a period of three years which is extendable. As per best practices, a manufacturer has to get a license before importation, and just the rate of yield that is input-output ratio is determined. No physical controls are required. The control and monitoring are through periodic statements and audits. Up to 40% of manufactured goods can be sold in the local market on payment of leviable duty and taxes.

The EOU scheme envisages complete exemption from duties and taxes on import of input goods including machinery imported into EOU under specified conditions laid down in the rules. This scheme also allows duty and tax-free import of coal, diesel, gas, furnace oil, and coke of coal used in the manufacture of output goods. The rate of yield is prescribed to keep track of goods manufactured out of duty-free inputs. Exporters can engage the services of vendors as well and can supply their goods to other exporters availing schemes like EOU, manufacturing bond, and duty and tax remission for export (DTRE). The manufacturers operating under this scheme can sell up to 20% of their production in the local market on payment of duty and taxes. The throughput period which is the period required to process the input goods imported duty-free is specified in the rules. The licensee is required to maintain a record of importation, exportation, production, and wastages that occurred during the process. However, when it comes to practice, some interesting points emerge regarding the schemes of manufacturing bonds and EOUs. The number of units availing of these schemes is low. The percentage of units who cease to use these schemes is quite high. If we take the number of units (in percentage terms) who keep availing of these schemes after getting a license of manufacturing bond or EOU as a proxy for the survival rate of export firms, then it becomes very obvious that the rate of export firms who fail to survive as exporters are as high as 12% and over 25% respectively for EOU and manufacturing bond licenses.[87] Such a high ratio of casualty speaks of some inherent problems with these export-oriented schemes.

DTRE scheme is based on the simple concept of no duty and taxes at the import stage and no duty drawbacks and refunds at the export stage. This facility is available for imported inputs, locally purchased tax-paid goods, and taxable/excisable services including gas, electricity, diesel, furnace oil, and coal. Theoretically, this scheme has got wide coverage. Sales tax registered persons and commercial exporters can also avail of this scheme. It also covers supplies made against international tender, EPZs, and projects entitled to duty and tax-free inputs and supplies made by indirect to direct exporters. For DTRE approval, a valid contract should be in the hand of the exporter and DTRE approval is granted to the extent of the order in hand. So, this scheme is comparatively simpler than EOU and manufacturing bonds schemes where the licensee is required respectively to at least export 80% and 60% of the production of the factory and in case of non-availability of export orders or some uncertainty, may fail to meet the requirement of a minimum threshold of production set for exports. Moreover, the DTRE scheme allows commercial exporters to purchase and export goods in the same state subject to 5% value addition. The import of goods by commercial exporters for subsequent export is, however, not allowed under DTRE. The schemes of manufacturing bonds, export-oriented units, and DTRE have now been merged into a comparatively more liberal scheme of "export facilitation scheme (EFS)" with a focus on post-customs clearance compliance checks.

The schemes under suspensive regimes or export promotion schemes are, however, characterized by low utilization. In FY 2018–2019, 16.45% of total exports were made availing export promotion schemes which gradually increased to 26.28% in 2022–2023 (see Table 13.4). I divide the exporters arbitrarily into five categories based on the quantum of their transactions or volume of exports under suspensive regimes or export promotion schemes Those who export merchandise of up to Rs. 10 million are categorized as "small exporters" whereas those who export merchandise of Rs. 11 to 50 million, Rs. 50 to 75 million, and Rs. 76 to 100 million are respectively bracketed as "low-medium category exporters", "medium category", and "upper medium category exporters". Large exporters are categorized as those who export merchandise of Rs. 100 million or above. In 2018–2019, all four categories of exporters (except large exporters) constituted 43.75% of the exporters who availed of the export promotion schemes but overall exported 1.14% of the total volume of exports under the said schemes. The number of the four categories of exporters decreased to 33.88% with exports of 0.54% (see Table 13.5). It simply means that existing export promotion schemes tend to focus on well-established and large exporters and smaller firms are unable to utilize the benefits of export promotion schemes.

Even small exporting firms are on average more productive than the local firms which do not export. According to a World Bank analysis, firms that systematically export are 25% more productive than those

Table 13.4 Exports 2018–2019 to 2022–2023

(Rs.& US$ in million)

Period	*Exports availing export promotion schemes (Rs.)*	*Exports under export schemes (%of total)*	*Exports other than under export promotion regime (Rs)*	*Total Exports Value (Rs.)*	*Total Export Value (US$)*
FY 2018–19	506,188	16.45	2,570,800	3,076,988	22,770
FY 2019–20	721,011	21.94	2,565,268	3,286,279	20,870
FY 2020–21	962,246	23.28	3,170,684	4,132,930	25,865
FY 2021–22	1,425,059	23.41	4,663,235	6,088,294	34,242
FY 2022–23	1,814,005	26.28	5,088,568	6,902,573	28,085

Source PRAL, FBR

that have never exported.[88] It is due to learning by exporting. The presence of a reasonable number of exporters, though having a small contribution toward total exports, has an important policy insight. These exporters are exposed to the dynamics of international trade, can handle export-related documentation, and are able to search for buyers in the international market. They may be credit-constrained or wary of using export promotion schemes. Presently, there is no separate duty and tax incentives scheme for small and medium-sized exporters. A differentiated policy catering to the requirements of different firm categories—by size, location, and sector—would help tap the potential of the small and medium-sized exporters.

Pakistan predominantly trades with the EU, USA, and China. Despite the huge scope of intraregional trade, Pakistan like other countries of the region has not capitalized on the geographic proximity. The South Asian region, home to one-fifth of the globe, is the least integrated region in the world. Hardly 5% of trade takes place among regional partners whereas half of the total trade in the South East and Pacific region takes place among the regional partners. Even in Sub-Saharan Africa, over one-fifth of total trade is intraregional.[89] Contrary to this, the South Asian

Table 13.5 Export promotion schemes (DTRE, EFS & EOU)

Slab		*Up to 10 million*	*11 to 50 million*	*50 to 75 million*	*76 to 100 million*	*Above 100 Million*	*Grand Total*
2018–2019	Total No of Exporters (Units)	46 (11.7%)	76 (19.34%)	24 (6.11%)	22 (9.78%)	225 (57.25%)	393
	No GDs	121 (0.13%)	593 (0.64%)	306 (0.33%)	412 (0.45%)	91,543 (98.46%)	92,975
	Total Export Values	254 (0.05%)	1999 (0.39%)	1538 (0.30%)	1986 (0.4%)	500,411 (98.86%)	506,188
2019–2020	Total No of Exporters (Units)	47 (10.38%)	92 (20.31%)	26 (5.74%)	19 (7.06%)	269 (59.38%)	453
	No GDs	102 (0.03%)	738 (0.63%)	523 (0.44%)	388 (0.33%)	116,306 (98.52%)	118,057
	Total Export Values	233 (0.03%)	2,602 (0.36%)	1,622 (0.22%)	1,672 (0.23%)	714,881 (99.15%)	721,010
2020–2021	Total No of Exporters (Units)	52 (9.2%)	111 (19.65%)	35 (6.19%)	30 (5.31%)	337 (59.65%)	565
	No GDs	179 (0.13%)	873 (0.62%)	475 (0.34%)	658 (0.47)	139,066 (98.45%)	141,251
	Total Export Values	262 (0.03%)	3025 (0.31%)	2248 (0.23%)	2572 (0.27%)	954,139 (99.16%)	962,246
2021–2022	Total No of Exporters (Units)	55 (8.62%)	110 (17.24%)	40 (6.27%)	29 (4.55%)	404 (63.32%)	638
	No GDs	115 (0.08%)	838 (0.55%)	824 (0.54%)	423 (0.28%)	150,718 (98.56%)	152,918
	Total Export Values	261 (0.02%)	3,032 (0.21%)	2,448 (0.17%)	2,585 (0.18%)	1,416,733 (99.42%)	1,425,059
2022–2023	Total No of Exporters (Units)	39 (5.33%)	118 (16.12%)	54 (7.38%)	37 (5.05%)	484 (66.12%)	732
	No GDs	106 (0.08%)	529 (0.4%)	457 (0.34%)	378 (0.28%)	131,807 (98.9%)	133,277
	Total Export Value	199 (0.01%)	3,065 (0.17%)	3,303 (0.18%)	3,160 (0.17%)	1,804,278 (99.46%)	1,814,005

Source Based on data retrieved from PRAL, FBR

region is unable to capitalize on the proximity of geography. “In South Asia, trade among the largest economies, particularly Bangladesh, India, and Pakistan, is below potential. The latest gravity estimates suggest that total potential merchandize trade in South Asia may be valued at around US$67 billion, almost three times the current trade value of US$23 billion”.[90] For Pakistan–India trade, the potential is around fifteen times the current level of bilateral trade as per estimates of the gravity model of trade.

Trade as Vent of Growth

From an economic perspective, the volume of trade between two partners is mainly influenced by three broad factors and those are the nature of comparative advantage, internal trade policies, and deep mutual distrust. Analysis of South Asian regional trade in the light of comparative advantage theory shows that most of the member countries enjoy similar comparative advantages. Their comparative advantage is restricted to a limited number of products. India has a comparative advantage in more categories of products as compared with other member countries, so India is expected to be a gainer with the liberalization of trade in the region. Factor endowments theory also points toward the limited scope of complementarity of trade among South Asian countries as economies of all the partners are predominantly labor-intensive.

Intra-industry trade model also shows limited chances of trade enhancement in the South Asian region as per capita income is very low in these countries. Intra-industry trade model does explain the trade pattern of high-income level countries. Linder Hypothesis of trade, which in contrast to other trade models with supply-side orientation is a demand-side oriented model and does explain trade among South Asian countries to a large extent. This model postulates that the pattern of trade is derived from overlapping demands. According to this model, in a world of imperfect knowledge, entrepreneurs produce goods for domestic needs. As the business firm grows, it extends trade across national frontiers. Trade would most likely take place, as per this model, among countries with similar tastes and income levels.[91]

The second factor is the trade policies of the trading partners. For example, the level of tariffs, paratariff barriers, and non-tariff barriers are important determinants of trade across borders. Initiatives like the South Asian Preferential Trade Agreement (SAPTA) and the South Asian Free

Trade Agreement (SAFTA) failed to increase intraregional trade in South Asia despite significant trade liberalization or tariff reduction. Lengthy sensitive lists (goods out of tariff rationalization list under regional trade agreement), and application of non-tariff measures are some pertinent examples of restrictive trade policies. Non-tariff measures include antidumping duties, countervailing duties, quota restrictions, packaging and labeling requirements, certifications, testing quarantine certification et cetera. "South Asian trade regimes discriminate against neighbors. In South Asia, protection is greater in the case of imports from within the South Asia region than from the rest of the world, as reflected in the overall trade restrictiveness index. This index measures the uniform tariff equivalent of a country's tariff and non-tariff barriers that would generate the same level of import value for the country in a given year. In the two largest economies in the region, India and Pakistan, the indexes are nine and six times higher, respectively, for imports from the South Asian region than for imports from the rest of the world".[92]

Pakistan and India have a troubled past which includes four wars and a number of skirmishes. And it is highly improbable to keep smooth trade relations in an environment of conflict and mistrust. For example, the most-favored nation (MFN) status which is purely a concept of international trade is opposed in Pakistan mainly on political grounds.[93] When Pakistan announced in 2013 that India was being granted MFN status, powerful political lobbies created a political controversy stalling all progress. It was argued that strategically it was not in the interest of the country to improve trade relations. And that trust deficit between the two countries can't be bridged (discussion on this point in next chapter titled "The Militancy Challenge") unless the Kashmir issue is resolved. Trade ties even if they improve for the time being would be broken with the slightest degree of strain in relations due to the Kashmir conflict. In such a scenario, trade relations are not likely to improve on a sustained basis. Undoubtedly, the Kashmir conflict is the biggest hindrance in the normalization of relations including trade relations between India and Pakistan and economic issues cannot be practically divorced from political and security issues. But the limited trade between the two countries is also rooted in managerial, bureaucratic, transportation, and low trade facilitation. Restricted exportable items, poor logistics, and connectivity are big impediments.

The infant industry argument is also advanced to oppose trading with India on MFN basis. It is argued that opening up the Pakistani market for all Indian goods will hurt the domestic manufacturing sector. The manufacturing sector of India is more diversified compared to Pakistan. It is apprehended that cheap Indian goods will flood Pakistani markets and Pakistani manufacturers and producers will not be able to compete with Indian counterparts due to lower prices of Indian goods. In this regard, it is said that the domestic auto and electronics industry may face stiff competition from the Indian industry as that industry is relatively more established and efficient. The textile sector may also be affected badly due to low-cost textiles of India which may wipe out Pakistani textile production. These apprehensions are connected to the third broad category and that is high mutual distrust. "Trust promotes trade, and trade fosters trust, interdependency, and constituencies of peace. In South Asia, a complicated history and asymmetries in the size of economies, perpetuated by insufficient people-to-people interactions, have rendered trust a fragile commodity".[94]

The theoretical arguments like those of similar comparative advantage and low desire for intraregional trade weaken when it comes to practical realities. Pakistan traded with India on the basis of the positive list (more restrictive) but now Pakistan has moved to a negative list of tradable items with India. Despite tensions, the quantum of trade has increased with the passage of time. A number of tradable items has registered a progressive and gradual increase, reflective of the desire and potential for expanding trade between the two countries. The force of gravity that is the attraction of trade between the neighboring countries due to the benefits of proximity is manifest in the informal trade between South Asian countries. Informal trade is taking place by land, sea, and air. "Informal trade has been estimated at about 50% of formal trade in South Asia, aggregating assessments of various studies for years between 1993 and 2005. India's informal trade with Nepal was as large as the formal trade; with Pakistan, it was 91% of the formal trade; with Sri Lanka, it was about 30%, and with Bhutan, it was almost three times the formal trade. More recent bilateral estimates of trade between India and Pakistan indicate that informal trade between the two countries in 2012–2013 was almost double the value of formal trade, and most of it was routed through a third country".[95]

Informal traders in India and Pakistan have developed efficient mechanisms for contract enforcement, information sharing, risk sharing, and risk mitigation.[96] Contrary to skeptics and anti-trade lobbyists, maximizing India–Pakistan trade would be a win-win situation. India has a huge middle class with rising purchasing power and even a 10% share of the Indian middle-class market is expected to double the market size of Pakistani companies and businesses. Myths and misperceptions that have taken root in public discourse with regard to trade with India need to be dispelled through dispassionate discussions and analysis. "A frequent accusation by Pakistani businessmen and traders is that India has numerous Pakistan-specific NTBs. A more honest examination, however, shows that claim is highly exaggerated and proves little more than an excuse by Pakistani businessmen and traders to not make the most of India's fairly open trade environment. Some hindrances, inefficiencies, and constraints from the Indian side at the Wagha-Attari border have Pakistan-specific consequences. Others, however, such as regulatory regime to administer imports or sanitary or phytosanitary standards affect all countries. Nevertheless, it has been pointed out that many land border issues and visa regimes are clearly specific to Pakistan (and India). This consequent lack of movement and information exchange is cited as a major reason why many otherwise commonly known protocols for trade are not well known between Indian and Pakistani traders".[97]

Unlocking the potential of trade between neighboring countries can turn out to be an important stimulator of economic growth. Informal trade between India and Pakistan and Pakistan and Iran (*Case Study trade* via *Zambad*) points toward the huge potential of regional trade. Progress toward regional integration or deepening of bilateral trade relations would inevitably generate pressure for cooperation in other spheres. Summing up, Pakistan needs to revisit its export promotion schemes to make them palatable for small and medium enterprises and explore opportunities of boosting trade with its neighboring, as part of its long-term growth strategy, to capitalize on the geographical proximities. The story of growth would, however, not be complete without analyzing the nexus between militancy and economic growth as terrorism and militancy have adversely impacted Pakistan at least in the last five decades. The next chapter is devoted to a discussion on the structural factors of militancy and terrorism (endogenous as well as exogenous) and the big impact terrorism and militancy had on the economy, economic growth, and society of Pakistan.

CHAPTER 14

The Militancy Challenge

Dilating upon the motivation and consequences of terrorism in '*What makes a Terrorist?*', Krueger points out that economists are divided on both the said aspects of the issue (as they are on other issues as well!). Their views about the impact of terrorism on the economic growth can be broadly divided into two categories, called by Krueger "small effect view" and "big effect view".[1] The proponents of the small effect view posit that terrorism has little impact on the amount of physical and human capital available in the economy for the production of goods and services that is economic growth. The argument is marshaled as follows. In the modern economies, it is the human capital which primarily matters for economic growth and as such the terrorist attacks do not cause much damage to the said capital (number of casualties are very small compared to overall population). As regards infrastructural damage or losses resulting from terrorist attacks, same can be recovered as done in case of other disasters. Moreover, a lot of scope of substitution among factors of production also exists. If terrorism damages some kinds of business activities, it at the same time stimulates productive activities in other sectors of the economy like defense and counterterrorism industries. For example, Robert Borrow writing on the triggers of terrorism in one of his articles in Business Week wrote that a silver lining in 9/11 attacks was that they would probably end the 'near-recession' in the US economy by loosening constraints on deficit spending by the government.[2]

J. Nasir, *Development Challenges of Pakistan*,
https://doi.org/10.1007/978-981-97-3064-3_14

The big effect view, however, looks at terrorism as a big threat to the economy and economic growth. For example, Milton Friedman in an interview with the Wall Street Journal rated terrorism as the biggest threat to the world economy.[3] According to Krueger, this view is based on three broad arguments. First, although industries adjust their strategies of survival and profit in response to terrorism but some industries like tourism are significantly affected. Second line of argument supporting the big effect view is the overreaction of the people and the government in the wake of terrorist acts. This overreaction may be rational as well as irrational. At the level of the people, the patterns of consumption may dramatically change due to uncertainty and fear caused by the terrorist acts while overreaction of the government could cause big effect on the economy due to its missteps. For example, developed countries like USA could crack down on immigration and could thus muzzle an important source of economic growth that is the energy and ingenuity of the immigrants. Third argument brought in favor of the big effect view is the element of uncertainty induced by terrorist attacks, resulting in business slowdown and at least "pausing when it comes to investment and hiring". The said arguments and propositions are theoretical in nature. Do we have some empirics or counterfactual to gage the impact of terrorism on the economy?

The studies conducted on the Basque region of Spain provide an objective analysis about the impact of the terrorist attacks by providing a counterfactual. The Basque in Northern region witnessed serious conflict during the period 1959–2011. The Basque conflict, also known as Spain-ETA conflict, had both political and military dimensions. It did not turn violent till late 1960s and was not violent on massive scale until the mid-1970s. Some researchers[4] studied the impact of violence and terrorism on the economy of the Basque region using a case study method and construction of counterfactual. What these researchers did was to identify some other regions of Spain which matched with the Basque region economically and demographically. Before onset of terrorism on wide scale that is till mid-1970s, the comparison regions and Basque were growing almost at the same rate but after the outbreak, roads diverged. The gap between Basque and comparison regions kept on increasing with the intensification of terrorist activities and reached to about 10% of GDP by the late 1970s. What can be inferred from the said investigation? First, terrorism has big effect on the economy. Second, the small effect view may hold only in case terrorist attacks are few and far between, are not

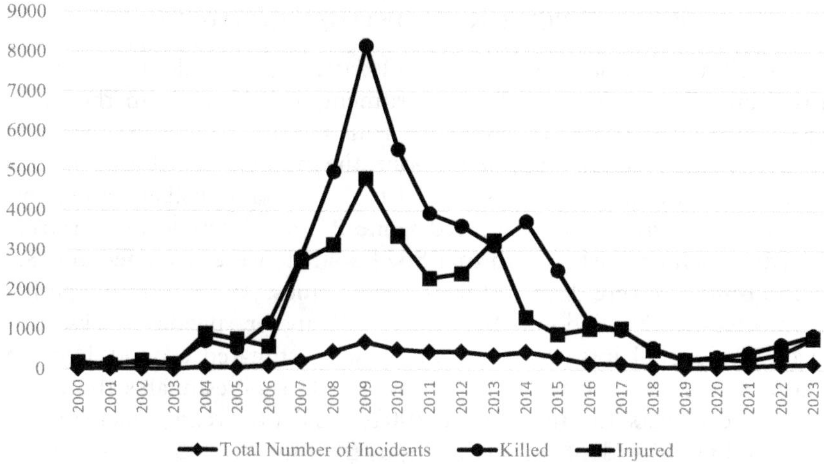

Fig. 14.1 Major incidents (*Source* South Asia Terrorism Portal (SATP)—https://www.satp.org/datasheet-terrorist-attack/major-incidents/pakistan)

widespread, and do not persist for longer time. Third, impact on economy increases with increase in terrorist incidents.

Terrorism and militancy have got serious adverse consequences for the economic growth, both in the short-run as well as long-run, inter alia, by reducing productivity, economic activity, and business confidence, and by eroding positive benefits which peacefulness can have on the macroeconomic performance of a country. According to the finding of a report,[5] based on data since year 2000, the countries which improved in peacefulness witnessed on average higher per capita GDP growth compared to countries which became less peaceful as measured by the Global Peace Index (GPI). Pakistan is engulfed in terrorism and militancy at least since the invasion of Russia on Afghanistan in 1979. The severity of terrorism in Pakistan can be well imagined from the fact that it witnessed over 4000 major terrorist attacks during the period 2000–2016 respectively killing and injuring 42,556 and 28,094 persons (Fig. 14.1).

The impact of militancy and terrorism on economic growth and the economy of Pakistan is very huge, which even the official accounts do not capture fully.

Big Effect on Economic Growth

On the 10th anniversary of 9/11 terrorist attacks, the Wall Street Journal carried an advertisement of the Government of Pakistan with the headline "which country can do more for your peace".[6] This advertisement contained some crucial numbers about the human casualties and loss to the economy of Pakistan. Some 21,672 Pakistani civilians either lost their lives or were seriously injured while 2795 soldiers were martyred. The advertisement further said that 8671 soldiers were wounded and 3.5 million residents were displaced from their homes. And during the period of one decade, 3486 bomb blasts and 283 major suicide attacks took place. The overall loss to the economy was estimated around US$ 68 billion. The Economic Survey of Pakistan 2016–17 estimates the direct and indirect costs for the period 2001–2017 (16 years), incurred by Pakistan due to incidents of terrorism, to the tune of US$ 123.13 billion (Rs. 10,373.93 billion). The estimated economic costs include losses to the country's exports, compensation to those affected by terrorism, lost foreign investments, decreased industrial output, decrease in tax collection, and damage to infrastructure, etc. A number of costs are not quantified by the Economic Survey of Pakistan. For example, downsizing of programs run by international and non-governmental agencies, missed educational opportunities due to denials of technology transfers, decreased foreign investments due to heightened risk assessments, and more stringent visa restrictions are some of the escaped costs.[7] These costs are real and serious. If we are able to calculate and put dollar value on the escaped costs, the economic losses due to terrorism would be far higher than the official estimates.

The Economic survey of Pakistan[8] undertook an analysis of the consequences war in Afghanistan had on the politics, internal security, economy, environment, and on overall society of Pakistan. According to the survey, impact of war on the economy was huge in the form of slowdown of economic growth in major sectors, disruption in economic activities and international trade, increase in the cost of doing business, and inordinate delays in meeting export orders. A substantial amount of resources, both men and material, was diverted to meet the challenge of security and for repairing the damaged infrastructure. In addition to said economic losses, cross-border terrorism in Pakistan multiplied human sufferings due to ferocious and indiscriminate terrorist attacks on the civilian population. Pakistan is still target of terrorism including foreign-sponsored terrorism, survey emphasizes.

Some other studies, undertaken to evaluate the impact of terrorism on the economy and economic growth of Pakistan, confirm huge negative impact on the economy and economic growth of Pakistan. For example, an investigation,[9] covering the period of 1973–2008, suggests that terrorism has cost Pakistan 33.02% of its real national income during the said period due to fall in domestic investment and remittances. This loss approximately is equivalent to 1% of real GDP per capita growth every year. Another empirical investigation,[10] based on time period of 1973–2010, also confirms negative relationship between terrorism and long-run economic growth. This investigation finds bidirectional causality between terrorism and capital, trade openness and capital, and terrorism and trade openness while unidirectional causality runs from economic growth to terrorism. The unidirectional causality running from economic growth to terrorism implies that low growth or inegalitarian distribution of its dividends may contribute to terrorism (deprivation hypothesis of terrorism). Another study,[11] covering the period 1972–2014, finds that 1% increase in terrorism reduces FDI by 0.104%, domestic investment by 0.039%, and economic growth by 0.002%. Another investigation exploring the relationship between terrorism and FDI,[12] based on data for the period 1980–2015, also confirms significant negative relationship between the said variables for Pakistan. Terrorism impacts the economy of a country through different channels in the short-run, medium-run, and long-run. The short-run impact is in the form of destruction of the factors of production. The medium-term impact operates through loss in consumer and investor confidence while in the long-run, transaction costs rise due to higher risk premiums and counterterrorism related expenditures, and reduced productivity.[13]

The negative impacts of terrorism are felt in the society, at the micro level as well as macro level. At the macro level, it reduces economic growth, investment, and savings while at the micro level, terrorism or violence may deter parents to send their children to schools. Using the data from the Global Terrorism Database and Pakistan's Social and Living Standards Measurement Survey, some researchers[14] have found that persistent exposure to terrorism significantly reduces the likelihood that parents will continue their children's education. Their results suggest that for every one million people, an increase in terrorist incidents causes 26,501 fewer children to continue education at the primary school level.

According to the said research, the impact of terrorist incidents meant that approximately 520,000 children chose not to continue education in schools during 2015 alone. During the outbreak of militancy in Swat, militants gained control of the most of the Swat valley and an estimated 80,000 girls were forced out of schools. In South Waziristan, out of total 814 schools, 410 were destroyed by the militants and in KPK province more than 900 educational institutions were closed and remained non-functional till eradication of the TPP terrorist activities.[15] A large number of houses were destroyed in terrorist-hit areas. According to some estimates, 105,744 houses were damaged—66,989 destroyed and 38,754 partially damaged—due to various factors associated with militancy in FATA.[16]

The other costs of terrorism include the value of goods and services devoted to prevention of terrorism, cost of human lives, cost incurred for the treatment of the injured or wounded, and costs associated with apprehending and prosecuting terrorists. Terrorism generates significant negative multiplier effects on the economy, besides lowering of economic growth, via low accumulation of human capital, lower participation in the workforce, and low productivity on the job, etc., which all impact current as well as future productivity. The damage done by terrorism can be visualized from another perspective. According to Paul Collier, a conflict qualifies as a civil war if it involves 1,000 or more than 1,000 combat-related deaths in a year, each side incurring at least 5% of these deaths (it is also called Michigan definition of civil war).[17] During the period 2006–2017, more than 1000 fatalities occurred per year in incidents of killings in Pakistan, which consumed civilians, terrorists, and personnel of security forces. A civil war, according to Collier, tends to reduce economic growth by around 2.3% per year which means Pakistan became 25.3% poorer just during the said period of 11 years (Fig. 14.2).

Motivation for Militancy

Now the question is: what are the underlying factors of militancy and terrorism and why people carry out terrorist attacks? Krueger is of the view that deprivations like poverty and low education do not explain terrorism as terrorism is either uncorrelated or is positively correlated with per capita GDP and level of education. Krueger derives support for the said claim from the profiles of the terrorists who conducted transnational terrorist attacks. The profiles suggested that a terrorist was less likely to

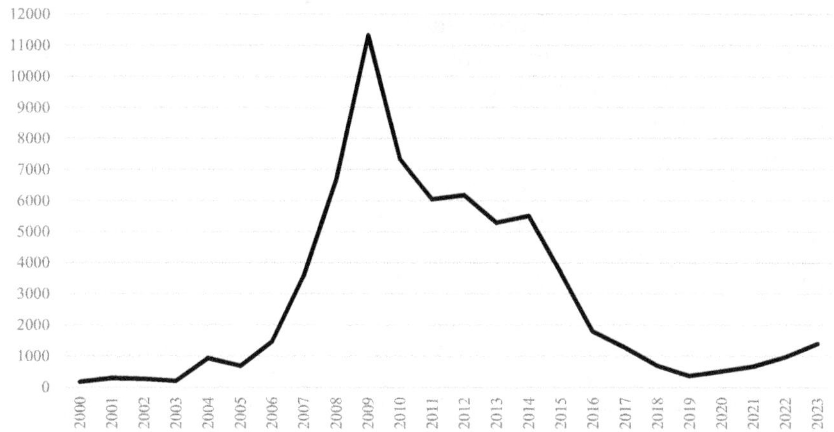

Fig. 14.2 Yearly Fatalities (*Source* South Asia Terrorism Portal (SAPT)—https://www.satp.org/datasheet-terrorist-attack/fatalities/pakistan)

come from an impoverished family background and was more likely to be well-educated. Krueger writes: "People presume that terrorism would be carried out by people who are poor and uneducated because they think of it as similar to other types of crime. I think a more appropriate analogy is voting. Terrorism is a violent and inappropriate form of political expression".[18] Terrorists generally come from the nations having low civil liberties and political rights.[19] Abadie also holds that the levels of political freedoms do explain terrorism. The countries in the medium range of political freedoms are likely to be more prone to terrorism compared to countries with high levels of political freedoms or countries with strict authoritarian regimes.[20]

Collier and Hoeffler whose work is mainly on internal conflicts in African countries hold greed as the motivating factor for conflicts. According to Collier-Hoeffler (CH) theory, opportunities for capturing resources and loot seeking cause civil wars.[21] Collier and Hoeffler, based on several case studies, also suggest that overall high GDP per capita, developed human capital (measured by secondary education), and high economic growth reduce the risk of civil war though there are some obvious deviations as well.[22] For example, in Pre-war Yugoslavia, per capita income was two to three times the average compared to civil war countries though unemployment had surged in some regions and had reached up to 40% of the adult population.[23] Similarly, the case of secondary education fails in several countries. Lebanon is a case in point. Its literacy rate was much higher than, say, of Saudi Arabia but Lebanon's civil war was among the longest but Saudi Arabia witnessed no civil war despite far lower literacy.

Moreover, some countries experiencing high economic growth may also get entrapped in civil war due to sub-optimal social and redistributive policy choices. Pakistan, as discussed somewhere else in detail, enjoyed good economic growth rates in 1960s but grievances in East Pakistan deepened during the same period of high growth. Neighbors also matter as the spillover effects from the neighborhood can induce conflict in a country through various mechanisms. "The presence of ethnic kin across the border may be one of the principal mechanisms that transmit civil wars across borders.---Another possible mechanism of contagion occurs through the accumulation of war-specific capital in regions experiencing wars, making it easier for other wars to start".[24] Refugee flows also increase risk of civil war by making cross-border movements of the insurgents easier with access to refugee camps.[25]

The phenomenon of militancy or terrorism is very complex and hard to explain by a single theory or model. For example, civil wars in African countries may be the result of greed (fight over diamonds) as postulated by Collier. And when it comes to transnational terrorism, it may be a type of voting through violent expression against the policies of the superpowers perceived to be unjust and exploitative. In some cases militancy may have roots in the territorial disputes left unresolved by the colonial powers or demarcating boundaries without consideration for the ethno-linguistic or religious composition of the region. In other contexts, it may be the manifestation of deprivations like poverty, inequality, social exclusion, and denial of political rights and freedoms, etc. The nexus between poverty and lack of opportunity and militancy is bit complex. Economists like Collier and Krueger do not see much truth in the argument that poverty is the root cause of militancy. According to them, even if some nexus exists between poverty and militancy, that is indirect and tenuous. Poverty hypothesis of terrorism has been tested through micro-level approach as well as cross-country analysis. At the micro level, characteristics of the militants (as done by Krueger) and of those who support militancy have been studied and overall results suggest that neither the militants nor those who support militancy (do not carry out militant acts themselves) predominantly come from the poor. Such investigations suffer from two deficiencies.

First, they invariably cover the militants hailing from the Middle East region and secondly, they concentrate on international terrorism. Some researchers[26] have come up with similar results for militancy in Pakistan as well. They conducted interviews of 6000 persons in the urban areas of Pakistan. Their results suggested little evidence of the support of the militancy by the poor. The results sound logical as the urban poor are more exposed to the negative externalities of militancy, so they, in most probability, would not support militant organizations. The findings, however, are not definitive due to selection bias as the sample did not cover the rural areas where in actual the poverty resides. The cross-country analysis approach also shows weak relationship between militancy and poverty. For example, Dipak Gupta tested the relationship between militancy and poverty for 110 countries using the aggregate data of deaths and injuries resulting from militant attacks and the percentage of people living below poverty. The results showed weak correlation.[27] The empirics thus dispute the deep-rooted belief that poverty, powerlessness, and deprivations generate terrorism.

It is a puzzle. Gupta writes: "When terrorists are interviewed, they all talk about their resentment towards the extant political system; they complain about factors of poverty and income inequality. They talk about the lack of economic opportunities, injustice, discrimination, repression, and intolerance facing their communities. Even when they are themselves from a well-off background, they tell researchers that they have been moved by the plight of their fellow community members. Why then these factor do not show up in our empirical analyses?"[28] Do deprivations not cause or induce terrorism? Perhaps this may not be the case. Militant acts are not random acts. Perhaps none of the acts in the universe is random. There is always a cause for an effect, an action for reaction. A militant act is caused by some deprivation or grievance of a collective nature. The question, however, is why an individual indulges in a militant act at the cost of his life for a collective group or community? The traditional model of rational choice does not capture such an act. After all, a rational human being would not take his life by indulging in a militant act. Masooda Bano in '*The Irrational Believer*'[29] has attempted to rationalize seemingly an irrational militant behavior by mapping the reasons of religiously motivated militancy. The axis of her analysis revolves around the major standoff in 2007 between the state and clerical leadership of the Red Mosque and female students of Jamia Hafsa in Islamabad.

Bano raises some crucial questions like follows: (1) How Pakistani young women demand Sharia despite limited women agency? (2) Why did the ulama and the students adopt apparently irrational preferences of advocating disengagement with modernity and calling for the replacement of civil law (designed to meet the needs of modern life) with the old times law of Shariat? (3) How does one explain the dramatic reversal of preferences within the Red Mosque? (4) And why religious actors in Pakistan adopt an exclusionary identity that is jihadist identity to the exclusion of other identities? Bano is of the view that finding answers of these questions merely in the indoctrination of madrassa education would not be fair. And it is also not correct that majority of the madrassas are involved in the political violence as only a small segment of madrassa population supports violent jihad. Local and global factors like Kashmir dispute, struggle for justice within Pakistan, and political activism on behalf of the Muslims globally, make fertile ground where exclusionary identities like jihadi identity flourish. We fail to understand the rationality of the acts because the traditional classical model of utility fails to account for non-material factors like altruism, commitment, and sacrifice. And if non-material factors are included in the model, then it appears that participation in jihad at times appears to be viable rational choice.

Terrorism is a type of voting by bullet as argued by Krueger. Disentangling the impact of deprivations as motivation for militancy, however, becomes difficult to analyze mainly due to three factors. First, variables like poverty and inequality are slow-moving variables. Their impact is felt at the collective level with a large time lag. Second, people suffering from deprivations like poverty and inequality suffer from collective action problem. Participation in a political violence entails an opportunity cost which is high for the poor as they are engaged, on day-to-day basis, in making both ends meet. Third, 'political entrepreneurs' are needed to aggregate the grievances of the community or population to create a separate collective identity. The political entrepreneurs weave a story around such identity by connecting the dots and borrowing threads from religion, mythology, and history to strengthen the belief of their followers in the new collective identity. The factors of deprivation like poverty constitute the necessary condition for militancy or political violence. For meeting the sufficient condition, political entrepreneurs are needed who can articulate the issue and can create a strong collective identity.[30] Several examples can be cited.

The untouchables (called Harijan i.e. children of God by Gandhiji) have historically suffered hugely. According to Gupta: "Very few groups, if any, have suffered as much in the hands of a larger society as so called "untouchable" castes in India. The humiliation and total degradation that the society imposed on the hapless people remain unparalleled in human society-----until the Maoists gave them leadership and fomented a violent insurgency".[31] The grievances of the Bengalis is another case in point which started simmering immediately after the creation of Pakistan over status of Bengali language, power sharing between the center and the provinces, distribution of resources, and increasing economic disparities. The growth rates in West Pakistan were about two percentage points higher than East Pakistan and the gap of per capita income increased from 17% in 1949–1950 to 60% in 1969–1970.[32] The political militancy, however, intensified when the issue of disparities was articulated by the Bengali leadership.

Lack of the rule of law, weak state (lack of capacity or will to exercise territorial control and maintain monopoly over violence), rapid modernization (with rapid economic growth from natural resources and emergence of new radical ideologies based on religion or nostalgia of the glorious past), extremist ideologies (both secular and religious are at least the intermediate cause; people adopt such ideologies as a consequence of some deep-rooted political or social deprivations or grievances), hegemony and inequality of power, illegitimate or corrupt governments, or powerful external factors supporting illegitimate governments, and experience of social injustice, etc., are some other factors responsible for militancy.[33] The militancy in Pakistan is also a result of multiple factors which can broadly be bracketed in four categories namely, Kashmir dispute, emphasis on the religious identity to the exclusion of other ethno-linguistic identities, spillover effects from Afghanistan and Iran, and structural imbalances arising out of socio-economic disparities and ungoverned spaces.

Deep-Seated Conflict

Pakistan was born in 1947 with pangs of bloodshed, migration, and a deep sense of grief and cheat over distribution of assets and resources. Over seven million refugees were to be absorbed and settled in the newly created country. The transportation system, communication networks, and trade which existed under the British got disrupted. But most importantly, Pakistan developed serious grievances over Kashmir. The issue precipitated with the decision of Hindu ruler Maharaja Hari Singh, in October 1947, to amalgamate Kashmir with India. This decision created bitterness of the worst kind between the two countries. Wars of 1948 and 1965 and several other conflicts arose out of the Kashmir dispute. "Undoubtedly, Kashmir is the bitterest legacy of the partition of the Indian subcontinent having serious consequences via growth of terrorism and sectarian violence in Pakistan as well as Kashmir".[34]

The grievances over Kashmir are, however, rooted in history. The Kashmiri Muslims were quite dissatisfied with the rule of Maharaja Hari Singh who was "an ineffectual, authoritarian and unpopular ruler, especially with his Muslim subjects".[35] The Muslims, who were in majority in Kashmir, were treated poorly by the administration of Maharaja. "In fact, so bad was the discrimination and mistreatment of the Muslim poor that, in 1929, one of the Maharaja's Hindu officials resigned his post because of the ill-treatment of the Muslim majority, whom he described as illiterate and poverty-stricken, and who were 'governed like dumb driven cattle'---- in 1941, a Hindu stated that: 'The poverty of Muslim masses is appalling. Dressed in rags and barefoot, a Muslim peasant represents the appearance of a starving beggar'. Opposition to Maharaja's government grew in 1930s".[36] The Muslims in Punjab had concerns about the maltreatment of Kashmiris and agitation started in 1930s, much before partition, in Punjab. It was a spontaneous expression of sympathy and solidarity with Kashmiri Muslims against the Maharaja administration. "The grievances of Kashmiri Musalmans comprised the appropriation by the state of a number of mosques, graveyards, and other places sacred to Muslims, the exclusion of Muslims from public places, the restrictions imposed on the observance of their religious ceremonies and the absence of a properly constituted legislature in which Muslims could be represented in accordance with their numerical proportion in the State".[37] A campaign, in the press, about said grievances resulted in communal riots in Sri Nagar on 30th July, 1931. The Majlis-i-Ahrar-i-Islam (founded on 4th May, 1931) led a band of one hundred volunteers from Sialkot in Punjab into Jammu territory.[38] The mystery shrouding the signing of accession document by Maharaja and dubious role of Mountbatten deepened the sense of deception and cheat in newly created Pakistan. It was in this context that several thousand Pashtun tribals from NWFP (now KPK) moved into Kashmir.

The Kashmir dispute has remained a thorn in the Indo-Pakistan bilateral relations. India alleges Pakistan of state-sponsored militancy in Indian-administered Kashmir while Pakistan alleges India of human rights violations and of ignoring resolution of the Kashmir dispute in accordance with UN resolution. For example, commenting on 1989–90 Kashmir insurgency, Sumit Ganguly writes about the allegations on both sides of the border as follows: "What explains the abrupt rise of violent ethno-religious fervor in 1989 in India's only Muslim majority state? Apologists for the Indian position have contended that the insurgency is the result of Pakistani propaganda and logistic support and training for the insurgents. Pakistani apologists, in turn, argue that the insurgency represents the spontaneous rise of ethno-religious sentiment among the oppressed Muslim community of Jammu and Kashmir".[39] Several serious attempts for mitigating tensions and conflict between Pakistan and India failed. The Agra Summit is a case in point. Sumit Ganguly in '*Deadly Impasse*' illustrates the critical role played by Indian leaders L.K. Advani and Sushma Swaraj in the failure of Agra Summit. He writes: "The Agra Summit's infelicitous conclusion also underscores the significance of critical policy differences within Indian policy-making elites. Despite Home Minister Advani's claim that he had no differences of opinion with Prime Minister Vajpayee, there is evidence that their positions on the question of Pakistan's abetment of terror were hardly identical. In fact, it is more than apparent that the two of them had fundamental differences on questions pertaining to the significance of the Kashmir dispute and issue of Pakistan's involvement in terror. Not surprisingly, these led to an internal deadlock on the Indian side and thereby helped to undermine progress at the Summit".[40]

The war against terror further deteriorated Pakistan–India relations. "Both India and Pakistan since long blame each other of carrying out terrorist attacks against each other. Charges of cross-border terrorism from both sides caused severe setback to their normalization process. The November 26, 2008 terrorist attacks in Mumbai and other terrorist events in different cities of Pakistan, and India made things worse in Indo-Pak relations".[41]Warmongers are in plenty on both sides and the primary bone of contention between the two countries is the dispute over Kashmir. "The anti-India narrative starts with anti-Hindu sentiment before partition (the very reason for which was the fear of domination by a Hindu majority), extends to unfair division of assets immediately following partition, to India's role in Bangladesh's secession from Pakistan, and to its unyielding stance on Kashmir. Pakistanis consider India to be a bully and Pakistan a victim".[42] The reason for the very existence of several religious militant groups[43] is the non-resolution of the Kashmir dispute. The pangs of partition had several other unintended consequences. The leaders of the new state assumed power in a heightened sense of insecurity due to acrimony of partition. The insecurity and threat perceived by the leadership in Pakistan diverted greater resources toward military capacity besides adoption of a national security prism for overall governance. Besides a sense of deep wrong and injustice on Kashmir, Pakistan faced a dilemma of identity and nation building.

Multiple Ethnic Identities

In 1947, Pakistan inherited at least five distinct identities, four in the West and one in the East. A distance of 1000 miles separated the east from the west. The eastern part was comparatively a homogenous province in ethnic and linguistic terms. The western part had huge ethnic and linguistic diversity. Moreover, none of the four provinces in the west could claim to have a single ethno-linguistic group. For example, Balochistan had Balochs and a significant number of Pakhtuns in the northern part of the province. Punjab was dominated by the Punjabis with significant population of Seraikis in the Southern part. KPK (then NWFP) was inhabited by the Pashtuns and Hindko-speakers. Sindh was distinctly divided between Sindhi-speaking local population and Urdu-speaking Mohajirs who had migrated from India and had settled in the urban areas. The dilemma Pakistan faced was: how to gel and integrate the multiple ethno-linguistic identities in view of the fact that practically ethnicity had remained the primary marker of identity in large parts of the country both before and after 1947.

It is perhaps one of the myths that all the ethno-linguistic communities which became part of Pakistan were the flag-bearers of the Pakistan movement. For instance, Pakhtuns in the Peshawar valley region generally supported congress-allied Khudai Khidmatgars (Servants of God), led by Bacha Khan. After the creation of Pakistan, Pakhtun nationalism did not die down in the Pakhtun-dominated areas like Peshawar valley and northern Balochistan. As regards Sindh, the provincial assembly of Sindh though passed a resolution to join Pakistan but the protest of ethnic

Sindhis against economic marginalization by the migrants and allottees of state land in Sindh dates back to pre-partition days. Balochistan always had an "ambivalent relationship" with the state of Pakistan.[44] Moreover, the regions and provinces which constitute Pakistan were largely associated with particular ethnic groups in the British India before partition of the subcontinent. Large-scale migration as a result of partition and demarcations of the boundaries changed demographic composition of these regions and political power configurations, thus creating instability and tensions.

Two-nation theory provided the intellectual foundation for the creation of new state which simply meant that Pakistan had to be different based on some metaphysical notion. Impliedly, it could not be a secular state. Rather it was to evolve as an ideological state with an overriding supremacy of religious identity over other identities. Evolution of nationhood on the basis of religious identity was easier said than done as religion could be interpreted by different people and sects in their own way. So the elite of that time decided that the ideological evolution would not be practically left to the will of the people. Rather institutions of the state would steer and control the process of nation building. The logical corollary was that the institutions of the state would be supreme even over the will of the people.[45] Moreover, centralization of power by implication required suppression of regional and provincial aspirations. Downplaying the regional identities had serious unintended consequences. The pitfalls of religion-based politics and nation-building started surfacing soon after the birth of Pakistan. A major manifestation was seen in January 1953, when ulama (clerics) of various sects demanded that the Ahmadi sect be legally declared non-Muslim. "Widespread riots soon followed, resulting in dozens of deaths and considerable loss to property. Reflecting what has been a consistent pattern in Pakistan's history, the religious demand also had a worldly purpose. Punjabi politicians had instigated the clerics in the hope of dislodging the government of Bengali prime minister, Khawaja Nazimuddin".[46]

The Munir Inquiry Commission was appointed to enquire into the Punjab disturbances of 1953. The commission interviewed number of ulama from various sects. The commission observed that no two ulama agreed on the fundamental definition of a Muslim. It noted the sharp sectarian differences as follows: "According to the Shias all Sunnis are kafirs, and Ahl-i-Quran, namely, persons who consider hadith to be unreliable and therefore not binding, are unanimously kafirs and so are all independent thinkers. The net result of all this is that neither Shias nor Sunnis nor Deobandis nor Ahl-i-Hadith nor Barelvis are Muslims and any change from one view to the other must be accompanied in an Islamic State with the penalty of death if the Government of the State is in the hands of the party which considers the other party to be kafirs. And it does not require much imagination to judge of the consequences of this doctrine when it is remembered that no two ulama have agreed before us to the definition of a Muslim. If the constituents of the each of the definitions given by the ulama are given effect to, and subjected to the rule of 'combination and permutation' and the form of charge in the Inquisition's sentence on Galileo is adopted mutatis mutandis as a model, the grounds on which a person may be indicted for apostasy will be too numerous to count".[47]

More emphasis on religious commonality under the constant supervision of the institutions of the state (bureaucratic-military establishment) simply meant that ethnic heterogeneity and cultural pluralism were threats to the country. The threats on ethnic front which existed and manifested their presence from the very inception of Pakistan were simply brushed aside as "regionalism" or "provincialism". "By dismissing ethnic heterogeneity and demands for provincial autonomy, devolution of power, decentralization and equitable policies governing relations with the center, the ruling elite have sought refuge in administrative, ad hoc measures and no comprehensive plan has been undertaken to coopt such plural forces through bargaining and appropriate politico-economic measures".[48] The issues of ethnicity emerged soon after independence. In the Eastern part, ethnicity reflected itself in the Bengali language movement. The Bengalis started emphasizing the primacy of language as their identity. "Bengal was culturally, linguistically, and religiously unique. Bengalis had very little in common with the Punjabis, Sindhis, and other ethnic groups living in the West".[49] The differences of language coupled with other deprivations provided a fertile ground for the Bengali separatist movement which culminated in creation of Bangladesh.

Emphasis on the religious identity and ideology continued with the same fervor even after separation of Bangladesh from Pakistan. For example, the subject of Pakistan studies and Islamiyat were declared compulsory even for medical and engineering students in 1981 and in the same year the University Grants commission (predecessor of HEC) issued instructions to the authors of the Pakistan Studies books that the books were "to demonstrate that the basis of Pakistan is not to be founded in racial, linguistic, or geographical factors, but, rather, in the shared experience of a common religion. To get students to know and appreciate the Ideology of Pakistan and to popularize it with slogans. To guide students towards the ultimate goal of Pakistan - the creation of a completely Islamic State".[50] The anti-Soviet jihad in Afghanistan, efforts to curb Shia militancy in response to Iran's 1979 revolution, and the Zia's Islamization program prepared the ground for organizations with sectarian agendas to flourish.[51]

Triple Whammy

In 2010, as many as 232 militant religious organizations were operating in Pakistan with multiple agendas like transformation of the society according to their ideologies, enforcement of Sharia law, establishment of caliphate system, fulfillment of their sectarian objectives, and achievement of Pakistan's strategic and ideological objectives through militancy.[52] The majority of the militant groups were established in the wake of Soviet-Afghan war in 1980s. The militants from different regions of the world came to Pakistan to fight against Russia. These militants assembled in the Northern part of the country and became source of the future troubles of Pakistan. After exit of Russian forces from Afghanistan, Talibans got ascendency in Afghanistan. And then 9/11 changed everything by adding new dimensions to the problems of militancy and terrorism.

What happened is that most of the warriors who had fought war against Russia were not disbanded once the war was over. Some of them found safe sanctuaries in the tribal Areas of Pakistan near Pak-Afghan border. They had accumulated war-specific capital during fight in Afghanistan. The USA and its coalition partners had no plan of dealing with them. Hillary Clinton acknowledged this fact in an interview as follows: "We have walked away from Pakistan and Afghanistan in the past --- we had helped to create the problem we are fighting when the Soviet Union invaded Afghanistan--- we had a brilliant idea to come to Pakistan and create a force of mujahedeen, equipped them – to go inside Afghanistan, and we were successful. Soviets left Afghanistan and we said goodbye leaving these people who were fanatical and armed, in Afghanistan and Pakistan".[53] Huge build-up of arms during so called jihad in Afghanistan became available to jihadi organizations, ethnic groups, sectarian groups, criminals, and even student bodies "who often outgunned the corrupt and demoralized police force".[54]The Afghan jihad also fueled sectarian violence in Pakistan due to increase in the influence and power of the extremist religious groups.[55] Huge influx of refugees in the wake of Afghan war also had consequences for the economy and society of Pakistan. According to UNHCR data, in 1987, the number of refugees had crossed three million. Till 1991, it was above three million for long five years (Fig. 14.3).

Moreover, the conflict in Afghanistan created an open war economy which not only affected Afghanistan but its surrounding areas as well. Afghanistan became the world's largest opium producer and a center of arms dealing besides supporting multibillion-dollar trade in goods smuggled from Dubai to Pakistan. In this way, Afghan conflict weakened legal economies throughout the region.[56] After 9/11, both internal and external funded terrorist activities started in Pakistan in reaction to Pakistan's decision to give logistics support to USA. Some militant groups even decided to fight alongside the Afghan Taliban against the international coalition forces in Afghanistan, "Pakistan's security establishment realized for the first time that religion was an area where it could not be certain of its control over these groups".[57] The TTP was established in 2007 which remained a critical force from 2007 to 2014 with varying degrees of influence. It established its chapters in different agencies of FATA, Balochistan, and Karachi. It became so formidable that it established a virtual state in Swat. It maintained close ties with Al-Qaeda, the

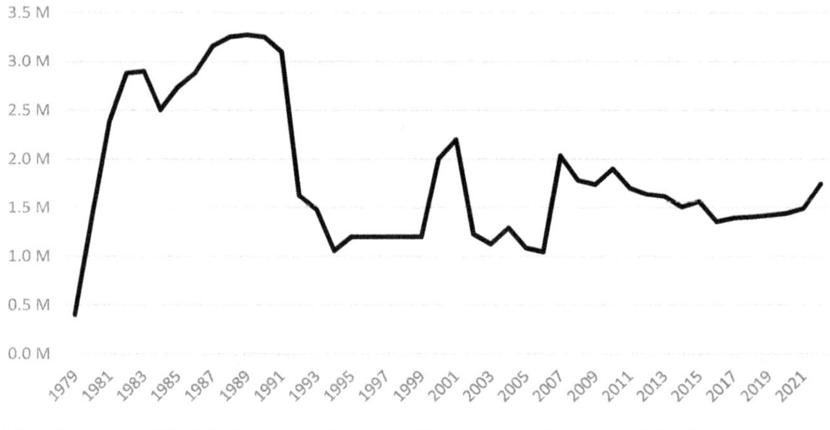

Fig. 14.3 UNHCR Refugees from 1979 to 2022 (*Source* UNHCR Population Statistics—https://doi.org/10.6068/DP18C0CB771F92)

Afghan Taliban, and host of other militant group and carried out some of the bloodiest terrorist attacks like assault on Pakistan Navy's largest Airbase in 2011, an attack on Karachi's international airport in 2014, and massacre at the Army public school in Peshawar in 2014 killing 150 persons mostly school children. An analysis of data[58] shows that with the establishment of TTP, Pakistan witnessed an abrupt surge in terrorist attacks, suicide bombings, and explosions. According to Global Terrorism Database (GTD), it was involved in 269 attacks between 2007 and 2009, primarily in erstwhile FATA and KPK. The TTP militants dispersed in the country and a significant number of terrorist attacks occurred in other parts particularly Balochistan and Sindh which respectively witnessed 98 and 108 attacks during the said period. They also established their links with militants in Punjab (called Punjabi Taliban). The Swat operation of 2009 and Zarb-e-azab operation of 2014 by the Pakistan Army in North Waziristan, however, dented its operations.

The Iranian revolution of 1979 was another big external factor which not only gave a new dimension to the politics of the Middle East and the Persian Gulf but its effects rippled across to Pakistan. The Shia-Sunni conflict became more pronounced with the revolution in Iran and the Islamizing dictatorship of General Zia as several Sunni militant groups took their roots during General Zia-ul-Haq's military government (1977–1988). The Iranian revolution increased Shia assertiveness in Pakistan who demanded representation in important government decision-making bodies and more freedom for commemoration of Muharram. At the same time, decision of exempting Shias from imposition of zakat angered Zia's Deobandi supporters. The seeds of Shia-Sunni schism, which existed in Pakistan from the very beginning and remained suppressed, became visible in a deadly fashion in 1980s. The militant groups were created and a spiral of violence started in the religion market which ultimately led to extreme violence and terrorism threatening the solidarity of the society. General Zia promulgated a series of ordinances to Islamize legal, fiscal, and monetary institutions of the country. The introduced amendments broadly included punishment of serious crimes under the sharia law, elimination of interest, introduction of profit loss sharing scheme, establishment of federal sharia court, and amendments for introduction of Islamic taxes of Zakat and Ushr. Introduction of Sharia law was basically a rent-seeking bargain in the religion market by General Zia to remain in power undemocratically and gather support for jihad in Afghanistan by appeasing the dominant religious players or sects while such religious factions were trying to expand their religious share in the legal, political, and judicial institutions.

Intervention in the religion market created huge negative externalities by creating and sharpening Shia–Sunni dissensions on several issues. All the amendments in the law were based on Hanafi jurisprudence and invited ire from the followers of jurisprudence of other schools of thought. For example, introduction of zakat (a taxation measure) earned the ire of the Shia community as according to Hanafi school, state is empowered to collect and distribute zakat (deduction could be made from an individual's bank account) while Shias maintained that state could not collect zakat forcibly by deducting it from the bank accounts rather Zakat would be paid or distributed to the needy (qualified for it under the Islamic injunctions) by the individuals themselves. In July 1980, the Shias from all over the country assembled in Islamabad demanding non-imposition of Zakat upon them. Zia's government though succumbed to the demand but interference in the religion market sharpened the misgivings among various sects of the Muslims in Pakistan. The damage done by Zia through his interventions in the religion market was huge. According to Ahmed Rashid "General Zia's eleven-year rule was to have the most long-lasting and damaging effect on Pakistani society, one still prevalent today. Zia, who seized power from Bhutto in a coup in 1977, dealt with Pakistan's identity crisis by imposing an ideological Islamic state upon the population. Many of today's problems—the militancy of the religious parties, the mushrooming of madrassas and extremist groups, the spread of drug and Kalashnikov culture, and the increase in sectarian violence took place during the Zia era".[59]

The Madrassa Factor

Zia's Islamization policy also contributed to the phenomenal growth of madrassas in 1980s. The madrassas are mostly concentrated in KP and Balochistan in areas bordering Afghanistan. Generally they cater to the needs of the poorest of the poor with certain exceptions in urban areas where children of some middle-class families also get religious education out of preference of the parents. Madrassas generally fill the void left by the state in some areas as they provide free lodging, boarding, and clothing to the students. Increase in the number of madrassas coincided with the rise of Sunni militancy in Pakistan which makes the madrassas an immediate and easy candidate for the rise of terrorist activities. In

1970s, the rise in madrassas is attributed to the flow of funds from the Persian Gulf monarchies, Governments of the Saudi Arabia, and United Arab Emirates as they viewed political developments with alarm due to tilt of politics toward the Left in late 1960s and early 1970s in Pakistan. In order to contain the influence of the Leftist politics in Pakistan and spilling over the leftist ideas to the Muslim monarchies, they funneled funds for establishment of madrassas in Pakistan and "supported all kinds of Islamic activities with the aim of strengthening Islamic Institutions and ideology as a bulwark against the Left".[60]

The financial assistance also increased from domestic sources with the liberal availability of Zakat funds. Formal recognition of degree awarded by the madrassas increased employment opportunities. The National Committee on Deeni Madaris produced a report in 1979 with the recommendation to encourage reforms in its curricula for catering to the needs of the changing society but the traditional ulama did not subscribe to the recommendation mainly on the argument that "madrassa education was to be judged in terms of the Islamic scholarship it produces and not its utility for the modern sectors of the economy".[61] The subsequent governments particularly the Musharraf regime also made attempts to reform madrassas but tangible success could not be achieved. The attempts of reforming madrassas are opposed by the ulama to date with the result that the graduates from these madrassas do not have marketable skill and cannot compete with the students of other streams of education. An analysis of enrollment of the students in madrasas shows that around 5% student get enrolled in religious schools. In 2004–2005, 1.54 million children were enrolled in madrassas compared to 27.76 million in public and private schools (see Table 14.1).

The enrollment data of schools reveals some interesting results. First, public sector enrollment is decreasing with the passage of time. Second, enrollment in private schools has consistently increased. Third, enrollment is Deeni Madaris has also increased but we see a quantum jump of almost 100% (from 2.2 million to 4.4 million) during the period 2015–16 to 2020–21 that is in the period when militancy and terrorism had subsided in Pakistan pointing toward tenuous link between madrasas and militancy. The financial incentives provided by the PTI government to madrassas with a view to allure them for reforms and bring them under government may be the factor for the rise in enrollment.[62]

The curriculum and pedagogy adopted in the madrassas is alleged to promote obscurantism and militancy. For example, Zahid Hussain, a

Table 14.1 Enrollment statistics

Year	*Enrollment (in millions) (% in Total)*				*% Growth in Enrollment (Base year 2004–2005)*		
	Public schools	*Private schools*	*Deeni Madaris*	*Public and private schools*	*Public schools*	*Private schools*	*Deeni Madaris*
2004–2005	19.86 (67.76)	7.9 (26.95)	1.54 (5.29)	27.76 (94.71)	–	–	–
2010–2011	21.79 (61.80)	11.74 (33.30)	1.72 (4.89)	33.53 (95.11)	9.72	48.61	11.69
2015–2016	22.25 (56.23)	15.11 (38.18)	2.2 (5.57)	37.36 (94.43)	12.03	91.27	42.86
2020–2021	23.72 (53.99)	15.8 (35.97)	4.4 (10.03)	39.52 (89.97)	19.44	100	185.71

Source (i) The National Education Census (NEC) 2005, (ii) Pakistan Education Statistics 2010–2011, 2015–2016, and 2020–2021, AEPAM, Government of Pakistan, Islamabad

senior journalist of Pakistan writes: "The education imparted by traditional madrassas often spawned factional, religious, and cultural conflict. It carried barriers to modern knowledge, stifled creativity, and bred bigotry thus laying the foundation on which fundamentalism—militant or otherwise—was bred. Divided by sectarian identities, these institutions were, by their very nature, driven by their zeal to outnumber and dominate rival sects. Promoting a particular sect inevitably implied the rejection of other sects, sowing the seeds of extremism in the minds of the students. The literature produced by their parent religious organizations promoted sectarian hatred and was aimed at proving the rival sects as infidels and apostates. The efforts by the successive governments to modernize the madrassa curricula and introduce secular subjects failed because of stiff resistance from the religious organs that control the religious schools".[63] Undoubtedly, there are issues with the inputs (curriculum and pedagogy, etc.) and the products of madrasas. The graduates of madrassas lack skills for gainful employment and have a factional worldview but madrasas, contrary to journalistic claims and reports suffused with lot of subjectivity and bias, are not involved in terrorism though some leaders of Taliban graduated from these religious schools. The elements of bias and subjectivity are so deep that even some well-reputed accounts and reports have grossly exaggerated the role and number of madrasa students. For example, Jessica Stern, while at Harvard, published a provocative article[64] in 2000 wherein she declared madrasas factories of jihad. She based her impression on some visits to Deobandi madrasas which had backed Afghan jihad against Russian invasion in 1979. The claims made and opinions expressed lack concrete data or evidence to support the validity of the assertions she made.

Similarly, the International Crisis Group (ICG) in its 2002 report asserted that one-third that is 33% of students in Pakistan (which ICG corrected in 2005) attend madrasas full time.[65] The number was a gross exaggeration pointing toward the bias and misperceptions about the role of madrassas in militancy and terrorism. The point simply is that a lot of fog and subjectivity is involved in the journalistic accounts and reports on madrassas, not only about the number but their role as well. Some non-journalistic accounts, on the contrary, suggest that predominantly militants do not come from madrassas. For example, some researchers,[66] based on analysis of the case files and detailed histories of 76 ex-militants at a rehabilitation and deradicalization center at Swat (where militancy was at its peak during 2007–2009), found that the madrasas were not significantly involved in militant recruitment as 63 (83%) out of 76 who joined Taliban had not attended any madrasa. Out of remaining 13 (17%), only three had got some training in weapon handling while the rest were involved in menial tasks or guard duties. And all the thirteen had joined militancy voluntarily without any coercion or push by the madrassas.

The cultivation of narrow and factional worldview is an overall problem of the entire education system of Pakistan. The regular education system also promotes a typical mindset. K.K. Aziz examined 60 text books on social studies, Pakistan studies, and History used in the schools and colleges of Pakistan and concluded that the text books emphasized on, among other things, support of military rule in Pakistan, glorification of wars, and hatred with India. The lies in the text books, as per K.K.Aziz, make the people hypocrite and liars, and promote a culture of rigidity and self-righteousness. "The natural result is intolerance. Views other than one's own are unwelcome, unpalatable, not worth a consideration. Argument or logic plays no part in his life. Self-righteousness conquers all".[67] Professor Hassan Askari writes in this regard as follows: "The skewed and emotional disposition has been created not only by madrasa education but also by the regular education system starting in the mid-1980s under the Zia regime. Zia-ul-Haq government also used state patronage to promote Islamist groups and militancy; the media was also used to propagate Islamic orthodoxy and militancy. The socialization of young people continued even after the death of Zia-ul-Haq.—This socialization downplays the notion of Pakistan as a territorial nation-state, Pakistani citizenship, and Pakistan as a political community. Their main reference points are transnational Muslim identity; western injustices against Muslims, non-resolution of the Palestine and Kashmir issues, the west as an adversary of Muslims, and the role of the Islamic movement rather than Muslim states as the liberators of Muslims from Western domination".[68]

And contrary to widely held belief in the outside world regarding rampancy of madrasas, Pakistan is not overrun by the religious schools. "At the national level, only 4% of the rural population lives in villages where a madrasa exists and there is no private school. In contrast, 32% of rural population lives in villages where there is a private school but not a madrasa. Thirteen percent of the population lives in a village where there is a madrasa but additional school choice exists in that a private school is present and importantly over half the rural population of Pakistan lives in villages where there is neither a madrasa nor a private school".[69] Moreover, madrasas are not a preferred option with the parents when it comes to the choice of a school. Even the poor people in all probability prefer a private school if they can afford it. The proposition that madrassas are not a preferred choice can be contested on the ground of ubiquity of public schools. It is true that public schools do not charge tuition fees and provide text books free of cost or at subsidized costs but they do not provide clothing, shelter, and food which madrasas provide. Moreover, quality and learning outcomes of the public schools are quite low and teacher absenteeism is high (discussed in detail in chapter on education) which may also work as disincentive for the poor families to get their children enrolled in the public school in some cases while making a choice between a public school and a madrassa. The people of Pakistan are not radicalized. Even in 2013, when terrorism was at its peak, 89% Pakistanis, according to a Pew Survey, said that violence was never justified.[70]

Some sections of the society particularly in the areas characterized by poor public service delivery and wide ungoverned spaces may sympathize with the militant organizations as several of them run social service delivery units and are engaged in philanthropic work. "Pakistanis' views of terrorist groups are not as extreme as you may think, but while Pakistanis are negative on militant groups and their violence writ large, their wider narratives surrounding these groups are far from simple. They clearly recognize extremisms is a problem --82% of respondents in 2015 said they were concerned about Islamic extremism in Pakistan—yet their narratives on extremism are muddied by a sense of national victimhood, by a blindness towards Pakistan's own faults, by anti-Americanism and anti-Indian sentiment and a deep-rooted struggle between Islam and the West".[71] Factors of militancy are deep-rooted. They are structural and historical. It would hardly be a matter of coincidence that militancy in Pakistan took roots in the areas where socio-economic disparities were deep and the ungoverned space was wide which the militant organizations exploited in their favor. Erstwhile FATA, Swat, South Punjab, urban Sindh, and Balochistan are the cases in point.

Religious Militancy in FATA and Swat

FATA, with inhospitable topography, has limited arable land. Public infrastructure, particularly health and education-related, is scant. People have to travel long distances to get basic health care. There is only one health care facility for every 4200 people and only one doctor for 7800 people.[72] Around 60% of the population remains below the poverty.[73] The development indicators of this region are very poor compared to the national average. The report of the committee, established by the Government of Pakistan, highlights the deprivations of FATA as follows: "Presently, there is a development deficit in FATA as the region is lagging behind regarding various socio-economic and development indicators. Access to health facilities in FATA is low and results in high infant and maternal mortality rates and low immunization coverage. Similarly, overall literacy rate is 33% (female adult literacy 12.7%) in FATA, as compared with the national average of 58%. Moreover, most of the households are engaged in subsistence farming and livestock rearing and there are very few livelihood opportunities available. The pervasive underdevelopment of the region due to persistent neglect and failure of successive governments to either introduce successful reforms or undertake substantial development efforts have created trust deficit between the residents of FATA and the state".[74] The per capita budget of FATA was lower in the range of 40–50% compared to per capita share of NFC.[75]

The region is characterized by neglect and political marginalization. Although constitutionally part of Pakistan, it was ruled under special law that is Frontier Crimes Regulation (FCR) designed and implemented since 1901. A handful of civil servants, called political agents (PAs), who wielded enormous powers under the FCR controlled the people of the area through local power brokers, the Maliks and Masharans. The political agents, the relic of the colonial rule, were responsible for carrying out the development functions in all the seven agencies of erstwhile FATA who hardly faced any accountability for their performance and were entrenched in the local rent-seeking relationships. "Such a system led to the concentration of power in the hands of a few, thereby giving rise to a non-representative, non-transparent and unaccountable system. The Soviet-Afghan war in the 1980s further aggravated the power equation, since "jihad" in Afghanistan raises the stature of local clergy or Mullah as another important factor in FATA. Owing to the paucity of modern state institutions, embedded in the FCR system, an unintended outcome, in the shape of political, economic, and security vacuum, surfaced in FATA. This vacuum was very adequately filled by the militants in the post-September 2001 (post -9/11)".[76] TTP exploited the grievances and socio-economic concerns of the local population. "It was less costly for local populations to acquiesce to the militant groups than actually confronting or opposing them".[77] A post-Crisis Needs Assessment of FATA region carried out by the World Bank and the Government of Pakistan concluded that: "substantial failures in governance and rule-of-law, and state failure to basic citizenship rights to the people of FATA were structural drivers of conflict".[78] According to an ADB report, absence of visible progress and perceived lack of interest both by the local and federal government in redressing acute economic deprivations and development disparities has contributed to widespread lack of trust in government institutions. "This creates opportunities for militant groups: they are known to frequently contextualize their calls to violence and popular recruitment in the language of redressing the substantial disparities which persist. It also enables them to present themselves as an emerging alternative to the state through direct and indirect provision of services".[79]

As regards militancy in Swat, Tehreek-e-Nafaz-e-Shariat-e-Mohammadi (TNSM) that is movement for the enforcement of Islamic laws, inter alia, exploited the underdeveloped and slow judicial system. Under the princely rule, Swat was known for cheap and quick dispensation of justice. After incorporation of Swat into Pakistan in 1969, the area was subjected to piecemeal judicial reforms and changes in its constitutional status. The dispensation of justice got slow like rest of the country. Local militant commanders established functional, though draconian, functions of police and dispute resolution. "The courts established in Swat, run by qazis, or Islamic jurists, required adding new qazis when the case load of a given court exceeded 150 cases. No such provision existed in the mainstream courts".[80] Moreover, TSNM also appealed to the marginalized sections of the society as majority of those who joined the said organization belonged to the landless families. And the presence of TSNM was felt more in the areas where landed aristocracy had its firm hold. The movement basically provided the disadvantaged (landless people) an opportunity to have their say in the socio-political affairs of the valley.[81] "The key to understanding the internal factors lies in understanding the composition of Maulana Fazlullah's supporters. The majority of the supporters belong to the lower rung of the social structure--- the vocational groups who do not have a share in the land distribution of the area. The supporters of the Maulana in the marginalized groups take a sense of empowerment in their state of powerlessness. Both the state and the traditional elites along with the political elites of the valley, unfortunately, have all along failed to respond to the aspirations of those who remained marginalized in an already marginalized society of Swat Valley".[82]

Impoverished South Punjab

The district Jhang of the Punjab province presents another example of socio-political deprivations. The Sipa-e-Sahaba Pakistan (SSP), a deadly militant Sunni organization took birth in 1986 in Jhang, a district of Punjab. The Shia landlords occupied around 65% of land and enjoyed political dominance in the area despite being in minority compared to Sunnis. As the SSP challenged the established but corrupt authority of the Shia landlords and Pirs, so it had appeal to the common and marginalized people.[83] The rise of SSP was an assertion of the Sunnis for share in the socio-political power. A large number of Sunni workers had gone to the Middle East particularly Saudi Arabia in 1970s and sent remittances to their families. With the financial conditions improved, they now had a pent-up demand for socio-political status. "The quest for social recognition attracted these newly affluent groups to the ideology of Sunni sectarian groups, particularly those who had been influenced by Wahhabism while away working in the Gulf states".[84] Later on, the influence of SSP penetrated into the districts of South Punjab. The Punjabi Taliban network which was a loose conglomeration of the members of the banned militant organizations had its stranglehold in South Punjab. It comprised of the sectarian militant organizations as well as those focused on conflict in Kashmir.[85]

The region of South Punjab is composed of three administrative divisions namely Bahawalpur, Dera Ghazi Khan, and Multan. Around 34.7 million people (32% of the Punjab population) live in South Punjab which covers 45% of the area of the province. South Punjab fares worse compared to Central and Northern Punjab on virtually every development metric. For example, in comparison with other regions of Punjab, literacy rate is 16% lower, the number of OOSC is 2.2 times higher, 40% fewer people have access to piped water facilities and sewerage, population per hospital bed is 50% higher, 44% more children experience stunted growth, and multidimensional poverty is 2.1 times higher.[86] About 55% of the population is living below 50% of median income per capita in the rural south region of Punjab whereas 31% is living below the national poverty line whereas this percentage is lower for the central and northern Punjab.[87] South Punjab has the highest proportion of child labor averaging 19.1% compared to 11.4% in the Northern Punjab. Around 20% of the girls get married before the age of 18 (this figure is 13% for rest of Punjab).[88] According to a Human Rights Commission report on South Punjab, child marriage is a serious concern and often goes unreported like other gender-based violence for fear of reprisals by tribal elders, local administrations, and political leaders.[89] The tribal belt bordering Balochistan area particularly remains vulnerable to obnoxious practices like wani, Karo kari, and swara. The revenge rape of Mukhtar Mai in 2002 is a case in point. Mai, an illiterate and poor woman, hails from a remote village of Muzaffargarh, a district with very poor human development indicators. She was subjected to rape on the orders of a village council. She, however, survived, fought back, and is now working as a human rights activist.[90]

Health and education infrastructure is woefully low. Inadequate, poorly staffed, and poorly resourced health centers are unable to meet the demand of the population. The gap between supply and demand creates severe distortions in the system. For example, according to HRCP the women were reported to pay bribe to the hospital staff to avail medical treatment. Similarly, due to lack of education infrastructure, literacy rates are low. Schools are located far away from the residential places particularly having more negative consequences for the female education. It partly explains huge variation, on the basis of gender, in school enrollment. The point, in a nutshell, is that South Punjab is the most deprived region of the Punjab province. Such deprivations coupled with ungoverned space provide a fertile ground to the militant organizations.

Contestations in the City of Light

Karachi is traditionally known as the city of lights, a city which never sleeps. It is the business hub of Pakistan. It accounts for over 50% of the tax revenues of the Federal Government and contributes around 25% of the GDP of Pakistan, handles 95% of the internal trade, contributes 30% to the manufacturing sector, and holds 50% of its bank deposits.[91] The economic performance of the city is both a result and a driver of large-scale migration. Initially, migrants moved to Karachi from India on creation of Pakistan. The city has a large-scale heterogeneity on ethnic and political lines. It is capital of a largely rural Sindh province but majority of its residents are non-Sindhi speakers. The dominant community is of Mohajirs who emerged from the ethnic mobilization of Urdu speakers by the MQM. They constitute about half of the population of Karachi. Other main ethnic groups include Pashtuns and Balochs. Since 1980s, Karachi witnessed spurts of violence along ethnic lines. "The presence of large-scale heterogeneity, political organization of ethnic identity and heightened competition over urban resources have all acted as strong drivers of conflict".[92] Nothing is bad with ethnic diversity if the institutions are of the high-quality (reflected in rule of law, bureaucratic quality, and enforcement of contracts, etc.). However, ethnic diversity negatively affects the prosperity if the institutions are poor.[93]

Karachi has faced multiple forms of militancy. Ethno-political, sectarian, militant, and criminal violence claimed 7000 lives between 2008 and 2011 in Karachi and the politically motivated violence alone accounted for 9.6% of all violent deaths in 2011.[94] The armed wings of political parties were the main perpetrators of violence which clashed over city resources and funds generated through extortion. City-wide outbreaks of violence caused daily losses of Rs. 3 billion (US$ 31.5 million) and Rs.7 billion (US$ 73.6 million) to trade and industry respectively due to routine closure of markets and industries.[95] Conflicts in Karachi generally owe to contestations over political and economic power, Heightened electoral competition for national and provincial legislative constituencies create political contestation among various parties and factions. As regards control over resources, disputes over land are the biggest source of conflict. Large-scale migration to Karachi, existence of huge ungoverned space, and high rents attached to real estate sector have made land grabbing very lucrative for the land grabbers. The land grabbers have to have pat of the politicians and the powerful to survive in the business of grabbing. They use such connections to regularize squatter dwellings and gain permissions to convert amenity plots that is plots allocated for parks and community centers into commercial and residential plots. "The 'riots' of April 1985 and December 1986-----which were only the deadliest and most reported incidents in the long series of disturbances---were intimately linked with land conflicts, and more specifically with the changing dynamics of real estate development in the city's kachi abadis".[96]

The problems of Karachi are deeply connected to poor governance. Some big failures of governance include sub-optimal provision of public goods (like law and order) and social services like decent housing. The city is facing housing crisis since 1947 when large-scale migration took place from India. In the last couple of decades, informal settlements (kachi abadis) have witnessed mushroom growth which now accommodate almost 50% of the population of Karachi. If we only consider this one variable, we can say that at least 50% space in Karachi is ungoverned leaving aside the points that 42% of water supply is in the hands of taker mafias and 45% of the electricity is siphoned off from the regular supply lines through kunda installation (a way of stealing electricity). "This prevalence and tolerance of the informal provides political and violent entrepreneurs with numerous opportunists of brokerage between the state (the bureaucracy, the judiciary, and the police) and the populations the most exposed to informality and uncertainty (the residents of the squatter settlements)".[97] The city government can hardly raise 10% of the potential revenue to finance development. "Due to segregated basis of political support, the provincial government has also shown little interest in enhancing local revenue capacity and has chosen to direct provincial revenue collected from the city to other areas".[98]

The local police apparatus remains heavily compromised due to rampant corruption, incompetence, and political interference.[99] Afghan jihad had also got nexus with militancy in Karachi. During 1983–87, arms supply to afghan mujahidin increased massively to the tune of 600%.[100] Karachi, being the port city, became an entry point for the arms and ammunition destined for the mujahidin out of which a large part pilfered during transit to Afghanistan and ended up in the hands of criminals, drug-traffickers, slumlords, and student activists. Religious groups also added to the complex landscape of militancy in Karachi. Escalation of war against terror, volatility in FATA and Balochistan, and Pakistan military operation against the terrorists compelled many a militant to run from those areas and take refuge in densely populated areas of Karachi. Between 2009 and 2013, Karachi witnessed dozens of terrorist attacks by the TTP. In 2014, the Federal government launched a large-scale paramilitary operation to deweaponize Karachi which has met huge success and Karachi has now almost returned to normalcy. "Unlike other situations of prolonged urban warfare, such as those witnessed in Beirut in the 1980s or in some Colombian cities during the 1980 or 1990s, Karachi's ordered disorder has stood the test of time".[101]

Grievances of Balochistan

Balochistan is the largest province of Pakistan covering 43% of the land mass. It offers some of the best assets for development. It is bestowed with natural and locational resources. Being a frontier province, it is ideally situated for trade with Iran, Afghanistan, Central Asia, and the Gulf countries. Over the last several decades, it has supplied cheap natural gas to the economic centers of Pakistan and has thus supported country's industrialization.[102] The population density is low which partly makes infrastructure development and public service delivery in per capita terms quite costly. The major ethnic groups inhibiting the province are Balochs and Pashtuns. Balochistan is the least developed province with very poor human development indicators compared to national average. From the very beginning, relations of the center with Balochistan got into difficulties. The center continued for all practical purposes with the two-legged governance model of the British in Balochistan which simply was to grant subsidies to the tribal chiefs (Leg one) and to provide them certain degree of autonomy as long as they were loyal and acquiesced to the imperial directives (Leg two). In the said two-legged model, inclusion of the people in the governance and development figured nowhere.

Pakistan continued with the same strategy. Instead of ensuring broader inclusion of the people of Balochistan in the politico-economic development, the central government handpicked tribal chiefs who were allowed to exercise some amount of autonomy as long as they did not defy the will and the directives of the center. The province is dependent on federal transfer grants for its budgetary and development needs. The grievances of Balochistan from an economic angle can broadly be described under three categories. First category of grievances pertains to development deficit in Balochistan compared to other provinces. Incidence of Poverty and unemployment is high compared to other provinces. For instance, according to UNDP's Multidimensional Poverty Index, 71% of the households in the province are poor compared to national average of 37%. In the rural areas the incidence of poverty is around 85%. While the overall multidimensional poverty dropped by 18 points from 55% to 37% of households between 2004 and 2015, Balochistan's incidence fell by only 10 points, from 81% to 71%. In some districts of Balochistan, poverty even increased during this period. Out of the five poorest districts of Pakistan, 4 are in Balochistan.[103]

Second category of grievances relates to transfer of resources from Balochistan to other provinces (particularly the Gas Grievance). Kaiser Bengali, a Pakistani economist who represented Balochistan in the National Finance Commission (NFC), constitutional body mandated to distribute resources from the central government to the provinces, estimates that other provinces were subsidized to the tune of Rs. 7.69 trillion between the period 1955 and 2014 due to distortions in gas pricing.[104] The gas was discovered in the province of Balochistan in 1952 but it was made available to the province in 1983 while other provinces benefitted out of it for decades. According to Bengali, per capita GDP of Balochistan declined by 5.2% in 1970s and that decline has continued. Third set of grievances is about low development allocations to the Balochistan province. Bengali writes: "While Balochistan has suffered from resource transfers in the form of gas pricing and neglect in the form of abysmally low development allocations, leading to high levels of poverty and deprivation, it has also been ignored in terms of distribution of social security coverage. Even in the Benazir Income Support Program, Balochistan's share stands significantly lower than its population share".[105]

The governance issues are also comparatively severe in Balochistan compared to other provinces. The government structures are weak and riddled with huge inefficiencies, corruption, and lack of capacity reflected in poor public service delivery and human development indicators. The provincial user satisfaction with public goods like health, education, and law and order, etc., is the lowest of the four provinces. Factors like size and structure of the provincial bureaucracy, extent of merit-based recruitment, the quality of career management, political fragmentation, and tribal identity, are some cross-cutting issues which limit the ability of Balochistan's public administration to deliver goods and services.

Balochistan's bureaucracy is biased toward low grades as 28% of public sector jobs are in the lowest skill category (Grade 1) compared to 18% in three other provinces.[106] Loot of public money and rampancy of corruption can be well gaged from the corruption scam, reported in the press in 2016, regarding recovery of Rs.730 million ill-gotten money from the house of finance secretary of the province. By its very design, provincial government in Balochistan is very weak and ineffective. It happens most often that all the legislators of the provincial Assembly, with the exception of very few, are the Ministers and advisors of the executive. So with no opposition, the treasury benches indulge in loot and plunder of the public money and are least interested in the amelioration of the conditions of the people.

Balochistan's ethnic composition further complicates the quandary. The ethnic groups in Balochistan are mostly segregated regionally. Northern and eastern districts, bordering FATA and Afghanistan, are dominated by the Pushto-speaking people while the Southern part is dominated by the Balochi-speaking. Brahui-speakers occupy a north–south corridor along the center of the province. Some concentration of Sindhi-speaking people exist in the Southeast (Lasbela) and the Karachi plain area. Balochistan is not entirely unique for its ethnic or linguistic diversity as sizeable linguistic minorities exists in other provinces as well like Seraikis in Punjab, Hindko-speaking in KPK, and Urdu speakers in Sindh. Ethnic identity can assume two important political dimensions in Balochistan (and Sindh) in two respects compared to other provinces. First, ethnic or linguistic minorities are large in size even to the extent that the major ethnic group might not constitute a majority. Second, the representatives of main ethnic group feel that they are at political disadvantage vis-à-vis the minority ethnic groups.[107]

Ethnic considerations in Balochistan complicate the business of arriving at agreements or consensus on provincial priorities regarding development. Agreements are generally result of concessions to the ethnic groups causing sub-optimum use of resources and development outcomes. Ethnicity also plays role in the placement of civil servants in government's administrative organization. Competition over resources and polarization at the provincial level are well-established trends. "Balochistan's geographical spread, degree of backwardness and marginalization, low population density, complex political landscape, and consistent neglect pose key challenges to the advent of modernity".[108]

Deprivations (vast inequalities, poverty, and low development), and perception of exploitation of resources of the province without payment of due share of receipts have created a sense of resentment and alienation among the people of Balochistan. "The grievances of the Baloch citizens are economic and political, and they are as old as Pakistan itself. High-handed policies in Balochistan including an emphasis on military solutions have aggravated the feeling of alienation among the Baloch. The issue of missing persons is a central point in Balochistan-center ties; the resolution of this issue is the Baloch nationalist leadership's primary demand".[109] The religious landscape of Balochistan has also got more complex in the last few decades. The traditional religious structures, which used to be responsible only for performing religious and social rituals, are becoming socio-political force. The Baloch clerics, sub-nationalist in character, now feel a sense of empowerment due to increase in religious influence and institutions (religious seminaries) in the province. They lacked this feel of empowerment in the traditional social structures. There are around 10,000 small and big madrassas in Balochistan, roughly one madrassa for 1200 to 1300 people (for Sindh and KPK one madrassa respectively caters to 45,000 to 50,000 and 10,000 to 12,000 people).[110]

Baloch also live on the other side of the border that is in Iran. Tehran's harsh treatment of the Baloch fueled Sunni radicalism in Siestan-o-Baluchistan. Several organizations and splinter groups, mainly sectarian, are operating on both sides of the border and their subversive activities sometimes become a big sore in the relationship between the two countries. "Even before the Iranian revolution, ethnic Baloch from Iran migrated to Balochistan and Karachi, engaging in political activities against the Shah of Iran. Over time, the diaspora turned more religious, diminishing the once prominent factor of nationalism seen as a challenge by Iran and Pakistan in 1970s".[111]

In 1970s, Baloch politics in Pakistan and Iran tended toward leftist ideologies. Progressive Baloch and Pakhtun leaders formed government under the banner of National Awami party (NAP) in Balochistan and erstwhile NWFP in the early 1970s until Bhutto disbanded the NAP government in February 1973. The history of ethnic conflict in Pakistan, both before 1971 and post-1971, amply vindicates at least one point and that is, Pakistan instead of resolving these conflicts through political strategies of inclusion, accommodation, and compromise, tried to find solutions by the use of state power. "Even when accommodation and compromise have been applied, they have been largely symptomatic of the state's contrivance in co-opting radical ethnic elites and their respective ethnic organizations without attending to the larger political, social, and economic problems that non-dominant ethnic groups face. This state of affairs and the employment of despotic powers carry the disadvantage of leaving ethnic groups aggrieved in post-conflict situations with the added possibility of further radicalization on the part of a younger generation of ethnic activists in the future".[112]

Summing up the discussion on the challenge of militancy, it can be concluded that militancy, religious as well as ethnic, has badly impacted long-term economic growth and development of Pakistan. The costs of militancy and terrorism are far higher than the official estimates. The phenomenon is quite complex involving both external and internal factors. Externally, Kashmir dispute, Russian-Afghan War, revolution of Iran, and 9/11 are some of the incidents of the history which intensified militancy while internally structural factors such as uneven regional development, sharp socio-economic disparities, less focus on human resource development, bad governance, and interventions by the state in the religion market to strengthen an Islamic identity to the exclusion of other ethno-linguistic identities fomented militant activities. Undoubtedly, Pakistan has achieved a tangible success in containing high level non-state militancy through its counter-militancy strategy mainly through military operations in the militancy-infested areas. However, it is feared that this success would be hard to sustain unless structural divers of militancy and fragility are addressed for sustainable economic growth and prosperity. Negotiations, inclusion, and political bargaining through debate and democratization, and not coercion and opportunism, would set the rules for the massive empowerment of the people and eradication of militancy.

CHAPTER 15

Conclusion

Economic growth generates resources for the individuals which they can invest to improve their lives. It provides resources to the government in the form of taxes which it can spend on the welfare of the citizens. Growth has several other economic and social virtues as discussed in chapter one of this book. High economic growth, for some longer period of time, is critical to pull the people out of misery. The development experience of Asian Tigers and in the very recent past that of China confirm that high economic growth is at least a necessary condition for poverty alleviation. With a growth rate of over 7%, Pakistan can become a middle-income country by 2050 and once it joins the club of middle-income countries, it will just require one decade more to become a developed economy if it maintains the said rate of growth. We have a robust case for high economic growth but the question is how to initiate and then sustain a growth rate of over 7% for three to four decades. The East Asian experience provides some insights which were unfortunately ignored by the South Asian Region in general and Pakistan in particular. The growth miracle of Asian Tigers can briefly be attributed to four factors that are investment in human resource, low initial inequalities, quality public service delivery, and strong state for collection of taxes and rents and making credible commitments. All the said four factors which formed the cornerstone of East Asian development strategy remained lacking in the growth policies and strategies of Pakistan.

J. Nasir, *Development Challenges of Pakistan*,
https://doi.org/10.1007/978-981-97-3064-3_15

Intimate causal connections exist between economic growth, human resource development, learning, health care, quality of public services, and socio-economic equities. A sufficient amount of empirical evidence confirms deep relationship among said variables as discussed at various places in this book. The complementarity between production and productivity cannot be ignored for long-term growth. It is quite intuitive that productivity of labor comes from quality education and better health care. Poor learning outcomes and bad health have huge costs for GDP. Prioritizing human resource development is highly significant for economic growth. Regrettably, Pakistan neglected the human resource development badly. A large number of children of school age are out of school and progress, over the years, for bringing them to school is not that impressive. The problem of the out of school children is not an administrative problem. It is an economic problem (argued at length in the chapter on education).

Majority of the children who are out of school belong to low-income households. Sending them to school has got an opportunity cost for the poor families. Some financial assistance, above the opportunity cost, would be required to bring the OOSC to schools and retain them. Education in Pakistan is a story of expectation failures particularly for the poor due to disconnect between the skills imparted in schools and those needed in the labor market. An entire overhaul of pedagogy and curriculum would be required to make education relevant for economic growth and socio-economic mobility. Single National Curriculum (SNC) is not sufficient to address educational inequities. Curriculum is not just books. It is an overall learning environment. Moreover, learning needs to be distinguished from schooling. It is learning which matters for economic growth. The education policy needs reorientation toward the productive knowledge that is the knowledge of science and technology, which becomes the input for producing goods and services.

Public health care is another area which is deeply connected to human resource development. In the 1960s, China had lower life expectancy than Pakistan but now it is far ahead against this variable. Similarly Bangladesh had lower life expectancy when it separated from Pakistan. Now it enjoys several additional years of life expectancy compared to Pakistan. The public health care system of Pakistan is simply not delivering. It is characterized by sharp inequities. The coverage of basic services like immunization widely differs with region and SES. Analysis of disaggregated data at the district-level reveals glaring gaps in this regard. Half of the population of children is still unvaccinated in number of districts particularly in the provinces of Sindh and Balochistan. Literature on health guides us that early interventions are more effective as formation of health capital begins before birth with fetal development. It means that child health is closely linked with the health of the mother. So, there is a robust case for prioritizing investment in the education and health of the females for effective use of women agency. Bangladesh reaped enormous benefits for the health of children and economic growth by enhancing women agency.

All focus of the existing health care system is on curative health. Preventive health care is badly neglected despite the point that it is more cost-effective compared to curative health. If preventive health care becomes the focus, the health care situation can improve dramatically even with existing resources. Besides focusing on preventive health care, some baby steps like making it mandatory for the doctors to prescribe medicine with the generic names can reduce the burden of out-of-pocket health expenditure. Doing so shall also help abolish malpractices like over-prescription of drugs by the doctors. Legislation on generic drugs was introduced in the 1970s but the said piece of legislation was not implemented effectively. It became victim of vested interests of the doctors and pharmaceutical companies. Revival of the said piece of legislation, with suitable amendments, where so required, can be a starting point for implementation of the said proposal.

We need fundamental changes in the public health care system to make it work for the poor. The Sehat Sahulat Card scheme is a good initiative. Vietnam, an emerging economy has moved toward universal coverage of health care in a short span of time with a similar health scheme. The sustainability of Sehat Sahulat Card shall, however, remain an issue due to political and fiscal factors. A credible commitment to the continuity of this scheme is needed from all political parties. Health care needs to be declared a constitutional entitlement. The right to health is connected to the right to life (Article 9) and right to dignity (Article 14), recognized by the constitution as fundamental rights. There can be no life and dignity without protection of human health. Accordingly, the right to health is squarely covered under the fundamental right which can be made enforceable by the courts through amendment in the Constitution.

Technology can be a big game-changer in improving access of public services cost-effectively particularly in education and health sectors. For instance, data bank about the health of all citizens can be developed through use of technology for preventive health care interventions. Village community dispensaries and rural health centers can be linked to big hospitals where specialist and consultant doctors can provide prescriptions to the patients online to avoid unnecessary visits to city hospitals. In education, customized content can be prepared by the well qualified teachers which can be delivered through technology. China is a pertinent example. It educated more than 100 million children through satellite intervention. Similarly, quality of education can be improved by replicating customized courses offered in the top universities of the world in class rooms where teachers can act just as facilitators.

Quality education could become a vehicle for economic growth and socio-economic mobility but unfortunately, it badly suffers from lack of relevance and quality. Education, instead of working as leveler in the society, is perpetuating stratification due to different education systems. Further, initial inequalities were high in the country due to inequitable distribution of productive resources. Economic inequalities created inequalities of voice and power. The privileged and the powerful dominated the politics and the public policy. They used power and public policy in their favor through tax concessions, exemptions, and subsidies. Domination of the elite over public policy and narratives also caused neglect of the issues concerning the lives of the common people like education, health care, rural non-farm economy, and subsistence agriculture.

The said factors could become big stimulators for economic growth and poverty alleviation but discussions on the real-life issues like public health care, quality and relevance of education, public sector accountability, low intergenerational mobility, economic growth, and reallocation of productive assets are entirely missing from the policy discourse and mainstream media. False narratives built over the years regarding development, nation building, and the state–society interactions have trapped the country in a fog of confusion. Misery, exploitation, poverty, exclusions, and indignity in the society seem to the poor inescapable situations. It is a historical fact that struggle by the people and not benevolence of the state dictated pro-poor and pro-people changes in the system and policies. The French Revolution uprooted the feudal system in France and paved the way for equal rights for all human beings. The peasants and laborers stood up against the Czarist regime and the result was the Bolshevik Revolution in Russia in 1917. The extension of franchise in the West, for example, was due to the threat of revolution as argued by Acemoglu and his colleagues. A series of reforms were introduced in education, health care, and local governance in UK with the empowerment of people.

The case in this book against inequalities is not on moral or ethical grounds. It is rather economic. Inequalities have multiple manifestations. Inequalities of income and gender are in particular big constraints on economic growth. The distribution of income in a society impacts aggregate demand. In case income is widely distributed, aggregate demand via consumption shall be high which shall boost economic growth. An analysis shows that Palma ratio has persistently remained over 3 since the 1980s in Pakistan with slight decrease in few intervening years which means that the top 10% have more than 300% income in comparison with the bottom 40% of the population. The aggregate inequality indicators like Gini and Palma in Pakistan are not worse compared to majority of the countries and regional comparators. These aggregate indicators of income inequality, however, mask the severity and depth of the real issue. For instance, provision of public services to various income groups differs in access and quality but this variation is not captured by the aggregate indicators of inequality. Severity of the issue does not become visible without deep analysis of the disaggregated household data. Persistence of almost same value of aggregate indicators of inequality since decades means that factors of income inequality are structural in nature. Limited intergenerational mobility also confirms existence of the structural nature of the inequality problem.

Structural inequalities are rooted in inequitable distribution of productive assets especially land. Misallocation of land is an economic issue with severe negative implications for economic growth. Pakistan has a valid case for reallocation of land from efficiency, equity, and legal angles as elaborated in the chapter on misallocation of land. The only argument against reallocation of private land in Pakistan would be that it is against the zeitgeist. Ideas, however, never die. Some ideas get shelved in libraries as they are inimical to the interests of those who control narratives and discourse in the society. Some ideas even being beneficial for the society and development do not materialize due to vested interests. In case of reallocation of land, the big land owners will be the losers not only in terms of economic power but socio-political power as well. Reallocation of property rights is an idea which was put on the backburner by the privileged and the powerful. It does not mean that the idea has become irrelevant or redundant.

A comparatively equitable society is a must for long-term economic growth. Japan, South Korea, and Taiwan introduced land reforms in the initial stages of their economic takeoff. In the very recent past, productivity of agriculture and economic growth increased when China introduced land reforms to rationalize land allocation since 1978. Besides reallocation of private land, a large amount of agricultural land is also available with the state. If the state land is distributed among the landless through a transparent process, about half a million households can be lifted out of poverty. Poverty alleviation and economic growth are connected. Both complement each other. When economic growth takes place, it lifts people out of poverty. And when people are out of poverty (poverty is alleviated) they do chores and businesses which have multiplier effect. Consequently economic growth increases. Transfer payments though contribute to aggregate demand but do not have transformative impact. A big push is needed to lift the people above a certain threshold level. Most of the poverty alleviation strategies do not work because they fail to overcome the threshold effects. Some productive assets are needed to initiate a stream of stable income.

A huge capital in the form of government buildings and clubs is lying dormant in the posh metropolis areas. Such capital, if put to commercial use, can create huge dividends in the form of economic growth and employment generation. Misallocation of talent is another area besides misallocation of productive assets which needs policy focus for economic growth. Educated youth, instead of becoming entrepreneurs, prefer to become rent-seekers. There are multiple reasons for this misallocation. Besides difficulties in setting up new businesses, due to high cost of sludge and corruption, norms and culture of the society are also responsible. If rent-seeking is more profitable business than entrepreneurship and social norms do not castigate rent-seeking, people would join rent-seeking professions instead of becoming wealth creators. The right person for the right job can produce enormous benefits for economic growth. If all placements, particularly in the public sector, are done on the said criterion, losses to the economy arising out of red tape and inefficiency can be reduced significantly.

Gender inequalities are also a big constraint on economic growth in addition to misallocation of land and talent. The female labor force participation is an important indicator of the contribution of women to economic growth. The Second Industrial Revolution (1870–1914) in the West owed a lot to the participation of women in the labor market. According to some estimates of the World Bank, if Pakistan improves female labor participation just to equalize it with Bangladesh, huge economic benefits via increase in economic growth are likely to accrue. Opportunities of quality education and female participation in the labor market are important for capitalizing on the potential of women. All sorts of gender discriminations are connected to economic disempowerment. Even discriminations due to cultural and social factors shall decrease with increase in earning power of women. The world experience as well as empirics confirm the said proposition. Selective affirmative action like allocation of seats in the National Assembly or civil services shall not make much difference from the angle of economic growth. Wider participation of the woman in the labor market would be required to alleviate poverty and boost economic growth.

The tax system also plays a vital role for poverty alleviation and inequality reduction. Taxes are primarily a function of economic growth and fiscal capacity of a country. The tax-to-GDP ratio of Pakistan is lower in comparison with countries of the same income level. Pakistan has huge tax potential even at the existing rate of economic growth. Tax collection can at least be doubled given the quantum of consumption component in GDP if leakages in sales tax are plugged. Pakistan is, however, unable to realize the tax potential due to weak fiscal capacities. Rampant tax evasion, corruption in tax machinery, low fiscal effort by the provinces, concessions, and exemptions due to political economy factors are some perennial issues responsible for low tax collection. Resultantly, Pakistan is unable to end its dependence on IMF loans with all negative consequences of the conditionality for long-term economic growth. It is now caught up in a deadly trap of low growth and high debt. Debt servicing expenditure on interest payments leaves little for investment in human development. The only viable option, besides enhancing economic growth, is domestic resource mobilization by strengthening fiscal capacity to control widespread evasion in existing taxes. Moreover, new sources of taxes need to be explored. Wealth tax, real estate tax, and inheritance tax are some sources with huge potential of revenue. The said taxes can be collected even with low fiscal capacity as it is difficult to hide the sources. Effective use of technology and data integration can help in plugging tax evasion and in enhancing collection efficiency of the tax machinery.

Overall accountability of the public sector, besides enhancing capacity of the tax bureaucracy, is required to improve public sector performance.

Contrary to popular perception, public sector employees enjoy significant amount of wage premium over their private sector counterparts. So the issue is not low wages. Rather real issues are weak accountability, disconnect between wages and performance, and inequities arising out of 'in-kind' benefits to public sector employees. Accountability of the entire system, which currently does not punish indecision, lethargy, incompetence, and even corruption, is needed. A new cadre of the public sector employees on the pattern of Japan's MITI or Taiwan's CEPD needs be created with the mandate of economic planning, management, fiscal governance, and formulation of sectoral growth strategies. The ownership of this cadre would be from the top so it does not become victim of civil service intrigues. It would be directly answerable to the Cabinet and the Prime Minister. Improving the capacity of civil servants and overall accountability of the public sector shall make the state strong. Institutions undoubtedly matter for economic growth and development.

Serious introspection is also required about the state–society relations. State and society are not inimical to each other. Both rise and fall together. A strong society is reflective of a strong state and vice versa. And strong state here does not mean a state like that of North Korea. A strong state means a state which is competent to raise taxes, enjoys monopoly over violence, and delivers public goods and services efficiently. Public service delivery is the prime tool of nation building. The tools like threat of the common enemy or bogey of existential threat would not work in a globalized world. Moreover, nation building through public service delivery has got multiple dividends in the form of increase in social capital and decrease in extremism and militancy.

Present socio-economic and governance structures of Pakistan hinder competition and promote monopolies. For instance, entry of new firms is difficult into the market due to corruption and sludge. These factors demotivate the youth to become entrepreneurs, so they prefer to join rent-seeking occupations. Restrictions, both implicit and explicit, on the entry of new firms into the market strengthen monopolies with all attendant negative consequences for efficiency. Competition is relevant not only for businesses and firms; it is also relevant for organizations and institutions. There is need not only to promote healthy competition inside the organizations through a transparent process of performance evaluation but some type of competition would be required from the outside. If an organization or public service delivery department does not have outside pressure, it would not be pushed to reform and improve particularly in an environment of weak internal accountability.

Judiciary and lawyers are pertinent examples to make the point. There is competition among the lawyers for delivering legal services. They argue cases against one another before the judges but as a group they do not face any competition. Neither does the judiciary as an institution. So any initiative for reforming the judicial system or legal service delivery may face resistance. Licensing private adjudicators, creating linkages between the formal and informal justice systems, and improving implementation of administrative laws can be some of the options to introduce competition and induce change in the judicial system. Similarly, absenteeism and low productivity are two perennial issues of the public sector school system. Inducing competition between public and private schools through introduction of school voucher programs can take care of the said issues. Introduction of school vouchers shall give an option to the parents to enroll their children in private schools if the quality of a public school is low.

Existing narratives on economic growth and development need to be debated and challenged for reimagining Pakistan as a progressive and economically developed country. Close collaboration between research institutions, think tanks, and universities is needed to generate ideas and develop new narratives. In the West, 'Economic Societies' were created in the late eighteenth century which facilitated creation, diffusion, and adoption of economic ideas. The said societies had positive long-term effect on development through knowledge spillovers and innovation. Pakistan needs such societies as it badly suffers from what Romer calls 'idea gaps'. Thematic research, on real-life issues concerning Pakistan, needs to be prioritized by the academia and the universities. Encouragement of horizontal networks, cutting across professional and political lines, is vital to deliberate, debate, and disseminate economic ideas to make Pakistan a developed country in the next 20–30 years.

Case Study 1

Misallocation of Talent

The public sector jobs are still the most sought-after jobs in Pakistan. Instead of becoming entrepreneurs, majority prefer to become cogs in the government machinery. Every year, federal and provincial public service commissions conduct recruitment tests for various categories of jobs in the public sector. A large number of candidates appear for the central superior services examination, out of whom, around 2% finally get a job after passing through the rigmarole of written and oral examination, in various service groups and departments like the foreign service, Police, Customs, District administration, Internal revenue service, and Accounts. A major proportion of those who entered the civil service, in the last three decades, had earned academic degrees in medicine and engineering, though they would work, in all probability, as generalists after entry into public sector jobs. They invariably perform supervisory roles in organizations. They are career civil servants and every one of them has bright chances to rise to the top of the organization with the caveats of some work (not necessarily hard work or smart work), luck (matters in every field and sphere of life), professionalism or a semblance of professionalism, connections (shoulder rubbing with politicians or guys of other power circles), and conservatism (revolutionaries, Marxists, those imbued with destructive ideas even if the destruction is creative, or having high enthusiasm to reform the public sector are not required!).

J. Nasir, *Development Challenges of Pakistan*,
https://doi.org/10.1007/978-981-97-3064-3

The second tier of the bureaucracy consists of frontline workers. They are the implementers or what Professor Ang calls "street-level bureaucrats". After independence, for long 50–60 years, they were recruited in the public sector on the basis of political considerations or connections. Since the last decade or so, some change has taken place in the process. Merit is now the professed criterion for their recruitment. Job vacancies or positions are now advertised in the newspapers and public service commission conducts examination. The process is comparatively transparent and merit-based. The frontline workers are the face of the public sector, as the majority of people come into contact with them for obtaining public services like driving licenses, registration of sale deeds and mutations in the land record, registration of complaints, customs clearance of baggage and goods.

The perceptions of corruption are very high in the public sector in general and about the frontline workers in particular. The concerns about the over-bloated public sector and the fiscally unviable pension burden are also expressed, from time to time, by the economists and foreign consultants. Firing of existing workers (recruited on considerations other than merit) from jobs was not possible administratively as well as politically, despite the prevalence of deep rot and incompetence that politically recruited workers had introduced in the public sector. And the novel idea for reducing the size of the public sector and corruption was thus to stop fresh recruitments of frontline workers and abolish the posts or to leave it vacant when any worker retired on attaining the age of superannuation.

Pakistan Customs is a case in point. No recruitments at the level of appraisers, examiners, or other support staff were made in the Customs Department for almost two and a half decades. Resultantly, two problems emerged. First, Pakistan Customs had an aging workforce, which was depleting fast due to retirements. Second, the skills of the old workforce were becoming redundant with emerging technology which was replacing paper and files with machines and computers. In this context, the government of Pakistan recruited about 500 appraising officers and inspectors of Customs in 2017 through a transparent and merit-based process by the FPSC. An analysis of the registration forms and related information submitted by the said employees at the time of entry into the public sector was conducted by this author. Data about their academic qualifications is tabulated in Table A.1.

Face-to-face interviews were also conducted. As a result, it transpired that almost half of the recruited officers were employed in private sector

Table A.1 Analysis of educational background

Sr. No.	*Degree/discipline*	*No (% of total)*
1	Engineers	134 (26.8%)
2	Pharmacists and Veterinary Scientists	13 (2.6%)
3	Law Graduates	36 (7.2%)
4	Economics Graduates	46 (9.2%)
5	Trained as Business Managers	62 (12.4%)
6	With M.Phil. Degrees	19 (3.8%)
7	Dual Degree	16 (3.2%)
8	With degrees social Sciences or general education	174 (34.8%)
	Total	500

jobs before joining the Customs Department. The average age of the entrants was 26–27 years. Interestingly, none of them embarked on an entrepreneurial journey after graduation from the college or university. Those who were working in the private sector before joining the Customs Department were fetching invariably more salary compared to the salary they were supposed to get in the public sector. Some had also accumulated reasonable experience working in the private sector. It needs to be kept in view that the officers who enter the Customs Department as Appraisers or Inspectors do not have a defined career path. Very few rise to the level of an Assistant Collector, after putting in more than three decades of service. The position of an Assistant Collector is an entry level position for a Customs officer who joins the department through the national competitive examination.

The motivation to join the Customs Department, by the Appraisers and Inspectors, for pursuing a career has little probability. Further, the pay structure is fixed according to the grades in the government job. For instance, an employee in Basic Pay Scale 16 (appraisers and inspectors join in this scale) shall fetch the same salary irrespective of the government department one joins. Since the last decade or so, the Federal Board of Revenue (FBR), under the umbrella of which the Customs Department works, has given a performance allowance across the board to its employees. This performance allowance, however, is not supposed to be included in the benefits and emoluments at the time of retirement from service and may be discontinued by the government at any time. The performance allowance is not linked to performance for practical purposes. It is a type of bonus that the department provides to its employees to compensate for the rising cost of living.

Cash rewards can be another possible source of incentive. Cash rewards are currently provided in two forms. The first category of rewards is technically called "Meritorious rewards," given on a quarterly or yearly basis at the close of the quarter or financial year. This reward is generally given to supervisory officers. Practically, nothing is meritorious about this. It is a type of income supplement or bonus. It is not necessarily connected to the performance and productivity of the officers. It is explicitly connected to the grade and position of an employee in the organization. This reward is tilted toward the senior management of the organization. Frontline workers like appraisers and inspectors are generally left out of the scheme of meritorious rewards. The second category of rewards is case-specific, which is given on detection and recovery of tax evasion in cases where special efforts seem to have gone into the detection and recovery of the evaded amount of tax. It is given once in a blue moon. Reward cases remain pending for years even after recovery, and in most of the cases, the reward is not paid. The said reward does not meet the criteria of being quick and significant.

So what were the motivations for the Appraisers and Inspectors to join the public sector? Almost 50% of them were already employed, and to their extent unemployment is not a factor. Those with a background in engineering, pharmacy, or veterinary science education had good chances of a career in the private sector. Those trained in business education had some competitive advantage to become entrepreneurs due to their peculiar training. On the contrary, they preferred to become rent-seekers and not wealth creators. There are multiple sources of motivation for joining the public sector. Factors like widespread unemployment and low prospects of getting a decent job in the private sector are certainly big factors. The security of a job is also an important incentive for joining public sector jobs. A study[1] undertaken by this author to determine the factors affecting the performance of Sales Tax Auditors working in the FBR suggested that job security was one of the important variables for seeking a public sector job.

The misallocation of talent, however, cannot be explained just by the consideration of job security, or economic variables like constraints of credit and high costs of entry into business. Non-economic factors are also at play. Social status and the rules of the game determine, to a large extent, the allocation of talent in a society. And social status may not necessarily correlate with the activities that are growth-enhancing. Priests, lawyers, civil servants, and military officers enjoy higher social status in a society like Pakistan despite the fact that these occupations are not productive from the perspective of wealth creation in the society. Engineers, technicians, and entrepreneurs are more important for economic growth, but their social status is not like that of a civil servant or an army officer.

"In a culture that emphasizes social status, occupational and educational choices are influenced not only by pecuniary rewards but also by non-monetary rewards such as social esteem. The relative weight that a person may put on these two rewards is likely to depend on his non-wage income. Consequently, the distribution of wealth in society affects the incentives to seek high-status activities-----social status is gained by association with a particular group or occupation and all members share the same status irrespective of their ability and non-wage income. Generally, a person's esteem throughout society can depend on his deeds or talents. However, except for exceptional cases, the specific merits of each individual are hard to verify. Schooling and occupation are two easily recognized signals for individual accomplishments-------Since social status depends on relative amount of human capital, it is impossible to increase the status of one occupation without reducing the status of the other".[2] It means social status in a society is not a win–win situation for all groups and avocations. Institutions that are the rules of the game also determine talent allocation.

In a society with strong institutions, talent will be attracted toward productive activities, whereas weak institutions will encourage rent-seeking. Entry into civil service, even for engineering and medical graduates, is considered a big achievement in Pakistan. The situation is similar to the one that existed in Mediaeval China. Those who entered the imperial service were given high rank in the bureaucracy. The competitive examination revolved around subjects like Confucian philosophy and calligraphy. The high social standing enjoyed by the civil servants was denied to the people engaged in trade or industry even if they were able to amass much material wealth. Economic growth and poverty reduction were missing from the entire story of human capital in ancient China.

Another example is that of ancient Rome, where there were only three primary sources of income: landholding, usury, and political payments. Occupations in industry and commerce were at the bottom of the social hierarchy and were often taken up by freedmen that is ex-slaves. Inventions and innovations were despised and discouraged. Economic effort was not a route to wealth prosperity.[3] We observe a similar situation in modern-day Pakistan. Professions and jobs with the potential for rent-seeking are attractive avocations not only due to their rents (in monetary terms) but also due to the social status attached to them. There are many instances where engineers, doctors, and even PhDs entered into the civil service and became cogs in the colonial-era working machine of bureaucracy.

Things changed in modern China. According to some estimates, human capital explains 38% of China's economic growth between 1978 and 2008, and if this period is shortened to 1999 to 2008, the percentage contribution of human capital goes much higher.[4] The allocation of talent can be improved in Pakistan as well by introducing changes in power structures and status symbols. The rules of the games can be altered with a view to reward productive activities and by discouraging rent-seeking.

Case Study 2

Imposed Reforms

Pakistan is among the very few countries which have received high dose prescriptions from the foreign consultants to reform its tax structure. "Indeed, an International Monetary Fund (IMF) technical mission led by Vito Tanzi in the late 1970s was the first to broach the issue of value-added tax".[1] Traditionally Pakistan relied, like other developing and poor countries, heavily on trade and excise taxes till the 1990s. The history of sales tax in Pakistan is, however, very old. After independence in 1947, the Government of Pakistan adopted the Government of India Act, 1935 which assigned sales tax on goods to the states or provincial governments. The Constituent Assembly changed the assignment from the provincial governments to the federal government through Pakistan General Sales Tax Act on March 31, 1948. This law came into effect on April 1, 1948. The tax under the said law was a multi-stage tax which was leviable whenever a sale was effected at a standard rate of six pies per rupee. The dealers having turnover up to Rs. 5000 were not subject to this levy. This was in fact a turnover tax. It led to protests and representations form the trade. The Government constituted a committee to examine the representations and demands of the trade and to give recommendations. The present Sales Tax Act was enacted on the recommendations of the said committee which came into force on July 1, 1951. The Sales Tax Act, 1951 applied only to consumption. The manufacturing and trade

J. Nasir, *Development Challenges of Pakistan*,
https://doi.org/10.1007/978-981-97-3064-3

of goods were brought under the ambit of sales tax by the Taxation of Goods Order, 1960.

Under the Sales Tax Act, 1951, implementation remained with the officers of income tax for long three decades which was transferred to the Central Excise and Customs Department (now Customs) on April 25, 1981 by amending the Sales Tax Act, 1951 through the Sales Tax (Amendment) Ordinance, 1981. In the year 1981–1982, sales tax collection was Rs. 3251.6 million against total collection of Rs. 38,544.4 million by the Central Board of Revenue (now FBR). In 1986–1987, Rs. 6408.8 million were collected from Sales Tax whereas total collection of FBR in that year was Rs. 65,701.7 million. The sales tax collection thus registered an increase of 97% during 1981–1982 to 1986–1987 but overall collection from sales tax remained very low. For instance, in the mid-1980s, Pakistan fared worse in terms of collection from sales tax and income tax even in comparison to other developing countries known for weak collection of inland revenues. Bulk of the revenue was collected from imports (42%). An analysis[2] by Ahmad and Stern of developing countries with different bands of per capita income confirms the above assertions (Table A.2).

The General Sales Tax (GST) was introduced in the country vide Sales Tax Act, 1990 (Act No. III of 1951 as amended by Act VII of 1990).

Table A.2 Pakistan's Tax collection in an international context (in mid-1980s)

All per capita income (US$) *Countries*						
	Pakistan	*In sample*	*0–349*	*350–849*	*850–1699*	*1700+*
% of GDP						
Customs	5.46	5.02	4.94	6.62	5.31	3.19
Sales and VAT	0.91	20.07	1.87	1.43	1.89	3.10
Excises	2.99	1.97	1.64	2.24	1.91	2.16
Income and Corporate	1.90	5.60	2.66	5.50	5.75	8.08
	11.26	14.66	11.11	15.79	14.86	16.53
% of total taxes						
Customs	42	31	39	38	29	15
Sales and VAT	7	12	15	9	10	13
Excises	23	12	13	16	11	10
Income and Corporate	14	29	20	30	30	36

Source Ahmad and Stern (1991)

The sales tax was implemented at the retail stage in 1996. The officers of Customs were responsible for the implementation of the said Act. A reasonable number of officers of Customs were posted just after their specialized training in the Sale Tax offices to manage the said tax and thus they developed a good amount of fiscal capacity to collect sales tax. Things changed in 2009. The administration of sales tax was entrusted to the income tax officers, the advice of the World Bank consultants, under the Tax Administration Reforms Program (TARP). It was a change in tax administration from "indirect vs. direct taxes" to "inland revenue versus trade taxes". Theoretically fair enough. But what was the outcome? The cost of collection increased. The Inland Revenue bureaucracy expanded on the justification that entrustment of new tax to income tax department (now Inland Revenue Service) required additional resources, both physical and human.

Expansion in positions at senior level in the tax bureaucracy is a good proxy for increase in the cost of collection. Creation of an additional position at the senior level means that the number of frontline taxmen also increases. And more offices, more equipment, more vehicles, and more infrastructural paraphernalia are required. If we take number of positions at the senior level as a proxy variable for costs, the policy prescription of the World Bank increased cost of collection at least by 120%.[3] The impact on collection of sales tax was, however, negative. A rudimentary analysis shows that growth of domestic sales tax deteriorated after above said change, as the income tax officers did not have training to manage sales tax and the Customs officers showed reluctance to join Inland Revenue Service (IRS).

The income tax officers started managing the sales tax in 2009. Let us analyze the period of 2014–2015 to 2017–2018 (with base year of 2013–2014) to assess the impact of reform introduced under TARP program of the World Bank. The assumptions for analyzing this period are as follows. First, the period 2009–2010 to 2013–2014 was a bit turbulent period due to multiple factors like bad law and order situation, terrorism, and serious energy crisis. Second, the period from 2014–2015 to 2017–2018 was comparatively a stable period, both economically and politically. Third, PMLN, a political party with long experience of running the country, was in power during the said period (Fig. A.1).

The growth in nominal GDP was 37% during the period 2014–2015 to 2017–2018 (with base year 2013–2014) whereas the impact of additional revenue measures, as per budgetary documents, was 42%. Thus, the total

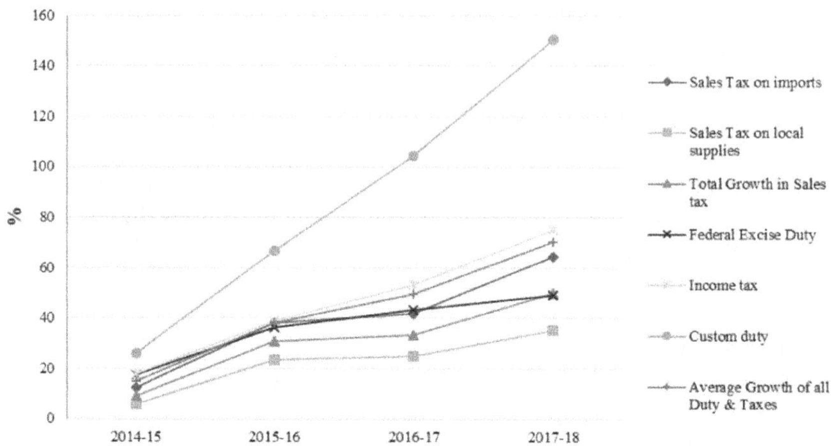

Fig. A.1 Growth in Revenue Collection (2014–2015 to 2017–2018) (*Source* FBR Year 2013–2014 to 2017–2018)

impact comes to 79% but domestic sales tax just registered an increase of 35%, less than even half of what would have been at the minimum collected. Overall growth in FBR revenue during this period was 70.4%, while growth in Customs duty and sales tax at import stage was respectively 150.4% and 64. 5%. The sales tax at import stage is collected by the Customs. So the result, in terms of domestic sales tax collection, for which all reforms like increase in the number of posts at the senior level, physical infrastructure, provision of machines, etc., were introduced under TARP, was simply disappointing.

The issue with the World Bank prescription was that it was imposed without factoring in the local realities. Rather than building on existing capacities, it started afresh. The foreign consultants failed to appreciate that it takes time to build fiscal capacities. The so-called reform is still haunting FBR. According to PBS, Pakistan's nominal GDP for the financial year 2022–2023 was Rs. 67 trillion,[4] out of which GDP from the component of consumption is Rs. 63 trillion which, theoretically speaking, is liable to sales tax at the standard rate of 17%. FBR collects sales tax on goods whereas sales tax on services is the domain of the provinces. FBR collected Rs. 2530 billion as sales tax on goods ending June 2022. The sales tax collection on services during this period by all provinces is Rs. 350 billion. FBR also collects FED (in sales tax mode) and the amount collected under FED was Rs. 320 billion. Collection of all three taxes comes to Rs. 3200 billion against consumption of Rs. 63 trillion.

If all consumption transactions were captured at the standard rate of GST, collection would have been Rs. 10,710 billion which is over 200% more than the collection for 2022–2023. Certainly, it cannot be the case as there are certain items which are exempt from GST like unprocessed crops, animals, meat etc., and certain supplies are subject to reduced rates. In addition to that, there are goods and services which the poor people consume from the informal sector. Let us assume that one-third consumption is not practically liable to sales tax due to said two factors. Simple back of the envelope calculation shows that an amount of Rs. 7140 billion revenue of the Government of Pakistan would be from the sales tax collection, after factoring in exemptions, concessions, and consumption by the poor, thus a gap of over 100% between the potential and revenue collection in actual. Imposed solutions from the foreign consultants (that is planners) often turn out destructive and harmful for the developing countries as local conditions are not taken into account. The change of sales tax administration and consequent fall in the trend of domestic sales tax collection in Pakistan is a little manifestation of the said assertion.

There are big stories as well. Bali's story is a pertinent example to make the point. Lansing gives an interesting account in '*Priests and Programmers*' of a well-intentioned disaster. The story goes that water, central to the lives of the people of Bali, originates from the volcanic Crater Lake, located in the mountain of the island, where the water goddess Devi Danu lives. Bali developed a system of irrigation and water use over the years for rice terraces where temples acted as irrigation managers. This complex irrigation system coevolved with the geological, ecological, social, and religious systems which shaped the landscape of Bali. Farmers were organized in groups called 'subaks'. Most subaks consisted of around 100 farmers who obtained water from a common source usually canal. A complex system of 'water rites' was an important aspect of the social life of the Balinese. Things, however, changed in Bali in the 1970s with the advent of Green Revolution. "In Bali, the Green revolution was accompanied by new government agricultural policies that promoted continuous cropping in an effort to boost rice production. Farmers were encouraged to plant rice as quickly as possible without regard to traditional irrigation schedules. But immediate gains in rice yields produced by this policy soon began to offset by water shortages and unprecedented outbreaks of rice pests and diseases".[5] The moral of the story is that spiritual beliefs and religious rituals which coincided with the planting decisions were beneficial and served to control pests. And poor understanding of the local customs and culture led to policy interventions that did more harm than good.

William Easterly in *'White Man's Burden'* also argues that the imposed solutions by the aid agencies and aid consultants result in sub-optimal outcomes for development and poverty alleviation in the aid recipient countries.[6] Moreover, imported solutions of the local problems devised in the West in the tradition of benevolent despotism and Whiteman's burden trample upon the rights of the people of the poor countries, he argues in the '*The Tyranny of Experts*'. "The global double standard of rights for the rich and not for the poor is very much alive in the technocratic worldview of development. --- The disrespect for poor people shown by agencies such as the World Bank and the Gates Foundation, with their stereotypes of the wise technocrats from the West and helpless victims from the Rest, may become increasingly untenable. Development has to give up its authoritarian mind-set to survive".[7] Easterly is right. The typical consultants and staff who accompany foreign aid are generally narrowly trained technicians from Europe and the USA lacking an understanding of the socio-cultural environment and institutions of the recipient countries and arrogate themselves the role of experts.[8] Foreign aid and advice of foreign consultants most often turn out to be counterproductive as the case study on sales tax shows. Foreign consultants also crowd out local expertise. The technical assistance often brings low-quality consultants.[9] The consultants employed in lender institutions are neither renowned intellectuals, nor big policy experts, and nor are they accomplished academics. The planners are often not exposed to local conditions, culture, traditions, institutions, and political dynamics. The asymmetries of power, information, and knowledge between the donors and the recipients also make the aid ineffective.

Stereotyped solutions generally on the assumption of one-size-fits-all are prescribed and the aid recipient country is coerced to implement such prescriptions how bitter they may be. Such prescriptions are, most often, the perfect recipe for a disaster. The so-called foreign experts eat a reasonable chunk of the aid money in lieu of their consultancy services and crowd out local expertise having negative implications for state capacity. Mazzucato and Collington in '*The Big Con*' point toward the adverse impacts of consultancies and consultants (not related to the aid projects only) on businesses and governments even in the developed countries like the UK. They argue that consultancies have weakened businesses and hollowed out state capacity. "The more governments and businesses outsource, the less they know how to do it",[10] they write. And the solution, they suggest and suggest rightly, is investment by the governments in its own people for creating capable organizations and bureaucracy, instead of wasting money on external consultancies.

Case Study 3

Trade via Zambad

The province of Balochistan is the largest province of Pakistan in terms of area. It is endowed with natural resources and contains about two-thirds coastline of Pakistan. There are huge opportunities of livelihoods in terms of trade but said comparative advantage could not be capitalized due to a host of internal and external factors. Overall human resource development is very low in Balochistan compared to other provinces and regions of the country. Incidence of poverty and food insecurity are high. According to the results of a survey conducted by the Government of Balochistan in collaboration with several aid giving agencies around 74% of the households are moderately or severely food insecure whereas 22% are severely food insecure. Balochistan borders around 900 km with Iran. Trade with Iran can help improve the livelihoods of the people of Balochistan. Pakistan has a preferential trade agreement (PTA) with Iran since 2004 (which became operational in 2006) but practically formal trade is very low rather its volume has decreased over time.[1] Due to trade sanctions against Iran and non-existence of commercial banking channels for payment, both countries are unable to realize the potential of formal trade. Some evidence, based on exporter-level Customs data of Iran, suggests that Iranian firms diverted trade from the USA and EU to Asian, African, and Latin American destinations and successfully managed the negative impact of USA and EU sanctions since 2008. Volume of Pakistan–Iran trade is, however, low and Iran has consistently maintained

J. Nasir, *Development Challenges of Pakistan*,
https://doi.org/10.1007/978-981-97-3064-3

positive balance of trade with Pakistan. The real part of the trade with Iran is the trade taking place through informal channels particularly of Iranian diesel. According to reports, Iranian diesel caters to 20–25% needs of Pakistan.

Drums of petrol and diesel come every day from Iran through "Zamyads", blue pickup trucks which locals call "Zambad". These vehicles are manufactured in Tehran and are non-custom duty paid. While this author was conducting interviews for this case study, some sources on the condition of non-attribution told that record of these vehicles and their drivers is now maintained in the offices of the local administration. The offices of the local administration of the concerned districts issue a list of registered drivers and vehicles every day granting permission to transport diesel via around nine different crossing points.[2] Local administrations for all practical purposes manage the process of registration of local persons and Zamyads and boats (Kayaks) for allowing specified quantity of Iranian oil for local consumption. In-depth interviews revealed that there is an elaborate mechanism to regulate this informal trade. The local administration offices issue token numbers and each individual is allowed to transport 3,000 liters of oil in his vehicle on rotation basis with 2 to 3 trips per month. Around 18,000 vehicles are registered in Ketch District of Balochistan alone, and around 600 vehicles, each carrying 3000 liters cross from one crossing point at Pak–Iran border daily. Similar situation may be observed for District Panjgoor where informal trade of oil takes place through two crossing points. Over 7000 Zamyads are registered in Washuk District for transport of oil from Mashkail in Rakshan Division. Zamyad is a symbol of gray economy and Pak–Iran border dynamics.

The trade is quite regulated except for the point that government revenue in the form of duty and taxes at the import stage is not collected from the informal trade. The amount of revenue which Pakistan can collect at import stage if informal trade of oil from Iran is converted to formal or legal trade is estimated at Rs. 240 billion. The report of an Inquiry commission on shortage of Petroleum products in Pakistan observed in this regard as follows: "Rs.240 billion is not an amount to be overlooked. The question arises as to how such a huge amount gets across the Taftan Border and further across the country with multiple agencies working to curb the menace. Interestingly, inquiry by the Commission has revealed that this huge quantity is brought in 50,000-liter tankers on road from Iran. The border check-posts are primarily manned by Frontier Corps (South), assisted by Pakistan Customs. It is not possible that these huge tankers can cross Iran borders on any other route or on the bare-backs of mules or humans. On condition of non-attribution, sources revealed that the smuggling is carried out in connivance of the government agencies. Once the smuggled goods are inside Pakistani territory, they are further transported to Sindh, Punjab, and KPK. The rate of delivery, however, varies with destination".[3] Manipulations are done in the customs documents such as Goods Declarations (GDs) of LPG and other POL products for the transportation of High Speed Diesel (HSD) to the other provinces of the country. The oil is carried from Iran through Zambads. Rarely HSD crosses the border in tankers. The HSD transported in Zambads is shifted into tankers once it has entered Balochistan for carrying it to other parts of the country.

In Pakistan, informal trade of Iranian oil connotes smuggling, corruption, and cartels of politicians. These perceptions are not untrue. Number of reports appear time and again in the press confirming said perceptions.[4] Even otherwise poor conditions of hospitals and schools in comparison with other provinces speak volumes about rampancy of corruption, bad governance, and low accountability in the province of Balochistan. Instances[5] of outright embezzlements from the public sector development fund (PSDP) have been reported in the press. Balochistan is a tribal society and perhaps socio-cultural norms explain why corruption is a way of life in Balochistan (it does not mean that other parts of the country are corruption-free). The cultural approach to corruption emphasizes that genesis of corruption lies in the socio-cultural norms of the society. Patrimonialism which is human propensity to favor family and friends, argued by Fukuyama, is the main stumbling block to the principle of the supremacy of law and accountability. In a traditional society where people are more attached to their clans and extended families, corruption levels will be high. The interviewees of this case study all were unanimous in their perceptions about corruption attached with informal trade of Iranian oil. Some of them even gave their estimates of the quantum of corruption, names of the agencies involved, point of collection, and method of collection of money on the condition of non-attribution. Revenue foregone and corruption associated with the informal trade of oil are undisputed facts. There are other aspects of the informal trade phenomenon which should not be ignored. Livelihoods of a large number of people who are victim of inhospitable geography depend on informal trade from Iran. Some guesstimates suggest that livelihoods of 2.2 million people are attached with smuggling of Iranian oil.[6]

The phenomenon of informal oil trade is, however, viewed predominantly as an enforcement issue in Pakistan. Viewing smuggling as an enforcement issue, Pakistan has adopted a very wide definition of smuggling.[7] Anti-smuggling operations are conducted in every nook and corner of the country. Businesses may be asked to prove that goods warehoused by them are bona fide imports. The country-wide operation launched in the year 2021 on POL outlets allegedly supplying Iranian oil is reflective of an enforcement approach to combat smuggling. Before the launch of the operation, data was collected from over 2000 illegal petrol retail outlets operating in Pakistan. "As per estimates, the highest number of illegal petroleum outlets are in the Punjab province at 1317, followed by 343 in KPK, 336 in Sindh and 98 in Islamabad Capital Territory and Rawalpindi Division", reported a leading newspaper of Pakistan.[8] Action was initiated against 1612 petrol pumps. Oil valuing rupees one billion (approx.) was seized and cases were instituted and strangely an amount of Rs. 17.5 billion was shown as recoverable on account of fines and penalties.[9] The exaggeration about the success of the operation can be judged alone from the said figure. Perhaps there can be no convincing argument for the recovery of fine and penalty, 17.5 times higher than the value of seized oil. Moreover, no penalty or fine can be recovered unless finally imposed by the court of law.

The crackdown on petrol outlets benefited the Oil Marketing Companies (OMCs), owned either by the state or the elite. Cases were made out on the presumption that the oil being sold at the outlets had been smuggled from Iran. The outlets against which cases were made out were generally small and in few cases medium-sized. The big gasoline pumps were not touched despite complaints that they also sold Iranian oil by mixing it with the oil purchased from OMCs to maximize their profits. At the end of the day even a single penny was not recovered out of the said amount by FBR. The cases landed in the courts of law where actions of the seizing agency were declared illegal. Finally nothing tangible was achieved except infliction of some suffering on the people associated with the POL outlets which were temporarily closed during the crackdown. Informal trade of oil with Iran is more than an enforcement issue. It has got socio-economic, political, and governance angles. The Iranian government provides oil at subsidized rates to its population in the bordering region. They sell it to Pakistani buyers for whom Iranian oil is hugely attractive due to price differential between the two countries with Iran being a net oil exporter having huge reserves and Pakistan being a net importer.

There are hardly any OMC authorized gasoline stations in the bordering districts of Balochistan, so population of Balochistan overwhelmingly relies on Iranian Oil for agriculture, transport, and fishing boats. Economic backwardness and lack of employment opportunities in the bordering districts of Balochistan also make informal trade of Iranian oil attractive. Currently POL products are highly regulated in Pakistan. Only approved oil marketing companies can import petrol and diesel. Due to price differential and monopoly of OMCs over import of oil, supply of Iranian is not confined to the bordering areas and has expanded to the rest of the country. Possibilities exist for converting the informal trade into formal and legal business. For example, quota-based import of diesel and petrol through land routes from Iran can be allowed to private firms and persons at reduced rates of duty and taxes. The PTA in place between Pakistan and Iran can be renegotiated for such an arrangement. Other petroleum products like bitumen, paraffin wax, and LPG are formally imported from Iran on payment of customs duty and taxes. Establishment of "Border Sustenance Markets" at the border in collaboration with Iran would also create livelihood opportunities on both sides.

Notes

Chapter 1: The Case for Equitable Growth

1. Rosenstein-Rodan, P.N. (1961), "International Aid for Underdeveloped Countries", Review of Economics and Statistics, Vol. 43, No. 2, pp. 107–138; Rosenstein-Rodan is known for his 'Big push' theory of development. In this paper, he predicted economic growth for the periods 1961–1966, 1966–1971, and 1971–1976 for all underdeveloped countries. Pakistan was expected to growth at almost double the growth rate of South Korea and Taiwan but in actual their growth rate was much higher than that of Pakistan. Per capita income in South Korea grew at 4.6%, 7.2%, and 6.3% while Taiwan showed growth of 6.8%, 8.1%, and 7.1% during the said three phases.
2. Papanek, Gustav F., 'Pakistan's Development: Social Goals and Private Incentives', 1967.
3. White, Lawrence J., 'Industrial Concentration and Economic Power in Pakistan', Chapter 3.
4. Referred to by the British High Commissioner in his communiqué dated April 9, 1969 (FCO ref: FSP 5/7) to the Secretary of State for Foreign and Commonwealth Affairs. This communiqué related to situation in East Pakistan and distributed among High Commissioners posted in various countries by C.S. Pickard (High Commissioner in Pakistan). Mr. Pickard also referred to his earlier despatches wherein he highlighted the continuing low standard of

J. Nasir, *Development Challenges of Pakistan*,
https://doi.org/10.1007/978-981-97-3064-3

the majority of the population and to the excessive concentration of newly produced wealth in remarkably few hands.

5. Table 14.9, p. 1023, in D. Kumar & M. Desai (Eds) 'The Cambridge History of India'.
6. Ibid., p. 1025.
7. For details see 'Industrial Concentration and Economic Power in Pakistan'.
8. Dr. Haq referred originally to 20 families in his article published in the Business Recorder on April 25, 1968. Haq's 20 families in later discussions expanded to 22 families and the overall concentration problem came to known as the problem of '22 families'.
9. Planning Commission "Socio-Economic Objectives of the Fourth Five Year Plan (1970–1975)", November 1968.
10. Haque & Hussain "A small Club: Distribution, Power and Networks in Financial Markets of Pakistan", PIDE Working Paper No. 2021:3, Islamabad.
11. The Next Convergence—in countries like USA, Canada, Australia, New Zealand, etc., income on average increased from $500 to $10,000.
12. Pilling, David, 'The Growth Delusion: Wealth, Poverty, and the Well Being of Nations', 2018. This book provides an incisive critique of economic growth and GDP in an entertaining and journalistic style.
13. Bhagwati & Panagariya 'Why Growth Matters—How Economic Growth in India Reduced Poverty and the Lessons for Other Developing Countries', 2013.
14. Moyo, Dambisa 'Edge of Chaos-Why Democracy Is Failing to Deliver Growth-and How to Fix it', 2018, Basic Books, New York (pp. 18–21).
15. Friedman, Benjamin M. 'The Moral Consequences of Economic Growth', 2006.
16. Ibid.
17. Dollar, David & Kraay, Aart (2002), "Growth Is Good for the Poor", Journal of Economic Growth, Vol. 7, No. 3, pp. 195–225; this investigation was based on sample data of 92 countries spanning over four decades. These findings of Dollar and Kraay have now been disputed by some poverty economists. The poor do benefit from the affluence and do suffer from economic contraction as well but relationship is not one-to-one. A sizable variation

exists around typical outcomes due to factors like initial inequalities, location, social exclusion, etc.

18. Warr, P (2000), "Poverty Reduction and Economic Growth: The Asia Experience", Asian Development Review, Vol. 18, No. 2, pp. 131–142.
19. Polyani, Karl, 'The Great Transformation'.
20. Quoted by Robert J. Gordon in 'The Rise and Fall of American Growth', p. 72.
21. Quoted by Easterly, William in 'The Elusive Quest of Growth-Economists Adventures and Misadventures in the Tropics', p. 21.
22. Ibid., p. 108.
23. Harari, Noah Yuval 'Sapiens: A Brief History of Humankind', pp. 344–345.
24. Cerra, Valerie, Eichengreen, Barry, El-ganainy, Asmaa, & Schindler, Martin, 'How to Achieve Inclusive Growth', 2022.
25. Hirschman, Albert "The Changing Tolerance for Income Inequality in the Course of Economic Development", in Essays in Trespassing, 1981.
26. Sen, Kunal (2014), "Inclusive Growth: When We May Expect It? When We May Not?" Asian Development Review, Vol. 31, No. 1, pp. 136–162.
27. According to Ha-Joon Chang, growth rate of 5% is considered good while a growth rate of 6% means that a country is entering a miracle territory as growth rate above 10% for a period of over one decade may occur either through some resource bonanza or recovery from war (Economics: The User's Guide by Ha-Joon Chang, 2014).
28. Talbot, Ian, 'Pakistan A New History', pp. 233.
29. See 'Uncertain Glory: India and its Contradictions' for details.
30. See 'India Is Broken—A People Betrayed, Independence to Today', Chapter 1.
31. See article "Measuring Growth Democratically" by Kemal Dervis published on Dec 6, 2019 (Project syndicate).
32. David Card et al. (2012), "Inequality at Work: The Effect of Peer Salaries on Job Satisfaction", American Economic Review, Vol. 102, No. 6, pp. 2981–3003.
33. Mark Vandevelde in his article "What Is Wrong with Inequality?" *Financial Times*, October 17, 2014.

34. Rodrik, Dani (1999), "Institutions for High Quality Growth: What They Are and How to Acquire Them", prepared for the delivery at the IMF conference on Second Generation Reforms.
35. Quinn & Woolley (2001), "Democracy and National Economic Performance: The Preference for Stability", American Journal of Political Science, Vol. 45, No. 3, pp. 634–657.
36. Cuberes & Jerzmanowski (2009), "Democracy, Diversifications and Growth Reversals", Economic Journal, Vol. 119, No. 540, pp. 1270–1302.
37. Jared Diamond, "Four Threats to American democracy".
38. Dr. B.R. Ambedkar is considered the principal architect of the Indian Constitution and was first law Minister of independent India.
39. *The Economist*, "What Has Gone Wrong with Democracy", March 2014.
40. Professor Dani Rodrik, "Rethinking Democracy", Project Syndicate, June 11, 2014.
41. Lipset, Seymour Martin (1959), "Some Social Requisites of Democracy: Economic Development and Political Legitimacy", The American Political Science Review, Vol. 53, No. 1, pp. 69–105.
42. Acemoglu et al. (2003), "Institutional Causes, Macroeconomic Symptoms: Volatility, Crises, and Growth", Journal of Monetary Economics, Vol. 50, No. 1, pp. 49–123.
43. Alesina, Alberto et al. "Political Instability and Economic Growth", NBER Working Paper, September 1992.
44. Aisen & Francisco (2011), "How Does Political Instability Affect Economic Growth?" IMF Working Paper No. 2011/012.
45. World Bank (2013), "Inclusion Matters: The Foundation for Shared Prosperity", Washington, D.C.
46. OECD (2012), "Perspectives on Global Development: Social Cohesion in a Shifting World", OECD.org.
47. See blog "Social Cohesion—Why It Matters?" http://www.imd.org.
48. Estimates by the World Bank for per capita income in year 2021.
49. 'The Next Convergence: The Future of Economic Growth in a Multispeed World', e-Edition.
50. Refer to Lant Pritchett's "Poverty Reduction and Economic Growth", Econofact, February 2, 2020.

51. Dani Rodrik "Growth Strategies", NBER Working Paper No.10050.
52. According to World Bank estimates, there are over 3.2 million SMEs in Pakistan which constitute about 90% of the private enterprises in the industrial sector, employ nearly 78% of the non-agriculture labor force, and contribute over 30% to the GDP. The estimation of number of SMEs and their contribution to GDP may differ depending upon the definition of SME as hardly some consensus exists on the definition of a SME.
53. Parente, Stephen L; Prescott, Edward C. (1999), "Monopoly Rights: A Barrier to Riches", American Economic Review, Vol. 89, No. 5, pp. 1216–1233.
54. The contribution of exports to GDP fell from 16% in 1999 to 10% in 2020. Pakistan exported 0.19% of the global exports in 1990, which fell to 0.12% by 2019.
55. See Box 3.1 of the "Pakistan Development Update April 2021", report of the World Bank.
56. See Pakistan Development Update November 2017; these figures are for the FY 2016–2017.
57. This analysis was conducted for the paper titled "The Tariff Tripod of Pakistan", presented at the conference held on March 11, 2020, under the auspices of PIDE, Islamabad.
58. Joseph E. Stiglitz, "Some Lessons from the East Asian Miracle", World Bank Research Observer (August 1996); also refer to 'The Making of an Asian Tiger by Jamil Nasir', The News International, July 27, 2013.
59. Deininger, Klaus, Jin, Songqing & Nagarjan, Hari K., "Land Reforms, Poverty Reduction, and Economic Growth: Evidence from India", The World Bank, December 2007.
60. Hassan, Javid "Class, Power, and Patronage: The Landed Elite and Politics in Pakistani Punjab", A thesis submitted to the Department of Sociology of the London School of Economics for PhD Degree, London, June 2012.
61. 'Strategy Not Tactics: Better Governance for Social Stability in Pakistan', Institute for Policy Reforms (IPR), Lahore, September 2014.
62. See PIDE's survey "Desire to Live in Pakistan: Stay or Leave", November 2022, Basics Notes No.4; According to reports, 765,000 people left Pakistan in 2022, nearly three times of the

people who left the country in 2021 and 2020. In 2019, 625,000 Pakistanis left the country (report by Express Tribune, December 12, 2022).

63. See IOM's survey "Pakistan: Survey on Drivers of Migration", 2020 (Available Online).
64. See Special report "Why Our Graduates Are Mass Migrating" by Henna Ahsan and Muhammad Jehangir Khan, April 23, 2023; according to this report unemployment rate among the engineers was 11% in 2018–2019 which more than doubled just in two years. The unemployment rate within the medical profession has also increased drastically i.e. by 68% within 2 years.
65. Mentioned by Jamil Nasir with reference to Kofi Annan, former UNO Secretary General in his article "Governance and Human development" published in the Daily Times on August 3, 2011.
66. See "To make the state strong", Jamil Nasir (The News, Op-Ed, May 27, 2014).
67. The Library of Congress country studies; CIA World Fact Book.

Chapter 2: How Deep Are the Deeper Determinants?

1. North, Douglass C. 'Institutions, Institutional Change and Economic Performance', p. 3.
2. Acemoglu, D., Johnson, S., & Robinson, J.A. (2001), "Colonial Origins of Comparative Development: An Empirical Investigation", American Economic Review.
3. Banerjee, Abhijit & Iyer, Lakshmi (2005), "History, Institutions, and Economic Performance: The Legacy of Colonial Land Tenure Systems in India", American Economic Review.
4. Sokoloff, Kenneth L. & Engerman, Stanley N. (2000), "History Lessons: Institutions, Factor Endowments, and Paths of Development in the New World"; this paper explains in detail how factor endowments created inequality and how long shadows of history are haunting the current-day institutions and development trajectories.
5. Tharoor, Shashi, 'Inglorious Empire—What the British did to India'.
6. Dell, Melissa (2010), "The Persistent Effects of Peru's Mining Mita", Econometrica, Vol. 78, No. 6, pp. 1863–1903.

7. Hochschild, Adam, 'King Leopard's Ghost—A Story of Greed, Terror, and Heroism in Colonial Africa', 1999.
8. Ibid., p. 166.
9. Lowes, S., & Montero, E. (2016), "Blood Rubber: The Effects of Labour Coercion on Development and Culture in the CRC", Working Paper.
10. Dell, Melissa & Olken, Benjamin (2020), "The Development Effects of the Extractive Colonial Economy: The Dutch Cultivation System in Java".
11. De Zawart, P., & Soekhradj, P. (2023), "Sweet Equality, Property Rights and Land Distribution in Colonial Java", Explorations in Economic History (also CEPR Discussion Paper DP 17278).
12. De Zawart, P., Gallardo-Albarran, D., & Rijpma, A. (2022), "The Demographic Effects of Colonialism: Forced Labour and Mortality in Java", Journal of Economic History, Vol. 82, No. 1, pp. 211–249.
13. Quoted by Benjamin Jones et al. in their article "Does Climate Change Affect Economic Growth", June 6, 2009, VoxEU.
14. Ibid.
15. Rodrik, Dani, 'In Search of Prosperity—Analytic Narratives on Economic Growth'.
16. Diamond, Jared, 'Guns, Germs, and Steel'.
17. Sachs, Jaffrey D., 'The End of Poverty—Economic Possibilities for Our times'.
18. Galore, Oded, 'The Journey of Humanity', 2022.
19. Gallup, John Luke, & Sachs, Jeffery D. (2001), "The Economic Burden of Malaria".
20. Dell, Melissa, Jones, Benjamin F., & Olken, Benjamin A. (2012), "Temperature Shocks and Economic Growth: Evidence from the Last Half Century", American Economic Journal: Macroeconomics, Vol. 4, No. 3, pp. 66–95.
21. Baumol, William J., Litan, Robert E., Schramm, Carl J., 'Good Capitalism, Bad Capitalism, and the Economies of Growth and Prosperity', 2007.
22. 'The Prisoners of Geography' by Tim Marshall, published in 2015.
23. The Bottom Billion, Paul Collier.
24. Ibid.
25. Talbot, Ian, 'Pakistan: A Modern History', 2010.
26. IMF country Report No. 23/260, July 2023.

27. See report on climate change in the "New Humanitarian", May 19, 2022.
28. See Box 1 of the IMF country Report.
29. See WWF-Pakistan report "Climate Change Adaptation in the Indus Ecoregion: A Micro-Econometric Study of the Determinants, Impact, and Cost-Effectiveness of Adaptation Strategies", produced in collaboration with LSE and LUMS.
30. www.ogimet.com.
31. Climate Country Risk Profile, Pakistan, 2021.
32. 'Good Capitalism, Bad Capitalism, and the Economics of Growth and Prosperity', 2007.
33. Krugman, Paul, 'The Age of Diminished Expectations', 1997, Paperback Edition.
34. Ibid.
35. Lucas, Robert E. (1990), "Why Doesn't Capital Flow from Rich to Poor Countries?" American Economic Review, Vol. 80, No. 2, Papers and proceedings of the Hundred and Second Annual Meeting of the American Economic Association (May 1990), 92–96.
36. For detailed formulation and mathematical exposition of the argument, see "Why Does Capital Flow from Poor to Rich Countries?" August 26, 2013 (http://voxeu.org).
37. Alfaro, Laura, Kalemli-Ozcan, Sebnem, & Volosovych, Vadym (2008), "Why Doesn't Capital Flow from Rich to Poor Counties? An Empirical Investigation", Review of Economics and Statistics, Vol. 90, No. 2, May, pp. 347–368.
38. The World Bank has abandoned publishing this report since 2021 after almost two decades; First report was published in 2003. Before its discontinuation, it covered around 190 economies of the world including Pakistan.
39. ADB "Potential Growth, Misallocation, And Institutional Obstacles: Firm-level Evidence", ADB Economics Working Paper Series No. 480 (April 2016).
40. Bates, Robert H., 'Markets and States in Tropical Africa—The Political Basis of Agricultural Policies', 1981.
41. Hall, Robert E. & Jones, Charles I. (1999), "Why Do Some Countries Produce So Much More Output per Worker than Others?" Quarterly Journal of Economics, Vol. 114, No. 1, pp. 83–116.

42. PIDE (2020), "Total Factor Productivity and Economic Growth in Pakistan: A Five Decade Overview", PIDE Working Paper No. 2020:11, Islamabad.
43. Chen, Kaiji & Irarrazabal, Alfonso (2015), "The Role of Allocative Efficiency in a Decade of Recovery", Review of Economic Dynamics; productivity gains of same quantum are estimated for Mexico during the period 2003 to 2012 due to improvement in allocative efficiency by Meza et al. (2019).
44. World Bank (2020), "Import Duties and Performance: Some Stylized Facts for Pakistan", Report No. AUS 0001593; the effective rates of protection are for the year 2019.
45. Lova, Stefania & Varela, Gonzalo (2020), "Internationally Linked Firms, Integration reforms and Productivity-Evidence from Pakistan", Policy Research Working Paper No. 9349, World Bank, Washington, D.C.
46. Malik, Adeel & Duncan, William (2022), "Obfuscated Liberalization: How Special Interest Groups Capture Trade Policy in Pakistan", PIDE-RASTA (Available Online).
47. Nasir, Jamil (2020), "The Tariff Tripod of Pakistan: Protection, Export Promotion, and Revenue Generation", PDR, Vol. 59, No. 3.
48. The idea of hyperbolic discounting was developed by Richard Herrnstein, a psychologist at Harvard who conducted experiments with pigeons and found that behavior was strongly biased toward immediate rewards. He also found that value of reward and delay to reward are inversely connected.
49. 'The Economics of Self-destructive Choices', p. 12.
50. As per World Bank data for 2021, the investment ratio for Sub-Saharan African region is 23.64%.
51. Sudden Stop refers to a situation when a country experiences abrupt reduction in capital inflows with danger of insolvency; Calvo is professor of Columbia University.
52. See Noah Smith's post "Why Would Pakistan grow", June 25, 2021 (Available Online).
53. Arshad, Zaman, "Social Origins of Debt Crises—Reflections on Pakistan's Experience", December 28, 2022, unpublished manuscript.
54. Alfred Marshall calls it a habit of mind which he says is not common among human beings. "It requires the habit of distinctly

realizing the future, of regarding a distant event as of nearly the same importance as if it were close at hand (discounting the future at a low rate of interest)" (Ref. Principals of Economics).

55. Sunde, Uwe, Dohmen, Thomas, Enke, Benjamin, Falk, Armin, Huffman, David & Gerrit Meyerheim (2022), "Patience and Comparative Development", Review of Economic Studies, Vol. 89, No. 5, October 2022, pp. 2806–2840.
56. The Economics of self-destructive choices.
57. A study undertaken by Banerjee et al. mentioned in the section on poverty.
58. See "The Political Economy of Growth without Development: A Case Study of Pakistan" by William Easterly included in "In search of Prosperity—Analytic Narratives on Economic growth", edited by Dani Rodrik, 2003.
59. Like Sheikh Rasheed (called father of socialism), Miraj Muhammad Khan, etc.
60. Refer to summary of proceedings on PIDE Webinar on "Electoral Reforms in Pakistan", Brief 52:2021 (Available Online).
61. See 'Leadership and Growth', edited by David Brady and Michael Spence, Commission on Growth and Development, 2010, World Bank.
62. Kissinger, Henry, 'Leadership', 2022, Penguin Press, New York.
63. Ibid.
64. The Bottom Billion, Paul Collier.
65. Jones, Benjamin F. & Olken, Benjamin A. (2005), "Do Leaders Matter? National Leadership and Growth since World War II", The Quarterly Journal of Economics, Vol. 120, No. 3 (August 2005), pp. 835–864.
66. Rodrik, Dani, Subramanian, Arvind & Trebbi, Francesco (2002), "Institutions Rule: The Primacy of Institutions over Geography and Integration in Economic Development", NBER Working Paper No. 9305.
67. From 2nd lecture of the Ho RIH HWA Public Lecture Series at Singapore on Asian leadership, October 11, 2014.
68. See "Do Leaders Matter for Growth?" included in 'Political Economy of Bad Governance' by Jamil Nasir, 2021.
69. See 'The Next Convergence'.
70. See 'Leadership and Growth', p. 110.

Chapter 3: Culture and Growth

1. Marx, Karl (1859), 'A Contribution to the Critique of Political Economy', 1979 Edition, New York, International Publishers.
2. See Max Weber's 'The Protestant Ethic and the Spirit of Capitalism'. This was a path-breaking thesis put forth by Weber which helped explain the material rise of the West.
3. Landes, David (1998), 'The Wealth and Poverty of Nations', p. 179.
4. Ibid., pp. 375–376.
5. Polyani, Karl, Avensberg, Conrad M., & Pearson, Harry W., 'Trade and Market in the Early Empires—Economies in History and Theory', p. 250.
6. Ibid., p. 355.
7. Landes, David (1998), p. 269.
8. Guiso, Luigi, Sapienza, Paolo, & Zingales, Luigi (2006), "Does Culture Affect Economic Outcomes?" Journal of Economic Perspectives, Vol. 20, No. 2, pp. 23–48; also refer to "Does Culture Matter for Development?" WPS 7092, November 2014 and NBER Working Paper No. 16368 titled "Culture, Institutions, and Wealth of Nations", September 2010 for discussion of various channels through which culture impacts economic outcomes and behaviors.
9. Mokyr, Joel, 'A Culture of Growth—The Origin of the Modern Economy', 2017.
10. Ibid., p. 19.
11. Ibid., p. 21.
12. Ibid., pp. 120–121.
13. Nelson, Mathew J. (2006), "Muslims, Markets, and the Meaning of 'Good' Education in Pakistan", Asian Survey, Vol. XLVI, No. 5, September/October 2006.
14. Pervez Hoodbhoy in his article 'Why attempts to reform Pakistani education fail?' in Dawn on October 27, 2018.
15. Ibid.
16. Quoted by Professor Abdus Salam in his speech "Islam and Science—Concordance and Conflict", delivered in Paris at the UNESCO House on April 27, 1984.
17. Landes, David (1998), 'The Wealth and Poverty of Nations' p. 185.

18. Acemoglu, Daron & Robinson, James A. (2012), 'Why Nations Fail', Crown Business New York, 1st Edition,(p. 78).
19. Meisenzahl & Mokyr (2011), 'The Rate and Direction of Invention in the British Industrial Revolution: Incentives and Institutions', NBER Working Paper 16993.
20. 'Proceedings of the Pakistan Educational Conference' held at Karachi (from 27th November to 1st December 1947), Government of Pakistan, Ministry of the Interior (Education Division), p. 16.
21. "Report of the Commission on National Education", Ministry of Education, Government of Pakistan, January–August 1959, p. 14.
22. Mokyr, Joel, 'The Lever of Riches—Technological Creativity and Economic Progress', 1990, p. 26.
23. Ibid., p. 124.
24. World Bank (2008), "The Growth Report—Strategies for Sustained Growth and Inclusive Development", p. 41.
25. For detailed discussion see NBER Working Paper No. 3271 by Paul. M. Romer, February 1990; and Charles J. Jones paper "Paul Romer: Ideas, Non-Rivalry, and Endogenous Growth", Scandinavian Journal of Economics, Vol. 121, No. 3, pp. 859–883.
26. See "How We Create and Destroy Growth: The 2018 Nobel Laureates", https://voxeu.org, October 11, 2018.
27. Romer, Paul (1993), "Idea Gaps and Object Gaps".
28. Johnson, Steven, 'Where Good Ideas Come From—The Natural History of Innovation', 2010.
29. See "Flow of Ideas: Economic Societies and the Rise of Useful Knowledge", paper by Francesco Cinnirella and others, June 2022. This paper examines the role of economic societies in the industrial rise of Germany.
30. For detailed discussion, see Reinert, Erick S. (2007), 'How Rich Countries Got Rich—And Why Poor Countries Stay Poor'.
31. Koren, Miklos & Tenreyro, Silvana (2007), "Volatility and Development".
32. Hamna, Ahmed, "Patterns of Export Diversification: Evidence from Pakistan".
33. The Observatory of Economic Complexity, MIT.
34. Hausmann, Ricardo, Hwang, Jason & Rodrik, Dani (2006), "What You Export Matters", NBER Working Paper No. 11905.
35. The Observatory of Economic Complexity, MIT.

36. Hidalgo, Cesar, 'Why Information Flows'.
37. Ibid., p. 152.
38. Gordon, Robert J. (2012), "Is U.S. Economic Growth Over? Faltering Innovation confronts the Six Headwinds", NBER Working Paper No. 18315.
39. Cowen, Tyler 'The Great Stagnation—How America Ate All the Low-Hanging Fruit of Modern History, Got Sick, and Will (Eventually) Feel Better', 2011, Dutton.
40. Aghion, Philippe, Antonin, Celine & Bunel, Simon, 'The Power of Creative Destruction—Economic Upheaval and the Wealth of Nations', 2021, pp. 142–144.
41. Moscona, Jacob & Sastry, Karthik A. (2022), "Inappropriate Technology: Evidence from Global Agriculture", October 7, 2022.
42. The Power of Creative Destruction (2021), pp. 138–142.
43. Refer to "The World Management Survey at 18: Lessons and the Way Forward", Oxford Review of Economic Policy, Vol. 37, No. 2, 2021, pp. 231–258.
44. Other factors which have consistently been rated at the top are political instability, policy uncertainty, corruption, macroeconomic instability, and hurdles in access to finance.
45. Nasir, Jamil (2020), 'Development for an Equitable Society', pp. 110–111.
46. Michael Porter, "Competitiveness in a Globalized World: Michael Porter on the Microeconomic Foundations of the Competitiveness of Nations, Regions and Firms".
47. Andrea Boltho, 'The Assessment of International Competitiveness', Oxford Review of Economic Policy, Vol. 12, No. 3, Autumn 1996.
48. 'Why Nations Fail', p. 77.
49. Romer, Paul M. (1994), 'Economic Growth and Investment in Children', Daedalus, Vol. 123, No. 4, Health and Wealth, pp. 141–154.
50. Nasir, Jamil, "Economic Development and Structural Transformation: Analyzing Pakistan's Case", Criterion Quarterly.
51. Rashid Amjad, Nadeem ul Haque & Christopher Colclough (2005), "Skills and Competitiveness: Can Pakistan Break Out of the Low-Level Skills Trap?" Pakistan Development Review, PIDE, Islamabad.

52. Giavazzi, Francesco, Petkov, Ivan & Schiantarelli, Fabio (2014), "Culture: Persistence and Evolution" NBER Working Paper 20174.
53. 'The Wealth and Poverty of Nations'.
54. Eswaran, Mukesh, Ramaswami, Bharat & Wadwha, William (2013), 'Status, Caste, and the Time Allocation of Women in Rural India', Economic Development and Cultural Change, Vol. 61, No. 2, pp. 311–333.
55. See World Bank's "Human Capital Review", 2022.
56. Ibid.

Chapter 4: The Question of Education

1. This quotation is from Alfred Marshall's Principles of Economics, e-Book Edition by Palgrave Macmillan, New York (p. 179).
2. Becker, Gary S. (1995) "Human Capital and Poverty Alleviation", HRO Working Paper 14458, World Bank.
3. An Uncertain Glory.
4. Piketty, Thomas, 'Capital in the Twenty-First Century'.
5. Rohner and A Saia (2019), "Education and Conflict: Evidence from a Policy Experiment in Indonesia", CEPR Discussion Paper.
6. Glaeser, Edward L., Ponzetto, Giacomo A.M., & Shleifer, Andrei (2007), "Why Does Democracy Need Education", Journal of Economic Growth, Vol. 12, pp. 77–99.
7. This figure is taken from the Highlights of the report on Pakistan Education Statistics, released in January 2024 (complete report is not publicly available). According to said report around 39% children are out of school at the national level. As complete report is not available so, analysis is based on previous publicly available report and PSLM survey. The figures about out of school children have remained under dispute. For example, Alif Ailaan in its report '25 million promises broken' published in 2014 estimates the number of out of school children at 25 million. The absence of true estimates points towards the confusion and lack of focused policy for bringing OOSC children to school.
8. These figures are based on official version of the Federal Ministry of Education and Professional Development, Government of

Pakistan, presented in the meeting of the Federal Cabinet held on March 9, 2021.

9. The National Education Policy 2009 recognizes commitment gap and implementation gap as two top factors for poor state of education. While discussing commitment gap, the NES 2009 says that commitment gap was mainly due to two factors, i.e. lack of belief in education's role in socio-economic development and second lack of belief in the goals set out in the education policies per se.
10. "Schooling and Labor Market Consequences of School Construction in Indonesia: Evidence from an Unusual Policy Experiment", Esther Duflo, NBER Working Paper. This is called INPRES program. The findings of Duflo suggest that children aged 2–6 in 1974 got 0.12–0.19 years of more schooling for each new school built per 1,000 children. A significant proportion of population was able to complete primary education. The wages witnessed an increase of 1.5–2.7% for each additional school. The cost–benefit analysis confirmed that the discounted lifetime gains in the wages of the generation exposed to this program of school building were more than the cost of the program.
11. Akresh, R., Halim, D., & Kleemans, M. (2018), "Long-Term and Intergenerational Effects of Education: Evidence from School Construction in Indonesia", NBER Working Paper 25265.
12. 'Proceedings of Pakistan Educational Conference', held at Karachi from 27th November to 1st December 1947, Ministry of the Interior (Education Division), Government of Pakistan (p. 28).
13. See Report of the Commission on National Education, 1959 (known as Sharif Commission report).
14. 'The New Education Policy of the Government of Pakistan', Ministry of Education and Scientific Research, Government of Pakistan, Islamabad, March 1970, p. 4.
15. 'The Education Policy 1972–1980', Government of Pakistan, Ministry of Education, Islamabad, March 1972.
16. National Education Policy and Implementation Programme, Government of Pakistan, Ministry of Education, Islamabad, 1979.
17. Pak Alliance for Maths and Science (2021), "The Missing Third: An Out of School Study of Pakistani 5–16 Year Olds".

18. "Overriding Social Inequality? Educational Aspirations versus the material realities of rural families in Pakistan", chapter included in 'Reforming Education and Challenging Inequalities in Southern Contexts', edited by Pauline Rose et al., 2021, Routledge.
19. The statistics pertain to year 2017–2018.
20. In 2013–2014 survival rate was 67% which went down to 63% in 2017–2018, the latest figures available as per Education Statistics.
21. "Causes of Dropout Rate at Primary Level in School", IJCI (2019).
22. Mentioned by Natalie Basu and Jishnu Das in their article "The Analytical Angle: Do Children Really Learn in Schools in Pakistan?" Dawn, July 16, 2021, with reference to a LEAPS study. The LEAPS data tracked and tested children who dropped out between grades 5 and 6.
23. EBA (2016), "Education in Developing Countries: What Policies and Programs Affect Learning and Time in School", Rapport 2016:02 (can be accessed online).
24. Quoted in 'The Rebirth of Education', Lant Pritchett, Centre by Global Development, 2013.
25. Why Nations Fail, p. 79.
26. OECD (2006), "Education at a Glance: OECD Indicators"; The Gini coefficient is almost double in countries with more private schooling compared to countries where primary and secondary education is provided by the public sector.
27. de la Croix, David & Doepke, Matthias (2007), "To Segregate or to Integrate: Education Politics and Democracy", CEPR Discussion Papers No. 5799.
28. Andrabi, Tahir et al. (2006), "A Dime a Day—The Possibilities and Limits of Private Schooling in Pakistan", WPS 4066.
29. Das, Jishua et al., "Learning Levels and Gaps in Pakistan", WPS 4067.
30. Ghuman, Sharon & Liyod, Cynthia (2010), "Teacher Absence as a Factor in Gender Inequalities in Access to Primary Schooling in Rural Pakistan", Comparative Education Review.
31. "Pakistan: Can Private Schools Catering to the Poor Increase Access and Improve Learning?" World Bank
32. Felipe Barrera-Osario and Dhushyanth Raju, "Teacher Performance Pay—Experimental Evidence from Pakistan", 2015, WPS 7307.

33. An Uncertain Glory, p. 132.
34. Shahid Kardar in his article "Private Sector in Education", included in Pakistan at 70, Routledge, 2019.
35. AEPAM (2018), "Public Financing in Education Sector", Ministry of Federal Education and Professional Development, Islamabad; the latest figures are for the Year 2016–2017 (Table 21). These figures seem to be on the lower side. The latest figure quoted by an Ex-Finance Minister of Pakistan are bit higher. According to him the province of Punjab spends over Rs. 2500 per month (Rs. 31,000 per annum), KP spends over Rs. 3000 (Rs. 38,000 per annum), Sindh over Rs. 3300 per month (Rs. 40,000 annually) and Balochistan over Rs. 5000 per month (Rs. 61,000 per annum) (refer to Dawn, December 22, 2022).
36. See "Our failure to educate", an opinion piece by Miftah Ismail, former Finance Minister of Pakistan, in Dawn, December 22, 2022.
37. An Uncertain Glory (pp. 141–142).
38. "Crowding in Private Quality: The Equilibrium Effects of Public Spending in Education", by Tahir Andrabi et al., NBER Working Paper 30929, February 2023.
39. Alderman, Harold et al. (2001) "School Quality, School Cost, and the Public/Private School Choices of Low-Income Households in Pakistan".
40. Case, Anne, & Deaton, Angus (1999), "School Inputs and Educational Outcomes in South Africa".
41. ASER, 2019.
42. Dang, Hai-Anh et al. (2020), 'What Explains Vietnam's Exceptional Performance in Education Relative to Other Countries? Analysis of the 2012 and 2015 PISA Data', Risc Working Paper 20/036, March 2020.
43. In urban areas 70% of the children enrolled in Grade-V could read in the local language, 67% can read sentences in English and 66% can do division whereas for rural areas these figures respectively are 59%, 55% and 57%. ASER Pakistan2019 (p. 14).
44. TIMMS, 20119.
45. Kalil, Ariel (2014), "Inequality Begins at Home: The Role of Parenting in the Diverging Destinies of Rich and Poor Children", NSFI, Vol. 5.

46. Hoff, Erika (2003), "The Specificity of Environmental Influence: Socioeconomic Status Affects Early Vocabulary Development via Maternal Speech", Child Development, September/October 2003, Vol. 74, No. 5, pp. 1368–1378.
47. Das, J. (2018), "Should I Stop Kidding Myself That Learning Leads to Educational Opportunity?"
48. Lupien, S.J., King, S., Meaney, M.J., & McEwan, B.S. (2000), "Child's Stress Harmone Levels Correlate with Mother's Socioeconomic Status and Depressive State", Biological Psychiatry, Vol. 48, No. 10, pp. 96–980.
49. Akmal, Maryam & Pritchett, Lant (2019), "Learning Equity Requires More Than Equality: Learning Goals and Achievement Gaps Between the Rich and the Poor in Five Developing Countries", www.cgdev.org.
50. Gust, Sarah, Hanushek, Eric A., & Woessmann, Ludger (2022), "Global Universal Basic Skills: Current Deficits and Implications for World Development", NBER Working Paper 30566; basic skills are defined by these researchers as skills needed to participate effectively in modern economies, i.e. the most basic level of the international PISA test (PISA Level 1 Skills).
51. Pritchett, Lant & Viarengo, Martina (2023), "The Learning Crisis of Developing Country Elites: Lessons from PISA-D", World Bank Economic Review, pp. 1–28.
52. Ibid.; quoted with reference to Stern et al. (2021).
53. "Where Has All the Education Gone", Pritchett, Lant, World Bank Economic Review, Vol. 15, No. 3, 2001.
54. 'Education and Economic Growth', Benos, N., & Zotou, S. (2013), World Development.
55. See article "Rethinking the Received Wisdom on Education: Alternative Policy Lessons", January 6, 2016, http://voxeu.org.
56. 'The Role of Education Quality in Economic Growth', WPS 4122, February 2007.
57. "Economic Growth in Developing Countries: The Role of Human Capital" by Eric A. Hanushek Economics of Education Review, 2013.
58. "Schooling, Cognitive Skills, and the Latin American Growth Puzzle", NBER Working Paper 15066, 2009.
59. "Measuring Human Capital Using Global Learning Data", Angrist et al. (2021).

60. This database is publically available and can be downloaded and analyzed. The data is one of the core ingredient of World Bank's Human Capital Project (HCP). In case of Pakistan, it contains score of reading only while in case of many other countries, scores for mathematics and science are also included.
61. The Human Capital Index (HCI) is composed of three components. First component is survival which is measured using under 5 mortality rates taken from the UN Child Mortality Estimates. Second component is 'Expected Learning—Adjusted years of schooling' and as such this component combines information of quantity and quality of education. The quantity is measured as number of years which out of three components of its composition contains one component about education. The component of education is composed of two sub-components, i.e. expected years of schooling a child can obtain by the age of 18 in a country and the quality of education determined from harmonized test scores from major international student achievement testing programs. Third component is health related. The latest data available is for the year 2020.
62. Quoted by Nicole Torpey-saboe in "Measuring Education Inequality in Developing Countries", 2019, Palgrave Macmillan.
63. "The Effect of Increasing Human Capital Investment on Economic Growth and Poverty", World Bank Policy Research Working Paper 8590, 2018.
64. "What Capital Is Missing in Developing Countries?" American Economic Review: Papers and Proceedings (May 2010).
65. The Rebirth of education.
66. "Improving School Education Outcomes in Developing Countries: Evidence, Knowledge, Gaps, and Policy Implications", Paul Glewwe & Karthik Muralidharan, RISE Working Paper 15/001, October 2015.
67. "What Really Works to Improve Learning in Developing Countries? An Analysis of Divergent Findings in Systematic Reviews", David K. Evans & Anna Popova, 2016.
68. "How Much Can We Remedy Very Low Learning Levels in Rural Parts of Low-Income Countries? Impact and Generalizability of a Multi-Pronged Para-Teacher Intervention from a Cluster-Randomized Trial in Gambia", Alex Eble et al., 2020, Journal of Development Economics.

69. "Education in Africa: What Are We Learning?" Working Paper 542, Centre for Global Development, August 2020.
70. Banerji, Rukmini (2015), "How Do Systems Respond to Disruptive Pedagogic Innovations? The Case of Pratham in Bihar", RISE-WP-15/002. This paper discusses in detail through case study approach as to what works effectively for improving learning outcomes and concludes that fixing pedagogy is the most effective theory of change for improving learning outcomes.
71. Banerjee et al., 'Remedying Education: Evidence from Two Randomized Experiments in India'.
72. Silliman, Mikko & Vitranen, Hanna (2021), 'Labour Market Returns to Vocational Secondary Education', American Economic Journal Applied Economics.
73. "Hard and Soft Skills in Vocational Training: Experimental Evidence from Colombia", NBER Working Paper 2548 (2020).
74. Young Omang, "Mapping of Life Skills Based Education in Punjab's Curriculum and Text Books".
75. "Skill for Growth and Development: A Technical and Vocational Education and Training (TVET) Policy for Pakistan" (2018), Ministry of Federal Education and Professional Training, Government of Pakistan, Islamabad (p. 21).
76. Muralidharan, Karthik & Singh, Abhieet (2020), "Improving Public Sector Management at Scale? Experimental Evidence on School Governance in India", NBER Working Paper 28129. This paper presents results from a large-scale experimental evaluation of an intervention to improve management in Indian public schools. The intervention adopted several best global practices including comprehensive assessments, detailed school ratings and customized school improvement plans but results of the evaluation suggest that intervention had no impact on school functioning as well as student outcomes which means that even well-designed programs based on administrative measures of compliance may be ineffective in practice. The most plausible reason of failure lies in weak bureaucratic incentives which generally reward paperwork and appearance of activity rather than improved outcomes.
77. 'Creativity in Schools: A 21st Century Need', PIDE Policy Viewpoint No. 21 (2020); The policy viewpoints are not based on rigorous research but are based on opinions and views of the

people expert of their areas and working on ground, so policy viewpoints contain practical policy insights.

78. 'An Investigation into the Factors Enhancing or Inhibiting Primary School Children's Creativity in Pakistan', Doctoral Dissertation, University of Birmingham.
79. The Murder of History by K. K. Aziz.
80. Quoted from Faisal Bari's opinion piece "Education Plans: A Suggestion", Daily Dawn, May 13, 2022.
81. NEMIS-PIE (2023), "Pakistan Education Statistics 2020–2021", February 2023, Ministry of Education and Professional Development, Islamabad.
82. Dissecting National Single Curriculum by Dr. A.H. Nayyar, Dawn, EOS, July 31, 2020.
83. Promoting anti-science via text books by Pervez Hoodbhoy, Dawn, December 3, 2016.
84. This one man commission was constituted in the context of a Supreme Court judgement given in 2014 which required the federal government to set up a task force for inter alia devising a strategy on religious tolerance and revisiting curriculum for the promotion of a culture of tolerance. The report of the commission was, however, not acceptable to both the Council of Islamic Ideology (CII) and the National Commission on Minorities.
85. This concept is associated with Carl Rogers, a human psychologist. The term is basically used to describe a client-centered therapy technique which impliedly means that uniqueness of each person should be appreciated and valued.
86. Lant Pritchett has argued it at length in his papers.
87. "School Feeding Programs and Development: Are We framing the Question correctly?" World Bank Research Observer.
88. "Raising the Floor on Learning Levels: Equitable Improvement Starts with the Tail", RISE Insight Note, August 28, 2017.
89. The 10th grade examination has total marks of 1100 and number of students in the year 2021 got 1100/1100 marks and if we go by the proposition that marks earned in the examination are true test of the intelligence and learning, then the students who got 1100 should not be less genius than Einstein and Newton but majority of them could not pass basic test of writing and comprehension conducted by the colleges for admission into first year

which speaks volumes about the examination system and learning outcomes in Pakistani schools.

90. Shehzad Roy, singer and education activist quoted by Nadia Naviwala in his article "Thoughts on the World Bank's Learning Poverty", Asia Program, Wilson Centre, February 25, 2020.
91. Aziz, Mehnaz et al. (2014), "Education System Reform in Pakistan: Why, When, and How? IZA Policy Paper No. 76.
92. British Council (2020), "The University Research System in Pakistan", available on line on PIDE website.
93. See "Our universities have turned into junk factories" by Pervez Hoodbhoy (MIT Technology Review, Pakistan); "Let us stop promoting Corruption in Pakistan's Universities" (The Express Tribune, June 4, 2013) and; "Plagiarism is but one Symptom" by Dr. Nadeem Ul Haque (The News, July 23, 2015); Please also refer to Pervez Hoodbhoy (2009), "Pakistan's Higher Education System—What Went Wrong and How to Fix It", PDR, Vol. 48, No. 4, Part II, Winter, pp. 581–594.
94. Soraya, S.H. et al. (2022), "Exploring the Research Landscape in a Developing Country: Gauging the Prospects of Growth, Research Impact and Innovation", Transforming Government: People, Process and Policy, Vol. 16, No. 4, pp. 567–581.
95. Known economist Ronald Coase is an example who hardly wrote 10 papers in his entire life but he is known for his two papers 'The Nature of Firm (1937)' and 'The problem of Social Cost (1960)' which had profound impact on economic thought and helped establish discipline of 'Law and Economics'. Similarly, John N. Nash wrote few papers but his contribution to game theory set in motion big changes in economic thought and in the disciplines of mathematics. Both Coase and Nash won Nobel prizes for their original contribution to knowledge.
96. Cohen, Stephen P. and others 'The Future of Pakistan', 2001, Brookings Institution Press, Washington, DC (p. 17).
97. "Improving Education in the Developing World: What Have We Learned from Randomized Evaluations?" Michael Kremer & Alaka Holla (2009), Annual Review of Economics Vol. 1, pp. 513–542.
98. "The Effect of Computer-Assisted Learning on Students', Long-Term Development", Nicola Bianchi et al. (2020).

99. "Beyond the Basics: Improving Post-Primary Content Delivery Through Classroom Technology" (2019), NBER Working Paper 25704.
100. In 2014–2015, share of education spending in the budgets of Punjab, Sindh, KP, and Balochistan in percentage terms was respectively 24, 21, 26, and 21. In 2018–2019, it was respectively 19, 18, 26, and 18% as per latest available statistics. Per student cost has also declined in case of Province of Punjab (from Rs. 18,222 in 2014–2014 to Rs. 16,069 in 2018–2019). In case of other three provinces there is increase in per student cost in rupee terms. Per student cost is considered at least a crude measure of the quality of education but it remains doubtful whether with increase in per student cost in three provinces quality of education has improved.
101. These figures have been taken from the Webinar Brief No. 3: 2020 available on PIDE website.
102. World Economic Forum, "Schools of the Future: Defining New Models of Education for the Fourth Industrial Revolution", January 2020, www.weforum.org.
103. PEC Report, March 2019, http://www.pec.org.pk.
104. The data is available on website of Punjab Bar Council (http://pbbarcouncil.com); other provinces also maintain data for the advocates registered with the respective Bar councils.
105. Murphy et al. (1991). "The Allocation of Talent: Implication for Growth", Quarterly Journal of Economics, Vol. 106. No. 2, pp. 3–530.
106. Maloney et al. (2017), "Engineers, Innovative Capacity and Development in the Americas", CESifo Working Paper No. 6339.
107. Olson, Mancur (1992), "Do Lawyers Impair Economic Growth?" Law and Social Inquiry, Vol. 17, No. 4, pp. 625–633.
108. Baumol, William J. (1990)," Entrepreneurship: Productive, Unproductive, and Destructive", Journal of Political Economy, Vol. 98, No. 5, Part 1, pp. 893–921.
109. Baumol, William J., 'The Free-Market Innovation Machine: Analyzing the Growth Miracle of Capitalism', 2002, Princeton University Press, Princeton, New Jersey, USA (p. 76).
110. North, Douglas, 'Institutions, Institutional Change, and Economic Performance', 1990.

Chapter 5: The Problem of Public Health Care

1. The report said that returns to investment in health in developing countries were as high as 500%. Accordingly, the report recommended that more investment is needed in particular poor and developing countries to scale up access of the poor to health facilities and thus made a case for foreign aid to the poor countries.
2. Bloom, D.E. & Canning, D. (2002), "The Health and Wealth of Nations", Science Vol. 287, pp. 1207–1209; also refer to Currie J., & Vogel, T. (2012), "Lasting Effects of Childhood Health in Developing Countries", VoxEU.org, November 15, 2012.
3. Cervellati & Sunde (2011), "Life Expectancy and Economic Growth: The Role of Demographic Transition", Journal of Economic Growth, Vol. 16, pp. 99–133; This paper highlights impact of greater life expectancy in post-demographic transition and also postulates that greater life expectancy accelerates the process of demographic transition.
4. Bloom et al. (2020), "The Contribution of Female Health to Economic Development", Economic Journal, Vol. 130, pp. 1650–1677.
5. See "Health and Economic Growth: Reconciling the Micro and Macro Evidence" by David Bloom et al., VoxEU, September 7, 2022; In this article the authors have reconciled both micro and macro evidence about role of health in economic growth and have concluded that both type of evidences confirm positive role of better health on economic growth and development.
6. Hoyt Bleakley in paper 'Health, Human Capital, and Development' has discussed a wide range of micro evidence to show that health is human capital per se as well as an input for producing several forms of human capital. Health and development are connected though health may not necessarily be single factor for development.
7. See "Worms: Identifying Impacts on Education and Health in the Presence of Treatment Externalities", Econometrica, Vol. 72.
8. There exists strong correlation between health and happiness and health includes both physical and mental health. According to WHR, 2013, on average 10% of the population of the world suffers from clinical depression or anxiety disorders.
9. Pritchett & Summers (1993), "Wealthier Is Healthier", The Journal of Human Resources, Vol. 31, No. 4, pp. 841–868.

10. See report of Commission on Growth and Development formed under the chairmanship of Michael Spence. Also refer to Chapter 3 on Health and Economic Growth by David. E Bloom and David Canning and Samuel Preston's paper 'The Changing Relation Between Mortality and Level of Economic Development" (1975).
11. In South Asian region, Sri Lanka has always remained an outlier which despite low income had on average high life expectancy at birth compared to other regional counties. More literacy rate and use of women agency may be some plausible reasons. The income-health relation also defies the experience of Pakistan which witnessed good rates of economic growth but increase in life expectancy was not commensurate with increase in income levels which points towards neglect of health in national priorities.
12. Here is an egg and chicken issue; the effect may be from good health to economic growth and from economic growth to improvements in health. Some papers have even disputed the claim that increase in life expectancy has any significant impact on GDP. Please see "Disease and Development: The Effect of Life Expectancy on Economic Growth" by Daron Acemoglu and Simon Johnson (NBER Working Paper No. 12269) and "When Does Improving Health Raise GDP?" by Quamrul H. Ashraf et al. (NBER Working Paper No. 14449).
13. See for details World Bank's Policy Research Working Paper No. 9418, September 2020.
14. "Mortality Inequality" by Sam Peltzman (2009), Journal of Economic Perspectives, Vol. 23, No. 4.
15. See 'The Evolution of Longevity: Evidence from Canada', NBER Working Paper 24929, August 2018. Comparing evolution of longevity between US and Canada, this paper finds that longevity gradient in Canada has shifted uniformly across earnings distribution meaning thereby all segments got benefitted equally from gains in income but same is not the case with evolution of longevity in US. Implication is that policies do determine the gains of income which shall not automatically accrue uniformly to all segments of the society.
16. "The Relationship Between Life Expectancy and Income in the United States, 2001–2014" by Raj Chetty et al. NBER Working Paper (2015).

17. Dwyer-Lindgren et al. in "Inequalities in Life Expectancy Among US Countries, 1980 to 2014 Temporal Trends and Key Drivers".
18. For details, see "The Causal Effects of Place on Health and Longevity", NBER Working Paper 29321, October 2021.
19. "Situation Analysis of Health Care System of Pakistan: Post 18 Amendments" by S.A. Khan (2019), available on line.
20. This data is available on line on the official Website of WHO.
21. "When Do Newborns Die? A Systemic Review of Timing of Overall and Cause-Specific Neonatal Deaths in Developing Countries" by Sankar, M.J. et al., Journal of Perinatology (2016). This review says that 6.3 million children under the age of 5 die globally annually out of which 44% deaths occur in the neonatal period. Accordingly authors of the review recommend that interventions should begin in the antenatal period.
22. Low percentage of post-natal consultation is also partly due to cultural norms. Traditionally, after the birth of the baby, woman is confined to home for 40 days especially in the rural areas.
23. The province of Punjab showed remarkable improvement in immunization coverage. Variations, though not as stark as in the provinces of Sindh and Balochistan, can be seen among districts. These variations can partly be explained by geographic and economic factors but variations among adjoining districts is also attributable to effectiveness of district management of the immunization program.
24. Almond & Currie (2011), "Killing Me Softly: The Fetal Origins Hypothesis", Journal of Economic Perspectives, Vol. 25, No. 3, pp. 153–172.
25. Almond & Mazumder (2011), "Health Capital and the Prenatal Environment: The Effect of Ramadan Observance During Pregnancy", American Economic Journal: Applied Economics, Vol. 3, October, pp. 56–85.
26. Cejka, T., & Waseem, M. (2022), "Long-term Impacts of In-Utero Ramadan Exposure: Evidence from Administrative Tax Records", CEPR Discussion Paper No. 17176.
27. See "The Long-Lasting Health Effects of Severe Shocks During Pregnancy" by Gabriella Conti et al., VoxEU, February 21, 2022.
28. Kelly, Elaine (2009), "The Scourge of Asian Flu: In Utero Exposure to Pandemic Influenza and the Development of a Cohort of

British Children", Institute of Fiscal Studies, Working Paper 09/17, University College London.

29. Foureaux Koppensteiner, M., & Manacorda, M. (2016), "Violence and Birth Outcomes: Evidence from Homicides in Brazil", CEP Working Paper DP1323.
30. Quoted by Pritchett and Summers in "Wealthier Is Healthier" WPS 1150, June 1993.
31. Bjorkegren et al., 2020, NBER Working Paper 28214.
32. Foster & Rosenzweig, "Missing Women, the Marriage Market, and Economic Growth", 1999, mimeo, University of Pennsylvania.
33. Wei, Shang-Jin (2011), "The Competitive Saving Motive in China: Evidence from Rising Sex Ratios and Savings Rate in China", Journal of Political Economy; Also see "A Theory of the Competitive Saving Motive", 2013, NBER Working Paper 18911.
34. Qian, Nancy (2008), "Missing Women and the Price of Tea in China: The Effect of Sex-Specific Earnings on Sex Imbalance".
35. Jensen, Robert T. (2010), "Economic opportunities and Gender Differences in Human Capital: Experimental Evidence from India".
36. "The Economic Consequences of Undernutrition in Pakistan: An Assessment of Losses", a study conducted by the Ministry of Planning, Development, and Reforms of Pakistan in collaboration with WFP in 2017. This is available on line on the official website of the Ministry.
37. "Why Are Indian Children So Short? The Role of Birth Order and Son Preference", American Economic Review, 2017.
38. WDI does not give comparative data of countries on stunting and wasting, so not mentioned.
39. Raju, Dhushyanth & D'Souza, Ritika (2017), "Child Undernutri tion in Pakistan: What Do We Know?" WPS 8049, World Bank, Washington, DC.
40. Review undertaken by Muhammad Asim and Yasir Nawaz in 2018 and is available online www.mdpi.com/journal/children.
41. Ministry of National Health Services, Regulations and Coordination, UNICEF Pakistan, 2018.
42. Ministry of Planning of Pakistan "Minimum Cost of the Diet (CoD) Pakistan", 2016.
43. Quoted by National Nutrition Survey 2018, Vol. 1.

44. Available on the official website of the Ministry of Food Security and Research, Government of Pakistan www.mnsfr.gov.pk.
45. The Returns to Prenatal Health: Evidence from Indonesia, NBER Working Paper 24304.
46. For details please see Maternal and Child Nutrition Series of Lancet in particular "Evidence-Based Interventions for Improvement of Maternal and Child Nutrition: What Can Be Done and at What Cost", Zafar A. Bhutta et al., Lancet, 2013 (Available Online).
47. "Stature and Status: Height, Ability, and Labour outcomes" by Anne Case and Christina Paxon, 2006, NBER Working Paper No. 12466.
48. "The Effect of Height on Earnings—Is Stature Just a Proxy for Cognitive and Non-cognitive Skills?" 2017, Policy Working Research Paper 8254, World Bank
49. See for details "Health Expenditure and Economic Growth-A Review of the Literature and an Analysis Between the Economic Community for Central African States (CEMAC) and Selected African countries' by Piabou et al., Health Economic Review, Vol. 7, No. 23 (2017).
50. Deaton, Angus (2006), NBER Working Paper 12735.
51. The Great Escape, p. 123 (Paperback Edition).
52. A Study of Registered Cases of Suicide—Last Five Years in Sindh Province 2016–2020, http://smha.sindh.gov.pk.
53. refer to report on "Psychological Autopsy of Suicide Cases Registered at District Tharparkar", http://smha.sindh.gov.pk.
54. "Mental Health Care in Pakistan" by Javed Afzal et al. (2020), Taiwanese Journal of Psychiatry.
55. World Happiness Report, 2013.
56. Case, Anne & Deaton, Angus, 'Deaths of Despair and Future of Capitalism', 2020.
57. See PIDE report on Beneficiaries' Experience, Satisfaction, and Hospital Utilization Under BISP's Waseela-e-Sehat Scheme.
58. Actuarial Analysis of the Federal Sehat Scheme, ILO, 2019; previously this scheme was called Prime Minister's National Health Program. This scheme was initially launched in KP province and being expanded gradually to other regions.
59. Health insurance is likely to attract persons who are more prone to illness with the result that insurance premiums are driven up. In such a case, insurance companies may screen their clients and doing

so runs against the principle of equity in health and this screening may exclude those who are in the greatest need of health care.

60. Insured patients and insurance companies have little incentive to contain the cost with the result that treatment provided may turn out to be costly and inefficient at the end of the day.
61. A Dozen Facts About the Economics of US Health-Care System, March 2020, The Hamilton Project Brookings; also see NBER's Paper "Is American Health Care Uniquely Inefficient?" by Alan M. Garber and Jonathan Skinner, 2008.
62. Filmer, Deon et al. (2000), "Weak Links in the Chain: A Diagnosis of Health Policy in Poor Countries", World Bank Observer.
63. Primary Health Care Systems (Primasys)—Comprehensive Case Study from Pakistan, WHO, 2017; also refer to "Analysis of the Health Care System of Pakistan: Lessons Learnt and Way Forward", by Kurji et al. published in Journal of Ayub Medical College Abbottabad in 2016 (Publicly Available Online).
64. National Health Accounts 2017–2018, Pakistan Bureau of Statistics, Government of Pakistan, released in June 2021.
65. The Role of Public Health Improvements in Health Advances: The Twentieth Century United States, 2005.
66. See Poor Economics.
67. The Great Escape, p. 123.
68. Banerjee et al. (2008) "Putting a Band-Aid on Corpse: Incentives for Nurses in the Indian Health Care system".
69. Callen, Michael et al. (2013), "Improving Public Health Delivery in Punjab, Pakistan: Issues and Opportunities", The Lahore Journal of Economics, Vol. 6, No. 2–3.
70. Farooq, Umar et al. "Doctors Perceptions About Staying in or Leaving Rural Health Facilities in District Abbottabad", Journal of Ayub Medical College, Vol. 16, No. 2.
71. Peng, Yuelan et al. (2019), "Evaluating the Efficiency and Determinants of Efficiency of Rural Health Centres Situated in Punjab, Pakistan", Health, pp. 630–645.
72. Punjab Health Facilities Management Company. In its quick overview, it gives some information about its basic health units and monitoring staff of year 2017. The author accessed the website in October 2021 which means that even basic information has not been updated in last four years.

73. People's Primary Health care Initiative; It claims to provide basic health care services in 22 rural districts of Sindh. It started its operations in 2007 from Kishmore District.
74. According to District level PSLM 2019–2020, only 26% children of the age 12–23 months were immunized based on record.
75. Pascaline Dupas, 'Health Behaviour in Developing Countries', 2011.
76. Letter sent by Federal Government to all provinces on 16th of April 2021.
77. The Act provided a mechanism for preparation of a list of generic drugs. The list of drugs was called National Formulary which was to be prepared by a committee called National Formulary Committee (Section 4) consisting inter alia of professors of medicine and dentistry, representatives of provincial governments and Federal Government. The committee was to prepare National Formulary which was to be notified by the Federal Government and Section 14 of the Act prescribed huge penalty, both criminal and pecuniary, for contravention of provisions of Section 7 which prohibited prescription and sale etc. under any patent name.
78. Mentioned in "Prizes, Not Patents", article by Joseph Stiglitz published on March 6, 2007 (Project Syndicate).
79. Brazil's Primary Health Care strategy, World Bank Paper No. 74957, January 2013.
80. Twenty Years of Health Reform in Brazil, World Bank, 2013.

Chapter 6: Multiple Inequalities

1. See Kanbur, Ravi (2012), "Does Kuznets Still Matter?" Working Paper.
2. Lewis, Arthur, "Development and Distribution", in 'Employment, Income Distribution and Development Strategy: Problems of the developing Countries (Essays in honour of H.W. Singer)', edited by Alan Cairncross and Mohinder Puri, 1976, Holmes & Meir Publications, New York.
3. Does Kuznets Still Matter? Ibid.
4. This novel written in 1854 conveys the conditions of industrial towns through a fictive industrial city Coketown besides dilating upon the dangers industrialization poses for turning human

beings into machines having implications for the development of their emotions and imaginations.

5. Glaesar, Edward L. (2006), "Inequality", Faculty Research Working Paper Series, JFK School of Government, Harvard University.
6. Tuominen, Alina (2015), "Reversal of the Kuznets Curve—Study on the Inequality-Development Relation Using Top Income Shares Data", WIDER Working Paper 2015/036.
7. According to thesis of Acemoglu et al., it was due to threat of revolution that the elite extended franchise to the people.
8. Acemoglu, Daron & Robinson, James A. (2002), "The Political Economy of the Kuznets Curve", Review of Development Economics, Vol. 6, No. 2, pp. 183–203.
9. Bavel, Bas Van, 'The Invisible Hand? How Market Economies Have Emerged and Declined Since AD 500', 2016.
10. Kaldor, N. (1956), "Alternative Theories of Distribution", Review of Economic Studies, Vol. 23, pp. 83–100.
11. Zattler, Jurgen K. (2015), "The Debate on Growing Inequality—Implications for Developing Countries and International Cooperation".
12. Benabou, Ronald (1996), "Inequality and Growth", NBER Working Paper 5658.
13. Deininger, Klaus & Squire, Lyn (1998), "New ways of Looking at Old Issues: Inequality and Growth", Journal of Development Economics, Vol. 57, No. 2, pp. 259–287; Alesina and Rodrik also empirically show negative correlation between land inequality and subsequent economic growth in their paper "Distributive Politics and Economic Growth", Quarterly Journal of Economics, May 1994.
14. Barro, Robert J. (2000), "Inequality and Growth in a Panel of Countries", Journal of Economic Growth, Vol. 5, pp. 5–32.
15. Berg, Andrew G. & Ostry, Jonathan D. (2011), "Inequality and Unsustainable Growth: Two Sides of the Same Coin?" IMF Staff Discussion Note (SDN/11/08).
16. Rodrik, Alesina (1994), "Distributive Politics and Economic Growth", Quarterly Journal of Economics, Vol. 109, No. 2, pp. 465–490.
17. Ostry et al. (2014), "Redistribution, Inequality and Growth", IMF Staff Discussion Note.

18. White & Anderson (2001), "Growth Versus Distribution: Does the Pattern of Growth Matter?" Development Policy Review, Vol. 19, No. 3, pp. 267–289.
19. Glaesar, Edward, Scheinkman, Jose & Shleifer, Andrei, "The Injustice of Inequality", 2002.
20. The Price of Inequality, p. 191.
21. See 'Third Pillar'.
22. "Addressing Inequality in South Asia", World Bank Group, 2015.
23. Oxfam, "Asia at the Crossroads: Why the Region Must Address Inequality Now", Briefing Note, January 20, 2015.
24. McAdams, Richard H. (2007), "Economic Costs of Inequality", University of Chicago Law School Paper.
25. "Even It Up—Time to End Extreme Inequality", Oxfam International Report, October 2014.
26. Oxfam (2014), ibid.
27. "Inequality Is Bad for the Growth of the Poor (But Not for That of the Rich)", World Bank Policy Research Working Paper No. 6963, July 2014.
28. "Aspirations and Inequality", NBER Working Paper No. 19976; also refer to Debraj Ray's paper "Aspirations, Poverty and Economic Change", March 2003.
29. See Robert Skidelsky's article "Happiness, Equality, and the Search for Economic Growth", Guardian, October 22, 2012.
30. "Why We All Care About Inequality (But Are Loath to Admit It)", Challenge, Vol. 50, No. 6, November–December 2007; The illustration/example has been borrowed from this article but presented here in bit modified form.
31. 'The Spirit Level—Why Greater Equality Makes Societies Stronger', 2009.
32. The Spirit Level, ibid.
33. The Spirit Level, ibid.
34. Flanney & Marcus, 'The Creation of Inequality: How Our Prehistoric Ancestors Set the Stage for Monarchy, Slavery, and Empire', 2012.
35. Wisman, John D. (2022), "The Origin and Dynamics of Inequality—Sex, Politics, and Ideology".
36. See Pistor, Katharina (2019), "The Code of Capital", p. 11.

37. "Sindh Rural Development Project—Final Report Prepared for Planning and Development", Government of Sindh and ADB, October 2000, Agrodev Canada Inc.
38. Piketty, Thomas, 'Capital and Ideology', 2020, Harvard University Press.
39. Ibid.
40. Williams, L.F. Rushbrook, 'The State of Pakistan', 1966, pp. 139–140.
41. Armytage, Rosita, 'Big Capital in an Unequal World: The Micropolitics of Wealth in Pakistan', 2020.
42. During the nineteenth century, the Western societies extended voting rights which in turn led to unprecedented redistributive programs and reforms as argued by Acemoglu and Robinson in their paper "Why did the West Extend the Franchise? Democracy, Inequality, and Growth in Historical Perspective".
43. 'Reimagining Pakistan—Transforming a Dysfunctional Nuclear State', 2018.
44. Toynbee, 'Pakistan as a Historian Sees Her', in Crescent and Green: A Miscellany of Writings on Pakistan, p. 2.
45. 'Reimagining Pakistan'.
46. See BBC report by Caroline Davies, February 26, 2024.
47. Jinns are invisible creatures who are possessed of power like men as per belief system of the Muslims. In the Zia regime, a conference was held on science where papers were presented on generation of electricity. These papers, according to Hoodbhoy, included a paper proposing a model for generation of electricity from the power possessed by the jinns (genie electricity). See Hoodbhoy's article "Jinns Invade Campuses", Dawn, October 10, 2015.
48. See Declan Walsh article in the New York Times, August 4, 2012.
49. Sen, Amartya, 'Identity and Violence—The Illusion of Destiny', p. 14 (Paperback edition).
50. Reimagining Pakistan, ibid.
51. Yousafzai, Malala & Lamb, Christina, 'I am Malala', 2013.
52. Sidhwa, Bapsi, 'The Pakistani Bride'.
53. Durrani, Tehmina, 'My Feudal Lord', 1994.
54. See page 41 of the PSLM 2017–2018 which gives province-wise and gender-wise education statistics of out of school children.

In every province/ region, the number of female out of school children is quite high compared to male children.

55. See VOXEU column "The Gap Between Law and Practice in Gender Rights", by Simeon Djankov, June 8, 2023.
56. See "Pakistan Demographic and Health Survey 2017–18", NIPS and ICF.
57. Agarwal, Bina, 'A Field of One's Own', pp. 15–16.
58. Najum-Us-Saqib & Arif, G.M. (2012), "Time Poverty, Work Status and Gender: The Case of Pakistan", Pakistan Development Review, Vol. 51, No. 1, pp. 23–46.
59. Yellen, J. (2020), "The History of Women's Work and Wages and How It Has Created Success for Us All", Brooking Institution.
60. "HERSTORY: The Rise of Self-Made Women", CEPR Discussion Paper 15736.
61. Macy, S., 'Wheels of Change: How Women Rode the Bicycle to Freedom (with Flat Tires Along the Way)', 2017, National Geographic Kids, Washington, D.C.
62. See FOPAH report on official website of the secretariat (https://www.fospah.gov.pk); also see special report of Dawn with the title "Predators in the Workplace" published on March 22, 2023.
63. Williams, G.L. (1947), "The Legal Unity of Husband and Wife", Modern Law Review, Vol. 10, pp. 16–31.
64. "Women's Liberation, Household Revolution", CEPR Discussion Paper 16838.
65. See article titled "Women's Rights: What's in It for Men", May 26, 2008 (https://voxeu.org).
66. Burde & Linden (2013), "Bringing Education to Afghan Girls: A Randomized Controlled Trial of Village-Based Schools", American Economic Journal.
67. Kim, Jooseop, Alderman, Harold & Peter, Orazem (1999), "Can Private School Subsidies Increase Enrollment for the Poor? The Quetta Urban Fellowship Program", World Bank Economic Review, Vol. 13, No. 3, pp. 443–465.
68. Mentioned in Seema Jayachandran's paper "The Roots of Gender Inequality in Developing Countries", NBER Working Paper 20380.
69. Ramakrishan et al. "Gender Differences in the Utilization of Surgery for Congenital Heart Disease in India", Heart, BMJ Journals.

70. 'Global Inequality: A New Approach for the Age of Globalization', Branko Milanovic, 2016.
71. This custom is prevalent in many countries of Africa and Asia; in Pakistan particularly in the ethnic communities having cultural influence of Hinduism, quite contrary practice prevails. The parents of the girl are required to make payments (generally in the form of goods) called dowry.
72. Ashraf, Nava et al. (2020), "Bride Price and Female Education".
73. The standard labor supply models postulate that as countries economically grow, education levels improve for male as well as female. Rising levels of education enhance earning capacity of the women. Both income and substitution effects are at play. Substitution effect means that more women would join the market labour force whereas income effect works in opposite direction (depressing work hours and withdrawal from the labour market) due to earned wages of the women and unearned income they can get from the wages of their husbands.
74. FLFP first declines as countries develop because male-dominated industrialization leaves behind women in subsistence farming. When education improves and norms about gender change, FLFP rises again.
75. World Bank, "Returns to Marriage in the Marriage Market", January 2023, Policy Research Working Paper 10288.
76. Afzal, Uzma et al., "Gender and Agency within the Household: Experimental Evidence from Pakistan", CEPR Discussion Paper No. 11464.
77. World Bank, "From Swimming in Sand to High and Sustainable Growth", Pakistan' s country Economic Memorandum (www.worldbank.org/pakistan), 2022.
78. Eswaran et al. (2013), "Status, Caste, and the Time Allocation of Women in Rural India", Economic Development and Cultural Change, Vol. 61, No. 2, pp. 311–333.
79. World Bank (2022), ibid.
80. "Gender Equality and Economic Growth: A Framework for Policy Analysis", VoxEU, April 24, 2013.
81. Galor & Maov (2004), "From Physical to Human Capital Accumulation: Inequality and the Process of Development", Review of Economic Studies, Vol. 71, No. 4, pp. 1001–1026.
82. Global Inequality: A New Approach.

83. "Global Inequality of Opportunity: How Much of Our Income Is Determined by Where We Live?" Review of Economics and Statistics, Vol. 97, No. 2, pp. 452–460.
84. "Unequal Opportunity, Unequal Growth", 2016, World Bank Policy Research Paper Series 7853.
85. World Bank, 'Measuring Inequality of Opportunities in Latin America and the Caribbean', 2009, Washington, D.C.
86. Gladwell, Malcolm, 'Outliers—The Story of Success', 2008.
87. Roemer, John E., 'Equality of Opportunity', 1998, Harvard University Press.
88. Ibid.
89. Kanbur, Ravi, "The Standard of Living: Uncertainty, Inequality and Opportunity", in 'The Standard of Living', edited by G. Hawthorn, 1987, Cambridge University Press, pp. 59–69.
90. Atkinson, Anthony B., 'Inequality—What Can Be Done', 2015, Harvard University Press.
91. World Bank, 'Fair Progress? Economic Mobility Across Generations Around the World', 2018, Washington, D.C.
92. World Bank (2018), ibid.
93. World Bank (2021), "Intergenerational Mobility Around the World", Policy Research Working Paper 9707.
94. "Multiple Inequalities and Policies to Mitigate Inequality Traps in Pakistan", Oxfam Research Report, 2015.
95. "Wealth Inequality, Poverty and Mobility: Evidence from a Panel Survey in Rural Pakistan", Mimeo, World Bank, 2018.
96. Corak, Miles (2013), "Income Inequality, Equality of Opportunity, and Intergenerational Mobility", Journal of Economic Perspectives, Vol. 27, No. 3, Summer.
97. See "The One Percent Republic", an op-ed article published in Dawn on November 20, 2022.
98. PILDAT, "Four Years of the 15th National Assembly of Pakistan—A Citizens' Report on Performance", August 2022, Islamabad, Pakistan.
99. See PIDE Webinar brief on "Electoral reforms in Pakistan", Webinar 52: 2021.
100. Mendoza et al. (2012), "An Empirical Analysis of Political Dynasties in the 15th Philippine Congress", Asian Institute of Management Policy Centre Research Paper.

101. Galasso & Nannicini (2009), "Competing on Good Politicians", CEPR Discussion Paper 7363.
102. UNDP "Pakistan National Human Development Report 2020", Islamabad, Pakistan.
103. Djankov et al. (2003), "Who Owns the Media?" Journal of Law and Economics, Vol. XLVI.
104. See PIDE Knowledge Brief No. 2021: 35 with the title "The Electronic Media Economy in Pakistan: Issues and Challenges", August 13, 2021.
105. See Media Ownership Monitor (MOM), https://www.mom-gmr.org/, information is publicly available.
106. For example content analysis report for the month of October 2022 says that 58% opinion articles were about politics; Health constituted just 2% while education did not figure in at all in the main topics of discussion. And security, law and order, and science and technology, each constituted less than 1% share in the topics of discussion.
107. Khalid Ahmed in "The Media in Pakistan", included in 'Pakistan at Seventy—A Handbook on Developments in Economic, Politics, and Society', edited by Shahid Javed Burki et al., 2019.
108. Acemoglu et al. (2018), "The Power of the Street: Evidence from Egypt's Arab Spring", The Review of Financial Studies, Vol. 31, pp. 1–42.
109. Hendel et al. (2017), "Consumer activism: The Cottage Cheese Boycott", The RAND Journal of Economics, Vol. 48, pp. 972–1003.
110. Zhuravskaya et al. (2020), "Political Effects of the Internet and Social Media", Annual Review of Economics, www.annualreview s.org
111. Vosoughi et al. (2018), "The Spread of True and False News Online", Science, Vol. 359, No. 6380, http://ww.science.org
112. Graeber et al. (2022), "Stories, Statistics, and Memory", CEPR Discussion Paper 17683.
113. Mercier, Hugo & Sperber, Dan, 'The Enigma of Reason—A New Theory of Human Understanding', 2017.
114. 'The Third Pillar', pp. 11–12 (e-Edition).
115. Cobham, Alex & Sumner, Andy (2013), "Putting the Gini Back in the Bottle? The 'Palma' as a Policy Relevant Measure of Inequality", March 15, 2013.

116. Palma, Gabriel (2011), "Homogenous Middles vs. Heterogeneous Tails, and the End of Inverted U".
117. Alex Cobham & Andy Sumner (2013), ibid.
118. Krozer, Alice (2015), "The Inequality We Want—How Much Is Too Much?" WIDER Working Paper 2015/015, January.
119. Gethin, Amory, Mehmood, Sultan & Piketty, Thomas (2020), "Social Inequality and the Dynamics of Political and Ethnolinguistic Divides in Pakistan, 1970–2018", WID. World Working Paper N 2020/16; This paper has documented in detail the changing structure of Pakistan's political cleavages using data of exit polls covering all elections held in Pakistan between 1970 and 2018. The paper inter alia points towards weakening of leftist parties in the country.
120. Baland, Jean-Marie & Robinson, James A. (2008), "Land and Power: Theory and Evidence from Chile", American Economic Review.
121. Scheidel, Walter, 'The Great Leveler—Violence and the History of Equality from the Stone Age to the Twenty-First Century', 2017.
122. Ibid.
123. Ibid.; Somalia's Gini for 1997 was 0.4, lower than its neighboring countries (0.47).
124. Ibid.
125. Ibid.
126. Oxfam (2015).
127. Segall, Shlomi, 'Equality and Opportunity', 2013, Oxford University Press, UK.
128. Henderson, David R., "Rent Seeking", Library of Economics and Liberty.
129. Murphy, Kevin M. , Shleifer, Andrei & Vishny, Robert W. (1993), "Why Is Rent-Seeking So Costly to Growth", AEA Papers and Proceedings, Vol. 83, No. 2, May.
130. UNDP, "Pakistan Human Development Report 2020".
131. See Tax Expenditure Report, 2023 available at official website of FBR; these figures are for FY 2021–22. In absolute terms, the amount of tax expenditure is estimated at Rs. 2239.63 billion. The tax expenditure has increased both in absolute terms as well as in terms of GDP. In FY 2020–21, it was Rs. 1499.17 billion (2.69% of GDP).

132. The supreme court of Pakistan confirmed the findings of the Competition Commission of Pakistan (CCP) regarding cartelization in poultry sector in its first-ever judgement on the issue in December 2022.
133. See report of the Commission of the Inquiry constituted by the Prime Minister of Pakistan, in 2020, to probe into the sugar crisis. This report was made public by the Government of Pakistan.
134. These figures are quoted in Pakistan National Human Development Report, 2020, UNDP.
135. Edwards, Sebastian & Marin, Alvaro Garcia (2014), "Constitutional Rights and Education: An International Comparative Study", NBER Working Paper No. 20475, September.
136. See op-ed article by one of the Finance Ministers of Pakistan published in Dawn with the title "The One Percent Republic" on November 10, 2022.
137. "Historical Inequality and Intergenerational Educational Mobility: The Dynamics of Change in Rural Punjab", Lahore Journal of Economics, No. 18, September 2013, pp. 211–231.
138. See "The Economics of Inequality", Vol. 10, No. 3, Criterion Quarterly, 2015.
139. 'Capitalism and Ideology', 2020.

Chapter 7: Misallocation of Land

1. 'A Punjabi Village in Pakistan—Perspectives on Community, Land, and Economy', p. 288.
2. Ibid., p. 60.
3. A Field of One's Own, 1994.
4. Deininger & Squire (1998), "New Ways of Looking at Old Issues: Inequality and Growth", Journal of Development Economics, Vol. 57, No. 2, pp. 259–287.
5. "The Colonial Roots of Land Inequality: Geography, Factor Endowments, or Institutions", Economic History Review, Vol. 63, No. 2, pp. 418–451.
6. Sen, Amartya (1962), "An Aspect of Indian Agriculture", Economic Weekly, Annual Number, February 1962; also see "Size of Holdings and Productivity", Economic Weekly, Annual Number, February 1964. The studies on farm management were

initiated in UP, Punjab, Bombay, Madras, Madhya Pradesh and West Bengal in 1954–55.

7. Sen, Amartya (1966), "Peasants and Dualism with or Without Surplus Labour", Journal of Political Economy, Vol. 4, No. 5, October.
8. Bhagwati & Chakravarty (1969), "Contributions to Indian Economic Analysis: A Survey", American Economic Review, Vol. 59, No. 4; this discussion is spread over pages 41–43 of the said paper.
9. See "Farm Size, Productivity and Returns to Scale", Economic and Political Weekly, June 28, 1969, Vol. 4, No. 26.
10. Srinivasan (1972), "Farm Size and Productivity Implications of Choice Under Uncertainty", Sankhya, Indian Journal of Statistics, Series B (1960–2002), Vol. 34, No. 4.
11. "Farm Size and Land Productivity Relationships in Pakistan", PDR, Vol. 18, No. 1, PIDE.
12. Moazam Mahmood & Nadeem-Ul-Haque (1981), "Farm Size and Productivity Revisited", PDR, Vol. 20, No. 2.
13. Helfand & Levine (2004), "Farm size and the Determinants of Productive Efficiency in the Brazilian Centre-West", Agricultural Economics, Blackwell, Vol. 31, No. 2–3, pp. 241–249.
14. See "Size-Productivity Relationship in Pakistan's Agriculture in the Seventies (with Comments)", PDR, Vol. 24, No. 3/4, Papers and Proceedings of the Second Annual General Meeting of the Pakistan Society of Development Economists (May 12–14, 1985), PIDE.
15. See "Farm-size Productivity Relationship—Recent Evidence from Central Punjab", Pakistan Economic and Social Review, Vol. 50, No. 2, Winter, 2012; all the districts included in the study are comparatively more fertile districts and farmers with landholdings less than 12.5 acres have been treated as small farmers whereas farmers with landholdings above 12.5 acre as big farmers.
16. E.F. Schumacher, 'Good Work', 1980.
17. Kay, Cristobal (2002), "Why East Asia Overtook Latin America: Agrarian Reform, Industrialization and Development", Third World Quarterly, Vol. 23, No. 6; This paper explains why Latin America lagged behind East Asian region despite the point that Latin American region started to industrialize much before East Asian countries. Sequencing of agrarian reforms is cited as one of the top factors in divergence of paths between the two regions.

18. Aresvik, Odvar. "Reflections on the Socio-Economic Objectives of the Fourth Five Year Plan—Agricultural Strategy", Agriculture Department, Government of Pakistan, November 1968 (Mimeo).
19. Alvi, Hamza (1976), "The Rural Elite and Agricultural Development in Pakistan", Pakistan Economic and Social Review, Vol. 14, No. 1/4, Department of Economics, University of the Punjab.
20. Ibid.
21. Alvi, Hamza (1973), "Elite Farm strategy and Regional Disparities in the Agricultural Development of Pakistan", Economic and Political Weekly, March 31, 1973, Vol. 8, No. 13.
22. Amjad, Rashid (1972), "A Critique of the Green Revolution in West Pakistan", MPRA Paper No. 39275; also refer to "Agriculture Price Policy and the Development of West Pakistan" by Gotsch and Falcon Vol. 1, Final Report (AIDS/OSTI MIMEO) who wrote 'the momentum of growth in West Pakistan has been largely confined to the medium to large scale farmers in the irrigated areas of the province'.
23. Dorosh, Paul et al. (2003), "Distributional Impacts of Agricultural Growth in Pakistan: A Multiplier Analysis", PDR Vol. 42, No. 3, pp. 249–275.
24. Javid, Hassan, "Class, Power, and Patronage: The Landed Elite and Politics in Pakistani Punjab", A Thesis Submitted to the Department of Sociology of the London School of Economics for the Degree of Doctor of Philosophy, London, June 2012.
25. Gersbach et al. (2010), "Land reforms and Economic Development", Macroeconomic Dynamics, Vol. 14, pp. 527–547 (http://www.cambridge.org/core).
26. See 'Muslim League: Memorandum for Economic Development', 3 September 1944; also quoted by Hassan Javid in his thesis, June 2012.
27. G.M. Syed gave his note of dissent and urged that tenancy rights should be granted to all haris without any stipulation. The batai system should altogether be abolished and replaced with a state-controlled tenancy system and land should be gradually nationalized by expropriation of large estates without any compensation to its owners.
28. Government of Sindh. Hari Enquiry Committee: Minute of Dissent by M. Masud I.C.S (Pak). Karachi, April 1949.

29. Pakistan Muslim League, "Report of the Agrarian Committee appointed by the Working Committee of the Pakistan Muslim League", Karachi, June 1949. The convener of the Agrarian Committee was Mian Mumtaz Mohammad Daultana and other members included Begum Shah Nawaz, Khan Abdul Qayyum Khan, Qazi Mohammad Isa, and Haji Ali Akbar Shah. The final report, however, does not contain signatures of Haji Ali Akbar Shah.
30. See page 186 of PIDE's document titled "Land Reforms in Pakistan: A Historical Perspective" (1987), edited by Syed Nawab Haider Naqvi and others, 1987. Mr. Ishaque who later became President of Pakistan proposed that landholding should not exceed 150 acres in case of individuals and 300 acres in case of family (family defined as husband and wife and dependent children). He also opposed the argument that leadership in rural areas can only be maintained through holding of big estates. He was of the view, and correctly so, that there may be other ways to build leadership in the rural areas.
31. Khan, Mahmood Hasan, 'Underdevelopment and Agrarian Structure in Pakistan', 1981, p. 162.
32. Ibid., p. 169.
33. Jalal, Ayesha, 'The State of Martial Rule', 1990.
34. See West Pakistan Land Reforms Regulation (MLR-59/64), Land Reforms Regulation, 1972 (MLR-115/72) and Land Reforms Act, 1977 (II of 1972) for details.
35. PIDE (1987) ibid., p. 36.
36. See for details Hassan, Javid (2012), p. 257.
37. See judgement reported as PLD 1981 FSC23, PLD 1990 SC99 (Qazalbash Waqf and others—Appellants Versus Chief Land Commissioner, Punjab, Lahore and others—Respondents) and 1993 SCMR 1697.
38. Waqf means permanent dedication of any property moveable or immovable by a person professing Islam for any purpose recognized by Islam. Still large number of properties/land are attached to shrines and are practically in use of religious elite. Such landed property helps in perpetuating stranglehold of the descendants of the religious and spiritual leaders on the political landscape of the country.

39. The big landholdings in Pakistan are not the result of hard work rather in majority cases big landholdings were bestowed upon the landlords by the British in lieu of their services with regard to recruitment of locals in the Army and consolidation of British rule in India. So there is valid case for redistribution of big lands-holdings irrespective of their status.
40. It is not possible in fiscal terms to pay compensation on market price; it simply amounts to demolishing entire scheme of land reforms.
41. The FLC drafted the Land Reforms (Amendment) Bill 2004 which sought to re-impose limits on individual landholdings, exempt Waqf lands and lands acquired through inheritance, provide for the payment of compensation for the resumed land and enable provincial governments to utilize the resumed land for public purposes. The bill was placed before the cabinet in 2005 but the cabinet did not approve it for placing before the Parliament and asked the Ministry of Law and Justice to look into the issue afresh and hold consultations with the stakeholders. It was in a way denial in a polite way. The FLC remained shuffling to different ministries. Between 2012 to 2018 it was transferred from Cabinet Division to Heritage Division, then to Information and Broadcasting Division, and lastly in 2018 to the Inter-Provincial Coordination Division. Reportedly, a bill of Land Reforms (Amendment) Act, 2021 was prepared by the FLC but could not get through the cabinet for tabling it in the Parliament.
42. Caprettini, B., Casburi, L. & Venturini, M. (2021), "The Electoral Impact of Wealth Redistribution: Evidence from the Italian Land Reform", available at SSRN 3767181.
43. This discussion is based on Imran Ali's arguments in 'The Punjab Under Imperialism 1885–1947', Princeton University Press, 1988.
44. Quoted by Dr. Hasan Askari Rizvi in his article "Land Allotments and the Military", December 15, 2009 (http://defence.pk).
45. Rizvi, Hasan Askari , 'Military, Society and State in Pakistan', 2000.
46. Ibid.
47. Biswanger & Deininger (1997), "Explaining Agricultural and Agrarian Policies in Developing Countries", Journal of Economic Literature, Vol. XXXV, December, pp. 1958–2005.
48. See para 28 of the judgment of the Supreme Court of Pakistan in case titled 'Federal Government Employees Housing Foundation

v. Ghulam Mustafa', Supreme Court Monthly Review, Vol. LIV, 2021, pp. 275–288. The judgement was authored by Justice Qazi Faez Isa.
49. Ibid., para 29.
50. Ibid., para 30.
51. Ibid., para 26.
52. "The opportunity of Dead Capital", published in P&R, Vol. 2, No. 1, 2021.
53. Haque, Nadeem Ul, 'Looking Back—How Pakistan became an Asian Tiger', 2017, p. 116.
54. This matter also came under discussion in the PAC. According to reports the Sindh government has also claimed ownership of the land and one of the case landed in the Supreme Court of Pakistan which reportedly cancelled the lease.
55. Husain, Ishrat, 'Pakistan-The Economy of an Elitist State', 2020 (2nd Edition).
56. Mentioned by Jamil Nasir in 'Political Economy of Bad Governance', p. 272.
57. Dixit, Avinash (2009), "Governance Institutions and Economic Activity", American Economic Review, Vol. 99, No. 1, pp. 5–24.
58. Besley, Timothy (1995), "Property Rights and Investment Incentives: Theory and Evidence from Ghana", Journal of Political Economy, Vol. 103, No. 5, pp. 903–937.
59. Goldstein & Udry (2008), "The Profits of Power: Land Rights and Agricultural Investment in Ghana", Journal of Political Economy, Vol. 116, No. 6, pp. 981–1022.
60. Field (2005), "Property Rights and Investment in Urban Slums", Journal of the European Economic Association, Vol. 3, No. 2–3, pp. 279–290.
61. "The Formation of Beliefs: Evidence from the Allocation of Land Titles to Squatters", Quarterly Journal of Economics, Vol. 122, No. 1, pp. 209–241.
62. De Soto, Hernando (2000), "The Mystery of Capital—Why Capitalism Triumphs in the West and Fails Everywhere Else".
63. Field (2005); also refer to Di Tella, Rafael et al. (2007), "The Formation of Beliefs: Evidence from the Allocation of Land Titles to Squatters", Quarterly Journal of Economics, Vol. 122, No. 1, pp. 209–241.

64. For empirics, refer to Besley, Timothy (1995), "Property Rights and Investment Incentives: Theory and Evidence from Ghana", Journal of Political Economy, Vol. 103, No. 5, pp. 903–937.
65. "Measuring Property Rights Institutions", LSE Financial Markets Group Discussion Paper 813, September 2020.
66. See PIDE's Knowledge Brief "Land Titles in Punjab—Overview, Problems, and Suggestions", No. 2022:91, December 2022.
67. Chang, Ha-Joon, "Understanding the Relationship between Institutions and Economic Development—Some Key Theoretical Issues", UNU-WIDER Discussion Paper No. 2006/05.
68. Wade, Robert, 'Governing the Market-Economic Theory and the Role of Government in East Asian Industrialization', 1990.
69. Figures of land Gini are quoted by Mahmood Hasan Khan in 'Underdevelopment and Agrarian Structure of Pakistan'.
70. 'Poverty Traps', 2006.
71. This example is borrowed from Adam Przeworski's paper "The Last chance: Are Institutions the Primary Cause of Economic Development?" Paper Prepared for a Meeting on Institutions, Behaviour, and Outcomes, CEBRAP, Sao Paulo, March 12–14, 2003.
72. Piketty, Thomas, 'Capital and Ideology', 2020.

Chapter 8: Constraints on Rural Growth

1. Rural population (63.6%), labour force participation (38.49%), GDP contribution (19.3% and as per PBS 22.6%), Rural poverty (40.2%) and women labour force in agriculture (67%).
2. Thirtle et al. (2003), "The Impact of Research Led Agricultural Productivity Growth on Poverty Reduction in Africa, Asia, and Latin America", World Development, Vol. 31, No. 12, pp. 1959–1975.
3. Datt & Ravallion (1998), "Farm Productivity and Rural Poverty in India", Journal of Development Studies, Vol. 34, No. 4, pp. 62–85.
4. Ravallion & Chen (1997), "What can New Data Survey tell us about RECENT Changes in Distribution and Poverty ?" World Bank Economic Review, Vol. 11, p. 2.

5. Ravallion & Datt (1996), "How Important to India's is the Sectoral Composition of Economic Growth", World Bank Economic Review, Vol. 10, p. 1.
6. Ravallion & Datt (1996) ibid.
7. See "Agricultural Development and Food Security" (2009), PDR.
8. "How Well do the Poor Connect to the Growth Process", Discussion paper No.17, Harvard Institute for International Development (HIID), Cambridge, 1997.
9. Fan, S. C, Chan-Kang & Mukherjee, A. (2005) "Rural and Urban Dynamics and Poverty: Evidence from China and India", IFPRI.
10. Marden, S. (2014), "The Agricultural Roots of Industrial Development: Forward linkages in Reform-era China", mimeo.
11. Diwakar, Vidya et al. (2019), "Economic Transformation and Poverty", Supporting Economic Transformation (SET) paper of DFID and ODI.
12. John W. Mellor, Ijaz Nabi & Tusneem, M. E. (2009), "Agriculture Development and Food Security", The Pakistan Development Review, Vol. 47, No. 4, Islamabad.
13. Sidhu, R. S. & Bhullar, A. S. (2005), "Patterns and Determinants of Agricultural Growth in the Two Punjabs", Economic and Political Weekly, Vol. 40, No. 53.
14. Table 5 of the paper ibid.
15. All banks in Indian Punjab were mandated to supply a minimum of 18% of the bank credit to agriculture sector; refer to Sidhu & Bhullar (2005).
16. For example, in 1999–2000 agricultural subsidies in India amounted to 3% of GDP; refer to Sidhu and Bhullar.
17. Rinku Murgai et al. (2001), "Productivity Growth and Sustainability in Post-Green Revolution Agriculture: The Case of Indian and Pakistan Punjabs", World Bank Research Observer, Vol. 16, No. 2, Fall 2001.
18. See "Trends in Total Factor Productivity in Pakistan Agriculture Sector", 2008, Pakistan Economic and Social Review, Vol. 46, No. 2, pp. 117–132.
19. "Two Blades of Grass: The Impact of the Green Revolution", NBER Working Paper No. 24744, June 2018.
20. Jayachandran, Seema (2006), "Selling Labor Low: Wage Response to Productivity Shocks in Developing Countries", Journal of Political Economy, Vol. 114, No. 3.

21. Sibiko, S. W., Qasim, M. (2017), "Weather Index Insurance, Agricultural Input Use, and Crop Productivity in Kenya", Global Food Discussion Paper 94, University of Gottingen.
22. See Chapter V (pages 91 onwards) of the Ministry of Food and Agriculture (Agriculture Division)'s Report titled 'Resport of the Pakistan Agricultural Inquiry Committee 1951–52', First Edition, published by the Manager of Publications, Karachi.
23. This movie is based on Rabindranath Tagore's Bengali poem "Dui Bigha Jomi" and stars Balraj Sahni (played role of Shambu Maheto) and Nirupa Roy in lead roles. Meena Kumari gave her maiden guest appearance in this movie. The family of Shambhu owed Rs. 235 as debt to the local money-lender and the movie sheds light on the trials and tribulations this family had to face due to debt.
24. Khandkar, Shahidur R. & Faruqee, Rashidur R. (2001), "The Impact of Farm Credit in Pakistan", Policy Research Working Paper 2653, World Bank, Washington D.C.
25. See State Bank of Pakistan's Annual Report 2020–21 on the state of Pakistan's Economy which can be reached at sbp.org.pk/reports/annual/arFY21 /Complete.pdf; According to SBP, out of 1,461,889 borrowers, Rs. 292 billion was disbursed among 2707 borrowers out of total disbursement of Rs. 637 billion to farm sector. Similarly, out of total Rs.576 billion for non-farm activities, Rs. 266 billion were disbursed among 11,077 borrowers. The total number of non-farm borrowers was 1,638,083. These figures point towards deep inequities in access of credit from formal sources in rural Pakistan.
26. "The Structure of Informal Credit Market in Pakistan", Research Report No.168, PIDE, 1999.
27. Report of the Committee on Rural Finance, SBP (sbp.org.pk/report/contents.html).
28. Shehla Amjad & SAF Hasnu (2007), "Smallholders's Access to Rural Credit: Evidence from Pakistan", Lahore Journal of Economics, Vol. 12, No. 2, pp. 1–25.
29. See article "Downside of Informal Agricultural Credit" by Jamil Nasir, Dawn, October 17, 2007.
30. Banerjee & Duflo (2007), "The Economic Lives of the Poor", Journal of Economic Perspectives, Vol. 21, No. 1, pp. 141–167. The survey included Pakistan as well.

31. A lender has less information than the borrower about the capacity of the borrower to pay back the loan.
32. Further disaggregation shows that 15% farms are under just one acre, 28% between 1 to 2.5 acres, 21% are between 2.5 to 5 acres, 14% (5 to 7.5 acres), and 11% (7.5 to 12.5 acres) as per Agricultural Census of 2010.
33. Dhingra & Tenreyro (2020), "The Rise of Agribusinesses and the Distributional Consequences of Policies on Intermediated Trade", CEP Discussion Paper No. 1677.
34. Gaspart & Platteau (2012), "The Perverse Effect of Cheap Aid Money", CRED working paper, Belgium, Centre for Research in Economic Development, University of Namur.
35. Alvi, Hamza (1975), "India and the Colonial Mode of Production", Economic and Political Weekly, Vol. 10, No. 33/35, Special Number pp. 1239 and 1240.
36. Alain Lefebvre, 'Kinship, Honour and Money in Rural Pakistan—Subsistence Economy and the Effects of Internal Migration', p. 166.
37. Quoted in "Off-Farm Employment and Income of Farm Families in Rural Punjab" with reference to Khan Muhammad, Pakistan Economic and Social Review, Vol. 35, No. 2, Winter, 1997.
38. See Table 9.1 of Mauza Census, 2020, PBS.
39. See article "Is Rural Non-farm Economy worth neglecting", included in 'Political Economy of Bad Governance' by Jamil Nasir, 2021.
40. See "Stylized Facts of Household Savings: Findings from the HIES 1993–94" PDR Vol. 3, No. 4—According to this paper, average income of the urban households is 2% higher than the overall income of Pakistan. The rural households on average enjoy 3% more income than rural households but rural savings are 15% higher than the urban savings and 5% higher than overall savings. Another paper titled "Rural Saving: Their Magnitude, Determinants, and Mobilization" (1995), PDR, 34:4 also pints towards similar situation of rural savings. According to this paper, despite more incidence and intensity of poverty in rural areas, data on rural incomes and family budgets show that average propensity of rural households to save is much higher than urban areas.
41. See "Explanation of Off-farm Work Participation in Rural Pakistan", PDR, Vol. 34, No. 2, Summer, 1995.

42. William Foster et al. (2011), "The Constraints to Escaping Rural Poverty: An Analysis of the Complementarities of Assets in Developing Countries", Applied Economic Perspectives and Policy, Vol. 33, No.4.
43. Marcel Fafchamps & Agnes R. Quisumbing (1999), "Human Capital, Productivity, and Labour Allocation in Rural Pakistan", The Journal of Human Resources, Vol. 34, No. 2, pp. 369–406.
44. "Non-farm Income, Inequality, and Poverty in Rural Egypt and Jordon", Policy Research Working Paper No. 2527, World Bank, 2001.
45. Leones, J. P., & Feldman, S. (1998), "Nonfarm Activity and Rural Household Income: Evidence from Philippine Microdata", Economic Development and Cultural Change, Vol. 46, No. 4, pp. 789–806.
46. "Agricultural Productivity and Poverty Reduction: Linkages and Pathways", Evans School Review, Vol. 1, No. 1, Spring, 2011.
47. See "Distributional Impacts of Agricultural Growth in Pakistan: A Multiplier Analysis" (2003), Pakistan Development Review.
48. Anriquez & Valdes (2006), "Determinants of Farm Revenue in Pakistan", PDR, Vol. 45, No. 2, pp. 281–301; the income from farm operations ranges from 65 to 83%. The households with less than 4 acres of land earn 65% of their income from farm operations, those with 4 to 20 acres 83% while households with land over 20 acres earn 78% of their income from farm operations. The farm income here includes income from crops as well as livestock.

Chapter 9: The Challenge of Poverty

1. "Attacking Poverty", World Development Report 2000–2001, p. 3 (Box1).
2. 'Poor Economics', pp. 20–21.
3. The estimated poverty line for the 2013–14 was Rs. 3030 per adult equivalent per month which is estimated at Rs. 3776 for 2018–19 as per calculations of PIDE. The updated poverty line was applied on the aggregate consumption expenditure obtained from HIES 2018–19 micro-data for arriving at said poverty line. The aggregate nominal expenditure includes all food and non-food expenditure incurred on a recurrent basis. For details see PIDE Knowledge

Brief on National Poverty Estimates, May 2020, available online on the official website of PIDE.

4. Sen, Amartya (1979), "Issues in the Measurement of Poverty", Scandinavian Journal of Economics, Vol. 81, No. 2, Measurement in Public Choice (1979), pp. 285–307.
5. The Basic needs approach attempts to define some basic requirements in terms of consumption goods necessary for physical wellbeing. The basic needs approach to poverty measurement and alleviation is advocated inter alia on the ground that consumers are not always efficient optimizers especially with regard to health and nutrition and there is misdistribution within households and between households. Refer to Paul P. Stretton's "Basic Needs: Premises and Promises", for detailed discussion, reprinted by the World Bank from Journal of Policy Modelling, 1979.
6. Hick, Rod (2012), "The Capability Approach: Insights for a New Poverty Focus", Journal of Social Policy.
7. Margret Thatcher is said to have described poverty as a personality defect (in developed countries) in an interview with Richard Dowden; refer to "The Thatcher Philosophy", Catholic Herald, December 22, 1978 (http://www.margretthatcher.org/document/103793).
8. Quoted by Martin Ravallion in "Awareness of Poverty Over Three Centuries", February 14, 2011, https://cepr.org.
9. Schultz, Theodore W. (1979), "The Economics of Being Poor", Lecture in the memory of Alfred Nobel, December 8, 1979.
10. Banerjee & Duflo (2007), "The Economic Lives of the Poor", Journal of Economic Perspectives, Vol. 21, No. 1, pp. 141–167.
11. HIES 2018–19; The poorest quintile spends Rs. 1263.34 out of total monthly per capita expenditure of Rs. 2680.07 compared to Rs. 3418.91 out of Rs. 12,341.68 per capita consumption out of the richest quintile.
12. Glewwe et al. (2009), "Many Children Left Behind? Textbooks and Test scores in Kenya", American Economic Journal: Applied Economics, Vol. 1, No. 1, pp. 115–135.
13. Portfolios of the Poor—How the World's Poor Live on $2 a day, p. 16, Princeton University.
14. Poor Economics.

15. Karlan et al. (2019), "Debt Traps? Money Vendors and Moneylender Debt in India and Philippines", AER, Vol. 1, No. 1, pp. 27–42.
16. For example, if a vendor buys fruit and vegetables of worth Rs. 10,000, and pays 10% in the evening, he would be paying on yearly basis 3650% interest (payment of Rs. 375,000) and if he pays weekly, then the simple interest amount on yearly basis comes to Rs. 62,000 (520% interest arte). And if rate of interest is on compound basis, and say, it is compounded on weekly basis, the interest rate at the end of the year would be 7419.10% and if compounded daily it would turn into horrendous amount running into billions.
17. Ashraf et al. (2006), "Tying Odysseus to the Mast: Evidence from Commitment Savings Product in the Philippines", Quarterly Journal of Economics, Vol. 121, No. 2, pp. 635–672.
18. See World Bank's Policy Research Paper "Does Africa Need a Rotten Kin Theorem?—Experimental Evidence from Village Economies", WPS 6085, 2012; This paper measures the economic impact of social pressure to share income with kin and neighbours in rural settings of Kenya and results suggest that such sharing distorts investment incentives as social pressure to share encourages hiding of income rather than investing it in visible schemes.
19. Poor Economics, pp. 199–200.
20. Becker& Tomes (1976), "Child Endowments and the Quantity and Quality of Children", Journal of Political Economy, Vol. 84, No. 4, pp. 143–162.
21. Angrist et al. (2005), "New Evidence on the Causal Link Between the Quantity and Quality of Children", NBER Working Paper No. 11835.
22. Qian, Nancy (2009), "Quantity-Quality and the One Child Policy: The Only Child Disadvantage in School Enrollment in Rural China", NBER Working Paper.
23. Mullainathan & Shafir 'Scarcity: Why Having Too Little Means So Much', 2013.
24. See "Money in the Mental Lives of the Poor", Social Cognition, Vol. 30, No. 1, pp. 4–19.
25. Anandi Mani et al. (2013), "Poverty Impedes Cognitive Function", Science, Vol. 341, No. 976. (www.sciencemag.org).

26. Ridley et al. (2020), "Poverty, Depression, and Anxiety: Causal Evidence and Mechanisms", NBER Working Paper 27157.
27. "How Research Affects Policy: Experimental Evidence from 2,150 Brazilian Municipalities", American Economic Review, 2021, Vol. 111, No. 5, pp. 1442–1480.
28. See Declaration of Microcredit Summit held in Washington D.C in 1977.
29. Banerjee et al. (2015), "The Miracle of Microfinance? Evidence from a Randomized Evaluation", American Economic Journal: Applied Economics, Vol. 7, No. 1, pp. 22–53.
30. Banerjee et al. (2019), "Can Microfinance Unlock a Poverty Trap for Some Entrepreneurs?" NBER Working Paper w26346.
31. ATM Jahiruddin et al. (2011), "Can Microcredit Worsen Poverty? Cases of Exacerbated Poverty in Bangladesh", Development in Practice, Vol. 21, No. 8, pp. 1109–1121.
32. Shirazi et al. (2009), "Role of Pakistan Poverty Alleviation Fund's Micro Credit in Poverty Alleviation: A case of Pakistan", Pakistan Economic and Social Review, Vol. 47, No. 2, pp. 215–228.
33. Tahir Mehmood et al. (2016), "Impact of Microfinance on Income Generation and Living Standards: A Case Study of Dera Ghazi Khan Division", Pakistan Economic and Social Review, Vol. 54, No. 1, pp. 73–80.
34. Zahoor Khan & Jamalludin Sulaiman (2015), "Does Microcredit Help the Poor and Financially Marginalized Communities? Experience of Pakistan", Economic Studies in Inequality, Social Exclusion, and Well-Being in: 'Poverty Reduction in Policies and Practices in Developing Asia' edited by Almas Heshmati & Esfandiar Maasoumi & Guanghua Wan.
35. See article "Microfinance: To What End? Findings from Pakistan", Economic and Political Weekly, Vol. 49, No. 10, March 8, 2014, pp. 63–67.
36. "Exploring the Impact of Microfinance in Pakistan", Research Report No. 77, SPDC.
37. Abid Hussain et al. (2016), "Impact of Credit on Education and Healthcare Spending in Rural Pakistan", Pakistan Development Review, Vol. 55, No. 4, pp. 853–870.
38. "Women's Empowerment through Microcredit: A Case Study of District Gujrat, Pakistan", Academic Research International, Vol. 1, No. 2 (Available Online).

39. Priyadarshee et al. (2011), "The Andra Pradesh Microfinance Crisis in India: Manifestation, Causal Analysis, and Regulatory Response", Brooks World Poverty Institute Working Paper 157, University of Manchester.
40. Jayati Ghosh (2012), "Microfinance and the Challenge of Financial Inclusion for Development", Ensayos Economicos, Central Bank of Argentina, Economic Research Department, Vol. 1, No. 67, pp. 7–34.
41. Banerjee et al. (2015), "Six Randomized Evaluations of Microcredit", American Economic Journal: Applied Economics, Vol. 7, No. 1, pp. 1–21.
42. Field & Pande (2008), "Repayment Frequency and Default in Microfinance: Evidence from India", Journal of the European Economic Association, Vol. 6, No. 2, pp. 501–509.
43. Beeman et al. (2021), "Selection into Credit Markets: Evidence from Agriculture in Mali", NBER Working Paper 20387.
44. Haushofer (2016), "The Short-term Impact of Unconditional Cash Transfers to the Poor: Experimental Evidence from Kenya", Quarterly Journal of Economics, Vol. 131, No. 4, pp. 1973–2042.
45. "Cash as Capital", Stanford Social Innovation Review, 2017.
46. "Conditional Cash Transfers: Reducing Present and Future Poverty", World Bank Policy Research Report, Washington, D.C.
47. "Cash Transfer and Formal Labour Markets: Evidence from Brazil", 2021, CEPR Press Discussion Paper No.16286.
48. Parker & Tom (2018), "Do Conditional Cash Transfers Improve Economic Outcomes in the next Generation? Evidence from Mexico", NBER Working Paper 24304.
49. Almas et al. (2016), "Measuring and Changing Control: Women's Empowerment and Targeted Transfers", IZA Discussion Papers, No.9779, Institute for the Study of Labor (IZA).
50. "The Politics of Distributing Social Transfers", edited by Tom Lavers, 2022.
51. "Rethinking Poverty—Report on the World Social Situation 2010", Department of Economic and Social Affairs, ST/ESA/324, pp. 140–141.
52. See chapter with the title "Cash and Care".
53. 'Unjust Conditions—Women's work and the Hidden Cost of Cash Transfer Programs', 2018.

54. It became the largest social safety net program covering around 5.7 million households. The quarterly stipend is Rs. 6000 per household i.e. Rs. 2000 per month (US$10) is an unconditional cash transfer which the beneficiaries receive after on the spot biometric verification.
55. See "The Effects of Fiscal Policy on Inequality and Poverty in Pakistan", World Bank Working Paper, 2022.
56. See "Unconditional Cash Transfers and Poverty Alleviation in Pakistan—BISP's Impact on Households' Socioeconomic Wellbeing", PIDE Policy Viewpoint No. 18: 2020.
57. "Frameworks for a Developmental Welfare State: Lessons from Pakistan's Ehsas Programme", CDDRL Working Papers, June 2022, p. 72.
58. See World Bank Blog "What have We Learned about Cash Transfers", May 10, 2021.
59. Jennifer Ward-Batts (2008), "Out of the Wallet and into the Purse: Using Micro data to Test Income Pooling", Journal of Human Resources, University of Wisconsin Press, Vol. 43, No. 2, pp. 325–351.
60. Arif & Faiz Bilquees (2007), "Chronic and Transitory Poverty in Pakistan: Evidence from a Longitudinal Study", Pakistan Development Review, Vol. 46, No. 2, pp. 111–127.
61. Weiss, John (edited), 'Poverty Targeting in Asia', a joint publication of ADB and Edward Elgar Publishing, 2005, p. 25.
62. See "A Phoneful of Dollars", The Economist, November 16, 2014.
63. 'Portfolios of the Poor—How the World's Poor Live on $2 a Day', 2009, Princeton University Press.
64. Beck et al. (2007), "Finance, Inequality and the poor", Journal of Economic Growth, Vol. 12, pp. 27–49.
65. Shirazi et al. (2018), "The Interlinkage between Social Exclusion and Financial Inclusion: Evidence from Pakistan", Available at SSRN: https://ssrn.com/abstract=3183623
66. Burgess & Pande (2005), "Do Rural Banks Matter? Evidence from the Indian Social Banking Experiment", American Economic Review, Vol. 95, No. 3, pp. 780–795.
67. Ayyagari et al. (2020), "Finance, Law and Poverty: Evidence from India", Journal of Corporate Finance, Vol. 60.
68. Agarwal et al. (2017), "Banking the Unbanked: What Do 255 Million New Bank Accounts Reveal about Financial Access?"

Columbia Business School Research Paper No. 17–12, Available at SSRN: http://dx.doi.org/10.2139/ssrn.2906523
69. "Financial Inclusion under Microscope", IMF Working Paper, September 2018.
70. Dupas & Robinson (2009), "Savings Constraints and Microenterprise Development: Evidence from a Field Experiment in Kenya", NBER Working Paper 14693.
71. Prina (2015), "Banking the poor via savings accounts: Evidence from a field experiment", Journal of Development Economics.
72. Dupas & Robinson (2013), "Why Don't the Poor save more? Evidence from Health Savings Experiments", American Economic Review, Vol. 103, No. 4, pp. 1138–1171.
73. Somville & Vandewalle (2018), "Saving by Default: Evidence from a Field Experiment in Rural India", American Economic Journal: Applied Economics, Vol. 10, No. 3, pp. 39–66.
74. "The Foundations of Financial Inclusion: Understanding Ownership and Use of Formal Accounts", World Bank Policy Research Working Paper 6290, 2012.
75. Max M. Nino-Zarazua & James Copestake (2008), "Financial Inclusion, Vulnerability and Mental Models: From Physical Access to Effective Use of Financial Services in a Low—Income Area of Mexico City", Savings and Development, Vol. 32, No. 4, pp. 353–379.
76. Fonseca, Julia & Adrein Matray (2022), "The Real Effects of Banking the Poor: Evidence from Brazil", NBER Working Paper No. 30057.
77. Azariadis, Costas (1996), "The Economics of Poverty Traps Part One: Complete Markets", Journal of Economic Growth, Vol. 1, No. 4, pp. 449–486.
78. Dasgupta, Partha (1993), "An Inquiry into Well-Being and Destitution", Oxford University press.
79. See 'Good Economics for Hard Times', Chapter 9 (Cash and Care).
80. Balboni et al. (2022), "Why do people Stay Poor", Quarterly Journal of Economics, Vol. 137, No. 2, pp. 785–844.
81. Banerjee et al. (2021)," Long-Term Effects of Targeting the Ultra Poor Program", American Economic Review: Insights, Vol. 3, No. 4, pp. 471–486.

82. Faisal Bari et al. (2021), "Asset-based microfinance for microenterprises: Evidence from Pakistan", CEPR Discussion Paper No.15768 http://cepr.org/publications/dp15768
83. Banerjee et al. (2015), "A Multifaceted Program causes lasting progress for the very poor: Evidence from Six countries", Science, Vol. 348, pp. 772.
84. "Social Development in Pakistan towards Poverty Reduction", SPDC, 2001, Annual Review.
85. Dorosh et al. (2003), "Distributional Impacts of Agricultural Growth in Pakistan: A Multiplier Analysis", Pakistan Development Review, Vol. 42, No. 3, pp. 249–275.
86. Ahmad et al. (1993), "Participation of Rural Women in Agricultural and Household Activities: A Micro-Level Analysis" in 'Agriculture Strategies in the 1990s: Issues and Policies' edited by A. S. Haider, Z. Hussain, R. McConnen, and S. J. Malik. Islamabad: Pakistan Association of Agricultural Social Scientists.
87. See 'Asia's Next Giant—South Korea and Late Industrialization', p. 38.
88. Quoted by Robert Wade in 'Governing the Markets—Economic Theory and the Role of the Government in East Asian Industrialization', p. 241.
89. See 'The Economics of Poverty' by Martin Ravallion, Oxford University Press, and p. 460.
90. Asian Development Bank (2002), pp. 2–3.
91. See' Land Reforms in Developing Countries—Property Rights and Property Wrongs', 2009.
92. "Letter Grading Government Efficiency", NBER Working Paper No. 18268.
93. See Mouza Census 2020, PBS.
94. Asian Development Bank (2002), "Poverty in Pakistan—Issues, Causes, and Institutional Response", Asian Development Bank Resident Mission, Islamabad, pp. 16–17.
95. Cheema, Ali (2007), "Governance Impediments to Pro-Poor Change in Pakistan", Asian Development Bank, Pakistan Resident Mission, Islamabad.

Chapter 10: The Public Sector Performance Conundrum

1. Evans, Peter, 'Embedded Autonomy—States and Industrial Transformation', 1995.
2. Higgs, Robert, 'Crisis and Leviathan: Critical Episodes in the Growth of American Government', 1987.
3. Dixit, Avinash (2002), "Incentives and Organizations in the Public Sector: An Interpretive Review", Journal of Human Resources, Vol. 37, No. 4, pp. 697–727.
4. 'Good Economics for Hard Times', Chapter 8 (LEGIT.GOV).
5. Fukuyama, Francis, 'Political Order and Political Decay: From Industrial Revolution to the Globalization of Democracy', 2014.
6. 'What Money can't buy—The Moral Limits of Markets', 2013.
7. Lerner, Melvin J., 'The Belief in a Just World—A Fundamental Delusion', 1980 (p. 193).
8. Rawls, John, 'A Theory of Justice', 1999, Revised Edition (p. 118).
9. Sen, Amartya, 'The Idea of Justice', 2009.
10. Sandel, Michael J. 'The Tyranny of Merit—What's Become of the Common Good'.
11. Tirole, Jean, 'Economics for the Common Good', 2017 (p. 15).
12. Ibid.
13. R. H. Tawney, 'Equality', Reprint Edition, 1931.
14. See blog "Aligning Elites with Development" by Alice Amsden et al., WIDER Angle Newsletter, August 2009.
15. Emergence and persistence of inefficient States by Acemoglu et al.
16. Mohmand, Shandana K., 'Crafty Oligarchs, Savvy Voters: Democracy under Inequality in Rural Pakistan', 2019.
17. Dixit, Avinash & Londregan, John (1996), "The Determinants of Success of Special Interests in Redistributive Politics", The Journal of Politics, Vol. 58, No. 4.
18. See Pande Rohini's article "Can Democracy Work for the Poor?" Science, Vol. 369, pp. 1188–1192, September 4, 2020.
19. Mohmand, Shandana K., 2019 (p. 27).
20. 'Understanding Policy Change: How to Apply Political Economy Concepts in Practice', 2013, World Bank (p. 57).
21. Lodhi, Maleeha (editor), 'Pakistan Beyond the Crisis State', 2011 (p. 74).
22. See Gerald E. Caiden's article "A Parabolic Theory of Bureaucracy or Max Weber through the Looking Glass" (Chapter 6) included in 'Bureaucracy and Administration', edited by Ali Farazmand, 2009.

23. See "Bureaucracy and Development" by Tim Besley et al., article published on VOX (http://voxeu.org), November 8, 2021.
24. For details see Chapter 7 of Robert wade's 'Governing the Market' (1990).
25. Johnson, Chalmers, 'MITI and the Japanese Miracle—The Growth of Industrial Policy, 1925–1975', Stanford University Press, Stanford, California, 1982 (p. vii); This book presents a well-documented institutional genealogy of MITI and central thesis is that MITI was central to the economic and political history of modern Japan.
26. Ibid., p. 266.
27. Cheng et al. (1998), "Institutions and Growth in Korea and Taiwan: The Bureaucracy", Journal of Development Studies, Vol. 34, No. 6, pp. 87–111.
28. Ang, Yuen Yuen, 'How China Escaped Poverty Trap', 2016.
29. Ibid., p. 251.
30. Barone (2023), "Place-Based Policies in the Italian Case, Part 1: A Lot of Money for Little or No Growth", VoxEU, January 31, 2023.
31. Quoted by Shahid Kardar in article "Governance Reforms anchored in civil service reforms", published in Business Recorder on February 8, 2023.
32. For details see Jamil Nasir's "Analyzing Pakistan's National Competitiveness", Criterion Quarterly, March 2015.
33. RASTA-PIDE (2022)," PIDE Sludge Audit Vol. 1", available online on the official website of PIDE, Islamabad.
34. Sludge is basically opposite of nudge. Contrary to nudge (which makes choices for the people easier to take decisions) sludge makes a process difficult, wastes time, increases red tape and bogs down people in many work settings. According to Sunstein sludge is a grab bag of "paper work requirements, waiting time, reporting requirements, clearance processes and the like". See 'Sludge: What Stops us from Getting Things Done and What to Do about it', book by Cass R. Sunstein, 2021, MIT Press.
35. Rand, Ayn, 'Atlas Shrugged', published in 1957.
36. Hanna & Wang (2017), "Dishonesty and Selection into Public Service: Evidence from India", American Economic Journal: Economic Policy 2017, Vol. 9, No. 3, pp. 262–290.

37. See FPSC Annual Report of 2019 available online on the official website of FPSC.
38. The Tyranny of Merit.
39. Watch address of the Director General, Civil Services Academy to 44th STP of PAS available on YouTube (https://youtu.be/WF1dGTb20a8); address is in Urdu Language.
40. Prosocial behaviour includes things like helping, cooperating, sharing, donating or showing altruism and empathy.
41. See Heckman et al. (1996), "What Do Bureaucrats Do? The Effects of Performance Standards and Bureaucratic Preferences on Acceptance into the JTPA Program", NBER Working Paper 5535.
42. Francois, Patrick (2000), "Public Service Motivation as an Argument for Government Provision", Journal of Public Economics, Vol. 78, No. 3, pp. 275–299; also refer to "Building Theory and Empirical Evidence about Public Service Motivation" by Perry & Hondeghem (2008), International Public Management Journal, Vol. 11, No. 1, pp. 3–12.
43. Nava Ashraf et al. (2014), "No Mission, No Margin? A Field Experiment on Incentives for Public Service Delivery", Journal of Public Economics, Vol. 120, pp. 1–17; In this experiment public health extension workers were randomly assigned to either different categories of financial rewards with margins of 10% or 90% on each condom sale or to a non-financial reward like additional star for each sale. The results were that non-financial rewards were more effective.
44. 'The Moral Economy: Why Good Incentives are not Substitute for Good Citizens', 2016 (p. 40).
45. Ibid., p. 43.
46. Ibid., p. 44.
47. See Alumlund, Mathilde et al. (2011), "Personality Psychology and Economics", NBER Working Paper No. 16822.
48. "Public Service through the Eyes of Civil Servants", PIDE Series on Governance and Institutions (Available Online) http://pide.org.pk.
49. Husain, Ishrat, 'Governing the Ungovernable-Institutional Reforms for Democratic Governance', 2018 (p. 222).
50. See "In the Bureaucracies of Bangladesh and Pakistan, the Raj lives on", June 20th, 2020 Edition of the Economist.

51. Quoted by Eric Gustafson in "Economic Reforms under the Bhutto Regime", Journal of Asian and African studies, July–October 1973.
52. See article "These 3 barriers make it hard for policymakers to use the evidence that development researchers produce" by Michael Callen et al., published in the Washington Post on August 13, 2017.
53. Bo et al. (2013), "Strengthening State Capabilities: The Role of Financial Incentives in the Call to Public", Quarterly Journal of Economics, pp. 1169–1218.
54. See PIDE Policy Viewpoint "The Pension Bombs and Possible Solutions", 2020, PIDE, Islamabad (Available Online). The share of pensioners as percentage of current expenditures for the FY 2019–20 stood at around 7.6% which PIDE estimates that in business as usual scenario, it shall be 56% of the current expenditure by 2050. The share of military pensions stands at 75.67% of the Federal Pension Budget 2019–20 though the number of the Federal and Military retirees stands at around 1.2 million each. The bigger expenditure of the military is due to early retirement of soldiers compared with federal employees who retire at the age of 60.
55. Finan et al. (2015), "The Personnel Economics of the State", NBER Working Paper 21825 (http://www.nber.org/papers/w21825).
56. See commentary on WWBI "Three Lessons from the World Bank's new Worldwide Bureaucracy Indicators Database", December 15, 2018 (https://www.cgdev.org/blog/three-lessons-world-banks-new-worldwide-bureacracy-indicators-database).
57. Van Rijckeghem & Weder (2001), "Bureaucratic Corruption and the Rate of Temptation: Do Wages in the Civil Service Affect Corruption, and by How Much?" Journal of Development Economics, Vol. 65, pp. 307–331.
58. "Cash Poor, Perk Rich Civil Service Compensation: Incentives, Dissatisfaction, and Costs", 2021, PIDE (Available Online).
59. Ibid.; a senior officer here means an officer of BPS-21.
60. Ibid., p. 17.
61. Ibid., p. 8.
62. Quoted by Abdul Wajid Rana with reference to Justice Durab Patel (Chairman 1991 Service Reform Commission) in "PACE

Policy Research Paper: Civil Service Reforms in Pakistan", paper presented at the 34th Annual Conference of Pakistan Society of Development Economics (PSDE), December 12–14, 2018, Islamabad, Pakistan.

63. Refer to World Bank's Report "Innovating Bureaucracy for a more Capable Government" (p. xi).
64. See PIDE Working Paper "Foreign Training of Government officers and Public Sector Capacity in Pakistan", PIDE Working Paper No. 2020:19.
65. See blog post "Five Assumptions about Bureaucracies that our data dispute", November 6, 2017 published on Governance for Development (Available Online).
66. See PIDE Policy Viewpoint No.07/2017 "Strengthening Public Sector Capacity for Improved Governance in Pakistan", available online on the official website of PIDE.
67. Foarta & Morelli (2021), "Complexity and the Reform process", CEPR Discussion Paper No. DP16522 (available at SSRN).
68. Sasso & Morelli (2021), "Bureaucrats under Populism", Journal of Public Economics, Vol. 202, October 2021, 104497.
69. Bellodi & M. Vannoni (2021), "The Costs of Populism for the Bureaucracy and Government Performance: Evidence from Italian Municipalities", CEPR Discussion Paper 1592; the empirics show that probability of non-expert bureaucrats replacing experts increase by 11%. So it is hypothesized that effects are significant. The empirical results are based on Italian municipalities but such an impact cannot be ruled out in the provincial and national bureaucracies in a country like Pakistan.
70. Gratton et al. (2021), "From Weber to Kafka: Political Instability and the Overproduction of Laws", American Economic Review, Vol. 111, No. 9.
71. See FPSC Annual Report, 2019 (Available Online) http://www.fpsc.gov.pk.
72. See WEF's International Competitiveness Reports of last one decade for the most problematic factors responsible for low competitiveness of Pakistan.
73. Ayesha Hanif et al. (2016), "Performance Management in Public Sector: A Case of Civil Service of Pakistan", South Asia Studies, Vol. 31, No.1. pp. 99–116.

74. Xu, Guo (2018), "The Costs of Patronage: Evidence from the British Empire". *American Economic Review*, Vol. 108, No. 11, pp. 3170–98.
75. Bertrand et al. (2020)," The Glittering Prizes: Career Incentives and Bureaucrat Performance", Review of Economic Studies, Vol. 87, No. 2.
76. Aditya Dasgupta and Devesh Kapur in their paper "The Political Economy of Bureaucratic Overload: Rural Development Officials in India" identify a different pathology for the failure of rural development programs or poor public service delivery which they name bureaucratic overload which simply means that local level bureaucrats are often heavily under-resourced compared with the responsibilities they have to discharge. Based on nationwide survey of rural local development officials across India, they conclude that local state capacity is weak due to underinvestment and bureaucratic overload crowds out managerial focus. This paper was published in American Political Science Review in 2020. These findings may be relevant to Pakistan as well to some extent but low productivity of frontline workers is mainly due to culture of patronage, rent-seeking, and weak local state institutions.
77. Colonnelli et al. (2019), "Patronage and Selection in Public sector Organizations", CEPR Discussion Paper 13697; This paper is in the context of Brazilian public sector but in Pakistan it is also an open secret that whenever some political party provided jobs to the individuals outside the sphere of public service commission, same were not provided on ideological considerations but on the consideration of political support to the party or against some other considerations.
78. See "Patronage and Selection in Public sector Organizations", CEPR Press Discussion Paper No. 13697, 2019.
79. See VOXEU article "The Problem of Public sector absenteeism", August 21, 2016 http://voxeu.org.
80. See Centre of Global Development's paper "Capability Traps? The Mechanisms of Persistent Implementation Failure" by Lant Pritchett et al., Working Paper 234, December 2010 (www.cgd ev.org); also refer to World Development Report 2011 background paper "Fragile States: Stuck in a Capability Trap?" by Lant Pritchett et al., 2010; isomorphic mimicry is a type of camouflage in the animal world for survival. For example, some flies look like bees

and even create buzz like a bee but actually do not have stings. The organizations also indulge in isomorphic mimicry for survival through forms but in actual they do not have functional capability.

81. "How has Isomorphic Mimicry contributed to the Failure of Fulfilling the Educational Objectives of the UNA Laptop POR NINO Program in Peru", http://blogs.lse.ac.uk: This essay highlights how failure of laptop program in Peru was a pertinent manifestation of isomorphic mimicry.
82. Tax-to-GDP ratio is almost stagnant since many years and hovers around 10%.
83. "The Tariff Tripod of Pakistan: Protection, Export Promotion and Revenue Generation", Pakistan Development Review (PDR), Vol. 59, No. 3, pp. 517–551.
84. See Clair Yang's paper "On Determinant of State Capacity: Wars, Goods, and Economic Shocks", written on February 22, 2022 and available on SSRN.
85. Dittmar & Meisenzahl (2016), "State Capacity and Public Goods: Institutional Change, Human Capital and Growth in Early Modern Germany", CEP Discussion Paper No. 1418.
86. See VOXEU column "Policymaking, trust, and the demand for public services: Evidence from a nationwide family planning program", July 15, 2022 (https://voxeu.org).
87. Spence, Michael (1973), "Job Market Signalling", Quarterly Journal of Economics, Vol. 87, No. 3, pp. 355–374.
88. Quoted by Andrew Wilder in "The Politics of Civil Service Reform in Pakistan", 2010, Journal of International Affairs, SIPA, Columbia.

Chapter 11: A Noisy Legal System

1. The Code of Capital, p. 229; this book basically answers the question as how the law creates wealth and inequality.
2. See "The Judiciary and Economic Development", John M. Olin Law and Economics Working Paper 287, 2006, University of Chicago Law School.
3. "Do More Transparent Governments Govern Better?" Policy Research Working Paper 3077, World Bank

4. See Dr. Faqir Hussain's report "The Judicial System of Pakistan" (4th Edition), May 2015; available on the website of the supreme court of Pakistan. Dr. Faqir Hussain has worked as the Registrar of the Supreme Court of Pakistan and Director General of Federal Judicial Academy of Pakistan.
5. Hadfield 'Rules for a Flat World: Why Humans Invented Law and How to Reinvent it for a Complex Global Economy', 2017.
6. "The Political Economy of Rule of Law Reform in Developing Countries", Michigan Journal of International Law, Vol. 26, No. 1, 2004.
7. See article "The End of the Feast" published in the Economist on July 27, 1996.
8. "Justice: Not a Fundamental Right", PIDE, 2022.
9. Siddique, Osama (2011), "Approaches to Legal and Judicial Reform in Pakistan: Post-colonial Inertia and the Paucity of Imagination in Times of Turmoil and Change", DPRC Working Paper No. 4, LUMS.
10. See "Trust in State and Non-State Actors: Evidence from Dispute Resolution in Pakistan" (2018); In the paper Acemoglu and his colleagues focusing on dispute resolution in rural Punjab have found that providing information on reduced delays in state courts increases willingness of the citizens to use the state courts more. The implication is that the citizens like rational human beings choose between the formal and informal mechanism of dispute resolution, where they can, depending on delays and costs involved.
11. The World Justice Project ranks Pakistan at 120 (out of total 128) in 2020 on rule of law index with score of 0.39.
12. Out of total 190 countries, Pakistan stands at 156 in terms of enforcing contracts as per World Bank's Doing Business ranking of 2020.
13. See copy of the speech of Justice Jawwad S. Khawaja available on the website of the Supreme Court of Pakistan.
14. Klein, R. Crawford & Alchian, A. (1978), "Vertical Integration, Appropriate Rents, and the Competitive Contracting Process", Journal of Law and Economics, Vol. 21, pp. 297–326.
15. Chemin, M. (2020), "Judicial Efficiency and Firm Productivity: Evidence from a World Database of Judicial Reforms", Review of Economics and Statistics, Vol. 102, No. 1, pp. 49–64.

16. This study was conducted by Umar Gilani and Usher Qazi in 2011 and is available in the library of the Supreme Court. Another study conducted in 2016 under the auspices of the European Union's Access to Justice program also came up with similar results of inordinate delay; Another report (of Legal Society) on the trial courts of Karachi, based on data for the period May 2013 to March 2016, found that at any given date there was 58.65% chance that the case would be adjourned.
17. "Economic Analysis of Law in Pakistan", PIDE Knowledge Brief No. 6/2020.
18. Chemin, Matthieu (2010), "Does Court Speed Shape Economic Activity? Evidence from a Court Reform in India", Journal of Law, Economics and Organization.
19. Mentioned in C.M.A filed in Constitutional Petition No.5/2018 under Article 184(3) of the Constitution of the Islamic Republic of Pakistan; The said petition has been filed by some members of the legal community with the prayer that the Supreme court should issue directions to the High Courts for reducing delays.
20. See Daily Dawn, October 24, 2016.
21. See Daily Tribune May 19, 2019.
22. Jayaraman & Simroth (2015), "The Impact of School Lunches on Primary School Enrollment: Evidence from India's Midday Meal Scheme", The Scandinavian Journal of Economics, Vol. 117, No. 4, pp. 1176–1203.
23. Refer to Suo Moto case No.13 of 2009 (PLD 2011 SC619) where the supreme court held that "right to life—implies the right to food, water, decent environment, education, medical care and shelter—"; Similarly in case "Messers Al-Raham Travels and Tours (Pvt.) Ltd" (reported at 2011 SCMR 1621), the supreme court held that: "a man cannot think of individual or collective development when he cannot meet the basic necessities of life such as minimum food, clothing and housing. The Right to those basic necessities of life are basically and fundamentally economic right—".
24. Hamid Khan, 2016.
25. See Miss Benazir Bhutto case reported as PLD 11988 SC416.
26. Maulana Abul Kalam Azad's statement on January 24, 1922 in the court of the Fourth Presidency Magistrate in Calcutta when he was

charged with sedition; translation taken from A. G. Noorani's 'The Trial of Bhagat Singh-Politics of Justice'.

27. See Arif Hasan's article "Courts and the Poor", published in Dawn on June 20, 2021.
28. See International Crisis Group's report "Reforming Pakistan's Criminal Justice System", 2010, p. 18 (Available Online).
29. PIDE Webinar Brief No.1: 2020 with title "Case Management as an Approach to Improve Judicial System", available on line on the website of PIDE.
30. CP No. 5620 of 2021 etc. The apex court converted the petitions into appeals and held that fixation of wage of Rs. 25,000 by the Sindh Government was not legal; The minimum wage of Rs. 25,000 is even lower than calculated by Wage Indicator Foundation which estimates the minimum wage for Pakistan around Rs. 28,700.
31. Card & Krueger (1994), "Minimum Wages and Employment: A Case study of the Fast-Food Industry in New Jersey and Pennsylvania", American Economic Review, Vol. 84, No. 4, pp. 772–793.
32. Card & Krueger 'Myth and Measurement: The New Economics of the Minimum Wage', p. 394.
33. This observation is based on face-to-face interviews of 50 Lawyers mainly providing legal services in the Sindh High Court and Lahore High court.
34. Hamid Khan, 'A History of the Judiciary in Pakistan', 2016, Oxford University Press (p. 547).
35. 'Noise—A Flaw in Human Judgment', 2021, p. 221.
36. Ibid., pp. 69–78 for detailed discussion on the analysis of noise.
37. Ibid., p. 89.
38. Ibid., pp. 90–93 for discussion on occasion noise.
39. Ibid., p. 351; for detailed discussion on pros and cons of standards and rules, refer to Chapter 28.
40. Hamid Khan, 2016.
41. 'Noise: A Flaw in Human Judgment', p. 226.
42. Thaler & Sunstein, 'Nudge—Improving Decisions about Health, Wealth, and Happiness', 2008; for examples and discussion on two systems of thinking, refer to pages 27–30.
43. Mehmood, Sultan (2020), "Judicial Independence and Development: Evidence from Pakistan", AMSE Working Paper 2041, Aix-Marseille School of Economics, France.

44. See 'Public Administration in East Asia—Mainland China, Japan, South Korea, and Taiwan', edited by Berman et al., 2010, CRC Press, New York, USA (pp. 368–369).
45. Sindh Judicial Academy (2008), "Study on Informal Justice in Pakistan"; this study was conducted by SJA in collaboration with Law and Justice Commission and UNICEF. The investigating team included Justice Saleem Akhtar and Justice Mushir Alam. The report inter alia recommended for establishing linkages between the formal and informal justice system.
46. This excerpt is from the Report of the Secretary General of UN on "Legal Empowerment of the poor and eradication of poverty", July 2009 (publicly available).
47. See 'Pakistan's Experience with Formal Law'.
48. Porta, Rafael La, Lopez-de-Silanes, Florencio & Shleifer, Andrei (2008), "The Economic Consequences of Legal Origins", Journal of Economic Literature, Vol. 46, No. 2, pp. 285–322.
49. "Judicial Checks and Balances", Journal of Political Economy, Vol. 112, No. 2, pp. 445–476.
50. Mahoney, Paul (2001), "The Common Law and Economic Growth: Hayek Might be Right", Journal of Legal studies, Vol. 25, No. 2, pp. 229–255.
51. Djankov et al. (2003) "Courts", Quarterly Journal of Economics, Vol. 118, No. 2.
52. Naveed Ahmad Shinwari (2015), "Understanding the Informal Justice System: Opportunities and Possibilities for Legal Pluralism in Pakistan", CAMP; this quote is from Chapter 1 (introductory chapter written by Dr. Osama Siddique).
53. Ibid, p. 118.
54. "Legal Advisory and Representational Services in South Punjab: Base Study of Availability and Priority Needs", 2015, Report of the Punjab Access to Justice Project Funded by the EU.
55. 'Pakistan's Experience with Formal Law: An Alien Justice', 2014, Chapter 2, p. 129; Sample was reasonably representative consisting of 440 litigants.
56. Ibid., p. 139.
57. Ibid., p. 143.
58. Ibid., Chapter 3, p. 195.
59. 'The Locust Effect—Why the End of Poverty requires the End of Violence', 2014, OUP.

60. Ibid.
61. Ibid.
62. Ibid.
63. Hamid Khan, 2016.
64. Acemoglu et al. (2018), "Trust in State and Non-state Actors: Evidence from Dispute Resolution in Pakistan", NBER Working Paper No. 24611.
65. Nadeem Ahmad Shinwari (2015) Chapter 2, pp. 32–64; Dr. Osama estimates that around 81.5% of the respondents show their lack of faith in formal justice system and 80–90% disputes are resolved through informal mechanisms.
66. Ibid., pp.16–32.
67. Ibid., Chapter 4.
68. Ibid., Chapter 5.
69. Lieven, Anatol 'Pakistan—A Hard Country' 2011, p. 96.
70. Diamond, Jared, 'The World until Yesterday—What We can learn from Traditional Societies', 2012.
71. Ibid., p. 109.

Chapter 12: Social Capital and Corruption Incorporated

1. Banefield, Edward, 'The Moral Basis of a Backward Society', 1958.
2. Ibid., pp. 166–167.
3. Ibid., pp. 33–35.
4. Refer to World Values Survey Wave 7 (2017–2020) Study # WVS-2017.
5. Knack & Keefer (1997), "Does Social Capital have an Economic Payoff?" Quarterly Journal of Economics, November 1997.
6. Arrow, Kenneth (1973), "Gifts and Exchanges", Philosophy and Public Affairs, 1, p. 357.
7. Fukuyama, Francis, 'Trust—The Social Virtues and the Creation of Prosperity', 1995, pp. 27–28.
8. Jose De Sousa et al. (2023), "Trust and Specialization in Complexity: Evidence from US States".
9. Zak & Knack (2001), "Trust and Growth", pp. 295–321.
10. Khanna, Tarun, 'Trust—Creating the Foundation for Entrepreneurship in Developing Countries', 2018.
11. Putman, Robert, 'Bowling Alone', 2000.

12. Coleman (1988), "Social Capital in the Creation of Human Capital", American Journal of Sociology, Vol. 94, Supplement: Organizations and Institutions: Sociological and Economic Approaches to the Analysis of Social Structure.
13. "Dinner Table Human Capital and Entrepreneurship", NBER Working Paper 24198, 2018.
14. Helliwell & Wang, "Trust and Well-being", NBER Working Paper 15911, 2010.
15. Putman, Robert, 'Making Democracy Work-Civic Traditions in Modern Italy', 1993.
16. See PIDE's Basic Notes Number 5 "Pakistanis: Who Are We? Social and Civic Engagement: Building Community or "Bowling Alone"? January 2023, PIDE (Available Online on PIDE website).
17. Bertrand & Schoar (2006), "The Role of Family in Family Firms", Journal of Economic Perspectives, Vol. 20, No. 2, pp. 73–96.
18. Nunn & Wantchekon (2011), "The Slave Trade and the Origins of Mistrust in Africa", American Economic Review, Vol. 101, No. 7, pp. 3221–3252.
19. Alesina & Ferrara (2002), "Who Trusts Others?" Journal of Public Economics, Vol. 85, No. 2, pp. 207–234.
20. Ananyev & Guriev (2018), "Effect of Income on Trust: Evidence form the 2009 Economic Crisis in Russia", EBRD Working Paper No. 209.
21. Rothstein & Stolle (2008), "The State and Social Capital: An Institutionalized Theory of Generalized Trust", Comparative Politics, Vol. 40, No. 4, pp. 441–459.
22. Quoted by Jamil Nasir in 'Political Economy of Bad Governance' p. 211.
23. World Happiness Report, 2015.
24. Competitive authoritarian regimes are neither democracies nor authoritarian regimes; in such regimes elections may be fought bitterly but electoral process may not be fair.
25. Cheema et al. (edited), 'Power Sector-An Enigma with No Easy Solution', 2022, PIDE, Islamabad.
26. For example, for the year 2021, the estimates for the said variables are respectively −0.79, −0.40, −0.73, −0.64, and −0.84.
27. Leff, Nathaniel H. (1964). "Economic Development through Bureaucratic Corruption", The American Behavioral Scientist (Pre-1986); November 1964; 8, 3; ABI/INFORM complete.

28. "An Equilibrium Queuing Model of Bribery", Journal of Political Economy, Vol. 93, 760–781; also refer to Lui, F. T. (1986), "A Dynamic Model of Corruption Deterrence", Journal of Public Economics, Vol. 31, pp. 215–236.
29. Beck and Maher, M. W. (1986). "A Comparison of Bribery and Bidding in Thin Markets", Economic Letters, Vol. 20, pp. 1–5.
30. Shleifer & Vishny (1993), "Corruption", Quarterly Journal of Economics, Vol. 108, No. 3.
31. Bardhan, Pranab. (1997). "Corruption and Development: A Review of Issues", Journal of Economic Literature, Vol. 35, No. 3, pp. 1320–1346, September; this paper also discusses the concept of 'centralization of bribery' which does explain why countries like South Korea and China grew despite corruption. The quotation about civil servants is in this context.
32. Ang, Yuen Yuen, 'China's Gilded Age—The Paradox of Economic Boom and Vast Corruption', 2020.
33. Fisman & Svensson (2007). "Are Corruption and Taxation Really Harmful to Growth? Firm Level Evidence", Journal of Development Economics, Vol. 83, No. 1, pp. 63–75.
34. Sequeria & Djankov, "An Empirical Study of Corruption in Ports", MPRA Paper 21791, 2010.
35. Bates, Roberts, 'Markets and States in Tropical Africa', 1981.
36. De Soto, Hernando, 'The Other Path', 1989.
37. Olken, Benjamin A. (2006), "Corruption and the Costs of Redistribution: Micro Evidence form Indonesia", Journal of Public Economics, Vol. 90, No. 4–5, pp. 853–870.
38. Gupta et al. (2000), "Corruption and the Provision of Health Care and Education Services", IMF Working Paper WP/001/116.
39. Ferraz et al. (2010), "Corrupting Learning: Evidence from Missing Federal Education Funds in Brazil", mimeo, Berkley.
40. Khawaja & Mian (2005). "Do Lenders Favour Politically Connected Firms? Rent Provision in an Emerging Financial Market", Quarterly Journal of Economics, Vol. 120, No. 4, 1371–1411.
41. Delavallade, Clara. (2006), "Corruption and Distribution of Public Spending in Developing Countries", Journal of Economics and Finance, Vol. 30, No. 2, Summer.

42. Yang, D. (2008), "Integrity for Hire: An Analysis of a Widespread Customs Reform", Journal of Law and Economics, Vol. 51, No. 1, pp. 25–57.
43. Dr Husain, Ishrat in his article "Retooling Institutions", included in 'Pakistan Beyond the Crisis State', 2011.
44. Ibid.
45. Olken & Pande (2011), "Corruption in Developing Countries", NBER Working Paper No. 17398 (for detailed discussion on this proposition).
46. Van Rijckeghem & Weder (2001), "Bureaucratic Corruption and The Rate of Temptation: Do Wages in the Civil Service Affect Corruption, and by How Much?" Journal of Development Economics, Vol. 65, No. 2, pp. 307–331.
47. The share of public sector expenditure in terms of GDP increases over time.
48. Haque, Nadeem Ul. & Sahay, Ratan (1996), "Do Government Wage Cuts Close Budget Deficits? Costs of Corruption", IMF Staff Papers, Vol. 43, No. 4, pp. 754–778.
49. Muralidharan & Sundararaman, "Teacher Performance Pay: Experimental Evidence from India", NBER Working Paper 15323, 2009.
50. "The Tariff Tripod of Pakistan: Protection, Export Promotion, and Revenue Generation", PIDE, 2020.
51. These examples are mentioned in IDB's report titled "Digitalizing Public Services – Opportunities for Latin America and the Caribbean", November 2022.
52. Abhijit et al. (2020), "E-governance, Accountability, and Leakage in Public Programs: Experimental Evidence from a Financial Management Reform in India", American Economic Journal: Applied Economics, Vol. 12, No. 4, October, pp. 39–72.
53. Callen, M., "Data and Policy Decisions: Experimental Evidence from Pakistan", CEPR Discussion Paper No. 15169, 2020 (http://cepr.org/publications/dp15169).
54. See 'Good Economics for Hard Times', Chapter 8.
55. According to Transparency survey, 2022, judiciary is perceived to be the second most corrupt institution after police.
56. Shaikh, Farzana, 'Making Sense of Pakistan', 2009, Columbia University Press.

Chapter 13: Weak Fiscal and Trade Capacities

1. From lecture in 1755, quoted in Dugald Stewart, Account of the Life and Writings of Adam Smith LLD, Section IV.
2. Besley & Persson, 'Pillars of Prosperity—The Political Economics of Development Clusters', 2011.
3. Ibid.; Chapter 2; also refer to Besley et al. (2013), "Weak States and Steady States: The Dynamics of Fiscal Capacity", American Economic Journal: Macroeconomics, Vol. 5, No. 4, pp. 205–236.
4. Rotberg, Robert I. (edited), 'When States Fail: Causes and Consequences', 2004, p. 101.
5. Dal Bo, E., Hernandez, P., & Mazzuca, S. (2015), "The Paradox of Civilization: Pre-Institutional Sources of Security and Prosperity", NBER Working Paper 21829.
6. Mc Neill, W. H. 'The Pursuit of Power: Technology, Armed Forces and Society Since AD 1000', 2013.
7. Fukuyama, Francis, 'Political Order and Political Decay-from the Industrial Revolution to the Globalization of Democracy', 2014.
8. Tilly, 'The Formation of National States in Western Europe', 1975.
9. Scheve, K., & Stasavage, D. (2012), "Democracy, War, and Wealth: Lessons from Two Centuries of Inheritance Taxation", American Political Science Review, Vol. 106, No. 1, pp. 81–102.
10. Stasavage, David, 'The Decline and Rise of Democracy: A Global History from Antiquity to Today', 2020.
11. Sanchez de la Sierra, R (2020), "On the Origin of States: Stationary Bandits and Taxation in Eastern Congo", Journal of Political Economy, Vol. 128, No. 1, pp. 32–74.
12. Besley & Persson (2014), "Why Do Developing Countries Tax So Little?" Journal of Economic Perspectives, Vol. 28, No. 4, pp. 99–120.
13. Chambru, C., Henry, E., & Marx, B., "The Dynamic Consequences of State-Building: Evidence from the French Revolution", CEPR Discussion Paper 16815, 2021.
14. Acemoglu et al. (2020), "The Perils of High-Powered Incentives: Evidence form Colombia's False Positives", American Economic Journal: Economic Policy, Vol. 12, No. 3, pp. 1–43.
15. Dell, M., & Querubin, P., "Nation Building Through Foreign Intervention: Evidence from Discontinuities in Military Strategies", NBER Working Paper No. 22395, 2016.

16. See Pablo Querubin and Melissa Dell's article "More Bombs, More Shells, More Napalm: Nation Building Through Foreign Intervention", August 16, 2016, VoxEU.
17. Rohner & Zhuravskaya (edited), 'Nation Building: Big Lessons from Successes and Failures', 2023, Centre for Economic Policy Research, e-Book (www.cepr.org).
18. Hayek, F.A., 'The Road to Serfdom', 1944, p. 64.
19. Migdal, Joel S., 'Strong Societies and Weak States: State-society Relations and State Capabilities in the Third World', 1988.
20. Acemoglu, D. & James Robinson, 'The Narrow Corridor', 2019, Penguin Books, p. kv.
21. Ibid., p. xv.
22. Armytage, Rosita, 'Big Capital in an Unequal World', 2020.
23. Uslander, E.M. 'Tax Evasion, Trust, and the Strong Arm of the Law', Paper at Conference on Tax Evasion, Trust, and State Capacity, University of St Gallen, Switzerland, 17–19 October 2003.
24. Acemoglu et al. (2011), "Emergence and Persistence of Inefficient States", Journal of the European Economic Association, European Economic Association, Vol. 9, No. 2, pp. 177–208.
25. Baum et al. (2017), "Corruption, Taxes and Compliance", IMF Working Paper.
26. Stiglitz, Joseph E. (1998), "Development Oriented Tax Policy", Initiative for Policy Dialogue, Columbia University.
27. Best et al. (2015), "Production vs. Revenue Efficiency with Limited Tax Capacity: Theory and Evidence from Pakistan", Journal of Political Economy, Vol. 123, No. 6, pp. 1311–1355.
28. De Neve et al. (2021), "How to Improve Tax Compliance? Evidence from Population—Wide Experiments in Belgium", The Journal of Political Economy, Vol. 129, No. 5, pp. 1425–1463.
29. Jorge Martinez-Vazquez (2006), "Pakistan: A Preliminary Assessment of the Federal Tax System", Working Paper 06–24, International Studies Program, Andrew Young School of Policy Studies.
30. Alstadsaeter et al. (2019), "Tax Evasion and Inequality", American Economic Review, Vol. 109, No. 6, pp. 2073–2103.
31. Muhammad Ashfaq Ahmed (2020), "Pakistan: Witholdingisation of the Economic System—A Source of Revenue, Civil Strife, or Dutch Disease?" Pakistan Development Review, Vol. 59, No. 3, Islamabad.

32. World Bank (2022), "The Effects of Fiscal Policy on Inequality and Poverty in Pakistan", Working Paper.
33. It is measure of progressivity of tax. A positive value of Kakwani index means that tax is progressive and a negative value means it is regressive. A value close to zero means it is neutral.
34. World Bank (2023), "Pakistan Federal Public Expenditure Review 2023", Chapter 5, p. 15.
35. Allingham, Michael G. & Sandmo, Agnar (1972), "Income Tax Evasion: A Theoretical Analysis", Journal of Public Economics, Vol. 1, pp. 323–338.
36. Aisen et al. (2005), "The Political Economy of Seigniorage", IMF Working Paper 05/175.
37. Easterly W. & Fischer, Stanley (2001), "Inflation and the Poor", Journal of Money, Credit and Banking, Vol. 33, No. 2, pp. 160–178.
38. Moore et al., 'Taxing Africa: Coercion, Reform and Development', 2018, Zed Books.
39. Albers et al., "The Fiscal State in Africa: Evidence from One Century of Growth", African Economic History Working Paper 55/2020, 2020.
40. Martin, Lucy (2016), "Taxation, Loss Aversion, and Accountability: Theory and Experimental Evidence for Taxation's Effect on Citizen Behavior", University of North California Paper (Available Online).
41. Moyo, Dambisa, 'Dead Aid—Why Aid Is Not Working and How There Is a Better Way for Africa', 2009.
42. Ibid.
43. Anderson et al. "Elite Capture of Foreign Aid—Evidence from Offshore Accounts", World Bank Policy Research Working Paper No. 9150, 2020.
44. Anderson et al. (2017), "Petro Rents, Political Institutions, and Hidden Wealth: Evidence from Offshore Accounts", Journal of European Economic Association, Vol. 15, No. 4, pp. 818–860.
45. Saez & Zucman, 'The Triumph of Injustice—How the Rich Dodge Taxes and How to Make Them Pay', 2019.
46. Alstadsaeter et al. (2018), "Who Owns the Wealth in Tax Havens: Macro Evidence and Implications for Global Inequality", Journal of Public Economics.

47. 11.5 million Documents which uncovered an intricate network of offshore entities involved in huge tax evasion by making transactions with several tax havens simultaneously pointing towards a complex interconnected structure of tax evasion of the super-rich at the global level. For details refer to paper "The Political Economy of Big Data leaks: Uncovering the Skeleton of Tax evasion'", by Pier Luigi Sacco et al.
48. As a result of an investigation undertaken by more than 600 investigative journalists, offshore dealings of for many world leaders, politicians, and public officials were unearthed. The Pandora Papers unmask the hidden owners of offshore companies, secret bank accounts, and other properties.
49. These papers are also result of the investigations by ICI J and reveal secrets of offshore law firms and other company registries in secret jurisdictions.
50. Bhagwati (1982), "Directly Unproductive, Profit-seeking (DUP) activities", Journal of Political Economy 90, 988–1002.
51. Pritchett, Lant (2023), "Multilateralism and Development Cooperation: The End of an Interesting Era?" Global Perspectives, Vol. 4, No. 1, 72711.
52. This figure is referred to in Webinar Brief No. 10: 2020 on Foreign Aid to Pakistan, available online on the official website PIDE.
53. Nasir, Jamil (2012), "IMF Programs in Pakistan (1988–2008)—An Analysis", Criterion Quarterly, Vol. 2, No. 4.
54. Dr. Ashfaq Hassan Khan (2019), "Pakistan's Experience with the IMF", Strategic Thought, 2019 (Issue 1).
55. Quoted by Daily Nation, September 3, 2001, Islamabad.
56. The Dawn, September 19, 2001, Karachi.
57. IMF (2002), "Evaluation of prolonged Use of IMF Resources", Independent Evaluation Office Report, p. 131.
58. Ibid., p. 119.
59. Refer to "PIDE Interviews Arshad Zaman", P & R Vol. 1, No. 3, 2020 (https://pide.org.pk).
60. Ibid.
61. Hudson, Michael, 'The Bubble and Beyond', September 2012, e-Book Edition.
62. The public debt servicing stands at 35% of total spending of the federal government (as on June 30, 2022). Debt and publicly guaranteed debt constitutes 78% of the GDP of Pakistan (for details

see Pakistan Federal Public Tax Expenditure Review 2023 by the World Bank).

63. See UN note "A World of Debt—A growing burden to global prosperity", July 2023; According to this note 3.3 billion people live in countries which spend more on interest payments than on education and health. And that public debt has increased more than fivefold since year 2000 and almost 30% of the global public debt is owed by the developing countries.
64. See "Pakistan Federal Public Expenditure Review 2023", Chapter 2 (p. 8), World Bank.
65. See "How to Avoid a Debt Crisis in Sub-Saharan Africa", 2023.
66. Kelton, Stephanie, 'The Deficit Myth—Modern Monetary Theory and the Birth of the People's Economy', 2020, Public Affairs.
67. See Box 3.1 in World Bank (2021), "Pakistan Development Update", April 2021; the analysis is based on the estimation of a gravity model of trade, with focus on countries with at least 5 million inhabitants and covering 80% of international trade flows.
68. See World Development indicators of the World Bank.
69. See Heiko Hesse.
70. See Atlas of Economic Complexity of Harvard (atlas.cid.harvard.edu).
71. Hartmann, Dominick et al. (2017), "Linking Economic Complexity, Institutions, and Income Inequality", World Development, Vol. 93, pp. 75–93.
72. Hausmann, Ricardo; Hwang, Jason & Dani Rodrik (2007), "What You Export Matters", Journal of Economic Growth, Vol. 12, No. 1.
73. Krugman, Paul & Taylor, Lance (1978), "Contractionary Effects of Devaluation", Journal of International Economics, Vol. 8, pp. 445–456.
74. Bader, Sadia, "Determining Import Intensity of Exports for Pakistan", State Bank of Pakistan SBP Working Paper Series, Karachi, 2006.
75. Felipe, Jesus & Lim, Joseph, "An analysis of Pakistan's Macroeconomic Situation and Prospects" ADB Economics Working Paper Series No. 136: ADB, Manila, 2008.
76. Gita Gopinath et al. (2020), "Dominant Currency Paradigm", American Economic Review, Vol. 110, No. 3, pp. 677–719.

77. Martin Brun et al. (2020), "Slow Rockets and Fast Feathers or the Link between Exchange Rates and Exports: A Case Study for Pakistan", World Bank Policy Research Working Paper No. 9353.
78. See "Determinants of Export Growth at the Extensive and Intensive Margins", WB Policy Research Working Paper No. 6341, January 2013.
79. Moberg, Lotta (2018), "Liberalizing Rent-seeking: How Export Processing Zones can save or sink an Economy", Journal of Private Enterprise, Vol. 33, pp. 61–89.
80. See Dani Rodrik's Paper "Industrial Policy for the Twenty-First Century", 2004.
81. See PIDE Research Report, "Special Economic Zones in Pakistan: Promises and Perils", 2020, PIDE, Islamabad.
82. Ibid.
83. Haque, Nadeem Ul & Kemal, M. Ali, "Impact of Export Subsidies on Pakistan's Exports", PIDE Working Paper 2007: 26, Islamabad, 2007.
84. Panagariya, Arvind (2000), "Evaluating the Case for Export Subsidies", Policy Research Working Paper 2276, World Bank.
85. Mah, Jai S. (2007), "Duty Drawback and Export Promotion in China", Journal of Developing Areas, Vol. 40, No. 2.
86. See Reviving Exports Section of "Pakistan Development Update October, 2021", World Bank.
87. Based on data analysis by the author for the period 2015–2022.
88. See World Bank paper "Internationally linked Firms, Integration Reforms and Productivity: Evidence from Pakistan", 2020.
89. Direction of Trade Statistics, IMF.
90. World Bank, 'A Glass Half Full-The Promise of Regional Trade in South Asia', 2018.
91. See Jamil Nasir, 'SAFTA: Potential, Prospects, and Limitations' for Discussion on Various Trade Models, 2007, LCCI.
92. World Bank, 'A Glass Half Full'.
93. See Jamil Nasir, SAFTA, 2007.
94. World Bank, 2018.
95. Ibid.
96. See Nisha Taneja & Samridhi Bismal (2016), "India's Informal Trade with Pakistan", ICRIER.
97. See Akbar Zaidi et al. (2017), "Misperception About India-Pakistan Trade—Beyond Politics", USFP, www.usfp.org.

Chapter 14: The Militancy Challenge

1. Krueger, Alan B., 'What Makes a Terrorist—Economics and the Roots of Terrorism', Tenth Anniversary Edition, 2018, Princeton University Press.
2. See Robert Barrow's article "The Myth that Poverty Breeds Terrorism", Bloomberg Businessweek New York, June 10, 2002.
3. Shared by the *Wall Street Journal*'s email exchanges with the Nobel Laureate; interview was granted in 2006, the year Friedman died.
4. Abadie, Alberto & Gardeazabal, Javier (2003), "The Economic Costs of Conflict: A Case Study of the Basque Country", American Economic Review, Vol. 93, No. 1, pp. 113–132.
5. Institute for Economics and Peace (IEP), "Economic Value of Peace 2021: Measuring the Global Economic Impact of Violence and Conflict", Sydney, January 2021.
6. See the *Wall Street Journal*, Saturday/Sunday, September 10–11, 2011, http://online.wsj.com/public/resources/documents/WSJ.pdf.
7. Greig, J. Andrew, "Riding the Tiger—The Threat to Pakistan from Terrorism", included in 'Pakistan's Political Labyrinths—Military, Society, and Terror', edited by Ravi Kalia, 2016, Routledge.
8. Economic Survey 2013–2014, Ministry of Finance, GOP.
9. Mehmood, Sultan (2013), "Terrorism and the Macroeconomy: Evidence from Pakistan", Defence and Peace Economics, 10.1080/10242694.2013.793529.
10. Shahbaz, Muhammad et al. (2013), "An Analysis of the causal Relationship between economic growth and terrorism in Pakistan", Economic Modelling, Vol. 35, pp. 21–29.
11. Zakaria, Muhammad et al. (2019), "Effect of Terrorism on Economic Growth of Pakistan: An Empirical Analysis", Economic Research-Ekonomska Istraživanja, Vol. 32, No. 1, pp. 1794–1812, https://doi.org/10.1080/1331677X.2019.1638290.
12. Ali, Hashmat et al. (2017), "How Terrorism Affects Foreign Direct Investment in Pakistan", International Journal of Economics and Financial Issues, Vol. 7, No. 3, pp. 625–631.

13. Oscal, N. & Yildrim, J. (2010), "Effects of Terrorism on Economic Growth in Turkey: A Geographically Weighted Regression Approach", Journal of Peace Research, Vol. 47, No. 4, pp. 477–489.
14. Javeid, Umer et al. (2023), "The Effect of Terrorism on Continuing Education: Evidence from Pakistan", Education Economics, Vol. 31, No. 3.
15. See "War on Terror: The Impact of Tehreek-e-Taliban Pakistan on the Education in South Waziristan", 2022, PJTR 4:2.
16. Annual report 2015–16 of the Rehabilitation and Reconstruction Unit (PRU) of the FATA Secretariat.
17. Paul Collier, 'The Bottom Billion: Why the Poorest Countries are Failing and What Can Be Done About It', 2007, Oxford University Press.
18. See 'What Makes a Terrorist', 2018 Edition.
19. Ibid.
20. Abadie, Alberto (2006), "Poverty, Political Freedom, and the Roots of Terrorism", American Economic Review, Vol. 96, No. 2, pp. 50–56.
21. Collier, Paul & Hoeffler, Anke (2004), "Greed and Grievance in Civil War", Oxford Economic Papers, Vol. 56, No. 4, pp. 563–595.
22. Collier, Paul & Nicholas Sambanis (Eds.), "Understanding Civil War—Evidence and Analysis", Volume 2: Europe, Central Asia, and Other Regions, 2005, World Bank.
23. Ibid.
24. Ibid.
25. Ibid.
26. Blair, Graeme, Fair, C. Christine, Neil, Malhotra, & Shapiro, Jacob N. (2013), "Poverty and Support for Militant Politics: Evidence from Pakistan", American Journal of Political Science, Vol. 57, No. 1, pp. 30–48.
27. Gupta, Dipak K., 'Understanding Terrorism and Political Violence—The Life Cycle of Birth, Growth, Transformation, and Demise', 2008, Routledge.
28. Ibid.
29. Bano, Masooda, 'The Rational Believer: Choices and Decisions in the Madrasas of Pakistan', 2012, Cornell University Press.
30. Gupta, 2008.

31. Ibid.
32. Griffin, Keith & Rahman Kahn, Azizur (Eds.), 'Growth and Inequality in Pakistan', 1972, Palgrave Macmillan.
33. Bjorgo, Tore (Eds.), 'Root Causes of Terrorism: Myths, Reality, and Ways Forward', 2005, Routledge.
34. Eamon Murphy, 'The Making of Terrorism in Pakistan—Historical and Social Roots of Extremism', 2013, Routledge, New York.
35. Ibid.
36. Ibid.
37. Report of the Court of Inquiry constituted under Punjab Act II of 1954 to enquire into the Punjab Disturbances of 1953 (commonly known as Munir Commission report).
38. Ibid.
39. Ganguly, Sumit (1996), "Explaining the Kashmir Insurgency—Political Mobilization and Institutional Decay", International Security, Vol. 21, No. 2, pp. 76–117.
40. Ganguly, Sumit, 'The Deadly Impasse—Kashmir and Indo-Pakistani Relations at the Dawn of a New Century', 2016, Cambridge University Press, p. 51.
41. Ahmer, Moonis (2011), "The Impact of the War Against Terror on Pakistan", Project Muse.
42. Afzal, Madiha 'Pakistan Under Siege: Extremism, Society, and the State', 2018, Paperback Edition, Brookings Institution Press.
43. Like Jaish-i-Mohammad and Lashkar-Taiba; There have been allegations from India that these groups fought proxy war for Pakistan in India-administered Kashmir.
44. Akhtar, Aasim Sajjad, 'The Politics of Common Sense—State, Society, and Culture in Pakistan', 2018, Cambridge University Press.
45. Hussain Haqqani 'Reimagining Pakistan' for detailed discussion on this point.
46. Ibid.
47. Munir Commission Report, 1954.
48. Malik, Iftikhar H., 'State and Civil Society in Pakistan—Politics of Authority, Ideology and Ethnicity', 1997, Palgrave Macmillan.
49. Murphy, Eamon, 'The Making of Terrorism in Pakistan—Historical and Social Roots of Extremism', 2013, Routledge.
50. Quoted by Madiha Afzal, 2018.

51. International Crisis Group, 'A New Era of Sectarian Violence in Pakistan', 2022, Brussels, Belgium.
52. Rana, Muhammad Amir (2011), "Evolution of Militant Groups in Pakistan", Conflict and Peace Studies, Vol. 4, No. 2.
53. Fox News, July 17, 2010.
54. The Making of Terrorism in Pakistan, 2013.
55. Ibid.
56. Rubin, Barnett R. (2000), "The Political Economy of War and Peace in Afghanistan", World Development, Vol. 28, No. 10.
57. Rana, Muhammad Amir (2018), "Pakistani-Based Militant Groups and Prospects of Their Reintegration: A Structural Analysis", Mantraya Occasional Paper, No. 6, March 12.
58. Data is available in Global Terrorism Data (GTD) base as well as South Asian Terrorism portal (SATP). It is mentioned in United States Institute of Peace Special Report No.494 with the title "The Evolution and Potential Resurgence of the Tehrik-i-Taliban Pakistan", May 2021.
59. Rashid, Ahmed, 'Descent into Chaos'.
60. Nasr, S.V.R. (2000), "The Rise of Sunni Militancy in Pakistan: The Changing Role of Islamism and the Ulama in Society and Politics", Modern Asian Studies, Vol. 34, No. 1.
61. Ibid.
62. During the said period, the PTI government in KPK and at the center, in a bid to reform madrassas, provided financial incentives. For example, in 2016, PTI government in KPK allocated Rs. 300 million for Darul Uloom Haqqania. In 2019, a separate Directorate General of Religious Education was inaugurated with a plan of 16 regional offices country-wide to regulate madrassas in the country and a budget of Rs. 2 billion was allocated.
63. Hussain, Zahid, 'Frontline Pakistan', 2007, Columbia University Press.
64. Stern, Jessica (2000), "Pakistan's Jihad Culture", Foreign Affairs, Vol. 79, No. 6, pp. 115–126.
65. International Crisis Group (ICG), 'Pakistan: Madrasas, Extremism and the Military', 2002, ICG Asia Report No. 36, Islamabad/Brussels.
66. NACTA (2021), "Misconception About the Relationship Between Militancy and Madrasas in Swat", Pakistan Journal of Terrorism Research, Vol. 3, No. 2, July–December.

67. See Aziz, K.K., 'Murder of History'.
68. See Hassan Askari Rizvi's article "Can Pakistan Cope with Terrorism", *Daily Times*, April 12, 2007.
69. Andrabi et al., "Madrasa Statistics Don't Support the Myth", included in 'Under the Drones', edited by Shahzad Bashir and Robert D. Crews, 2012, Harvard University Press.
70. Quoted by Madiha Afzal in Pakistan under Siege.
71. Ibid.
72. Quoted by USIP Special Report No. 421, March 2018, www.usip.org.
73. Ibid.
74. Government of Pakistan (2016), "Report of the Committee on FATA Reforms", August 2016.
75. Ibid.; NFC is an institutional arrangement under the Constitutions of Pakistan for providing monetary transfer from the federal divisible pool of duties and taxes collected by the Federation among the four provinces of Pakistan. The underlying principle is that such allocations create a symmetry in the per capita allotments to ensure equitable development and economic growth.
76. FATA Research Centre Report (2016), "Governance Reforms in Federally Administered Tribal Areas: A People's Perspective", Islamabad, www.frc.org.pk.
77. Jones, Seth G., & Christine Fair, C., 'Counterinsurgency in Pakistan', 2010, RAND Corporation www.rand.org.
78. GOP, 'FATA: Post-Crisis Needs Assessment', 2010, FATA Secretariat, Government of Pakistan, Islamabad.
79. See ADB Technical Assistance Consultant's report titled "Pakistan: Post-Conflict Needs Assessment", September 2010.
80. Counterinsurgency in Pakistan, 2010.
81. Hussain, Khadim, 'The Militant Discourse', Narratives, Islamabad, Pakistan.
82. Ibid.
83. Zaman, Muhammad Qasim (1998), "Sectarianism in Pakistan: The Radicalization of Shi 'i and Sunni Identities", Modern Asian Studies, Vol. 32, No. 3, pp. 689–716.
84. Eamon Murphy, 2013.
85. Abbas, Hassan (2009), "Defining the Punjabi Taliban Network", CTC SENTINEL, Vol. 2, No. 4, April.

86. See "South Punjab Deep Dive Report 2022", https://pakistan.un.org/en/177830-south-punjab-deep-dive-report.
87. Ibid.
88. See report, "South Punjab Regional SDGs Indicators Comparison with Centre and North', Prepared by UNDP in Collaboration with South Punjab Secretariat, February 2022.
89. HRCP (2022), "South Punjab—Excluded, Exploited", Human Rights Commission of Pakistan, Lahore.
90. See Mukhtar Mai, Wikipedia.
91. Laurent Gayer, 'Karachi—Ordered Disorder and the Struggle for the City', 2014, Oxford University Press.
92. Javed, Umair & Nabi, Ijaz "Heterogeneous Fragility in Pakistan", included in 'State Fragility—Case Studies and Comparisons', edited by Nematullah Bizhan, 2023, Routledge.
93. Easterly, William (2000), "Can Institutions Resolve Ethnic Conflict?" World Bank Policy Research Working Paper 2482.
94. USIP Report, "Conflict Dynamics in Karachi", 2012, www.usip.org
95. Ibid.
96. Laurent Gayer, 2014.
97. Ibid.
98. Umair Javed and Ijaz Ghani (2023).
99. Ibid.
100. See Zahid Hussain's article "War Within", Herald, August 1987.
101. Laurent Gayer, 2014.
102. World Bank, 'Balochistan Economic Report—From Periphery to Core', Report No. 40345-PK, May 2008, p. 1.
103. UNDP (2015), "FATA Sustainable Return and Rehabilitation Strategy", FATA Secretariat Support Program, UNDP Pakistan office, Islamabad.
104. See 'A Cry for Justice', OUP.
105. Ibid.
106. World Bank, May 2008, p. 24.
107. See background paper Social Structures and Migration (for Balochistan Economic Report) by Haris Gazdar, 2007.
108. Rumi, Raza (2012), "Pakistan: Ungoverned Spaces", Barcelona Centre for International Affairs, http://www.cidob.org.
109. See Amir Rana's article "Reconciliation in Balochistan?" in Dawn, published on July 11, 2021.

110. See Amir Rana article "Religion, Nationalism, and Insurgency in Balochistan", Dawn, July 14, 2019.
111. See Kiyya Baloch's article with the title "Trust Issues: Why Are Pakistan and Iran Up in Arms?" Dawn, January 19, 2024.
112. Siddique, Farhan Irfan, 'The Politics of Ethnicity in Pakistan—The Baloch, Sindhi and Mohajir Ethnic Movements', 2012, Routledge.

Case Study 1

1. Nasir, Jamil (2007), "Factors Affecting Performance of Sales Tax Audit Workforce of the Central Board of Revenue", Pakistan Management Review, Vol. XLIV, No. 3, Karachi.
2. Fershtman et al. (1996), "Social Status, Education, and Growth", Journal of Political Economy, Vol. 104, No. 1, pp. 108–132.
3. Quoted by William J. Baumol (1990).
4. Whalley, John & Zhao, Xiliang (2010) "The Contribution of Human Capital to China's Growth", NBER Working Paper 16592.

Case Study 2

1. Ahmad, Ehtisham (2010), "Why It Is so Difficult to Implement a GST in Pakistan?" Lahore Journal of Economics, Vol. 15, SE, pp. 139–169.
2. Ahmad, E. & Stern, N. 'Theory and Practice of Tax Reforms in Developing Countries', 1991.
3. The tax bureaucracy working in BPS-20, 21 and 22 is the senior level bureaucracy. The posts of BPS-20 increased from 70 to 170, of BPS-21 from 29 to 49 and some additional posts of 22 were also created. If BPS-20 and 21 posts are taken into account, increase was of 120%.
4. Exact number is Rs. 66,950 billion.
5. Lansing, 'Priests and Programmers', 1991.
6. William Easterly expresses similar arguments in his other book 'Tyranny of Experts' where he argues that the neglect of people's rights in aid receiving countries has become a moral tragedy of development and technocratic approach has served the interests of

the autocrats and so-called development experts. The world aid apparatus ignores the individual rights, imposes solutions which fail to take into account the historical experiences, value system, and the local conditions of a community.

7. Easterly (2013), 'The Tyranny of Experts—Economists, Dictators and the Forgotten Rights of the Poor', Basic Books, p. 320.
8. Altaf, Samina Waleed, 'So Much Aid, So Little Development—Stories from Pakistan', 2011; This books gives firsthand account of aid machinery as to how aid has failed to bring any tangible change and how it creates a dependency culture.
9. PIDE "Foreign Aid Effectiveness: The Relationship Between Aid Inflows and Economic Growth", September 2022, Knowledge Brief, Available online of PIDE's official website.
10. Mazzucato & Collington, 'The Big Con: How the Consulting Industry Weakens Our Businesses, Infantilises our Governments and Warps Our Economies', 20.

Case Study 3

1. In 2011, Pakistan's exports to Iran were US $ 219 which decreased to just to US $ 3.2 thousand; imports have also declined from US $ 568 million (in 2011) to US $ 352 million in 2020 (refer to note No. G & RS-08 dated March 24, 2023, Islamabad).
2. Kuntani Bay, Abdoi, Jalagi, Jeerak, and Perago (in Makran Division) and Tump, Judhar, Guzar Derpan, and Rajhay (in Rakshan Division).
3. GOP (2020), "Report of the Inquiry Commission on the Shortage of Petroleum Products in Pakistan", http://cabinet.gov.pk.
4. See "Oil, Sweat and Tears", Dawn, June 23, 2019 and "Senior Police Officers Smuggling Iranian Oil", Dawn, September 7, 2015.
5. For example, incident of recovery of Rs. 730 million cash and jewelry of worth Rs.40 million from the Finance Secretary of Balochistan, Report by Dawn, May 6, 2016.
6. Press report published in Nikkei Asia on March 26, 2021.
7. Smuggling includes to bring into or out of country any goods in breach of prohibitions and restrictions, or carrying, transporting, removing, depositing, harboring, keeping, concealing, and even

retailing. The smuggling also includes any goods brought to country through any route other than the approved as Customs-station.

8. "PM Orders Action Against fuel Smuggling Across Iran Border", Dawn, January 3, 2021.
9. This is administrative data of FBR which appeared in the press as well.

Bibliography

Abadie, Alberto & Gardeazabal, Javier (2003), "The Economic Costs of Conflict: A Case Study of the Basque Country", American Economic Review, Vol. 93, No. 1, pp. 113-132.

Abadie, Alberto (2006), "Poverty, Political Freedom, and the Roots of Terrorism", American Economic Review, Vol. 96, No. 2, pp. 50-56.

Abbas, Hassan (2009), "Defining the Punjabi Taliban Network", CTC SENTINEL, Vol. 2, No. 4, April.

Acemoglu, D., Hassan, T.A., & Tahoun, A. (2018), "The Power of the Street: Evidence from Egypt's Arab Spring", Rev. Financ. Stud., Vol. 31, pp. 1–42.

Acemoglu, D., Johnson, S., & Robinson, J.A. (2001), "Colonial Origins of Comparative Development: An Empirical Investigation", American Economic Review, Vol. 91, No. 5.

Acemoglu, Daron & Johnson, Simon, "Disease and Development: The Effect of Life Expectancy on Economic Growth", NBER Working Paper No. 12269.

Acemoglu, Daron & Robinson, James (2000), "Why Did the West Extend the Franchise? Democracy, Inequality, and Growth in Historical Perspective", Quarterly Journal of Economics, Vol. 115, No. 4.

Acemoglu, Daron & Robinson, James A. (2002), "The Political Economy of the Kuznets Curve", Review of Development Economics, Vol. 6, No. 2.

Acemoglu, Daron & Robinson, James A., 'The Narrow Corridor', 2019, Penguin Books.

Acemoglu, Daron & Robinson, James A., 'Why Nations Fail', 2012, Crown Business, New York, USA

J. Nasir, *Development Challenges of Pakistan*,
https://doi.org/10.1007/978-981-97-3064-3

Acemoglu, Daron & Simon Jonson, 'Power and Progress: Our Thousand-Year Struggle Over Technology and Prosperity', 2023, Public Affairs. New York, USA

Acemoglu, Daron, Cheema, Ali, Khawaja, Asim I., & Robinson, James A. (2018), "Trust in State and Non-State Actors: Evidence from Dispute Resolution in Pakistan", NBER Working Paper 24611.

Acemoglu, Daron, Fergusson, Leopoldo, Robinson, James, & Vargas, Juan F. (2020), "The Perils of High-Powered Incentives: Evidence form Colombia's False Positives", American Economic Journal: Economic Policy, Vol. 12, No. 3.

Acemoglu, Daron, Johnson, Simon, Robinson, James, & Thaicharoen, Yunyong (2003), "Institutional Causes, Macroeconomic Symptoms: Volatility, Crises, and Growth", Journal of Monetary Economics, Vol. 50, No. 1.

Acemoglu, Daron, Vindigni, Andrea, & Ticchi, Davide (2011), "Emergence and Persistence of Inefficient Sates", Journal of the European Economic Association, Vol. 9, No. 2.

Adams, Richard H. (2001), "Non-farm Income, Inequality, and Poverty in Rural Egypt and Jordon", Policy Research Working Paper No. 2527, World Bank, Washington, D.C.

ADB (2016), "Potential Growth, Misallocation, and Institutional Obstacles: Firm-level Evidence", ADB Economics Working Paper Series No. 480, April, 2016

AEPAM (2018), "Public Financing in Education Sector", Ministry of Federal Education and Professional Development, Government of Pakistan, Islamabad.

Afzal, Uzma, Adda, Giovanna D., Fafchamps, Marcel, & Said, Farah (2016), "Gender and Agency Within the Household: Experimental Evidence from Pakistan", CEPR Discussion Paper No. 11464.

Agarwal, Bina, 'A Field of One's Own', 1994, Cambridge University Press.

Agarwal, Sumit, Alok, Shashwat, Ghosh, Pulak, Ghosh, Soumya, Piskorski, Tomasz, & Amit Seru (2017), "Banking the Unbanked: What Do 255 Million New Bank Accounts Reveal about Financial Access?" Columbia Business School Research Paper No. 17-12, Available at SSRN: https://doi.org/10.2139/ssrn.2906523.

Aghion, Philippe, Antonin, Celine, & Bunel, Simon, 'The Power of Creative Destruction—Economic Upheaval and the Wealth of Nations', 2021, Harvard University Press, Cambridge, USA.

Ahmad, E. & Stern, N., 'Theory and Practice of Tax Reforms in Developing Countries', 1991, Cambridge University Press.

Ahmad, Ehtisham (2010), "Why It Is so Difficult to Implement a GST in Pakistan?" Lahore Journal of Economics, Vol. 15, SE.

Ahmad, Khalil, Chaudhary, M. Aslam, & Ilyas, Muhammad (2008), "Trends in Total Factor Productivity in Pakistan Agriculture Sector", Pakistan Economic and Social Review, Vol. 46, No. 2.

Ahmad, Munir, Chand, Asghar & Alam Khan, Nasir (1993), "Participation of Rural Women in Agricultural and Household Activities: A Micro-Level Analysis", included in 'Agriculture Strategies in the 1990s: Issues and Policies. Islamabad: Pakistan Association of Agricultural Social Scientists', edited by A.S. Haider, Z. Hussain, R. McConnen, and S.J. Malik.

Ahmer, Moonis (2011), "The Impact of the War against Terror on Pakistan", Project Muse.

Aisen, Ari & Veiga, Francisco Jose (2011), "How Does Political Instability Affect Economic Growth?" IMF Working Paper No. 2011/012.

Aisen, Ari, & Veiga, Francisco Jose (2005), "The Political Economy of Seigniorage", IMF Working Paper 05/175.

Akhtar, Aasim Sajjad, 'The Politics of Common Sense—State, Society, and Culture in Pakistan', 2018, Cambridge University Press.

Akmal, Maryam & Pritchett, Lant (2019), "Learning Equity Requires More Than Equality: Learning Goals and Achievement Gaps Between the Rich and the Poor in Five Developing Countries", www.cgdev.org.

Akresh, R., Halim, D., & Kleemans, M. (2018), "Long-Term and Intergenerational Effects of Education: Evidence from School Construction in Indonesia", NBER Working Paper 25265.

Alain Lefebvre, 'Kinship, Honour and Money in Rural Pakistan: Subsistence Economy and the Effects of Internal Migration', 1999 Edition, Curzon Press.

Albers, T, Jerven, M., & Suesse, M. (2020), "The Fiscal State in Africa: Evidence from one Century of Growth", African Economic History Working Paper 55/2020.

Alderman, Harold & Bundy, Donald (2011), "School Feeding Programs and Development: Are We Framing the Question Correctly?" World Bank Research Observer.

Alderman, Harold, Orazem, Peter F., & Paterno, Elizabeth M. (2001), "School Quality, School Cost, and the Public/ Private school choices of low-Income Households in Pakistan", Journal of Human Resources, Vol. 36, No. 2.

Alesina, Alberto & Ferrara, Eliana La (2002), "Who Trusts Others?" Journal of Public Economics, Vol. 85, No. 2.

Alesina, Alberto & Rodrik, Dani (1994), "Distributive Politics and Economic Growth", Quarterly Journal of Economics, Vol. 109, No. 2.

Alesina, Alberto, Ozler, Sule, Roubini, Nouriel, & Swagel, Philip (1996), "Political Instability and Economic Growth", Journal of Economic Growth, Vol. 1, No. 2.

Alex Cobham & Andy Sumner (2013), "Putting the Gini back in the bottle? The 'Palma' as a policy relevant measure of inequality", Mimeograph, London: London King's College.

Alex, Eble, Chris Frost, Alpha Camara, Baboucarr Bouy, Momodou Bah, Maitri Sivaraman, Pei-Tseng Jenny Hsieh, Chitra Jayanty, Tony Brady, Piotr Gawron, Stijn Vansteelandt, Peter Boone and Diana Elbourne (2021), "How Much Can We Remedy Very Low Learning Levels in Rural Parts of Low-Income Countries? Impact and Generalizability of a Multi-Pronged Para-Teacher Intervention from a Cluster-Randomized Trial in the Gambia", Journal of Development Economics, Vol. 148, No. C.

Alfaro, Laura, Kalemli-Ozcan, Sebnem, & Volosovych, Vadym (2008), "Why Doesn't Capital Flow from Rich to Poor Counties? An Empirical Investigation", Review of Economics and Statistics, Vol. 90, No. 2.

Ali, Hashmat, Qingshi, Wang, Ullah, Irfan & Ali, Zulifqar (2017), "How Terrorism Affects Foreign Direct Investment in Pakistan", International Journal of Economics and Financial Issues, Vol. 7, No. 3.

Ali, Imran, 'The Punjab Under Imperialism 1885–1947', 1988, Princeton University Press.

Alina Tuominen (2015), "Reversal of the Kuznets Curve—Study on the Inequality-Development Relation Using Top Income Shares Data", WIDER Working Paper 2015/036.

Allingham, Michael G. & Sandmo, Agnar (1972), "Income Tax Evasion: A Theoretical Analysis", Journal of Public Economics 1 (1972).

Almas, Ingvild, Armand, Alex, Attanasio, Orazio, & Carneiro, Pedro (2016), "Measuring and Changing Control: Women's Empowerment and Targeted Transfers", IZA Discussion Papers, No. 9779, Institute for the Study of Labor (IZA), Bonn.

Almond, Douglas & Currie, Janet (2011), "Killing Me Softly: The Fetal Origins Hypothesis", Journal of Economic Perspectives, Vol. 25, No. 3.

Almond, Douglas & Mazumder, Bhashkar (2011), "Health Capital and the Prenatal Environment: The Effect of Ramadan Observance during Pregnancy", American Economic Journal: Applied Economics, Vol. 3, October.

Alstadsaeter, Annette, Jahannesen, Niels & Zucman, Gabriel (2018), "Who Owns the Wealth in Tax Havens: Macro Evidence and Implications for Global Inequality", Journal of Public Economics, Elsevier, Vol. 162, No. C.

Alstadsaeter, Annette, Johannesen, Niels & Zucman, Gabriel (2019), "Tax Evasion and Inequality", American Economic Review, Vol. 109, No. 6.

Altaf, Samina Waleed, 'So Much Aid, So Little Development—Stories from Pakistan', 2011.

Alumlund, Mathilde, Duckworth, Angela Lee, Heckman, James J. & Kautz, Tim D. (2011), "Personality Psychology and Economics", NBER Working Paper No. 16822.

Alvi, Hamza (1973), "Elite Farm strategy and Regional Disparities in the Agricultural Development of Pakistan", Economic and Political Weekly, Vol. 8, No. 13, March 31.

Alvi, Hamza (1975), "India and the Colonial Mode of Production", Economic and Political Weekly, Vol. 10, No33/35, Special Number.

Alvi, Hamza (1976), "The Rural Elite and Agricultural Development in Pakistan", Pakistan Economic and Social Review, Vol. 14, No. 1/4, Department of Economics, University of the Punjab.

Amjad, B., Carrasco, H., & Meyer, M. (2022), "The Effects of Fiscal Policy on Inequality and Poverty in Pakistan", World Bank Working Paper.

Amjad, Rashid (1972), "A Critique of the Green Revolution in West Pakistan", MPRA Paper No. 39275.

Amjad, Rashid, ul Haque, Nadeem, & Colclough, Christopher (2005), "Skills and Competitiveness: Can Pakistan Break Out of the Low-Level Skills Trap?" Pakistan Development Review, PIDE, Islamabad.

Amjad, Shehla & Hasnu, S.A.F. (2007), "Smallholders' Access to Rural Credit: Evidence from Pakistan", Lahore Journal of Economics, Vol. 12, p. 2.

Amsden, Alice H., 'Asia's Next Giant: South Korea and Late Industrialization', 1989, Oxford University Press.

Ananyev, Maxim & Guriev, Sergei (2018), "Effect of Income on Trust: Evidence form the 2009 economic crisis in Russia", EBRD Working Paper No. 209.

Anderson, Jorgen Juel, Johanneson, Niels, & Rijkers, Bob (2020), "Elite Capture of Foreign Aid—Evidence from Offshore Accounts", World Bank Policy Research Working Paper No. 9150.

Anderson, Jorgen Juel, Johanneson, Niels, Lassen, David Dryer, & Paltseva, Elena (2017), "Petro Rents, Political Institutions, and Hidden Wealth: Evidence from Offshore Accounts", Journal of European Economic Association, Vol. 15, No. 4.

Andrabi, Tahir, Bau, Natalie, Das, Jishnu, Karachiwalla, Naureen, & Khwaja, Asim Ijaz (2023), "Crowding in Private Quality: The Equilibrium Effects of Public Spending in Education", NBER Working Paper 309209.

Andrabi, Tahir, Das, Jishnu, & Khawaja, Asim Ijaz (2008), "A Dime a Day—The Possibilities and Limits of Private Schooling in Pakistan", Comparative Education Review, Vol. 52, No. 3.

Andrabi, Tahir, Das, Jishnu, & Khawaja, Asim Ijaz, "Madrasa Statistics Don't Support the Myth", included in 'Under the Drones', edited by Shahzad Bashir and Robert D. Crews, 2012, Harvard University Press.

Ang, Yuen Yuen, 'China's Gilded Age: The Paradox of Economic Boom and Vast Corruption', 2020, Cambridge University Press.

Ang, Yuen Yuen, 'How China Escaped Poverty Trap', 2016, Cornell University Press.

Angrist, Joshua, D., Lavy, Victor & Schlosser, Analia (2005), "New Evidence on the Casual Link between the Quantity and Quality of Children", NBER Working Paper No. 11835.

Angrist, Noam, Djankov, Simeon, Goldberg, Pinelopi K., & Patrinos, Harry A. (2021), "Measuring Human Capital Using Global Learning Data", Nature, Vol. 592.

Anriquez, Gustavo & Valdes, Alberto (2006), "Determinants of Farm Revenue in Pakistan", Pakistan Development Review, Vol. 45, No. 2.

Anuj, Shah K., Zhao, Jiaying, Mullainathan, Sendhil, & Shafir, Eldar (2018), "Money in the Mental Lives of the Poor", Social Cognition, Vol. 30, No. 1.

Aresvik, Odvar (1968), "Reflections on the Socio-Economic Objectives of the Fourth Five Year Plan—Agricultural Strategy", Agriculture Department, Government of Pakistan, Nov. 1968 (Mimeo).

Arif, G.M & Faiz Bilquees (2007), "Chronic and Transitory Poverty in Pakistan: Evidence from a Longitudinal Study", Pakistan Development Review, Vol. 46, 2.

Armytage, Rosita, 'Big Capital in an Unequal World: The Micropolitics of Wealth in Pakistan', 2020, Berghahn Books, New York, USA.

Arrow, Kenneth (1973), "Gifts and Exchanges", Philosophy and Public Affairs.

Arshad, Zaman, 'Social Origins of Debt Crises—Reflections on Pakistan's Experience', December, 2022, Unpublished Manuscript.

ASER (2020), "Annual Status of Education Report 2019", January.

Ashraf, Nava, Bau, Natalie, Nunn, Nathan, & Voena, Alessandra (2020), "Bride Price and Female Education", Journal of Political Economy, Vol. 128, No. 2.

Ashraf, Nava, Oriana, Bandiera, & Jack, B. Kelsey (2014), "No Mission, No Margin? A Field Experiment on Incentives for Public Service Delivery", Journal of Public Economics, Vol. 120, Issue C.

Ashraf, Nava; Karlan, Dean & Wesley Yin (2006), "Tying Odysseus to the Mast: Evidence from Commitment Savings Product in the Philippines", Quarterly Journal of Economics, Vol. 121, No. 2.

Ashraf, Quamrul H., Lester, Ashley, & Weil, David N. (2008), "When Does Improving Health Raise GDP?" NBER Working Paper No. 14449.

Asian Development Bank (2002), "Poverty in Pakistan—Issues, Causes, and Institutional Response", Asian Development Bank Resident Mission, Islamabad.

Atkinson, Anthony B., 'Inequality-What Can Be Done', 2015, Harvard University Press.

Ayyagari, Meghana, Beck, Thorsten, & Hoseini, Mohammad (2020), "Finance, Law and Poverty: Evidence from India", Journal of Corporate Finance, Vol. 60.

Azariadis, Costas (1996), "The Economics of Poverty Traps Part One: Complete Markets", Journal of Economic Growth, Vol. 1, No. 4.

Azhar, B.A. (1995), "Rural Saving: Their Magnitude, Determinants, and Mobilization", Pakistan Development Review, Vol. 34, No. 4 Part II -1995.

Aziz, K.K., "The Murder of History', 1993, Vanguard Books, Lahore, Pakistan.

Baland, Jean-Marie & Robinson, James A. (2008), "Land and Power: Theory and Evidence from Chile", American Economic Review, Vol. 98, No. 5.

Balboni, Clare, Bandiera, Oriana, Burgess, Robin, Ghatak, Maitreesh, & Heil, Anton (2022), "Why Do People Stay Poor", Quarterly Journal of Economics, Vol. 137, No. 2.

Banefield, Edward C., 'The Moral Basis of a Backward Society', 1958, Free Press, Glencoe, Illinois, USA.

Banerjee, Abhijit & Duflo, Esther (2007), "The Economic Lives of the Poor", Journal of Economic Perspectives, Vol. 21, No. 1.

Banerjee, Abhijit & Duflo, Esther, 'Poor Economics', 2011, Public Affairs, USA.

Banerjee, Abhijit & Iyer, Lakshmi (2005), "History, Institutions, and Economic Performance: The Legacy of Colonial Land Tenure Systems in India", American Economic Review, Vol. 95, No. 4.

Banerjee, Abhijit V. & Duflo, Esther, 'Good Economics for Hard Times', 2019, Public Affairs, New York, USA.

Banerjee, Abhijit V., Cole, Shawn, Duflo, Esther, & Lindon, Leigh (2007), "Remedying Education: Evidence from Two Randomized Experiments in India", Quarterly Journal of Economics, Vol. 122, No. 3.

Banerjee, Abhijit, Breza, E., Duflo, Esther & Kinnan, Cynthia (2019), "Can Microfinance unlock a Poverty Trap for Some Entrepreneurs?" NBER Working Paper w26346.

Banerjee, Abhijit, Duflo, Esther, & Zinman, J. (2015), "Six Randomized Evaluations of Microcredit", American Economic Journal: Applied Economics, Vol. 7, No. 1.

Banerjee, Abhijit, Duflo, Esther, and Sharma, Garima (2021), "Long-Term Effects of Targeting the Ultra Poor Program", American Economic Review: Insights, Vol. 3, No. 4.

Banerjee, Abhijit, Duflo, Esther, Glennerster, Rachel & Kinnan, Cynthia (2015), "The Miracle of Microfinance? Evidence from a Randomized Evaluation", American Economic Journal: Applied Economics, Vol. 7, No. 1, pp. 22–53.

Banerjee, Abhijit, Duflo, Esther, Goldberg, Nathanael, Karlan, Dean, Osei, Robert, Pariente, William, Shapiro, Jeremy, Thuysbaert, Bram & Christopher Udry (2015), "A Multifaceted Program Causes Lasting Progress for the Very Poor: Evidence from Six Countries", Science, Vol. 348, 772.

Banerjee, Abhijit, Esther, Duflo, Imbert, Clement, Mathew, Santosh & Pande, Rohini (2020), "E-governance, Accountability, and Leakage in Public Programs: Experimental Evidence from a Financial Management Reform in India", American Economic Journal: Applied Economics, Vol. 12, No. 4, October.

Banerjee, Abhijit, Glennerster, Rachel, & Duflo, Esther (2008), "Putting a Band-Aid on Corpse: Incentives for Nurses in the Indian Public Healthcare system", Journal of European Economic Association, Vol. 6 Nos. 2–3.

Banerji, Rukmini (2015), "How Do Systems Respond to Disruptive Pedagogic Innovations? The Case of Pratham in Bihar", RISE-WP-15/002.

Bano, Masooda, 'The Rational Believer: Choices and Decisions in the Madrasas of Pakistan', 2012, Cornell University Press.

Baqai, Huma & Wasi, Nausheen (Eds.), 'Pakistan–Afghanistan Relations: Pitfalls and the way Forward', 2021, FES Pakistan Office, Islamabad.

Barber, Michael & Shahzad, Muqeet (2022), "Frameworks for a Developmental Welfare State: Lessons from Pakistan's Ehsas Programme", CDDRL Working Papers, June.

Bardhan, Pranab (1997), "Corruption and Development: A Review of Issues", Journal of Economic Literature, Vol. 35, No. 3, September.

Bari, Faisal, Malik, Kashif, Meki, Muhammad & Quinn, Simon (2021), "Asset-Based Microfinance for Microenterprises: Evidence from Pakistan", CEPR Discussion Paper No. 15768 http://cepr.org/publications/dp15768.

Barone, Guqlielmo & de Blasio, Guido (2023), "Place-Based Policies in the Italian Case, Part 1: A Lot of Money for Little or No Growth", VoxEU, January 31.

Barrera-Osario, Felipe and Raju, Dhushyanth (2015), "Teacher Performance Pay—Experimental Evidence from Pakistan", WPS 7307.

Barrera-Osorio, Felipe; Adriana D., Kugler, & Silliman, Mikko I. (2020), "Hard and Soft Skills in Vocational Training: Experimental Evidence from Colombia", NBER Working Paper 2548.

Barro, Robert J. (2000), "Inequality and Growth in a Panel of Countries", Journal of Economic Growth, Vol. 5.

Bates, Robert H., 'Markets and States in Tropical Africa—The Political Basis of Agricultural Policies', 1981, University of California Press, USA.

Baum, Anja, Gupta, Sanjeev, Kimani, Elijah, & Tapsoba, Sampawende Jules (2017), "Corruption, Taxes and Compliance", IMF Working Paper.

Baumol, William J. (1990), "Entrepreneurship: Productive, Unproductive, and Destructive", Journal of Political Economy, Vol. 98, No. 5, Part 1.

Baumol, William J., 'The Free-Market Innovation Machine—Analyzing the Growth Miracle of Capitalism', 2002, Princeton University Press, Princeton, New Jersey, USA.

Baumol, William J., Litan, Robert E., & Schramm, Carl J., 'Good Capitalism, Bad Capitalism, and the Economics of Growth and Prosperity', 2007, Yale University Press, New Haven & London.

Beck, P.J. & Maher, M.W. (1986), "A Comparison of Bribery and Bidding in thin Markets", Economics Letters, Vol. 20, No. 1.

Beck, T, A Demirguc & R Levine (2007), "Finance, Inequality and the poor", Journal of Economic Growth, Vol. 12.

Becker, Gary & Tomes, Nigel (1976), "Child Endowments and the Quantity and Quality of Children", Journal of Political Economy, Vol. 84, No. 4.

Becker, Gary S. (1995), "Human Capital and Poverty Alleviation", HRO Working Paper 14458, World Bank.

Beeman, Lori, Dean Karlan, Bram, Thuysbaert, & Udry, Christopher (2021), "Selection into Credit Markets: Evidence from Agriculture in Mali", NBER Working Paper 20387.

Beg, Sabrina A., Lucas, Adrienne, Halim, Waqas, & Saif, Umar (2019), "Beyond the Basics: Improving Post-Primary Content Delivery through Classroom Technology", NBER Working Paper 25704.

Bellodi, L., Morelli, M., & Vannoni, M. (2021), "The Costs of Populism for the Bureaucracy and Government Performance: Evidence from Italian Municipalities", CEPR Discussion paper 1592.

Benabou, Ronald (1996), "Inequality and Growth", NBER Working Paper 5658.

Bengali, Kaiser, 'A Cry for Justice—Empirical Insights from Balochistan', 2018, Oxford University Press.

Benos, N & S Zotou (2014), "Education and Economic Growth: A Meta—Regression Analysis", World Development, Elsevier, Vol. 64, No. C.

Berg, Andrew G. & Ostry, Jonathan D. (2011), "Inequality and Unsustainable Growth: Two Sides of the Same Coin?" IMF Staff Discussion Note (SDN/11/08).

Berman, Evan (Eds.), 'Public Administration in East Asia—Mainland China, Japan, South Korea, and Taiwan', 2010, CRC Press, New York, USA.

Bertrand, Marianne & Schoar, Antoinette (2006), "The Role of Family in Family Firms", Journal of Economic Perspectives, Vol. 20, No. 2.

Bertrand, Marianne, Burgess, Robin, Chawla, Arunish, & Xu, Gao (2020), "The Glittering Prizes: Career Incentives and Bureaucrat Performance", Review of Economic Studies, Vol. 87, No. 2.

Besley, Timothy & Persson, Torsten (2011), 'Pillars of Prosperity—The Political Economics of Development Clusters', Princeton University Press, New Jersey, USA.

Besley, Timothy & Persson, Torsten (2014), "Why Do Developing Countries Tax So Little?" Journal of Economic Perspectives, Vol. 28, No. 4.

Besley, Timothy (1995), "Property Rights and Investment Incentives: Theory and Evidence from Ghana", Journal of Political Economy, Vol. 103, No. 5.

Besley, Timothy, Ilzetzki, Ethan, & Persson, Torsten (2013), "Weak States and Steady States: The Dynamics of Fiscal Capacity", American Economic Journal: Macroeconomics, Vol. 5, No. 4, pp. 205–236.

Best, Michael, Brockmeyer, Anne, Kleven, Henrik, Spinnewijn, Johannes, & Waseem, Mazhar (2015), "Production vs. Revenue Efficiency with Limited

Tax Capacity: Theory and Evidence from Pakistan", Journal of Political Economy, Vol. 123, No. 6.

Bhagwati, J.N. (1982), "Directly Unproductive, Profit-Seeking (DUP) Activities", Journal of Political Economy, Vol. 90.

Bhagwati, Jagdish & Panagariya, Arvind, 'Why Growth Matters', 2013, Council on Foreign Relations, New York, USA.

Bhagwati, Jagdish N. & Chakravarty, Sukhamoy (1969), "Contributions to Indian Economic Analysis: A Survey", American Economic Review, Vol. 59, No. 4.

Bhutta, Zafar A., Das, Jai K., Rizvi, Arjumand, Gaffey, Michelle F., Walker, Neff, Horton, Susan, Webb, Patrick, Lartey, Anna & Black, Robert E. (2013), "Evidence-Based Interventions for Improvement of Maternal and Child Nutrition: What Can Be Done and at What Cost?" Lancet

Bianchi, Nicola, Lu, Yi, & Song, Hong (2020), "The Effect of Computer-Assisted Learning on Students' Long-Term Development", NBER Working Paper 28180.

Bina Agarwal, 'A Field of One's Own', 1994, Cambridge University Press.

Biswanger, Hans P. & Deininger, Klaus (1997), "Explaining Agricultural and Agrarian Policies in Developing Countries", Journal of Economic Literature, Vol. XXXV.

Bizhan, Nematullah (Eds.), 'State Fragility—Case Studies and Comparisons', 2023, Routledge.

Bjorgo, Tore (Ed.), 'Root Causes of Terrorism: Myths, Reality, and Ways Forward', 2005, Routledge.

Blair, Graeme, Fair, C. Christine, Neil, Malhotra, & Shapiro, Jacob N. (2013), "Poverty and Support for Militant Politics: Evidence from Pakistan", American Journal of Political Science, Vol. 57, No. 1.

Bleakley, Hoyt (2010), "Health, Human Capital, and Development", Annual Review Economics.

Bloom, D.E., & Canning, D. (2002), "The Health and Wealth of Nations", Science, Vol. 287.

Bloom, D.E., Kuhn, M., & Prettner, K. (2020), "The Contribution of Female Health to Economic Development", Economic Journal, Vol. 130.

Bo, Ernesto Dal, Finan, Frederico, & Rossi, Martin A. (2013), "Strengthening State Capabilities: The Role of Financial Incentives in the Call to Public", Quarterly Journal of Economics.

Boltho, Andrea (1996), "The Assessment of International Competitiveness", Oxford Review of Economic Policy, Vol. 12, No. 3.

Bowles, Samuel, 'Poverty Traps', 2006, Princeton University Press.

Bowles, Samuel, 'The Moral Economy: Why Good Incentives Are Not Substitute for Good Citizens', 2016, Yale University Press.

Brady, David & Spence, Michael (Eds.), 'Leadership and Growth', 2010, Commission on Growth and Development, 2010, World Bank, Washington, D.C.

British Council (2020), "The University Research System in Pakistan", Available on Line on PIDE Website.

Bruhn, Miriam, Karlan, Dean, & Schoar, Antoinette (2010), "What Capital Is Missing in Developing Countries?" American Economic Review, Vol. 100, No. 2.

Brun, Martin, Gambetta, Juan Pedro, & Varela, Gonzalo J. (2020), "Slow Rockets and Fast Feathers or the Link Between Exchange Rates and Exports: A Case Study for Pakistan", World Bank Policy Research Working Paper No. 9353.

Brynjolfsson, Erick & McAfee, Andrew, 'The Second Age Machine—Work, Progress, and Prosperity in a Time of Brilliant Technologies', 2014, W.W. Norton and Company, New York, USA.

Burde, Dana & Linden, Leigh L. (2013), "Bringing Education to Afghan Girls: A Randomized Controlled Trial of Village-Based Schools", American Economic Journal: Applied Economics, Vol. 5, No. 3.

Burgess, R., & Rohini, Pande (2005), "Do Rural Banks Matter? Evidence from the Indian Social Banking Experiment", American Economic Review, Vol. 95, No. 3.

Burki, Abid S., Memon, Rashid, & Mir, Khalid (2015), "Multiple Inequalities and Policies to Mitigate Inequality Traps in Pakistan", Oxfam Research Report.

Burki, Shahid Javed (Eds.), 'Pakistan at Seventy—A Handbook on Developments in Economic, Politics, and Society', 2019, Routledge, New York.

Callen, M (2020), "Data and Policy Decisions: Experimental Evidence from Pakistan", CEPR Discussion Paper No. 15169, http://cepr.org/publications/dp15169.

Callen, Michael; Gulzar, Saad; Hasnain, Ali; Rehman Khan, Abdur; Khan, Yasir, & Mehmood, Muhammad Zia (2013), "Improving Public Health Delivery in Punjab, Pakistan: Issues and Opportunities", Lahore Journal of Economics, Vol. 18, SE.

Canuto, Otaviano & Agenor, Pierre-Richard (2012), "Gender Equality and Economic Growth: A Framework for Policy Analysis", VoxEU, 24 April 2013.

Caprettini, Bruno, Casaburi, Lorenzo, & Venturini, Miriam (2021), "The Electoral Impact of Wealth Redistribution: Evidence from the Italian Land Reform", SSRN 3767181.

Card, David & Krueger, Alan B. (1994), "Minimum Wages and Employment: A Case Study of the Fast-Food Industry in New Jersey and Pennsylvania", American Economic Review, Vol. 84, No. 4.

Card, David & Krueger, Alan B., 'Myth and Measurement—The New Economics of the Minimum Wage', 1995, Princeton University Press, Princeton New Jersey, USA.

Card, David, Mas, Alexandre, Moretti, Enrico, & Saez, Emmanuel (2012), "Inequality at Work: The Effect of Peer Salaries on Job Satisfaction", American Economic Review, Vol. 102, No. 6.

Case, Anne & Deaton, Angus (1999) "School Inputs and Educational Outcomes in South Africa", Quarterly Journal of Economics Vol. 114, No. 3.

Case, Anne & Paxon, Christina (2006), "Stature and Status: Height, Ability, and Labor Outcomes", NBER Working Paper No. 12466.

Cejka, T., & Waseem, M. (2022), "Long-Term Impacts of In-Utero Ramadan Exposure: Evidence from Administrative Tax Records", CEPR Discussion Paper No. 17176.

Centre for Global Development (2020), "'Education in Africa: What Are We Learning?" Working Paper 542, August, http://www.cgdev.org.

Cerra, Valerie, Eichengreen, Barry, El-Ganainy, Asmaa, & Schindler, Martin, 'How to Achieve Inclusive Growth', 2022, Oxford University Press, London, UK.

Cervellati, Mattio & Sunde, Uwe (2011), "Life Expectancy and Economic Growth: The Role of Demographic Transition", Journal of Economic Growth, 16.

Chambru, C., Henry, E., & Marx, B. (2021), "The Dynamic Consequences of State-Building: Evidence from the French Revolution", CEPR Discussion Paper 16815.

Chang, Ha-Joon (2006), "Understanding the Relationship Between Institutions and Economic Development—Some Key Theoretical Issues", UNU-WIDER Discussion Paper No. 2006/05.

Charles J. Jones (2019), "Paul Romer: Ideas, Non-Rivalry, and Endogenous Growth", Scandinavian Journal of Economics, Vol. 121, No. 3.

Chaudhary, Muhammad Azam, 'Justice in Practice: Legal Ethnography of a Pakistani Punjabi Village', 1999, Oxford University Press, New York, USA.

Cheema, Ali & Naseer, Muhammad Farooq (2013), "Historical Inequality and Intergenerational Educational Mobility: The Dynamics of change in Rural Punjab", Lahore Journal of Economics, No. 18.

Cheema, Ali (2007), "Governance Impediments to Pro-Poor Change in Pakistan", Asian Development Bank, Pakistan Resident Mission, Islamabad.

Cheema, Tahir Bashir, Haque, Nadeem Ul & Malik, Afia (Eds.), 'Power Sector: An Enigma with No Easy Solution', 2022, PIDE, Islamabad.

Chemin, M (2020), "Judicial Efficiency and Firm Productivity: Evidence from a World Database of Judicial Reforms", Review of Economics and Statistics, Vol. 102, No. 1.

Chemin, Matthieu (2008), "The Impact of the Judiciary on Entrepreneurship: Evaluation of Pakistan's Access to Justice Programme", Journal of Public Economics, Vol. 93, Nos. 1–2.

Chemin, Matthieu (2010), "Does Court Speed Shape Economic Activity? Evidence form a Court Reform in India", Journal of Law, Economics and Organization.

Chen, Kaiji & Irarrazabal, Alfonso (2015), "The Role of Allocative Efficiency in a Decade of Recovery", Review of Economic Dynamics.

Cheng, Tun-Jen, Haggard, Stephen, & Kang, David (1998), "Institutions and Growth in Korea and Taiwan: The Bureaucracy", Journal of Development Studies, Vol. 34, No. 6.

Chetty, Raj, Stepner, Michael, Abraham, Sarah, Lin, Shelby, Scuderi, Benjamin, Turner, Nicholas, Bergeron, Augustan & Cutler, David (2015), "The Relationship Between Life Expectancy and Income in the United States, 2001–2014", NBER Working Paper PRC NB 15-01.

Chong, Alberto, Porta, Rafael La, Lopez-de-Silanes, Florencio & Shleifer, Andrei (2012), "Letter Grading Government Efficiency", NBER Working Paper No. 18268.

Cinnirella, Francesco, Hornung, Erick, & Koschnick, Julius (2022), "Flow of Ideas: Economic Societies and the Rise of Useful Knowledge", CESifo Working Paper No. 9836.

Clair Yang (2022), "On Determinant of State Capacity: Wars, Goods, and Economic Shocks", Available on SSRN.

Cohen, Stephen P. (2011), "The Future of Pakistan", Brookings Institution Press, Washington, D.C.

Coleman, James S. (1988), "Social Capital in the Creation of Human Capital", American Journal of Sociology, Vol. 94, Supplement: Organizations and Institutions: Sociological and Economic Approaches to the Analysis of Social Structure.

Collier, Paul & Hoeffler, Anke (2004), "Greed and Grievance in Civil War", Oxford Economic Papers, Vol. 56, No. 4 pp. 563–595.

Collier, Paul & Sambanis, Nicholas (Eds.), "Understanding Civil War—Evidence and Analysis", Volume 2: Europe, Central Asia, and Other Regions, 2005, World Bank.

Collier, Paul, 'The Bottom Billion: Why the Poorest Countries Are Failing and What Can Be Done About It', 2007, Oxford University Press.

Collin, Daryl, Morduch, Jonathan, Rutherford, Stuart, & Ruthven, Orlanda, 'Portfolios of the Poor—How the World's Poor Live on $ 2 a Day', 2009, Princeton University Press.

Colonnelli, E., Prem, Mouno, & Teso, Edorado (2019), "Patronage and Selection in Public Sector Organizations", CEPR Discussion Paper 13697.

Cookson, T.P., 'Unjust Conditions: Women's Work and the Hidden Cost of Cash Transfer Programs', 2018, University of California Press, Oakland.

Corak, Miles (2013), "Income Inequality, Equality of Opportunity, and Intergenerational Mobility", Journal of Economic Perspectives, Vol. 27, No. 3, Summer.

Corduneanu-Huci, Cristina, Hamilton, Alexander & Ferrer, Issel Masses (2013), "Understanding Policy Change: How to Apply Political Economy Concepts in Practice", World Bank, Washington, D.C.

Cowen, Tyler, 'The Great Stagnation—How America Ate All the Low-Hanging Fruit of Modern History, Got Sick, and Will (Eventually) Feel Better', 2011, Dutton Adult, New York.

Cuberes, Davis & Jerzmanowski, Michal (2009), "Democracy, Diversifications and Growth Reversals", Economic Journal, Vol. 119, No. 540.

Cutler, David & Miller, Grant (2005), "The Role of Public Health Improvements in Health Advances: The Twentieth-Century United States", Demography, Vol. 42, No. 1.

Dal Bo, E., Hernandez, P. & Mazzuca, S. (2015), "The Paradox of Civilization: Pre-institutional Sources of Security and Prosperity", NBER Working Paper 21829.

Dang, Hai-Anh; Glewwe, Paul, Lee, Jongwook, & Vu, Khoa (2020), "What Explains Vietnam's Exceptional Performance in Education Relative to Other Countries? Analysis of the 2012 and 2015 PISA Data", Rise Working Paper 20/036, March.

Daniels, Ronald J. & Trebilcock, Michael J. (2004), "The Political Economy of Rule of Law Reform in Developing Countries", Michigan Journal of International Law, Vol. 26, No. 1.

Daron, Acemoglu, Koster, Hans & Ozgen, Ceren (2023), "Robots and Workers: Evidence from the Netherlands", NBER Working Paper 31009.

Das, Jishua, Pandey, Priyanka & Zajonc, Tristan (2013), "Learning Levels and Gaps in Pakistan", WPS 4067.

Dasgupta, Aditya & Kapur, Devesh (2020), "The Political Economy of Bureaucratic Overload: Rural Development Officials in India", American Political Science Review, Vol. 114, No. 2.

Dasgupta, Partha, 'An Inquiry into Well-Being and Destitution', 1993, Oxford University Press.

Datt, G. & Ravallion, M. (1998), "Farm Productivity and Rural Poverty in India", Journal of Development Studies, Vol. 34, No. 4.

de la Croix, David & Doepke, Matthias (2007), "To Segregate or to Integrate: Education Politics and Democracy", CEPR Discussion Papers No. 5799.

De Neve, J.E., Imbert, C., Spinnewijn, J., Tsankova, T. & Luts, M. (2021), "How to Improve Tax Compliance? Evidence form Population—Wide Experiments in Belgium", The Journal of Political Economy, Vol. 129, No. 5.

De Soto, Hernando (2000), 'The Mystery of Capital—Why Capitalism Triumphs in the West and Fails Everywhere Else", Basic Books, New York, USA

De Soto, Hernando, 'The Other Path', 1989, New York: Harper and Row.

De Sousa, Jose, Guillin, A., Lochard, J., & Silve, A. (2023), "Trust and Specialization in Complexity: Evidence from US States", Journal of Economic Behavior and Organization.

de Zawart, Pim & Soekhradj, P. (2022), "Sweet Equality, Property Rights and Land Distribution in Colonial Java", CEPR Discussion Paper No. 17278.

de Zawart, Pim, Daniel, Gallardo-Albarran & Rijpma, Auke (2022), "The Demographic Effects of Colonialism: Forced Labor and Mortality in Java", Journal of Economic History, Vol. 82, No. 1.

Deaton, Angus (2006), "Global Patterns of Income and Health: Facts, Interpretations, and Policies", NBER Working Paper 12735.

Deaton, Angus, 'The Great Escape: Health, wealth and the Origins of Inequality', 2013, Princeton University.

Debraj Ray (2003), "Aspirations, Poverty and Economic Change", March.

Deininger, Klaus & Squire, Lyn (1998), "New Ways of Looking at Old Issues: Inequality and Growth", Journal of Development Economics, Vol. 57, No. 2.

Deininger, Klaus, Jin, Songqing & Nagarjan, Hari K. (2007), "Land Reforms, Poverty Reduction, and Economic Growth: Evidence from India", World Bank, December.

Delavallade, Clara (2006), "Corruption and Distribution of Public Spending in Developing Countries", Journal of Economics and Finance, Vol. 30, No. 2, Summer.

Dell, M. & Querubin, P. (2016), "Nation Building Through Foreign Intervention: Evidence from Discontinuities in Military Strategies", NBER Working Paper No. 22395.

Dell, Melissa & Olken, Benjamin (2020), "The Development Effects of the Extractive Colonial Economy: The Dutch Cultivation System in Java", Review of Economic Studies 87, No. 1.

Dell, Melissa (2010), "The Persistent Effects of Peru's Mining Mita", Econometrica, Vol. 78. No. 6.

Dell, Melissa, Jones, Benjamin F. & Olken, Benjamin A. (2012), "Temperature Shocks and Economic Growth: Evidence from the Last Half Century", American Economic Journal: Macroeconomics, Vol. 4, No. 3.

Deryugina, Tatyana & Molitor, David (2021), "The Causal Effects of Place on Health and Longevity", NBER Working Paper 29321.

Dhingra, Swati & Tenreyro, Silvana (2020), "The Rise of Agribusinesses and the Distributional Consequences of Policies on Intermediated Trade", CEP Discussion Paper No. 1677.

Di Tella, Rafael, Galiani, Sebastian.& Schargrodsky, Ernesto (2007), "The Formation of Beliefs Evidence from the Allocation of Land Titles to Squatters", Quarterly Journal of Economics, Vol. 122, No. 1.

Diamond, Jared (2014), "Four Threats to American Democracy", Governance: An International Journal of Policy, Administration, and Institutions.

Diamond, Jared, 'Guns, Germs, and Steel—A Short History for Everybody for the Last 13,000 Years', 2005, Vintage Books, London.

Diamond, Jared, 'The World Until Yesterday—What We Can Learn from Traditional Societies', 2012, Penguin, New York, USA.

Dittmar, Jeremiah & Meisenzahl, Ralf R. (2016), "State Capacity and Public Goods: Institutional Change, Human Capital and Growth in Early Modern Germany", CEP Discussion Paper No1418.

Diwakar, Vidya, Lemma, Alberto, Shepherd, Andrew & te Velde, Dirk Willem (2019), "Economic Transformation and Poverty", Supporting Economic Transformation (SET) paper of DFID and ODI.

Dixit, Avinash & Londregan, John (1996), "The Determinants of Success of Special Interests in Redistributive Politics", Journal of Politics, Vol. 58, No. 4.

Dixit, Avinash (2002), "Incentives and Organizations in the Public Sector: An Interpretive Review", Journal of Human Resources, Vol. 37, No. 4, pp. 697–727.

Dixit, Avinash (2009), "Governance Institutions and Economic Activity", American Economic Review, Vol. 99, 1.

Djankov, S., Glaeser, E., Perotti, V. & Shleifer, A. (2020), "Measuring Property Rights Institutions", LSE Financial Markets Group Discussion Paper 813, September.

Djankov, Simeon Porta, Rafael La, Lopez-de-Silanes, Florencio. & Shleifer, Andrei (2003), "Courts", Quarterly Journal of Economics, Vol. 118, No. 2.

Djankov, Simeon, Mcliesh, Caralee, Nenova, Tatiana & Shleifer, Andrei (2003), "Who Owns the Media?" Journal of Law and Economics, Vol. XLVI.

Dollar, David & Kraay, Aart (2002), "Growth Is Good for the Poor", Journal of Economic Growth, Vol. 7 No. 3.

Dorosh, Paul, Niazi, Muhammad Khan & Nazli, Hina (2003), "Distributional Impacts of Agricultural Growth in Pakistan: A Multiplier Analysis", Pakistan Development Review, Vol. 42, 3.

Dorosh, Paul, Niazi, Muhammad Khan, & Niazi, Hina (2003), "Distributional Impacts of Agricultural Growth in Pakistan: A Multiplier Analysis", PDR Vol. 42, No. 3, pp. 249–275.

Dreze, Jean & Sen, Amartya, 'Uncertain Glory: India and Its Contradictions', 2013, Princeton University Press.

Du, Qingyuan & Wei, Shang-Jin (2013), "A Theory of the Competitive Saving Motive", NBER Working Paper 18911.

Duflo, Esther (2000), "Schooling and Labor Market Consequences of School Construction in Indonesia: Evidence from an Unusual Policy Experiment", Esther Duflo, NBER Working Paper No. 7860.

Dupas, Pascaline & Robinson, Jonathan (2009), "Savings Constraints and Microenterprise Development: Evidence from a Field Experiment in Kenya", NBER Working Paper 14693.

Dupas, Pascaline & Robinson, Jonathan (2013), "Why Don't the Poor Save More? Evidence from Health Savings Experiments", American Economic Review, Vol. 103, No. 4.

Dupas, Pascaline (2011), "Health Behaviour in Developing Countries", Annual Reviews of Economics, Vol. 3.

Durrani, Tehmina, 'My Feudal Lord', 1994, Transword Publishers, London.

Dwyer-Lindgren, Laura, Bertozzi-Villa, Amelia, Stubs, Rebecca W., Morozoff, Chloe, Mackenbach, Johan P., Van Lenthe, Frank J., Mokdad, Ali H. & Murray, Christopher J.L. (2017), "Inequalities in Life Expectancy Among US Countries, 1980 to 2014:Temporal Trends and Key Drivers", JAMA Intern. Med., Vol. 177, No. 7.

Easterly, William & Fischer, Stanley (2001), "Inflation and the Poor", Journal of Money, Credit and Banking, Vol. 33, No. 2.

Easterly, William (2000), "Can Institutions Resolve Ethnic Conflict?" World Bank Policy Research Working Paper 2482.

Easterly, William, 'The Elusive Quest of Growth-Economists Adventures and Misadventures in the Tropics', 2001, MIT Press, Cambridge.

Easterly, Williams, 'The Tyranny of Experts: Economists, Dictators and the Forgotten Rights of the Poor', 2013, Basic Books.

EBA (2016), "Education in Developing Countries-What Policies and Programmes Affect Learning and Time in School", Rapport 2016:02 www.eba.se.

Edward, Miguel & Kremer, Michael (2004), "Worms: Identifying Impacts on Education and Health in the Presence of Treatment Externalities", Econometrica, Vol. 72, No. 1.

Edwards, Sebastian & Marin, Alvaro Garcia (2014), "Constitutional Rights and Education: An International Comparative Study", NBER Working Paper No. 20475.

Eglar, Zekiye, 'A Punjabi Village in Pakistan—Perspectives on Community, Land, and Economy', 2010, Oxford University Press.

Eswaran, Mukesh, Ramaswami, Bharat & Wadwha, William (2013), "Status, Caste, and the Time Allocation of Women in Rural India", Economic Development and Cultural Change, Vol. 61, No. 2.

Eswaran, Mukesh, Ramaswami, Bharat, & Wadwha, Wilima (2013), "Status, Caste, and the Time Allocation of Women in Rural India", Economic Development and Cultural Change, Vol. 61, No. 2.

Evans, Peter, 'Embedded Autonomy: States and Industrial Transformation', 1995, Princeton University Press.

Evans,David K. & Popova, Anna (2016), "What Really Works to Improve Learning in Developing Countries? An Analysis of Divergent Findings in Systematic Reviews", World Bank Research Observer.

Fan, S., Chan-Kang, C., & Mukherjee, A. (2005), "Rural and Urban Dynamics and Poverty: Evidence from China and India", IFPRI, Washington, D.C.

Farazmand, Ali (Eds.), 'A Parabolic Theory of Bureaucracy or Max Weber Through the Looking Glass', 2009, CRC, New York, USA.

Farooq, Umar, Ghaffar, Abdul, Narru, Iftikhar Ahmed, Khan, Dilawar & Irshad, Romana (2004), "Doctors Perceptions About Staying in or Leaving Rural Health Facilities in District Abbottabad", Journal of Ayub Medical College, Vol. 16, No. 2.

FATA Research Centre Report (2016), "Governance Reforms in Federally Administered Tribal Areas: A People's Perspective", Islamabad, www.frc.org.pk.

Federal Public Service Commission Report (2022), "FPSC Annual Report 2020", FPSC Secretariat, Islamabad, Pakistan.

Ferraz, C., Finan, F., & Moreira, D.B. (2010), "Corrupting Learning: Evidence from Missing Federal Education Funds in Brazil", Mimeo, Berkley.

Fershtman, Chaim, Murphy, Kevin M., & Weiss, Yoram (1996), "Social Status, Education, and Growth", Journal of Political Economy, Vol. 104, No. 1.

Field, Erica & Pande, Rohini (2008), "Repayment Frequency and Default in Microfinance: Evidence from India", Journal of the European Economic Association, Vol. 6, No. 2.

Field, Erica (2005), "Property Rights and Investment in Urban Slums", Journal of the European Economic Association, Vol. 3, Nos. 2–3.

Filmer, Deon, Hammer, Jeffrey S. & Pritchett, Lant (2000), "Weak Links in the Chain: A Diagnosis of Health Policy in Poor countries", World Bank Observer.

Finan, Frederico, Olken, Benjamin A. & Pande, Rohini (2015), "The Personnel Economics of the State", NBER Working Paper 21825, http://www.nber.org/papers/w21825.

Fioramonti, Lorenzo, 'Gross Domestic Problem—The Politics Behind the World's Most Powerful Number', 2013, Zed Books, London.

Fisman, R. & Svensson, Jakob (2007), "Are Corruption and Taxation Really Harmful to Growth? Firm Level Evidence", Journal of Development Economics, Vol. 83, No. 1, pp. 63–75.

Flanney, Kent & Marcus, Joyce, 'The Creation of Inequality: How Our Prehistoric Ancestors Set the Stage for Monarchy, Slavery, and Empire', 2012, Harvard University Press.

Foarta, D.D.D., & Morelli, Massimo (2021), "Complexity and the Reform Process", CEPR Discussion Paper No. DP16522.

Fonseca, Julia & Matray, Adrein (2022), "The Real Effects of Banking the Poor: Evidence from Brazil", NBER Working Paper No. 30057.

Foster, Andrew D. & Rosenzweig, Mark R. (1999), "Missing Women, the Marriage Market, and Economic Growth", Stanford Center for International Development, Working Paper No. 49.

Foster, William, Valdes, Alberto, Davis, Benjamin & Anriquez, Gustavo (2011), "The Constraints to Escaping Rural Poverty: An Analysis of the Complementarities of Assets in Developing Countries", Applied Economic Perspectives and Policy, Vol. 33, No. 4, Oxford University Press.

Francois, Patrick (2000), "Public Service Motivation as an Argument for Government Provision", Journal of Public Economics, Vol. 78, No. 3.

Frankema, Ewoud (2010), "The Colonial Roots of Land Inequality: Geography, Factor Endowments, or Institutions", Economic History Review, Vol. 63, No. 2.

Friedman, Benjamin M., 'The Moral Consequences of Economic Growth', September 2006, First Vintage Book Edition, New York.

Fujiwara, Thomas (2015), "Voting Technology, Political Responsiveness, and Infant Health: Evidence from Brazil", Econometrica, Vol. 83, No. 2.

Fukuyama, Francis, 'Political Order and Political Decay: From Industrial Revolution to the Globalization of Democracy', 2014, Farrar, Straus and Giroux, New York, USA.

Fukuyama, Francis, 'Trust—The Social Virtues and the Creation of Prosperity', 1995, Penguin Paperback Edition.

Galasso, V. & Nannicini, T. (2009), "Competing on Good Politicians", CEPR Discussion Paper 7363.

Gallup, John Luke & Sachs, Jeffery D. (2001), "The Economic Burden of Malaria", Am. J. Trop. Med. Hyg., Vol. 64, Nos. 1–2.

Galor, Oded & Maov, Omar (2004), "From Physical to Human Capital Accumulation: Inequality and the Process of Development", Review of Economic Studies, Vol. 71, No. 4.

Galore, Oded, 'The Journey of Humanity', 2022, Penguin Random House.

Ganguly, Sumit (1996), "Explaining the Kashmir Insurgency—Political Mobilization and Institutional Decay", International Security, Vol. 21, No. 2.

Ganguly, Sumit, 'The Deadly Impasse-Kashmir and Indo-Pakistani Relations at the Dawn of a New Century', 2016, Cambridge University Press.

Garber, Alan M. & Skinner, Jonathan (2008), "Is American Health Care Uniquely Inefficient?" NBER Working.

Gaspart, F. & Platteau, J.P. (2012), "The Perverse Effect of Cheap Aid Money", CRED Working Paper, Belgium, Centre for Research in Economic Development, University of Namur.

Genicot, Grance & Ray, Debraj (2014), "Aspirations and Inequality", NBER Working Paper No. 1997.

Gerard, F., Naritomi, J., & Silva, J. (Eds.) (2021), "Cash Transfer and Formal Labor Markets: Evidence from Brazil", CEPR Press Discussion Paper No. 16286.

Gersbach, Hans & Siemens, Lars, H.R. (2010), "Land Reforms and Economic Development", Macroeconomic Dynamics (http://www.cambridge.org/core).

Gethin, Amory, Mehmood, Sultan, & Piketty, Thomas (2020), "Social Inequality and the Dynamics of Political and Ethnolinguistic Divides in Pakistan, 1970–2018", WID. World Working Paper N 2020/16.

Ghosh, Jayati (2012), "Microfinance and the Challenge of Financial Inclusion for Development", Ensayos Economicos, Central Bank of Argentina, Economic Research Department, Vol. 1, No. 67.

Ghuman, Sharon & Lloyd, Cynthia (2010), "Teacher Absence as a Factor in Gender Inequalities in Access to Primary Schooling in Rural Pakistan", Comparative Education Review, Vol. 54, No. 4.

Giavazzi, Francesco, Petkov, Ivan & Schiantarelli, Fabio (2014), "Culture: Persistence and Evolution", NBER Working Paper No. 20174.

Gladwell, Malcolm, 'Outliers—The Story of Success', 2008, Little, Brown and Company, New York.

Glaesar, Edward L. (2006), "Inequality", Faculty Research Working Paper Series, JFK School of Government, Harvard University.

Glaesar, Edward, Scheinkman, Jose, & Shleifer, Andrei (2002), "The Injustice of Inequality", NBER Working Paper 9150.

Glaeser, Edward L., A.M. Ponzetto, Giacomo, & Shleifer, Andrei (2007), "Why Does Democracy Need Education", Journal of Economic Growth.

Glewwe, Paul & Muralidharan, Karthik (2015), "Improving School Education Outcomes in Developing Countries: Evidence, Knowledge, Gaps, and Policy Implications", RISE Working Paper 15/001.

Glewwe, Paul, Kremer, Michael & Moulin, Sylvie (2009), "Many Children Left Behind? Textbooks and Test Scores in Kenya", American Economic Journal: Applied Economics, Vol. 1, No. 1, pp. 115–135.

Goldstein, Markus & Udry, Christopher (2008), "The Profits of Power: Land Rights and Agricultural Investment in Ghana", Journal of Political Economy, Vol. 116, No. 6.

Gollin, Douglas, Hanse, Casper W., & Wingender, Asger (2018), "Two Blades of Grass: The Impact of the Green Revolution", NBER Working Paper No. 24744.

GOP (2010), 'FATA--Post-Crisis Needs Assessment', 2010, FATA Secretariat, Government of Pakistan, Islamabad.

GOP (2015), "Annual Report 2015–16", Rehabilitation and Reconstruction Unit of the FATA Secretariat.

Gopinath, Gita, Boz, Emine, Casas, Camila, Diez, Federico J., Gourinchas, Pierre-Olivier & Plagborg-Moller, Mikkel (2020), "Dominant Currency Paradigm", American Economic Review, Vol. 110, No. 3.

Gordon, Robert J. (2012), "Is U.S. Economic Growth Over? Faltering Innovation Confronts the Six Headwinds", NBER Working Paper No. 18315.

Gordon, Robert J., 'The Rise and Fall of American Growth', 2016, Princeton University Press.

Government of KPK (2021), "Development Statistics of Khyber Pakhtunkhwa", Planning and Development Department, Government of KPK.

Government of KPK (2021), "Multiple Indicator Cluster Survey (MICS) 2017–18", Planning and Development Department, Government of KPK and UNICEF.

Government of Pakistan & UNICEF (2018), "National Nutrition Survey 2018", Ministry of National Health Services, Regulations and Coordination, Government of Pakistan.

Government of Pakistan (1947), "Proceedings of Pakistan Educational Conference", Ministry of the Interior (Education Division), Government of Pakistan, Karachi.

Government of Pakistan (1951–1952), "Report of the Pakistan Agricultural Inquiry Committee 1951–52", Ministry of Food and Agriculture (Agriculture Division), Karachi.

Government of Pakistan (1959), "Report of the Commission on National Education", Ministry of Education, Government of Pakistan, Karachi.

Government of Pakistan (1968), "Socio-Economic Objectives of the Fourth Five Year Plan (1970–1975)", Planning Commission, November 1968.

Government of Pakistan (1970), "The New Education Policy of the Government of Pakistan", Ministry of Education and Scientific Research, Government of Pakistan, Islamabad, March.

Government of Pakistan (1972), "Agriculture Census Report 1972", Agriculture Census Organization, 1972, Pakistan Bureau of Statistics, Government of Pakistan.

Government of Pakistan (1972), "The Education Policy 1972–80", Ministry of Education, Islamabad, March.
Government of Pakistan (1979), "National Education Policy and Implementation Programme", Government of Pakistan, Ministry of Education, Islamabad.
Government of Pakistan (1980), "Agriculture Census Report 1980", Agriculture Census Organization, Pakistan Bureau of Statistics, Government of Pakistan.
Government of Pakistan (1990), "Agriculture Census Report 1990", Agriculture Census Organization, Pakistan Bureau of Statistics, Government of Pakistan.
Government of Pakistan (2000), "Agriculture Census Report 2000", Agriculture Census Organization, Pakistan Bureau of Statistics, Government of Pakistan.
Government of Pakistan (2010), "Agriculture Census Report 2010", Agriculture Census Organization, Pakistan Bureau of Statistics, Government of Pakistan.
Government of Pakistan (2016), "Minimum Cost of the Diet (CoD)", Ministry of Planning, Government of Pakistan.
Government of Pakistan (2016), "Report of the Committee on FATA Reforms", August.
Government of Pakistan (2017), "The Economic Consequences of Undernutrition in Pakistan: An Assessment of Losses", Ministry of Planning, Development, and Reforms, Government of Pakistan.
Government of Pakistan (2018), "Skills for Growth and Development—A Technical and Vocational Education and Training (TVET) Policy for Pakistan", Ministry of Federal Education and Professional Training, Government of Pakistan, Islamabad.
Government of Pakistan (2019), "Pakistan National Nutrition Survey (PNNS)", Nutrition Wing, Ministry of National Health Services, Regulations and Coordination, Government of Pakistan.
Government of Pakistan (2020), "Pakistan Social and Living Standards Measurement Survey (PSLM) Provincial/ District-2019–20", Pakistan Bureau of Statistics, Government of Pakistan.
Government of Pakistan (2020), "Pakistan Social and Living Standards Measurement Survey (PSLM) National/ Provincial-2018–19", Pakistan Bureau of Statistics, Government of Pakistan.
Government of Pakistan (2020), "Punjab Mouza Census 2020", Agricultural Census Wing, Pakistan Bureau of Statistics, Ministry of Planning, Development & Special Initiatives, Government of Pakistan.
Government of Pakistan (2020), "Report of the Inquiry Commission on the Shortage of Petroleum Products in Pakistan", http://cabinet.gov.pk.
Government of Pakistan (2021), "National Health Accounts 2017–18", Pakistan Bureau of Statistics, Government of Pakistan, Islamabad.
Government of Pakistan (2022), "Labor Force Survey 2020–21 (Annual Report)", Pakistan Bureau of Statistics, Ministry of Planning, Development, and Special Initiatives, Government of Pakistan.

Government of Pakistan (2023), “Pakistan Education Statistics 2020–2021”, Ministry of Education and Professional Development, Government of Pakistan.

Government of Pakistan, “FBR Revenue Division Year Book 2004–2005 to 2021–2022”, Directorate of Research and Statistics, Federal Board of Revenue, Islamabad.

Government of Punjab (1953), “Munir Commission Report”.

Government of Punjab (2020), “Punjab Development Indicators 2020”, Planning and Development Department, Government of Punjab, Lahore.

Government of Sindh (1949), “Hari Enquiry Committee”, Karachi, April.

Government of Sindh (2000), “Sindh Rural Development Project—Final Report prepared for Planning and Development”, Government of Sindh and ADB, Agrodev Canada Inc., October.

Government of Sindh (2021), “Multiple Indicator Cluster Survey (MICS) 2018–19”, Sindh Bureau of Statistics, Planning and Development Department, Government of Sindh and UNICEF.

Graeber, T., Roth, C. & Zimmermann, F. (2022), “Stories, Statistics, and Memory”, CEPR Discussion Paper 17683.

Gratton, Gabriele, Guiso, Luigi, Michelacci, Claudio, & Morelli, Massimo (2021), “From Weber to Kafka: Political Instability and the Overproduction of Laws”, American Economic Review, Vol. 111, No. 9.

Griffin, Keith & Rahman Kahn, Azizur (Eds.), ‘Growth and Inequality in Pakistan’, 1972, Palgrave Macmillan.

Guiso, Luigi, Sapienza, Paolo, & Zingales, Luigi (2006), “Does Culture Affect Economic Outcomes?” Journal of Economic Perspectives, Vol. 20, No. 2.

Gupta, Dipak K., ‘Understanding Terrorism and Political Violence—The Life Cycle of Birth, Growth, Transformation, and Demise’, 2008, Routledge.

Gupta, Sanjeev, Davoodi, Hamid, & Tiongson, Erwin (2000), “Corruption and the Provision of Health Care and Education Services”, IMF Working Paper WP/001/116.

Gust, Sarah, Hanushek, Eric A., & Woessmann, Ludger (2022), “Global Universal Basic Skills: Current Deficits and Implications for World Development”, NBER Working Paper 30566.

Gustafson, Eric (1973), “Economic Reforms Under the Bhutto Regime”, Journal of Asian and African Studies.

Hadfield, Gillian K., ‘Rules for a Flat World—Why Humans Invented Law and How to Reinvent it for a Complex Global Economy’, 2017, Oxford University Press, New York, USA.

Hall, Robert E. & Jones, Charles I. (1999), “Why Do Some Countries Produce So Much More Output Per Worker Than Others?” Quarterly Journal of Economics, Vol. 114, No. 1.

Hamna Ahmed (2014), "Patterns of Export Diversification: Evidence from Pakistan", Lahore Journal of Economics, Vol. 19, SE.

Hanif, Ayesha, Jabeen, Nasira, & Jadoon, Zafar Iqbal (2016), "Performance Management in Public Sector: A Case of Civil Service of Pakistan", South Asia Studies, Vol. 31, No. 1.

Hanna, Rema & Wang, Shing-Yi (2017), "Dishonesty and Selection into Public Service: Evidence from India", American Economic Journal: Economic Policy 2017, Vol. 9, No. 3.

Hanushek, Eric A. (2009), "Schooling, Cognitive Skills, and the Latin American Growth Puzzle", NBER Working Paper 15066.

Hanushek, Eric A. (2013), "Economic Growth in Developing Countries: The Role of Human Capital", Economics of Education Review, Vol. 37.

Haqqani, Husain, 'Reimagining Pakistan—Transforming a Dysfunctional Nuclear State', 2018, HarperCollins Publishers.

Haque, Nadeem Ul & Hussain, Amin (2021), "A Small Club: Distribution, Power and Networks in Financial Markets of Pakistan", PIDE Working Paper No. 2021:3, Islamabad.

Haque, Nadeem Ul & Sahay, Ratan (1996), "Do Government Wage Cuts Close Budget Deficits? Costs of Corruption", IMF Staff Papers, Vol. 43, No. 4.

Haque, Nadeem Ul, 'Looking Back—How Pakistan became an Asian Tiger', 2017, p. 116.

Harari, Noah Yuval, 'Sapiens—A Brief History of Humankind', 2011, Vintage, London.

Hasnain, Zahid, Rogger, Daniel Oliver, Walker, Daniel John, Kay, Kerenssa Mayo, & She, Rong (2019), "Innovating Bureaucracy for a More Capable Government", World Bank, Washington, D.C.

Hassan Javid, "Class, Power, and Patronage: The Landed Elite and Politics in Pakistani Punjab", a Thesis Submitted to the Department of Sociology of the London School of Economics for PhD degree, London, June 2012.

Hassan Khan, Ashfaq (2019), "Pakistan's Experience with the IMF", Strategic Thought—2019 (No. 1), Islamabad.

Haugen, Gary A., & Boutros, Victor, 'The Locust Effect—Why the End of Poverty Requires the End of Violence', 2014, Oxford University Press.

Haushofer, Johannes & Shapiro, Jeremy (2016), "The Short-Term Impact of Unconditional Cash Transfers to the Poor: Experimental Evidence from Kenya", Quarterly Journal of Economics, Vol. 131, No. 4.

Hausmann, Ricardo, Hwang, Jason, & Rodrik, Dani (2006), "What You Export Matters", NBER Working Paper No. 11905.

Hayek, F.A., 'The Road to Serfdom', 1944, Routledge & Sons.

Hazan, Moshe, Weiss, David & Zoabi, H. (2021), "Women's Liberation, Household Revolution", CEPR Discussion Paper 16838.

Heckman, James J., Smith, Jeffrey A., & Taber, Christopher (1996), "What Do Bureaucrats Do? The Effects of Performance Standards and Bureaucratic Preferences on Acceptance into the JTPA Program", NBER Working Paper 5535.

Helfand, Steven M. & Levine, Edward S. (2004), "Farm Size and the Determinants of Productive Efficiency in the Brazilian Centre-West", Agricultural Economics, Vol. 31, Nos. 2–3, Blackwell.

Helliwell, John F. & Wang, shun (2010), "Trust and Well-Being", NBER Working Paper 15911.

Hendel, I., Nyhan, B., & Reifler, J. (2017), "Consumer Activism: The Cottage Cheese Boycott", RAND J. Economics, Vol. 48, Nos. 972-1003.

Heshmati, Almas, Maasoumi, Esfandiar, & Wan, Guanghua (Eds.), 'Poverty Reduction in Policies and Practices in Developing Asia', 2015, Economic Studies in Inequality, Social Exclusion, and Well-Being (EIAP), Asian Development Bank, Springer Open.

Hick, Rod (2012), "The Capability Approach: Insights for a New Poverty Focus", Journal of Social Policy, Cambridge University Press.

Hidalgo, Cesar, 'Why Information Flows', 2015, Basic Books, New York, USA.

Higgs, Robert, 'Crisis and Leviathan: Critical Episodes in the Growth of American Government', 1987, Oxford University Press, New York, USA.

Hirschman, Albert (1981), "The Changing Tolerance for Income Inequality in the Course of Economic Development", in Essays in Trespassing, Cambridge University Press, Cambridge, UK.

Hjort, Jonas, Diana, Moreira, Gautam Rao, & Santini, Juan Francisco (2021), "How Research Affects Policy: Experimental Evidence from 2, 150 Brazilian Municipalities", American Economic Review, Vol. 111, No. 5.

Hochschild, Adam, 'King Leopard's Ghost—A Story of Greed, Terror, and Heroism in Colonial Africa', 1999, Houghton Mifflin Company, Boston New York.

Hoff, Erika (2003), "The Specificity of Environmental Influence: Socioeconomic Status Affects Early Vocabulary Development via Maternal Speech", Child Development, Vol. 74, No. 5, September/October.

Hoodbhoy, Pervez (2009), "Pakistan's Higher Education System—What Went Wrong and How to Fix It", PDR 48:4 Part II.

Hotte, K., Somers, M. & Theodorakopoulos, A. (2022), "Technology and Jobs: A Systematic Literature Review", Oxford Martin Working Paper Series on Technology and Economic Change No. 2022-2.

Hudson, Michael, 'The Bubble and Beyond', September 2012, e-Book Edition.

Husain, Ishrat, 'Governing the Ungovernable-Institutional Reforms for Democratic Governance', 2018, Oxford University Press.

Husain, Ishrat, 'Pakistan—The Economy of an Elitist State', 2020, Second Edition, Oxford University Press.

Hussain, Abid, Khan, Muhammad Jehangir, & Ahmad, Iftikhar (2016), "Impact of Credit on Education and Healthcare Spending in Rural Pakistan", Pakistan Development Review, Vol. 55, 4.

Hussain, Faqir (2017), "The Judicial System of Pakistan", Federal Judicial Academy, Islamabad.

Hussain, Khadim, 'The Militant Discourse', Narratives, Islamabad, Pakistan.

Hvide, H.K. & Oyer, P. (2018), "Dinner Table Human Capital and Entrepreneurship", NBER Working Paper 24198.

ICG (2010), "Reforming Pakistan's Criminal Justice System", http://www.crisisgroup.org.

IDB (2022), "Digitalizing Public Services—Opportunities for Latin America and the Caribbean", November.

IJCP (2017), "Judicial Statistics of Pakistan 2017", Law and Justice Commission of Pakistan, Islamabad www.ijcp.gov.pk.

IJCP (2021), "Judicial Statistics of Pakistan 2020", Law and Justice Commission of Pakistan, Islamabad www.ijcp.gov.pk.

Ikeda, Shinsuki, 'The Economics of Self-Destructive Choices', 2016, Springer, Japan.

IMF (2002), "Evaluation of Prolonged Use of IMF Resources", Independent Evaluation Group (IEG) Review, IMF, Washington, D.C.

IMF (2018), "Financial Inclusion Under Microscope", IMF Working Paper, September.

IMF (2023), "How to Avoid a Debt-Crisis in Sub-Saharan Africa", https://www.imf.org/en/News/Articles/2023/09/26/cf-how-to-avoid-a-debt-crisis-in-sub-saharan-africa.

Institute for Economics and Peace (IEP), 'Economic Value of Peace 2021: Measuring the Global Economic Impact of Violence and Conflict', Sydney, January 2021.

International Crisis Group (ICG), 'Pakistan: Madrasas, Extremism and the Military', 2002, ICG Asia Report No. 36, Islamabad/ Brussels.

International Crisis Group, 'A New Era of Sectarian Violence in Pakistan', 2022, Brussels, Belgium.

IPR (2014), "Strategy not Tactics: Better Governance for Social Stability in Pakistan", Institute for Policy Reforms, Lahore.

ITA (2020), "Mapping of Life Skills Based Education in Punjab's Curriculum and Textbooks", Young Omang Project, http://itacec.org.

IZA (2014), "Education System Reform in Pakistan: Why, When, and How?", IZA Policy Paper No. 76), Bonn.

J. Andrew Greig, "Riding the Tiger—The Threat to Pakistan from Terrorism", included in 'Pakistan's Political Labyrinths—Military, Society, and Terror', edited by Ravi Kalia, 2016, Routledge.

Jahiruddin, A.T.M, Short, Patricia, Dressler, Wolfram & Adil Khan, M. (2011), "Can Microcredit Worsen Poverty? Cases of Exacerbated Poverty in Bangladesh", Development in Practice, Vol. 21, No. 8.

Jalal, Ayesha, 'The State of Martial Rule', 1990, Cambridge University Press, UK.

Jamal, Haroon (1995), "Explanation of Off-farm Work Participation in Rural Pakistan", Pakistan Development Review, Vol. 34, No. 2.

Jamal, Haroon (2008), "Exploring the Impact of Microfinance in Pakistan", Research Report No. 77, Social Policy and Development Centre, Karachi.

Javed, Afzal, Khan, Muhammad Nasar Sayeed, Nasar, Amina & Rasheed, Alina (2020), "Mental Healthcare in Pakistan", Taiwanese Journal of Psychiatry.

Javeid, Umer, Pratt, Stephan, Li, Han & Zao, Guochang (2023), "The Effect of Terrorism on Continuing Education: Evidence from Pakistan", Education Economics, Vol. 31, No. 3.

Javid, Hassan, "Class, Power, and Patronage: The Landed Elite and Politics in Pakistani Punjab", a thesis submitted to the Department of Sociology of the London School of Economics for the Degree of Doctor of Philosophy, London, June 2012.

Jayachandran, Seema & Pande, Rohini (2017), "Why Are Indian Children so Short? The Role of Birth Order and Son Preference", American Economic Review, Vol. 107, No. 9.

Jayachandran, Seema (2006), "Selling Labor Low: Wage Response to Productivity Shocks in Developing Countries", Journal of Political Economy, Vol. 114, No. 3, University of Chicago Press.

Jayachandran, Seema (2014), "The Roots of Gender Inequality in Developing Countries", NBER Working Paper 20380.

Jayaraman, Rajshri & Simroth, Dora (2015), "The Impact of School Lunches on Primary School Enrollment: Evidence from India's Midday Meal scheme", The Scandinavian Journal of Economics, Vol. 117, No. 4.

Johnson, Chalmers, 'MITI and the Japanese Miracle: The Growth of Industrial Policy, 1925–1975', 1982, Stanford University Press.

Johnson, Steven, 'Where Good Ideas Come From: The Natural History of Innovation', 2010, Riverhead Books, New York, USA.

Jones, Benjamin F. & Olken, Benjamin A. (2005), "Do Leaders Matter? National Leadership and Growth Since World War II", Quarterly Journal of Economics, Vol. 120, No. 3.

Jones, Seth G. & Christine Fair, C., 'Counterinsurgency in Pakistan', 2010, RAND Corporation www.rand.org.

Kahneman, Daniel, 'Thinking Fast and Slow', 2011, Farrar, Straus and Giroux, New York, USA.

Kahneman, Daniel, Sibony, Olivier, & Sustein, Cass R., 'Noise—A Flaw in Human Judgment', 2021, William Collins, UK.

Kaldor, N (1956), "Alternative Theories of Distribution", Review of Economic Studies 23.

Kalil, Ariel (2014), "Inequality Begins at Home: The Role of Parenting in the Diverging Destinies of Rich and Poor Children", NSFI, Vol. 5, Spring Link.

Kanazawa, Kyogo, Kawaguchi, Daiji, Shigeoka, Hitoshi, & Watanabe, Yasutora (2022), "AI, Skill, and Productivity: The Case of Taxi Drivers", NBER Working Paper 30612.

Kanbur, Ravi & Wagstaff, Adam (2014), "How Useful Is Inequality of Opportunity as a Policy Construct?" Policy Research Working Paper 6980, World Bank, Washington, D.C.

Kanbur, Ravi (1987), "The Standard of Living: Uncertainty, Inequality and Opportunity", in G. Hawthorn (Ed.) The Standard of Living, Cambridge University Press.

Karlan, Dean; Mullainathan, Sendhil, & Roth, Benjamin N. (2019), "Debt Traps? Money Vendors and Moneylender Debt in India and Philippines", AER, Vol. 1, No. 1.

Kate, Pickett & Wilkinson, Richard, 'The Spirit Level—Why Greater Equality Makes Societies Stronger', 2009, Bloomsbury Press, New York.

Kay, Cristobal (2002), "Why East Asia Overtook Latin America: Agrarian Reform, Industrialization and Development", Third World Quarterly, Vol. 23, No. 6, Taylor & Francis, Ltd.

Kelly, Elaine (2009), "The Scourge of Asian Flu: In Utero Exposure to Pandemic Influenza and the Development of a Cohort of British Children", Institute of Fiscal Studies, Working Paper 09/17, University College London.

Kelton, Stephanie, 'The Deficit Myth—Modern Monetary Theory and the Birth of the People's Economy', 2020, Public Affairs.

Khan, Ashfaque Hassan & Nasir, Zafar (1998), "Stylized Facts of Household Savings: Findings from the HIES 1993–94", Pakistan Development Review, Vol. 3, No. 4.

Khan, Mahmood Hasan (1979), "Farm Size and Land Productivity Relationships in Pakistan", PDR, Vol. 18, No. 1, PIDE, Islamabad.

Khan, Mahmood Hasan, 'Underdevelopment and Agrarian Structure in Pakistan', 1981, Westview Press Inc., USA.

Khan, S A. (2019), "Situation Analysis of Health Care System of Pakistan: Post 18 Amendment".

Khan, S., Sajid, M.R. & Hafeez-ur-Rehman (2011), "Women's Empowerment Through Microcredit: A Case Study of District Gujrat, Pakistan", Academic Research International, Vol. 1, Issue.2.

Khandkar, Shahidur R. & Faruqee, Rashidur R. (2001), "The Impact of Farm Credit in Pakistan", Policy Research Working Paper 2653, World Bank, Washington, D.C.

Khanna, Tarun, 'Trust—Creating the Foundation for Entrepreneurship in Developing Countries', 2018, Berrett-Koehler Publishers, Oakland.

Khawaja, Asim Ijaz & Mian, Atif (2005), "Do Lenders Favor Politically Connected Firms? Rent Provision in an Emerging Financial Market", Quarterly Journal of Economics, Vol. 120, No. 4.

Kim, Jooseop, Alderman, Harold & Peter, Orazem (1999), "Can Private School Subsidies Increase Enrollment for the Poor? The Quetta Urban Fellowship Program", World Bank Economic Review, Vol. 13, No. 3.

Kissinger, Henry, 'Leadership', 2022, Penguin Press, New York.

Klein, R., Crawford, R.G., & Alchian, A. (1978), "Vertical Integration, Appropriate Rents, and the Competitive Contracting Process", Journal of Law and Economics, Vol. 21.

Knack, Stephen & Keefer, Philip (1997), "Does Social Capital Have an Economic Payoff?" Quarterly Journal of Economics, November.

Koppensteiner, Martin Foureaux & Manacorda, Marco (2016), "Violence and Birth Outcomes: Evidence from Homicides in Brazil", CEP Working Paper DP1323.

Koren, Miklos & Tenreyro, Silvana (2007), "Volatility and Development", Quarterly Journal of Economics, Vol. 122, No. 1.

Kremer, Michael & Holla, Alaka (2009), "Improving Education in the Developing World: What have We Learned from Randomized Evaluations?" Annual Review of Economics.

Krozer, Alice (2015), "The Inequality We Want—How Much Is Too Much?" WIDER Working Paper 2015/015.

Krueger, Alan B., 'What Makes a Terrorist—Economics and the Roots of Terrorism', Tenth Anniversary Edition, 2018, Princeton University Press.

Krugman, Paul & Taylor, Lance (1978), "Contractionary Effects of Devaluation", Journal of International Economics, Vol. 8.

Krugman, Paul, 'The Age of Diminished Expectations, 1997, Paperback Edition, MIT University Press.

Kumar, D. & Desai, M. (Eds.), 'The Cambridge History of India', 2005, Cambridge University Press.

Kurji, Zohra, Premani, Zahra Shaheen & Mithani, Yasmin (2016), "Analysis of the Health Care System of Pakistan: Lessons Learnt and Way Forward", Journal of Ayub Medical College Abbottabad, Vol. 28, No. 3.

Landes, David, 'The Wealth and Poverty of Nations', 1999, Abacus Edition, London.

Lansing, Stephen J., 'Priests and Programmers', 1991, Princeton University Press.

Laurent Gayer, 'Karachi—Ordered Disorder and the Struggle for the City', 2014, Oxford University Press.

Lavers, Tom (Eds.), 'The Politics of Distributing Social Transfers—State Capacity and Political Contestation in Sub-Saharan Africa and South Asia', 2022, Oxford University Press.

Leff, Nathaniel H. (1964), "Economic Development through Bureaucratic Corruption", The American Behavioral Scientist (Pre-1986); Nov.1964; 8, 3; ABI/INFORM complete.

León-Ciliotta, Gianmarco, Zejcirovic, Dijana, & Fernandez, Fernando (2022), "Policymaking, Trust, and the Demand for Public Services: Evidence from a Nationwide Family Planning Programme", Working Paper 1352, Barcelona School of Economics.

Leones, J.P. & Feldman, S. (1998), "Nonfarm Activity and Rural Household Income: Evidence from Philippine Microdata", Economic Development and Cultural Change, Vol. 46, No. 4.

Lerner, Melvin J., 'The Belief in a Just World—A Fundamental Delusion', 1980, Plenum Press New York, USA.

Lewis, Arthur (1976), "Development and Distribution", included in 'Employment, Income Distribution and Development Strategy: Problems of the Developing Countries' (Essays in Honour of H.W. Singer), edited by Alan Cairncross and Mohinder Puri, 1976, Holmes & Meir Publications, New York.

Lieven, Anatol (2011), 'Pakistan—A Hard Country', Penguin Books.

Lipset, Seymour Martin (1959), "Some Social Requisites of Democracy: Economic Development and Political Legitimacy", American Political Science Review, Vol. 53, No. 1.

Lipton, Michael, 'Land Reforms in Developing Countries: Property Rights and Property Wrongs', 2009, Routledge, New York.

Lodhi, Maleeha (Eds.), 'Pakistan Beyond the Crisis State', 2011, Oxford University Press.

Lova, Stefania & Varela, Gonzalo (2020), "Internationally Linked Firms, Integration Reforms and Productivity—Evidence from Pakistan", Policy Research Working Paper No. 9349, World Bank, Washington, D.C.

Lowes, S & Montero, E. (2016), "Blood Rubber: The Effects of Labor Coercion on Development and Culture in the CRC", working Paper.

Luca, Dara Lee & Bloom, David E. (2018), "The Returns to Prenatal Health: Evidence from Indonesia", NBER Working Paper 24304.

Lucas, Robert E. (1990), "Why Doesn't Capital Flow from Rich to Poor Countries?" American Economic Review, Vol. 80, No. 2.

Lui, F.T. (1985), "An Equilibrium Queuing Model of Bribery", Journal of Political Economy, Vol. 93, No. 4.

Lui, F.T. (1986), "A Dynamic Model of Corruption Deterrence", Journal of Public Economics, Vol. 31, No. 2.

Lupien, S.J., King, S., Meaney, M.J., & McEwan, B.S. (2000), "Child's Stress Hormone levels Correlate with Mother's Socioeconomic Status and Depressive State", Biological Psychiatry, Vol. 48, No. 10.

Macy, S. (2017), "Wheels of Change: How Women Rode the Bicycle to Freedom (with Flat Tires Along the Way), National Geographic Kids, Washington, D.C.

Madiha Afzal, 'Pakistan Under Siege: Extremism, Society, and the State', 2018, Brookings Institution Press.

Mahmood, Moazam & Nadeem-Ul-Haque (1981), "Farm Size and Productivity Revisited", PDR, Vol. 20, No. 2.

Mahoney, Paul (2001), "The Common Law and Economic Growth: Hayek Might Be Right", Journal of Legal studies, Vol. 25, No. 2.

Malik, Adeel & Duncan, William (2022), "Obfuscated Liberalization: How Special Interest Groups Capture Trade Policy in Pakistan", PIDE-RASTA, Islamabad.

Malik, Iftikhar H., 'State and Civil Society in Pakistan—Politics of Authority, Ideology and Ethnicity', 1997, Palgrave Macmillan.

Maloney, W.F. & Caicedo, F. Valencia (2017), "Engineers, Innovative Capacity and Development in the Americas", CESifo Working Paper No. 6339, Munich.

Mancur, Olson (1992), "Do Lawyers Impair Economic Growth", Law & Social Inquiry, Vol. 17, No. 4.

Mani, Anandi, Mullainathan, Sendhil, Shafir, Eldar, & Zhao, Jiaying (2013), "Poverty Impedes Cognitive Function", Science Vol. 341, 976, www.sciencemag.org.

Mansuri, Ghazala & Slesh Shrestha (2018), "Wealth Inequality, Poverty and Mobility: Evidence from a Panel Survey in Rural Pakistan", Mimeo, World Bank.

Marcel Fafchamps & Agnes R. Quisumbing (1999), "Human Capital, Productivity, and Labor Allocation in Rural Pakistan", Journal of Human Resources, Vol. 34, No. 2.

Marden, S. (2014), "The Agricultural Roots of Industrial Development: Forward linkages in Reform—Era China", mimeo.

Marrero, G.A., Rodriguez, J.G. & van der Weide, R. (2016), "Unequal Opportunity, Unequal Growth", World Bank Policy Research Paper Series 7853.

Marshall, Alfred, 'Principles of Economics', 1890, First Edition, Palgrave Macmillan, New York.

Marshall, Tim, 'The Prisoners of Geography', 2015, Elliot & Thompson, UK.

Martin, Lucy (2016), "Taxation, Loss Aversion, and Accountability: Theory and Experimental Evidence for Taxation's Effect on Citizen Behaviour", University of North California Paper.

Martinez-Vazquez, Jorge (2006), "Pakistan: A Preliminary Assessment of the Federal Tax System", Working Paper 06-24, International Studies Program, Andrew Young School of Policy Studies.

Marx, Karl (1859), 'A Contribution to the Critique of Political Economy', 1979 Edition, New York, International Publishers.

Mazzucato, Mariana & Collington, Rosie, 'The Big Con: How the Consulting Industry Weakens our Businesses, Infantilises our Governments and Warps our Economies', 2023, Penguin Press.

Mc Neill, W.H., 'The Pursuit of Power: Technology, Armed Forces and Society Since AD 1000', 2013, University of Chicago Press.

McAdams, Richard H. (2007), "Economic Costs of Inequality", University of Chicago Law School Paper.

Mehmood, Sultan (2013), "Terrorism and the Macroeconomy: Evidence from Pakistan", Defence and Peace Economics. https://doi.org/10.1080/10242694.2013.793529.

Mehmood, Sultan (2020), "Judicial Independence and Development: Evidence from Pakistan", AMSE Working Paper 2041, Aix-Marseille School of Economics, France.

Mehmood, Tahir, Arby, Muhammad Farooq, Hussain, Touqir & Sattar, Abdul (2016), "Impact of Microfinance on Income Generation and Living Standards: A Case Study of Dera Ghazi Khan Division", Pakistan Economic and Social Review, Vol. 54, No. 1, pp. 73–80.

Meisenzahl, R. & Mokyr, J. (2011), "The Rate and Direction of Invention in the British Industrial Revolution: Incentives and Institutions", NBER Working Paper 16993.

Mellor, John W., Nabi, Ijaz & Tusneem, M.E. (2009), "Agriculture Development and Food Security", Pakistan Development Review, Vol. 47, No. 4, Islamabad.

Mendoza, RU, E Beja, V Venida & D Yap (2012), "An Empirical Analysis of Political Dynasties in the 15th Philippine Congress", Asian Institute of Management Policy Centre Research Paper.

Mercier, Hugo & Sperber, Dan, 'The Enigma of Reason—A New Theory of Human Understanding', 2017, Harvard University Press.

Migdal, Joel S., 'Strong Societies and Weak States: State-society Relations and State Capabilities in the Third World', 1988, Princeton University Press.

Milanovic, Brank (2015), "Global Inequality of Opportunity: How Much of Our Income Is Determined by Where We Live?" Review of Economics and Statistics, Vol. 97, 2.

Milanovic, Branko (2007), "Why We All Care About Inequality (But Are Loath to Admit It)", Challenge, Vol. 50, No. 6.

Milanovic, Branko, 'Global Inequality—A New Approach for the Age of Globalization', 2016, Harvard University Press, Cambridge.

Milligan, Kevin & Schirle, Tammy (2018), "The Evolution of Longevity: Evidence from Canada", NBER Working Paper 24929.

Mody, Ashoka, 'India is Broken', 2023, Stanford University Press.

Mohmand, Shandana K., 'Crafty Oligarchs, Savvy Voters: Democracy Under Inequality in Rural Pakistan', 2019, Cambridge University Press.

Mokyr, Joel, 'A Culture of Growth—The Origin of the Modern Economy', 2017, Princeton University Press.

Mokyr, Joel, 'The Lever of Riches—Technological Creativity and Economic Progress', 1990, Oxford University Press, New York, USA.

Mokyr, Joel, Vickers, Chris & Ziebarth, Nicholas L. (2015), "The History of Technological Anxiety", Journal of Economic Perspectives, Vol. 29, No. 3.

Moore, M., Prichard, W., & Fjeldstad, O.-H., 'Taxing Africa: Coercion, Reform and Development', 2018, Zed Books.

Moscona, Jacob & Sastry, Karthik A. (2022), "Inappropriate Technology: Evidence from Global Agriculture", November.

Moyo, Dambisa, 'Dead Aid—Why Aid Is Not Working and How There Is a Better Way for Africa', 2009, Farrar, Straus and Giroux, New York, USA.

Moyo, Dambisa, 'Edge of Chaos', 2018, Basic Books, New York.

Muhammad Ashfaq Ahmed (2020), "Pakistan: Witholdingisation of the Economic System: A Source of Revenue, Civil Strife, or Dutch Disease?" Pakistan Development Review, Vol. 59, 3, Islamabad.

Mullainathan, Sendhil and Shafir, Eldar, 'Scarcity: Why Having Too Little Means So Much', 2013, Times Books.

Muralidharan, K. & Sundararaman, V. (2009), "Teacher Performance Pay: Experimental Evidence from India", NBER Working Paper 15323.

Muralidharan, Karthik & Singh, Abhijeet (2020), "Improving Public Sector Management at Scale? Experimental Evidence on School Governance in India", NBER Working Paper 28129.

Murgai, Rinku, Ali, Mubarak, & Byerlee, Derek (2001), "Productivity Growth and Sustainability in Post-Green Revolution Agriculture: The Case of Indian and Pakistan Punjabs", World Bank Research Observer, Vol. 16, No. 2, Fall.

Murphy, Eamon, 'The Making of Terrorism in Pakistan—Historical and Social Roots of Extremism', 2013, Routledge, New York.

Murphy, Kevin M., Shleifer, Andrei, & Vishny Robert W. (1991), "The Allocation of Talent: Implication for Growth", Quarterly Journal of Economics, Vol. 106. No. 2.

Murphy, Kevin M., Shleifer, Andrei, & Vishny, Robert W., (1993) "Why Is Rent-Seeking so Costly to Growth", American Economic Review, Vol. 83, No. 2.

NACTA (2021), "Misconception About the Relationship Between Militancy and Madrasas in Swat", Pakistan Journal of Terrorism Research, Vol. 3, No. 2, July–December.

NACTA (2022), "War on Terror: The Impact of Tehreek-e-Taliban Pakistan on the Education in South Waziristan", PJTR, Vol. 4, p. 2.

Najum-Us-Saqib & G.M. Arif (2012), "Time Poverty, Work Status and Gender: The Case of Pakistan", Pakistan Development Review, Vol. 51, No. 1.

Nancy Qian (2008), "Missing Women and the Price of Tea in China: The Effect of Sex-Specific Earnings on Sex Imbalance", Quarterly Journal of Economics, Vol. 123, No. 3.

Naqvi, Syed Nawab Haider, Hasan Khan, Mahmood & Chaudhary, M. Ghaffar (1987), "Land Reforms in Pakistan: A Historical Perspective", PIDE, Islamabad.

Nasir, Jamil (2007), "Factors Affecting Performance of Sales Tax Audit Workforce of the Central Board of Revenue", Pakistan Management Review, Vol. XLIV, No. 3, Karachi.

Nasir, Jamil (2012), "IMF Programs in Pakistan (1988–2008)—An Analysis", Criterion Quarterly, Vol. 2, No. 4, Islamabad.

Nasir, Jamil (2015), "Analyzing Pakistan's National Competitiveness", Criterion Quarterly, Vol. 10, No. 1, Islamabad.

Nasir, Jamil (2015), "Economic Perspectives on Corruption", Criterion Quarterly, Vol. 10, No. 4, Islamabad, Pakistan.

Nasir, Jamil (2015), "The Economics of Inequality", Criterion Quarterly, Vol. 10, No. 3, Islamabad, Pakistan.

Nasir, Jamil, 'Development for an Equitable Society', 2020, Jumhoori Publications, Lahore, Pakistan.

Nasir, Jamil (2020), "The Tariff Tripod of Pakistan: Protection, Export Promotion, and Revenue Generation", PDR, Vol. 59, No. 3, Islamabad.

Nasir, Jamil, 'Political Economy of Bad Governance' 2021, Jumhoori Publications, Lahore, Pakistan.

Nasir, Jamil, 'SAFTA: Potential, Prospects, and Limitations' for Discussion on Various Trade Models, 2007, LCCI.

Nasr, S.V.R. (2000), "The Rise of Sunni Militancy in Pakistan: The Changing Role of Islamism and the Ulama in Society and Politics", Modern Asian Studies, Vol. 34, No. 1.

Nekoei, Arash & Sinn, Fabian (2021), "HERSTORY: The Rise of Self-Made Women", CEPR Discussion Paper 15736.

Nelson, Mathew J. (2006), "Muslims, Markets, and the Meaning of 'Good' Education in Pakistan", Asian Survey, Vol. XLVI, No. 5, September/October.

Nino-Zarazua, Max M. & Copestake, James (2008), "Financial Inclusion, Vulnerability and Mental Models: From Physical Access to Effective Use of Financial Services in a Low—Income Area of Mexico City", Savings and Development, Vol. 32, No. 4.

NIPS (2020), "Pakistan Maternal Mortality Survey 2019", National Institute of Population studies, Islamabad, Pakistan and Rockville, Maryland, USA, NIPS and ICF.

NIPS, Pakistan & ICF (2019), "Pakistan Demographic and Health Survey 2017–18", Islamabad, Pakistan, and Rockville, Maryland, USA: NIPS and ICF.

Noorani, A.G., 'The Trial of Bhagat Singh-Politics of Justice', 1996, Oxford University Press.

North, Douglass C., 'Institutions, Institutional Change and Economic Performance', 1990, Cambridge University Press.

Noy, Shakked & Zhang, Whitney (2023), "Experimental Evidence on the Productivity Effects of Generative Artificial Intelligence", Working Paper, March.

Nunn, Nathan & Wantchekon, Leonard (2011), "The Slave Trade and the Origins of Mistrust in Africa", American Economic Review, Vol. 101, No. 7.

OECD (2006), "Education at a Glance: OECD Indicators", Paris.

OECD (2012), "Perspectives on Global Development: Social Cohesion in a Shifting World", OECD.org.

Olken, Benjamin A. & Pande, Rohini (2011), "Corruption in Developing Countries", NBER Working Paper No. 17398.

Olken, Benjamin A. (2006), "Corruption and the Costs of Redistribution: Micro Evidence form Indonesia", Journal of Public Economics, Vol. 90, Nos. 4–5.

Oscal, N. & Yildrim, J. (2010), "Regional Effects of Terrorism on Economic Growth in Turkey: A Geographically Weighted Regression Approach", Journal of Peace Research, Vol. 47, No. 4.

Ostry, Jonathan D., Berg, Andrew & Tsangarides, Charalambos G. (2014), "Redistribution, Inequality and Growth", IMF Staff Discussion Note.

Oxfam (2014), "Even It Up—Time to End Extreme Inequality", Oxfam International Report, October.

Oxfam (2015), "Asia at the Crossroads—Why the Region Must Address Inequality Now", Briefing Note.

Pak Alliance for Maths and Science (2021), "The Missing Third: An Out of School Study of Pakistani 5–16 Year Olds", Islamabad, Pakistan.

Palma, Gabriel (2011), "Homogenous Middles vs. Heterogeneous Tails, and the End of 'Inverted U': The Share of Rich Is What It's All About", Cambridge Working Papers in Economics, University of Cambridge.

Pande, Rohini (2020), "Can Democracy Work for the Poor?" Science.

Papanek Gustav F., 'Pakistan's Development—Social Goals and Private Incentives', 1967, Harvard University Press, Cambridge.

Parente, Stephen L. & Prescott, Edward C. (1999), "Monopoly Rights: A Barrier to Riches", American Economic Review, Vol. 89, No. 5.

Parker, Susan W. & Vogl, Tom (2018), "Do Conditional Cash Transfers Improve Economic Outcomes in the Next Generation? Evidence from Mexico", NBER Working Paper 24304.

Pasha, Hafiz A., 'Leading Issues in the Economy of Pakistan', 2023, FES, Islamabad, Pakistan.

Peltzman, Sam (2009), "Mortality Inequality", Journal of Economic Perspectives, Vol. 23, No. 4.

Peng, Yuelan, Akbar, Muhammad Waqas, Anwar, Sofia & Hafeez, Muhammad (2019), "Evaluating the Efficiency and Determinants of Efficiency of Rural Health Centres Situated in Punjab, Pakistan", Health.

Perry, J.L. & Hondeghem, A. (2008), "Building Theory and Empirical Evidence about Public Service Motivation", International Public Management Journal, Vol. 11, No. 1.

Peter, Timmer C. (1997), "How Well Do the Poor Connect to the Growth Process", Discussion Paper No. 17, Harvard Institute for International Development (HIID), Cambridge.

Piabou, S.M. & Tieguhong, J.C. (2017), "Health Expenditure and Economic Growth-a Review of the Literature and an Analysis Between the Economic Community for Central African States (CEMAC) and Selected African Countries", Health Economic Review Vol. 7, No. 23.

PIDE (1985), "Size-Productivity Relationship in Pakistan's Agriculture in the Seventies (with Comments)", PDR, Vol. 24, No3/4, Papers and Proceedings of the Second Annual General Meeting of the Pakistan society of Development Economists, PIDE, Islamabad, May 12–14.

PIDE (1999), "The Structure of Informal Credit Market in Pakistan", Research Report No. 168, PIDE, Islamabad.

PIDE (2007), "Public Service Through the Eyes of Civil Servants", PIDE Series on Governance and Institutions (Available Online) http://pide.org.pk.

PIDE (2017), "Strengthening Public Sector Capacity for Improved Governance in Pakistan", Policy Viewpoint No. 07/2017, Pakistan Institute of Development, Islamabad.

PIDE (2020), "Case Management as an Approach to Improve Judicial System", Webinar Brief No. 1, PIDE, Islamabad.

PIDE (2020), "Creativity in Schools: A 21st Century Need", PIDE Policy Viewpoint No. 21.

PIDE (2020), "Economic Analysis of Law in Pakistan", PIDE Knowledge Brief No. 6/2020.

PIDE (2020), "Foreign Training of Government officers and Public Sector Capacity in Pakistan", PIDE Working Paper No. 2020:19.

PIDE (2020), "National Poverty Estimates", Knowledge Brief, Pakistan Development Institute, Islamabad, Pakistan.

PIDE (2020), "The Pension Bombs and Possible Solutions", Policy Viewpoint, Pakistan Institute of Development Economics, Islamabad.

PIDE (2020), "Total Factor Productivity and Economic Growth in Pakistan: A Five Decade Overview", PIDE Working Paper No. 2020: 11, Islamabad.

PIDE (2020), "Unconditional Cash Transfers and Poverty Alleviation in Pakistan—BISP's Impact on Households' Socioeconomic Wellbeing", PIDE Policy Viewpoint No. 18: 2020.

PIDE (2021), "Cash Poor, Perk Rich Civil Service Compensation: Incentives, Dissatisfaction, and Costs", https://pide.org.pk

PIDE (2021), "Electoral reforms in Pakistan", Webinar 52: 2021.

PIDE (2021), "The Electronic Media Economy in Pakistan: Issues and Challenges", Knowledge Brief No. 2021: 35.

PIDE (2022), "Desire to Live in Pakistan: Stay or Leave", Basics Notes No. 4, PIDE, Islamabad, November.

PIDE (2022), "Foreign Aid Effectiveness: The Relationship between Aid Inflows and Economic Growth", Knowledge Brief, PIDE, Islamabad, September.

PIDE (2022), "Justice: Not a Fundamental Right but a Neoclassical Economic Commodity?" PIDE Knowledge Brief No. 59, Islamabad.

PIDE (2022), "Land Titles in Punjab – Overview, Problems, and Suggestions", Knowledge Brief No 2022: 91.

Piketty, Thomas, 'Capital and Ideology', 2020, Harvard University Press.

Piketty, Thomas, 'Capital in the Twenty-First Century', 2014, Harvard University Press.

PILDAT (2022), "Four Years of the 15th National Assembly of Pakistan—A Citizens' Report on Performance", Islamabad, Pakistan, August.

Pilling, David, 'The Growth Delusion: Wealth, Poverty, and the Well-Being of Nations', 2018, Penguin Random House.

Pistor, Katharina, 'The Code of Capital: How the Law creates Wealth and Inequality', 2019, Princeton University Press.

Polyani, Karl, 'The Great Transformation', 2001, Second Beacon Paperback Edition.

Polyani, Karl, Avensberg, Conrad M., & Pearson, Harry W. (1957), 'Trade and Market in the Early Empires—Economies in History and Theory', The Free Press Glencoe, Illinois.

Porta, Rafael La, Lopez-de-Silanes, Florencio & Shleifer, Andrei (2008), "The Economic Consequences of Legal Origins", Journal of Economic Literature, Vol. 46, No. 2.

Porta, Rafael La, Lopez-de-Silanes, Florencio, Pop-Eleches, Cristian, & Shleifer, Andrei (2004), "Judicial Checks and Balances", Journal of Political Economy, Vol. 112, No. 2.

Preston, Samuel H. (1975), "The Changing Relation Between Mortality and Level of Economic Development", Population Studies, Vol. 29, No. 2.

Prina, Silvia (2015), "Banking the Poor via Savings Accounts: Evidence from a Field Experiment", Journal of Development Economics.

Pritchett, Lant & Matt, Andrews (2010), "Capability Traps? The Mechanisms of Persistent Implementation Failure", Centre for Global Development, Working Paper 234, December, www.cgdev.org.

Pritchett, Lant & Viarengo, Martina (2023), "The Learning Crisis of Developing Country Elites: Lessons from PISA-D", World Bank Economic Review.

Pritchett, Lant (2001), "Where Has All the Education Gone", World Bank Economic Review, Vol. 15, No. 3, Washington, D.C.

Pritchett, Lant (2013), "The Rebirth of Education", Centre for Global Development.

Pritchett, Lant (2020), "Poverty Reduction and Economic Growth", Econofact, February.

Pritchett, Lant (2023), "Multilateralism and Development Cooperation: The End of an Interesting Era?" Global Perspectives, Vol. 4, No. 1.

Pritchett, Lant, & Summers, Lawrence H. (1993), "Wealthier Is Healthier", Journal of Human Resources, Vol. 31, No. 4.

Priyadarshee, Anurag & Ghalib, Asad K. (2011), "The Andra Pradesh Microfinance Crisis in India: Manifestation, Causal Analysis, and Regulatory Response", Brooks World Poverty Institute Working Paper 157, University of Manchester.

Przeworski, Adam (2003), "The Last Chance: Are Institutions the Primary Cause of Economic Development?" Paper Prepared for a Meeting on Institutions, Behaviour, and Outcomes, CEBRAP, Sao Paulo, March 12–14.

Punjab Bureau of Statistics (2021), "Multiple Indicator Cluster Survey (MICS) 2017–18", Planning and Development Department, Government of Punjab and UNICEF.

Putman, Robert D., "Bowling Alone', 2000, Simon and Schuster, New York, USA.

Putnam, Robert D. (1993), "Making Democracy Work: Civic Traditions in Modern Italy', Princeton University Press.

Qian, Nancy (2009), "Quantity-Quality and the One Child Policy: The Only –Child Disadvantage in School Enrollment in Rural China", NBER Working Paper.

Quinn, Dennis P., & Woolley, John T. (2001), "Democracy and National Economic Performance: The Preference for Stability", American Journal of Political Science, Vol. 45, No. 3.

Raghuram Rajan, 'Third Pillar: How Markets and States Leave the Community Behind', 2019, Penguin Random House.

Raju, Dhushyanth & D'Souza, Ritika (2017), "Child Undernutrition in Pakistan: What Do We Know?" WPS 8049, World Bank, Washington, D.C.

Rama, Martin, Beteille, Tara, Li, Yue, Mitra, Pradeep K. & Newman, John Lincoln (2015), "Addressing Inequality in South Asia", World Bank Group.

Ramakrishan, S., Khera, R., Jain, S., Saxena, A. & Kailash, S. (2011), "Gender Differences in the Utilization of Surgery for Congenital Heart Disease in India", Heart, BMJ Journals.

Rana, Muhammad Amir (2011), "Evolution of Militant Groups in Pakistan (1)", Conflict and Peace Studies, Vol. 4, No. 2.

Rana, Muhammad Amir (2018), "Pakistani-Based Militant Groups and Prospects of Their Reintegration: A Structural Analysis", Mantraya Occasional Paper No. 6, March 12.

Rand, Ayn, 'Atlas Shrugged', 1957.

Rashid, Ahmed, 'Descent into Chaos', 2009, Penguin Books.

RASTA-PIDE (2022), "PIDE Sludge Audit Vol. 1", Pakistan Institute of Development Economics, Islamabad.

Ravallion, Martin & Chen, Shaohua (1997), "What Can New Data Survey Tell Us About Recent Changes in Distribution and Poverty?" World Bank Economic Review, Vol. 11.

Ravallion, Martin & Datt, Gaurav (1996), "How Important to India Is the Sectoral Composition of Economic Growth", World Bank Economic Review, Vol. 10.

Ravallion, Martin, 'The Economics of Poverty: History, Measurement, and Policy', 2015, Oxford University Press.

Ravi Kanbur (2012), "Does Kuznets Still Matter?" Working Paper Charles H. Dyson School of Applied Economics and Management, Cornell University.

Rawls, John, 'A theory of Justice', 1999, Revised Edition, Harvard University Press.

Reinert, Erick S., 'How Rich Countries Got Rich—And Why Poor Countries Stay Poor', 2007, Constable & Robinson Ltd. London, UK.

Reis, Jose Guilherme & Taglioni, Daria (2013), "Determinants of Export Growth at the Extensive and Intensive Margins—Evidence from Product and Firm-Level Data for Pakistan", Policy Research Working Paper, World Bank, Washington, D.C.

Ridley, Matthew W., Rao, Gautam, Schilbach, Frank, & Patel, Vikram H. (2020), "Poverty, Depression, and Anxiety: Causal Evidence and Mechanisms", NBER Working Paper 27157.

RISE (2017), "Raising the Floor on Learning Levels: Equitable Improvement Starts with the Tail", RISE Insight Note.

Rizvi, Hasan Askari, 'Military, Society and State in Pakistan' 2000, Macmillan Press ltd.

Robert T. Jensen (2010), "Economic Opportunities and Gender Differences in Human Capital: Experimental Evidence from India", NBER Working Paper No. 16021.

Robert Wade, 'Governing the Market: Economic Theory and the Role of the Government in East Asian Industrialization', 1990, Princeton University Press.

Rodrik, Dani (1999), "Institutions for High Quality Growth: What They Are and How to Acquire Them", Paper presented in IMF conference on Second Generation Reforms.

Rodrik, Dani (2003), "Growth Strategies", NBER Working Paper No. 10050.

Rodrik, Dani (Ed.), 'In search of Prosperity—Analytic Narratives on Economic growth', 2003, Princeton University Press, New Jersey, USA.

Rodrik, Dani, 'In Search of Prosperity—Analytic Narratives on Economic Growth', 2003, Princeton University Press.

Rodrik, Dani, Subramanian, Arvind & Trebbi, Francesco (2002), "Institutions Rule: The Primacy of Institutions Over Geography and Integration in Economic Development", NBER Working Paper No. 9305.

Roemer, John E. (1998), 'Equality of Opportunity', Harvard University Press.

Rohner, D. & Saia, A. (2019), "Education and Conflict: Evidence from a Policy Experiment in Indonesia", CEPR, Discussion Paper 13509.

Rohner, Dominic & Zhuravskaya, Ekaterina (Eds.), 'Nation Building: Big Lessons from Successes and Failures', 2023, Centre for Economic Policy Research, e-Book, www.cepr.org.

Romer, Paul (1993), "Idea Gaps and Object Gaps in Economic Development", Journal of Monetary Economics, Vol. 32, No. 3.

Romer, Paul M. (1994), "Economic Growth and Investment in Children", Daedalus, Vol. 123, No. 4, Health and Wealth, Fall.

Rose, Pauline (Eds.), 'Reforming Education and Challenging Inequalities in Southern Contexts', 2021, Routledge.

Rosenstein-Rodan, P.N. (1961), "International Aid for Underdeveloped Countries", Review of Economics and Statistics, Vol. 43, No. 2.

Rotberg, Robert I. (Eds.), 'When States Fail: Causes and Consequences', 2004, Princeton University Press.

Rothstein, Bo & Stolle, Dietlind (2008), "The State and Social Capital: An Institutionalized Theory of Generalized Trust", Comparative Politics, Vol. 40, No. 4, pp. 441–459.

Rubin, Barnett R. (2000), "The Political Economy of War and Peace in Afghanistan", World Development, Vol. 28, No. 10.

Rumi, Raza (2102), "Pakistan: Ungoverned Spaces", Barcelona Centre for International Affairs, http://www.cidob.org.

Sacco, Pier Luigi, Arenas, Alex, & De Domenico, Manlio (2023), "The Political Economy of Big Data Leaks: Uncovering the Skeleton of Tax evasion", Chaos, Solitons & Fractals, Vol. 168, 113182, March 23.

Sachs, Jaffrey D., 'The End of Poverty—Economic Possibilities for Our times', 2005, Penguin Press, New York, USA.

Saez, Emmanuel & Zucman, Gabriel, 'The Triumph of Injustice—How the Rich Dodge Taxes and How to Make Them Pay', 2019, W.W. Norton.

Saini, G.R. (1969), "Farm Size, Productivity and Returns to scale", Economic and Political Weekly, Vol. 4, No. 26.

Sana Ashraf, 'Finding the Enemy Within—Blasphemy Accusations and Subsequent Violence in Pakistan', 2021, Australian National University Press.

Sanchez de la Sierra, R. (2020), "On the Origin of States: Stationary Bandits and Taxation in Eastern Congo", Journal of Political Economy, Vol. 128, No. 1.

Sandel, Michael J., 'The Tyranny of Merit: What's Become of the Common Good?' 2020, Farrar, Straus, and Giroux.

Sandel, Michael, J., 'What Money Can't Buy: The Moral Limits to Market', 2013, Farrar, Straus and Giroux, New York.

Sankar, M.J., Natarajan, C.K., Das, R.R., Agarwal, R., Chandrasekaran, A., & Paul, V.K. (2016), "When Do Newborns Die? A Systemic Review of Timing of Overall and Cause-specific Neonatal Deaths in Developing Countries", Journal of Perinatology.

Sasso, Greg & Morelli, Massimo (2021), "Bureaucrats Under Populism", Journal of Public Economics, Vol. 202, 104497, October.

Scheidel, Walter (2017), 'The Great Leveler—Violence and the History of Equality from the Stone Age to the Twenty-First Century', Princeton University Press, Princeton, New Jersey.

Scheve, K & Stasavage, D (2012), "Democracy, War, and Wealth: Lessons from Two Centuries of Inheritance Taxation", American Political Science Review Vol. 106, No. 1.

Schneider, Kate & Gugerty, Professor Mary Kay (2011), "Agricultural Productivity and Poverty Reduction: Linkages and Pathways", Evans School Review, Vol. 1, No. 1.

Schumacher, E.F., 'Good Work', 1980, Harper Collins Publishers.

Scur, Daniela, Sadun, Raffaella, Reenan, John Van, Remos, Renata, & Bloom, Nicholas (2021), "The World Management Survey at 18: Lessons and the Way Forward", Oxford Review of Economic Policy, Vol. 37, No. 2.

Segall, Shlomi (2013), 'Equality and Opportunity', Oxford University Press, UK.

Sen, Amartya (1962), "An Aspect of Indian Agriculture", Economic Weekly, Annual Number, February.

Sen, Amartya (1966), "Peasants and Dualism with or Without Surplus Labor", Journal of Political Economy, Vol. 4, No. 5.

Sen, Amartya (1979), "Issues in the Measurement of Poverty", Scandinavian Journal of Economics, Vol. 81, No. 2, Measurement in Public Choice.

Sen, Amartya, 'Identity and Violence—The Illusion of Destiny', 2006, Penguin Books.

Sen, Amartya, 'The Idea of Justice', 2009, Allen Lane, London.

Sen, Kunal (2014), "Inclusive Growth: When We May Expect It? When We May Not?" Asian Development Review, Vol. 31, No. 1.

Sequeria, S. & Djankov, S (2010). "An Empirical study of Corruption in Ports", MPRA Paper 21791, University Library of Munich, Germany.

Shahbaz, Muhammad; Shabbir, Muhammad Shabaz; Malik, Muhammad Nasir & Wolters, Mark Edwards (2013), "An Analysis of the Causal Relationship Between Economic Growth and Terrorism in Pakistan", Economic Modelling, Vol. 35, pp. 21–29.

Shaheen, Rubina (2010), "An Investigation into the Factors Enhancing or Inhibiting Primary School Children's Creativity in Pakistan", Doctoral Dissertation, University of Birmingham.

Shaikh, Farzana, 'Making Sense of Pakistan', 2009, Columbia University Press.

Shinwari, Naveed Ahmad (2015), "Understanding the Informal Justice System: Opportunities and Possibilities for Legal Pluralism in Pakistan", CAM.

Shirazi, Nasim Shah; Javed, Sajid Amin; Ashraf, Dawood (2018), "The Interlinkage Between Social Exclusion and Financial Inclusion: Evidence from Pakistan", SSRN https://ssrn.com/abstract=3183623.

Shirizi, Nasim Shah & Khan, Aman Ullah (2009), "Role of Pakistan Poverty Alleviation Fund's Micro Credit in Poverty Alleviation: A Case of Pakistan", Pakistan Economic and Social Review, Vol. 47, No. 2, pp. 215–228.

Shleifer, Andrei & Vishny, Robert W. (1993), "Corruption", Quarterly Journal of Economics, Vol. 108, No. 3.

Sial, M.H., Iqbal, S. & Sheikh, A. (2012), "Farm-Size Productivity Relationship—Recent Evidence from Central Punjab", Pakistan Economic and Social Review, Vol. 50, No. 2.

Sibiko, S.W. & Qasim, M. (2017), "Weather Index Insurance, Agricultural Input Use, and Crop Productivity in Kenya", Global Food Discussion Paper 94, University of Gottingen.

Siddique, Farhan Irfan, 'The Politics of Ethnicity in Pakistan—The Baloch, Sindhi and Mohajir Ethnic Movements', 2012, Routledge.

Siddique, Osama (2011), "Approaches to Legal and Judicial Reform in Pakistan: Post-colonial Inertia and the Paucity of Imagination in Times of Turmoil and Change", DPRC Working Paper No. 4, LUMS, Lahore, Pakistan.

Siddique, Osama (2015), "Legal Advisory and Representational Services in South Punjab: Base Study of Availability and Priority Needs", Report of the Punjab Access to Justice Project.

Siddique, Osama, 'Pakistan's Experience with Formal Law: An Alien Justice', 2014, Cambridge University.

Sidhu, R.S. & Bhullar, A.S. (2005), "Patterns and Determinants of Agricultural Growth in the Two Punjabs", Economic and Political Weekly, Vol. 40, No. 53.

Sidhwa, Bapsi, 'The Pakistani Bride', 1983, St Martins Pr.

Silliman, Mikko & Virtanen, Hanna (2022), "Labor Market Returns to Vocational Secondary Education", American Economic Journal: Applied Economics, Vol. 14, No. 1.

Sindh Judicial Academy (2008), "Study on Informal Justice in Pakistan" SJA, Karachi

Snowdon, Brian & Stonehouse, George (2006), "Competitiveness in a Globalized World: Michael Porter on the Microeconomic Foundations of the Competitiveness of Nations, Regions and Firms", Journal of International Business Studies, Vol. 37.

Social Policy Development Centre (2001), "Social Development in Pakistan Towards Poverty Reduction", Annual Review, Oxford University Press.

Sokoloff, Kenneth L. & Engerman, Stanley N. (2000), "History Lessons: Institutions, Factor Endowments, and Paths of Development in the New World", Journal of Economic Perspectives, Vol. 14, No. 3.

Somville, Vincent & Vandewalle, Lore (2018), "Saving by Default: Evidence from a Field Experiment in Rural India", American Economic Journal: Applied Economics, Vol. 10, No. 3.

Soraya, S.H. (2022), "Exploring the Research Landscape in a Developing Country: Gauging the Prospects of Growth, Research Impact and Innovation", Transforming Government: People, Process and Policy, Vol. 16, No. 4.

Spence, Michael (1973), "Job Market Signaling", Quarterly Journal of Economics, Vol. 87, No. 3.

Spence, Michael, 'The Next Convergence: The Future of Economic Growth in a Multispeed World', 2011, E-edition.

Srinivasan, T.N. (1972), "Farm Size and Productivity Implications of Choice Under Uncertainty", Indian Journal of Statistics, Series B (1960–2002), Vol. 34, No. 4.

Stasavage, David, 'The Decline and Rise of Democracy: A Global History from Antiquity to Today', 2020, Princeton University Press.

Stern, Jessica (2000), "Pakistan's Jihad Culture", Foreign Affairs, Vol. 79, No. 6.

Stiglitz, Joseph E. (1996), "Some Lessons from the East Asian Miracle", The World Bank Research Observer, August.

Stiglitz, Joseph E. (1998), "Development Oriented Tax Policy", Initiative for Policy Dialogue, Columbia University.

Stiglitz, Joseph E., 'The Price of Inequality', 2012, W.W. Norton, New York, USA.

Stiglitz, Joseph E., Sen, Amartya & Fitoussi, Jean-Paul, 'Report of the Commission on the Measurement of Economic Performance and Social Progress', 2009.

Stretton, Paul P. (1979), "Basic Needs: Premises and Promises", Reprinted by the World Bank from Journal of Policy Modelling, 1979.

Sumit Ganguly, 'The Deadly Impasse—Kashmir and Indo-Pakistani Relations at the Dawn of a New Century', 2016, Cambridge University Press.

Sunde, Uwe, Dohmen, Thomas, Enke, Benjamin, Falk, Armin, Huffman, David & Meyerheim, Gerrit (2022), "Patience and Comparative Development", Review of Economic Studies, Vol. 89, No. 5, October.

Sustein, Cass R., 'Sludge: What Stops Us from Getting Things Done and What to Do About It', 2021, MIT Press.

Talbot, Ian, 'Pakistan - A New History', 2011, Oxford University Press.

Talbot, Ian, 'Pakistan: A Modern History', 2010, Second Edition, Palgrave Macmillan.

Taneja, Nisha & Bismal, Samridhi (2016), "India's Informal Trade with Pakistan", ICRIER.

Tawney, R.H., 'Equality', 1931, Reprint Edition, London: Unwin Books, 1964.

Thaler, Richard H. & Sunstein, Cass R. (2008), 'Nudge-Improving Decisions About Health, Wealth, and Happiness', Yale University Press.

Tharoor, Shashi, 'Inglorious Empire—What the British Did to India', 2016, Scribe Publications.

Thirtle, Colin, Lin, Lin, & Piesse, Jenifer (2003), "The Impact of Research-led Agricultural Productivity Growth on Poverty Reduction in Africa, Asia, and Latin America", World Development, Vol. 31, No. 12.

Tilly, C. (1975), 'The Formation of National States in Western Europe', Princeton University Press.

Tirole, Jean, 'Economics for the Common Good', 2017, Princeton University Press.

Torpey-Saboe, Nicole, 'Measuring Education Inequality in Developing Countries', 2019, Palgrave Macmillan.

Toynbee, Arnold, J, "Pakistan as a Historian Sees Her", included in 'Crescent and Green: A Miscellany of Writings on Pakistan', 1955, London and Cassell & Co. Limited.

UNDP (2015), "FATA Sustainable Return and Rehabilitation Strategy", FATA Secretariat Support Program, UNDP Pakistan office, Islamabad.

UNDP (2020), "Pakistan Human Development Report 2020", http://www.undp.org.

UNDP (2022), "South Punjab Deep Dive Report 2022", https://pakistan.un.org/en/177830-south-punjab-deep-dive-report.

UNIDO (2022), "Industrial Report 2022: The Future of Industrialization in a Post-Pandemic World", United Nations Industrial Development Organization, Vienna.

United Nations Organization (2009), "Rethinking Poverty—Report on the World Social Situation 2010", Department of Economic and Social Affairs, ST/ESA/324.

UNO (2009), "Legal Empowerment of the Poor and Eradication of Poverty", July.

USIP (2012), "Conflict Dynamics in Karachi", www.usip.org.

USIP (2018), "Special Report No. 421", March, www.usip.org.

Uslander, Eric M. (2003), "Tax Evasion, Trust, and the Strong Arm of the Law", Paper for the Conference on "Tax Evasion, Trust, and State Capacity", University of St. Gallen, Switzerland, October.

Van Bavel, Bas (2016), "The Invisible Hand? How Market Economies Have Emerged and Declined since AD 500", Oxford University Press, London, UK.

Van Rijckeghem, C., & Weder, B. (2001), "Bureaucratic Corruption and the Rate of Temptation: Do Wages in the Civil Service Affect Corruption, and by How Much?" Journal of Development Economics, Vol. 65, No. 2.

Vosoughi, Soroush, Roy, Deb & Aral, Sinan (2018), "The Spread of True and False News Online", Science, Vol. 359, No. 6380, http://ww.science.org.

Wade, Robert, 'Governing the Market-Economic Theory and the Role of Government in East Asian Industrialization', 1990, Princeton University Press.

Ward-Batts, Jennifer (2008), "Out of the Wallet and into the Purse: Using Micro Data to Test Income Pooling", Journal of Human Resources, University of Wisconsin Press, Vol. 43, No. 2.

Warr, P (2000), "Poverty Reduction and Economic Growth: The Asia Experience", Asian Development Review, Vol. 18, No. 2.

Wasif, Mazhur-ul-Haq Maryam & Wasif Siddique, M. (1997), "Off-Farm Employment and Income of Farm Families in Rural Punjab", Pakistan Economic and Social Review, Vol. 35, No. 2.

WDR (2001), "Attacking Poverty", World Development Report 2000–2001, World Bank, Washington, D.C., USA.

Weber, Max (1904–1905), 'The Protestant Ethic and the Spirit of Capitalism', translation of Tallcot Parsons, September 1958, Angelico Press, Cambridge MA.

Wei, Shang-Jin & Zhang, Xiaobo (2011), "The Competitive Saving Motive in China: Evidence from Rising Sex Ratios and Savings Rate in China", Journal of Political Economy, Vol. 119, No. 3.

Weide, Roy Van der & Milanovic, Branko (2014), "Inequality Is Bad for the Growth of the Poor (But Not for That of the Rich)", World Bank Policy Research Working Paper No. 6963, July.

Weiss, John (Ed.), 'Poverty Targeting in Asia', 2005, A Joint Publication of ADB and Edward Elgar Publishing.

Whalley, John & Zhao, Xiliang (2010), "The Contribution of Human Capital to China's Growth", NBER Working Paper 16592.

White, Howard & Anderson, Edward (2001), "Growth Versus Distribution: Does the Pattern of Growth Matter?" Development Policy Review, Vol. 19, No. 3.

White, Lawrence J., 'Industrial Concentration and Economic Power in Pakistan', 2016, Princeton University Press.

WHO & Alliance for Health policy and Systems Research (2017), "Primary Health Care Systems (Primasys): Comprehensive Case Study from Pakistan", World Health Organization (WHO-HIS-HSR-17.37-eng-pdf).

Wilder, Andrew (2010), "The Politics of Civil Service Reform in Pakistan", Journal of International Affairs, SIPA, Columbia.

Williams, G.L. (1947), "The Legal Unity of Husband and Wife", Modern Law Review, Vol. 10.

Williams, L.F. Rushbrook, 'The State of Pakistan', 1966, Faber and Faber.

Wisman, John D. (2022), 'The Origin and Dynamics of Inequality—Sex, Politics, and Ideology", Oxford University Press.

Wolff, Jonathan & De-Shalit, Avner, 'City of Equals', 2023, Oxford University Press.

World Bank (2007), "The Role of Education Quality in Economic Growth", WPS 4122, February.

World Bank (2008), "Balochistan Economic Report—From Periphery to Core", Report No. 40345-PK, May.

World Bank (2008), "The Growth Report—Strategies for Sustained Growth and Inclusive Development", Report of Commission on Growth and Development, World Bank, Washington, D.C.

World Bank (2009), "Measuring Inequality of Opportunities in Latin America and the Caribbean", Washington, D.C.

World Bank (2009), "Conditional Cash Transfers: Reducing Present and Future Poverty", World Bank Policy Research Report, Washington, D.C.

World Bank (2012), "Does Africa Need a Rotten Kin Theorem? Experimental Evidence from Village Economies", World Bank Policy Research WPS 6085, 2012.

World Bank (2012), "The Foundations of Financial Inclusion: Understanding Ownership and Use of Formal Accounts", Policy Research Working Paper 6290.

World Bank (2013), "Brazil's Primary Health Care Strategy", World Bank Paper No. 74957, January 2013.

World Bank (2013), "Inclusion Matters: The Foundation for Shared Prosperity", Washington, D.C.

World Bank (2017), "The Effect of Height on Earnings—Is Stature Just a Proxy for Cognitive and Non-Cognitive Skills? Policy Working Research Paper 8254, World Bank.

World Bank (2018), 'Fair Progress? Economic Mobility Across Generations Around the World', Washington, D.C.

World Bank (2018), "Pakistan: Can Private Schools Catering to the Poor Increase Access and Improve Learning?" World Bank, February.

World Bank (2018), "The Effect of Increasing Human Capital Investment on Economic Growth and Poverty", World Bank Policy Research Working Paper 8590.

World Bank (2020), "Import Duties and Performance: Some Stylized Facts for Pakistan", Report No. AUS 0001593.

World Bank (2020), "Internationally linked Firms, Integration Reforms and Productivity: Evidence from Pakistan". World Bank, Washington, D.C

World Bank (2021), "Intergenerational Mobility around the World", Policy Research Working Paper 9707, World Bank, Washington, D.C.

World Bank (2021), "Pakistan Development Update-Reviving Exports", October.

World Bank (2022), "From Swimming in Sand to High and Sustainable Growth", Pakistan's Country Economic Memorandum, www.worldbank.org/pakistan.

World Bank (2022), "Pakistan Human Capital Review", World Bank Group, Washington D.C, USA.

World Bank (2022), "The Effects of Fiscal Policy on Inequality and Poverty in Pakistan", Working Paper.

World Bank (2022), "The Global Findex Database 2021: Financial Inclusion, Digital Payments and Resilience in the age of Covid-19", World Bank, Washington, D.C.

World Bank (2023), "Pakistan Federal Public Expenditure Review 2023", World Bank, Washington D.C

World Bank (2023), "Returns to Marriage in the Marriage Market", Policy Research Working Paper 10288, January.

World Bank, 'A Glass Half Full—The Promise of Regional Trade in South Asia', 2018, South Asia Development Forum.

World Bank, 'Twenty Years of Health Reform in Brazil', 2013, World Bank.

World Economic Forum, "Schools of the Future: Defining New Models of Education for the Fourth Industrial Revolution", January 2020, www.weforum.org.

Xu, Guo (2018), "The Costs of Patronage: Evidence from the British Empire", American Economic Review, Vol. 108, No. 11, 3170-98.

Yang, D. (2008), "Integrity for Hire: An Analysis of a Widespread Customs Reform", Journal of Law and Economics, Vol. 51, No. 1, 25–57.

Yellen, J (2020), "The History of Women's Work and Wages and How It Has Created Success for Us All", Brookings Institution.

Yousafzai, Malala & Lamb, Christina, 'I am Malala', 2013, Weidenfeld & Nicolson, UK.

Zahid Hussain, 'Frontline Pakistan', 2007, Columbia University Press.

Zaidi, Akbar Ṣ; Saba, Aslam & Ghaffar, Farheen (2017), "Misperception About India-Pakistan Trade—Beyond Politics", USFP, www.usfp.org.

Zak, Paul J. & Knack, Stephen (2001), "Trust and Growth", The Economic Journal, Vol. 111, No. 470.

Zakaria, Muhammad, Jun, Wen & Ahmed, Haseeb (2019), "Effect of Terrorism on Economic Growth of Pakistan: An Empirical Analysis", Economic Research-Ekonomska Istraživanja, Vol. 32, No. 1, pp. 1794-1812, https://doi.org/10.1080/1331677X.2019.1638290.

Zaman, Muhammad Qasim (1998), "Sectarianism in Pakistan: The Radicalization of Shi 'i and Sunni Identities", Modern Asian Studies, Vol. 32, No. 3.

Zattler, Jürgen K. (2015), "The Debate on Growing Inequality—Implications for Developing Countries and International Cooperation", Courant Research Centre, Gottingen, Germany.

Name Index

A
Abadie, Alberto, 413, 550, 551
Abdul Sattar Edhi, 172
Acemoglu, Daron, 27, 28, 159, 371, 376, 378, 446, 476, 478, 484, 497, 503, 505, 536, 540, 544, 545
Advani, L.K., 419
Agarwal, Bina, 174, 210, 506
Ahmed, Mushtaq, 190
Akhtar, Shoaib, 190
Akram, Waseem, 190
Alvi, Hamza, 214, 513, 520
Ambedkar, B.R., 15, 476
Anthony, Susan B., 177
Armytage, Rosita, 169, 505, 545
Arrow, Kenneth, 349, 540
Asim, Khawaja, 362
Azad, Maulana Abdul Kalam, 330, 537
Aziz, K.K., 101, 429, 493, 554

B
Bandaranaike, Srimavo, 177
Banefield, Edward, 347, 348, 351, 540
Banerjee, Abhijit, 98, 146, 147, 152, 246, 261, 262, 264, 268, 269, 271, 274, 366, 478, 482, 492, 501, 519, 522, 524, 525, 527, 528
Bano, Masooda, 415, 416, 551
Bates, Robert H., 41, 361, 480, 542
Baumol, William J, 39, 112, 479, 556
Becker, Gary S., 73, 486, 523
Bengali, Kaiser, 438
Bhagwati, J.N., 5, 385, 474, 512, 547
Bhutto, Benazir, 177, 198, 537
Borrow, Robert, 407
Boutros, Victor, 341, 342
Bowles, Samuel, 231, 306, 307

C
Calvo, 46, 481
Card, David, 331, 475, 538
Chang, Ha-Joon, 230, 475, 517
Christina, Queen, 177
Chung-hee, Park, 50

J. Nasir, *Development Challenges of Pakistan*, https://doi.org/10.1007/978-981-97-3064-3

Cleopatra VII, 177
Coleman, James S., 350, 541
Collier, Paul, 35, 412–414, 479, 482, 551
Collington, Rosie, 465, 557
Cookson, Tara Patricia, 274
Cowen, Tyler, 66, 485

D
Darwin, Charles, 103
Deaton, Angus, 139, 142, 147, 489, 500
Dervis, Kemal, 13, 475
De Soto, Hernando, 229, 361, 516, 542
Diamond, Jared, 32, 345, 476, 479, 540
Dickens, Charles, 158
Disraeli, Benjamin, 16
Dreze, Jean, 13, 73
Dr. Yunus, Muhammad, 268
Duflo, Esther, 146, 147, 152, 246, 261, 264, 274, 366, 487, 519, 522
Durrani, Tehmina, 173, 505

E
Easterly, William, 464, 475, 482, 546, 555–557
Edison, Thomas, 70
Eglar, Zekiye, 209
Elizabeth, Queen, 177
Engerman, Stanley N., 29
Errera, Roger, 195
Evans, Peter, 98, 289, 529

F
Flannery, Kent, 166, 167
Friedman, Milton, 408
Fujimori, Alberto, 318
Fukuyama, Francis, 351, 469, 529, 540, 544

G
Galor, Oded, 33
Gladwell, Malcolm, 184, 508
Gandhi, Indira, 177
Gandhiji, 417
Ganguly, Sumit, 419, 552
Gates, Bill, 83, 184
General DePuy, William, 374
General Zia-ul-Haque, 198, 425, 429, 430
Ghazali, Imam, 57
Gladstone, William, 16
Gordon, Robert J., 65, 66, 181
Gupta, Dipak, 415, 417, 542, 551
Gust, Sarah, 91, 490

H
Hadfield, Gillian, 322, 536
Harari, Yuval Noah, 9, 475
Haugen, Gary A., 341, 342
Hayek, Friedrich, 374
Hidalgo, Cesar, 64, 485
Higgs, Robert, 290, 529
Hirschman, Albert, 10, 475
Hoeffler, Anke, 413, 551
Hoodbhoy, Pervez, 56, 103, 483, 493, 494, 505
Hudson, Michael, 387, 547
Hussain, Ishrat, 227, 302, 365, 516, 531, 543
Hussain, Zahid, 427, 553, 555

J
Jalal, Ayesha, 220, 514
Joan of Arc, 177

K

Kafka, Franz, 344
Kahneman, Daniel, 333
Kakwani, 381, 546
Kanbur, Ravi, 164, 185, 502, 508
Kaunda, Kenneth, 34
Kelton, Stephanie, 389, 548
Khaddarposh, Masud, 218
Khaldun, Ibn, 32
Khan, Abdul Wali, 170
Khan, Ashfaq Hassan, 386, 547
Khan, Ghulam Ishaque, 219
Khan, Hamid, 329, 332, 335, 537, 538, 540
Khan, Mishal, 170
Khanna, Tarun, 349, 540
King Leopard II, 30
King, Martin Luther, 172
Krueger, Alan, 187, 331, 407, 408, 412–414, 416, 538
Krugman, Paul, 39, 480, 548
Kuznets, 158, 159

L

Landes, David, 54, 56, 57, 71, 483
Lansing, Stephen J., 463, 556
Leff, Nathaniel H., 355, 357, 541
Lewis, Arthur, 157, 502
Lockwood, Sarah, 349
Lodhi, Maleeha, 298, 529
Lucas, Robert E., 40, 480

M

Macaulay, 58
Mai, Mukhtar, 434, 555
Malthus, 265
Mandela, Nelson, 51, 172
Marcus, Joyce, 166, 167, 504
Marshall, Alfred, 48, 73, 481, 486
Marshall, Tim, 35, 479
Marx, Karl, 53, 483
Mazzucato, Mariana, 465, 557
Mian, Atif, 362
Migdal, Joel, 375, 376, 545
Milanovic, Branko, 179, 507
Modi, Narendra, 199
Mody, Ashoka, 13
Mohammad, Mahathir, 51, 52
Mokyr, Joel, 55, 56, 58, 483, 484
Montesquieu, 32
Moss, Robert, 260
Moyo, Dambisa, 384, 474, 546
Mullainathan, Sendhil, 266, 523
Murphy, Eamon, 552, 554
Murphy, Kevin M., 110, 510
Musharraf, 365, 367, 427

N

Nazimuddin, Khawaja, 421
Nekoei, Arash, 175
North, Douglas, 27, 112, 478, 495

O

O'Connell, Steve, 35
Olson, Mancur, 49, 111, 495
Orwell, George, 331

P

Palma, Gabriel, 196, 510
Panagariya, Arvind, 5, 474
Papanek, Gustav, 1, 2, 473
Perez Alfonso, Juan Pablo, 34
Piketty, Thomas, 169, 200, 207, 486, 505, 510, 517
Pistor, Katharina, 321, 504
Polyani, Karl, 7, 54, 475, 483
Porter, Michael, 70, 485
Pritchett, Lant, 19, 83, 92, 93, 97, 116, 317, 476, 488, 490, 493, 499, 534, 547
Putman, Robert, 350, 540, 541
Puzo, Mario, 342

Q

Qian, Nancy, 131, 180, 499
Quaid-e-Azam, 65

R

Rajan, Raghuram, 162, 195
Rand, Ayn, 303, 530
Rashid, Ahmed, 426, 553
Rawls, John, 294, 529
Rizvi, Hasan Askari, 224, 515, 554
Rodrik, Dani, 16, 19, 476, 477, 479, 482, 484, 548, 549
Roemer, John E., 184, 185, 508
Romer, Paul, 60, 70, 451, 484, 485
Rosenstein-Rodan, P.N., 1, 2, 473
Roy, Bismal, 243

S

Sachs, Jeffrey, 32–34, 115, 479
Saez, Emmanuel, 385
Saini, G.R., 211
Sandel, Michael, 292, 529
Sappho, 177
Scheidel, Walter, 200, 201, 510
Schultz, Theodore W., 260, 522
Schumacher, E.F., 212, 512
Sen, Amartya, 130, 210, 259, 505, 511, 512, 522, 529
Shafir, Eldar, 266
Sheikh, Farzana, 367, 543
Sidhwa, Bapsi, 173, 505
Singh, Maharaja Hari, 418
Smith, Adam, 53, 369, 544
Sokoloff, Kenneth L., 29, 478
Solow, Robert, 39, 93
Spence, Michael, 50, 482, 497, 535
Stasavage, D., 371, 544
Stern, Jessica, 429, 460, 490, 553
Stiglitz, Joseph, 7, 19, 160, 338, 477, 502, 545
Suharto, 77, 352
Sultana, Razia, 177
Summers, Lawrence H., 116, 496, 499
Swaraj, Sushma, 419

T

Talbot, Ian, 11, 36, 475
Tanzi, Vito, 459
Taseer, Salman, 170
Teresa, Mother, 172
Tirole, Jean, 295, 529
Toynbee, Arnold, 170, 505

U

Ul Haq, Mahbub, 3
Ul Haque, Nadeem, 226, 485, 494

V

Vajpayee, Atal Bihari, 419

W

Wade, Robert, 299, 517, 528, 530
Weber, Max, 53, 71, 483, 529
Williams, Rushbrook, 169, 505

X

Xiaoping, Deng, 50
Xu, Guo, 316

Y

Yang, Yuen Yuen, 300, 301
Yew, Lee Kwan, 51
Yousaf, Muhammad, 190
Yousafzai, Malala, 173, 505

Z

Zaman, Arshad, 386, 387, 481, 547
Zedong, Mao, 201
Zucman, Gabriel, 385

Subject Index

A

Accountability, 6, 10, 22, 51, 86, 87, 98–100, 109, 140, 147, 148, 152, 194, 298, 302, 308, 310, 316, 337, 350, 351, 355–357, 364, 365, 384, 432, 446, 449–451, 469

Afghan war, 423, 424, 432, 441

Agricultural productivity, 28, 33, 212, 214, 236, 237, 239, 240, 242, 248, 254, 361, 521

Allocation of property rights, 230, 232

B

Big effect view, 407, 408

C

Capital formation, 2, 43, 45, 48, 95, 96, 276

Cash transfers, ix, 82, 146, 268, 272–277, 283, 284

Centralization of bribery, 359, 360, 542

Civil service, 22, 52, 113, 171, 179, 288, 292, 299–302, 304, 305, 307–309, 312, 313, 315, 316, 319, 336, 357, 449, 450, 453, 457, 458, 530

Clientelism, 273, 296–298, 354

Climate change, 36, 37, 480

Cognitive overload, 266

Collection efficiency ratio (CEF), 318

Common good, 293–296, 529

Competition, 20, 42, 43, 50, 62, 66, 101, 169, 170, 183, 185, 190, 205, 290, 301, 302, 317, 322, 362–364, 366, 371, 374, 404, 435, 439, 450, 451

Competitiveness, vii, 11, 17, 34, 40, 41, 44, 67, 68, 70, 71, 303, 315, 392, 393, 485, 533

Complexity of tariffs, 43

Contract enforcement, x, 31, 240, 321, 339, 369, 404

J. Nasir, *Development Challenges of Pakistan*,
https://doi.org/10.1007/978-981-97-3064-3

Corruption, 16, 46, 47, 145, 162, 166, 191, 194, 203, 226, 233, 274, 287, 297, 298, 303–305, 307, 310, 314, 316, 323, 340, 342, 343, 352, 353, 355–368, 370, 378–380, 384, 385, 436, 438, 439, 448–450, 454, 469, 485, 542
Cost-benefit analysis, 365
Credit constraints, 182
Customs duty, 43, 382, 462, 471

D
Dead capital, 160, 205, 226, 227, 229, 231, 312
Debt, v, 30, 46, 49, 168, 204, 243, 264, 276, 295, 368, 377, 383, 386–389, 449, 519, 547, 548
Democracy, viii, 6, 15, 16, 34, 49, 52, 74, 155, 159, 191, 194, 297, 299, 353, 354, 371, 372, 374, 375, 377, 378, 385, 476
Demographic dividend, 66, 71, 72
Devaluation, 392, 393
Developmental bureaucracy, 112, 299, 303
Dividends of Education, 104–105
Dividends of growth, ix, 4–8, 71–72, 304, 448
Duty and tax remission scheme, 206
Duty drawback, vi, 21, 395, 396, 398

E
Economic complexity, 8, 64, 484, 548
Educational technology, 108
Education policy, 77–79, 99, 100, 444
Emotional closure, 343, 345, 346
Empirics of Poverty, 261
Equitable growth, ix, 19, 21, 213
Ethnic identity, 435, 439
Export facilitation, 399
Export Oriented Units Scheme (EOU), 206, 396, 398, 399, 401
Export processing zones (EPZ), vi, 21, 393–395, 398
Exports, vi, 20, 21, 34, 63, 64, 70, 161, 237, 238, 241, 247, 253, 384, 388–401, 405, 410, 477

F
Federal Excise duty, 380
Financial exclusion, 278
Food security, 125, 237, 253, 273
Foreign aid, 3, 34, 368, 383, 385, 464, 496, 547
Formal justice system, 323, 325, 340, 342–345, 353

G
Gender inequality, 173, 179, 180
Generalized trust, 351–354
General Sales Tax (GST), 459, 461, 463
Generic drugs, 149, 445, 502
Geography, viii, ix, 25, 30, 32–35, 38, 52, 101, 402, 469
Gini coefficient, 161, 197, 202, 231, 488
Governance indicators, 355
Green revolution, 212–214, 240, 249, 250, 252, 253, 298, 463

H
Harmonized tests, 94, 95, 491
Health inequities, 121, 126, 144
Human Capital Index (HCI), 94–96, 491
Human factor, ix, x, 68, 71

I
Ideas, v, 8, 20, 51, 52, 54, 55, 58–62, 65, 71, 100, 106, 107, 171, 174, 190, 191, 201, 233, 260, 265, 267, 302, 322, 384, 427, 447, 451, 453
Identity, 51, 54, 170–172, 179, 192, 195, 374, 416, 417, 420–422, 426, 430, 438, 441
Imitation, 65, 67, 96
Imports, 21, 43, 46, 206, 363, 379–381, 389, 394–399, 403, 462, 468, 471
Inclusion, ix, 8–11, 49, 54, 101, 103, 206, 242, 267, 268, 277–282, 284, 437, 440, 441
Inclusiveness, 4, 8–10, 13–15, 51, 52, 139
Industrialization, 3, 16, 38, 158, 230, 299, 393, 437, 502, 507, 512
Inequalities of media, 191
Inequality, 5, 6, 10, 11, 16, 17, 28–31, 66, 73, 74, 84, 91, 118, 142, 157–169, 172, 179, 180, 182, 183, 185, 186, 190, 191, 193, 196–203, 205, 207, 210, 213, 225, 230, 231, 233, 255, 256, 275, 279, 287, 297, 352, 360, 392, 414–417, 447, 449, 478, 503, 504, 508, 509, 535, 546
Inequality of opportunity, 182, 183
Informal justice system, 325, 340, 343–346, 451, 539
Inheritance tax, 204, 205, 371, 449
Initial endowments, vi, 161, 282–284
Innovation, ix, 4, 7, 8, 35, 39, 42, 52, 59–62, 65, 66, 68, 70, 71, 96, 97, 99, 100, 205, 317, 318, 329, 349, 393, 451, 494
Institutions, v, vi, viii–x, 1, 6, 11, 16, 17, 19, 21, 22, 25, 27–33, 38, 40, 41, 46, 49–52, 59, 61, 70, 83, 84, 89, 102, 106–108, 146, 158, 162, 167, 201, 203, 212, 226, 228–230, 244, 246, 247, 249, 254, 264, 267, 268, 270, 271, 276, 278, 280–282, 287, 291, 295–297, 300, 301, 306, 308, 318, 321, 325, 327, 339, 341, 343, 348, 353, 355, 363, 365, 367, 370, 373–376, 378, 384–386, 395, 412, 421, 422, 425, 426, 428, 432, 435, 440, 450, 451, 457, 464, 478, 534, 543
Integrity, 52, 100, 305, 313, 315, 316, 335, 341, 363
Intergenerational mobility (IGM), xi, 8, 103, 185–187, 446, 447
International Monetary Fund (IMF), vi, 4, 11, 46, 378, 385–387, 389, 449, 459, 476, 479, 480, 527, 542, 546, 547, 549
Investment, vi, vii, x, 2, 8, 24, 39–47, 49, 54, 55, 66, 67, 72, 73, 81, 96, 115, 119, 130, 131, 146, 159–161, 164, 178, 179, 227, 229–231, 241, 248, 254, 255, 269, 273, 276, 280, 281, 299, 300, 303, 304, 321, 327, 349, 350, 360, 371, 384, 387, 394, 395, 408, 411, 443, 445, 449, 465, 481, 485, 496, 523
Isomorphic mimicry, 317, 318, 534, 535

J
Judicial efficiency, 327, 536
Justice system, 22, 162, 173, 321, 322, 331, 341, 342, 540

K
Kashmir conflict, 403
Kuznets curve, 157, 159, 503

L
Labor force participation rate (LFPR), 175, 176
Land conferrals, 223–226
Land reforms, vi, 20, 21, 161, 201, 202, 210, 217–223, 230, 231, 283, 285, 286, 330, 448, 515, 528
Leaders, 38, 47, 49–52, 102, 169, 170, 177, 190, 335, 347, 350, 352, 375, 376, 383, 384, 419, 420, 428, 434, 440, 514, 547
Learning, vii, ix, 8, 52, 54, 55, 61, 62, 65, 67, 68, 74, 82, 85, 89–94, 98–101, 104, 108, 109, 129, 195, 282, 314, 318, 323, 350, 390, 400, 444, 490, 491, 493
Learning outcomes, 86, 89–94, 97, 98, 104, 105, 318, 430, 444, 492, 494
Legal origins, 340
Life expectancy, 18, 115–118, 125, 144, 155, 166, 174, 444, 496, 497
Lorenz curve, 196
Low-cost private schools, 84, 85, 89

M
Madrassa, 93, 416, 426–430, 440, 553
Mental health, 141, 142, 267, 496, 500
Microcredit, ix, 19, 268–272, 283
Militancy, x, 36, 405, 409, 412, 414–417, 419, 423, 426, 427, 429–432, 435–437, 441, 450
Misallocation, ix, x, 34, 41, 42, 65, 226, 227, 284, 360, 385, 447, 448, 456
Modern education, 56, 57
Monopoly, 20, 101, 150, 169, 191, 205, 246, 322, 323, 340, 362, 364, 368, 370–374, 377, 383, 417, 450, 471
Most-favored nation (MFN), 403
Multidimensional poverty, 259, 434, 438

N
Negative externalities, 35, 162, 166, 415, 426
Noise, 332–335, 341, 343, 538
Nutrition, xi, 5, 8, 91, 105, 118, 121, 129, 132, 134–136, 138, 139, 141, 146, 154, 155, 259, 260, 329, 500, 522

O
Opportunity cost, 20, 79, 80, 82, 86, 99, 131, 163, 175, 391, 416, 444
Out of school children (OOSC), 8, 75–77, 79–82, 92, 104, 173, 434, 444, 486, 505, 506

P
Palma ratio, 118, 196–200, 382, 447
Patience, v, 43, 44, 48, 50, 358
Patronage, 50, 217, 276, 297, 298, 314, 316, 317, 367, 370, 378, 429, 534
Positive externalities, 49, 87, 118, 132, 249, 291, 321, 352
Preventive health care, 145, 146, 445, 446
Primary health care, 142, 145, 148, 501, 502

Productive assets, vii, ix, x, 10, 31, 48, 173, 174, 200, 208, 260, 266, 276, 277, 282–285, 295, 330, 446–448
Productivity, vii, ix, 8, 11, 20, 21, 24, 39–44, 48, 53, 61, 66–68, 70, 71, 83, 85, 94, 96, 104, 112, 115, 116, 167, 210–212, 217, 219, 237, 239, 240, 242, 247–249, 253, 255, 273, 301, 302, 304, 307, 308, 312, 313, 316, 324, 327, 352, 370, 373, 392, 409, 411, 412, 444, 448, 451, 456, 481, 534
Professionalism, 100, 314, 315, 317–319, 335, 453
Prosociality, 304, 305, 307
Public good, vi, 13, 16, 23, 30, 42, 54, 59, 84, 152, 154, 155, 163, 191, 293, 295, 321, 322, 338, 340, 363
Public health care, ix, 444
Public schools, 77, 82, 84–87, 89, 90, 99, 101, 104, 138, 206, 207, 261, 291, 292, 316, 355, 430, 492
Public sector, viii, x, 10, 22, 46, 51, 67, 85–87, 89, 101–103, 110, 148, 163, 226, 287–290, 293, 296, 298, 302, 304–317, 319, 353–355, 362, 365–367, 427, 439, 446, 448–451, 453–456, 469, 488, 534, 543
Public service(s), vii, x, 6, 10, 20, 22–24, 33, 87, 141, 142, 163, 170, 172, 173, 182, 183, 190, 195, 207, 277, 286, 287, 292, 297–299, 302, 305–309, 312, 313, 315, 317–319, 351, 353, 354, 364, 368, 373, 375–378, 430, 437, 438, 443–445, 447, 450, 453, 454, 534, 535

Q
Quality of research, 106

R
Redistribution, vi, 3, 5, 10, 21, 110, 157–161, 200, 210, 213, 217, 221, 223, 231, 232, 285, 286, 291, 292, 378, 515
Rent-seeking, 24, 41, 52, 68, 110, 112, 113, 166, 191, 204–206, 225, 227, 231, 233, 305, 315, 370, 377, 380, 383, 385, 396, 425, 432, 448, 450, 457, 458, 510, 534
Right to health, 155, 156, 294, 445
Rural growth, 235, 247, 253
Rural non-farm economy, 21, 254–256, 446
Rural poor, 241, 250, 253, 285

S
Savings, 2, 21, 43–46, 48, 72, 131, 159, 160, 182, 236, 247, 254, 261, 263–265, 278, 280, 281, 284, 384, 411, 520, 527
Scarcity, 50, 145, 158, 240, 260, 266, 296–298
Security of property rights, 31, 168, 228, 230–233, 339
Sehat Sahulat Program (SSP), 143
Self-regulation, 337, 339
Single National Curriculum (SNC), 84, 101, 102, 104, 105, 444
Size-efficiency relation, 210
Small and medium enterprises, 405
Small farms, 210–213, 215, 237, 241, 247, 248, 250, 285, 286, 296
Social capital, viii, x, 17, 142, 158, 229, 249, 346–348, 350–354, 367, 384, 450
Social cohesion, 11, 17, 24, 52, 195

Social inclusion, 17
Social media, 149, 194, 195
Socio-political stability, vii, ix, 15
Stabilization, 385, 386
State building, 172, 372–374, 383
State-in-Society approach, 375
Stunting, 121, 132–136, 186, 499
Suspensive regime, 396, 397, 399

T

Taxation, xi, 30, 166, 197, 203–205, 231, 295, 359, 360, 371–374, 379, 384, 426, 460
Tax structure, 377–382, 459
Terrorism, 36, 356, 386, 405, 407–416, 418, 419, 423, 425, 427–430, 441, 461, 550, 553
Trade, viii, x, 21, 33, 35, 36, 43, 65, 112, 163, 275, 314, 352, 372, 373, 382, 387, 389, 391–393, 400, 402–405, 410, 411, 418, 424, 435, 437, 457, 459, 461, 467–471, 548, 549
Traditional education, 56
Transaction costs, x, 242, 256, 268, 271, 281, 282, 349, 353, 411
Transparency, 49, 106, 364, 543
Trust, vii, x, 9, 17, 65, 165, 166, 195, 206, 318, 319, 321, 328, 343, 347–354, 373, 377, 403, 404, 431, 432, 535

U

Undernutrition, 132, 135, 139, 499
Underweight, 121, 129, 132–135
Useful knowledge, 59, 64

V

Village community dispensaries, 151, 152

W

Wage premium, 310, 450
Wealth creation, 168, 230, 457
Weather insurance, 242
Women agency, 133, 416, 445, 497
World Bank, 5, 12, 14, 18, 36, 37, 41, 42, 46, 50, 71, 85, 94–96, 117, 118, 135, 139, 140, 142, 147, 181, 186, 239, 275, 278, 303, 318, 325, 355, 357, 381, 386, 389, 393, 396, 399, 432, 449, 461, 462, 464, 476, 477, 480–482, 484, 486, 488, 490, 491, 493, 494, 497, 499–502, 504, 507, 508, 517–519, 521–523, 525–527, 529, 532, 533, 535, 536, 546, 548, 549, 551, 555